The
Jefferson Image
in the
American Mind

The
Jefferson Image
in the
American Mind

MERRILL D. PETERSON

OXFORD UNIVERSITY PRESS
New York   Oxford

Oxford University Press

Oxford   New York   Toronto
Delhi   Bombay   Calcutta   Madras   Karachi
Kuala Lumpur   Singapore   Hong Kong   Tokyo
Nairobi   Dar es Salaam   Cape Town
Melbourne   Auckland

and associated companies in
Beirut   Berlin   Ibadan   Mexico City   Nicosia

Library of Congress Cataloging-in-Publication Data
Peterson, Merrill D.
The Jefferson image in the American mind.
Bibliography: p.
Includes index.
1. Jefferson, Thomas, 1743-1826—Influence.
I. Title.
E332.2.P4   1985   973.4'6'0924   85-15502
ISBN 0-19-500698-4 (pbk.)

Printing (last digit): 9 8 7 6 5 4 3 2 1

Printed in the United States of America

For JEAN

THE AUTHOR WISHES TO THANK Allen Tate and *The Sewanee Review* for permission to quote "On The Father of Liberty"; Harcourt, Brace and Company, Inc., for permission to quote from Vernon L. Parrington, *Main Currents in American Thought;* Charles Scribner's Sons for permission to quote from Lawrence Lee, "Monticello," in *Monticello and Other Poems,* and James Truslow Adams, *The Living Jefferson;* Random House, Inc., for permission to quote from Karl Shapiro, "Jefferson," in *V-Letter and Other Poems,* and Robert Penn Warren, *Brother to Dragons;* Alfred A. Knopf, Inc., for permission to quote from Carl Becker, *The Declaration of Independence;* Dodd, Mead & Company for permission to quote from Hendrik Willem Van Loon, *Thomas Jefferson;* Rinehart & Company, Inc., for permission to quote from Elizabeth Page, *The Tree of Liberty;* Little, Brown & Company for permission to quote from Gilbert Chinard, *Thomas Jefferson, Apostle of Americanism;* The University of North Carolina Press for permission to quote from Charles W. Dabney, *Universal Education in the South; The American Historical Review* for permission to quote from Andrew C. McLaughlin, "American History and American Democracy"; George Gaylord Simpson and the *Proceedings of the American Philosophical Society* for permission to quote from his "The Beginnings of Vertebrate Paleontology in the United States"; Ellen C. Masters for permission to quote stanzas of Edgar Lee Masters' "Jefferson," in *Poems of the People;* the Macmillan Company for permission to quote from Alfred North Whitehead, *Symbolism, Its Meaning and Effect,* Herbert Croly, *The Promise of American Life,* and Charles A. Beard, *The Economic Origins of Jeffersonian Democracy.*

The poem "Thomas Jefferson," by Stephen Vincent Benét, quoted in part, is from *A Book of Americans* by Rosemary and Stephen Vincent Benét, copyrighted by them and published by Rinehart & Company, Inc., in 1933.

An earlier version of a part of Chapter I was published as "The Jefferson Image, 1829," in *The American Quarterly,* III (Fall 1951); similarly, "Parrington and American Liberalism," *The Virginia Quarterly Review,* XXX (Winter 1954) is a more extended treatment of a section of Chapter VI; and "Bowers, Roosevelt, and the 'New Jefferson,'" *The Virginia Quarterly Review,* XXXIV (Autumn 1958) is a different version of a part of Chapter VII. I am grateful to these journals for freedom to incorporate here materials that they first published.

PREFACE

THIS IS NOT a book on the history Thomas Jefferson made but a book on what history made of Thomas Jefferson. I have attempted to chart Jefferson's course in American thought and imagination, beginning with the moment of his death nearly one hundred and thirty-four years ago. For very few historic figures would the posthumous course be worth running at all. Jefferson is one of the few chiefly because of his compelling relationship to the American experiment in democracy.

The guiding concept, *the Jefferson image*, may be defined as the composite representation of the historic personage and of the ideas and ideals, policies and sentiments, habitually identified with him. The image is highly complex, never uniform and never stationary. It is a mixed product of memory and hope, fact and myth, love and hate, of the politician's strategy, the patriot's veneration, and the scholar's quest. My concern is not primarily with the truth or falsity of the image either as a whole or in its parts, but rather with its illuminations of the evolving culture and its shaping power. It is posterity's configuration of Jefferson. Even more, however, it is a sensitive reflector, through several generations, of America's troubled search for the image of itself.

Jefferson himself has always been an elusive subject; his shadow must prove more elusive still. I am acutely aware of the difficulties of rendering it intelligible. Confronting the massive record of America's affair with Jefferson, I have tried to report it honestly and, at the same time, to make sense of it in the light of my own reason. Another historian might have elected another approach, used methods and formed interpretations different from mine; nevertheless, I am confident that his report would agree in most essential respects with the history charted in the following pages. I have included a *Guide to Sources,* which is intended to serve both as a select bibliography and as a running commentary on the materials that form the basis of my discussion in each chapter and section.

This work has been a solitary preoccupation of mine over the past dozen years. But in my slow and halting progress I have accumulated several scholarly debts, and I am happy to acknowledge the most important of them here. I am deeply grateful to those so often unsung heroes of the scholar's enterprise, the directors and staffs of some forty research libraries, who put their collections at my disposal and helped me to ferret out obscure items of Jeffersonia. Unfortunately, they must remain anonymous. Professor Perry Miller of Harvard University introduced me to the fascinating realms of the American imagination. He, too, together with Professor John Gaus, guided an initial study submitted for my doctorate in the History of American Civilization at Harvard in 1950. My good friends Sherman Paul of the University of Illinois and Leonard Levy of Brandeis University have been such unfailing sources of intellectual stimulation that any work of mine must reflect their different influences. Professor Julian Boyd, Editor of *The Papers of Thomas Jefferson,* has done me the inestimable kindness of reading the book in galleys and spotting my errors. And I shall always remain grateful to the late Nathan Schachner, who made Jefferson come alive for me at Monticello when I first saw it more than a decade ago.

A grant from the Penrose Fund of the American Philosophical Society made it possible for me to pursue research in numerous libraries that would otherwise have been beyond my reach. My appointment as Bicentennial Preceptor in History at Princeton University, 1955-58, furnished me a year free from academic responsibilities, and thus enabled me to complete the final manuscript. The Princeton University Research Fund provided further financial assistance.

M. D. P.

Brandeis University
November 10, 1959

CONTENTS

Book Two

The
Jefferson Image
in the
American Mind

THE APOTHEOSIS

Evening in majestic shadows fell upon the fortress' walls;
Sweetly were the last bells ringing on the James and on the Charles.
'Mid the choruses of freedom two departed victors lay,
One beside the blue Rivanna, one by Massachusetts Bay.
He was gone, and night her sable curtain drew across the sky;
Gone his soul into all nations, gone to live and not to die.*

THOMAS JEFFERSON died in his eighty-third year, at Monticello, fifty minutes past meridian, July Fourth 1826. "Is it the Fourth?" the old man asked anxiously sometime during the night. From his bedside came reassuring nods of assent. "Ah," he murmured with satisfaction and went serenely to rest. Many hundreds of miles away in Quincy, Massachusetts, the friend, sometimes foe, of fifty years was also dying. John Adams survived Jefferson by five hours; but his last words, "Thomas Jefferson still survives," became the most famous he ever uttered.

The triumphal anthem of American Independence rose across the broad land on this fiftieth anniversary. A patriotic rite, a festive holiday, a day of booming cannon, parades, picnics, and oratory—the Fourth of July already belonged to Jefferson, author of the Declaration of Independence, acclaimed on the Jubilee "the most important event, humanly speaking, in the history of the world." The Sage of Monticello weighed upon the minds of Americans in this epic year for an unhappy reason as well. Crushed by debt, he had obtained permission from the state in February to dispose

* Hezekiah Butterworth, "The Death of Jefferson," *Songs of History* (Boston, 1887).

of much of his property by lottery. The lottery was suspended, however, when friends and admirers learned of his plight and organized subscription funds in many cities for his relief. It was hoped the Fourth would bring to fruition "this affecting tribute of public gratitude."

The charmed death of Jefferson and of his venerable friend made the Jubilee a solemn monument in American memory and opened a remarkable season of patriotism. "There was a living and dying for you!" Monticello's earth received its master without pomp or ceremony, as he had directed, on July 5. Black-craped students, followed by the local citizenry, trudged through a downpour up the mountain's slope to pay last respects to the Father of the University of Virginia. "I never saw young men so deeply affected by any circumstance in my life," one of the professors reported. The news crossed the Potomac the next day. "A strange and very exciting coincidence," President John Quincy Adams jotted in his diary. Three days later, having just set out to reach his aged father, the President felt the full force of the coincidence. Where the tidings from Massachusetts and Virginia crossed, the shock was electrifying. "Great God! Thy ways are inscrutable!" exclaimed a New York editor. On the tenth Boston again tolled its bells and lowered its flags, while in Jefferson's Albemarle a Republican with a long memory, as legend had it, greeted the Northern report in disbelief and then announced in a huff, "It's a damned Yankee trick."

Over the next several weeks, from New Orleans to Portland, Americans raised a swelling hymn of praise to Jefferson and Adams. Military stations conferred honors; courts, legislative bodies, and learned societies held commemorative exercises; communities in untold number set aside days of public homage, "the unbought offering of an independent people." Virtually the whole populace of Richmond turned out for the mock funeral procession and Governor John Tyler's eulogy of Jefferson in Capitol Square. Thirty thousand witnessed the services in Baltimore's Howard Park, where Charles Carroll, the last of the Signers of the Declaration, was the guest of all the dignitaries of state and city. On a hot August afternoon, Bostonians jammed famed Faneuil Hall, and listened for two and one-half hours to one of the greatest orations of Daniel Webster's career.

But nothing that Webster or any of his peers said in this season of eulogy would be as well remembered as Jefferson's personal valedictory. Only ten days before he died, barely able to hold the pen in his hand, he had declined an invitation to attend the Independence Day ceremonies in Washington, D. C. Seizing as if in foreknowledge this last opportunity to embellish a legend, Jefferson labored to make his letter an inspiring last testament to the American people. And so it became, printed in newspapers, engraved as a souvenir, and pronounced all over the country. May the Jubilee be to the world, Jefferson wrote, "the signal of arousing men to burst the chains" of their oppression, "and to assume the blessings and security of self-government."

All eyes are opened, or opening, to the rights of man. The general spread of the light of science has already laid open to every view the palpable truth, that the mass of mankind has not been born with saddles on their backs, nor a favored few booted and spurred, ready to ride them legitimately, by the grace of God. These are grounds of hope for others. For ourselves, let the annual return of this day, forever refresh our recollections of these rights, and an undiminished devotion to them.

The passing of Jefferson and Adams was a dramatic moment in the growth of American self-consciousness. The imagination, working upon the event, made of it a fable of the republic. The fable explained the miraculous, brought men into a community of loyalty and belief, and turned the nation's loss into a triumph. It was the creation of a pervasive national faith reaching for justification and here finding it. Providence, Union, Heritage: these were three of the emotion-laden ideas composing the patriotic faith. In the "double apotheosis" of 1826 they were confirmed with awesome finality, and formed into a fabled story of America.

An event so wonderful, President Adams declared in an official proclamation, certified that the work of these illustrious men in founding the republic was "Heaven directed," and furnished "a new seal" to the belief that the nation was under the special care of a kind Providence. This was the instantaneous and uniform reaction.

"In this most singular coincidence, the finger of Providence is plainly visible! It hallows the Declaration of Independence as the Word of God, and is the bow in the Heavens, that promises its principles shall be eternal, and their dissemination universal over the Earth." Americans in 1826 looked back with Jefferson upon 1776 as "the auspicious commencement of the political salvation of the world," and saw in his death the sign of "divine approval of the course of freedom."

The spectacle of a whole people blending their grief "in the funeral trains of their rival chieftains" was a fitting symbol of the Era of Good Feelings. The era's glow had vanished from politics in 1826 when the apotheosis caught and held its flickering light. Orators sought to make the event a monument to the idea of Union; and not just in the restricted *federal* sense, but in the sense of a uniform republican *faith* that transcended the antagonisms of men and parties and theories. The remarkable parallels in the lives of the two patriots, which Webster developed most fully, gave the impression of a surpassing harmony of purpose. Copartners in the struggles of the revolutionary era, they had become political enemies in the party warfare of Federalists and Republicans, only at last to renew their friendship in the glorious intellectual fellowship of their autumnal years. The patriots' "sublime example" of reunion, the eulogists said, was "at the head of the catalogue of their praises."

Nevertheless, the memory of antagonism was "calculated to embarrass the eulogist." The faithful Federalist, Horace Binney of Philadelphia, remarked that for those who were partisans of Jefferson or Adams in 1798, "the most extraordinary feature in their history is that of a joint or consociated celebration. Their tempers and dispositions toward one another would at one time have made a very tolerable salad . . . [and] it never entered into my conception that it would ultimately settle down into such a homogenous mixture as to admit one and the same apotheosis." Similarly, a Jacksonian satirist looked upon the obsequies with amazement:

> Not half an age has roll'd its winter o'er,
> Since hate of *Adams* spread to every shore.
> Now how revers'd in love they seem to melt,
> And feign an adoration they never felt!

However, young men such as Edward Everett, who had come to political maturity in the national era after 1812, knew the patriots "not as opponents but as friends to each other," and they revered both. Jefferson and Adams might be interpreted as representing opposite poles of republicanism—liberty and law, the popular will and its restriction—but both were essential. The problem was one of balance. It had been solved, or practically so, by the melting of old partisan loyalties into the synthetic republicanism of the Era of Good Feelings. And if, said one eulogist, "the relique of the bitterness of long past times could possibly have survived in any bosom till now . . . here is the place to bury it." Bury the "doctrines of '98," bury Hartford Convention Federalism, bury the "regalism" of Adams and the "demagogism" of Jefferson—bury them all under this sublime symbol of Union.

Turning aside the memories of division and discord, the eulogists cemented the legend of a noble Heritage. Providence, Everett declared, "seems to have appointed that the revolutionary age of America should be closed up, by a scene as illustriously affecting, as its commencement was appalling and terrific." The apotheosis, said another, "marked the solemn termination of one great epoch of our Republic—it is the sublime commencement of another." With mingled emotions of sorrow and exaltation at this conclusive moment in their history, Americans made the discovery that they were heirs of a glorious national past.

The history of Adams and Jefferson was written throughout the first epoch of the nation, whose "political fathers" they were. By laying up "the images of their virtues in our hearts," the eulogists declared, Americans might lighten the future. Adams and Jefferson were classic models of civic virtue. Neither warriors nor priests nor kings, the illustrious dead were philosopher-statesmen whose only weapons were reason and truth and love. Phideas had had no models such as these. The nation did itself honor, the eulogists said, by freely appreciating their services and by understanding that recurrence to their lives was a civic obligation. "The Republic will cease to be, when it ceases to remember, to revere, and to imitate the virtues of its founders. The Revolution is to us what the golden age was to Greece and Italy—what chivalry was to England and France."

With the passing of the last great heads of the American family, patriot-orators called for a ritual of ancestor-worship. Samuel Knapp instructed the young men of Boston to adopt the custom of the Roman youth, who had yearly sought inspiration at the tomb of Numa, founder of religious rites and civil institutions. "Go, ye young men of my country, oftener than once a year, to visit the tombs of your fathers. No man was ever great who did not live much among the dead." The apotheosis of 1826 joined this piety of remembrance to the idea of an eternally valid heritage from the founders. In "the age of commemoration," the imagery of The Signers, The Heroes and Sages of the Revolution, The Founding Fathers was a fixture of the American mind.

This fable of the republic entered into the fabric of patriotism, but it also assumed significance in American politics. Politicians took up the habit of looking backward to oracles and landmarks, and thus drew the fabled past into contemporary myth. Venerable principles became weapons in the struggle for power. Patriarchs became symbols of parties and causes. No name was more important in this way than Jefferson's. His was the compelling image of the fable. The habits of patriotic ritual combined with the force of his thought and example kept Jefferson's memory green. Ironically, this rebel against the past was fated to become the great idol of republican tradition.

Could Americans make a patriarchal hero of Jefferson? A man tall and virile, yet radiating grace and mind, as in Rembrandt Peale's portrait, he lacked the dominant personal aspect upon which prototypes are made. Gilbert Stuart painted Washington and stamped his personal image indelibly on the American mind. But Jefferson would perhaps be viewed in the Mather Brown (a cosmopolitan young dandy in tie-wig) or the Bass Otis (a plain weathered old schoolmaster) as in Peale's or in Stuart's stately portraits. As Henry Adams later wrote, not as a painter but as a historian, Jefferson could not be portrayed with "a few broad strokes of the brush . . . only touch by touch with a fine pencil, and the perfection of the likeness depended upon the shifting and uncertain flicker of its semi-transparent shadows." Jefferson lacked the openness and earthiness of Franklin, the dignified austerity of Washington, the oratorical brilliance of Henry. He had known none of the surpassing glories of battle nor the blessings of martyrdom. He had written no autobiography to instruct the young; no Parson Weems endeared him to the morality of the age; no Herndon sat at his feet and recorded his inmost life.

Jefferson was a baffling series of contradictions: philosopher and politician, aristocrat and democrat, cosmopolitan and American. He authored the nation's birthright, but he also wrote the Kentucky Resolutions of "nullification." He was the friend of Washington, but the enemy of his administration. Americans remembered his Presidency for the achievement of the Louisiana Purchase and the disaster of the Embargo. None of the ordinary categories of the hero— lawgiver, chieftain, prophet—sufficed for Jefferson. As his character was somewhat labyrinthian, so his mind was bewildering in its range and complexity. Later generations comprehended his thought only in fragments, crossing and colliding with each other, until it seemed that the protean figure, if ever he had genuine historical existence, must never be rediscovered.

Everyman was his own Jeffersonian. This was due not only to the enigma of the man, but also to partisan memories and to some mysterious attraction that caused men in every generation to interpolate Jefferson in their living worlds. It was Jefferson's lot, his first important biographer wrote, "to be at once more loved and praised by his friends, and more hated and reviled by his adversaries, than any of his compatriots." The ambivalence continued far into the future.

The dominant recognition of Jefferson in the encomium of 1826 was as the Apostle of Liberty. "The life of Jefferson," Nicholas Biddle said in a masterful eulogy before the American Philosophical Society, where the president's chair Jefferson had once occupied was draped in black, "was a perpetual devotion, not to his own purposes, but to the pure and noble cause of public freedom," "which shed its hues over all the studies and actions of his life." None of the eulogists, not even Biddle, took the full measure of his "impassioned devotion to freedom." They tended to focus instead its apex, the Declaration of Independence. Webster, for instance, gave one-third of his oration to this immortal moment of Jefferson's life.

Liberty was the quintessence; but liberty in what sense? If the

eulogies are read with an eye to their theoretical purport, they associated Jefferson with two contrasting, some may say contradictory,
types of political liberty. One derived from the English legal heritage: the Whiggish liberty of individual rights. The other partook
strongly of American and French revolutionary ideology: the democratic liberty of popular rule. Was Jefferson the conservative guardian of the law or the flaming prophet of democracy? The eulogists
gave no clear-cut answer to the question. Nor was one requisite,
since it was, after all, the fundamental question, the irresoluble
ambiguity, in the American polity. Jefferson could be imaged in
either way. He embodied the ambiguity. Repeatedly in his posthumous history he was to be caught up in the dilemma of a nation
committed both to a system of constituted rights and to the sovereignty of the people. While one eulogist in 1826 defined the fundamental premise of Jefferson's politics as "the people could do no
wrong," another viewed him as the model Whig, whose respect for
the law and whose aristocratic pride of self enabled him to resist
the fatal tendency of republican rulers to degenerate into "the slaves
and victims of that mysterious fascination, the love of popularity."
The two views often occurred in one and the same encomium: at
one moment Jefferson is ready "to hazard all for liberty," at the next
moment his passion is "curbed by practical wisdom." John Tyler
named Jefferson "a mighty reformer." "He was born to overturn
systems and pull down establishments." The legend of Jefferson's revolutionary overturn in Virginia was already rooted in the mind.
Tyler not only attributed to Jefferson the abolition of entail and
primogeniture, but also said that it had accompished the destruction
of the Virginia aristocracy and the virtual equalization of landed
property.

Another legend, "the revolution of 1800," posed the problem of
defining Jefferson's true political character. The traditional Republican view, mildly restated in 1826, was consistent with the reformer
image: Jefferson overturned the Federalist system and erected his
own democratic system in the central government. William A. Duer
of Federalist lineage, on the other hand, found the key to Jefferson's
Presidency in the fact that "notwithstanding the warfare between
the parties had seemed to threaten the peace of the nation, no violent

change of measures or of system followed" the Republican accession. About Jefferson's Presidency, the eulogists were not very articulate. The Louisiana Purchase assured its fame; but the veil of the past had not yet fallen over it. Alternately interpreted in moderate and in radical terms, it revealed Jefferson's capacity to appeal to men of diverse political temperaments and persuasions. As his devotion to liberty could not be comprehended in either the Whig or the democratic frame of reference, neither did his administration lend itself to strictly partisan interpretation.

Although the unity motif checked the natural tendency to contrast Jefferson and Adams, several of the eulogists intimated the historical issue between them, and in doing so heightened the democratic tones of the Jefferson image. Adams was Roman, Jefferson was Grecian; Adams was practical, Jefferson was theoretical; Adams was a Whig of the old school, Jefferson belonged to the modern liberal school; Adams's politics were essentially English, Jefferson's French; Adams wished to restrain the popular will, Jefferson to ensure its supremacy. Adams believed in institutions. Jefferson believed in man. Altogether, the contrast suggested that Jefferson's greatness lay not so much in work done as in ideas advanced.

And yet, as everyone knew, it was the idealist Jefferson, not Adams, who had succeeded in America. His startling theories were embodied in institutions and received as truths by posterity. Was there something about America which armed the prophet and dismissed the mere preceptor of history? Or perhaps Jefferson was actually a hard-headed and practical man of affairs. He possessed, one eulogist said, "all the elements which unite to compose a beautiful system-maker and imposing theorist," but, he quickly added, none of these influenced Jefferson's politics. "He would admit of no innovating speculations into the business of government. He was, if any man was, a practical man. He at all times built, as the wise of all the ages had done, on history and experience." How he had managed to operate on *both* mental tracks without apparent collision, and upon which track posterity ought to ride, were puzzling questions. In Biddle's astute analysis the two tracks converged. It was Jefferson's peculiar genius "to unite the retired love of science with the practical energy of the world," and thus to deserve "that most illustrious of all names

—a philosophical statesman." It would take generations of study and controversy to test and balance the eulogists' varying estimates of Jefferson's genius, and even then the enigma remained.

A public apotheosis of Jefferson permitted no impious reflections. Did the eulogists really believe, as some of them said, that Jefferson, the revered Sage of Monticello for seventeen years after his retirement, had outlived all the hatred and calumnies of his enemies? Had the governor of Virginia outlived the accusation of pusillanimous weakness in the crisis of Benedict Arnold's invasion? Was the party leader invulnerable to the hereditary hatred of New England's Federalist sons? Was the "infidel" safe from the cant of Christians? The eulogists either ignored or passed lightly over the vexed memories from which death itself offered no escape. Between the Apostle of Liberty who gave voice to the American political ideal in 1776 and the admirable Sage of Monticello, Jefferson was entangled in a web of history that was proof against the apotheosis.

In their mourning Americans were exalted. "The grief that such a man is dead," as Nicholas Biddle said, "may be well assuaged by the proud consolation that such a man has lived." The coincidence of the Jubilee dramatized the meaning of American history, refreshed memory and hope, and renewed the sense of participation in the fabled adventure. The death of Jefferson and his compatriot consecrated the ideal of 1776 and fixed it as the unifying theme.

But the hope that the consecration would issue in a new canon of patriotic sensibility was not to be realized. Fifty years later, on the Centennial of American Independence, a distinguished elder citizen of Massachusetts dredged up his memories of the first Jubilee and complained that this "most striking, most impressive, most memorable coincidence in American history, or even in the authentic records of mankind, is without a visible monument anywhere." However, not even the late reunion of Massachusetts and Virginia furnished the incentive to commemorate in bronze or stone an event emptied of significance, except as irony, in the conflict of the intervening fifty years.

More an apotheosis of ideals than of persons, the Jubilee nevertheless seemed to open the portals of Olympus to Jefferson. (Not to Adams: Americans too readily concurred in the old Federalist's own judgment that "Mausoleums, statues, monuments will never be erected to me . . . nor flattering orations spoken to transmit me to posterity in brilliant colors.") Jefferson, it was thought, would command an influence over posterity surpassed only by Washington. As Washington was the symbol of nationality, so Jefferson would be the symbol of republican liberty. The difficulty, however, was at once suggested by the inability of the eulogists to prefigure a simple and coherent image of Jefferson. He remained an enigma, a figure of contradiction, a man of many faces. Unlike Washington— the savior by the sword, the godlike being, exalted in life as in death —Jefferson assailed the conventions of heroism. His triumph was of the mind. His character was not crystalline. He was a man of phrases, doctrines, and causes. And, most important, the ideas and ideals he exemplified could not be enshrined on Olympus. They addressed the future; they were bound into the living tissues of a growing democracy; they bred contention and strife. As history extended his life far into the future, Jefferson was fated to endure these struggles and agonies.

Monuments, the eulogists said, were superfluous to his fame. The sentiment reverberated down the years, but in the presence of Jefferson's death many Americans wished for some permanent memorial of gratitude and remembrance. One proposed the erection of a statue from the subscription fund (now erroneously thought unnecessary to save the estate); another called upon Congress to purchase Monticello as both a shrine and a summer executive mansion; still another wanted a vast government edition of Jefferson's writings so that his thought might be "diffused throughout the land for the enlightenment of new generations." Nothing materialized. In Virginia the *Richmond Enquirer* found little support for its plan to raise a statue to accompany that of Washington in the state Capitol.

The federal government showed no more interest than Jefferson's state. Edward Everett of Massachusetts failed in his efforts to induce Congress to purchase a valuable bust, later destroyed by fire, and other priceless relics from Jefferson's estate. Several years later, in 1834, Lieutenant Uriah P. Levy, who had recently acquired Monticello, made a gift to Congress of a bronze statue by David d'Angers.

Congress, after some haggling, spurned the gift. Congressmen questioned the propriety of accepting it, argued that a monument to Washington must take precedence, and simply did not like the statue. "By God," a Southerner swore, "it makes old Tom a negro!"

Monticello, the great love of Jefferson's life, was lost to his heirs forever. Frustrated in their efforts to save Monticello, Jefferson's friends turned instead to the fulfillment of his last wish that Martha, his only living child, be cared for. "I resign myself to my God, and my child to my country" were his reported last words. Congress declined relief on general principle, an action some believed to justify the common reproach of "the notorious ingratitude of republics." However, the generosity of two states, South Carolina and Louisiana, went far toward accomplishing the object. In Washington, where she lived most of her remaining years, Mrs. Randolph was a leading lady of official society. "Her father's image," an intimate wrote, "is seldom absent from her mind."

Monticello passed into the hands of a Charlottesville citizen in 1831, then from him to Lieutenant Levy. Only the burial ground, with a monument made to Jefferson's own design, was retained by the family. "All is dilapidation and ruin," wrote a visitor one year later; and this was the common report for many decades. One eulogist had looked forward to the day when Monticello would be a consecrated spot, where "the advocates of the rights of man, from all quarters of the globe will perform a pilgrimage, like the Jews to their holy city." So it had been, and so in a sense it would become, but only after a century.

If, as has been said, "It is the quality of great men that they continue to live long after they are gone," Jefferson was pre-eminently great. More than any other American, he impressed himself on the nation's future. His apotheosis in consociation with Adams summed up an epoch; but Jefferson—his ideas and ideals, his prophesies and legacies—was also engaged in the great campaigns of history to come. The successive generations of American experience testified, "Thomas Jefferson still survives." And thus he could not be finished off in eulogy or enclosed in a pantheon. Events soon proved the apotheosis of 1826 was premature.

BOOK ONE

One

RESURRECTION

What principle in the political ethics of our country might not be sanctioned AND refuted by the writings of Mr. Jefferson? *

AMERICAN POLITICS were in turmoil when Jefferson died. In the decade since the Peace of Ghent, the Federalist party had faded away and the Republican order Jefferson had founded drew into itself most of the men and many of the principles of its once hated adversary. The young Republican leaders, who rose to leadership in the late war and who set the political tone during the administration of President Monroe, attempted to fashion nationalistic solutions for the new problems which the return of peace and reaction abroad and unparalleled expansion at home forced upon the United States. The general name given to their program was "the American System." Infused with the political "good feelings" of the Monroe era, the system contemplated American withdrawal from the Old World— no longer believed capable of nurturing either the material prosperity or the political ideals of the New—and the planned development of the nation's internal resources under the fostering hand of the federal government. The Monroe Doctrine, of which Jefferson was one of the architects, fixed the strategy in American foreign policy. In domestic affairs the National Republicans advocated a national bank to manage the country's finances, protective tariffs to encourage its manufactures, a vast transportation network to effect a "home market" both for eastern manufactures and for the agricultural surplus no longer wanted abroad, a revenue-producing public lands

* *Niles' Register,* April 7, 1832.

policy, and support of the arts and sciences. The program was partially enacted; but in the process it revived old fears of the national authority, fomented sectional discord, and split the Republican party. The political storm engulfed Monroe's successor, John Quincy Adams.

The younger Adams, who had abandoned the die-hard Federalists in 1808 and then risen to leadership under the Virginia presidents, exemplified the career of party amalgamation—"all federalists, all republicans"—foretold by Jefferson in 1801. Keying his administration to the national spirit, Adams warmly applauded the break-up of parties. Events foreign to the United States, he said in his Inaugural Address, had been the principal source of party division. After the Peace of Ghent, "this baneful weed of party strife was uprooted," and no new division of principle had arisen. Adams wished to institutionalize the "good feelings" of his predecessor, to unite all sections and factions in a common program of national betterment. He dwelt at length on the subject in his First Message to Congress in 1825. The great object of civil government, he declared, is "the improvement of those who are parties to the social compact." The failure of the federal government to exercise its powers in their fullness was a sin in the eyes of God and treachery to the people themselves. He proposed, therefore, to extend the American System to objects of moral and intellectual improvement, urging appropriations for a national university, a naval academy, scientific surveys, and astronomical observatories—"lighthouses of the skies." In these matters America lagged dangerously behind the Old World. The Constitution presented no obstacle; and, as for the people, let us not, Adams said, "be palsied by the will of our constituents."

The Adams message threw the Sage of Monticello back to the Federalist decade. These new Republicans, Jefferson confided to an old friend, "having nothing in them of the feelings and principles of '76, now look back to a single and splendid government of an aristocracy, founded on banking institutions, moneyed incorporations under the guise and cloak of their favored branches of manufacture, commerce and navigation, riding and ruling over the plundered plowman and beggared yeomanry." Ravaged by debt, stirred by the Missouri Compromise to doubt the perpetuation of the Union, dreading the effect of the American System on the reserved rights of the states, Jefferson was haunted by the specters of departed Federalism in his final years; and, as before, he counseled Virginia to ready its defenses. Adams said, "Liberty is power." Jefferson believed liberty is the jealous restraint of power. He had stated the fundamental imperative, moral and constitutional—"the sum of good government" —in his First Inaugural: "a wise and frugal government, which shall restrain men from injuring one another, which shall leave them otherwise free to regulate their own pursuits of industry and improvement, and shall not take from the mouth of labor the bread it has earned." He had not expected his appeal for harmony and union at that time, or his subsequent deviations from principle under the stress of circumstance, would end in the resurrection of Federalism under a second Adams.

The opposition to Adams and the National Republicans coalesced around Andrew Jackson. One of the prizes in the critical election of 1828 was the title to the republican tradition; and thus Jefferson, its author, was involved. Jacksonian Democracy won the prize, although the opposition party never ceased to contest the result. The Jackson movement attempted to knit together the two major commitments of the Jeffersonian political tradition, Democracy and State Rights. But this was awkward, since they represented the most characteristic American form of the dilemma of popular sovereignty and constituted rights which the eulogists had stumbled upon in the apotheosis of 1826. Coincident with Jackson's first administration, events in Virginia, the native ground of Jeffersonianism, sundered Democracy and State Rights. At the same time South Carolina pushed the latter to the heresy of nullification.

Within this shaping pattern of politics, *The Memoirs, Correspondence and Private Papers of Thomas Jefferson* made their appearance in 1829. Here, in four stout volumes, the Apostle of Liberty told his story and expanded his faith. His name again "went ringing through the newspapers of the country," invoking idolatrous praise as before but now also bitter recrimination. "Jefferson's posthumous works were very generally circulated whilst I was in America," said the captious Mrs. Trollope. "They are a mighty mass of mischief." Under the imposing sanction of the late apotheosized patriot, the *Memoirs* renewed old party feelings and fanned "the embers of a fierce con-

flagration, whose ashes are not yet quenched." Their appearance at
any time would have aroused curiosity and controversy; the work
was a unique event in 1829 because of Jefferson's compelling relationship to the swirling currents of American politics.

1. The Election of 1828

Martin Van Buren, United States Senator from New York, made
the pilgrimage to Monticello less than two years before the master's
death. For several days, as the two men drove through the neighborhood in the mornings and retired to the library in the afternoons,
the young disciple drank at the fountain of Republican faith. Jefferson's political ardor was as strong as ever. "Standing upon the very
brink of the grave," Van Buren recalled, "and forever excluded from
any interest in the management of public concerns that was not
common to all his fellow citizens, he seemed never to tire in his
review of the past and in explanations of the grounds of his apprehension for the future, both obviously for my benefit." From the New
Yorker's earliest memory, Jefferson had been, and would always remain, his *beau ideal* of statesmanship. He came away from Monticello assured of the apostle's benediction.

It was Van Buren's conviction that the degeneration of government
from the Republican standard took its course from the "fusion policy"
introduced by Monroe and supposed by Adams to have permanently
obliterated party distinctions. Adams did not believe in parties; they
were, as his hero Washington had thought, mischievous factions, the
bane and curse of the republic. Van Buren, on the other hand, believed parties were inseparable from free government and beneficial
to its progress. The "cant against parties," Van Buren thought, ema-
nated from a small minority, the privileged money class, who were
already consolidated by a common material interest and who, therefore, did not have the same need as the common people for party
organization. Parties were not mortal. They might change their
causes, go underground in a dry season, take a new name; but, Van
Buren said, "the cohesive influences and innate qualities which originally united them remain with the mass and spring up in their
former vigour with the return of propitious skies." This was true,
fundamentally, for the reason Jefferson had assigned: nature divided

men into Tories and Whigs, into those who always sought to concentrate power in the few and those who always sought to diffuse it among the many.

The New York Senator restated the old theory and applied it to the American situation in the course of a lengthy speech in 1828. The party warfare of the Federalist decade fixed the enduring form of the American political conflict. Hamilton (John Adams, others said) and Jefferson were the archetypal antagonists, whose opposite principles were the Monarchical and the Democratical. *"The former,"* Van Buren emphasized, *"has grown out of a deep and settled distrust of the people and of the states. . . . The antagonist principle has its origin in the jealousy of power, justified by all human experience."* The Federalist-Republican division was all-inclusive, perpetual, and, indeed, necessary. But the delusion arose in the Era of Good Feelings that parties had outlived their usefulness. Principles were obscured, old landmarks ignored, the unity of the Republican party shattered. From this delusion the "ultra latitudinarian doctrines" of Adams's First Message awakened the mass of Republicans and led to the speedy reunion of the party. The circle back to 1800, the Senator concluded, would be closed by Jackson's election; for the same impulse of radical change operated now as then: "a settled conviction in the minds of the people, that a deliberate plan had been formed by the men . . . in power, to change the government, from its true republican form."

This conception of American political conflict molded the ideology* of the Jackson party. The quest for power by the motley Jacksonian coalition was clothed in the righteous garments of Jeffersonian Republicanism. The major issues of the Adams administration offered the congressional opposition numerous opportunities to plot the newborn party struggle on the master plan of history. The second Adams, like the first, grasped for powers which properly belonged to Congress. The Jacksonians raised the ghosts of monarchy. Adams was

---

* The term *ideology* is given to that synthesis of ideas and representations designed to state an ideal and to motivate action. It may be true in some of its parts; but it is a gross oversimplification both of history and of the existing situation, the true recognition of which would not be an accord with the feelings and interests of the men who advance the ideology.

a spendthrift. The Jacksonians recalled Jefferson's maxim, "Economy and liberty, or profusion and servitude." His measures of public improvement threatened the constitutional liberties of the citizens and the rights of the states. Let us return to "the days of the Republic's glory" was the constant cry. The issues were more artificial than real, the allegations were often absurd; but the resurrection of the past, the sentiment of return, the theory of a rooted native tradition of political conflict—this was basic and it endured.

The Jacksonian polemics in the campaign of 1828 ripened the sense of the past in the deepening party struggle. The idea of "the history of parties," most fully developed by Van Buren, was repeatedly stated. Typical was the convention address of the New Hampshire Jacksonians. Quotations from John Adams's *Defense of the Constitutions* and Jefferson's First Inaugural exhibited the rival theories. Defeated in 1801, the Federalists went underground, only to emerge again in the Republican disguise during Monroe's placid administration. The election of the second Adams returned to power the party that fell with the first.

The campaign fell to a level of smear and vilification unknown since 1800. The Jacksonians drew the parallel and deduced the lesson: 1828 was but the second round in the struggle between "the people" and "the crafty aristocracy." Pursuing the parallel of the two Adamses, the Jackson press encountered the young John Quincy's canards against Jefferson. In *Publicola* (1791) Adams had named Jefferson "the Islam of Democracy"; in satirical verses many years later he had "laughed at the party Lama." And so, as he noted in his diary, these verses were "dragged into light twenty years afterwards, for political effect against me." The verses ridiculed Jefferson's ideas and scientific pretensions, insinuated infidelity in religion and also miscegenation with his female slaves. There was no question of Adams's authorship of the main item attributed to him, *On the Discoveries of Captain Lewis*. Often reprinted after 1828, it was used by Democrats in their unending campaign to stigmatize all opposition as anti-Jeffersonian.

No party wished to be cast in the role of anathematized Federalism. The National Republicans spurned the odious ancestry and covered

themselves in Jefferson's mantle. While the Jacksonians accented
Jefferson's party leadership, the National Republicans emphasized
the reconciliation of men and principles which, they believed, he had
invited in his First Inaugural and gone a long way toward accomplishing in his Presidency. After the War of 1812, they said, Federalists abandoned their aristocratic creed and Republicans abandoned
state rights. Henry Clay, who had entered politics under the banner
of the Kentucky Resolutions in 1798, became the architect of the
American System not because he was any less Jeffersonian, his advocates said, but because new conditions called for the expansion of
the national policies that Jefferson himself had wisely embraced
in the Republican design. The doctrine of "implied powers" may
have originated with Hamilton and Marshall; but the Louisiana Purchase, by Jefferson's own admission, made the Constitution "a blank
paper by construction." In 1806 Jefferson proposed a great system
of internal improvements. The constitutional scruples that caused
him to recommend an amendment specifically delegating the power
to Congress, the National Republicans said, had been vacated in
recent years by statutory action. Even without an amendment, he
was responsible for the National Road, the government's most substantial and continuing improvements enterprise. The issue of policy
was, in the National Republican view, one of opinion rather than of
principle. Jefferson's counsels were divided: one man's Jeffersonian
meat was another man's Jeffersonian poison.

The National Republicans thus imaged Jefferson as an enlightened
nationalist. The "plain and simple" Republicans snorted and fumed
when Adams asked an appropriation for astronomical observatories,
with which the United States might survey its coasts, promote science, and return "light for light" to the Old World. But according to
Samuel Southard, Secretary of the Navy, the policy had originated
with President Jefferson in 1807. Addressing the Columbian Institute
in Washington, Southard declared that Jefferson "did more for the
cultivation of knowledge, than was ever accomplished in any age
of the world, under similar circumstances." The dream of an American "empire of science" was born, not with John Quincy Adams,
but with Thomas Jefferson. Here again, in Southard's address, was
the national theme of the apotheosis with its same minor accent on

scientific progress. Largely drowned out by Jacksonian Democracy, it nevertheless echoed faintly down the years. "*He* was none of your statesman," an editor wrote in 1840, "who consider it the duty of government to do nothing for the improvement of the country or for the advantage of the People." He was, rather, "an enlightened practical statesman."

As to the protective tariff, the advocates of the American System studiously cultivated the idea that Jefferson had repudiated his agrarian and free trade doctrines. The idea took its rise from Jefferson's letter to Benjamin Austin in 1816. The Napoleonic wars and the American conflict with Britain had encouraged the growth of domestic manufactures and proved the vulnerability of an agrarian republic such as he had envisioned, Jefferson wrote. "We must now place the manufacturer by the side of the agriculturist." He permitted Austin to publish the letter. It soon became well known as his definitive opinion. Clay quoted it in Congress; the publicists Mathew Carey and Hezekiah Niles repeatedly printed it; and Friedrich List, the German economist, expounded it in his influential *Outlines of American Political Economy* in 1827. In the view of the leading free trade writer, Condy Raguet, the widespread assumption of Jefferson's approval was one of the protectionists' strongest weapons. Orthodox Republicans still quoted the Arcadian passages from Jefferson's *Notes on Virginia,* as if nothing had happened since the eighteenth century to change his mind. The mystery of his true opinion deepened soon after his death. Numerous letters on the Austin model, all written at about the same time, found their way into the newspapers. But among the last scratchings of his pen, also published, was an attack on the protective tariff and its companion measures as unconstitutional, unjust, and "the surest stepping stones" to monarchy.

The riddle of the Sage of Monticello's true opinion of the protective tariff was never adequately solved. The unique opportunity of America, he had believed, was to build a society at once prosperous and free on the simple economies of nature. But nature failed him, and the War of 1812 was the result. He breached his agrarian principles in order to make room for "domestic manufactures." Whether he meant to embrace the spirit and substance of an industrial society or merely the household-handicraft-mill manufacturing complex of advanced agricultural societies was the question at the heart of his, and America's, dilemma. When the Panic of 1819 broke banks and infant industries, bringing misery to people across the land, Jefferson seemed to take back whatever concession to circumstance he had made. The American System, which its advocates justified because of the Panic, he came to think a curse. "The great desideratum in political economy is the same as in private pursuits," Henry Clay declared in the tariff debate of 1824, "that is, what is the best application of the aggregate industry of the nation, that can be made to produce the largest sum of national wealth." The proposition, with its intimations of the positive state, violated Jefferson's deepest republican instincts.

Turning the light on Jefferson's nationalistic and progressive side, the National Republicans propagated the idea that he had, as it were, joined his republican faith to Hamilton's system of political economy. While Jefferson's career after 1800 furnished abundant evidence to support this idea, it also gave abundant evidence that he had not fundamentally changed his agrarian outlook. America inherited, to borrow Joseph Dorfman's words, Jefferson's own "inner struggle with respect to the values of the simple life and the rich economy."

The difficulty that Jacksonians experienced in consorting with Jefferson's principles was equaled by the problem of tying their hero to Jefferson. Jefferson had opposed Jackson's candidacy in 1824. Had he changed his opinion before July Fourth 1826? Much effort was spent, much ink spilled, to prove he had or had not. Of course the question had no bearing on the election's outcome. But it may be taken as the single most important instance of a curious phenomenon in the Jackson period: the acute sensibility of political leaders to the value of Jefferson's benediction.*

---

* Henry Clay is another instance. Soon after he became Secretary of State, in line for the Presidency, words of disapproval leaked to him from Monticello. In 1826 Thomas Mann Randolph stated in a public letter that Jefferson (his father-in-law) had constantly expressed "strong repugnance" to Clay. Three years later, when Clay was about to begin his campaign to unseat Jackson, his zealous supporter, the editor S. S. Southworth in Providence, Rhode Island, published what purported to be a letter written by Jefferson in 1823 to laud Clay and his work. The general style of the letter, to say nothing of its opinions, led to sus-

One of the main efforts of the Adams press was to depict Jackson as a "mere military chieftain." This appeared to accord precisely with Jefferson's opinion. In 1827 former governor Edward Coles of Illinois told of a conversation he had had with Jefferson in August 1825. Next to Crawford, Jefferson had preferred Adams in the previous election. He feared the popular enthusiasm for Jackson. "Sir," he confessed to Coles, "it has caused me to doubt more than anything that has occurred since our Revolution." Coles solicited and published supporting testimony from Thomas Gilmer, a local friend of Jefferson and editor of the *Charlottesville Advocate*. Prior to the election of 1824 Jefferson had exploded to Gilmer: "One might as well make a sailor of a cock, or a soldier of a goose, as a President of Andrew Jackson." Daniel Webster, who had visited Monticello at this time, made the same report.

The Jacksonians would not be outdone. Gilmer accused Coles of misrepresentation, for Jefferson's opinion underwent a radical change in 1825, he said. Thomas Mann Randolph publicly stated that Jefferson became friendly to Jackson's candidacy as early as July or August 1825, perhaps because of the "corrupt bargain" charge against Adams and Clay. Jefferson then saw in Jackson "the only hope left" of reversing the movement of consolidation. According to Randolph, he thought Jackson "an honest, sincere, clear-headed and strong-minded man; of the soundest political principles." Others testified to the same effect, but Randolph spoke as a former governor and Jefferson's son-in-law. Nevertheless, it was impossible for devoted friends such as Coles to believe that the pacific and enlightened Sage of

---

picions of a hoax. Southworth would not let Democratic editors see the alleged manuscript. Thomas Ritchie of the *Richmond Enquirer* reported that a check of Jefferson's files (presumably by one of the Randolph family) disclosed no trace of this letter. Ritchie nailed it an "unprincipled forgery." He raised such a fuss when he discovered it was being widely quoted by the National Republicans that he forced Clay to disclaim the "Southworth forgery." Clay, on his own, managed to obtain a confidential statement from Thomas Jefferson Randolph, a grandson and executor of the estate, testifying to Jefferson's esteem for him. "I am not insensible of the value of the good opinion of his [Randolph's] grandfather," Clay wrote to a Virginia associate. Randolph would not permit publication of his statement, since it contradicted the well-known testimony of his father, Thomas Mann Randolph. Clay apparently abandoned his efforts along this line; but the "Southworth forgery" was constantly turning up in the press.

Monticello had actually embraced the new popular hero. Although there was no way to establish Jefferson's true opinion, so important did it seem that men begged his grandson, Thomas Jefferson Randolph, to dig into his papers for that purpose.

As early as September 1827, William B. Giles concluded it was time to let Jefferson speak for himself. He released to the *Richmond Enquirer* Jefferson's boldest attack on the administration, written in hot reaction to the First Message. Here was Jefferson's definitive opinion, Giles insisted; and it showed that "his deepest affliction . . . was not produced by his *terrific alarms* at 'the election of a military chieftain' to the presidency, but by . . . the unprincipled usurpations of the practical government." This letter of December 26, 1825 to Giles was one of the most influential Jefferson ever wrote. Denouncing the central government's encroachments on the states, he advocated vigorous protest against every usurpation "as a temporary yielding to a lesser evil, until their accumulation shall outweigh that of separation." The letter was a boon to Virginia state-rightists; Adams men found it unbelievable except as a mark of senility; Jacksonians generally read it as proof of their re-enactment of "the revolution of 1800."

Alas, even this was not Jefferson's true opinion, nor did it exhaust the political effect of the Giles maneuver. The next year an Adams follower in Charlottesville learned that among Jefferson's last letters was one generously praising Adams's course at the time of the Embargo in 1808 and giving assurances of his continued respect. It is perfectly clear why T. J. Randolph broke his usual rule and honored the request for a copy of this letter: it was addressed to Giles one day previous to the vindictive letter already published! Giles had stacked the cards against Adams. Randolph soon collected and published all the correspondence related to the episode. The first letter, it appeared, had been intended for the public eye; the second was confidential, though in publishing it Giles had deleted this injunction as well as references to the previous letter.

The deception was forgotten in the storm raised by Jefferson's recollection of Adams's role in the crisis of the Embargo. It presented Adams in the odious light of an apostate from his party, one who carried tales to Jefferson of a disunion conspiracy among his friends,

the Massachusetts Federalists. Suddenly, by the disclosure of a few
scratches from the aged Jefferson's pen, Adams was thrown on the
defensive in his native land. New Englanders were astounded. It
was said that for some time when Adams "walked the streets of
Boston . . . he was generally passed without being spoken to, even
by his former acquaintances." The Federalists believed he had traded
his honor, the honor of his friends and his state, for a place in the
Republican fold. The Jacksonians, meanwhile, enjoyed Adams's predicament, which they supposed stemmed from his calculated policy
to "get hold of the Republicans, but not to let go of the Federalists."
To the end of his life, Adams believed Jefferson was the real "double-
dealer"—Jefferson, whose policies incited the New England disunion
conspiracy; Jefferson, whose "treacherous and inventive memory"
alienated Adams from part of his New England following.

The disclosure of Jefferson's private correspondence in an affair
of honor, pride, and power was a foretaste of the *Memoirs* and had
the same effect on his reputation. The sublime figure of 1826 was
degraded. The two letters to Giles seemed irreconcilable. One was
written for publication, the other in confidence. One soothed, the
other agitated. Both inflamed the ashes of memory.

The election of 1828, momentous on so many accounts, fixed the
main line of descent from Republican orthodoxy and assured that
the Jefferson symbol would be a force to reckon with for years to
come. An adroitly managed coalition of aggrieved factions and
interests, the Jackson party obtained a degree of unity, motivation,
and justification through its Jeffersonian ideology. The impassioned
rhetoric and clashing symbols recalled from the founders' era evoked
the dramatic picture of a political world in which heroes and villains
still battled on fundamental principles.

According to the ideology the victory of 1828 was a restoration.
But the popular democracy the Jacksonians championed clashed with
the republican order they professed to cherish; the party's label in
1828, Democratic Republican, suggested its ambivalent posture. The
proof of Jackson's orthodoxy was to be his adherence to the principles
of Jefferson, as if these constituted a fixed and coherent code of government. The Jacksonians believed the victory of 1828 secured their

title to the Republican tradition. More significantly, however, it secured a convention of political sensibility, "the touchstone of Jefferson," which was available to anyone. Parties, it was said a quarter century after Jefferson's death, "do not take sides for or against him, but contend, like children, as to their legitimate descent from the 'apostle of democracy.'"

2. Jefferson's Memoirs

The publication of the *Memoirs* in 1829 opened to public view for the first time not only the history of Jefferson's character and opinions but also a revelation of the momentous era in which he was a principal actor. Whether regarded from a historical or a political standpoint, it was, as reviewers on both sides of the Atlantic attested, "one of the most important publications ever presented to the world." The work could not be judged in the cooler shades of historical understanding. Memories were too fresh, political passions too ardent. No sooner had it appeared than the leading Jackson organ in the West declared that the *Memoirs* "must emphatically become the text-book of republicanism." But the Library Company of Philadelphia refused to place the volumes on its shelves; and a New York editor found their impiety and radicalism so shocking that he warned his readers away from them. Few, if any, publications of the period had a greater impact or importance than Jefferson's *Memoirs*. Men of letters tasted it, politicians swallowed it, historians digested it—or tried to.

Jefferson left his papers to his executor, Thomas Jefferson Randolph, subject to his entire discretion and control. "The greatest of the Godsends which heaven has granted me," Jefferson had said of his eldest grandson. Randolph managed the estate during the old man's declining years, gradually paid off the huge debt, and saved for his family the Edgehill plantation. He, like his father Thomas Mann Randolph, was a man of consequence in Virginia: a rector of the University, a champion of liberal causes in the Virginia Assembly, a Confederate colonel in the War. Randolph's last public act, in 1872, was to preside over the national convention of the beaten party he believed, with most Americans, his grandfather had founded.

He loved to talk of Jefferson, and many sounded him out for stories and testimony. Showing a visitor around Monticello, he would burst out, "You have heard the miserable lies the dirty . . . political enemies have told of my grandfather, Mr. Jefferson. Let me tell you, no better, purer man ever lived." Until the end, he, with some of his children, lived in the shadow of Jefferson's memory and did what he could to care for it. He died in 1875 gazing up at Monticello, "whose graceful profile was ever clear and distinct in the purple light of the early dawn."

The *Memoirs,* the first collected edition of Jefferson's writings, was a family enterprise under Randolph's editorship. He at first planned to publish only Jefferson's brief Autobiography, which sketched his career to March 1790. This was ready for the press a few months after the Jubilee. A small volume appearing before the recent fervor abated might find a large audience and help pay the debts. Madison wrote to Lafayette, with appropriate emphasis, that "*discreet* extracts" from the manuscripts "may perhaps prove a further pecuniary resource, from time to time." However, on the advice given to his mother by Boston publishers and men of letters, Randolph decided instead to prepare a substantial life and letters in several volumes. The work did not appear until eighteen months after it was announced. Selection from the mass of Jefferson's papers proved "a very delicate task," and the transcription of the correspondence from indistinct press copies was arduous. Of the latter, Martha gave an affecting account to her son-in-law, Joseph Coolidge, in Boston:

The originals themselves are in many places so faded as to be almost entirely obliterated. For pages together the girls have to take advantage of the broad light of a noonday sun, frequently unable to read them but with the assistance of a looking glass applied to the back, where alone the impression shows. A few lines will sometimes cost as many days. This is not the state of the *whole,* but a very *considerable* portion. . . . We are, the girls and myself, very closely employed from 5 to 8 hours a day with them, after which they go through a second examination by the editor, whose trouble is much lessened by our *pioneering* the way before him.

Randolph, moreover, had a hard time making advantageous arrangements for publication. He had six thousand copies printed by a

Charlottesville press in 1829; these were subscribed within a single year. The rights were sold to a Boston publisher, whose edition of three thousand came out a few months later but was not so rapidly exhausted. The demand in New England, the publisher complained, was "small, very small." A New York and a London edition appeared in 1830; one in Paris came three years later.

Several critics of the work were inclined to blame Jefferson for its explosive contents; but seven years later George Tucker, Jefferson's first major biographer, stated with authority that Randolph was alone responsible. Tucker, and probably Madison too, thought the editor showed a want of caution, owing to an exaggerated appreciation of the claims of the public and a naïve view of his grandfather's reputation. Jefferson left no instructions regarding publication of his papers. He had, however, more than once said his biography should be written from the private record of his life, and the care he bestowed on his papers expressed the wish that they might some day be ushered before the world. Short of wanton mutilation and distortion, no editor of the papers could have steered Jefferson's reputation into a safe harbor. Randolph certainly received assistance from Madison, from another grandson, Nicholas P. Trist, and perhaps from a few other Albemarle friends of the Sage. The story circulated in Virginia that Madison revised and censored the entire work, but no evidence supports it.

Comprising the edition were over three volumes of letters, the Autobiography, most of the Anas, and selected state papers. Randolph's editing was far short of present-day standards, but it was superior to Jared Sparks's editing of Washington and, in most respects, to the later Congress Edition of Jefferson. There were numerous errors (many of them repeated by subsequent editors), the serious ones most often caused by that pious exercise of caution critics generally missed. Randolph seemed particularly anxious not to offend John Marshall, who was the only living personage Jefferson may be said to have genuinely hated. He struck from the Anas the heated criticism of Marshall's *Life of George Washington*. In the correspondence, he deleted the Chief Justice's name from such phrases as "X.Y.Z. dish cooked up by Marshall" and "the visits of the Apostle Marshall to Kentucky." Randolph also drew the curtain over the tawdry James

Callender affair. None of the incriminating missives to this cheap libeler during "the terror of '98" were printed; and the editor struck from another letter Jefferson's instructions to an agent in Richmond to draw fifty dollars on his account in payment of Callender.

Several criticized the work for its apparently over-scrupulous selectivity. For the crucial years 1791 to 1794, the letters were entirely of an official or semi-official nature. For an even longer span of time, no letters to Madison appeared; and yet, as John Quincy Adams acutely observed, the alliance established between the two Virginians in this period was a turning point in American history. Charles Carter Lee, a champion Jefferson-hater, said that although the six months prior to the legislative session of 1798 were "epochal in Virginia Jeffersonianism," Randolph had found only six letters that would bear the light of day. Other readers were on sounder ground in charging the editor with the suppression of sentiments hostile to Washington and Adams. The notorious Mazzei letter, of course, could not be omitted. Jefferson's reputation for honor and loyalty would not soon recover from this poisonous missile of 1796—a sensation when it appeared—aimed at Washington and his administration.

The *Memoirs*, like Tucker's *Life of Jefferson,* so largely based upon it, was an exceedingly impersonal work. Nearly all the materials related to Jefferson's public career. The fascinating records of his domestic life at Monticello, along with travel accounts and scientific memoranda, Randolph either had not discovered or thought comparatively unimportant. The common Jefferson image was grave and austere, a political entity, and the *Memoirs* tended to strengthen this partial view. His politics, a writer observed many years later, "has so occupied the attention of his countrymen as to leave them little familiarity with his personal habits and history." Not until the arrival in 1858 of Henry S. Randall's colorful full-length biography did the portrait begin to be filled out.

"Have you seen Mr. Jefferson's *Works?*" Joseph Story asked a fellow judge.

If not, sit down at once and read his fourth volume. It is the most precious melange of all sorts of scandals you ever read. It will elevate your opinion of his talents, but lower him in point of principle and morals not a little.

His attacks on Christianity are *a la mode de Voltaire*. . . . Few public men have escaped his reproof; but the Federalists are dealt with in terms of unmeasured harshness.

Story was particularly agitated by the Anas, a collection of anecdote, gossip, and miscellaneous reflections on the men and politics of the Federalist period. The Autobiography was, with minor exceptions, non-controversial. Many of the letters caused complaint; some of them Jefferson had not trusted to the post when they were written. But the Anas aroused bitter controversy. For the Jacksonians it was a feast: the Federalists were served up as corrupt monarchists! For men in the Federalist lineage, and moderates generally, it seemed "truly a matter of wonder, astonishment and grief" that Jefferson had preserved, "calmly revised" in 1818, as he said, and finally sent forth to posterity this hodgepodge of gossip and slander, much of it emanating from the busybodies of the early republic whom Jefferson himself had distrusted. One diligent censor counted in the Anas serious charges against thirty-one persons in sixty-eight instances, seventeen against Alexander Hamilton alone.

Although the Anas did poor service to Jefferson's memory for a century to come, nothing was so obviously intended for publication. In the explanation he wrote for the finished collection in 1818, Jefferson said he would not have thought the old notes worth preserving "but for their testimony against the only history of the period which pretends to have been compiled from authentic and unpublished documents." This was Jefferson's testimony against Marshall's *Life of Washington*, "the five volumed libel," and especially against the fifth volume, still in 1829 the standard history of Washington's administration. Jefferson sought to prove that the Republicans were not simply "grumblers and disorganizers," but advocates of republican against kingly government. The party conflict manifested a fundamental disagreement on the *form* of the new government. The prevalence of monarchical sympathies among the Federalists, the evidence of privilege and hints of corruption, as documented in the Anas, gave credence to the Republican belief that the Hamiltonian measures and practices slowly spun a web of government indistinguishable from the English model.

The connection Jefferson made between a strong national government, fashioned by economic privilege, and anti-republicanism was
one of his most important legacies to politics. He condemned the
Federalists less because they were privileged capitalists than because
they were corrupt monarchists. In the continuing political struggle
between big capitalists and small, the stigmata of "monarchy" and
"aristocracy" were to hurt the former, just as the Jeffersonian rhetoric
of "cherish the people" was to help the latter. This ideological polar-
ity made the issue of more than economic consequence.

One of the ways the Anas rekindled partisan feelings was exhibited
in the vindication of the Delaware Federalist, James A. Bayard. The
Anas noted the word of Edward Livingston in February 1801, at the
height of the Presidential contest in Congress, that Bayard had offered
high office to Livingston and General Samuel Smith if they would
swing their votes to Jefferson's Republican rival, Aaron Burr. John M.
Clayton, of Delaware, brought this matter before the Senate in 1830.
Both Livingston and Smith were then in the Senate. Clayton asked
for their testimony. Neither had any recollection of a proposition from
Bayard. The inference was plain: Jefferson's solemn statement was a
falsehood. Thomas Hart Benton, who sprinkled Jefferson's holy water
on every issue from slavery to salt, denounced Clayton for smearing
the venerable name. The Delaware Senator replied that, although
"there were other charges in that volume equally unfounded," he
wished not to tarnish Jefferson's fame but to vindicate Bayard's.
James Madison came to Jefferson's defense in a letter to the *National
Gazette* of Philadelphia. Bayard's two sons zealously prosecuted the
case for years to come. Accumulating new evidence, they branded
the tale "an idle slander," and then turned on the accuser by reviving
the elder Bayard's charge that it was really Jefferson who had bargained with him to obtain the Presidency. The political conduct of
1801, thus re-examined thirty years later, was debated off and on
for the next several decades. It had another airing in the Senate in
1855, at the instigation of the younger James A. Bayard. Historians
never ceased wondering about it.

The defense of historic personages ranged from the luminaries—
Washington, Hamilton, Marshall—to such lesser lights as William
Hooper of North Carolina and General Henry Lee of Virginia. It

even included Aaron Burr, who, it was said, in the blackness of his
villainy was better than the Sage of Monticello—and much more
romantic! On Jefferson's account, the Revolutionary Heroes and
Founding Fathers were not the pure and distinterested patriots of
the mythic mind. For that reason alone, a conservative historian
wrote, Jefferson's tales should not be trusted. If the Fathers of the
Constitution were as Jefferson depicted them, another said, "he casts
a deep and discouraging shade on the hopes of mankind, that there
is honor, intelligence, and virtue enough in the world 'to assert and
maintain the rights of rational self-government."

The guardians of the law were more alarmed than before by
Jefferson's "loose and visionary" ideas. The letters amply proved
Jefferson's hostility to the independent judiciary, to the augmented
power of the Supreme Court, to judicial assumption of rules from
the English common law. Several dispatches to George Hay, chief
prosecutor in the treason trial of Aaron Burr, showed the President's
passionate dedicaticn to obtaining either Burr's head or Judge Marshall's bench. One of the interesting features of Justice Story's *Commentaries on the Constitution*, in 1833, was the running criticism of
constitutional doctrines set forth in the *Memoirs*. Marshall applauded this corrective of wayward opinions, though he had no
doubt that Story would be "stung in requital for . . . [his] skill and
industry."

In the political arena, the *Memoirs* became "the canon," "the Koran,"
"the textbook," "the Bible," "the touchstone," to which men turned as
they competed for the favors of the Jefferson symbol. Jefferson's utterances in private letters were quoted with the utmost alacrity, as if
they merited the same deference as the First Inaugural Address. Because of some strange power, his name did not cease to attract even
when its sanctions were irrelevant or confused. If some, like the editor
Hezekiah Niles, wished that the entire edition of Jefferson's writings,
plus every scrap left over, might be committed to the flames, most
men in politics regarded the *Memoirs* as a valuable legacy to
American government.

The work had a substantial, but very different, influence on historical literature. It made new claims for Jefferson's fame which, as in
the instance of his agency in drafting the memorable Declaration of

the Causes of Taking Up Arms in 1775, heretofore ascribed to John Dickinson, could not be graciously honored. It furnished the basis of Jefferson biography for the next twenty-five years. More widely read than Tucker's distinguished work was the compact *Life of Thomas Jefferson* by B. L. Rayner in 1834. Believing that the progress of free government required "an extensive dissemination" of Jefferson's writings, Rayner condensed the four volumes and interwove the selections with a biographical narrative. But the Randolph Edition was more prolific of anti-Jefferson volumes, being directly responsible for Matthew Davis's *Memoirs of Aaron Burr* in 1836, and a factor in the writing of innumerable books and essays. History in this period was largely patristic and pietistic. Authors were commemorating founders, fathers and friends, parties, states and sections; and in these matters there was no end to the refutation of Jefferson's "errors" and "slanders." Randolph's labor probably encouraged the publication of the writings or recollections of other eminent men. The works of Washington, Adams, and Hamilton followed, as did the memoirs of Story, Jay, and Wolcott. All were Federalists. The Jeffersonians got a poor show on the historical page. For the next century it seemed to many of them that the Federalists, defeated everywhere else, had retreated to the books, and there triumphed.

3. *Virginia: State Rights, Democracy, and Slavery*

The Senator from South Carolina, Robert Y. Hayne, loved to quote Jefferson, whose words came "in the garb of wisdom, invested with authority." Hayne introduced the *Memoirs* on the floor of Congress in January 1830, quarrying from the volumes the materials of his attack on New England Federalism and his defense of the doctrine of nullification recently advanced in his state. Let not the stone of "disunionism" be cast at the Southern states! Its true history, Hayne said, was documented by Jefferson in four chapters: first, the Federalist financial system; second, the conspiracy under the Embargo; third, the Hartford Convention; fourth, the American System consolidation. The protective tariff, by putting the burden of taxation on the Southern states and creating revenue for further expansions of power, called once again for the Jeffersonian remedy of nullification to save the Union. The alternatives were, as Jefferson had advised

Giles six months before his death, submission to unlimited government or resistance with separation the ultimate recourse. Hayne
read long passages from the Virginia and Kentucky Resolutions. They
represented "the most fixed and settled convictions" of Jefferson's
mind. South Carolina simply followed in his footsteps. "I should
think," Hayne concluded, "it would require more self-respect than
any gentleman here would be willing to assume, to treat lightly
doctrines derived from such high sources."

Hayne's powerful antagonist, Daniel Webster, did not defend Old
Federalism, but he gave eloquent statement to the national theory of
the Constitution. A generation of schoolboys in the North declaimed
his peroration—"liberty *and* Union, now and forever, one and inseparable!"—while in the South the state rights "doctrines of '98" held
equal sway. This most famous congressional debate dramatized the
long conflict on the Constitution that finally erupted in civil war.

By some process of division the Apostle of Liberty became, in the
generation after his death, the Father of Democracy and the Father
of State Rights. As the hostility between Democracy and State Rights
was uncovered in Jefferson's politics, he stood incongruously at the
head of two traditions which seemed to have less and less in common.
"How was it possible," the historian Richard Hildreth asked in 1852,
"to reconcile with the democratic theory of the sovereign power of
numerical majorities that doctrine of state rights of which ... Jefferson was the especial champion?" The dilemma forced itself upon
American consciousness chiefly because it impaled the very practical
question of Negro slavery. How the dilemma took shape, and with
what forebodings for Jefferson's reputation, may be best approached
through Virginia, where with two decisive strokes between 1829 and
1832 State Rights and Democracy were split asunder.

The movement to revive the Old Republican doctrines of '98 and
to rehabilitate Jefferson as the hero of state rights began in Virginia
around 1819. Jefferson himself, in reaction against the American
System, seemed to encourage it. It made vast strides after 1826 because the doctrines consorted with powerful interests in the South
and attained the emotional power of a political religion.

With one or two exceptions the key men in the Virginia revival of state rights were veteran Republicans of '98. John Randolph, whose political career began in that critical year, strutted and fumed in Congress. Jefferson's Louisiana Purchase and other national acts had, in Randolph's estimate, fastened a Nessus shirt on the triumphant Republicanism of 1800, but there was still a chance Hercules might live. Judge Spencer Roane, in decisions from the state's supreme bench, battled Marshall and the Supreme Court. Roane attacked the Court's Hamiltonian decisions, such as *McCulloch* v. *Maryland;* but his main aim was to break the federal judiciary's dominion over state court decisions involving the United States Constitution. His writings, if not instigated and counseled by "the great Lama of the mountain" as Marshall insisted, were nevertheless cheered from Monticello. "No man ranks before Tom Jefferson in my house!" Roane exclaimed from his deathbed. A third figure, the planter-philosopher John Taylor, kept the flame burning throughout the national period. Although there was no more doctrinaire state-rightist than Taylor, his contentious tomes had a libertarian spirit that widened his circle of influence. He brought under attack every advance of consolidation. The movement promised, in his sardonic judgment, "to reach the whole intercourse among men and even include the connubial." Jefferson pronounced Taylor's writings orthodox, but would not permit publication of his endorsement. Another leader, William B. Giles, it will be recalled, was the recipient of Jefferson's epistolary outburst against Adams in December 1825. Drawing upon the authority of that letter, Giles led the successful fight in the Virginia House of Delegates for resolutions against the constitutionality of the tariff and internal improvements.

Roane and Taylor preceded their mentor to the grave, Randolph was merely eccentric, and Giles had no influence beyond Virginia. But Thomas Ritchie, editor of the *Richmond Enquirer,* preached the doctrines in the South's most influential newspaper for the next two decades and lived to see them installed in the platform of the nation's dominant party. The wife of an Alabama senator later recalled that in her childhood she had been religiously taught three lessons: "To be proud alike of my name and blood and section; to read my Bible; and last, to know my *Richmond Enquirer.*" Democrats deferred to the *Enquirer* as if they believed its editor was the embodied spirit of Jeffersonian Republicanism. The newspaper began as a party organ in 1804 and, despite opposition charges to the contrary, had Jefferson's uninterrupted blessing. Ritchie claimed credit for the recovery, after twenty years in limbo, of the sacred texts of state rights: the Virginia and Kentucky Resolutions of 1798-99. In 1821 he broke one of the best kept secrets of American politics: Jefferson's authorship of the Kentucky Resolutions. Five years later, Ritchie published the first of many new editions of the combined texts. Politicians soon became as well versed in "The Book of State Rights" as in the Constitution itself.

By 1833 John Marshall felt an alien in his own state. "The word 'State Rights,' as expounded in the resolutions of '98 and the report of '99," he wrote, "has charm against which all reasoning is vain. These resolutions and that report constitute the creed of every politician, who hopes to rise in Virginia; and to question them ... is deemed political sacrilege." From Virginia the charm radiated through the South. According to a circuit-riding lawyer in the brawling Lower South of the eighteen-thirties, Virginians and men who mimicked Virginia opinion resolved every question into a question of the Constitution, resolved that into the "doctrines of '98," and spiced their arguments with allusions to "black cockades, blue lights, Essex Juntos, the Reign of Terror, and some other mystic entities." Nor were Jacksonian Democrats of the North and West immune to the Resolutions' charm. Identification of state rights with Jefferson helped to make the doctrines of '98 irresistible to a wide variety of politicians.

The state rights symbol first clearly confronted its democratic opposite in the Virginia Constitutional Convention of 1829-30. The Constitution of 1776 had never been to Jefferson's liking. A few months after its adoption, he entered the Assembly and attempted to achieve by legislation the reforms he had proposed to effect at one stroke through a revolutionary constitution. His persistent efforts met with some success, most notably in the Statute of Religious Freedom. Still not satisfied, he attacked the unrepublican features of the Constitution in the *Notes on Virginia* in 1785, urging then and again a decade later a thorough-going revision. But no strong movement for reform arose until 1816. It arose in the two western sections

of the state, the Valley and the Transmontane, which had a long
history of opposition to the dominant power of the Tidewater and
Piedmont. The people of the west advocated more state banking,
the protective tariff, and internal improvements; but existing constitutional arrangements, particularly the inequality of suffrage and
representation, left them virtually helpless. Their economic interests
and aims coincided, to a large extent, with Jefferson's long-standing
objections to the Constitution on political grounds. One of their
leaders, Samuel Kercheval, asked and received Jefferson's support.

The two letters of 1816 to Kercheval—little essays in political theory
—represented the furthest reach of Jefferson's democratic thought.
Seldom had he been so bold. He beseeched Kercheval not to publish
them—he was too old to suffer this controversy again—but Kercheval
knew their value too well to keep them secret. Jefferson recalled his
long-standing criticisms of the frame of government. But he now
confessed that even his own earlier proposals for reform had contained "gross departures ... from genuine republican canons." Governments, he wrote to Kercheval, "are republican only in proportion
as they embody the will of the people, and execute it." Applying this
"mother principle," he advocated several far-reaching reforms. First,
equality of representation in the legislature and enfranchisement of
virtually all adult white males. Second, abolition of the obstructive
executive council and popular election of the governor. Third, popular election of judges or, at least, their appointment by the governor
alone subject to removal on concurrence of the two elective branches.
Fourth, the overturn of the oligarchical "monopolies of county administration," the county courts, and the transfer of their functions to
the people in newly constituted local units called "wards." Finally,
believing that "laws and institutions must go hand in hand with the
progress of the human mind," Jefferson assailed the exaggerated
respect for the historic Constitution, and called again for regular
amendment and revision. The enactment of Jefferson's program
might have revolutionized Virginia government and, in time, the
whole society.

The wide circulation of Jefferson's opinions accelerated the convention movement. Thomas Ritchie soon became a convert, a rare
exception in the east, though he suspected the movement's nationalist

leadership and outlook. Of course constitutional revision was bound
to come and might have come sooner without Jefferson's intervention. The fear that democratic reforms would be enacted "under the
known influence of his name," George Tucker observed, "induced
many who would have otherwise desired a revision of the constitution to postpone it during his life." Jefferson was less important as
a cause of the convention than as its philosopher. He supplied the
westerners a philosophical rationale for their grievances, an ideology
that fixed the lines of debate and enabled a conflict of interests to
be conducted as a conflict of principle.

Hugh Blair Grigsby, both a member of the convention and its first
historian, had an acute understanding of Jefferson's role. The first
(the more important) letter to Kercheval was a conspicuous instance
of Jefferson's faculty "of putting great truths in a nutshell, of com-
pressing whole theories into an adage." When he wrote a letter or
paper on a political topic, Grigsby said, it became "the battleground
of the time ... part of the public mind." The brilliant phrases of
Jefferson's letter, Grigsby recalled, "were at once stereotyped in the
public voice." The fate of the first Virginia Constitution was sealed.

Jefferson's connection with democratic reform caused a crisis of
ideology and allegiance among the state rights Republicans who
made up the bulk of the eastern conservative opposition. The division
between the two great sections of the state in respect to reform was
almost perfect; and it represented only somewhat less perfectly the
division between state rights and consolidation in respect to the central government. The eastern state rightists, the Old Republicans, had
become the conservatives, the western nationalists of suspicious lineage the democratic reformers. The debates offered many striking
examples of the hostility between Old Republicanism and New Democracy. Madison joined Marshall to repudiate the identical principle
on tenure of judges he had helped Jefferson establish in 1802: that
the abolition of a court simultaneously deprives the judge of his office
and salary. Monroe opposed the election of the governor by the
people on the principle: "The less you give them to do in exercising
the elective privilege, the safer they will be." Giles was perplexed
that the same Jefferson who had written him a last testament of state
rights was also the potent agent of reform. Well, he shrugged, "No

man . . . is wise at all hours." Men who had been known as Federalists, always opposed to the Jeffersonian school of politics, had suddenly fallen upon Jefferson as their political saint. It was, as Giles said, "something anomalous."

This inverted attitude toward Jefferson signified the split in the tradition stemming from him. Reform imperiled not only the rule of the planter class but also Virginia's historic role in the Union. Within as little as ten years, the west would have a majority of the state's population. Under a democratic constitution, this prosperous and largely free labor section, possibly in combination with the commercial or propertyless classes of the eastern towns, would be able to use the resources of the state for economic developments and to align Virginia with the movement of national consolidation. It was perhaps the principal object, a conservative leader said, "of those who set this ball of revolution in motion, to overturn the doctrine of state rights, of which Virginia has been the very pillar . . . by so reorganizing the legislature that Virginia, too, may be hitched to the Federal car." Should the movement succeed, eastern interests in land and slaves—the whole plantation edifice—would be put in jeopardy. Eastern Virginia would stand to the state government as the commonwealth then stood to the federal government: exploited, after the manner of the protective tariff.

The conservatives, therefore, attempted to establish a theory which would safeguard the substantial landed interest of the commonwealth in the same way that the theory of state rights assured Virginia a concurring power in the Union. The most articulate of the young conservatives, Abel P. Upshur, stated the fundamental principle: "There is a majority in *interest*, as well as a majority in number." The federal principle of state concurrence was viewed as identical with the principle of interest representation. They stand or fall together, said Upshur. What would be the result, he asked, if an amendment to the federal Constitution abolished slavery and Virginia had, in this convention, abandoned the principle of a minority's concurring voice in government? "Would she not be told by those who abhor this species of property, and who are restive under the power which it confers, 'You have abandoned the principle in your own institutions, and with what face do you claim it in your connexions with us.'"

The debate thus turned on one of the enduring issues of American politics: should government collect mass opinion or balance and protect interests, reinforce the public will or fracture and resist it, let numbers or property rule? Some in the Jacksonian era saw in the issue the question of whether the United States was to be a republic or a democracy. Many thought it defined the basic difference of principle between Whigs and Democrats. The political theorist Francis Lieber later put it in terms of the conflict between the Anglican and the Gallican conceptions of liberty. The former, he said, was federal and practical, liberty consisting in an intricate system of laws and guarantees. The latter represented "the idea of equality founded upon or acting through universal suffrage, or . . . 'the undivided sovereignty of the people' with an uncompromising centralism." Similarly, Benjamin Watkins Leigh, the Randolph protégé who led the eastern forces in the Virginia convention, held that the Constitution of 1776 was English, while the proposed reform was founded upon "the rights of man as held in the French school." Leigh, by implication, linked Jefferson to "the wildest democracy and demented French jacobinism." This profound conflict of principle lay at the heart of the convention.

Jefferson's definition of republican government in terms of equal, direct, and constant control by the whole citizenry seemed to the conservatives not republican at all and actually destructive to the federal and agrarian elements of his politics. Jefferson's marvelous union of three political elements—provincial right, agrarian interest, and democratic idea—was split apart. Eastern conservatives associated the first two with a traditional way of life; the third they discarded as its outworn ideology, one which had in Jefferson's day secured Virginia's ascendancy in the Union but was now no longer compatible with it.

Ranging Jefferson's agrarian sentiments against reform, the conservatives argued that democracy would enfranchise the "potboilers and mechanics" of the towns and "the peasantry of the west." Leigh doubted the political competence of either class. I believe, Philip Nicholas told the convention, "if there are any chosen people of God, they are the cultivators of the soil. If there be virtue to be found any where, it would be amongst the middling farmers, who constitute the yeomanry, the bone and sinews of our country." Virtually a transcript of Jefferson's hymn to the yeomen, yet here used to shield the planter interest and to defeat his liberal aims! The petitioning non-freeholders of Richmond might deny that virtue and intelligence are "products of the soil" and declare Jefferson "ever foremost to assert the rights of his fellow-men"; still the agrarian prejudice of Old Republicanism strengthened the demand for retention of the freehold suffrage. In 1800 Northern capitalism menaced the landed order. In 1829, however, it was threatened by democracy itself.

Approaching the questions of suffrage and representation as social rather than moral, practical rather than theoretical, the conservatives attacked the groundwork of American government in natural rights philosophy. "In truth, Mr. Chairman," Upshur solemnly declared, "there are no original principles of government. Principles do not precede, but spring out of government." Another delegate attributed the equalitarian theory of natural rights to "the fancies of Rousseau ... the *ignis fatuus* of French politics ... the delusions of anarchy and atheism." Philip P. Barbour conceded that men are naturally free and equal, as stated in Article I of the Declaration of Rights; but under the compact of government, he said, natural rights are subject to modification according to the canons of "practical utility," "men and things as they are." Reformers pointed to the disparity between the Declaration and the Constitution, and cited Jefferson's exhortation to reduce the principles of the former to the practice of the latter. Conservatives denied the connection and suggested the drastic consequences of making it. Literal application of Article I, Barbour warned, could not stop short of emancipation of the slaves.

Half-way through the convention, a western delegate remarked that formerly "the Sage of Monticello would have stood against the world; now, there are 'none so poor as to do him reverence.' Then, was Burke regarded as the enemy of human rights and the firmest defender of aristocracy and monarchy—but now, Burke, Filmer, and Hobbes ... have become the textbook of our statesmen." The opposition of Jefferson and Burke went right to the point. The assault on natural right and abstract principle, the emphasis on prescriptive social rights, the reverence for the ancient, the historically validated, Constitution of 1776—in all this the conservatives were more Burkean than Jeffersonian. As Virginia and the South were thrown increasingly on the defensive because of their peculiar institution and waning power in the Union, the provincial, the agrarian, the legalistic elements of the Jeffersonian heritage were intermixed with the Burkean canons of thought.

Burke was the key to John Randolph's thought, as his early Virginia biographer recognized, and the violent spasms of his politics came from the effort of his life to reconcile Virginia Jeffersonianism with the philosophy of Burke. Already a legend, Randolph, with his emaciated frame and venomous tongue, cast a spell over all who heard him denounce the reformers. Conservatives commonly disparaged Jefferson as a theorist of the French type; but the acme in this line was Randolph's fantasy of the Sage's famous plow with the moldboard of least resistance. "We are not to be struck down by the authority of Mr. Jefferson. Sir, if there be any point upon which Mr. Jefferson might be considered as valid, it is the mechanism of the plough." Some time after the savants of Europe pronounced Jefferson's the best mold-board ever devised, Randolph continued,

an adversary brought into Virginia the Carey plough; but it was such an awkward ill-looking thing, that it would not sell; at length some one tried it, and though its mould-board was not that of least resistance, it beat Mr. Jefferson's plough as much as common sense will always beat theories and reveries. Now there is not in Virginia, I believe, one plough with the *mould-board of least-resistance. . . .* So much for authority!

The degeneracy of Virginia was one of the acrid themes of Randolph's old age. The intimate who wrote his biography, Hugh Garland, said Randolph attributed the decay to Jefferson's influence —his democratic ideas, the Embargo's blight on the plantations, and the abolition of entail and primogeniture. "The country is ruined, thanks to Mr. Jefferson and Mr. Ritchie." Eccentric, fretful, with a rare gift of sarcasm, Randolph confessed not long before his death, "I cannot live in this miserable, undone country, where as the Turks follow their sacred standard, which is a pair of Mahomet's green breeches, we are governed by the old red breeches of that prince of projectors, St. Thomas of Cantingbury; and surely Becket himself never had more pilgrims at his shrine, than the saint of Monticello." Randolph typified Randolph; yet he had an articulate if small following in Virginia. His Anglicized Jeffersonianism expressed the agony of Virginia Republicanism and heightened the Gallic tones of the Jefferson image.

Jefferson's proposed reforms fared with meager success in the convention. Despite a more equal representation, the apportionment continued to favor the east by hedging property against numbers. The suffrage was extended, but over thirty thousand adult white males still lacked the franchise. The General Assembly continued to elect the executive, with a smaller council, and slightly enlarged powers. The oligarchical county court system was untouched. Judicial tenure was loosened, but the principle of popular election found little support even among the reformers. Finally, the new constitution contained no provision for amendment. State rights Republicans brought to the Jeffersonian touchstone of democracy rejected it, and evolved from the old doctrines methods of resistance to centralizing democracy.

At bottom it was slavery that divided Virginia along the Blue Ridge Mountains. Most members of the convention might have agreed with the opinion of the distinguished delegate, James Monroe, that "if no such thing as slavery existed . . . the people of our Atlantic border, would meet their brethren of the west, upon the basis of a majority, of the free white population." But slavery existed, largely as an eastern institution; and it demanded protection from mere numbers both in the state and in the federal government. By-passed in the convention, the dreaded issue, swollen by the hopes and fears of a terrible torrent, soon locked Virginia in another great debate that ripped wide the seams of the Jeffersonian heritage.

The memory of Jefferson hung in the air of his Roman-styled Capitol in Richmond, where the legislature assembled in December 1831. Four months before, a fanatical slave preacher, Nat Turner, and his band massacred about sixty whites, many of them women and children, in Southampton County. The insurrection was by far the bloodiest in the annals of American slavery. Jefferson's jeremiad of half a century rang with poignant significance: "And can the liberties of a nation be thought secure when we have removed their only firm basis, a conviction in the minds of the people that these liberties are the gifts of God? That they are not to be violated but with his wrath? Indeed I tremble for my country when I reflect that God is just; that his justice cannot sleep forever." Converting crisis to opportunity, many Virginians hoped for the realization of Jefferson's cherished goal, a gradual emancipation, trusting as well that Virginia's lead would "impart a resistless impulse" to the whole South.

Once again Jefferson provided the moral justification for western interests, which coincided with emancipation. The House of Delegates referred the slavery question to a special committee dominated by eastern conservatives. But before the committee could submit its report, debate erupted in the House on two resolutions which instructed the committee to contradictory courses of action. Thomas Jefferson Randolph, for the liberals, asked the committee to report on the expediency of placing before the electorate a plan of gradual emancipation. Children of slaves born on or after July 4, 1840 would become the property of the state when they came of age, and would be colonized outside the United States when the return from their labor met the expenses of their removal. This was, in essence, "the plan of Mr. Jefferson," as everyone recognized; the plan broached by him in the *Notes on Virginia* and repeatedly advocated as late as 1824. Thus the Virginia slavery debate was also a debate on Jefferson.

Standing on the natural rights philosophy, the reformers argued that slavery was both an injustice to the Negroes and a curse to the whites. The principles of American liberty, they said, embraced the whole of humanity. Let the master debase the slave's humanity, pervert his feelings, muffle his reason, still "the idea that he was born to be free will survive it all. It is . . . a torch lit up in his soul by the hand of the Deity and never meant to be extinguished by the hand of man." The slave system weakened the moral restraints of Christianity. It made industry dishonorable. It retarded popular education and free inquiry. The educative effect of the master-slave relationship was graphically portrayed by George W. Summers:

Lisping infancy hears the vocabulary of abusive epithets, and struts the embryo tyrant of its little domain. The consciousness of superior destiny, takes possession of his mind at its earliest dawning, and love of power and rule "grows with his growth and strengthens with his strength." . . . Unless enabled to rise above the operation of powerful causes, he enters the world with miserable notions of self-importance, and under the government of an unbridled temper.

The description bore enough resemblance to the famous passage in Query XVIII of the *Notes on Virginia* to give some basis to Benjamin W. Leigh's charge that Summers was merely parroting Jefferson.* Actually, this was another example of how Jefferson's striking language became "stereotyped in the public voice." No other words from his pen, or perhaps from any pen, were more often quoted as gospel by anti-slavery men. Jefferson's "false picture" of Virginia society, Leigh complained in the press, "has gone forth to the world as our true character."

The defenders of slavery worked mainly with the ideas of their conservative predecessors in the convention of 1829; however, they introduced one important modification. They were forced to contend now not only for the supremacy of the landed class but also for the supremacy of the master race. Defending racial inequality and slavery as laws of nature, attested by all history, the eastern delegates superimposed a still nebulous ideology of white supremacy upon the older conservative ideology of property. The slaves, they said, were happy with their lot, and the whites were more equal and more republican because of this labor system. Increasingly, throughout the South, racial inequalities would be substituted for economic ones, color would become the badge of aristocracy,

---

* The pertinent parts of Jefferson's passage: "The whole commerce between master and slave is a perpetual exercise of the most boisterous passions, the most unremitting despotism on the one part, and degrading submissions on the other. Our children see this, and learn to imitate it; for man is an imitative animal. This quality is the germ of all education in him. From his cradle to his grave he is learning to do what he sees others do. . . . The parent storms, the child looks on, catches the lineaments of wrath, puts on the same airs in the circle of smaller slaves, gives a loose to the worst of passions, and thus nursed, educated and daily exercised in tyranny, cannot but be stamped by it with odious peculiarities. The man must be a prodigy who can retain his manners and morals undepraved by such circumstances."

and class issues would be smothered by the blanket appeal to racial solidarity. Pro-slavery ideology divided society not between the rich and the poor but between the whites and the blacks.

Having assailed the natural rights premises of the reformers, the conservatives went on to argue that emancipation was impractical. What better proof was wanted than Jefferson's own conduct! He never liberated *his* slaves, but "perpetuated their condition by the last solemn act of his life; which is sufficient . . . to put to flight all the conclusions that have been drawn from the expressions of his abstract opinions." His scheme of emancipation was only a "day dream." He never went before the public as its advocate. Posterity could not venture what he dared not attempt: "The fragments of a great man's thoughts are not only valueless but dangerous. The same genius which conceived them is necessary to fill up their details. . . . When Hercules died, there was no man left to lift his club."

On the contrary, the reformers replied, Jefferson explicitly made emancipation his legacy "to the younger generation, receiving their early impressions after the flame of liberty has been kindled in every bosom, and has become . . . the vital spirit of every American." These words appeared in a newly discovered letter to Edward Coles in 1814, which was read into the debate by T. J. Randolph and thus started on its career as a significant anti-slavery document. The letter reaffirmed sentiments Jefferson had first advanced as a young member of the Virginia Burgesses, and also pointedly distinguished between the wisdom of general emancipation and the error of individual manumissions. "It appears, then," Randolph concluded, "that in 1770, 1814, 1824, he still deemed abolition indispensable. . . . Those dreams of his lasted a long time—some sixty years."

Many things foredoomed the Jeffersonian plan to failure; none, however, was as significant for Jefferson's place in the Southern imagination as the doctrine of state rights. Jefferson, as its champion, had often condemned federal intervention of any sort with slavery in the states. Finally realizing in 1824 that Virginia could never bear the financial burden of compensation and colonization, he put aside his constitutional scruples and proposed the diversion to the states of federal revenue from the public lands in order to effect emancipation. Similar suggestions were made by the reformers in 1832. But a more inopportune time for this affront to state rights principle could scarcely be imagined. During the fight on the tariff, any measure increasing the state's subservience to the nation was cast in the shadows. Virginia conservatives, who had evoked state rights against democratic reform two years before, could not be expected to act any more kindly toward the western proposal for federal aid in emancipation. It was like the apple in the Garden of Eden, Thomas R. Dew wrote in his influential *Review* of the slavery debate. The price of the temptation was Virginia's "pure political principles." The whole movement of emancipation, he thought, "is but too well calculated to furnish the political *lever* by which Virginia is to be prised out of her natural and honorable position in the Union, and made to sacrifice her noble political creed." The reformers hoped that the flood of light turned upon slavery in 1832 would result in its early extinction. "The name of the Great Democrat is once more in the van:—a power that never failed in Virginia." But Carolina Nullification, not emancipation, was the absorbing issue of the succeeding session of the legislature, and from this state rights crisis the promising anti-slavery movement never recovered.

Dew's *Review*, the first formal treatise in defense of Southern slavery, underlined the cardinal significance of the debate. This Professor of Law at William and Mary declared the principles of the reformers false, their arguments wild, intemperate, and vicious, their proposals subversive of the rights of property and the order of society. Every conceivable plan of emancipation was "totally impracticable." African slavery was the norm of history, the natural condition of the race, the bulwark of Southern culture. Dew effaced Jefferson's intimate portrait of the manners and morals of slave society. The master was not "in a continual passion" but generous and over-indulgent toward his slaves; the master's children, instead of being "nursed, educated and daily exercized in tyranny," acquired "a more exalted benevolence . . . and elevation of soul"; and the slave, so far from feeling miserable because unfree, was indeed "happier than we are." Here, in Dew's work, was the beginning of a full-blown pro-slavery philosophy. Southern leaders, while they remained committed to the republican creed centered in the "doctrines of '98," discovered in popular democratic theory what the editor of the *Richmond Whig* sardonically named "Mr. Jefferson's Fatal Legacies." The double image pointed to the ironic recognition that the father of the symbolic creed which shielded the South and the father of the symbolic creed which threatened to destroy it were one and the same.

4. *South Carolina Nullification*

The nullification movement in South Carolina completed the transformation of Jefferson into the Father of State Rights. According to a legend, the South Carolina congressman and Jackson leader, James Hamilton, angry and downcast after the passage of the Tariff of Abominations in 1828, interrupted his homeward journey to talk with John Randolph at Roanoke. Randolph presented his visitor, who had only recently emerged from National Republicanism, with a tattered copy of the Virginia and Kentucky Resolutions. Hamilton studied the documents and all was light. In a speech to his constituents in Walterborough some months later, he advanced the doctrine of nullification as the South's salvation. "After all, we must come back to Mr. Jefferson's plain, practical, and downright principle, as 'our rightful remedy'—a nullification." John C. Calhoun applied to Hamilton for the rare pamphlet, embodied its principles in his authoritative *Exposition* of 1828, and so South Carolina nullification was born.

This was legend—with a core of truth. For the nullification movement was inwardly affiliated with the Virginia state rights reaction against democratic principles, not just nationalism. The inter-sectional debates in Virginia anticipated in miniature, as it were, the hardening sectional conflict within the Union, and pointed to the strategy of minority defense against majority power, which might be employed with the same success by the minority South. Nullification sprang from the identical impulse of Virginia conservatism: the defense of institutions condemned by democratic opinion. In the one case the idea of concurrence, the organic protection of great interests from great numbers, was employed in the state government with a constant eye on its federal implications. In the other case the federal problem was in the foreground; and Calhoun, the master-mind of nullification, developed an elaborate theory of government around the idea.

Calhoun, like his chief associates in South Carolina, had no compelling Jeffersonian antecedents. He and the trio of nullification governors—Hamilton, Hayne, and George McDuffie—were new converts to state rights. Until the Adams administration the leading state rights politician in the state was William Smith. The Calhoun faction turned Smith out of the Senate in 1823 for opposition to American System measures, and then again six years later because he was not a Nullifier! Two ardent Jeffersonian publicists, Thomas Cooper (friend of Jefferson and a college president) and Robert Turnbull (lawyer and planter) kept alive the almost forgotten language of state rights in powerful tracts against consolidation. But, though they expounded the Constitution and exhorted the South to resistance, they prescribed no remedy commensurate with the disease.

The remedy of nullification suggested in the Kentucky Resolutions seemed to meet the need. The Resolutions were published, together with those of Virginia, the Virginia Report, and documents pertinent to them, in Charleston in 1828. Hamilton first publicly espoused nullification. Calhoun took up the still vague idea and shaped it into an organic law of the federal system. The basic premises were laid in the historic Resolutions: the Union is a compact of independent states; the central government is limited to explicitly enumerated powers; when these are transcended each state, there being no common arbiter, judges for itself the mode and measure of redress. Calhoun added his own metaphysic of "sovereignty" and his fears of majority power; but he was orthodox in his view that the division of powers in the federal system was nugatory if one of the authorities possessed the exclusive right of judging the portion allotted to each. He then went on to describe with precision for the first time how nullification would work as a constitutional process. A convention of the people of a single state, as representing the indivisible sovereign authority, would suspend the operation of a federal law. Then, in a convention of the several states, the law would be declared unconstitutional and void by one-fourth of them. If three-fourths of the states granted the disputed power by amendment of

the Constitution, the aggrieved state would either acquiesce or withdraw from the compact, in the same way it had entered, by the
exercise of its highest sovereignty. This was the Carolina doctrine.

As the movement gained momentum in South Carolina and spread
into national politics, the Nullifiers made a concerted effort to identify their cause and doctrine with Jefferson and the Old Republican
party. Nullification was enhanced by the prestige of the Jefferson
symbol, the sanction of hallowed precedent, the fiction of its success
in "the revolution of 1800." Quite aside from their genuine response
to the historic Resolutions, the Nullifiers chanted Jefferson and '98
because it was the best possible strategy. From the Senate, Hayne
implored his friends at home to base their proceedings on the Resolutions of '98, confident that only in this way could they carry with
them the South and a large portion of the people in other quarters.
Jefferson was the Nullifier's armor of safety and flag of victory.
Chanting his name and doctrine, celebrating his birthday, showering him with oratory—this was a ritual in South Carolina politics
for several years.

Of course the Nullifiers also found support in Jefferson's *Memoirs*.
Chancellor William Harper had recently read the posthumous work.
Much might be objected to Jefferson on other scores, but, he professed, "for a true and thorough comprehension of the genius and
working of our confederate system, he alone appears to be the master." The *Memoirs* showed Jefferson to have been, another said,
"from the origin of the government, the able, untiring, and consistent
advocate of the rights of the states and constitutional liberty." Believing that the federal government was a derivative agency, properly
limited to the management of the country's external relations, Jefferson set about to dislodge the national party and return the government to the states. The Resolutions of '98 were but the culmination
of the decade-long struggle against monarchical Federalism. "Virginia was the mother of these doctrines, and Thomas Jefferson their
author," Hayne emphatically declared.

"In politics, he is a prophet—aye, greater than a prophet. He
stands confessedly, as the great light of the political world." This
was Turnbull's accolade of Jefferson in 1832. Five years before, in
his alarm-raising *The Crisis*, he had scarcely bothered to notice the

Resolutions of '98 and their author; now he thought it important to praise Jefferson as the "particular individual" elevated by Providence to light the fires of liberty. As Nullification became a monomania, so did the idolatry of Jefferson. Thanks to the Nullifiers, Turnbull said, "Mr. Jefferson's sun of truth has at last risen upon the people of these states, after a long, a dark, and a dreary night of consolidation and misrule." Nullification was "the groundwork" of Jefferson's faith, the "chief corner-stone" of South Carolina's principles. Supercharged with emotion, the movement repelled rational analysis and invited satire. In one of these satires, three South Carolina wizards conjure up "the Goddess Nullification" from a potion containing the writings of Jefferson, Turnbull, and other Nullifiers. "Goddess, arise! . . ." runs the incantation, "In the hallowed name of Jefferson, thy high priest." The symbolism was not inappropriate; for sorcery and charm were factors, conscious or unconscious, in the polemics of Nullification.

The Carolinians made their major bid for federal support in 1830, and again they counted on the association of Jefferson's name with nullification. Hayne made considerable progress in the great Senate debate: Democratic speakers in number allied themselves with state rights without, however, commitment to the Carolina doctrine. Thomas Hart Benton saw the opportunity thus presented to unite the party under the banner of Jefferson in opposition to the American System. Nothing would do so well as an imposing ceremony, so the histrionic Missouri Senator arranged a party celebration of Jefferson's birthday, April 13, in the capital. No such formal commemoration of Jefferson's birth had ever been held. While he lived he had refused to make his birthdate known to wishful celebrants; but he was helpless against his partisan admirers in 1830. Benton viewed the affair as the start of a party rite, an annual "recurrence to fundamental principles, and a declaration of adhesion to the republican doctrines of the great apostle of American liberty."

Taken together, the programmed toasts and addresses of the birthday dinner presented Jefferson as a state rights radical, if not indeed the Father of Nullification. Pennsylvania and Ohio congressmen walked out when they realized that the program celebrated the Jefferson of '98 and strengthened the hand of South Carolina. Hayne

addressed the assemblage. His state, he said, marched in the footsteps of Jefferson to the same end of saving the Constitution. The
historic Resolutions were repeatedly quoted; Georgia was praised
for her tenacious stand in the Cherokee case; and a Kentucky congressman went to such lengths defending the Carolina doctrine that
he was accused of treason by the *National Intelligencer.*

The opening volunteer toasts of Jackson and Calhoun climaxed
the celebration. The President, staring at the Vice-President, offered,
"Our [Federal] Union: It must be preserved." Calhoun supplied the
significant qualification: "The Union: Next to our liberties the most
dear." And thus was reproduced within the party the constitutional
issue between Webster and Hayne. Many years later Van Buren
recalled the electric effect of Jackson's maneuver: "The veil was rent
—the incantations of the night were exposed to the light of day."
The Nullifiers at first tried to save face by ingenious rationalizations
of Jackson's sentiment. They were not yet ready to renounce the
"second Jefferson," whose administration thus far was consistent with
state rights principles. Both opposition and administration spokesmen, on the other hand, at once turned Jackson's declaration against
South Carolina. The Nullifiers' incantations failed to work their spell
in the Jackson party. South Carolina was isolated. But the birthday
dinner helped to fix the stigma of nullification on Jefferson; and,
incidentally, it killed the idea of an annual party festival. The Pennsylvania protectionists, at a public dinner in Philadelphia a month
later, sought to free Jefferson "from the false impressions of the late
anniversary." Despite such vigorous counterthrusts, despite Jackson,
despite truth itself, the "false impression" was so insistently planted
in the mind that it could never be wholly rooted out.

The movement went rapidly forward in South Carolina until the
Nullifiers won a stunning victory in 1832. As the debate between
Nullifiers and Unionists rose in fury, one of the points at issue was
the relationship between the Resolutions of '98 and the Carolina
doctrine. Such was the respect accorded these historic documents
that the radicals used their phraseology, often verbatim and section
by section, in their own legislative papers. "We have hoisted an old

flag . . . but a proud one," A. P. Butler declared in 1830, "one that is associated with triumph and the glory of other days."

But for all the Nullifiers' insistence on Jefferson's patrimony, they had not yet established his use of the word "nullification." The word was important, for it compressed Calhoun's involved theory into a symbol and a slogan. It derived unmistakably from the Kentucky Resolutions of 1799, the second and stronger set. The Nullifiers maintained from the start that Jefferson wrote both sets, but as to the second this was mere inference. The Unionists actually had better proof from the *Memoirs* that Jefferson had nothing to do with the second document and, therefore, with "nullification." All parties admitting "the high authority of Mr. Jefferson," as Calhoun later explained, it became then "a point of great importance" to determine the authorship of the 1799 Resolutions.

Early in 1832 the *Richmond Enquirer* published Jefferson's manuscript draft of the Kentucky Resolutions of 1798. The responsibility for this development belonged, ironically, to James Madison, who had called the Carolina doctrine "a preposterous and anarchical pretension." He discovered at Montpellier the press copy of a draft Jefferson had enclosed in a letter to him in November 1799. The draft used the words "nullify" and "nullification." The information was relayed to T. J. Randolph, who rummaged in the piles of papers at Edgehill and came up with a rough and a fair manuscript, the original of Madison's copy, which appeared to be the draft composed for transmission to Kentucky in 1798. He released it to Ritchie for publication. Ritchie, like Madison and Randolph, had defended Jefferson from the nullification procedure adumbrated in the 1799 Resolutions, but he now frankly confessed "the *South Carolinians* were right as to Mr. Jefferson's opinions."

Jefferson's draft was more radical than either set of the Kentucky Resolutions, to say nothing of the milder Virginia Resolutions. The crucial eighth resolve contained two key passages omitted by the Kentucky legislature: first, "that every state has a natural right in cases not within the compact, (*casus non fœderis*) to nullify of their own authority all assumptions of power by others within their limits"; and second, that each state "will take measures of its own for providing that neither these acts [the Alien and Sedition Acts] nor any

others of the General Government not plainly and intentionally authorized by the Constitution, shall be exercized within their respective territories." Jefferson's closing statement, "Nullification . . . is the
rightful remedy," was incorporated in the Resolutions of 1799, but
in other respects that document simply repeated the sentiments of
the first.

Calhoun was elated by the discovery. So fully, he later said, did it
accord with his own statements that "had it been possible for him
to have had access to the manuscript, he might well have been
suspected of plagiarism." Jefferson's authority thus confirmed, the
opposition forced to admit its error, nullification "moved forward
with renovated energy and confidence in preparing for the great
issue."

But this was to mistake words for things. Jefferson's draft made
his opinion more ambiguous, his authority more uncertain than
before. For example, in the eighth resolve he called nullification a
natural right. If so, how could a state exercise it and still remain
in the civil compact? And if Kentucky could nullify on its own authority, what was the point of consultation with the "co-states"?
Kentucky wanted to hear "their sentiments," but was this all the
resolutions aimed to accomplish? Jefferson also clearly differentiated
assumptions of undelegated power from abuses of delegated power,
and reserved nullification for the former. Was the protective tariff
abuse or assumption? Jefferson's opinion was conjectural, though in
view of the relation between the tax power and protection, he would
probably have classified the tariff as an abuse. Who, in any event,
decided when a federal law was an abuse or an assumption of power?
Decision by a single state would not only disrupt the Union but also
paralyze the majority will, which Jefferson in his First Inaugural had
called "the vital principle of republicanism, from which there is no
appeal but to force."

Even these questions, all quite legitimate, barely skimmed the
surface of confusion. They were not easily clarified, but Madison's
efforts were more helpful than most. "You have been a pillar of
support to me through life," Jefferson wrote to his old friend in
1826. "Take care of me when dead." Hoping to lift the incubus of
nullification from Jefferson, Madison argued that despite apparent

differences between Jefferson's and his own Virginia Resolutions, between "nullification" and "state interposition," they were hatched together and meant essentially the same thing. The Carolina doctrine was heretical on several counts. The Resolutions of '98 were declaratory of opinion, Calhoun's doctrine was *ipso facto* executory; the former referred to the rights of the several states, the latter to the claim of a single state; the former was directed against usurpations, the latter against abuses as well; the former's ultimate appeal was to natural right, the latter disguised secession as a constitutional process. The Nullifiers, Madison fumed, seized upon particular expressions of Jefferson's "as the Shibboleth of their party, and almost a sanctification of their cause"; they omitted the evidence that showed his meaning to be entirely at variance with theirs. "Who can believe," he wrote privately in 1831, that Jefferson's doctrine contemplated "a Convention summoned at the pleasure of a single state, with an interregnum during its deliberations; and, above all with a rule of decision subjecting nearly ¾ to ¼. No man's creed was more opposed to such an inversion of the Repub[lican] order of things."

The South Carolina Unionists similarly combatted the Nullifiers' shibboleth. While no one could fathom the mysteries of 1798 or of Jefferson's mind, the Unionists agreed that, whatever his purpose, he recognized no intermediate right or recourse between protest under the Constitution and secession from it. On the evidence of the *Memoirs* he counseled moderation in 1798, and in 1825 continued protest as the only alternative to the *ultima ratio*.

The Unionists presented themselves as the true friends of Jefferson and state rights. Two alternative strategies were available to them. They might have followed some of the American System advocates and built Jefferson into a national figure. But this was politically unrealistic as well as against the opinion of the majority of Unionists. Or, as a second course, the Unionists might have repudiated Jefferson and the Resolutions of '98, in effect conceding this historical authority to the Nullifiers. It was not for love of Jefferson and his principles that several of the Unionist leaders of Federalist backgrounds rejected this course. "The politics of the immortal Jefferson! Pish!" Hugh Legaré exclaimed in the privacy of a letter; but in public even Legaré felt the necessity of bowing to "the holy father of democracy." Soon after the controversy subsided, J. Q. Adams remarked to a Charleston Unionist that his party had conceded too much to the Nullifiers. If so, the Unionist replied, "Mr. Jefferson was the cause of it, and . . . if the Union party had not held out a strong adhesion to State rights they would have been officers without an army."

South Carolina nullified the federal tariff in November 1832, "sanctified by the high authority of Thomas Jefferson." President Jackson's Proclamation a few days later denounced this proffered method of saving the Union a "mad project of disunion." Boldly nationalistic, closer to the Webster school than to anything Jeffersonian, the Proclamation startled Nullifiers and state rights men generally. The embattled Unionists, despite repeated assurances of Jackson's support, were equally surprised. One of them had remarked six weeks earlier, "The *old man* seems to be more than half a nullifier himself."

The Calhoun party now turned the Jefferson bogy on Jackson. What are the new doctrines of the President? "Why they are, that our history is false, and that Jefferson and Madison were fools." One Nullifier sketched an imaginary conversation between the President and the ghost of Jefferson. Jackson is reminded that he was elected with Jefferson's support and on the promise to govern according to the "simply and easily understood" doctrines of '98. Jackson pleads the master's own principle of majority rule. The phantom snaps back: "Good God, Sir! do you call that republican, the doctrines of Jefferson? Why the Federalists, with Tim Pickering at their head, never published a more offensive libel against me and my principles."

Governor Hayne readied the state's defenses and in a counter-proclamation appealed for justification to "the great apostle of American liberty." Quoting Jefferson's text of 1798, he fraudulently omitted the clause that designated the election machinery as the constitutional remedy for abuses of power. Previously, the Nullifiers had emphasized the Union-saving virtues of their remedy; now, with Hayne, they exalted the Jefferson who preferred dissolution to unlimited centralization. Previously, they had emphasized the sufficiency of the Constitution; now some of them named Patrick Henry a Cassandra, complained of the Constitution's centralizing features, and praised the old Confederacy as "the wisest system . . . which mankind had ever produced." Previously, the Republicans of '98 had been beyond criticism; but now they were censured for their failure in power to amend the Constitution, a failure by which "they have entailed upon the country evils not easy of eradication."

As the state governments, one after another, reported against South Carolina, the eyes of the nation turned on Virginia. "Much depends upon Virginia . . . upon her depends whether the country is involved in civil war, or the controversy is amicably settled." While the bulk of Virginia state rightists rejected nullification, they were unwilling to join the President in supplanting, as the Proclamation threatened, the doctrines of '98. Virginia sought to mediate the federal dispute, and also to define the correct state rights doctrine. The long debate in the House of Delegates reproduced the sectional division of the slavery debate in the preceding session. The west supported Jackson, while the eastern leadership of the House condemned both the President and South Carolina, reaffirmed the doctrines of '98, and deduced from them the right of peaceable secession. Was this Jeffersonian? The eastern leader and consistent conservative, William H. Broadnax, argued it was. T. J. Randolph denied it, pointing out that even in the famous letter to Giles, quoted by Broadnax, Jefferson's ultimate recourse was "stand to our arms." Nothing was settled as to the right of peaceable secession in the final compromise resolutions approved by the General Assembly. However, Virginia renewed its loyalty to the doctrines of '98, and declared the President to be in "direct conflict with them."

Virginia's defection from the administration in 1833 alarmed several of its leaders. Van Buren urged the President to reconsider certain "doctrinal points" of his Proclamation; within a year a so-called "authorized exposition" appeared in the administration organ, the *Washington Globe.* Although it did not, in strict logic, contradict the theory of the Proclamation, the exposition specifically sanctioned the Resolutions of 1798 and recognized the right of the people of the several states, in extreme cases of oppression, to resist the central government, "confiding in a good cause, the favor of heaven and the spirit of freedom to vindicate the right." The exposition was favorably received in the South, even called a recantation. But tempers were still ruffled by Jackson's heresy.*

The compromise which, by resort to the vague yet powerful shibboleth, "the doctrines of '98," slurred over the profound constitutional issue raised in the nullification crisis, was preceded by Henry Clay's legislative compromise, the Tariff of 1833. The Nullifiers were jubilant. At their Victory Ball in Charleston a great banner proclaimed the truth of Jefferson's assertion, "Nullification is the rightful remedy." Actually the specific remedy, though it forced upon Congress a moderate tariff, was defeated. South Carolina would not again employ the process, nor would any state ever succeed with it. In the South, nullification was the pivot upon which many state rights Jeffersonians swung toward the politics of sectionalism, slavery, and secession.

Jackson had every right to wonder if in killing nullification he had also killed secession. The two sprang from "the same poisonous root," Madison wrote in 1831; and men at either pole of opinion agreed on the close relationship. A young New York legislator, William H. Seward, saw the relationship with astounding clarity in 1833. The legislature had before it a report on South Carolina's action which, while it rejected nullification, endorsed the doctrines of '98. New York, Seward vainly argued against the report,

resolves against nullification, but adopts the text-book of the heresy to show that she is *not in earnest!* . . . Sir, South Carolina and the great party who favor nullification at the South ask nothing more of us than to waive the Constitution, and adopt those resolutions of Virginia and Kentucky. They are written in their heart's core. If we adopt them, the question is no longer whether nullification and secession are constitutional, but it is reduced to a question of construction of your political text-book.

* When Thomas Ritchie went to Washington for Van Buren's inauguration in 1837, the retiring President complained to him: "You Virginians will not do justice by my proclamation. I have read the political works of your Jefferson and Madison, and I cannot perceive how the principles of my proclamation as it was intended clash in the slightest with the principles of those illustrious men." Ritchie asked about the *Globe* exposition. He was satisfied when Jackson said it expressed his true opinion. Gravitating to the camp of his old enemy, Calhoun, the editor came to believe the Nullifier had merely "reasoned wrong from right premises" in wishing "to give ascendancy to the old Republican doctrines of '98."

The textbook, as Seward saw it, was the root of the problem. He had many an occasion in his future career to remember it. The doctrines of '98 were annexed to the dominant Democratic party and repeatedly declared before the Civil War "one of the main foundations of its political creed." While for Southern secessionists, such as the Charleston fire-eater Robert Barnwell Rhett, schooled by Turnbull and others in the nullification crisis, the Resolutions of '98 were held to "distinctly affirm ... the right of State interposition *or secession*."

The crisis had not yet cooled when Carolinians shifted the object of state rights resistance from free trade to slavery. Northern abolitionists and reformers felt the barrage previously directed at consolidation and the manufacturing interest. Under the doctrines of the Proclamation, it was feared, the majority power of the North might attack slavery. Jackson saw the turn. "The nullifiers in the South intend to blow up a storm on the slave question." He felt with some bitterness that their purpose was to destroy the Union and form a Southern confederacy. The defense of slavery had been a latent factor, if indeed not the covert basis, of the Southern attack on consolidation; and thus the transition to pro-slavery thought and politics was as logical as it was sudden, especially in South Carolina.

The strategy of organized sectional, as distinguished from state, resistance to Northern power developed more slowly but just as logically. For the lesson of South Carolina's experience was that no state alone, if pushed to the extremity, could succeed. This was, in fact, precisely the position of some men who called themselves Unionists in 1832 but were later revealed as Southern nationalists. Coincident with the state rights climax was the growing recognition of the minority section's fundamental solidarity. Calhoun clearly saw it in 1831, when he said that in the United States geographical interests determined the division of sovereign power and constituted the check on majority tyranny. Was South Carolina then a separate geographical interest? Of course not; but Calhoun had taken over from Old Republicanism the general principle of state rights, and built it into the theory of a union of *sovereign* states, which he then mixed up with the anti-democratic theory of "majority of interests" conceived in geographical terms. The theory of sectional interest and minority check, "the concurrent majority" as he called it, was

the passion of Calhoun's later career, although he continued to talk
state rights and employ the imagery of Jeffersonian Republicanism.

The Nullifiers made the same connection between democracy and
consolidation as the Virginia conservatives. State rights doctrine was
for them the means of fracturing the collective will of the people.
"If this be a Government of the people collectively, it must be a
government of the majority," Turnbull wrote. The analogue of the
majoritarian theory in federal relations was the nationalist theory
of a union of "one people." The opposite conception of a union
of sovereign states was a bulwark against both consolidation and
democracy.

These untoward developments had ominous consequences for Jefferson's reputation, since he was implicated, chiefly through the
doctrines of '98, in all of them. How deeply he was implicated, with
what mitigations, and whether by his own actions or by the constructions posterity put upon them, were questions which troubled
politicians and historians for decades to come. The chain of events
which led to Jefferson's reconstruction as the hero of state rights
culminated in South Carolina in his canonization as the Father of
Nullification.

No man may fairly be held accountable for all the twistings and
turnings of his intellectual offspring; yet the meaning of an idea
reaches beyond its original context and purpose. It is unfolded in
history. Jefferson's state rights doctrines afford an illuminating instance. They were capable of being appropriated for purposes alien
to his own in any crisis of federal relations that might arise, and
the power of the Jefferson symbol, combined with the political memory of 1798, made it expedient to appropriate them. The Resolutions
contained in embryo the idea of constitutional resistance by a single
state to federal laws which in the view of that state transcended the
compact of government. How far Jefferson meant to practice this
idea would never be known (perhaps he never knew himself) largely
because the election of 1800 made it unnecessary. The embryo, in
any event, nursed by interest, fraud, and deceit, grew into a monster.

The character of Jefferson's life and thought compounded the
errors and distortions produced by the idolatrous habit of the polit-

ical mind. His speculative and practical sides were frequently confused. Few men took into account that Jefferson's private self, as
expressed in his letters, might not coincide with his public self. Or
that his opinion at one time might not represent his opinion under
different circumstances. Or that a man of his intellectual temperament did not often bother to qualify felicitous generalizations.

The Nullifiers invested heavily in Jefferson's draft resolutions
of 1798, though they were never published in his lifetime. "Nullification is *purloined* ... from Jefferson's unuttered and undigested
thought," an editor remarked. "What a man *writes* and *never* publishes, is like what a man *thinks* and *never speaks*." Jefferson never
acknowledged his connection with the Virginia and Kentucky Resolutions until 1821, in a private letter, which suggests he did not regard
them as enduring dogma. They were, despite their other values,
maneuvers in the struggle for power, and partly for this reason were
purposely equivocal on the limits of state resistance.

The single mirror of '98 Republicanism gave an incredibly deficient
image of Jefferson. "Were State Rights ... with all their absurdities,
the true and only tests of Republicanism?" a Virginia legislator asked
in 1833. "If such was the understanding now, it was not so at the
period when parties were first divided by the distinction of Federal
and Republican." But the fractured conception had a power beyond
reason to dissuade. Turnbull called nullification "the groundwork"
of Jefferson's faith, while Calhoun thought it was "the fundamental
principle" of his system.

Calhoun absorbed just enough Jeffersonian doctrine in the nullification controversy to acquire a Jeffersonian reputation—even today
scholars laud him as "the spiritual heir of Jefferson." The Virginian
and the Carolinian shared, with most Americans, a belief in state
rights principle. But whereas Jefferson considered this principle derivative of the fundamental principles of individual liberty and self-
government, Calhoun reversed the relationship. Jefferson's doctrine
expressed his positive faith in local government, in domestic affections and individualism, all as civilizing agents; Calhoun's converted
state rights into an essentially defensive weapon against democratic
centralization. The dilemma of democracy and state rights lay hidden
in Jefferson's politics. Calhoun came to grips with it, but in the process

sacrificed the democratic element which had been an integral part of Jefferson's system. Jefferson conceived of state rights as a means of buttressing a union identified with his fundamental principles. Calhoun's doctrine worked toward the disruption of that union, along with the destruction of state rights, by the identification of the principle with the cause of slavery.

In the American political tradition, Calhoun vies with Jefferson as the leading exponent of the theory of strict construction. But nothing in the Constitution or, for that matter, in Jefferson's writings supported the theory of nullification as a normal constitutional process. "For the last fifty years," a South Carolina Unionist complained, "the advocates of honest and fair government have been denouncing the construction by implication its most dangerous enemy ... yet it has taken its seat in the high places of the advocates of State Rights." Given the canon of strict construction, as Jefferson seemed to recognize and as Madison understood him, there was no middle path of resistance between the Constitution's authorized procedures and the appeal beyond it to natural right.

The new state rights movement had as its fundamental aim the protection of exclusive state and sectional interests from the majority power of the Union. Men seemed to forget the very different purpose of the Resolutions against the Alien and Sedition Laws: to secure majority power at its source in freedom of thought, expression, and political agitation. None of the Nullifiers and few of their adversaries distinguished the two cases, 1798 and 1832, on the basis of the federal laws in controversy. What the Alien and Sedition Laws were in 1798, the tariff was in 1832; an encroachment on civil liberty was viewed as interchangeable with an encroachment on economic liberty. "Freedom of industry is as sacred as freedom of speech, or conscience or the press." Not only did the radicals extend the nullification principle far beyond the realm of palpable violations of individual rights; they actually employed the principle to deny these rights, in much the same way as state rights had been used in Virginia to ward off equality of suffrage and representation. The Unionist minority in South Carolina called the Nullification Ordinance "the mad edict of a despotic majority." The state raised an army of twelve thousand men, denied the protection of the federal courts to cases arising under the Ordinance, required of public officials an oath of allegiance to the state, and, in general, established a majority rule in South Carolina more tyrannical than any emanating from Washington. The ironic end of the Jeffersonian vision!

The state rights revival capped by nullification had two major effects on the Jefferson image. It exaggerated the state rights aspect, uncovered its contradictions with the democratic aspect, and burdened Jefferson with the incubus of the Southern cause. It also demonstrated the hazards of taking Jefferson as the oracle of political truth. "Great men are the guideposts and landmarks in the state," a wise philosopher had said. But in the clashing and refracted light of time, Jefferson's landmarks were enigmatic, and the guideposts pointed in several directions.

Of all his progenies none had been thought more transparent than the "doctrines of '98." Suddenly they were opaque. "Professing to be expositions of the Constitution, they already require expounders themselves." The editor of the *Richmond Whig* gave up exegesis and declared, "the boasted doctrines of '98 are not worth a pinch of snuff." Abstracted from their history and drained of their original meaning, they survived with a strange emotional power as counterfeit symbols of the Jeffersonian polity. Fortunately for Jefferson's fame the image was but partially compassed by state rights. Within the new political design of the Jackson era, he was transformed into a democratic saint.

Two

DEMOCRACY I

It may be confidently asserted, that the whole range of history does not exhibit any instance of baser subserviency, not only of the many, as individuals, but of the nation at large,—than the over-powering influence of the mere name of Jefferson.[*]

THE STORIES most often told about Jefferson suggested two separate persons: the plain republican and the visionary philosopher. "He used often, while President," one of the former type began, "to walk down to the navy yard, early in a summer's morning, and sitting him down upon an anchor or a spar enter into a familiar conversation with the surprised and delighted shipwrights .... 'There!' would cry one of his political opponents, 'see the demagogue! There's Long Tom, sinking the dignity of his station, to get votes, and court the mob.'" Few legends in political annals had the currency and persistence of the one started by the English traveler John Davis in 1803. In contrast to the imposing ceremony of his predecessors—the paneled carriages, liveried servants, gallant equipage, and military display—when Jefferson was inaugurated, Davis reported, "He tied his horse to the paling which surrounds the Capitol grounds, and without ceremony entered the senate chamber." This was his way for eight years—plain and simple Tom Jefferson, unconscious of pomp and station, receiving all and sundry while vulgarly dressed in heelless slippers, red breeches, and vest, a boorish fellow before the ambassadors of kings, a plebeian before his countrymen.

[*] Joseph Seawell Jones, *A Defense of the Revolutionary History of the State of North Carolina from the Aspersions of Mr. Jefferson* (Boston, Raleigh, 1834), p. 8.

A typical characterization of Jefferson as visionary philosopher was the tale of an ingenious saw mill. Jefferson supposedly invented a saw mill to be driven by vertical sails, and hired an engineer to build it on a windy height near Monticello. The work completed, the engineer agreed with Jefferson that it was the greatest improvement ever made in saw mills. Only one thing troubled him. "Ah! What's that?" Jefferson asked. "I have been wondering," the engineer replied, "how you are to *get up* your *saw logs*." Jefferson threw up his hands. "I never thought of that!" In satire and anecdote Jefferson appeared as a lofty speculator in pursuit of shadows and chimeras, learned in useless knowledge but devoid of common sense—the Jefferson who excavated the mammoth, who sent out the Lewis and Clark expedition and waxed eloquent over its discoveries of salt mountains and prairie dogs, who invented the gunboat system to fight the British Navy only to find the tiny craft submerged or stranded after a storm; the Jefferson whose library at Monticello, it was said, contained such impressive tomes of his authorship as a two-volume demonstration that the prairie dog is of the same species as the woodchuck, three folios on the colors of butterfly wings, five volumes on the agility of the flea, and so on.

No sizable quantity of folkish apochrypha and legend gathered about Jefferson, as it would about Lincoln. "Mr. Jefferson" gave off more light than warmth. Nevertheless, the two legends ran throughout the history of the Jefferson image. The political pedigree of both was Federalist. But, as it happened, the vulgar democrat of the first characterization changed into a hero of democracy, and the ludicrous philosopher of the second turned out to be much more practical than the Federalists who had fancied the portrait. Moreover, it was precisely because Jefferson combined, or seemed to combine, the traits of the man-of-the-people and the man-of-vision that he was capable of being mythicized as the Father of Democracy. Neither the politician nor the philosopher, as a type, was admirable. But the man whose iconoclastic theories were received as truths by posterity, and whose lofty mental perch did not keep him from cherishing the people and mingling with them, was not only generally admirable but endlessly useful in the new age of democracy. Although Jefferson's democratic character was chiefly defined by tenets and ideas, tales and legends limning the person assisted in the creation and supplied a soft human touch.

The matrix of the image was Jacksonian Democracy. To Jacksonian Democrats, and to their conservative antagonists in the Federalist tradition as well, Jefferson and Jackson explained each other, one the originator, the other the executor of democracy, both sainted or satanical according to preference. Although many Whigs and Republicans of the state rights school combated it, the dominant tendency was for the two movements, Jeffersonian and Jacksonian, to fuse into one. Accordingly, the Jefferson image registered the progress of democracy.

1. *The Jacksonians*

Jefferson's Republican party expired with him sometime around 1826. The party of Jackson was a distinctive new creation. The first organized party of modern democracy, it marked a historic change in the relationship of the people to their government and, in the light of this, introduced forms and techniques of popular government of which Jefferson had only the vaguest premonition. But from the first, as earlier explained, the Jacksonians advertised their party as the re-creation of Jefferson's. Imaging Jefferson as the founder both of democracy and of the Democratic party, its advocates became the main conveyors of the Jefferson symbol in politics. So tight was the association of these three elements—the Jefferson symbol, democracy, and the Democratic party—that one scarcely existed in the public mind apart from the others and attempts to disengage them met with fleeting success.

Every political party has, in some measure, its canonized texts and doctrines, its fabled heroes and demons, its legend and tradition and ritual, its moral posture, its emotive rhetoric, its ideological distortions and disguises. The total composition is the party's myth, an imaginative projection of the party's history and destiny. It invokes commonly shared values and ideals, inspires sentiments of loyalty, and induces the widest possible response in its support. Symbols are objective representations and vehicles of the myth, most successful when they are charged with its whole emotional background. They make the abstract vivid, the chaotic symmetrical, the drab colorful, the sordid struggles of interests struggles of high principle. No myth is true in the sense of correspondence to objective reality; but this does not diminish the importance of its shaping power in history, which is "determined no more by what is true than by what men believe to be true."

The political myth of Jacksonian Democracy formed around the idea of return to the Jeffersonian foundations and of continuing popular struggle in the image of Jeffersonian politics. Jefferson appeared not only as the sainted Father of Democracy but also as the symbol of a pure and noble way of life. Most Jacksonians were intellectually and emotionally predisposed to view their world through the Jeffersonian categories of government and society. While these prepossessions enabled the Jacksonians to obtain insights that were otherwise unobtainable and to focus issues that were otherwise blurred, they at the same time induced what the sociologist Karl Mannheim has called "false consciousness," an orientation to traditional norms with which action in the existing situation cannot comply. Whether conscious or unconscious, ingenuous or manipulative, the Jefferson symbol played a major role in the Jacksonian mind.

The party myth arrayed Jefferson as "the highest democratic authority in America." His *Memoirs* were "text-books of liberal political principles and axioms from which the modern politician deduces present applications and solutions." Nothing, editorialized the national party organ, "can be so efficacious in preserving the purity of our institutions as the dissemination of the views of Mr. Jefferson's luminous mind." The Jackson press constantly circulated his opinions. James K. Polk of Tennessee did not merely read the *Memoirs* but, according to his recent biographer, copied out long extracts for instruction and use. Democratic politicians developed the habit of answering their opponents "by squirting Jefferson's opinions into their eyes." His name attached to any opinion was warrant that it was sound. And why was this? Because, in the commonplace view, "his convictions went along with the national mind," his name was "identified with the democratic feelings of the people," his peculiar power kindled "in their bosoms that glow of feeling by which the true votary of liberty has ever been distinguished."

The *Memoirs* were quoted in Congress almost as readily as ministers quoted Scripture. Thomas Hart Benton, a conspicuous example, quoted or cited Jefferson's writings to sanction his position on nullification, fishing bounties, the salt tax, the tariff, the United States Bank, currency, internal improvements, westward expansion, public lands policy, foreign missions, specific appropriations, civil pensions, and sundry other matters. After observing the Jefferson fetish for several years, a Whig congressman, William Cost Johnson of Maryland, rose in 1837 to satirize its worshippers:

They call themselves the true State rights Old Dominion republican democrats of the Jeffersonian school, and quote the name of that person to every partisan purpose, numberless times, in every speech with which they favor the House. . . . Gentlemen . . . quote slips from, and fragments of, his letters written some fifty years ago. . . . One descants upon constitutional law, and all eagerly listen, in hope to hear some idea which may impinge upon something which Mr. Jefferson may have loosely written or said, believing it will be his political destruction at home. Quick as thought a messenger is sent to the library to produce a letter or conversation of Mr. Jefferson. The orator ends, and another begins with anticipated victory joyously illuminating his features. . . . [But] he soon runs afoul of some other opinion of Mr. Jefferson, on some other and foreign subject. . . . Then another State rights Jeffersonian Old Dominion true republican democrat arises, and with the merciless vengeance of a Samson, he routs and vanquishes the political Philistines before him, behind him, and around him, horse, foot, and dragoons. These gentlemen regard it high treason, verily, to differ in the minutest particular from Mr. Jefferson. What a bombastic Englishman once said of Homer, they think of Jefferson:

> "Read Homer once, and you can read no more,
> For all other books else read so mean, so poor,
> Verse will seem prose; but still persist and read,
> And Homer will be all the books you need."

Johnson thought this a curious way to honor the man who dethroned all authorities save reason alone. ("It is remarkable," one of Jefferson's first biographers wrote, "that he never quotes the opinion of any other as the foundation or motive of his own.") But congressmen gave no evidence of appreciating the humor, nor could Johnson shake off the spell. He concluded his speech with the assertion of Jefferson's benediction on the United States Bank!

The Democratic "history of the parties" followed, with one later to be noted exception, the outlines of Van Buren's speech in the Senate in 1828. After the Revolution, it was said, there was a dangerous relapse into Toryism. Jefferson saw the issue and determined to act. "He perceived, at once, that the work of the revolution was unconsummated;—that the guarantee against a retrograde movement was yet wanting;—and that unless his fellow-citizens were made aware of this danger" they would lose their liberties. The aroused populace succeeded in shaping the Tory-inspired Constitution to the principles of '76, notably by the addition of the first ten amendments, only to witness the Federalist betrayal in the next decade. The frustrated monarchists, "taught by experience the danger of openly avowing their designs, without at all faltering in their purposes, sought to accomplish their object by adroit and insidious means"—the Hamiltonian financial system. Jefferson again came to the rescue. He founded, organized, and led the party of the people against entrenched Federalism. The victory of 1800 was the people's "first authentic and emphatic ratification of the entire Democratic creed." Jefferson in power did what he could to restore "the primitive purity of our system." Political principles slackened under his successors, however, and the "monied aristocracy," with the leverage of economic privilege, raised itself again to power. 1828 repeated 1800. Jacksonian Democracy sought to finish the work begun by Jefferson.

This may be taken as a synthetic statement of the Jacksonian rationale of political conflict, which was also the historical framework of the myth. It was argued, much extended and embellished with quotations from Jefferson and lesser luminaries, in newspapers and tracts, in convention addresses and orations, on the floors of Congress and state legislatures. Jackson himself accepted the dramatic role, "the second Jefferson," it assigned to him in history. He wrote in 1835:

I have long believed, that it was only by preserving the identity of the Republican party as embodied and characterized by the principles introduced by Mr. Jefferson that the original rights of the states and the people could be maintained as contemplated by the Constitution. I have labored to reconstruct this great party and bring the popular power to bear with full influence upon the Government, by securing its permanent ascendancy.

Thinking men regardless of party were keenly interested in "the history of the parties." This was, in fact, the mental design of most writing on the history of the United States under the Constitution. But though the design was historical, its value for many was philosophical. When men as diverse as Van Buren and Adams, Alexander Everett and William Sullivan, wished to state their theoretical views on American government, they cast them in the form of party history. The history of the parties was the common American substitute for formal political theory.

George Camp's little volume, *Democracy*, in 1836, was the first formal treatise on democracy as a *theory* of American government. Camp complained that Americans lived "in the rich experience and practical enjoyment of democratic freedom, but in entire and reckless indifference to its abstract principles." No native school of theorists to combat the European speculators followed Camp, despite his prediction of dire results from this indifference to theory; and partly for the reason Camp recognized, that is, the active bent of American life and satisfaction with the "rich experience." But there were two additional reasons why Americans lacked or did not need a *theory* of democracy, and the Jefferson image illumined both of them. For one thing, as Harriet Martineau observed, Americans were imaginatively possessed with the idea of the Declaration of Independence. This was The Word, *the* American idea, "their high democratic hope, their faith in man." And all the necessary principles to the nation's farthest horizons were enfolded in and unfolded from that idea. Equally important was "the history of the parties," conceived as a rationale of enduring conflict of principle within the American system.

A simple theory was implicit in the history. As a leading Massachusetts Jacksonian declared, "if ever history was 'philosophy teaching by example,' we have that philosophy teaching us in the history of the great parties that have divided the country." The division was held to be radical, uniform, and continuous. The Jacksonians believed with Jefferson that the division of conservative and liberal, aristocratic and republican, was rooted in the nature of man. "One fears most the ignorance of the people; the other the selfishness of rulers independent of them." The Federalist-Republican conflict permanently set this natural division of temperament and principle in American politics. And therefore, as Van Buren said, there were no better tests of the creeds and motives of the present parties than "the characters and dispositions of those by whom the parties themselves were founded and, in their earlier stages, guided." In America, as in no other country, he continued, everyone is a disciple of Hamilton or of Jefferson. The picture of these two colossuses contending for the nation's future almost from the hour of its birth was the dramatic center of the Jacksonian myth. Political debate was carried on in the reflection of the epic struggle. The struggle must go on, the Jacksonians believed, "as long as ours remains a free government, and as long as the characters and dispositions of men remain what they are."

An ideology of conflict derived from a vivid past was thus incorporated into American politics. On the one side, the Jeffersonians were those who cherished the people, obeyed the Constitution, and left everyone free to enjoy the honest fruits of his own industry. On the other side were those who feared the people, made the Constitution an instrument of aristocratic privilege, and took "from the mouth of labor the bread it has earned." Needless to say, this was not an accurate representation of politics in the Jacksonian era or at any time. Whether corporate privileges and bank monopolies were good or bad—the crucial issue of that time—was not, after all, a fundamental issue of principle and interest such as divides genuinely aristocratic and democratic parties. Yet what is *fundamental* depends upon the standards and expectations of a given society. In America, where the extent of freedom and equality was a patriotic boast and a puzzle to Europeans, they were higher than in any other time or place. The relative unity of ideals and uniformity of conditions furnished, paradoxically, the basis of deep and on-going political conflict. The conditions of agreement were accompanied by the disturbing inability to agree upon practical meanings and applications of principles. And the existence of a climate of free opinion, in which the conflict could be carried on, assured its generous development.

No one wrote more persuasively of equality and uniformity in America than the young Frenchman, Alexis de Tocqueville, in Jackson's reign. From his vantage point, the party divisions seemed trifling; yet Tocqueville also saw that the passions and heroics of the new democracy were not empty delusions.

The hatred which men bear to privilege increases in proportion as privileges become more scarce and less considerable, so that democratic passions would seem to burn most fiercely at the very time when they have least fuel. . . . When all conditions are unequal, no inequality is so great as to offend the eye; whereas the slightest dissimilarity is odious in the midst of general uniformity: the more complete is this uniformity, the more insupportable does the sight of such a difference become. Hence it is natural that the love of equality should constantly increase together with equality itself, and that it should grow by what it feeds upon.

How much more so did this seem to be the case of democracy when democracy was related to the storied Jeffersonian past!

"Words [or names] are things," someone had said, and members of both parties saw in this slight phrase the style or even the genius of democratic politics. The axiom conveyed a sense of the added importance of evocative rhetoric and symbols to the engineering of consent within a broad and diffuse electorate. The Jackson party took the name "Democracy," and therein acquired a potent political asset. It was, as a conservative publicist wrote, a "talisman" against which rational argument was vain. "The fate of the country is sealed up in this SINGLE word, and there is no escape from its influence. It is dear to the native born of the land, and every immigrant comes here for the sake of DEMOCRACY. DEMOCRACY all the world over is the proud name of the people's sovereignty, and so it is destined to be." The word had once had a fairly precise meaning. The Federalists had used it as a Jacobinical stigma on the Jeffersonians in 1800. Dictionaries commonly distinguished a *republic*, in which "the exercise of sovereign power is lodged in representatives of the people," from a *democracy*, in which "the whole people exercise the power of sovereignty in person." By 1840, however, common usage had blurred the distinction: a government republican in form became in the public imagination a democracy, in the vague sense of "will of the people." Since Jefferson, though he never applied the name to himself, was associated historically with the popular struggle, his metamorphosis into a democrat (and Democrat) followed naturally once the dominant ideology described that struggle and the spirit of American government as democratic.

The names, the slogans, the symbols—the whole Jacksonian myth—were much denounced, but the opposition was seriously divided on what to do about it. One group considered hostility to democracy and its supposed progenitor, Jefferson, a badge of honor and pride. It was reduced to impotence by 1840. Another and ascendant group of Whig politicians sought to beat the Jacksonians at their own game. The original National Republican position was to transcend the old party conflict in the spirit, the true spirit as Adams had believed, of Jefferson's First Inaugural. After 1828, however, there was no return to this bland view of the parties.

The Bank War epitomized Jacksonian Democracy partly because it made manifest the myth of return to the Jeffersonian landmarks. "We once more stood on the old democratic ground." The creation of the first United States Bank in 1791 was commonly thought, as Jefferson averred in the Anas, the first great party issue to arise under the Constitution. The first Bank ran its course in 1811, but five years later the slack Republicans chartered its successor. Jackson determined to destroy this Federalist hydra. The first Bank no less than the second was on trial. The clashing images of Jefferson and Hamilton hovered in the background of Jackson and Nicholas Biddle, the Bank's director.

In Jeffersonian usage, the Bank was Hamilton's permanent engine of moneyed influence and corruption, an adroit back door to monarchy, a vast, secret, intricate power beyond the people's understanding or control, unconstitutional, centralizing, aristocratic. The Jacksonian attack was couched in this familiar language, and it evoked all these dangers, real or imaginary. The question was not simply one of policy—of how the government should manage its finances—nor was it simply one of economics. The Jeffersonians had enmeshed the Bank in fears of monarchy and aristocracy from which it could never be entirely freed. While their successors were more restive under the Bank's economic power, they nevertheless reaffirmed

Jefferson's belief that the fundamental issue was one of the *form* of government.

Jackson suddenly opened the new debate on the Bank in December 1829, coincident with the appearance of Jefferson's *Memoirs*. The work presented a rather full conspectus of Jefferson's opinions on federal finances. Aside from the Anas, the most important anti-Bank item was a letter to Albert Gallatin in 1803. "This institution," Jefferson wrote to his Secretary of Treasury, "is one of the most deadly hostility existing, against the principles & form of our Constitution . . . . I deem no government safe which is under the vassalage of any self-constituted authorities, or any other authority than that of the nation, or its regular functionaries." The letter was widely printed in the administration press following Jackson's lead in 1829, and regularly for several years thereafter. When Jackson first suggested a Treasury bank to assume the governmental functions of the condemned corporation, and until the establishment of the Independent Treasury several years later, Jefferson's observation to Gallatin that the government should "make a beginning towards an independent use of our own money" was often cited as the germinal conception. There were other attempts, all conjectural or imaginary, to dignify the Independent Treasury as Jeffersonian.

In October 1829, Van Buren's party organ in New York, the *Albany Argus,* rescued from obscurity Jefferson's report in 1791 against the constitutionality of the Bank. Jackson held the same position on the constitutional question, although the Supreme Court had ruled to the contrary. The report noted, moreover, that the power of Congress to charter corporations had been specifically rejected in the Constitutional Convention. Additional testimony in the Anas from two members of the Convention seemed to place the point beyond cavil. All this was forgotten history in 1829; the Jacksonians were glad to have the benefit of it.

As always, however, the "orthodoxy" of Jefferson's opinions was weakened by the "heresy" of his actions. Three months after he wrote Gallatin of the Bank's "deadly hostility" to republican government, he approved the establishment of the New Orleans branch of the institution. In his message vetoing recharter in 1832, Jackson dwelled at length on the danger of the Bank's foreign stockholders; but, as a congressman exulted, the Apostle of Liberty himself "sold to foreigners all the stock which the United States held in the existing Bank." The fact that Jefferson did not disturb Hamilton's Bank, or consistently advocate a different system, suggested his practical acceptance. Biddle's friends circulated rumors of Jefferson's "deathbed conversion" to the Bank idea. These were unfounded, but they rested on reasonable suppositions. The second Bank was a Republican measure; the Sage of Monticello's attack on the American System was not aimed primarily at the Bank; and his disciples, once they turned to construction of an alternate system, were unable to agree on a "Jeffersonian solution."

In truth, there was no Jeffersonian solution. There were Jeffersonian sentiments: distrust of central banking, fear of privilege and moneyed influence in government, hostility to stock manipulation, to the soft and fickle values of paper money, and so on. The sentiments were mostly negative. They evoked the picture of a society in which men dealt in hard coin and banks were but ciphers. Many Jacksonians, including the President, had a "trained incapacity" to deal with the complicated problems of financial management in an expanding economy. They were obsessed by fears of Hamiltonian Federalism, trained in opposition to bank power as a matter of principle, incapable of dissociating paper and stock from corruptions of the Old Republican ideal. But other Jacksonians rejected this archaic attitude. They opposed the United States Bank precisely because it checked capitalist expansion through its power over state banks. Their "Jeffersonian solution" called for reliance on state banks for the custody of the government's money and for rapid credit expansion. The administration gave the system a trial, with most unsatisfactory results. The two groups could occupy common Jeffersonian ground in opposition to the principle of corporate privilege, of which the monstrous example was the Bank; but when one group looked backward to the plain Republican order and the other group looked forward to a free and fluid democratized capitalism, no constructive "Jeffersonian solution" was possible between them.

Thoughtful Jacksonians broached a theory of democracy, but succeeded only in intellectualizing elements of the myth. The theory, if such it may be called, consisted not so much of ideas as the emotional counterpart of ideas. Enveloped in Jeffersonian habit and feeling, Democratic speculations on society and government clustered around a few central concepts. Three of these of particular relevance for the Jefferson image were Nature, The People, and Genius.

Nature signified in the Jacksonian mind a set of beneficent principles at work in society, which if let alone would automatically secure the morals and the rights of all men. Jacksonians called for a return to "the natural system" governed by "the voluntary principle." The system was a social Newtonianism, "borrowed from the example of the perfect self-government of the physical universe, being written in letters of light on every page of the great Bible of Nature." This commonplace idea was especially associated with Jefferson, who had crystallized the whole eighteenth century philosophy of natural law and put it at the foundation of American government. The noted tragedian Edwin Forrest, in a much heralded oration, compared Jefferson to Bacon. As Bacon freed natural science from artificialities and subtleties and placed it on the firm basis of elementary truth, so Jefferson made politics a moral science by the discovery of "those eternal self-evident first principles of justice and reason on which alone the fabric of government should be reared." Jefferson was apparently the liberating scientist who had discovered the sum of political truth once and for all, and thus put an end to the habit of mind that led to the discovery!

The most persistent and dogmatic application of the Nature concept was expressed in the Jeffersonian maxim, "That government is best, which governs least," the motto of the party magazine, as its twin, "The world is too much governed," was the motto of the party newspaper. The "too much" that especially aroused the Jacksonians was economic privilege. Privilege, it was assumed, was the product of unequal laws, special interest legislation of which the Bank was the monstrous example. The central government was highly susceptible to this aristocratic disease because of its remoteness from the corrective action of popular opinion. Government should act only in respect to individuals, and such action was wholly negative: "to prevent the rights of citizens from being infringed or encroached upon." The best reliances of a healthy society, George Camp wrote, are "the strong natural impulses of self-interest," which he assumed with Jefferson no less than with the Concord philosopher of "self-reliance" to be rooted in a moral sense and made agreeable to the interests of society by the beneficent design of nature. Jackson could speak of reducing the government to "a simple machine" because of his assumptions about the ordered health and freedom of society. It had been his fixed purpose, he said in 1834,

to persuade my countrymen, so far as I may, that it is not in a splendid government supported by powerful monopolies and aristocratical establishments that they will find happiness or their liberties protection, but in a plain system, void of pomp, protecting all and granting favors to none, dispensing its blessings, like the dews of Heaven, unseen and unfelt save in the freshness and beauty they contribute to produce.

The most articulate representative of this outlook was the journalist and voice of the radical wing of New York Democracy, William Leggett. Young Walt Whitman looked upon Leggett as the intellectual successor of Jefferson. If any article of our faith is heterodox as tried by Jefferson's standard, Leggett challenged, "let it be pointed out, and we promise to renounce it at once." Interested in the equal rights of property and the rational conduct of government, Leggett thought both could be achieved if politics were sealed off from the scramble for rewards and privileges. Let everyone manage his own prosperity. Let the action of government be limited to common concerns, which reason might arbitrate.

This was the meaning of the First Inaugural. It enshrined for all time, in Leggett's view, "the fundamental maxim of democracy *and* political economy." The doctrine of Jefferson and the doctrine of Adam Smith were "twin sisters," both "the natural champions of freedom," the former looking to the kind of government that assured the harmonious and equalizing movement of the latter. And so Leggett called for the total disengagement of government from the economy: repeal usury laws, abolish government inspection in every branch of trade, return the postal service to private enterprise. Leggett's sharp recoil from the abuses of government economic activity led him to the conviction that no power in this field could ever be exercised for the benefit of the community. "Experience will show, that this power has always been exercized under the influence and for the exclusive benefit of wealth."

The psychic shock of the Hamiltonian alliance of wealth and government set up in the tradition stemming from Jefferson an ideological block to the recognition of economic inequalities and abuses that arose outside of politics. One of the main effects of the Jacksonian war on privilege, as recent historians have shown, was to liberate capitalism and to check the only power of surveillance over it, on the assumption that such a power was inherently un-democratic. The social outlook of most Jacksonians was pre-capi-talistic. Their Jeffersonian vision of society contemplated neither great capital formations nor great cities nor great classes of rich and poor. But since these Hamiltonian developments occurred in a society that was spiritually Jeffersonian, a democratic rationale for them at once suggested itself. The capitalist society, men could say, was the natural result of democratic principles, of individual freedom, equal rights of property, and limited government. "The distinction of wealth, so long as it confers no political privileges . . . is a peculiarly democratic distinction," Camp wrote, "since wealth may be said to be almost within every man's reach; at least, every man is free to strive in an equal competition to obtain it." At this point, the Jeffersonian heritage entered into capitalist ideology, finding its ironic fulfillment after the Civil War when Jefferson was linked to Spencerian *laissez faire* philosophy and the Supreme Court invoked the Declaration of Independence to put property rights beyond the reach of the people's sovereignty.

The concept of The People took two distinct forms in Jacksonian thought. One was summed up in the phrase "the sovereignty of the people." The People, in this sense, was a metaphysical entity: the will of the *whole* nation, the rule of the people *en masse*. Laws and institutions were good or bad according to their popular character. Jackson appealed to this pervasive sentiment in 1828 when he wrote, *"The people must themselves triumph*—a great principle is at stake, & if they do, then it can be said that all power flows from them." The second meaning referred to what Jackson once

called "the real people," that is, the great majority of producers in
the society. It embraced workers and small tradesmen—all whose
success depended upon their own virtue and industry—but particularly the cultivators of the soil. "The wealth and strength of a
country are its population," Jackson echoed Jefferson, "and the best
part of that population are the cultivators of the soil. Independent
farmers are everywhere, the basis of society, and the true friends
of liberty." Obviously, the *sovereignty* and the *agrarian* conceptions
of The People were incompatible. Both belonged, nevertheless, to
the Jeffersonian vision of an essentially rural society, in which men
were their own masters, vigilant of their rights, and constant to
express their will.

The resources of "popular sovereignty" were numerous and
notorious. The people had been enthroned and were anxious to
taste their power. No measure could succeed unless it made some
show of conformity to the popular will. As the mythicized Father
of Democracy, Jefferson figured prominently in this idealization of
the people. The Virginia reformers of 1829 sought a popular
suffrage under the sanction of his name. Over a decade later, the
Dorr rebels in Rhode Island justified their revolutionary action to
obtain a democratic constitution by appeal to the Jeffersonian idea
of "the sovereignty of the living generation." In the constitutional
conventions of Pennsylvania (1837) and Illinois (1847), elective
judiciaries were advocated on popular doctrines derived from
Jefferson.

Jackson enunciated the principle of "rotation in office" in his first
message to Congress. Under it administrative offices would be made
as fully responsive to the popular will as elective offices. The duties
of federal office, in Jackson's view, were so plain and simple that
the average citizen was competent to perform them. He was, in
fact, a better public servant than the man of trained intelligence,
since "in a free government the demand for moral qualities should
be made superior to that of talents." Many Democrats and some
Whigs traced the principle to Jefferson, as well as the practice of
partisan appointments it justified—the "spoils system." Like most of
the popular dogmas dignified with Jefferson's name, this one
stretched his principle so far as to alter its whole character and

intent. Jefferson advocated "rotation in office," but with respect to elective office, to the representative system, not to the administrative system; and he certainly never countenanced periodic assaults on the civil service. His concern for an educated leadership—a "natural aristocracy" he called it in a now famous letter—was dropped by the Jacksonians. His faith in the people as "bloodhounds of tyrants," "jealous guardians of their liberties," was transmuted into a faith in the omnicompetency of the people to rule.

Popular sovereignty might be exercised at two levels of government: in the making of a constitution, and in the regular processes under it. Everyone agreed as to the first case of "constituent power" that the people were sovereign, but men divided sharply on the question of how this sovereignty should be exercised. Do the people retain an elemental right to alter or destroy the constitution at will, or must changes be made under the terms stipulated by the constitution? Jefferson was invariably associated with the radical theory: the *right* of the community not only to institute government but also to alter its organic character, if need be by revolution. Conservative theorists bracketed him with French Jacobinism and "all modern red-republicanism, socialism, and communism."

Sovereignty as a normal process meant, in effect, the rule of the popular majority. Its implications frightened even some of the more advanced Democrats. The editor of *The Democratic Review*, John L. O'Sullivan, expressed the dilemma: "Though we go for the republican principle of the supremacy of the majority, we acknowledge . . . a strong sympathy with minorities. . . . This has ever been the point of the democratic cause most open to assault and difficult to defend." For how could the full measure of popular authority be exacted under the restraining apparatus of state rights, strict construction, separation of powers, and so on? O'Sullivan's simple way out of the dilemma was the Jeffersonian "least government" principle. So long as government was conducted in accordance with the present popular sentiment that "it should have as little as possible to do with the general business and interests of the people," O'Sullivan thought there was nothing to fear from majority rule.

But with other Jacksonians the will of the people acquired a transcendent and progressive power that could not be bound by mere historic and legal forms. George Bancroft, the philospher, historian, and Jackson leader, defined democracy as "the voice of God 'as it breathes through the people.'" It was "the collective reason and conscience of the people," rather like the Quaker "sense of the meeting," best approximated politically in the expedient of majority rule. Democracy, Bancroft said, "knows nothing, recognizes nothing, as a perpetuity, but the law of God," and it perfects its institutions "as fast as the increase of knowledge and uprightness shall demand." This was "the faith of Jefferson," whose proclamation to the world in 1801 was "Freedom of Inquiry, and the Power of the People . . . the right to discover new truth, and to embody it in legislation." J. Q. Adams had a different opinion of the fate of progress and improvement under Jefferson's system. Doctrinaires, whether of the Leggett or the Calhoun type, dissented from Bancroft's dynamic interpretation of the apostle they all acclaimed.

The great majority whose will the Jacksonians presumed to embody was composed of the producer classes. Jefferson had supplied the stereotyped image of the American conflict: the mass of toiling producers battling their exploiters in commerce, finance, and other speculative enterprises dependent upon the resources and favors of government. For Jefferson and his contemporary John Taylor, the producers were almost exclusively in agriculture. The Jacksonians embraced in the original conception the new working and small property classes of the eastern cities. Yet they were never reconciled to this, largely because of the enchanting Jeffersonian vision of an agrarian society, kept plain and pure by the mysterious values of rural life.

Jefferson's bucolic passages had helped to make "the true-hearted and independent yeoman" a fixture of the general American imagination, only the more firmly held by Democrats. It is a little curious, nevertheless, to see Van Buren's chief of the Boston Customs House, George Bancroft, complain of the "avarice and sensualism" of the market place, and insist that Democracy "rested for its support on villagers and country people." Van Buren himself later wrote, "It can only be when the agriculturists abandon the implements of the field of their labor and become . . . shopkeepers, manufacturers, carriers, and traders, that the Republic will be brought in danger of the influence of the money power." So fixed in their mind was the Jeffersonian equation of republican virtue and agricultural vocation that radical Jacksonians, such as George H. Evans and the young Orestes Brownson, saw no prospect of elevating the poor workers except by making each one an independent proprietor, preferably a farmer.

Although democratic in many of its effects, the agrarian dogma was inherently conservative. From the beginning, the anomaly of American politics was that the democratic tradition was the tradition of landed property. The two necessarily collided as democracy fused with capitalism and as the people were alienated and uprooted from the old landed order. The conflict was felt more strongly in the South, where democracy seemed to threaten the planter class which was always a pillar of agrarian politics. It was not unknown in the North, however, as the anti-rent wars on the great quasi-feudal estates along the upper Hudson revealed. In Congress, J. Q. Adams was the most vigorous assailant of the "old and long exploded doctrine" of Jefferson's. It was feudal and aristocratic, Adams thought. "It exhibited two great and *equal* interests [agriculture and commerce] in the community in the relative position and importance of master and slave. It could have originated only on a tobacco plantation. It was utterly incompatible with a government founded on equal rights."

Genius, the third concept in the Jacksonian political imagination, referred particularly to the nature of democratic leadership. In Jacksonian usage it had the same connotations as in the romantic literature and philosophy of the age. Genius was opposed to Talent, and a long series of distinctions followed: originative-imitative, intuitive-cognitive, untutored-trained, heart-head, natural-artificial. The man who possessed in uncommon measure the first qualities, it was believed, had the power in uncommon measure both to feel and to express the spirit of the age. Pre-eminence should be calculated not by what a man is or does, but by what he personifies, by his sympathy with the age. Since the conception assumed the superiority of Nature to Art and the existence of a collective will, it was a logical corollary of the two ideas already discussed. The Jacksonian thinkers derived their notion of Genius, or the Great Man, from such European romanticists as Victor Cousin.

The Great Man [Cousin said] is in fact nothing more than the people personified, and it is precisely on this account that the people sympathize with him; that they put confidence in him, that they are filled with love and enthusiasm for him, that they give themselves up to him. . . . The origin of the influence of Great Men is therefore something far more deeply seated than that of any mere external consent of their fellow citizens. . . . It is the deep, spontaneous, and irresistible conviction, that this individual is himself *the People,—the Age.*

The Boston scholar and editor, Alexander Everett, first introduced Cousin's work in America, and he applied this definition of greatness to Jefferson in 1834.

The followers of Andrew Jackson instinctively understood that he was the Great Man of the age. He was "the nursling of the wilds," possessed of a "fiery heart," "untutored genius," and "those great powers of the mind that can generalize with as much ease as the common man can go through detail." The image gained by contrast with his predecessor Adams: cold, effete, learned, timid. Cousin's definition was taken again and again as almost a literal description of Jackson. William Holland drew upon Cousin to distinguish between the two great parties. The mass of Whigs look to leaders of talent, for they wish to be governed. Democratic sympathies, Holland said, "are most strongly drawn toward the individual who can best embody and express the spirit of their own principles."

And so the process of generalization began which led some Jacksonians to make over the first democrat in their romantic image of Jackson. The aloof "Mr. Jefferson," the learned philosopher of reason, the prophet ahead of his time, was coerced under the canon of democratic genius. Bancroft's famous chapter on Jefferson in his *History of the United States* best illustrates the transformation. Bancroft believed the American Revolution owed more to the Quaker doctrine of the Inner Light than to the sensationalistic philosophy of John Locke. It was, therefore, important for him to adapt Jefferson and the Declaration of Independence to this thesis. The Revolution, he said, was the vindication of nature and the soul against the artificiality and skepticism of Europe. The Declaration consummated a long native development, and fixed the institutions and beliefs of a people who from the beginning "were near to Nature, listened willingly to her voice, and easily copied her forms." Jefferson was peculiarly fitted for his role in 1776. He loved to commune with nature; he took a never-failing delight in rural life; and music, the most spiritual of pleasures, was his favorite recreation. Not a "visionary devotee of abstract theories," but, said Bancroft, "the nursling of his country," Jefferson was gifted with "the sympathetic character . . . by which he was able with instinctive perception to read the soul of the nation."

The test of democratic Genius—"instinctive perception to read the soul of the nation"—justified the power of the leader. It was not *his* power but the people's. The dangers flowing from power in one man or many had always been uppermost in Jefferson's mind. The Whigs called Jackson's vigorous conduct of the Presidency "monarchical," and criticized it on what they assumed were Jeffersonian grounds. But it was part of Jackson's legend that he was only the sympathetic agent or grand tribune of the people. The concept was thus related to the shift, begun under Jackson, of democratic gravity from the legislative to the executive branch. There was no basis for it in Jeffersonian theory, nor in Jefferson's relation to his public. But it was inevitable that some of the gloss of the Jackson myth should be collected in his image.

2. *The Conservatives*

"Robespierre is not more detested in France, than Jefferson and Jackson are among the higher classes of America." So wrote the Austrian observer, Francis J. Grund, in *Aristocracy in America*. Grund mingled with the "aristocrats" (the usage was Jacksonian) and listened to their talk. In a New York bar frequented by merchants and bankers, he overheard a Virginian propose a toast to Thomas Jefferson. "Don't mention him for mercy's sake!" someone bellowed, "that vile blasphemer!—that infidel scoundrel!—that godless father of democracy, who has ruined the country." After a round of testimony on the insults all had suffered from the lower classes maddened by democracy, the whole company shouted, "Jefferson has ruined the country!" and drank it down.

The sentiment was prevalent in the Eastern cities, where the memory of aristocracy and the pride of Old Federalist families reinforced the natural tendency everywhere to couple Jefferson with Jackson. Jackson was more dangerous than Jefferson only because of his intrepidity. Jefferson was the original heretic, conservatives believed, and all the muddy tracks of the present led back to him and to the autocratic sway of his opinions. "No matter what evil invades the land, what dreadful ruin breaks up our institutions, what disgrace attaches and leaves its foul spots on our character, all may be traced to the damnable policy of Thomas Jefferson and his party." The root of the matter was the grip of Jefferson's "pedlar principles" on the American public. "The first symptoms of the elevation of our feelings as a nation, will be a complete revolution in our regard for his opinions, but until then, we shall only go on multiplying our dangers, and throwing obstacles in the way of our moral greatness."

The furtherance of this revolution in the public mind went on mainly under the color of history, but the assault also involved, usually within the history, a conserative theory of American government as a counterpoise to the reigning democratic theory. Like its opposite, the conservative theory was enmeshed in the party conflict; it was more a product of longing for a bygone age than of rational thought; and it made Jefferson the crucial figure in the discourse of ideas. The conservatives numbered such diverse individuals as: Orestes Brownson, whose disillusionment with *vox populi vox Dei* in the election of 1840 pitched him into the arms of the Catholic Church; Francis Lister Hawks, historian, editor, and one of the great preachers of his time; Taylor Lewis, classicist and theologian, who for many years conducted the "Editor's Table" in *Harper's Magazine;* Theodore Dwight, of the powerful Connecticut Federalist clan and editor of the *New York Advertiser;* Calvin Colton, friend and editor of Henry Clay and a prolific pamphleteer; Stephen Simpson, a renegade Jacksonian whose vigorous polemics won him the title of "the American Cobbett"; Horace Binney, leader of the Philadelphia bar; William Sullivan, a Boston survivor of

Massachusetts Federalism; and many others. The prominence of Old Federalists and the scions of Federalist families points up the influence of memory and pride on conservative thinking. Because these men had at their disposal literary talent and instruments of communication far out of proportion to their dwindling numbers, they made themselves heard despite their practical exclusion from active politics.

The web of conservative thought was spun out from the core principle that American government, rightly conceived, was republican rather than democratic. The form of the distinction varied, but the meaning was consistent: American government was a genetic growth from English institutions, and it established sovereignty in the permanent constitutional order of the state. Reasoning from this, the conservatives agreed with Edmund Burke that the American Revolution was "not a revolution, but a revolution prevented." As the Federalist historian, George Gibbs, explained, "What the people wanted, and what they took up arms to get, was not some new privilege, some new liberty, but the security of rights, privileges and immunities, which they had always had." Jefferson had, of course, in the Declaration of Independence thrown out the idea of a popular revolution; but this was *obiter dictum.* The Constitution and the Federalist party continued the sane and practical Whig tradition of 1776. The new government was republican; its chief function "to restrain, and control the popular will"; its chief purpose to set "principles, rules and laws, certain and permanent."

The real revolution occurred in 1800. Calvin Colton expressed the typical view:

From that moment, the history of the American republic has presented the singular spectacle of a republican Constitution, imposing salutary checks on the popular will . . . and yet, the popular will in the shape of a dynasty of opinion, has habitually triumphed over these provisions. The government has been republican in form, but democratic in fact; and the rising element of democracy has been constantly increasing in power and efficiency.

Conservatives believed that conditions would worsen "the more the idea spreads that this country was meant to be a democracy

and not a republic." The very life of the American people, Brownson
said, depended on the favorable outcome of the great struggle in
the background of everyday politics: the struggle between the
organic "constitutional order" and the alien "democratic order."

How had Jefferson managed to wreak such damage on American
institutions? By combining beyond parallel "visions of the imagination no age of the world has ever before witnessed" with talents that
made him "the most accomplished disciple of the great Florentine
politician." To the conservatives Jefferson was the visionary philosopher of democracy as Machiavelli!

Under the head of the former were Jefferson's democratic dogmas, "philosophic and sentimental fancies," whose only merit was
their attractive popularity. Brownson spoke for the generality of
conservatives when he said that Jefferson "believed it quite possible
to form the American people to the ideal model formed by the
infidel philosophers of France, and to change them from an English
to a continental people." The contrast to his rival, Hamilton, who
rapidly displaced John Adams as the antipodal symbol, was built
upon the theory-practice antithesis. Jefferson disdained "the tedious-
ness of induction" and "had an extravagant confidence in his
intuitive perceptions." Hamilton was the model practical statesman,
forming his opinions after "the closest inductive reasoning from the
experience of other nations." Jefferson the politician, on the other
hand, was exceedingly earthy and practical. He introduced into
American government the deceits of simplicity and the arts of
courting the people. He was, it was repeatedly said, "the father,
the founder, the establisher of demagogism in this country."

Jefferson doubled as theorist and practitioner of democracy. Perhaps the conservatives were merely confused. Hawks, on one page,
wrote that Jefferson "caught too eagerly at the visible, the tangible,"
but on the next page he, as opposed to Hamilton, was put down as
a "visionary." Brownson, on a single page, scorned Jefferson's
empirical philosophy and also said he was imprisoned by his
idealistic French theories. But this was, in fact, a confusion centered
in the paradox of Jefferson. The conservatives' double image
deviated from the norm only in its diabolic tones. If the two com-

mon types of anecdotes are an index of popular opinion, then Jefferson was both celestial and terrene.

The genius of Jefferson's politics was its assimilation of principles and ideals which in the whole range of modern history had been what the conservatives called them, "philosophic and sentimental fancies," to the kind of political knowledge and skill traditionally monopolized by conservatives: the kind that mastered reality. The conservatives sensed, in their wildly exaggerated way, that Jefferson had mastered reality for the dreams of democracy. "The conservative type of knowledge," it has been said, "originally is the sort of knowledge giving practical control." Yet Jefferson had stolen these mysteries and skills into a democratic system. In the Jacksonian era the conservatives were the impractical visionaries! How else was it possible to explain the idolatry of Jefferson, while Hamilton, "the greatest statesman of the eighteenth century," was reviled? Conservatives did not object to Jefferson's democracy because it was fantasy, but because it assumed the frightening forms of reality.

Jacksonian Democracy simply threw into relief the character and consequences of the Jeffersonian revolution. First of all, Jefferson implanted in the populace the gnawing doubt of its freedom and equality and the hunger for more and more. He, Simpson wrote, "bequeathed as a legacy to the people, *doubts* never to be dispelled by controversy, and broached principles that, while they cannot add to liberty or happiness, interrupt the calm enjoyment of both, by inspiring fallacious hopes in visionary dreams of political bliss." Second, it followed from this that Jefferson established a false and deceitful basis of politics. Once the multitude was rendered mad, there arose a class of political demagogues, who "like Cromwell, only shouts liberty to gain *power*, and cants *reform*, that it may successfully practice corruption." Third, since democracy was basically an opportunistic manipulation of popular whim and folly, it annihilated principle. How else explain Jefferson's numerous shiftings and turnings? The *Memoirs* left not "one stone upon another, or cement enough to bind together a fragment of principle or a pebble of policy." Fourth, the end result of popular supremacy was what Tocqueville called "the tyranny of the majority," which in practice meant the omnipotence of one man, "the grand tribune of the people." The Federalist executive was strong but responsible; the Democrats, Sullivan charged, converted the system of popular election "into the dangerous engine by which the people themselves may be enslaved, and made to rejoice in their chains, since it is their own act which puts them on." Finally, Jefferson's demagogic arts were responsible for the loss of dignity and intelligence in public life. American democracy was an odious thing, "without light or dignity, or refinement, or guarantee, or balance . . . of accident in its existence, impulse in its movement, and uncertainty in its object."

Those conservatives who went to the root of the problem presented by an alien "democratic order" imposed upon the "constitutional order" located it in the confusion surrounding the nebulous concept of sovereignty. Insofar as the Jacksonians had a theory as well as a rhetoric of sovereignty, it was in terms of the continuous will of the popular majority. Conservatives, on the other hand, believed that there must be a permanent will of the state above the transient will of its members and that this was formalized in the Constitution of 1787. Brownson traced the confusion to Jefferson's *obiter dictum* on the right of revolution in the Declaration of Independence. Following Locke, Jefferson failed to state whether the right to reform government belonged to the people under the constitution or outside of it. The French importations compounded this "fatal error," with the result that the people came to believe they had absolute power to rule. Similarly, Taylor Lewis attributed to Jefferson the idea "that the age of the State was about the same as the ordinary age of a horse, and that its vital functions could not much exceed thirty years." This doctrine of living sovereignty, Lewis said, robbed the state of any well-being "that cannot be resolved into something directly sensible or tangible to the present masses." Whether or not conservatives entered their reflections on the concept of sovereignty, they regarded Jefferson as the author of a theory of American government radical down to the ground.

The characteristic conservative tenet on the religious foundation of republican government clashed with the secularism that was one of Jefferson's richest legacies to democracy. The conflict flared up in the eighteen-thirties, as Jacksonians sought to raise higher Jefferson's "wall of separation between Church and State," and as conservatives looked to religious institutions to check the progress of democracy. In the conservative mind, democracy and infidelity were two sides of the same coin, a coin minted by Jefferson in the crucible of French radicalism and put into circulation during his war on the Episcopal establishment in Virginia. The obsession with the question of Jefferson's religion reflected a concern, not primarily for religion as such, but for government. It was an issue at the heart of democracy.

The conservatives labored to develop the figure of Jefferson the Infidel for several reasons. His name and opinion gave a color of respectability to all sorts of attacks on religion. Even his jottings on the Presbyterians—"the loudest, the most intolerant," "tyrannical" and "grasping at ascendancy"—supported a caustic anti-nativist attack in 1844: *The Warning of Thomas Jefferson . . . of the Dangers to be Apprehended to our Civil and Religious Liberties from Presbyterianism.* Conservatives were apprehensive of the Robert Owens and Fanny Wrights, reputed freethinkers, freelovers, and equalitarians of every variety, who linked atheism with socialistic projects. Thomas Paine was their patron saint; but they dedicated books to Jefferson, toasted his memory, and spread his radical ideas through their newspapers. The conservatives, furthermore, used Jefferson as the model of the mere politician, whose primary traits were irreverence of established authority and unconscionable conduct. The rejection of Christianity, Hawks observed, was the basis of all Jefferson's defects, for it deprived him of a *"principle of action sufficiently powerful to enable him to overcome human passion and prejudice."* Finally, and of utmost importance in the thought of some conservatives, the republic could not survive except on a religious foundation. This necessitated amendment of the theory and practice of separation of church and state.

"A commonwealth ought to be as one huge Christian personage," John Milton had said. Conservatives inclined to agree with the ideal, but knew it was impossible. Most of them accepted what was called the "voluntary system" of religious life in America, while holding that it was possible to maintain under it, if not a formal alliance, at least a connection between religion and government. Joseph Story, in his great *Commentaries on the Constitution,* doubted the permanence of republican government "where public worship of God, and support of religion, constitute no part of the policy or duty of the state in any assignable shape."

The opposite doctrine that religion and government have nothing to do with each other was, conservatives said, foreign to native institutions. "President Jefferson was the first American teacher of this sort of doctrine." Henry W. Warner, author of the influential *Inquiry into the Moral and Religious Character of American Government,* in 1838, argued that this doctrine of political irreligion was never accredited until Jefferson gave it currency, executed it in Virginia, and read it into the United States Constitution. The infidel President construed the valid guarantee of freedom in the First Amendment as placing religion entirely "independent of the powers of the General Government." Unlike his predecessors, and his successors until Jackson, he refused to proclaim fasts. His opinions on these matters contributed to the growing belief "that Christianity has no connexion with the law of the land." Nothing was more foreign to the American heritage, Warner said.

But the Christian conservatives knew that theirs was a rearguard action. During the cholera epidemic of 1832 numerous churches petitioned Jackson to appoint a day of fast, and Henry Clay, the opposition leader, got a resolution to this effect approved by Congress. Jackson rejected both the appeals and the resolution on Jeffersonian grounds. Simultaneously, the Democratic Governor of New York took the same position. The outcry against the Governor's action led the *Albany Argus* to a vigorous defense of Jefferson's principle, which it named "the one feature of our government more marked than any other." Here was additional proof, the editor wrote, that the anti-Jackson party was Federalist to the core. "Since the period when artful and profligate men sought to array the ... religious public against the immortal author of the Declaration of Independence, we have not known the old rant and spirit of Federal hypocrisy so hopelessly and recklessly abroad." The successful Jacksonian campaign for the Sunday Mail, the novel spectacle of "an unpraying legislature" in New York, the attacks on the religious oath in courtroom proceedings—all of these developments were frequently sanctioned and condemned as Jeffersonian.

The Sabbath might be desecrated, legislatures might not pray, fasts might not be proclaimed; but adherents of a Christian polity could always fall back upon the common law. Christianity had been recognized as part of the common law of England since the decision of Sir Matthew Hale at the Kings Bench in 1676. The identical principle was incorporated in American law after a similar precedent-making decision by Chancellor Kent, of New York, in 1811. In a blasphemy case, *People* v. *Ruggles*, Kent declared that Christianity is "part and parcel of the laws of the land." The ruling became the legal cornerstone of the conservative theory, with far-reaching implications.

The sole authoritative brief against this judge-made doctrine was Thomas Jefferson's. Two years before he died, he wrote an amiable letter to the English radical John Cartwright, in which he offered his explanation of when and how the judges "stole this law in upon us." The usurpation originated in 1613, when Sir Henry Finch in a famous work on the *Common Law* mistranslated a phrase in an opinion by Prisot contained in the Yearbook for 1458. The opinion held that the common law credited those laws of the Holy Church which were in ancient writing (*en ancien scripture*), that is, those practices and precedents in the canon law which were shown to be part of the common law. But Finch translated "*ancien scripture*" as "holy scripture," Jefferson said, thus taking Christian revelation into common law. Jefferson went on to trace Finch's error through Hale and to Blackstone and Mansfield, whence it came to America. He concluded his letter to Cartwright with a dare to any lawyer "to produce another scrip of authority for the judicial forgery. . . . What a conspiracy this, between Church and State! Sing Tantarara, rogues all, rogues all! Sing Tantarara, rogues all!"

This was a remarkable *tour de force*. Jefferson was the sole discoverer of this alleged origin of the legal rule. Learned lawyers generally assumed that it had no specific origin—Christianity had always been part of common law. Jefferson's opinion to the contrary thus had considerable importance. Cartwright at once, and to the author's distress, had the letter published in the London *Nation*. From there it was taken and printed in the *Boston Daily Advertiser* in 1824. Other newspapers copied it. Five years later it appeared in the *Memoirs*. The same year saw the publication of a legal compilation prepared by Jefferson, *Report of Çases Determined in the General Court of Virginia,* to which he appended a disquisition he had written in 1764 on "Whether Christianity is a Part of the Common Law?" The Cartwright letter added little to this brief set down when Jefferson was twenty-one years of age! Some unorthodox jurists at once accepted Jefferson's view of the subject. Thomas Cooper, for example, fully concurred and printed the letter to Cartwright in his *Treatise on the Law of Libel* in 1830.

Conservatives thought Jefferson's letter consistent with his whole outlook. It was but another of his attempts to undermine the integrity of the bench, demolish common law jurisdiction in state courts, and consecrate a godless state. Well aware of "the extensive influence which the opinions of Mr. Jefferson will exert upon his countrymen," conservative jurists were eager to expose him. Joseph Story's attention had been called to Jefferson's gloating letter when it was first published. After consulting the sources, and concluding that Jefferson's exegesis was "so manifestly erroneous" that it could not be excused as an "involuntary mistake," Story wrote out his opinion and later published it in the *American Jurist*. The questionable words in Prisot's opinion referred to a higher law, Story contended, rather than to an ancient written code of the Church. It seemed inconceivable to him that the erratic opinion of one man, a known infidel, should be given any weight in law. On his inauguration in 1829 as Dane Professor of Law at Harvard, Story reaffirmed the orthodox doctrine: the common law had always recognized Christianity as lying at its foundations.

Opportunities to test Jefferson's view of the law were rare, but one dramatically presented itself in 1834. Abner Kneeland, the leader of a substantial body of freethinkers in Boston and editor of *The Investigator,* was indicted for the publication of three impious, obscene, and blasphemous libels of God. Of these Kneeland had actually written one: "Universalists believe in a god which I do not. . . ." The trial was a *cause célèbre* in Boston. Most of the Democrats lined up on one side, the Whigs opposite. Kneeland was convicted and, after numerous appeals, sentenced to sixty days in 1838. The conviction was under a Massachusetts statute, but the issue at common law raised by Jefferson entered into the trial.

Kneeland's counsel, Andrew Dunlap, argued that the indictment did not fall within the statute against blasphemy, or if it did the statute was unconstitutional; and, to exclude the only alternative ground, he argued that the case could not be tried under common law. The second part of his brief was based entirely on the letter to Cartwright. The Sage of Monticello had shown conclusively that the accepted doctrine was "founded on a gross blunder or a gross fraud." Its importation to America muzzled civil liberty and restricted freedom of conscience. Moreover, on the crucial point in the indictment (the ambiguous statement about the god of the Universalists) Kneeland had said no more than Jefferson. Dunlap opened the fourth volume of the *Memoirs* to a letter addressed to John Adams, in which Jefferson said, "I can never join Calvin in addressing *his* God." "Are the publishers of the correspondence of the Apostle of Liberty indicted?" Dunlap asked. Jefferson, like Kneeland, did not consider this a profession of atheism but a denunciation of it. Dunlap concluded by repeating Jefferson's defiance to anyone to enter an authority to dispose of his.

Samuel D. Parker, Attorney for the Commonwealth, accepted the challenge. He based his defense of the precedent on Story's article in the *American Jurist* of the previous year, but he went considerably beyond it. Jefferson falsely assumed, Parker said, that because the common law antedated the Saxon conversion to Christianity, the link between law and religion was the work of the alien Normans. Actually, he continued, the link began in the sixth century, and Christianity was part of the law of England ten centuries before Finch made the alleged fraud or blunder. It was Jefferson who had willfully mistranslated Prisot. This "imbecile dart," Parker said contemptuously, was a gross libel on the nation's judiciary and religion—"the flippant and superficial judgment of the Virginia Voltaire."

Kneeland's martyrdom was successful: never again was a man convicted of blasphemy in Massachusetts, and rarely in any other state. And whatever the disagreement among jurists as to the merit of Jefferson's view of the law, he too was ultimately victorious in fact. The religious conditions and convictions of the American people made the orthodox doctrine a practical impossibility, as well as a perversion of the democratic creed. Compared to these massive forces of a liberal society, Jefferson's letter to Cartwright was of small significance; yet it gave libertarians high ground to stand on, almost their only judicial ground, in their struggles against the conservative judicial mind. The progress of Jefferson's principle went forward with slight interruptions until, in recent years, the Supreme Court has explicitly recognized his interpretation of the First Amendment—"a wall of separation between Church and State"—as the orthodox principle of American institutions.

The conservative image of Jefferson was the reverse face of the Jacksonian image. It too mythicized Jefferson as the Great Democrat; and the reciprocal action of these opposite forces of opinion made the conception virtually unassailable. For good or for ill, Jefferson was the Father of Democracy. Conservatives might have taken comfort in some of Jefferson's ideas and practices, as the enlightened Nicholas Biddle had in his eulogy of Jefferson; instead they rejected him entirely. Fearing the tyranny of the Jefferson symbol, they combatted it. Routed from the main political arenas by the Jacksonian revolution, they sought refuge in those institutions that were still free of direct popular control, especially the Church and the Judiciary. Even here, however, Jefferson haunted them.

One of the problems, of which conservatives often complained, was that they had no counter-symbol to Jefferson. First Jefferson and then Jackson had stolen the impersonal symbol of the Constitution from them. Hamilton was of course the great antagonist symbol; but Hamilton was in disrepute outside of conservative circles. Washington was, as with the Federalists of old, the god of conservative idolatry, and no American was so universally honored. The Bunker Hill Monument, as Webster declared on its completion, "by its uprightness, its solidity, its durability, is no unfit emblem of his character."

But a white, piercing granite obelisk did not generate heat or light unless in the nebulous realm of patriotism. The Washington image had the storied splendor of warfare, the dignity of aristocracy, the purity of a "Sunday school hero," the cautious conservatism of a venerable family guardian. "It might be set apart for individual homage," a conservative observed, but regrettably "the mass of a nation could neither conceive nor appreciate it." The conception was grand, but it had no political use.

The image of Jefferson, on the other hand, as Harriet Martineau said, lay "at the very heart of the people," chiefly because his ideas and opinions "went along with the national mind." "The people," conservatives wailed, "have placed him upon the throne of public opinion, and the statue of Washington is burnt, broken, and scattered into fragments." A body of political doctrine whose meanings could not be concentrated into images that evoked whole clusters of values and historic sentiments labored under a terrible handicap in a society given over to the sway of popular opinion. Conservatism found no solution to the problem, but a new group of democratic tacticians in the Whig party solved it with electrifying success in 1840 by the incorporation of Jefferson into its own priestcraft, in defiance of all the party's conservative members preached.

3. *The Whigs*

After Jackson destroyed the United States Bank by unprecedented use of the powers of the Presidency, the opposition reformed and rallied under the new banner—Whig. Clay had earlier proposed to retrieve the Republican name from its usurpers, upon whom he wanted to fix the "Federalist" stigma; but Adams dissuaded him, pointing out that the maneuver would not set well with their numerous patrons among the Old Federalists. The new name of 1834 was an appropriate choice. Lacking the connotations of the American System, which had suffered such humiliating defeats in the two previous presidential elections, it focused attention instead on "King Andrew," the tyrannical President. It put the party in touch with the Anglo-American tradition of the rule of law and, more particularly, of legislative opposition to royal prerogative from Magna Charta to the American Revolution.

The name also staked the party conflict from one of the Jeffersonian landmarks of 1800; for in America the Whig doctrine was
part of the Jeffersonian tradition. The Jacksonians had made the
most of this in 1828, when they attacked the American "House
of Stuart," whose reigning sovereign was the scion of the "monarchical tyrant" of '98, John Adams. Martin Van Buren had then argued
that the continuing party struggle arose in part from the opposing
principles, Tory and Whig, "the one seeking to absorb . . . all the
power from its legitimate sources, and to condense it in a single
head; the other . . . laboring assiduously to resist the encroachments, and limit the extent of our executive authority." Very soon,
however, the parties changed places on this historic issue; the
Whiggish segment of the Jeffersonian tradition split off from its
mass; and Van Buren, in 1840, had cause to regret the words he had
uttered as a party credo twelve years before.

So the Jackson opposition in its new guise entered into a vigorous
competition for the Jefferson symbol. The National Republicans had
appealed to the harmony sentiments of Jefferson's First Inaugural as
the guiding spirit of the parties. Some Whigs never abandoned this
course. In the heat of the 1840 campaign, the *National Intelligencer,*
a leading party organ, cursed the priestcraft of historic symbols "a
plague on both your houses." It was blasphemy, the editor wrote,
to invoke the name of Jefferson against any man or party "as a spirit
of inextinguishable wrath . . . little short of absolute extermination."
The *Memoirs* confirmed others in their belief that the battle was a
sham, and utterly futile, for Jefferson could be "quoted on any side
of almost any question."

The Whig leaders, Henry Clay at their head, gave up this approach
for sound political reasons. The party was, if anything, a more het-
erogeneous assemblage than its rival. It thus needed an ideology less
to define than to obscure specific issues of public policy, one sufficiently broad to unite factions and sufficiently attractive to encourage
popular support in its behalf. The forays of the President, "military
chieftain" become "monarch," cued the opposition's ideology. All the
former grounds of difference between the old parties have ceased,
Clay stated after the Bank Veto, "with the exception of ONE, and

that is the maintenance and increase of executive power." On this ground, he continued, "the true old democratic party, who were for resisting the encroachments of power, and limiting the executive patronage, [are] on our side of the senate, and not with . . . the Jackson-Van Buren democratic party . . . which does not hold a solitary principle in common with the republican party of 1798."

The administration's despoliation of the civil service offered the first of two major opportunities to test the ideology. The Democrats took refuge in Jeffersonian precedent; and as Webster observed of Jackson, "without the aid of that *precedent*, his acts would never have received the sanction of Congress." The alleged precedent was partly fact and partly myth. The Federalists had conjured up the monster of proscription from Jefferson's few and discreet removals; down through the years their apologists traced the beginnings of the "spoils system" to Jefferson's administration. Mingling Republican fact with Federalist fiction, Isaac Hill, the Jackson leader of New Hampshire, asserted that Jefferson definitely subordinated office to party. He went on to recall "the general turning out of federal postmasters in New England" after 1800. If any Republican in a New Hampshire town, Hill alleged, was unhappy with his postmaster, he wrote to the state leader, John Langdon, who contacted the Postmaster General, "and the removal was as sure to take place as the day is to succeed the night."

The Whigs defended Jefferson against his enemies on the right and his avowed friends on the left. They argued, first of all, that the analogy to 1800 was fatuous. Jefferson's election was a civil revolution; it could not have been executed had the appointive offices remained a monopoly of the defeated party. Clay spoke from bitter experience when he said that in the previous administration, so far was it from having a monopoly, the majority of officeholders supported Jackson. Jefferson's object was "to break down a pre-existing monopoly . . . and to establish an equilibrium between the two parties. The object of president Jackson appears to be to destroy an existing equilibrium . . . and to establish a monopoly." Moreover, the Whigs said, once the Federalist control was broken, Jefferson was guided by the high standard set forth in his answer to the New Haven

Remonstrance: "the only question concerning a candidate shall be—
Is he honest? Is he capable? Is he faithful to the Constitution?"

A clear test of party fidelity to Jeffersonian principle appeared to
present itself in the shape of a Whig measure to prohibit electioneering by certain classes of officials. The leading precedent was a circular Jefferson had caused the cabinet heads to issue in 1801. It
expressed his conviction that "the elective principle becomes nothing,
if it may be smothered by the enormous patronage of the General
Government." His apparent motive, in this instance, was to check the
political activity of Federalist officials kept on in the hope that they
might in time be converted to Republicanism; yet the Whigs made
the precedent their own and insisted the principle was more imperative than ever. When the bill came before the Senate, William C.
Rives of Virginia, who had just broken with the administration,
offered a substitute couched in the exact language of Jefferson's
circular. The Democratic majority assailed the bill as a "gag" in
the spirit of the Alien and Sedition laws. "They met the trial," Rives
acidly declared after the vote, "in the genuine spirit of modern *party
heroism*, and in spite of their professions did not hesitate to vote
down the *words* and *principles* of Thomas Jefferson!"

The Whig stratagems invariably failed, but in the process one of
the most bewildering problems of Jefferson's political career and
legacy was brought to the surface. Was he the older type republican
statesman, who conceived of public office as a public trust, to be
conferred "for the common good, and not for the benefit or gain of
the incumbent or his party"? The Whigs said he was, and thus distinguished Jefferson's revolution of principle from Jackson's revolution
of the party system. Or was Jefferson the first leader of a mass party,
the organizer of the demos, who brought the common man into the
circle of political competence, and was none too scrupulous in the
devices he used to serve his democratic ends? The Jacksonians said
he was; therefore, the Democratic party simply completed the revolution Jefferson began. Scholars of later times would never solve the
problem. Jefferson was one or the other, they said, republican statesman or democratic politician, and more than likely a little of both.
As for the Whigs, it was clear to them by 1841 that, whatever Jefferson's policy on patronage, the democratic government of which he

was the putative father required party control of the jobs if it was to function at all.

Since the President was the protagonist in each of the successive battles of the Bank War, it involved not only major issues of policy but also a terrific struggle between the executive and legislative branches of the government. The Whigs constantly elaborated their cardinal doctrine. Jackson used the veto power as a "royal prerogative," they said. He usurped the historic role of the legislative branch to determine policy and of the Supreme Court to judge its constitutionality. "Statutes are but recommendations, judgments no more than opinions," Webster solemnly declared. Jackson's dictation to the Treasury Department, which by the act of its creation in 1789 was made partly responsible to Congress, announced the reunion of the purse and the sword. Van Buren's Sub-Treasury plan, acclaimed by its sponsors as a separation of the government from the banking system, ordained a colossal government bank after "the system of Alexander Hamilton."

This, the Whigs cried, was Tory Federalism. Jefferson was schooled on Coke, Sidney, and Locke—the English assailants of kingly government. He went into power on the wave of popular reaction against the ministerial domination of Hamilton and the presidential usurpations of Adams. His Presidency was marked by the cautious avoidance of arbitrary action. All of his successors followed his rules of action until Jackson. He opened a new era of presidential power associated with the power of party. Even Old Federalists, William Sullivan for example, felt a pang of remorse that the strong executive of their creation had opened the way for democratic tyranny. It was the "one great error" of the Founding Fathers, Clay asserted, and he offered several constitutional amendments to correct it.

But Clay's proposals got nowhere. From the longer perspective of history the Whig tactics appeared to be "the rear-guard actions of the retreat of the old Republicanism that had begun its career resisting the Hamiltonian system with its executive initiative in legislation." If the Whigs exaggerated Jefferson's submissiveness to Congress, they were right, in the main, as to the Whiggish character of the Jeffersonian system. Not until Jackson did the Presidency become a popular organ of government. It was no empty boast by

Jackson that he was the first President nominated and elected by democratic processes. He could presume to represent the people, while his antagonists in Congress, Clay and Webster at front, were identified with Hamiltonian privilege. As Democracy superseded Republicanism, the nexus between legislative supremacy and popular government was broken. Jacksonian Democracy was rich in apostacy partly for this reason. Mentally, many politicians lingered in the world of Jeffersonian politics, and all were influenced by the convention of Jeffersonian landmarks. The Whigs claimed, and no doubt had convinced themselves, that they were leading a popular revolt against executive tyranny along the traditional lines of liberal progress. They did not see that the Whig and democratic principles were parting company.

Noah Webster, America's pioneer lexicographer, fired his final blast at American democracy during the Panic of 1837. The seventy-nine-year-old Webster was a household name because of his famous *Spelling Book.* Americans had forgotten his reputation four decades past as a Federalist journalist, just as they had outgrown the old party's fears of democracy; but Jacksonian rule and the Panic summoned Webster again to the political columns of the newspapers. America's disorders, he wrote, "are the genuine and natural consequences of *defects in the constitution,* and of the false and visionary opinions which Mr. Jefferson and his disciples have been preaching for forty years." Webster's indictment was in most respects typical of conservatism. He condemned the equalitarian theories, the flattery of the multitude, the elevation of numbers over property. The main corrective he proposed for most of these ills was an executive authority independent of the people. For nothing had done more harm, in Webster's view, than the dogma that monarchies are oppressive, since it had given rise to the more erroneous dogma that popular governments with elective chief magistrates are free.

William L. Stone, editor of the *New York Commercial Advertiser,* published one of Webster's essays under the pseudonym "Sidney." A loyal Federalist himself, Stone's newspaper was the successor, in fact and in spirit, of Webster's Federalist organ, *The American*

Minerva. As a leading Whig spokesman in New York, Stone claimed that the "Sidney" essay spoke for the party.

"Federalism Revived!" blasted the *Albany Journal,* the organ of the state's liberal Whigs, edited by the shrewd politician Thurlow Weed. "Sidney" (at first believed to be Stone) advocated the obnoxious and exploded theories of the high-toned Federalists. "In all that relates to the philosophy of Government, he has slept for fifty years as profoundly as Rip Van Winkle, and now wakes up, rubs open his eyes, and starts with the world as it was when he left it!" Weed and the realists around him practically read Stone out of the party. They had labored for several years to shake off the Federalist incubus and give the party a popular character, only now at the threshold of success to find themselves associated with the monarchical opinions of a stubborn Federalist. Advocacy of Federalism or tolerance of its historic trappings, another New York editor wrote, conceded the opposition's case against the Whigs. As he expected, the Democrats were quick to capitalize on the "Sidney" letter.

Seven months later, in July 1838, the political realists staged the Whig Young Men's State Convention at Utica, New York. Aside from stimulating enthusiasm in the forthcoming election, the convention's purpose was to declare the Whigs the present disciples of Thomas Jefferson. The formal address opened like any standard Democratic appeal. Jefferson came to power in 1800, it began, upon the overthrow of a party whose principles he execrated. "The leading features discoverable in the policy of that party were the design to perpetuate power in the hands of a few, to effect its centralization and consolidation in the Federal government, and to attach the fatal and fading splendors of monarchy to our Republican institutions." After a quarter century of Jeffersonian government, the Jackson party threw the nation back to Federalism. The aim of the Whigs was "to bring the Government back to its first principles"—the principles of Jefferson.

The young Whigs' manifesto caused a heated three-corner debate in the newspapers. The leading Democratic sheet, the *Albany Argus,* announced that the Democrats might "cheerfully endorse every word" of the address so far as it referred to party history. The *Argus* objected, of course, to the Whig artifice of presuming to speak "in the language of Mr. Jefferson and of truth." The maneuver also angered conservative Whigs. For the past several years, Charles King of the *New York American* explained, there had been a competition for the honor of Jeffersonian tutelage, accompanied by a revival of interest in the old parties. This was most unfortunate, he felt. The mass of Americans really knew nothing of the historic conflict, and their vision of present politics was confused by its grotesque shadows. "But," King concluded, "inasmuch as with the ignorant and unthinking, the Administration have made capital, by affecting to honor the name and adopt the principles of Thomas Jefferson ... certain Whig scribes seem bent upon the same experiment,—and by stealing the thunder of their opponents, to rule the Olympus of 'our fierce democracie.' "

Stone led the assault on this bald party stratagem, and several editors in and out of the state came to his support. In what false school of politics, he wondered, had the party's young leaders been educated? Never had there been a "fouler libel on Washington, and Adams, and Hamilton, and Jay, and the whole glorious array of patriots who framed the government." If the Whigs were ready to cut loose from them and "run a steeple chase for the loaves and fishes with the demagogues of the day," Stone would keep on the "up-hill road," the road of high principle and courage, in the track of the honored fathers.

The realists, from their corner, stepped up the verbal barrage on Stone and the "blue-lightists." To get rid of them, said the *Rochester Democrat,* "would be worth a Georgia gold mine to the Whigs." James Watson Webb, of the *New York Courier and Enquirer,* put the case candidly and cogently: "If the Whigs are to fight the battle of 1840, on the Federal grounds of 1800, the sooner they withdraw from the contest the better." As a further token of their conversion, the Whig managers set up a lavish campaign sheet, *The Jeffersonian,* under the editorship of young Horace Greeley, who had a hand in the Utica Address. "Jeffersonian, indeed!" the conservatives fumed. "In the name of all that is honorable in man, when did the Whig party discover the principles of Jefferson in their creed?"

The democratization of the Whig party was a general process, though nowhere was its significance for the Jefferson image so clearly disclosed as in New York. The Whig realists discovered around 1838 that they had been laboring in the shadow of Federalism while the Jackson party had pre-empted the democratic tradition. The appeal to Jefferson was a political gesture intended to efface the tracings of "aristocracy" on the Whig escutcheon and assume more popular bearings. To the Whigs on the political right it was a foolish and treacherous act. William Stone licked his wounds: "Woe to the man who dares to think that Thomas Jefferson was not the purest of saints and patriots."

The Whig "Log Cabin and Hard Cider Campaign" of 1840 passed into history as a ludicrous commentary on American democracy. The Whigs surpassed their tutors in the arts of electioneering. Issues were smothered under a blanket of invective, irrelevancy, catchword, and slogan. Great leaders were shunted to the wings and a popular hero brought forward. The successful campaign proved the party's legitimacy. It also offered an imposing demonstration of Jefferson's transformation into a democratic saint under the political pressures of the Jacksonian era.

The ideology of the ruling party was unchanged. New York Democrats met Weed's challenge by more frantic gestures and louder claims to Jefferson. Its answer to *The Jeffersonian* was *The Rough Hewer*: "Devoted to the Support of the Democratic Principles of Jefferson." Founded in the belief, it said, that these principles were fundamental, it constantly brought the parties to the Jeffersonian touchstone. The First Inaugural was the main text, with the one exception of Jefferson's appeal for party harmony, which *The Rough Hewer* silently eliminated. The startling declaration of the young Whigs in 1838 was offset the next year by turning the Democratic Young Men's Convention into a festival in honor of Jefferson's birth. Elder leaders sent letters of lavish praise. The chief orator of the occasion called the party back to the strict creed of 1798. In Jefferson's life and writings, the convention resolved, "we learn the great lessons of human rights and the true principles of self-government . . . adorned by every act and every effort of him whose memory we cherish and commemorate as the great advocate of Republican liberty."

Two leaders of the Massachusetts Democracy, Charles G. Greene of the *Boston Post* and Benjamin F. Hallett, mustered the facts to prove *Whiggery is Federalism*. Widely circulated as a pamphlet and in the press, this campaign blast accused the Whigs of a secret design to restore the Bank. The Jeffersonian smokescreen hid the Hamiltonian intention. Case histories of their leaders disclosed the fraud, the authors said. Daniel Webster, cast as Hamilton's Richelieu, had been an enemy of Jefferson's and Madison's administrations. The two surviving members of the Hartford Convention, plus its secretary, were prominent Whigs. From Richmond came the report that all the city's survivors of the election of 1800 who had voted for Adams were Whigs and all who had voted for Jefferson were Democrats. Greene also printed in the *Post* two letters which he alleged were written by an anonymous Old Federalist. "Is it strange that we should feel deeply humiliated," one of the letters read, "that the *pedlar principles* of Jefferson and Madison should now be sounded by those who are . . . at heart most strongly opposed to their prevalence in the councils of the nation?" But conservatives take heart! Bad as it was to use Jefferson's name, the Whigs could never seriously adopt his principles. "Those who fell with the elder and younger Adams, will assuredly rise with the Hero of Tippecanoe!"

Despite the conservative demurrer, the Whigs cheered for Jefferson and democracy. If their rivals, one scribe predicted, could be "stripped of the names Democracy, Jefferson, Madison, and the last war . . . there would scarcely be enough left to accompany Mr. Van Buren to Kinderhook on the 4th of March next." Jefferson was toasted in Whig celebrations: "the old and true Democracy of '98" or "the immortal author of the Declaration of Independence—we find no trace of the republican principles taught by him, in the practice of the last or present administration." Two could play at the game of old timers' allegiances. Thus the *Richmond Whig* said that of nine living men who had voted for the Virginia Resolutions of 1798, seven would vote for Harrison in 1840. Sergeant Jack Downing, the great creation of newspaper humor, inveterate Whig, sent an alarming report from Maine to "the Gineral" at the Hermitage. Uncle Joshua, the Democratic postmaster of Downingville, had deserted the party. Just as in 1800, the old man told Jack, "the Republican blood fairly biled over." "We are fighting over almost sich a battle as we did in the days of Jefferson and Adams."

The Whigs pressed their claim to Jeffersonian origins on the issue of legislative versus executive power. Clay's vigorous speeches for Harrison emphasized above all else the monarchical tendencies of the administration. The Old Hero himself, in spirited addresses to mammoth throngs, told how he had been reared on the "doctrines of '98." "I believe now, as I did then, with the patriarchs of the Jeffersonian school, that the seeds of monarchy were indeed sown in the soil of our Federal Constitution." They sprouted under Jackson. *"This government is now a practical monarchy!"* Harrison roared. His only important pledge was to reduce the power of the Presidency. "If the Augean stable is to be cleaned," he shouted at Dayton, Ohio, "it will be necessary to go back to the principles of Jefferson." The crowd raved. But Harrison's Jeffersonian credentials were not above suspicion. The Democrats charged, mainly on the strength of John Randolph's questionable statement in 1826, that Harrison had supported the Adams "black cockade administration." Harrison angrily denounced the libel, submitting evidence in the form of old letters and a record of long service under Jefferson and Madison to prove his attachment to "the old Jeffersonian school." When practically every politician was making the claim, Harrison's was not unreasonable.

But Jeffersonian cant from the lips of Daniel Webster was really too much! It was indeed pathetic: "Gentlemen, it did not happen to me to be born in a log cabin; but my elder brothers and sisters were born in a log cabin." Webster choked with emotion as he described his humble beginnings and his annual pilgrimage with his children to the natural fount of republican wisdom and virtue, the ancestral log cabin in the wilderness. In September 1840 the Massachusetts Senator carried the Whig message to the Old Dominion. He baited his speeches with polite allusions to the Sage of Monticello. On such questions as state rights, the powers of the executive, the wisdom of specific appropriations, Webster claimed fellowship with "the old-fashioned republicans of Virginia." Thomas Ritchie exploded: "In the whole course of this campaign, we have seen no humbug so audacious, no trick so absurd, as this attempt of the head of the Essex Junto to pass himself off as a Jeffersonian Democrat."

The democratization of the Whig party was one of several important factors in the triumph of 1840. The process involved party organization and electoral tactics responsive to the Jacksonian revolution in American politics. That revolution went on under the myth of return to Jefferson, and thus Jeffersonian symbol and doctrine passed into the democratic "spirit of the age." Coming to terms with this condition, the Whig realists perforce purged the party of its Federalist impurities and conspicuously embraced Jefferson, the Apostle of Democracy. So Jefferson was involved in the democratization process, though no one would suppose that the Whig gesture toward him was itself a major factor in the triumph.

The result was of utmost significance for the evolving Jefferson image. As the Tammany brave, Benjamin F. Butler observed, each party "inscribes on its banner the name of Jefferson." What a triumph! "What an illustration . . . of the vitality, the omnipotence of truth!" Greene of the *Boston Post* noted the same prodigious fact: "Jefferson is every where invoked, while about Hamilton people are as silent as the grave." Chicanery, demagoguery, hypocrisy were, as Greene reflected on the matter after the vote was in, gross and unsatisfactory explanations of Jefferson's ascendancy. The answer, he thought, was "that Jefferson thoroughly identified himself with the Democratic principle." The advance of democracy, however nebulous and shifting its meaning, swelled Jefferson's reputation; and throughout American history the image was one of the most sensitive reflectors of the democratic sentiment.

The politics of the age gave four clear faces to the Jefferson image: the intransigent Democrat of the Jacksonians, the ruthless demagogue of the conservatives, the liberal and practical statesman of the Whigs, the state rights constitutionalist of the Old Republicans. But all these visages tended to merge into the imposing figure of the Father or Apostle of Democracy. 1840 completed the first, and in a sense the decisive, stage of Jefferson's posthumous history. For, so far as politics determined the image, it was imbued with the mysterious qualities of democracy, and no one could ever quite escape its power. Only the state rights conception, as held in the South particularly, maintained for some years yet an integrity of its own.

After 1840 there was a noticeable slackening of Jeffersonian polemics in the party conflict. Democracy had triumphed, it seemed, and so had its Apostle. Men might continue to talk Jefferson, but it was in the nature of anticlimax and it added nothing to the generalized democratic image. Soon, however, the burgeoning slavery controversy changed the whole pattern of politics, its forces, ideas, and issues. The Jefferson image reflected the change. Jefferson assumed new and profound significance in American consciousness, for the tensions at the center of the slavery conflict were also at the center of the Jeffersonian heritage.

Three

HISTORY I

We are presented with the remarkable spectacle of a reputation more assailed by class and hereditary hatred than any other ... scarcely defended by a page where volumes have been written to traduce it— yet steadily and resistlessly spreading, until all parties seek to appropriate it—until not an American man between the Atlantic and Pacific dare place himself before a popular constituency with revilings of Jefferson on his lips. [*]

THE POLITICAL RAGE surrounding the Jefferson symbol was the principal obstacle to the discovery of the historical Jefferson. The symbolic function of great men, as Alfred North Whitehead observed, necessarily interferes with the *true* historical discovery. "There is the hysteria of depreciation, and there is the opposite hysteria which dehumanizes in order to exalt." In the instance of Jefferson before the Civil War, and for some time after, these twin hysterias virtually usurped the place of disinterested intelligence in the apprehension of the historical figure. The cycle which began with the *Memoirs* in 1829, which was propelled in its course more by the "hysteria of depreciation" than by its opposite, ended thirty years later in the resounding triumph of Henry S. Randall's three-volume *Life of Thomas Jefferson*. Although Randall's adulatory work was to become, for the better part of a century, the outstanding single influence in Jefferson historiography, it was also the capstone of an era. It rested upon the assumptions, and it embodied the feelings about the character of American history and of Jefferson's importance, that were

[*] Henry S. Randall, *The Life of Thomas Jefferson* (New York, 1858).

common to the era of the Jefferson image Randall experienced and consummated in historical literature.

Partisanship, it was commonly thought, was inescapable, perhaps even a moral obligation, where Jefferson was concerned. Randall fully identified himself with his idol, and conceived his work as a historical defense of the Democratic, *née* Republican, party, as well as a life of Jefferson. Because history ran into contemporary politics, he did not see how he or anyone could write dispassionately of the past. When the *New York Tribune* called his biography "a Campaign life, a political tract," Randall protested, "What American biography is not partisan, i.e. what biography of our political great men?" This was a rule with no significant exceptions, though Randall was keener in his avowal than most.

The outstanding narrative history of the early national period was the work of the Massachusetts Whig, Richard Hildreth. Although notable in its time for sober scholarship, its treatment of Jefferson read rather like a Federalist polemic. Of course, partisanship in retrospective writing was a matter of degree and different factors produced it. But chiefly because of antithetical feelings about the political symbol, every work tended to be for or against Jefferson. Even the defenses judicious writers, such as Randall's Virginia predecessor, George Tucker, raised against their feelings collapsed under the barrage of Jefferson's enemies.

"There is properly no history, only biography." Emerson's aphorism expressed the opinion of the age. Everyone believed "there were giants in those days." The history of the early republic, Hildreth premised, was essentially the biographies of a "few leading and conspicuous characters." Sometime earlier Tocqueville speculated that the effect of democracy on historical literature would be just the reverse. Historians of democratic times, he said, "attribute hardly any influence to the individual over the destiny of the race, nor to citizens over the fate of a people; but . . . assign great general causes to all petty incidents." In aristocracies a few great personages "occupy the front of the stage, arrest the observation, and fix it on themselves," while in democracies "all the citizens are independent of one another, and each of them is individually weak, [thus] no one is seen to exert a great, or still less a lasting power, over the community." This latter condition, Tocqueville thought, prompted the historian to search out vast causes and forces of which the individual actors were but the representatives or the effects. Some of Jefferson's interpreters—George Bancroft and Alexander Hill Everett, for instance—comported with Tocqueville's idea; but it did not describe the prevalent American conception of the national past. For the scene was dominated by a few great leaders, powerful, instructive, picturesque, who were believed to have acted as causes, made events, and fixed the destiny of a people. History tended always to become biography. And the explanation of past events easily became an exercise in moral judgment upon the men presumed to have made them. By Tocqueville's standard the historical mind of American democracy was aristocratic!

A third characteristic of this cycle in the historical literature was the manifest discrepancy between the dominant image it presented and Jefferson's towering prestige in public opinion. "Our opponents are far ahead of us in preparations for placing their cause favorably before posterity," Jefferson wrote in 1823. "History may distort truth," he continued, "and will distort it for a time, by the superior effort at justification of those who are conscious of needing it most." He expected an early reversal of the Federalist lead as private papers, such as his own, were opened to public view. But this did not occur. Thirty-five years later, Randall complained that despite Jefferson's unassailable public reputation, he had in the books "not one personal defender to every fifty personal assailants." Making allowance for extravagance, most informed men could agree with the estimate. Jeffersonian historians were thrown on the defensive. They wrote from a sense, as Tucker said, of great injustice to Jefferson's memory and injury to his principles of government. Federalist opinion ruled even in the schoolroom manuals and texts. Hamilton was lauded in the McGuffey *Readers,* while Jefferson was excluded from the entire series. The *Political Class Book* of William Sullivan, Story's *Constitutional Class Book,* the history texts of Noah Webster and the brothers Goodrich were all non-Jeffersonian, if not anti-Jeffersonian. The combative habit, once developed by Jefferson's friends in history, was not easily overcome. Even after the radical inequality between the public and the historical reputations was corrected, they wrote with feelings of resentment and with apprehension that Jefferson's memory and authority would be buried under the literary avalanche of his enemies, who, as Jefferson had said, made "the superior effort at justification" because they were "conscious of needing it most."

1. The Character of Jefferson: Virginia

Controversy about the historical Jefferson, stimulated by the *Memoirs*, reached its most significant development in Virginia and Massachusetts. Seizing the offensive, Jefferson's detractors attempted to dethrone the popular idol by critical examinations of his career and writings. They converged upon the vulnerable point, "the character of Jefferson," by which they meant both the distinctive quality of the man and his capacity for virtuous leadership. "Character" was rigidly split into public and private parts. With few exceptions, the historical critics avoided the latter in their published writings, unless religion qualifies as private. They were less concerned with Jefferson's public services than with his behavior in their performance, less concerned with his measures than with the motives behind them. They judged Jefferson's political leadership according to the canons of private morality, and demanded of his opinions the beautiful consistency of cloistered philosophy. All ideas and works were bad if their author was a bad man, one who lacked direct moral presence and fortitude under the stresses and temptations of public life.

Jefferson's defenders, on the other hand, judged him chiefly by his works and by the philosophy of his works. These, they believed, were the real objects of the assault upon his character. His personal defects, if admissible at all, weighed lightly in the balance against tremendous services of which the nation's history afforded irrefutable proof. Along the connecting axis between the two poles of interpretation were, of course, degrees of praise and blame, but writers generally gravitated to one pole or the other. And the lines of descent were pretty direct from the Virginians George Tucker and Henry Lee in the eighteen-thirties to the New Yorkers Henry S. Randall and John C. Hamilton a quarter century later.

No work in the literature takes higher rank for sheer malice than Henry Lee's *Observations on the Writings of Thomas Jefferson,* in

1832. Lee had gone abroad three years earlier to assume a consular post to which Jackson had nominated him in appreciation of his pamphleteering services in the recent election. Feeling some delicacy about Lee's morals, the Senate unanimously rejected the nomination. This scion of a famous Virginia family had been convicted of an odious crime, stripped of his estate and his social position. "Black Horse Harry" he came to be caᵁled. With the wreckage of his political prospects as well, he spent the rest of his life in an unhappy vagabondage abroad. Everything, he reported to a friend at home, "had turned to the bitterness of ashes on his taste." In this mood Lee wrote the *Observations*.

Most of the Lees of Virginia had some grudge against Jefferson. In the case of the younger Henry Lee, the immediate provocation was the "malicious slander" in the *Memoirs* on his father of Revolutionary fame, "Lighthorse Harry." The "slander" was twofold: that General Lee in 1796 was a "miserable tergiversator" dirtily employed to sow tares between Jefferson and Washington; and that in 1812 he revived all the old imputations of Jefferson's leadership during Benedict Arnold's invasion of Virginia by including them "among the romances of his historical novel," Lee's *Memoirs of the War in the Southern Department of the United States*. Filial obligation was thus the excuse for the *Observations*. The two major counts in the son's sweeping indictmen of Jefferson were unfaithfulness to Washington and pusillanimous conduct in the Virginia crisis of 1780-81. Strange to say, Lee had a high regard for Jefferson until he read the *Memoirs*. The Federalism of his father had led to political suicide, a debtor's prison, and a pauper's death in the West Indies. Despite the bitter memory, the son visited Monticello three days before Jefferson's death to look at the papers compiled in defense of his wartime governorship. Lee then virtually repudiated his father's censures on "this illustrious patriot" in a new edition of the *Memoirs of the War*. It did not occur to him that Jefferson was the fiend responsible for all the family misfortunes, including his own, until after the publication of Jefferson's writings.

The brief episode of the governorship had an importance for Jefferson's reputation far in excess of its historical merit. State pride was involved. Many Virginians far into the future believed Arnold's unresisted conquest of the state by a force estimated at nine hundred men "was the greatest disgrace that ever befell Virginia." Somehow the Governor was responsible, from incapacity or neglect or cowardice or all together. But the importance of Jefferson's war-governorship as history has always been tangential to its value for his critics as a demonstration of damnable traits of character. The younger Lee thought it "the most characteristic point in his career." H. J. Eckenrode, in this century, considered it the crowning proof that Jefferson was a "Rousseauist doctrinaire" incapable of firm and decisive action in a crisis. Jefferson's misfortunes in the crisis long retained the smear value the Federalists saw in them in 1800. A half-dozen pages in General Lee's *Memoirs* did more than anything else to set the pattern of later criticism; and the embellishments by his son, though too wild to be accepted on their face by any but hateful men, established the angry mode of treatment of the subject.

There were three main counts in the indictment: first, that Jefferson had failed to organize the forces at his disposal for the defense of the Lower James and Richmond against the sea-borne invasion about which he had adequate foreknowledge; second, that in the face of the invaders he acted a coward's part, abandoned archives, stores, and munitions, and fled the capital; third, that when the Assembly called him to account for his actions, Jefferson resigned his office and resorted to "grovelling diplomacy" in order to escape impeachment proceedings. (The famous adventure of Carter's Mountain—Jefferson's hairbreadth escape from Tarleton at Monticello—was a separate episode but one which also made Jefferson a quixotic object of ridicule.) Jefferson's defense to posterity was written by Louis H. Girardin for his *History of Virginia* from materials supplied at Monticello after the appearance of Lee's *Memoirs*. In the military situation then existing in Virginia, the argument ran, Arnold could not have been repelled; the Governor acted with courage and resourcefulness in the crisis; the Assembly fully vindicated his conduct; his withdrawal from the governorship in favor of a military leader was a patriotic act; and, it was suggested, the British surrender at Yorktown a few months later was closely connected with Jefferson's management of affairs. This formed the basis of all subsequent defenses in the Jefferson literature.

A calculated dupery of posterity, Henry Lee the younger branded Girardin's *History*. And yet, he complained, it was "received for gospel in Virginia." The affair betrayed, he thought, not only Jefferson's pusillanimous character but also "the nature of the spell which he casts over the public mind . . . and his own confidence in its endurance and tenacity." Jefferson lay utterly defeated in 1781 and oblivion descended over him; yet he rallied, and with the confidence of one practiced in the arts of popular deception "he determined to turn his escape from punishment into a title of glory."

Lee's examination of Jefferson's conduct toward Washington went far beyond his father's Federalist accusation of duplicity. With the *Memoirs* before him, he traced Jefferson's maneuvers to undermine the administration, first in the cabinet, and then from Monticello whither he had fled supposedly to enjoy the pleasures of farm and family but actually, Lee said, to pursue with more success his faithless campaign.*

The high point of Jefferson's campaign against Washington, according to Lee and every succeeding critic, was the notorious letter of April 1796 to Philip Mazzei, a former neighbor who had returned to Italy. No single writing from Jefferson's pen pursued him so remorselessly beyond the grave. Published successively in Florence and

* Lee gave only passing notice to the first severe strain between Jefferson and the President, which had its source in the newspaper warfare of the Federalist *Gazette of the United States* and the poet Freneau's *National Gazette*. Pro-Federalist writers charged that Jefferson enticed Freneau to Philadelphia by the award of a job in the State Department, in order to support him as editor of the Republican newspaper; that through the *National Gazette* Jefferson aroused opposition to the administration of which he was a leading member; that he countenanced, if indeed he did not write, its libelous attacks on Washington, and refused to stop them at the President's request. Jefferson's defenders generally denied these charges altogether, and pointed the accusing finger at Hamilton. Continually debated, the issue rested on dead center until 1854. Rufus Griswold then published what historians came to call "the Griswold story." In 1832, when he was seventy-eight years old, Freneau told Dr. John Francis (Griswold's source) that Jefferson had personally dictated or written most of the *National Gazette's* offensive articles on Washington. If the story was true, as Jeffersonians quickly pointed out, Freneau had perjured himself on his oath to the contrary at the time Hamilton first charged authorship to Jefferson. Dr. Francis himself soon discounted the story, and never was a particle of evidence found to support it. Yet it was taken for granted by many later historians, numbering such respectable names as John Bach McMaster, Edward Channing, and Paul L. Ford.

Paris, and then translated back into English for American publication in 1797, it accused the Federalist "Anglican monarchical and aristocratical party" of designs to "impose on us the *substance*, as they have already given us the *form*, of the British government." When at last in 1824 Jefferson wrote a defense of the letter, he insisted he had written *forms*, the difference between the singular and the plural amounting to the difference between monarchical government and President Washington's levées. His own copy of the letter appeared in the *Memoirs*, showing this and other slight variations from the original newspaper version. Lee, however, suspected tampering with the press-copy. Even if that had not occurred, he said, Jefferson's labored distinction was immaterial; it was substantially the same letter Jefferson's friends had denounced a forgery in 1797. (John Marshall took the same view in his new edition of the *Life of Washington*.) Equally fraudulent was the author's effort in 1824 to refer the remark about the monarchical heresies of late "Samson's in the field" to the Society of Cincinnati, and thus to remove the stigma from Washington. This was to deny the plain sense of the letter, Lee said, which was that these heresies had recently occurred in the highest places. Jefferson's construction of still other key expressions was the purest sophistry. Lee thus concluded his detailed indictment:

that the imputations contained in that letter, upon Gen. Washington, and his principal friends, were unfounded in fact, and calumnious in spirit; that the equivocating refusal to avow and explain it, betrayed at once pusillanimity, and malice; and that the gross and deliberate misstatements by which it is justified . . . are sufficient to deprive Mr. Jefferson's most solemn assertions, in all cases in which his interests are concerned, or his passions enlisted, of the slightest claim whatever to credit.

Jeffersonian historians read the letter differently, of course. It was neither intended to incriminate Washington nor understood by him in this light. Jefferson had a record of loyal service under Washington, and he expressed high praise and affection for him as a man above party. Following Jefferson's example, his defenders attempted to separate Washington from the Federalists. While this was a useful political fiction, Lee answered, it was as lacking in foundation and

as deceitful as the cries of monarchical heresy. Jefferson's later praise
of Washington, particularly the famous biographical sketch written
for Dr. Jones in 1814, was a kind of atonement, Lee said. He was
nevertheless determined it should not have its redeeming effect on
Jefferson's reputation. Where Jefferson qualified his praise, Lee
accused him of the old malice. Where the praise was full-blown, Lee
thought it further proof of Jefferson's duplicity, proof that he had
never believed his own defamations of Washington.

Another thorn in the nettle of Jefferson's relationship with Washington was sharpened by Charles Carter Lee in the 1837 edition of
his half-brother's *Observations*. For many years rumors had circulated in Alexandria of a late and acrimonious correspondence between the two great Virginians. After his retirement to Mount Vernon, the gossip said, Washington demanded an apology from the
author of the Mazzei letter. Timothy Pickering, the Massachusetts
Federalist, published and credited this report in 1824. Jefferson at
once denied it, and any contact whatsoever with Washington after
March 1797, in the letter to Van Buren which was also his defense
before posterity. No record of a correspondence survived. But Pickering, Henry Lee, and others suspected that the letters in question had
been clandestinely removed from Washington's papers by his secretary, Tobias Lear, whom Jefferson later appointed to office. Charles
Carter Lee obtained the first testimony of a living witness tending
to support the notion of a violent estrangement. Lawrence Lewis,
Washington's near relative and neighbor, explained to Lee how the
General's confidential clerk Rawlins had told him of recording several letters to Jefferson, one of them so severe "that his hair appeared
to rise on his head, as he recorded it, and he felt it must produce
a duel."*

* In 1836, in his edition of Washington's *Writings,* Jared Sparks stated that
the story of Pickering and others was commonly "reported and believed."
Approached by Randall two decades later, Sparks dismissed the story as a fabri-
cation. In the same volume of the *Writings,* Sparks put in circulation the mysterious "Langhorne Letter" of 1797. The fictitious Langhorne elicited from Washington political sentiments which might be used against him in Virginia. Washington evaded the trap. He was soon informed by a Charlottesville citizen that
the trapper was Jefferson. Sparks noted the assertion without affirming or denying
its accuracy. Numerous writers categorically charged the plot to Jefferson. Its real
perpetrator was probably Peter Carr, his nephew.

Out of such a mixture of exegesis and recrimination, of inference and gossip and legend, was the picture of Jefferson as the enemy of Washington made. The reason for the picture is clear. Federalist historians, as one who came at the end of that tradition observed, "have strenuously asserted that Jefferson forfeited Washington's confidence, as if this fact, if true, ought to involve a like withdrawal of confidence by everyone else. It has always seemed to the thorough Federalist," he continued, "that to question the perfect wisdom of Washington in matters political was a sort of secular profanity, and of this crime Jefferson was on some few occasions guilty." But Jeffersonian historians have just as strenuously denied the guilt as they have the conclusion drawn from it. Reluctant to acknowledge that Jefferson's opposition to Federalism was per- force opposition to Washington, quick to denounce the idea that Jefferson's Republican ardor stung and wounded Washington, they too have been sensitive to the "secular profanity" of unfaith- fulness to Washington and have gone out of their way to demonstrate the contrary.

The picture drawn by Henry Lee differed from the others only in its almost insane extravagance. Jefferson became in his eyes the greatest diabolist in history, one whose life-struggle was "to destroy the temple of American glory and to build of its rubbish, a shrine to the worship of his own image." Duplicity was his evil weapon: duplicity not only to Washington, but duplicity to the people by a hypocritical campaign to stigmatize all opposition to him "monarchical," duplicity to the Constitution as evidenced by nulli- fication and numerous other actions that belied his professions of "sacrosanct adherence to the Constitution," duplicity to posterity by his audacious attempt to rewrite history in the *Memoirs*. Luckily, said Lee, the last stroke of deceit failed. The *Memoirs* yielded the antidote to the poison, and thus in time the country would be "thankful for having escaped the mischief of Mr. Jefferson's con- trivances, rather than for having enjoyed the benefit of his services."

Unlike most other critics, Lee did not believe Jefferson's duplicity was due to a faulty understanding or a blunted moral sense. Having the capacity and the will purposely to deceive men and nations, Jefferson's entire public life was a calculated fraud. He was perfectly aware of this, Lee said. It was because he had a sense of guilt about his own conduct that, by a kind of psychic transference, he ascribed to others the base motives of which he knew he was the victim. His mind was of "a chameleon order," Lee said, rapidly taking the hue of the mind in juxtaposition to his own. His affinity to other men's desires was all the more efficient because united with the power "to instill, under the guise of disapproving,—to stimulate, while pretending to dissuade,—to urge on, while appearing to check,—and, a skillful rider of men as he was, to make the bridle perform the office of the spur." Such a man must necessarily fall into fantastic inconsistencies and contradictions. Inordinate egotism and ambition, the capacity to deceive, the chameleon order of mind, the want of honor and courage—these personal characteristics explained Jefferson to the Lees.

Henry Lee was in a unique position for a Virginia Jefferson-hater: he had nothing more to lose. He probably voiced the real, but largely suppressed, convictions of many Virginians. State pride and politics kept the better side of the Jefferson image forward. Lee's bitterness and malice, his clamorous insolence, his spiteful dispraise of every item in the calendar of Jefferson's fame, made the *Observations* a piece with the scandal his life had become. Jefferson's critics drew upon the *Observations* but shied from mentioning it as if it were poison, "a vial of rage" as Madison said. Tucker avoided direct answer to Lee, and Randall relegated his treatment to an appendix. The *Observations,* he said, were as unanswerable as Callender's libels and no more deserving of answer.

George Tucker began the pioneer work in Jefferson biography in 1830. Two brief lives, by B. L. Rayner and William Linn, appeared before his; but neither was important as history. Tucker ventured upon "the hazardous task" with two main objects in view. First, he wished to dispel the confusion and misunderstanding that surrounded the history and principles of the two great parties. A "dispassionate narrative" of Jefferson's life written in the "cool retrospect" of time would serve the cause of truth and sound government. Second, he wished to remedy the damage done to Jefferson's character by the *Memoirs* and the fresh impetus it gave to his antagonists. While not blind to Jefferson's errors and defects, Tucker said, he would draw a veil over these and place his virtues and services in a clear true light. *The Life of Thomas Jefferson* was, therefore, frankly partisan; but it was also temperate. Even C. C. Lee, whose revised edition of the *Observations* was prompted by Tucker's book, conceded it was "tolerably fair." And Randall was later to complain, "It was ice trying to represent fire!" Too calm and judicious for many Jeffersonians, it was too partisan and apologetic for most conservatives.

Before becoming Professor of Moral Philosophy at the University of Virginia in 1825, George Tucker had been a country gentleman, lawyer, politician, and man of letters. He possessed one of the most versatile minds in Virginia. He belonged, in the succession from Jefferson and Madison, to Virginia's liberal intellectual tradition. As it waned and "Mr. Jefferson's University" turned stuffy, Tucker grew restive and in 1845 left for the freer intellectual air of Philadelphia.

Tucker dedicated the *Life* to Madison, whose letter of acceptance and recommendation was the last act of his pen thirteen hours before he died. Madison gave freely of his own recollections, provided fugitive papers and documents, counseled the biographer on delicate points, and corrected the manuscript. Of the two Virginia Republicans, Madison was Tucker's favorite. Where their political opinions differed, Tucker agreed with the more conservative man. He admired Madison's amiable temper, the coolness of his mind, the moderation of his politics; and he consciously brought these qualities to his interpretation of Jefferson and his times. Between these two sober rationalists, Madison and Tucker, much of the grit and gravel of the real Jefferson was sifted out. The resulting image was a somewhat smoothed-down version of the original.

Believing that the great party conflict was the most important, yet least understood, part of the nation's history, Tucker devoted one third of his two volumes to the period 1788 to 1800. The parties divided on the question of the powers and limitations of the new central government. This constitutional division involved the more fundamental issue of republican government; for, in Tucker's view,

Jefferson and his party were on the whole correct in associating Federalist consolidation with anti-republicanism. The conflict was reinforced by the economic effects of Hamilton's measures and by the impact of the French Revolution. Educated to English ideas of government, anxious to remedy the genuine weaknesses of the confederation, wedded to special economic interests, the Federalists naturally sought to increase the power of the central authority, and some of the leaders hoped thereby gradually to change it into their ideal form. This was conspicuously true of Hamilton. It was, Tucker thought, "a fair presumption that those who admired him as a politician, and supported all his measures, could not have strongly objected to his principles." Hamilton had been falsely praised in history as a friend of the Constitution, Jefferson falsely condemned as an enemy of it. In fact, Tucker said, Jefferson at once accepted the Constitution, with a few minor reservations soon overcome by amendment and practice; Hamilton never accepted its substance or its finality. His strategy and that of his party was "to yield so far to popular prejudice as to forego the form they deemed best, but . . . to avail themselves of every opportunity of improving the existing government into that form."

Believing the republic in danger, Jefferson acted to save it. Tucker's Jefferson was a fighter, though an unusually self-controlled one. In retrospect, Jefferson's fears were exaggerated and his zeal sometimes blinded his judgment. The Anas were proof enough. Yet, Tucker thought, this did not deprive the fears of basis or the zeal of justification, nor should it be allowed to distract attention from the "unusual moderation" which distinguished Jefferson's political course. If he still held high ambitions after his retirement from Washington's cabinet in 1793, they were "tempered and regulated." It was untrue and unfair, Tucker said, to picture him as affecting a love for the tranquil pursuits of rural life and as disclaiming a leadership secretly coveted and insidiously developed. Jefferson practiced "no concealment" then or later. The Presidency only gradually came into view as Republicans forced the candidacy upon him. "Delicacy and forbearance" continued to mark his course until 1798. Even then, though at first inclined to extreme measures, Jefferson drew back, restrained his followers, and viewed the

Virginia and Kentucky Resolutions, Tucker said, as no more than
"a declaration of opinion, for the purpose of producing a moral
influence on the public sentiment."

Of Jefferson's Presidency, Tucker wrote, "it would be difficult to
adduce an instance in which a statesman in power more steadily
adhered to the principles he had previously professed." He thus
took issue with the interpretation which became popular with
Federalist-minded historians: that Jefferson's administration exploded all his principles and that he made no change in the system
of his predecessors. Not only did Jefferson adhere to principle, his
biographer said, but he actually laid a self-denying ordinance on
himself. Believing that concentration of power in the executive
tended toward monarchy, he reduced his own influence, as the
repeal of the internal taxes most clearly demonstrated. Had he
been as ambitious or as unprincipled as his enemies imagined him,
he would have kept these taxes and the substantial patronage their
collection placed at his disposal. It was precisely his stubborn, and
Tucker judged misguided, adherence to principle in maintaining
the Embargo that provoked the only significant opposition to his
administration. The outstanding achievement of Jefferson's administration was its subversion of power to republican forms in accordance with the maxim

that government was instituted for the benefit of the governed, and, consequently, that its power is not a *property* in those who administer it, but
a *trust* for the public good: that as power . . . always more or less conflicts
with the interests or the wishes of others, it should be as sparingly delegated and as forbearingly exerted as is consistent with the great purposes
of peace and security.

Tucker's view of Jefferson's public character was in striking
contrast to Lee's. Jefferson was seen, first of all, as a man of constant
and uncompromising principle. This explained, Tucker thought,
the remarkable fact that he was, in death as in life, both the most
worshipped and the most reviled of Americans. Second, he was
frank and open in his political opinions. As his words gave injury,
so he received it in return. It was easy enough to compile from
Jefferson's letters expressions at one time appearing to contradict

expressions at another time, and then to infer the disingenuousness of the whole performance. But, Tucker answered, whoever expects to find in the private letters of political leaders the same candor as marks "the confessions of the Catholic to his priest, or the young maiden to her lover" only exposes his own simplicity. Third, Jefferson was excessively optimistic and credulous on all matters promising utility and happiness for mankind. Thus his greatest virtues—confidence in the people to govern themselves and zeal for progress—involved his mind in his emotions, often misled his judgment, and opened him to attack. Fourth, in his adherence to principle Jefferson was capable of courage at the risk of his own popularity. His generous rescue of the notorious Paine from France, in 1802, scarcely accorded with the picture of a timid and calculating being obsessed with his own popularity. Finally, because of these qualities or in spite of them, Jefferson possessed a consummate skill in politics. The Federalists said he courted the people. No, Tucker replied, he was simply more sensitive to public opinion and wished its ascendancy, which was not a vice in a republican government. Only a "master spirit" could have molded the Republican party in ten years, accomplished the revolution of 1800, and vanquished the opposition.

If Jefferson's life was a fraud, Tucker reasoned, then so was the progress of mankind under republican institutions of government. His life was identified with this movement as much as Bacon's with free inquiry, Newton's with science, Columbus's with discovery. Revilers of Jefferson set themselves against the American people; for "beyond all his contemporaries . . . he impressed his opinions on the great mass of his countrymen." He paid the penalty of all men of vision. Misunderstood, reproached as a visionary and schemer, he wisely left his vindication to the future he grasped. The civilized world, Tucker concluded, "is every day approximating to opinions which he had deliberately formed fifty years ago."

Randall later criticized Tucker for failure to enter into the political feelings of his subject. The biography was partisan yet cold and reserved; the flat and circuitous style belied the agitation of ideas and parties; the warm human figure never emerged from the political abstraction. Although the most balanced history of Jefferson's public life written in the nineteenth century, it was not a work to arouse enthusiasm or command a large audience. The American edition was two thousand copies; it was never reprinted. The *Life* was most highly regarded in Virginia. Virginia Jeffersonians might disagree with Tucker on some points, but most of his reservations about Jefferson were also their own: radical democracy, extreme religious opinions, impatience of contradiction. They also found in the work a vindication of Virginia's course in federal politics under Jefferson's leadership. To this extent Edward Channing, the historian, was right some decades hence in calling Tucker's *Life* "the Virginia view." Elsewhere the biography had a mixed reception. The editor of the *New York Review and Quarterly Church Journal* wrote one of the most violent reviews ever accorded a serious work in this country. It broke down Tucker's wall of reserve and drew from him a forty-five page reply, which should be read as an appendix to the biography.

The editor was Francis Lister Hawks, already encountered as a spokesman for conservatism. Jefferson had no more diligent censor than this North Carolinian. His fifty-two page blast in 1837 was only the first of several in the *New York Review*. He was always taking aim on Jefferson in his historical writings, and possibly also from the Episcopal pulpit where he made his reputation. The 1837 article was in most respects a typical conservative indictment. Tucker had posed the great and intriguing question: Why was Jefferson the most loved *and* hated of men? But Tucker's answer, in terms of Jefferson's principles, Hawks said, was unacceptable. He either purposely concealed or could not see Jefferson's grave defects of character. "The lives of great men are beacon lights to those who come after them, but they are false lights if they do not tell the *whole* truth." Tucker did not tell the whole truth, but fortunately Americans were discovering it for themselves with the aid of Jefferson's writings and the new inquiries of historians. Since Hawks thought the rejection of Christianity was the foundation of all Jefferson's errors and crimes, he pounced upon this subject. Tucker, in rebuttal, offered the most comprehensive view of Jefferson's religious opinions that had yet appeared.

Hawks came at the subject fresh from his research for *The Rise and Progress of the Protestant Episcopal Church in Virginia,* published in 1836. Here he accused Jefferson of destroying the alliance of church and state in order to erect on its ruins "an alliance between the civil authority and infidelity." Jefferson was exulted by the defeat of an amendment to his famous statute which would have inserted the name "Jesus Christ" before the infidel phrase, "the holy author of our religion." The statute, Hawks charged, was a declaration, not of religious freedom, but against Christianity. Hawks also held Jefferson responsible for the final and fatal blow, the statutes of 1799 and 1802. These repealed all laws in any way associated with religion, confiscated the property of the Church, and directed the sale of glebe lands. Jefferson actually had no direct connection with this "plunder." Yet so powerful in Virginia were the legends of the "French infidel" and "mighty reformer" that the whole work of the disestablishment, with the ensuing degeneration of the Church, was repeatedly attributed to him.

Jefferson, according to Hawks, was not only a French infidel but an "infidel propagandist" to boot. His late professions of a Unitarian faith, emphasized by Tucker, were a mockery. While he hypocritically appealed to the religious sentiments of the American people, Jefferson was busily "poisoning the stream at the fountain." His instrument of proselytization was to be the University of Virginia. Its whole purpose was to teach the youth of the country "a refined and civilized heathenism." He imported infidel professors, prohibited religious instruction, and invited students to Monticello on the Sabbath, there at his table to hear sneers and scoffs at Jesus Christ. Fortunately, Hawks asserted, the experiment was already a failure.

"The pride of a nation is crushed, and trampled upon with insulting mockery," Tucker angrily replied to this latest emission of clerical spleen. Hawks, "this apostolic missionary of the faith of civilized Christendom," showed less compassion and justice than the pagan barbarian. Whatever his own religious feelings, Tucker rose in indignation against this vengeful pursuit of Jefferson beyond the grave by the Christian clergy. The supposed "great arch-demon of infidelity" practiced the convictions of his own mind and only wished the opportunity for others to do the same. Jefferson's religion was a matter of conjecture, Tucker said, precisely because he did not proselytize. But the motives of his Unitarian professions could not be fairly questioned. His neighbors saw him observe the Sabbath, sometimes in attendance at Charlottesville churches, and knew of his gifts to sectarian causes. As for the University, religion was neither excluded nor included. It was Jefferson's *"atrocious impartiality,"* his desire to keep this instrument of the state and citadel of learning free of sectarian influence, that called down Hawks's anathema. The students were perfectly free to worship as they pleased, and Jefferson's experiment flourished. (Actually, religion had already made some slight inroads. Virginians frequently spoke of the failure of the experiment. But the hostility to "Mr. Jefferson's University" on religious grounds persisted, and it contributed to the defeat of a student campaign for a monument to the founder a quarter century after his death.)

Clerics like Hawks were incapable of understanding how the same process of free inquiry that had led Jefferson to deny traditional Christianity could also lead him to affirm a freer religious faith. So to the old stereotype—infidel propagandist—they added another—Christian hypocrite—not stopping to realize the absurdity of his performing in both roles simultanously: "one moment a Mephistopheles, coolly shutting out heaven from the view of the unfortunate, and alluring him to a fatal compact with the Prince of Darkness, the next worldly hypocrite, claiming for himself the protecting mantle of a Christian sect!" This was Tucker's *coup de grace* to Hawks.*

---

* In 1840 an equally prominent Episcopal clergyman, Dr. Stephen Higginson Tyng of Philadelphia, while attending a convention in Charlottesville, implicated the local citizenry in his opinion of Jefferson's religious character. Monticello in decay appeared to Tyng a fitting monument to "a man who spent his life in opposing the cause dearest to my heart." That Jefferson was an unbeliever and subverter of Christianity was not just his opinion, Tyng said, but that of "the very neighborhood in which he lived and died." The local press denounced Tyng. Whig leaders, headed by William C. Rives, arranged a meeting of the Albemarle citizenry, which adopted resolutions disclaiming the sentiments of Dr. Tyng and renewing the community's testament of esteem made on Jefferson's retirement to Monticello in 1809.

Tucker was confident in 1838 that Jefferson's reputation was "as safe from the effusions of clerical hate as the fixed star from the influence of the earth's noxious exhortations." Yet assaults like those of Hawks were periodic over the next fifty or sixty years. Only in a more distant run of time was Tucker's assurance warranted. And this was equally true of class and political hatred. Virginians, especially, had cause to remember Jefferson; he had left his mark on the society, the government, the church, the academy. Great as his reputation was in Virginia, the state did almost nothing in the nineteenth century to perpetuate his fame. Washington, and later Robert E. Lee, won the consent of Virginians' hearts and the state's highest honors. Jefferson, the Virginian, would have to win his honors as the American.

2. The Character of Jefferson: Massachusetts

Daniel Webster's stirring eulogy of Jefferson and Adams in 1826 symbolized the amnesty New England Federalists had declared on the old partisan contests that still afflicted their minds and festered their hearts. Jefferson's assault from the grave, the *Memoirs*, broke the spell. At first, however, it appeared New England letters would absorb even this blow. Andrew Ritchie, in the *North American Review*, confessed his feelings against Jefferson vanished "as we advanced from page to page, [and] we gradually yielded to the proofs of the frankness of his character, his great learning, and his various genius." John Quincy Adams, in a letter to the *Review*'s editor, at once rebuked this dangerous tolerance of Jeffersonian heresies. He was reluctant himself to shake "the hornets' nest" that hung over Jefferson's name. But he desperately hoped someone would again take up "the Cause of the Cross, the Cause of *Justice*, and the Cause of the American Union" against Jefferson's effort to crowd American history with his own fame. Two veteran Federalist warriors, William Sullivan and Theodore Dwight, responded, and behind them the parade formed: Alden Bradford, minister of the gospel and Secretary of the Commonwealth from 1812 to 1824, author of the *History of the Federal Government* in 1840; George Gibbs, ethnologist, grandson of the Connecticut Federalist Oliver Wolcott, and author of *Memoirs of the Administrations of Washing-*

ton and John Adams in 1846; Samuel Goodrich, better known as the "Peter Parley" of children's stories, son of a prominent Federalist family, author of *Recollections of a Lifetime* in 1856. Nathan Dane, William W. Story, Rufus Griswold, and many others contributed to the New England Federalist case against Jefferson.

Sullivan's antidote to the *Memoirs* bore the unimpressive title, *Familiar Letters on Public Characters, and Public Events.* A lawyer, legislator, and many-sided public servant, Sullivan was prominent in the affairs of Boston and Massachusetts. His sole venture on the national political scene occurred in 1814, when he had the dubious honor with two others of bearing to Washington the resolves of the Massachusetts General Court based upon the report of the Hartford Convention. As the recollections of one who had been in the inner councils of Massachusetts Federalism during the greater part of its history, Sullivan's work was eagerly read and highly regarded in Old Federalist circles.

The *Letters* was written to defend, and if need be restore, the reputation of leading Federalists "maligned" by Jefferson. It was a full vindication of the Federalist party, particularly of that extremist Massachusetts wing Jefferson had labeled the "Essex Junto." It was a eulogy of New England's historic role in the Union, and a dirge on her shrunken estate under the politics of the Virginia leadership. It was, like so much of the Federalist literature, a nostalgic recollection of the "golden age," "the age of politeness," when "the old platform of religion and politics still stood strong," when gentlemen wore knee breeches and powdered their hair and those of Sullivan's stamp gave "the community its shaping quality, [and] as if by divine right, its social and political issues." It aimed to supply the background of conservative politics by showing in Jefferson the triple alliance of democracy, demagoguery, and despotism perfected by Jackson. "The perils, sufferings, and dread of the present hour" all stemmed, in Sullivan's judgment, from Jefferson. Finally, the *Letters* sought to reveal "the true character of the man," drawn, *mirabile dictu,* from Jefferson's own writings.

Sullivan's book and Dwight's *History of the Hartford Convention,* also recently published, brought the young editor of the *North*

American Review, Alexander Hill Everett, to Jefferson's defense.
His long article, "The Origin and Character of the Old Parties,"
excited unusual interest. It was hardly to be expected, a critic wrote
in the *Boston Courier,* "that this high note of praise and admiration
should be so soon sounded in New England." Sullivan published his
answer in a pamphlet. Everett's rebuttal was a second long article,
"The Character of Jefferson," and he reiterated his views in a
subsequent Forth of July oration. Coming at a time when public
admiration of Jefferson in Boston (and much of New England) was
a monopoly of the lowly Jacksonians, Everett's writings were
courageous, not to say surprising. His political mentor was J. Q.
Adams; his older brother Edward was a leading Whig; his own
political background was anti-Jacksonian. Yet, in 1834 this brilliant
member of Boston's leading literary and political circles went Jeffersonian. The next year he resigned the editorship of the *Review* and
embraced the Democratic party.

The main significance of the Everett-Sullivan debate for the
Jefferson image lay in its sharp definition of two opposed attitudes
toward history. Sullivan, keen to every personal fault, judged
Jefferson under absolute standards of right and wrong.   Everett
judged Jefferson in his larger relations to the spiritual movement of
the age in which he played a conspicuous part. Sullivan viewed
Jefferson as a detached person—what he *was*—and discovered this
by examination of his utterance and conduct. Everett viewed his
delegated quality—what he *represented*—and determined this from
a philosophical conception of modern history. For convenience' sake,
these two attitudes may be termed the moralistic and the philosophical. Both were present in some degree in nearly all interpretations
of Jefferson. Federalist-minded historians generally took the narrow
view of character, while Democratic-minded historians were more
inclined to the larger philosophical view. However, Everett's interpretation was unique in its time for its transcendence of the nettled
points of personal morality which beset Jefferson's reputation for
another century.

Fundamentally, Everett asserted, the party division of the early
republic mirrored the conflict then raging in the Christian world
between the forces of Liberty and Law. The movement of history

and the conditions of America brought these two essential principles of organized society into violent conflict. The need for a stronger government after the American Revolution led to an extension of the power of law beyond its capacity to sustain itself. For the progressive expansion of liberty and reform was, from Luther and Cromwell to Jefferson and Rousseau, *the spirit* of the age." It was all one vast movement. Liberty, first victorious in America, returned to complete its task in Europe—the French Revolution. Since the movement of liberated humanity was as beneficial as it was irresistible, Everett said, "the party which was acting under its influence—that is, the Democratic party . . . was mainly, as to its great objects, in the right; and the opposition party, which sustained the existing establishments with all their abuses, in the wrong."

Thus assimilated to the spirit of the age, Jefferson was put beyond the reach of moral censure or labored correction of error. He was a "great man," according to the definition from Cousin: one who felt with great energy the common impressions of the age, one who opened his mind to transcendent truth hidden from practical men bent on law and order. Luther was sometimes mad, as when he threw his inkstand at the devil, Everett recalled; but this did not detract from his greatness, which "must be settled not by a transient, optical or mental illusion, but by the labors of his life, the results of the reformation." Similarly, Jefferson's fame was inseparable from "the great intellectual and social movement of the age" he labored to advance. As this movement was good, so Jefferson's life was good. He believed in Liberty. One needed to search no further for the cause of his and his party's influence with the people. They felt he represented their highest being.

The conception of an abstract "spirit of the age," transporting Jefferson to ethereal regions on the wings of angels, seemed to Sullivan no more than an ingenious refuge for the scoundrel. There was, first of all, no single master movement in the three centuries since the Protestant Reformation. 1688, 1776, 1789—these were distinct events. The American Revolution was no kin to the French. The brutal course of the latter was fixed by the democratic philosophy, which Jefferson brought back to America where it must have the same effects. Not liberty but democracy was Jefferson's doctrine.

The Federalists opposed him because they believed with the ancient writers that democracy, the government of the whole people, passed directly into despotism by the demagogic process of "personification of the people" that Everett made Jefferson's highest claim to honor. Both Jefferson and Napoleon began as democrats; both eventually placed themselves above the law.

The division of Federalists and Republicans, Sullivan argued, was fundamentally between "the honorable, high-minded, and intelligent order of statesmen" and "the managing, contriving, and unprincipled class of politicians." Under these moral categories, statesman and politician, men and parties were judged by their measure of respectability, the means they employed, their tastes and habits of conduct. Prejudice and usage supported the distinction. Webster's *American Dictionary* defined a *statesman* as "A man versed in the arts of government." A *politician* might also be a statesman, but gentlemen agreed with Webster's alternate definition: "A man of artifice or deep contrivance." Federalist writers applied these categories to the old parties and their leaders. Jefferson, according to Sullivan, started the decline of the statesman and the rise of the politician. If "politics," in its odious sense, reigned in the Jacksonian years, then Jefferson had prepared the way; and no fair estimate could be made of him except by scrutiny of his political behavior, a task which Everett in his lofty superiority to Jefferson's four volumes of self-incrimination refused to undertake.

Sullivan took this position: *"to be truly great one must be good."* Jefferson was not deliberately wicked, as Lee said; but rather, because of some obliquity of perception or perversion of the moral sense, he was incapable of telling right from wrong. Since the great man influences those who come after him, he must be morally exemplary. He should not be praised for his accomplishments without regard to the motives and means that produced them. The Louisiana Purchase was, Sullivan said, "the least of all Mr. Jefferson's claims to an honorable fame," if judged by the "motives which *then* operated, and the *acts* then done." Since these involved enmity to New England, friendship for France, and wanton disregard of the Constitution, the "brilliant achievement" was iniquitous. Finally, the quality of greatness Everett assigned to Jefferson actually proved his demagogic character. No man in a republic, Sullivan asserted, could be "the people personified" unless he possessed "the art . . . to insinuate, and to teach, all that he chooses to have the people feel and think." Destitute of moral sense, gifted with these arts of the politician, Jefferson became America's first consummate demagogue.

The Everett-Sullivan debate exhibited two main approaches to Jefferson. Neither was satisfactory as history. Comprehension of Jefferson was as unavailable to the moralist as it was to the philosopher. The former, with preconceived bias, drew close and was repelled; the latter attained a more distant perspective but lost the man in the abstraction. The American people have always felt the abstraction, the symbol, to be more important than the man. It was Jefferson's great morality. The untold thousands who climb the steps of the Jefferson Memorial have never heard of the Mazzei letter or, if they have, it makes no difference in their feeling for Jefferson, the Apostle of Liberty. But historians have had to pass through the thicket of Jefferson's "character." For a century after his death many of them were unable to pass beyond it.

Two prominent New Englanders, in their different ways, achieved a loose synthesis of the traditional Federalist and the modern democratic interpretations. One was Richard Hildreth, whose masterful *History of the United States* was Hamiltonian yet liberal. The other was John Quincy Adams, over whose career both Jefferson and the Essex Junto cast dark shadows. Adams's interpretation must be pieced together from numerous speeches, discourses, and orations, supplemented by the more forthright speculations (one of them a history of the parties) he dared not publish. Both men wrote of American political history from a New England point of view, but neither was dominated by the inherited prejudice of the Federalist remnant whose concern with Jefferson was the vengeance "of a bygone party and a buried race."

Adams and Hildreth agreed with most of the Federalist criticism of Jefferson's character. Jefferson was deceptive and insincere, adroit and supple and insinuating. Duplicity was his characteristic vice, according to Adams, "a vice which originated in his overweening

passion for popularity, and his consequent desire to be all things
to all men." His political conduct and opinions were tattered tissues
of inconsistency. "To sympathize with popular passions seemed to
be his test of patriotism; to sail before the wind as a popular
favorite the great object of ambition." France strengthened his
natural enthusiasm, unbridled by religion, for theoretical ideas of
liberty and equality. "His imagination," Hildreth wrote, "so far
predominated over his reason as to lead him to see things, not as
they were, but as he hoped, wished, suspected they might be."
Jefferson developed "the strange hallucination of a monarchical
conspiracy for the destruction of the Constitution on the part of
those by whom its adoption had been secured." His political dogma-
tism, or bigotry as Hildreth thought, stood in marked contrast to his
penchant for free inquiry in other realms and, especially, to his
religious skepticism. Madison, by comparison, was a man of more
reason, cooler sensibility, and sounder judgment. Adams's funeral
eulogy of the "Father of the Constitution" in 1836 was a remarkable
performance: it was an apology for Madison's Jeffersonianism! In all
these views—duplicity, fanaticism, bigotry—the Federalist writers
concurred; yet Adams and Hildreth saw in Jefferson's politics a gross
consistency through all the twistings and turnings, a sympathy with
the people that was more than trickery, a generous vision for mankind that was creditable despite its follies.

The two Massachusetts Whigs underscored the negativism of
Jefferson's political system. Enthusiasm for liberty led illogically, as
Everett observed, to the negation of authority. Even Jefferson's
most creative work, the reform of the Virginia laws, suggested to
Adams his peculiar genius for destruction: "he could demolish,
deface, and cast down; he could not build up or preserve." The
same was true as to the central government. Jefferson took over
from the Confederation the false idea that the remedy for the
abuse of power was "stinginess of grant in its organization." Hildreth
pointed up the crucial French experience. While there, he said,
Jefferson's attention was exclusively drawn to the evils of power.
"Hence his political philosophy was almost entirely negative—his
sum total seeming to be the reduction of the exercise of authority
within the narrowest possible limits, even at the risk of depriving

government of its ability for good as well as for evil." Both writers
had great respect for the positive accomplishments of Washington's
administration. Jefferson raised against it, not the generous sentiments of the American people, but their coarse prejudices: the prejudice against Britain and all things British, the provincial animus
against the Union, the agrarian hostility to commerce and economic
improvement. State rights, strict construction, agrarian supremacy,
public economy—all these principles were negative. Jefferson went
into power on professions of reform, but "in truth reformed nothing." Hildreth concurred in Adams's judgment. However much the
Republicans excelled the Federalists in the arts of popularity, "the
best thing they could do, in the constructive part of politics, was
humbly to copy the models they had once calumniated."

The bankruptcy of Jeffersonian statesmanship was a standard
Federalist argument. Adams and Hildreth, however, did not believe
that Jefferson's professions were merely for electioneering, that the
"revolution of 1800" was vacuous, that the disparity between theory
and practice explained nothing but demagogic talents. It was illogi-
cal to condemn Jefferson, as Sullivan and Dwight did, both for
acceptance and for obliteration of the Federalist system. He ought
to be criticized, rather, for his failure to put the constructive force
of government behind his vision of liberty. Not despotism but
feebleness was the danger of Jefferson's politics.

The nadir of Jefferson's administration was the Embargo, as it
was also in New England eyes the most characteristic act of his
politics. The Federalist historians in their interpretation of the
causes of the War of 1812 were "revisionists"—that is, they attacked
the official version and charged it instead to the secret designs of
the men in power. Jefferson's Embargo of 1807-09, an interdict of
all American foreign commerce, was a major test of the thesis. It
revealed, Dwight, Sullivan, and the others charged, the governing
principle of Jefferson's system: *"Friendship for France and Enmity
to Great Britain."* Cleverly manipulating the anti-British prejudices
of the American people and teaching the false notion of France as
a kindred spirit, Jefferson ever deemed her the natural ally of the
United States and tried always to keep alive a controversy with
Britain.

When the Embargo was laid, the Federalists said, our differences with Britain were minor and subject to negotiation without endangering the profits of the neutral trade; our relations with France, on the other hand, were unpromising in every respect. Yet the Embargo could only be expected to hurt Britain by, in effect, making the United States a partner in Bonaparte's "continental system." From this simple fact, supplemented by suggestive items in Jefferson's correspondence and elsewhere, Dwight reasoned to the same conclusion as the Essex Federalists in 1808: the Embargo was agreed upon by Jefferson and Bonaparte "*as a measure to aid the common enemy.*" The President recommended the measure to Congress as the only way short of war to protect American men, ships, and goods from the depredations of the European powers. These were not, Dwight insisted, his real reasons. In addition to the French conquest of Britain—a prospect Jefferson once greeted with such jubilation that he thought he would be tempted to leave his land for a while "to go and hail the dawn of liberty and republicanism in that island"—Jefferson aimed to destroy New England commerce and the Federalist party allied with it. New England's resistance, spearheaded by the Essex Junto, was a defensive action to save her economy, save national honor, save the cause of liberty old England represented.

These strains of machination and plot were softened in the writings of Adams and Hildreth by notes of irony, even of compassion. The operative effect of the Embargo was to aid France, but this was not its cause. The measure was in the tradition of commercial retaliation: the remedy employed by the pre-revolutionary radicals and always advocated by the Republicans to force concessions from Great Britain. No secret or foreign cause was necessary to explain an act entirely consistent with Jefferson's domestic system. Protection of commerce was no part of that system. Agrarian prejudice, obsession with peace, and shortsighted views of public economy led Jefferson to abandon the infant navy started by his predecessor. As Adams saw it, this weakened his hand against Britain, aroused the New England states, and left the Embargo the only alternative to war. The measure displayed less the traits of the Gallomaniac or the demagogue than the bungling statesmanship of the Virginia planter. The main point against it was that it did not work. "Mr. Jefferson," Adams noted with keen irony, "pursued his policy of peace till it brought the nation to the borders of internal war."

Of the three approaches to Jefferson—the moralistic, the philosophical, and the ironical—only the last has enriched our understanding of the historical Jefferson. The two liberal-minded New Englanders, Adams and Hildreth, worked through the Federalist criticism to an appreciation of the truth Everett placed in the foreground. Hildreth's shrewd summing-up perfectly expressed their ambivalent attitude. Whatever Jefferson's defects of character and statesmanship, Hildreth said, there remains behind, after all, this undeniable fact:

He was—rarity, indeed, among men of affairs—rarity, indeed, among professed democratical leaders—a sincere and enthusiastic believer in the rights of humanity. And, as in so many other like cases, this faith on his part will ever suffice to cover, as with the mantle of charity, a multitude of sins; nor will there ever be wanting a host of worshipers—living ideas being of vastly more consequence to posterity than dead actions passed and gone—to mythicize him into a political saint . . . exalted, by a passionate imagination, far above the heads of contemporary men, who, if they labored, suffered, and accomplished more for that generation, yet loved and trusted universal humanity less.

Because Jefferson possessed this genius of humanity, this power as a symbol, he more than most great actors in history was accountable to posterity for his work. Men of small vision, whatever their accomplishments, were not similarly leagued with the future or responsible for it. Mythicization of Jefferson was inevitable but, Hildreth and Adams warned, the dross of his life and thought could be forgotten only at great peril. The historical Jefferson, an instructive figure of error and contradiction and irony, should not be lost in the enveloping abstractions of Liberty and Humanity. Though basically Federalist in their views, Adams and Hildreth were forerunners of an interpretation grounded in ambivalence and irony, of which the elaborate *History* by Henry Adams, John Quincy's grandson, half a century later was the masterpiece.

3. *Episodes: Mecklenburg and Burr*

Historical fact and fancy on a wide variety of subjects played on the image of Jefferson. Two of the most interesting examples in the wake of the *Memoirs* concerned the "Mecklenburg Declaration of Independence" and the reputation of Aaron Burr. They serve further to illustrate what quantities of malice and error Jefferson had to overcome on his way to Olympus.

The Declaration of Independence was a work of super-eminence. What could deface this great aegis of Jefferson's fame and influence? In the panegyrics of the Fourth of July, in the flood of patristic literature one form of which was *Lives of the Signers,* in the popularity of Trumbull's masterpiece of historical portraiture, "The Signing of the Declaration"—Jefferson's authorship of the American birthright was his certain title to immortality.

> But one great deed, part human, part divine
> Must fix with yon stars, throughout all time.

The great deed, to be sure, never lacked carping critics. The idea of the Declaration's unoriginality was already stale when Jefferson offered his definitive explanation in 1825. Rhetoricians found fault with its style; political enemies said the work was not Jefferson's but the committee's; Northern conservatives thought it an invitation to mob rule; and slaveholders grew increasingly restive under its principles. Men who feared the sway of his opinions complained that the Declaration gave "an éclat to Jefferson that continually held him up to the eye of the people" from which there was no satisfactory appeal. Part of the importance of the "Mecklenburg Declaration of Independence" was that it offered opportunities, supposedly founded in historical fact, to deface the ineffaceable: Jefferson's title to glory, July Fourth 1776.

The North Carolina document was first published in the *Raleigh Register* in 1819. John Adams soon read it with amazement. Jefferson, he wrote, "has copied the spirit, the sense, the expressions of it *verbatim* into his Declaration of the 4th of July, 1776." There were four verbatim expressions: "dissolve the political bands which have connected," "absolve from all allegiance to the British crown," "are, and of right ought to be," "pledge to each other our lives, our fortunes, and our sacred honor." These were in a series of five resolves apparently adopted by the militia officers of Mecklenburg County on May 20, 1775. The resolves clearly announced the county's separation from Great Britain. Adams called Jefferson's attention to this relic. If it was an authentic "Declaration of Independence," Jefferson wrote in a stinging reply, why had the Continental Congress never heard of it, and why had North Carolina only now discovered its existence? For good measure, he pinned the "tory" label on two of North Carolina's Revolutionary patriots.

Publication of Jefferson's letter in the *Memoirs* quickened into life a century-long controversy. In 1830 the state legislature resolved to supply the "solemn proof" Jefferson had demanded; the official defense appeared the next year. Then, in 1834, came the important work of Joseph Seawell Jones, *A Defense of the Revolutionary History of the State of North Carolina from the Aspersions of Mr. Jefferson.* Jones was a pompous character with all the conservative Whig's vehement feelings against Jefferson and democracy. Generally recognized as North Carolina's first historian, his *Defense* has been called "a landmark in the awakening of patriotic interest in the state's history." The authenticity of the Mecklenburg Declaration and the patriotism of William Hooper (one of Jefferson's "tories") were the main subjects of Jones's *Defense*. His brief for the former consisted of the depositions gathered by the legislature in 1830 from living witnesses of the event, the several copies of the document preserved, and the Royal Governor's proclamation of August 8, 1775 condemning the traitorous action of the people of Mecklenburg. Jones did not accuse Jefferson of plagiarism, but rather of vindictive envy. This little county had declared independence, he wrote, "fully a year before the Sage of Monticello had ceased his vows, or had surrendered his hope of inventing a plan of reconciliation; 'and for this they could never be forgiven.'"

On May 20, 1835 over five thousand people gathered in Charlotte for the first great celebration of the Mecklenburg Declaration. Most of the honored guests (the most distinguished assemblage in the state's history, the local press reported) were Whigs and Nullifiers, then allied in opposition to Jackson's administration. In the long round of toasts offered at the dinner, the Mecklenburg document was repeatedly acclaimed "the *first* declaration of American independence," and Jefferson's name was never mentioned. The *Washington Globe* charged that the Mecklenburg Declaration was a stalking horse "to get up a Southern *national* feeling" opposed to the American feelings for Jefferson, Democracy, and Union. Although this opinion must be discounted, the Mecklenburg Declaration was involved in politics at the very moment North Carolinians took it to their hearts.

George Tucker undertook to demolish the fable before it could bring serious injury to Jefferson's reputation. His careful analysis in the *Life* led to the conclusion that the Mecklenburg Declaration was plagiaristic. Passages from the national Declaration had been fraudulently interpolated in some North Carolina document of 1775. Tucker only succeeded in goading the Carolina enthusiasts. The plagiarist, Hawks charged, was Jefferson! Hawks had discovered the Royal Governor's proclamation book, in which it was stated the Mecklenburg resolves were published soon after adoption in the *Cape Fear Mercury* of Wilmington. All that remained to clinch the case was the particular issue of this newspaper. Hawks also cited other contemporary documents with words and passages remarkably similar to Jefferson's in 1776. Of these the Preamble to the old Virginia Constitution was the closest fit. But this was hardly surprising, as Tucker ably proved, since Jefferson was its author. None of the evidence furnished by Hawks or anyone else, in Tucker's judgment, established the authenticity of the Mecklenburg relic or discredited Jefferson's authorship of the Declaration of 1776.

The controversy took a new turn in December 1838. Peter Force, pioneer American archivist, announced the discovery in contemporary newspapers of a set of resolutions adopted at Mecklenburg on May 31, 1775. They did not declare independence and bore little resemblance to the supposed declaration of eleven days previous. Most sensible historians soon concluded that the Royal Governor's references, both in his proclamation and in his dispatch to the ministry in London, pertained to the resolutions of May 31. Somehow, they supposed, the Mecklenburg radicals had, in reconstructing the event several decades after it occurred, confused the language and intent of the American Declaration of Independence with this action a year earlier. Revelations at a later date gave additional support to this view.

The zealots' hope was sustained, however, by the missing issue of the *Cape Fear Mercury*. Word had come to Jones, he wrote in 1838, that the United States Minister to Great Britain, the Virginia Jeffersonian Andrew Stevenson, had been commissioned to explore the British archives for evidence against the Mecklenburg Declaration. Except for the sinister overtones, Jones's information was correct. Tucker, perhaps even President Van Buren, had asked Stevenson to aid in the vindication of Jefferson by a search of the archives. Nothing was ever reported from Stevenson on the subject. But a few years later Jared Sparks examined the Royal Governor's dispatch to the colonial secretary on the Mecklenburg action. He thought it referred to the resolutions of May 31. He could not be certain, however, since the newspaper clipping originally attached had been borrowed by the United States Minister, Stevenson, and never returned. Some North Carolina historians believed Stevenson had wantonly destroyed the only positive proof of the Declaration of May 20, 1775. In 1905, a pseudonymous article in *Collier's Magazine* contained what purported to be a photographic reproduction of the *Cape Fear Mercury* clipping, the original of which, it was said, was found in Stevenson's papers. This last bold effort to prove the existence of the Mecklenburg Declaration of Independence was quickly proven a hoax.

Belief in the "historical truth" of the Mecklenburg Declaration successfully withstood fact and logic in North Carolina. Many Fedderalist-minded historians before the Civil War—Hildreth, Washington Irving, Benson J. Lossing, along with the Carolinians Hawks and Jones—accepted the document as authentic. After the war, state pride alone kept it afloat. This was enough. Monuments were erected to the Mecklenburg signers; the legend was taught as fact in the schools; May 20 was made a state holiday, an inscription on the state seal and the state flag. A North Carolina Senator at the end of the century, having read a recent work on the humbug of the Mecklenburg Declaration, wrote to its author: "I believe you have sustained every point you have raised, and clearly made out your case, but I will kill you if you ever tell anybody I said so." Such was the legend's power in North Carolina.

Jeffersonian historians believed the thinly disguised object of the Mecklenburg advocates was, as Randall said, "to show that Mr. Jefferson was guilty of plagiarism." They viewed the controversy in the context of its origins: Jefferson's letter to Adams, which North Carolinians took as an insult and hurried to rebuke; the political overtones of the Mecklenburg celebrations; the hatred of Jefferson voiced by the document's leading advocates; the whole conservative campaign to discredit Jefferson's character. This context—the intimate relationship of the Mecklenburg Declaration to Jefferson's reputation —has long since been forgotten, partly because the Jeffersonian historians saw the relationship and attacked the legend. The Mecklenburg enthusiasm left no lasting scars on the Jefferson image.

"There never was a greater villain than Aaron Burr—never!" The simple cruel sentence from a widely read article in 1857 expressed the American judgment. Burr lived in the imagination as an ambitious, intriguing, thoroughly disreputable politician, as Hamilton's murderer, a monster of licentiousness, a reckless trifler with feminine hearts, a traitor to his country. He was Machiavelli, Don Juan, and Benedict Arnold rolled into one. Romantic, gracious, intelligent though he was, alive or dead there was "no speaking of him without a shudder." When Burr was laid in his grave, it was said, "decency congratulated itself that a nuisance was removed, and good men were glad that God had seen fit to deliver society from the contaminating contact of a festering mass of moral putrefaction." Fiction and poetry embellished the legend; history cemented its foundations. Sympathetic portrayals of Burr, especially James Parton's biography in 1858, evoked indignation and availed little against the force of opinion rapidly passing into myth.

Yet there were men who asked, Was Burr any worse than Jefferson? Was he not indeed the victim of Jefferson's vengeful fury? Was there a better test of the true character of Jefferson than the shabby part he played in the downfall of Aaron Burr? A convention arose in retrospective writing of mirroring Jefferson in Burr. Principally the work of men who wished to blacken Jefferson's fame or to avenge

Burr's, the practice has declined but not disappeared in recent historiography.

The crucial work was the two-volume *Memoirs of Aaron Burr,* published in 1836-37, one year after the subject's death. Its author was Matthew L. Davis, a friend and associate of many years, to whom Burr committed most of his papers. From the first appearance of Jefferson's writings, Davis stated in the Preface, Burr commissioned him to write his biography. To aid the task of vindication Burr sent to Davis his annotated copy of Jefferson's *Memoirs.* The Burr *Memoirs* thus had the air of authority and the promise of excitement. Although harshly reviewed in the press, it was reportedly "read with great interest and curiosity, and was for a time a leading topic of conversation in literary circles."

From beginning to end, Davis said, Jefferson was deceitful toward Burr. His letters showed that before the election of 1800 he insinuated himself into the favor of the Republican leader of New York. Then, after the contest between them in the House of Representatives, Jefferson turned on Burr, and soon recorded in the Anas that he had never trusted or befriended him. Henry Lee exhibited this as a case of duplicity. Hawks took it as an avowal on Jefferson's part of cultivating Burr solely to satisfy his presidential ambitions. While Jefferson extended one hand in friendship to this rival for power, as Davis saw it, he held the other ready to destroy him.

The conduct of the two candidates during the deliberations of the Representatives on the tie-vote of 1800 had been freshly aired with special reference to Bayard in 1830. Davis reviewed the subject. Jefferson alone, he said, bargained with the Federalists, but then transferred his own guilt to Burr by recording the lies of bargain and intrigue which posterity accepted as true. Davis also revived an obscure and forgotten incident of that election. This was the matter of the irregular Georgia vote, first publicized in 1802 by a Burr hireling in New York to prove the fraudulence of Jefferson's election. The Burrite cited a contemporaneous newspaper report, which said that when the state election certificates were opened in the Senate chamber the tellers remarked on some informality in the votes of Georgia but counted them anyway. Davis searched for an explanation. He obtained a statement from a member of that

Congress, who recalled how one of the tellers had told him that the Georgia votes, four for Burr and four for Jefferson, had not been authenticated by the electors. The tellers handed the certificates to the presiding officer, the Vice-President, who was Jefferson, expecting him to rule the votes out of order. Instead, Jefferson's countenance changed, the teller had testified, and he "rapidly declared that the votes of Georgia were *four* for Thomas Jefferson and *four* for Aaron Burr, without noticing this informality, and in a hurried manner put them aside, and then broke the seals and handed the tellers the package from the next state." What was the effect of this? As Davis observed, had the Georgia votes been declared invalid, no candidate would have had a majority; therefore the two Federalist candidates, Adams and Pinckney, would have been drawn into the contest. In a four-cornered fight, Davis surmised, Jefferson could not possibly have been elected.

Was Jefferson a usurper and a cheat? The reviewer of the *Memoirs* in the *Democratic Review* held he was not. A literal copy of the original Georgia document in the Senate files showed the votes, in his judgment, to have been properly authenticated by the electors and formal in every respect. This evidence went unchallenged, yet the story as revived by Davis persisted. Several reputable historians credited it. The prolific novelist and critic John Neal wrote in 1841 that Burr was, "if not actually swindled *out* of the presidential chair, so cunningly over-reached by Jefferson, in the management of the informal Georgia vote, that Jefferson was swindled in." On this accounting, Burr, for all his political talents, was no match for the supple Jefferson. In 1877, after another disputed presidential election, the matter of the Georgia vote came into congressional discussion, and the Burrite imputation was again set to Jefferson's account.*

* Senator Hannibal Hamlin of Maine reviewed the tradition of the Georgia vote in the debate on a bill to transfer the power of decision on disputed electoral votes, as they are counted in the joint session of Congress, from the Vice-President to the Congress. Hamlin was literally correct in asserting of the Georgia document of 1800: "There is no certificate that they met and balloted. There is no certificate that there was a vote given to anybody for President." The Governor certified the list of electors, but they did not, in strict compliance with Art. II, Sct. 1 of the Constitution, certify the ballot. The fact does not justify the imputation of Jefferson. It is also interesting, in connection with the contested election of 1876, that his great-granddaughter, Sarah N. Randolph,

After his election, Davis's narrative continued, Jefferson conspired with the Clinton faction in New York to destroy their mutual rival. Having forced him out of the party, they then falsely accused him of a dishonorable association with the Federalists. None of the Vice-President's key men were rewarded with office, as Davis bitterly remembered, for he had been one of the noisiest aspirants. Yet it was Burr who, by swinging the decisive vote in New York City, was responsible for the Republican victory in 1800. Wealth and talent, the power of patronage, the passions of ambition, combined to crucify him. Jefferson fixed upon Burr all his malignant hatred of competition, and it "never ceased but with his last breath." Burr's doom was sealed in 1801, Davis wrote. The utter disgracement eight years later was only the last act of the drama of revenge.

No one has ever quite fathomed the mystery of the Burr Conspiracy. The two opposed interpretations have usually been rooted in opposed attitudes toward Jefferson. Burr held, as have his defenders, that he only aimed to revolutionize Mexico. Jeffersonian historians held with their hero that Burr treasonously conspired to detach the Western states from the Union. But putting aside this difficult question, Jefferson's critics, including some of a friendly persuasion, believed he brought Burr to trial more from personal antagonism than from concern for the safety of the Union. Davis doubted if any analysis of the way Jefferson turned Burr's adventure into "an opportunity of shedding his blood, under the color of law" would have any effect upon the "public opinion of this philosopher." He accordingly despaired of the attempt. Others, however, undertook the task with enthusiasm.

The question of Burr's guilt or innocence tended to be replaced by the question of Jefferson's in hunting him down, prosecuting him, and sending him into exile. Critics exhibited the President's letters during and just after the celebrated trial at Richmond before Judge Marshall as brazen attempts to obstruct justice. Jefferson held Marshall chiefly responsible for the acquittal on the charge of treason,

---

submitted for publication in the *New York World* a bill Jefferson had drafted as Vice-President to give the power of decision to the Representatives of the state involved.

and proposed to lay the entire proceedings of the trial before Congress. Although his temper soon cooled, and he did nothing, Sullivan and others saw in his angry first reaction vicious designs to impeach the Chief Justice, overturn the independent judiciary, and subvert the administration of justice to executive dictation. "Here is one more proof that those who talk and boast most loudly of republican liberty, are the men least qualified to be trusted with power." Acquitted at the bar of justice, convicted at the bar of public opinion, hounded by Jefferson on lesser charges than treason, Burr was forced into exile in 1808.

A reviewer of Davis's book longed for an "American Plutarch" to execute a parallel on Jefferson and Burr. What instruction it might afford! Until about 1804 they were political rivals whose careers ran along the same lines and whose claims for success were nearly balanced. But then Jefferson's fortunes ascended until capped by a sanctifying death, while Burr fell, in Davis's words, "to a condition more mortifying and more prostrate than any distinguished man has ever experienced in the United States." Jefferson spent his last years compiling the Anas, "that malignant tissue of exploded calumny," as the reviewer thought; while Burr found no better use of his talents than, according to Davis, to compile an odious record of his affairs with women. Burr and Jefferson, others said, were "chips of the same block," children of the immoral father, democracy; yet by the irony or the caprice of democracy, one grew to become the revered Sage of Monticello, the other a reviled social outcast. Hard put to choose between the sacrificial priest and his victim, Federalist writers often declared their preference for Burr, and thus ratified the judgment of the bulk of Federalists who had cast their votes for Burr in the contest of 1801. "Bad as was the character of Col. Burr," wrote William Stone, "his election in preference to Jefferson would have been a blessing to the nation."

The stream of recollection ran through the partisan polemics of the age, and thus the plaints for Aaron Burr were of more than historical interest. "True to the instincts of Federalism," wrote Francis Blair in the *Washington Globe*, conservatives seized upon Davis's book to smear the Jeffersonian escutcheon. "The denunciations and calumnies of an exposed and disappointed criminal are seriously urged against the character of one whose duty it was to bring him to justice!" Unable to find in their political past a reputable hero for their creed, the Whig "Federalists" hoped to defame Jefferson by the blemish of Burr. They know, Blair said, "that, as long as the name and opinions of this illustrious patriot retain their influence with the people, they cannot accomplish their unconstitutional designs."

The prolonged vindication of Aaron Burr in historical literature did far more harm to Jefferson's reputation (without much help to Burr's) than the legend of Mecklenburg. Isaac Jenkinson's *Aaron Burr* and, in the main, Walter McCaleb's authoritative *Aaron Burr Conspiracy*, both at the beginning of this century, were in the tradition of Davis's *Memoirs*. The case of Burr, better than most others, continued to furnish a test of attitudes toward Jefferson, and to betray the disproportion between the figure of the historians and the hero of American democracy.

4. Henry S. Randall

Henry S. Randall's *Life of Jefferson* came toward the end of a burst of historical publication that included the most extensive treatments yet given to Jefferson's leading contemporaries: Washington, Adams, Hamilton, Burr, and Madison. Hildreth's *History*, George T. Curtis's *History of the Constitution*, and the collected writings of Adams, Hamilton, and Madison also helped to make the decade of the eighteen-fifties a brilliant climax to the first "age of commemoration." None of these conspicuous volumes in the galaxy, unless those on Madison, added luster to Jefferson's fame. No biography of him had appeared since Tucker's. While Randall was writing, however, two substantial additions were made to knowledge of Jefferson. Under the auspices of the Society of Alumni of the University of Virginia, the early history of that institution, as revealed in the correspondence between Jefferson and his leading associate, Joseph C. Cabell, was published. Two years earlier, in 1853-54, appeared the nine-volume Congress Edition of Jefferson's *Works*. This followed, after five years, the government's purchase from T. J. Randolph of Jefferson's *public* papers. Although the Congress Edition excited no unusual interest, it replaced the *Memoirs* as the standard work, and was not superseded for over forty years.*

Convinced that Jefferson was losing the battle of the books, Randall approached the biographer's charge in the spirit of a knight who, if he could not rout the entrenched foe, was nerved for the martyr's faggot and stake in the cause of his hero. "The north wind which sweeps without," he wrote in 1856, "is not at this moment more fearless & reckless than I, so far as Mr. Jefferson's political or personal enemies are concerned." Not the least interesting feature of the *Life* was the author's angry attack on Jefferson's detractors in history. Scarcely a blemish on the reputation escaped notice. In page after page, in lengthy footnotes and appendixes, Randall ran the gamut from the "petty and dirty allegations" of Henry Lee and his ilk to the more subtle imputations of respectable scholars. Hildreth's *History* was but a continuation of the Federalist smear of Jefferson, with every slander "as carefully preserved as the dead wasps in an entomological cabinet." Marshall's *Life of Washington* seemed to Randall the most insidious work of all, because of its author's esteem, its dry and colorless style, its veneer of judicious impartiality. This Federalist rubbish fouling the historical page, as Randall saw it, had to be cleared away if the heroic figure of Jefferson was to rise and if Americans were to understand the political principles essential to the nation's well-being.

Randall's *Life* was, as the reviewers noted, "a labor of love"; in a sense, it was also the labor of a lifetime. Oddly enough, Randall was raised in the traditions of Federalism. Around Hamilton's "trumpet-filling name," he recalled, "clustered all the admiring feelings of my boyhood." But soon after graduating from Union College in 1830, Randall became an active worker in the Democratic party of New York and an avid student of American political history. These influ-

---

* The Congress Edition was executed in a hurried and slipshod manner. The editor, Henry A. Washington, a Virginian and Librarian of the Department of State, added his own errors to Randolph's, misread and mishandled the manuscripts, and needlessly abridged the size of the *Works*. The editor's heart was not in it. Disgusted by the Anas, he finally printed them with reluctance. He thought the only fair ground of complaint against the edition was its inclusion of too many letters "scarce worthy" of preservation. Contact with "the dregs" of Jefferson's correspondence left a bad taste in Washington's mouth and greatly lowered his estimate of him.

ences set his mind to reflection on Jefferson nearly twenty years before he determined to write the biography in 1850. What he lacked in literary talent and historical training, he made up by partisan enthusiasm and passion for investigation. "I think I have a blood hound staunchness in *running down* game," he boasted not without some justification. He tried to enter into the feelings of his hero. His library, according to a visitor, was "a perfect magazine of personal mementos of Mr. Jefferson, manuscripts, pictures, views of Monticello, grand plans of its garden ... personal relics and other things not to be classed." Several first readers thought here at last was Jefferson's Boswell. Actually, however, Macaulay better fit the case; for like the great English Whig historian, Randall essayed to write the epic of a party. As he said at the outset to his good friend, Martin Van Buren, his major aim was an authentic history of the parties. Jefferson was the vehicle of this story, as indeed he was in most of the literature in which Randall had saturated himself since 1830.

While engaged with the biography, Randall's own politics underwent an important change. He had been affiliated for many years with the radical or Barnburner faction of the New York Democracy. It was largely responsible in 1848 for the Free Soil ticket headed by Van Buren. Randall had a hand in writing its anti-slavery platform. As the slavery crisis mounted, Randall did not follow the Free Soilers into the Republican party, but instead went over to the pro-Southern Democracy of the state. In 1860 he presided over the New York Breckenridge Convention. In the opinion of several observers this political about-face was related to his work on Jefferson. "The truth is," he wrote at the time of publication, "the work cannot suit sectionalists—or anybody affected with the Southern-phobia. That disease rages now in the North." He expected "old-fashioned State rights democrats" of the South vigorously to sustain his work. The expectation was gratified. In the pages of the *Richmond Enquirer,* it was acclaimed "a Southern book."

The spring of 1851 found Randall in Virginia in search of materials. The search was so fruitful that the single volume he had planned grew to three octavos totaling two thousand pages. T. J. Randolph, during the biographer's visit at Edgehill, discovered a forgotten hoard of private papers—memoranda, account books, garden books, meteorological records, and so on. These were put in Randall's hands, as also were stores of family correspondence, personal mementos, and reminiscences of grandchildren. The exquisite letters of Ellen Randolph Coolidge and the recollections of the manumitted slave, Wormley, helped Randall to write the first history of Jefferson's life at Monticello. Intimate family letters were worked into the narrative for nearly every year of Jefferson's life after his wife's death in 1782. All previous biography, with a modest exception for Tucker's, had been based upon official records and published writings, which dealt almost entirely with public affairs. Randall was the first to gain the full co-operation of the family and to exploit its treasures. He came to regard his *Life* as authorized by the family. It was so received by many of its readers.

With this mass of new material on the Sage's private life, making up about one fourth of the biography, Randall cracked, however slightly, the legend of the "man of bronze," and excited in his readers a sense of fresh discovery. For all the literature on Jefferson, one reviewer observed, he was not really known. "What he did can be gathered from it, but not what he was." The figure projected in nearly every book and statue and painting was the embodiment of a political principle. John Esten Cooke, the Virginia novelist, described its most popular form: "gigantic size, bronze, enveloped in a huge cloak; the hand holds the pen; the mighty head 'oppressive with its mind,' droops toward the breast, and 'we hold these truths to be self-evident' seems to issue from the bronzed lips." * Tucker's work had been in this mode. Admirable as it was, Grigsby wrote in a long review of Randall's biography, it bore the same relation to Jefferson as Marshall's *Life* bore to Washington. It appealed almost

---

* Cooke actually preceded Randall by four years in the humanization of Jefferson. His historical romance, *The Youth of Jefferson,* pictured the student at Williamsburg: a rebel against authority but an aristocrat in manners and taste, bent upon pleasure no less than learning, youthful companion of the Royal Governor at the Palace, where together they gambled, sipped sherry, and talked Deism into the wee hours of the morning, a gay and amorous young Virginian. "Mr. Thomas Jefferson..." Cooke said, "was the very last man whom any one would have regarded as the future leader of a great political party and the writer of the Declaration of Independence."

exclusively to the student of political history. Randall's wide and colorful panorama opened Jefferson to view, Grigsby thought, just as Irving's pages gave glimpses of Washington as a human being. This was not only history, it was biography in the truest sense. By first describing Jefferson's life at Monticello in some detail, Randall was the first historian to add sweet and mellow touches to the Jefferson image.

It was hard to believe that this man of domestic felicity and the political hero Randall crowned with laurel were one and the same. The brief yet delightful portrait of the young Jefferson was capped at the end of the biography by a much fuller portrait of the gentleman farmer and sage. Running throughout was the author's sentimental appreciation of his idol's parental virtues:

He was naturally fond of children; he was cautious and painstaking; his eye and ear were quick to watch over them and note their little wants; he had the feminine dexterity and delicacy of manipulation; he had the feminine loving patience; he appreciated instantly and correctly what was under all circumstances appropriate to them, with a feminine instinct.

Jefferson treasured to his death, Randall learned, locks of hair and other mementos of his deceased wife and children. The great man loved the soil and all that grew upon it. He was a kind master and a perfect gentleman, bowing to blacks and whites alike on the road. He loved the fiddle; men who heard his bow testified to his accomplishment. He never gambled, and cards were forbidden in his house. He had aversion to strong drink. His mouth was unpolluted by oaths and tobacco.

As readers snatched at these passages, discovering an interest they had not known before, it at once became apparent that Jefferson had a higher destiny than politics. He would serve posterity as an instructor in the arts of civility and a monitor of the young. "Jefferson as Student and Lover," "Jefferson's Daughter Wishes to Become a Nun," "Jefferson's Last Hours"—these were characteristic titles of passages from the *Life* most often reprinted in newspapers and magazines. The letters to his daughters were favorably compared to those of Chesterfield to his sons. "Modern daughters can learn many a lesson of parental obedience and duty by studying the history of the most admirable Martha Jefferson." The great mind unbended itself in the unreserve of the family and in the tranquil pursuits of literature and horticulture.

The revelation of the private life pointed the way to a better understanding of Jefferson's mind and thought. Aiming to write "the history of the mind as well as the public career," Randall showed keen perception of the former without, however, appreciating its interactions with the latter. He was dumbfounded by Jefferson's passion for detail—"the merest seeming trifles." How could a man "so constantly intent on small subjects . . . have taste, or time, or power, to master large ones?" Jefferson's exhaustless energy kept every faculty "constantly strained and in full play, each one a conduit which is pouring knowledge into the soul." None of the facts he so assiduously gathered and systematized was meaningless. He worked from fact to abstraction, from abstraction to practical innovation. This fertile genius applied to the problem of the moldboard of the plow led to a great utilitarian discovery; applied to the problem of government it made America the democracy nature destined her to be. Only against a mountain of evidence from Jefferson's everyday life would it any longer be permissible to scoff at him as an impractical visionary.

Randall felt somewhat uncomfortable with this mind caught in the tedium of fact and narrowed to utility. Jefferson scorned the more recondite branches of learning—Plato's "cloudland of hypothesis" and the romantic fancy of Scott. He lacked pure imagination and a sense of the beautiful. "Beauty with him was a utility, and he therefore sought it. But he apparently kindled into no fine imaginings as he gazed on it. He measured its heights and depths—duly estimated its components—counted its accessories." This was clear from the *Notes on Virginia;* Randall's excerpts from travel accounts accented the trait. Jefferson prized beauty for what it could do, for its place in the future scheme of things, which he contemplated with the same fervor as the metaphysician contemplates the cosmos or the sentimental dreamer the picturesque past.

All this, in Randall's view, simply added interest and charm to a man whose genius lay elsewhere. By its revelation of the private life, the biography opened a new phase in the quest for the historical

Jefferson. But this was merely "another field" quite apart from the primary field of Randall's interest: politics. Here Randall trod old ground in paths already well worn. Jefferson moved through the volumes at the author's bidding, first in one field and then in another, and the two seemed scarcely related. One was home, family, farm; the other was forum, party, Presidency. Writing of the former, Randall was gentle, calm, and leisurely. When he shifted to the political arena, his style became pungent, energetic, and argumentative. This was Randall's passion, the political history he had started out to write until the family led him into odd but fascinating byways. Although fuller and more triumphant than any preceding it, Randall's account of Jefferson's public career was in the tradition of Jeffersonian history.

The crux of Randall's *Life* was the decade of party struggle ending in the revolution of 1800. Eleven of the hero's eighty-three years consumed one third of the author's pages. What led up to 1790 was prologue, what followed 1800 was epilogue. In between lay the crucial decade of American history. It was therefore of the utmost importance to understand the party conflict in all its parts and relations. Jefferson's greatest achievement, Randall thought, was the establishment of "a party which permanently fixed the character of our institutions and the destiny of our country." The year 1800 was, in effect, the happy beginning of America. The new President guided the ship of state safely out of the fierce storm that had almost battered it to pieces into calm seas wafted by steady breezes. Randall went behind the scenes to show how the Federalists governed, tracing their every maneuver; but with respect to the Republican rulers after 1800, he was content to give "public political results." Suddenly all was clear, simple, and harmonious.

Randall sought to put upon the solid foundation of fact Jefferson's own belief in the existence of a monarchical party with Hamilton at its head. Despite the vigor and fulness of the argument, it did not allay the growing sense of the unreality of Jefferson's fears and accusations. On no other point was the book subjected to as much criticism. Even the New York Democrat, William Dorsheimer, thought Randall did Jefferson "great injury by reviving this absurd business." But if this belief was absurd, Randall pleaded, then Jefferson was absurd; for it was a settled dogma of his political creed and it colored his every political transaction. The question was "a naked one of veracity." If there was no party constantly at work to overthrow republicanism, then Jefferson was guilty as charged: a "monomaniacal fanatic" or a "cold-blooded demagogue."

As the vast panorama of the party conflict unfolded in Randall's pages, the numerous assemblage formed no more than a background for the giant protagonists, Hamilton and Jefferson. Hamilton, Randall argued, exploited every opportunity to destroy the republic. Dissatisfied with the Constitution, "the frail and worthless fabric" as he later called it, he nevertheless urged its ratification as a temporary bond until some crisis of state would enable him to seize power and establish a monarchical government. Under Washington he pursued his fixed course by devious and subtle means. The financial measures were not allowed to operate naturally, but were used as devices to promote Hamilton's larger ends. Jefferson complained, Randall said, not so much of the measures as of their administration. Hamilton's interference in the affairs of Jefferson's department and his intrigues with British agents looked to an alliance with Britain against France. The crisis he had anticipated and worked for came in the wake of the X.Y.Z. fury of 1798. Hamilton, not Adams, was the "prime engineer" of the terror, Randall said. But neither the hysteria of sedition nor the control of the army nor the plottings of electoral fraud accomplished Hamilton's aim; and Jefferson's triumphant administration left the would-be American Caesar politically impotent.

Randall was thus led to conclude with Hamilton himself that he was, indeed, an exotic in this American world. The epithets usually applied to Jefferson—"projector," "visionary," "foreign domination"—were peculiarly appropriate to his great adversary. He lacked the "practical wisdom" of Jefferson, who adapted his politics to the progress of ideas so that they might stand the test of civilization in America. "He certainly cannot be called wise in practice," Randall judged, "who 'props' his edifice till he crushes it with the buttresses he builds against it." By his immoderate efforts to establish his system, Hamilton forced the people to choose between it and democracy, "upbuilt democracy by his overaction against it," and compelled the opposition to sweep away nearly all his work. He could be credited with executive ability, but Randall quickly added, "The most efficient political executive is a despot."

The biographer looked upon Jefferson's administration as a virtual golden age:

The taxes were abolished, yet public credit was visibly and rapidly decreasing. Great treasury schemes were extinct, yet industry prospered. . . . Democracy was everywhere triumphant. . . . Great and expensive judicial "engines of government" had fallen, yet every man sat under his own vine and fig tree, and enjoyed his own in security. Never since the dawn of history was there a government which met all the ends of its institution better, or with less burden to the governed.

Enthralled by this vision, Randall ignored the Federalist mechanism that continued to turn the wheels of government and took Jefferson's ineffable contribution, "democracy," for the machinery of government itself. The vicissitudes of the administration were smoothed to unruffled and regular motion. Every problem was solved upon the principles Jefferson brought into power. The Louisiana Purchase? The magnificence of the triumph, in Randall's eyes, left no fair basis for criticism or detraction. And the Embargo? It was a statesmanlike measure taken to preserve peace, and would have succeeded but for the treacherous Junto men in Massachusetts. Using Federalist precedents to justify the Enforcing Act of 1808, Randall seemed to forget that Jefferson came into power to end just such infringements of individual liberty and latitudinarian constructions of the Constitution. He missed all the ironies of Jefferson's policy, including its erosive effects on the agrarian basis of Jeffersonian Democracy. Jefferson retired from office, Randall concluded, "unchanged, unchilled, unhardened," and "his hopes of the world's future had only grown brighter."

John Adams had made a concise characterization of Jefferson when the two first met in 1775: "Prompt, frank, explicit, and decisive!" This, declared Randall, was the key to Jefferson's whole public life and character. Even as he gloried in Jefferson's skillful political leadership, he sought to put it on the highest moral plane. He noticed, like Tucker before, traits of demeanor and style which lent themselves to tortuous misrepresentation. His natural amiability, his enemies converted into hollowness and insincerity. His habit in small affairs of "taking things by the smooth handle," they construed as weakness. His habit in large affairs of spurning all middle prudences, they took as tyrannical. Jefferson was above all a bold and passionate leader in language, thought, and action. "The mighty leader of mankind must be something more than a sage; something more than a skillful executive tactician—he must be, at heart, a hero." Thus the multitude would always regard him, Randall trusted, the Hero of Democracy.

The *Life of Jefferson* made a highly favorable impression on its first readers. Several reviewers ranked it with "the best historico-biographical works in English literature." The verdict of time, however, was suggested by the reviewer who said the work failed of being a masterpiece by the neglect of a few wholesome rules of rhetoric Randall must have learned as a schoolboy. The fact that the *Life* was otherwise generally thought to be a masterpiece suggests a broader area of acceptance for Randall's conception of Jefferson than might have been expected. "Dare nobody couch lances against the dead champion? Suddenly all *are praising Jefferson!!*" Randall exclaimed. He had expected a different reception. The lancers gradually came forward; even so, Randall's *Life* was a public triumph, one which represented the pinnacle of Jefferson's reputation in historical literature in the nineteenth century.

More than half a century after Callender published his libels to the world, the pious family view of Jefferson's private character was rarely questioned. An exception was the Reverend E. O. Dunning, of Connecticut, who wrote in response to an article, "Jefferson's Private Character," in the *North American Review*. The article (based upon the *Life* and additional reminiscences by Ellen Coolidge) premised that the grandchildren's testimony was definitive. The New England minister thought this foolish logic in the service of a "pious fraud." Dunning was especially alarmed by Randall's (and the grandchildren's) attempt to make the Sage of Monticello into a Christian. On this point, as on every other, Randall claimed much more for his idol than had the cautious Tucker. Most reviewers were tolerant without being convinced. Infidelity was fading from the image, but Jefferson's conversion to Christianity still lay in the future.

Randall's vindication of Jefferson's public character scored high with the reviewers. The shiftings and turnings of Jefferson's course seemed to diminish within the larger pattern of consistency Randall unfolded. The affairs of pride and honor—all those issues of "character" that had formed the substance of so much discussion—began to appear petty as their injuries ceased to be felt and the full measure of Jefferson's place in history came to be appreciated. While this was the general line of response, the "character" mode of interpretation still had many years to run. Just at the time Randall's *Jefferson* claimed the attention of the public, John C. Hamilton was writing the multi-volume life of his father that was to be one of the most comprehensive assaults ever made on Jefferson's character.

The ideology of Randall's book was the ideology of his party; as such it could not escape criticism. "It is not enough for Mr. Randall to exalt his hero into a demigod;" said Greeley's *New York Tribune,* "he must debase his antagonists into demons." Thirty years after men first read the Anas with amazement or disbelief, thirty years in which Jefferson was an oracle in politics and his dogmas of state rights and democracy formed the creed of a party, some men were simply unable to accept Randall's "history of the parties." The biographer's idolatry, though perhaps in keeping with the conventions of public opinion, the *Richmond Whig* observed, necessitated the opinion that "the whole people of the Union formed a perfectly inert, unthinking mass, and Thos. Jefferson did all the thinking for the whole of them. . . . There is such a thing as making a man ridiculous by overpraise!"

But was it overpraise? Could the *real* Jefferson have been very different from the Jefferson the people imagined? Indeed, could he be said to have existed at all apart from what American democracy revealed him to be? Again and again reviewers cited the unparalleled example of Jefferson's "extensive and continued control over the popular mind," the universal democracy that is "the work of his hands," the influence that has "shaped or modified the existing polity of the United States." It could no longer be gainsaid, the *New York*

Times declared, that Jefferson was "the political father of his country."

This recognition was the starting point for a distinguished essay on Jefferson's political thought by William Dorsheimer, who reviewed the *Life* in the *Atlantic Monthly*. Venturing much farther into the realm of ideas than Randall, Dorsheimer thought the key to Jefferson's political system was the doctrine of individual freedom, with its necessary corollaries of limited and decentralized government. Jefferson was the first man to see that the progress, even the splendor, of a nation came not from building up its governing power but from the release of its myriad individual talents and energies. An ardent patriot infused with the native genius—"He sympathized with all our national desires and prejudices, our enterprise and confidence, our love of dominion and boundless pride"—Jefferson did not, like the French philosophers, attempt to frame a political system for an ideal society or to expound principles in a social vacuum. "He was compelled to think because he had need to act,—to make laws for a real society," Dorsheimer wrote. Bound to the practical task of forming political institutions suitable to the sentiments and conditions of American society, Jefferson succeeded so magnificently that his system seemed now to have been "providentially designed" and his name forever connected with "the future progress of an agile and ambitious people." Developing this theme, which lay buried under the pretentious and partisan rhetoric of Randall's work, Dorsheimer concluded that Jefferson was more than the Apostle of Democracy—he was the first great American.

The confidence in the sufficiency of the Jeffersonian polity, as evidenced by the general reception of Randall's *Life* in 1858, was sharply assailed two years later when the biographer released to the press portions of his correspondence with Lord Macaulay, lately deceased. One of Macaulay's letters—recognized by his most telling metaphor, "Your Constitution is all sail and no anchor"—has since become famous; but his trenchant commentary on American institutions took on added significance in the context of Randall's book.

As an admirer of the great Whig advocate and historian, Randall sought an exchange of views with Macaulay on Jefferson in 1856. The Englishman replied in a friendly vein, but bluntly stated that

Jefferson was no hero of his and that he looked with apprehension on the Jeffersonian drift of American institutions. His temper somewhat ruffled, Randall pressed upon Macaulay a more sympathetic understanding of his subject. The cutting answer disclosed the wide gap between English Whiggery and American Democracy. Just why his opinion should have caused Randall any surprise puzzled Macaulay. He had never uttered a word of approval for the democratic institutions of equality and majority rule. They must, he thought, eventually destroy liberty or civilization or both. America's fate under them was no less certain for being temporarily deferred. Her progress to date was in no way the result of Jeffersonian principles but rather of vast land and resources. So long as this natural abundance existed, "the Jeffersonian polity may continue to exist without causing any fatal calamity." It would not be fairly tested until men crowded the land and grew hungry. With what means then, Macaulay asked, could the American government restrain the mad and ignorant majority? "Either some Caesar or Napoleon will seize the reins of government with a strong hand; or your republic will be . . . laid waste by barbarians in the twentieth century as the Roman Empire was in the fifth. . . . Thinking thus, of course I can not reckon Jefferson among the benefactors of mankind." One final exchange closed the correspondence on Macaulay's sour note.

So the disaster Macaulay predicted was a Jeffersonian disaster. He agreed with Randall's basic premise: democracy and Jefferson were synonymous and the polity was increasingly Jeffersonian. But he struck contemptuously at the American's almost religious faith in the beneficence of the Jeffersonian state. The reaction of the press was of course generally favorable to Randall. "Lord Macaulay," it was said, "stands just where Hamilton, Knox, Ames and Sedgwick stood three quarters of a century ago." Like most Englishmen, he had learned nothing from the success of the American experiment.

This was, nevertheless, 1860, when events imposed upon men's faith in the perpetuation of the American system. Interpreted in the light of an impending calamity other than the distant one he predicted, Macaulay's letters were pregnant with meaning; all the more so because Jefferson, "the political father of his country," was deeply implicated in that calamity.

Four

UNION

All honor to Jefferson—to the man who, in the concrete pressure of a struggle for national independence by a single people, had the coolness, forecast, and capacity to introduce into a merely revolutionary document, an abstract truth, and so to embalm it there, that to-day, and in all coming days, it shall be a rebuke and a stumbling block to the very harbingers of re-appearing tyranny and oppression.*

ON APRIL 6, 1859 Abraham Lincoln wrote a letter respectfully declining the invitation to address a Republican festival in Boston one week later in honor of Thomas Jefferson. The Jefferson the Republicans celebrated as their spiritual father on this one hundred and sixteenth anniversary of his birth was "the author of the Declaration of Independence, the father of the Ordinance of 1787, and the apostle of state rights." With his flair for appreciating the humorous side of even the gravest events, Lincoln magnificently captured the spirit of the occasion. Bearing in mind, his letter began, that Jefferson was the head of one of the original parties and Boston the headquarters of the other, it was "curious and interesting that those supposed to descend politically from the party opposed to Jefferson should now be celebrating his birthday in their own original seat of empire, while those claiming political descent from him have ceased to breathe his name everywhere." The two parties, he continued, had completely "changed hands as to the principle upon which they were originally supposed to have divided"—the issue between liberty and property. Then the unfailing anecdote:

* Abraham Lincoln to H. L. Pierce and others, April 6, 1859.

I remember once being much amused at seeing two partially intoxicated men engage in a fight with their great-coats on, which fight, after a long and rather harmless contest, ended in each having fought himself out of his own coat, and *into* that of the other. If the two leading parties of this day are really identical with the two in the days of Jefferson and Adams, they have performed the same feat as the two drunken men.

"But soberly"—Lincoln changed his demeanor—"it is now no child's play to save the principles of Jefferson from total overthrow in this nation." They had the same relation to "free society" as the proposi- tions of Euclid had to geometry. They were openly flouted by the guardians of slavery. Unless Americans could agree upón the truth of "the definitions and axioms" stated in the Declaration of Inde- pendence, no enduring Union was possible. Lincoln concluded with one of the most eloquent tributes to Jefferson (quoted at the head of this chapter) ever penned. Little noticed just after it was read at the Boston festival, Lincoln's letter circulated freely during the presidential campaign of 1860. It was a masterpiece, the *Cincinnati Daily Gazette* declared, "the most pointed and most forcible political letter ever written . . . a platform in itself."

"Barefaced humbuggery!" The Democrats denounced this Repub- lican appeal to Jefferson; as well they might, since they had renewed their historic allegiance to the party's patron saint only a few days before in imposing ceremonies at Salem, Massachusetts. Repeating the stale praises and slogans of a generation of party leaders, the leading orator of the day eulogized "the great apostle of civil free- dom, the embodiment of democratic truth, the friend and expounder of human rights, the fearless foe of every form of oppression." But nothing was said about Jefferson's hostility to that particular oppres- sion, slavery, which warmed the feelings of Lincoln and many other Republicans. They took the Democrats' omission as "a sign that the homage they render is to a name, hallowed in the popular memory, and not to the principles which the name represents."

Jefferson's double birthday honors in 1859 was only the most star- tling exhibition of his relationship to the gathering crisis. The great political parties whose antagonism was undoing the Union were, as a neutral observer wrote, like "two faces under the same hood," both "equally loud in celebrating the praises of the same man as the

recognized exemplar and representative of their distinctive sentiments." While this may be understood as a tribute to the power
of his name as a political watchword, it also points to the fact that
the Civil War, interpreted in the mirror Jefferson made for posterity,
was the outgrowth of a deep cleavage in the orthodox political tradition. There were two faces under Jefferson's hood because the elements of the tradition which should have worked in unison came into
irresoluble conflict. How this developed, and with what consequences
for Jefferson's reputation, may be told in three sections: first, the
changing geometry of Jeffersonian ideals and the new configurations
of the great geometer himself in the slavery agitation; second, the
appropriation of the Jefferson symbol by Free Soilers and Republicans in national politics; third, the reaction against Jefferson and
his teachings in the surge of nationalism produced by the War.

1. Slavery and Abolitionism

The Virginia slavery debate of 1831-32 represented the last stand
of liberal opinion in the South against its peculiar institution. In
the twilight of Nullification, "the road from Monticello" widened
throughout the South, which merged its cause, and the Jeffersonian
cause of state rights, with the cause of slavery. "Domestic slavery . . ."
Governor McDuffie declared before the South Carolina legislature
in 1835, "instead of being a political evil, is the cornerstone of our
republican edifice." At the same time Northern abolitionists built
upon the proposition of 1776 a mighty engine of reform. The shifting pattern of political beliefs came into focus in the Jefferson image.

The abolitionist onslaught gave the Southerners reason to fear the
power of Jeffersonian ideals. The incorporation of the idea of natural
equality into the Declaration of Independence seemed to Daniel K.
Whitaker, a Charleston publicist, the most grievous blunder in American history; for this flattering illusion, he wrote, was "now seized
upon by the abolitionists with greater avidity than it once was by
the ultra-democrats . . . and is likely seriously to be turned to the
account of fanaticism, and the great confusion of the whole country."
In the first novel by an American Negro, William Wells Brown's
Clotel, a slave who followed Nat Turner testifies during the trial:
"I will tell you why I joined the revolting negroes. I have heard my

master read in the Declaration of Independence 'that all men are created equal,' and this caused me to inquire why I was a slave." The poignant contradiction between the fundamental American commitment and the imperatives of slave society had found agonized expression in Jefferson's lament during the Missouri debate: "We have the wolf by the ears, and we can neither hold him nor safely let him go. Justice is in one scale, and self-preservation in the other." For most Southern leaders after Jefferson, the agony was unbearable. They did not, for some time, totally reject the sacred text of 1776, but rather tried in ingenious ways to render it tolerable—and harmless. Its equalitarian principle, some said, was a quirk of patriotic enthusiasm; others called it "a mere sentimental phrase," to be taken rather as the document's "ornament than its substance"; and still others denied that it was meant to apply to Negroes.

Viewing the Declaration of Independence in its historical context, pro-slavery thinkers argued that it referred not to the abstract rights of man but to the substantial rights of specific communities. "All men in their national, or state capacity, were equally entitled, and equally at liberty, to rid themselves of oppression, and act for themselves,— a right which as individual citizens, they did not possess and could not exercise, as against established government." This, Whitaker insisted, was the only justifiable interpretation. More than a convenient escape from an embarrassing moral commitment, the "separatism" theory of the Declaration conformed to the theory of the Union as a terminable compact. The American birthright, which could not be honored in its moral intent, might be used to sanction the delivery of the Southern people, in their state capacity, from an oppressive Union.

In its larger outlines the "separatism" theory was part of the general conservative attack on the legend of revolutionary origins. Jefferson planted the seed of the legend in the Declaration; it was entirely alien to American experience. This was the accusation, repeated again and again. The natural rights dogma was "absolute theory, excogitated from the brain of cyclopedists, resting on visions of dreamers"; Jefferson was "not a Christian, but a disciple of the French philosophy"; the Declaration preamble, "every jot and tittle, is the liberty and equality claimed by infidelity." The patriots of

1776, it was said, fought to preserve their English liberties, not to win new ones.

Rejecting the revolutionary legend, Southern thinkers developed in its place the legend of the Cavaliers. Southern liberties were "the entailed inheritance ... from the bosom of a haughty and exclusive aristocracy," which originated in the Cavalier migration of the mid-seventeenth century. *The Southern Literary Messenger* severely criticized those historians, such as Bancroft and Grigsby, who interpreted the revolution in Virginia as a democratic movement. It was in fact, said this sectional organ, "set in motion by the Cavaliers of the Tidewater," with no support whatever from the *demos*.

The source of Jefferson's "disastrous error," most of the pro-slavery writers agreed, lay in his confusion of the two categories, nature and society—as false as his identification of nature and God. W. J. Grayson called the Declaration an infidel production, because "it deduces rights in the social state from the state of nature; or in other words, appeals to nature for the exhibition of the principles of social science." Southern institutions proceeded from just the opposite grounds, from "the experience of the world," from "man as he really is, not as presented by the imagination of idealists." Jefferson's self-evident truth—"that all men are created equal"—seemed a senseless sophism to the slavery logicians, partly because they supposed the proposition referred to the birth of men in organized society. They usually altered it to read "that all men are *born* equal," as in the French Declaration of the Rights of Man. Chancellor Harper of South Carolina demonstrated how deceptively easy it was to dispose of Jefferson's bold dogma when its validity was made to depend upon empirical evidences drawn from history and social science. Would it not be nearer the truth to say that no man is ever born free and no two men ever born equal? Harper asked. "Low as we descend in combatting the theories of presumptuous dogmatists, it cannot be necessary to stoop to this." Given the endless diversity in the conditions of men, which increased with the progress of civilization, Harper thought that the equality dogma was fanciful, anarchical, and unjust. This was the Southern advocate's standard rejoinder, going stale with age.

To the argument of human inequality, pro-slavery theorists usually added the racist argument of Negro inferiority. The equalization of white suffrage and representation in the Southern states before the Civil War reflected the general drift toward the idea of democracy among all the whites, the ideology of white supremacy. Some support for this position could be found in Jefferson's thought. Even as he advocated emancipation in the *Notes on Virginia,* he voiced the "strong suspicion" that the Negroes "are inferior to the whites in endowments both of body and mind," and, moreover, that "this inferiority is not the effect merely of their condition of life." Deportation of the freed Negroes was an essential part of his plan of emancipation, for never was he able to envision a biracial society that would not end in "the extermination of one or the other race." In some pro-slavery literature his guarded remarks on Negro inferiority took their place beside the arguments of modern racial theorists. The explicit distinction he made in a private letter, sometimes cited by abolitionists, between *capacities* in which the races might differ, and *rights* in which they were equal, was commonly ignored by Southern spokesmen.

Slavery, it was argued, strengthened the foundations of republican government. Abel P. Upshur, the youthful spokesman of Virginia conservatism in 1829, made a thorough statement of the case a decade later. First, said Upshur, in slave society every white man was an aristocrat. The whites had status, a kind of rank and privilege, as Burke had said, which made them more zealous of personal liberty and social order than men whose craving for distinction found release only in the competition for office and wealth. Second, slavery served agriculture, the economic basis of Jeffersonian republicanism. Societies with uniform habits and fixed pursuits were most favorable to liberty. "We are all cultivators of the soil, and all owners of slaves." Third, the plantation system developed an educated class to rule, making needless the mischievous Jeffersonian project for the general diffusion of knowledge. "Only a few are necessary for the wise ordering of public affairs and for the safety and prosperity of the nation." Finally, slavery buttressed the institution of private property. It was impossible, the Southerners warned, for the Northern states under the wage system and majority rule permanently to secure property. When the outlet to the West closed and the laws of capitalist economics hardened, Northern society would be defenseless against the propertyless rabble, and, in line with Macaulay's prediction, Jefferson's "much lauded but nowhere accredited dogma . . . 'that all men are born equal' " would be proven a perilous delusion.

This fantastic mixture of racist democracy and planter aristocracy with the tradition of agrarian republicanism indicates how selected Jeffersonian sentiments and concepts survived in pro-slavery ideology. The most important Jeffersonian survival, however, was the doctrine of state rights. Slavery was the bulwark of state rights; state rights was the bulwark of slavery. The South was, in the phrase of the fiery Carolinian R. B. Rhett, "the balance-wheel of the confederacy." The natural tendency of Northern democracy toward consolidation of power in the central government was always counteracted by the South. "The South, on account of her institution of slavery, has been *the sentinel over the Constitution.*" State rights in American history was like a chameleon, inconstant in the interests it served and changing its color to suit shifting political environments; but the mark of the slave power upon it was indelible beyond any power of liberalism to erase and restore its original character.

Not until just before the War did a small group of Southern thinkers free themselves completely from the Jeffersonian heritage and make their task, not the revision of Jeffersonian symbols in the light of slavery, but the construction from the ground up of an ideology responsive to the system of slavery itself. Seeing the inescapable antagonism of Jeffersonian philosophy to slavery, these radicals discarded the one to save the other. If, as one of them observed, "The dissolution of the American Union was written in the Declaration of Independence," then it was foolhardy to equivocate with its philosophy. If Jefferson was "that visionary, theoretical, and fanatical political monomaniac, who . . . reasoned for Americans as 'if they were Frenchmen,' " then it was fatuous for the South to seek justification in him. If it was Jefferson who fathered "the spirit of slavery emancipation" and under whose "political influence this mental poison spread through our political sphere," then he was rightly the god of abolitionist idolatry.

The Virginian George Fitzhugh was the outstanding representative of this late radical phase of pro-slavery thought. Fitzhugh called the Declaration a collection of "powder-cask abstractions." His hatred of all things Jeffersonian was unbounded:

The true greatness of Mr. Jefferson was his fitness for revolution. He was the genius of innovation, the architect of ruin, the inaugurator of anarchy. His mission was to pull down, not to build up. He thought everything false as well in the physical, as in the moral world. He fed his horses on potatoes, and defended harbors with gunboats, because it was contrary to human experience and human opinion. He proposed to govern boys without the authority of masters or the control of religion, supplying their place with Laissez-faire philosophy, and morality from the pages of Laurence Sterne. His character, like his philosophy, is exceptional—invaluable in urging revolution; but useless, if not dangerous, in quiet times.

The criticism was novel not so much in what it said as in the violence of the rejection.

The great error of the age, Fitzhugh thought, was the *laissez faire* philosophy, of which Jefferson was the American apostle. It idealized the emancipated man selfishly competing against his fellows in an atomized society. Free society had already failed in England, Fitzhugh said, and eventual failure was certain in the Northern states. Southern society was based upon older and firmer foundations: the conception of man as a social animal, the virtues of order and balance, the organic theory of society. Fitzhugh advocated a kind of aristocratic communism, in which men of different degrees and stations labored for the common good.

With this general outlook, Fitzhugh went on to reject every major tenet of Jeffersonian Democracy. The unnatural individualism and self-sufficiency of agricultural societies fostered that backward state of civilization in which men believed "that government is best which governs least." Fitzhugh agreed with Carlyle's dictum: "the world is too little governed." The hierarchical organization of slave society was conducive to hereditary aristocracy; thus entail and primogeniture should be restored. "Social equality, liberty of speech and of press, separation of church and state, and the free exercise of religion, are, each and all, utterly inconsistent with the existence of social order, and of all government." Southern society was organic, its insti-

tutions were authoritarian; yet Southern statesmanship was liberal.
To close this dangerous gap, Fitzhugh urged the South to abandon
its antiquated Jeffersonian ideas, especially its blind trust in constitutional guarantees and remedies. Constitutions were useless except as
they reinforced a society's living institutions. Finally, hoping for the
survival of the Union, Fitzhugh advocated in 1860 an alliance between Southern slaveholders and Northern capitalists—a reversal of
the Jeffersonian strategy. The real conflict, he believed, was not
between North and South or consolidation and state rights or agriculture and manufacturing. It was a conflict of ideas kept in focus by
the issue of slavery and abolition. At the opposite poles were "Christians and infidels . . . law and order men and no government men . . .
friends of private property and socialists . . . the chaste and libidinous
. . . marriage and free love," and so on. In this great struggle, the
conservatives of the two sections had common interests upon which
to unite. If, on the other hand, the South courted Northern democracy, she courted her destroyer.

Fitzhugh's thought, with its brutal logic, undercut the shallow
efforts of those who in their need for some rapprochement with
Jefferson pruned and amended his principles. Wishing to rid the
Southern mind of its debris of Jeffersonianism, Fitzhugh seemed to
feel no responsibility to what he admitted to be the ruling tradition
of American politics. The radical assault on the eve of the war signified the rotting away of traditional loyalties; yet the Southern mind
remained divided. As Louis Hartz observes, the South appeared "to
divide its time between the world of Burke and the world of
Jefferson."

There were two sides of the Jefferson image in the ante-bellum
South. One was *republican*. Around it clustered the ideas of constitutional liberty, the sanctity of property, the agrarian order, state
rights, and home rule. The republican Jefferson, the Jefferson of '98,
had high claims to recognition, and pro-slavery ideology was in part
shaped to this tradition. The "fatal legacies" came from the *democratic* Jefferson, whose influence in the South was slowly extinguished
because of the need to defend slavery. Southern leaders well knew
the gulf separating the two. Democracy, either as a theory of government or as the name of a party, never had much status with Southern

leaders. It was not until 1840, one writer observed, "that decent persons could willingly stomach the name" democracy. Some Southerners could never stomach it. The great leader, Calhoun, always wanted to be known as a "Republican." The word "Democrat," he said, was Northern and "as usually understood means those who are in favour of the government of the absolute numerical majority to which I am utterly opposed and the prevalence of which would destroy our system and destroy the South." Calhoun felt the truth of Disraeli's axiom, "With words we govern men." Democracy was the symbol of the people's sovereignty; and attached to the historically conservative party of the Union, it set up a constant pressure against constitutional limitations. Northern abolitionism greatly expanded the internal pressure between republicanism and democracy in the Jeffersonian heritage.

During the tense congressional debate of 1854, an outspoken member of the abolitionist bloc in the Senate, Benjamin F. Wade of Ohio, rose to the defense of his principles:

I have been pointed at here as an Abolitionist. . . . But let me say to my northern Democratic friends, who are Jeffersonian Democrats, who make that their boast on every stump from Maine to Chicago, that no boast could be more glorious, for no one . . . more glorious has ever breathed the breath of life, even among that great galaxy of worthies of revolutionary memory. I have always admired him. I have endeavored to imitate him; and now, if I have abolitionism about me more than is due, I came very honestly by it, for he taught me. . . . Dispose of him, the giant of Democracy, first; and when you have completely buried his great and glorious deeds and name, I may be expected to attack, but not before.

The panegyric had become familiar by 1854. Congressmen no longer laughed at it. "Who taught me to hate slavery, and every other form of oppression?" one of the earliest abolitionist congressmen declared, "*Jefferson*, the great and good Jefferson." "Were I to write a history of American slavery," still another said, "I should be constrained, in all honesty and truth, to say, that Mr. Jefferson was entitled to the credit of first publicly expressing anti-slavery sentiments in this country; that he was the prime mover of the anti-slavery movement."

Northern abolitionists, from the commencement of their agitation, called Jefferson "an ultra abolitionist." His Declaration of Independence was the polestar of all American strivings. He had repeatedly denounced slavery as a crime against God and humanity. Theodore Parker thought there was no writer who could be more honestly and effectively quoted against slavery than Jefferson. Jefferson's antislavery record gave the signature of a great name to their crusade. Slowly pieced together from Jefferson's writings, public documents, private reminiscences, and scholarly findings, the record seemed one to warrant disciples of Jefferson becoming disciples of Garrison or Sumner. Emancipation, an admiring biographer wrote in 1834, "was the first public movement which he had the honor to originate, and the one in all probability, whose spirit and object were most congenial to his heart." Repeatedly the challenge was flung at the Southern leaders: Abolitionism was Jeffersonianism!

But the Jefferson image of the abolitionists had its negative as well as its positive side. Neither one nor the other but both together represented Jefferson's real legacy to the slavery controversy. Jefferson defined the theory of American institutions; but, the abolitionists complained, he never turned the theory to practice once the theory became uncomfortable. His political leadership established the supremacy of the "slave power" in the country he had dedicated to freedom. He fostered the myth of Negro inferiority. He was at least partly guilty of the scheme of colonization—a crime against the Negro second only to slavery itself. He penned the world's most eloquent testament on the morals of master-slave relations; but, sad to say, he was himself the victim, as well as the observer, of the system's tendency to inflame the worst passions. The ambivalence of the abolitionists toward Jefferson was well expressed by William Lloyd Garrison, editor of the *Liberator*, in his reflections on the Virginia slavery debate. After noting Jefferson's failures and correcting the "capital errors" of his plan of emancipation, after discovering in Jefferson the symbol of democracy's complicity in slavery, Garrison nevertheless praised him for declaring "that slavery was indefensible and disgraceful, and that strenuous efforts ought to be made for its extirpation." In this, Garrison said, Jefferson had shown more

sympathy and courage than all the other Presidents of the United
States together.

Abolitionism was steeped in the rich lore, the rhetoric, and the
imagery of the American Revolution. "One lived in the atmosphere
of the Stamp Act, the Tea Tax, and the Boston Massacre," Henry
Adams wrote in recollection of his Massachusetts boyhood during
the peak years of the agitation. Why shouldn't the slaves strike for
freedom! Garrison roared. Wasn't America founded in rebellion?
"Let Bunker Hill give the response! Let the plains of Concord, and
Lexington, and Yorktown answer!" The "Declaration" of the founding convention of the American Anti-Slavery Society appealed to the
gospel of 1776 and viewed the new enterprise as one "without which
the work of our fathers is incomplete." Abolitionism was simple
patriotism.

Of course the Declaration of Independence applied to slaves! Not,
to be sure, as a self-executing law but as a moral standard to which
the nation must repair. Every nation, Theodore Parker wrote, has
"a certain fundamental idea to unfold and develop." The American
idea is freedom; its providential task is "to organize the rights of
man." It was too late to recommit the Declaration to its author with
instructions to amend: for whites only. The revered patriots and
signers had thought slavery a monstrosity and had confidently believed it would sink under the tide of revolutionary enthusiasm.
John Quincy Adams, near the close of his life, asserted as a fact that
Jefferson had formed years before 1776 "a project ... for the total
abolition of slavery throughout the Union; and it is to be presumed
that all the delegates who affixed their names to the Declaration
entertained the same purpose." Both fact and presumption were
doubtless wrong; the abolitionists conformed the Declaration to their
beliefs. The moral aspect of the Revolution, rather than its diplomatic or constitutional aspect, was of foremost importance. "Take
away from the Declaration of Independence is self-evident truths,"
the elder Adams said, "and you rob the North American Revolution
of all its moral principle, and proclaim it a foul and unnatural rebellion." Although the colonies were declared independent in 1776, the

true revolution was the declaration of human rights and principles at the foundations of government.

While the abolitionists made the venerable idea of natural rights the core of their agitation, they changed its character by blending into it ideas and passions drawn from the heritage of militant Protestant Christianity. "The Bible and the Declaration of Independence constitute the two-edged sword with which we shall slay the monster." The partnership would have startled Jefferson, who, as Garrison complained, "had clearer views of the impolicy of the slave system than of its guilt." Abolitionists viewed slavery less as a crime against nature and reason than as a sin against God and conscience. The rational eighteenth-century concept of the rights of man was supplied with religious sanctions, translated into the Biblical idiom, and inspired by the prophetic tradition of Christianity. The whole vast movement of humanitarian reform which swept through the Northern states in the second quarter of the century rested upon intellectual premises and generated an emotional climate very different from the Enlightenment.

What had been an article of faith with Jefferson, for which, as he finally concluded, "Persuasion, perseverance, and patience are the best advocates," the abolitionists made into an engine of agitation and reform. They found it hard to understand why Jefferson, in his situation, could think moderation the wisest course. Extremes of opinion met on the judgment that his outbursts against slavery were but "temporary fits of inspiration." Had he practiced upon his theory, Garrison exclaimed, "what an all-conquering influence must have attended his illustrious example!" In the view of many Northern observers, not necessarily abolitionists, the South was still paying the cost of Jefferson's bad theories, such as the Embargo, while it was deprived of the benefit of his good theories, such as emancipation. Whether this was because the planter interest was essential to his system of politics or because of painful weaknesses of personal character, most abolitionists could agree with J. Q. Adams's judgment: "Mr. Jefferson had not the spirit of martyrdom."

But if Jefferson was not an agitator, abolitionists nevertheless discovered some signal evidences of moral courage on his part, which they publicized in partial justification of themselves. A striking instance was his letter to Richard Price, the English radical, in 1785. He had written to encourage Price's long-distance project for the dissemination of anti-slavery doctrine in the Southern states. Fifty years later abolitionists were jailed as libelers and incendiaries for doing what Jefferson had commended even of an Englishmen. "By the help of this letter," ran an acid comment, "as a sure signal we may ascertain what progress we have made in respect to liberty." A second instance was that of Dorothy Ripley, an obscure English sojourner in 1801-02, who solicited the President's support for her plan to establish a school for Negro girls in Washington. She described the interview in her journal, which Garrison, apparently, had discovered. "You have my approbation, and I wish you success," she quoted Jefferson's response. Garrison contrasted her good fortune with the fate of Prudence Crandall, forced to close her school for Negro girls in Canterbury, Connecticut, in 1834. "A 'Nigger School,' not in Canterbury, but in Washington, cheek by jowl with the elite of good society and democratic aristocracy—a Nigger School for 'sixty females'—and under the patronage not of Wm. L. Garrison . . . but of Thomas Jefferson." Items of this sort, some of them apocryphal, added to the image of Jefferson as abolitionist; still the opinion was prevalent on both sides of the Mason and Dixon Line that Jefferson's anti-slavery was more theoretical than practical.

David Walker, a free Negro who had wandered from North Carolina to Boston, published in 1829 a crude and fanatical exhortation for the liberation of his race: Appeal, in Four Articles, together with a Preamble, to the Colored Citizens of the World, but in Particular, and Very Expressly to those in the United States of America. The pamphlet ran through several editions. Peddling it in Virginia, Walker was branded an incendiary by the state authorities and, two years later, an accessory to the Southampton massacre. He attributed great influence to Jefferson's remarks in the Notes on Virginia on the inferiority of the Negro race, whose manhood Walker wished to vindicate. "Are we men!!—I ask you, O my brethren! Are we MEN!" How unjust Jefferson's argument that because the white slaves of Rome were noted for virtue and intelligence, the inferiority of the

American blacks must be due to nature rather than to condition! Roman slavery was "no more than a cypher, when compared with ours under the Americans." Jefferson symbolized for Walker the tyranny of a false opinion. "Mr. Jefferson's remarks respecting us have sunk deep into the hearts of millions of the whites and never will be removed this side of eternity." Because the world never knew a better philosopher than the Sage of Monticello, Walker thought the infamous Query XIV "has been as great a barrier to our emancipation, as any thing that has ever been advanced against us." He begged each of his brethren "to buy a copy of Mr. Jefferson's 'Notes on Virginia,' and put it into the hand of his son.... We, and the world wish to see the charges of Mr. Jefferson refuted by the blacks themselves."

These strictures, once laid in so sensational a manner, were frequently repeated in anti-slavery circles. Garrison charged that Jefferson first broached the vulgar opinion that "the negro is a distinct genus, inferior to the human race, and nearly allied to the *simia* species." It might one day be, Garrison thought, "that every drop of ink wasted in its support will cost a drop of human blood." Jefferson had, of course, softened his opinion in letters, one contained in the *Memoirs* and another printed in anti-slavery literature at a later date. Bits of testimony, published from time to time, further mitigated Jefferson's responsibility. For example, one Julius Melbourne, a North Carolina freedman who had emigrated to England, told in his memoirs of a visit he had made to Monticello as a young man in 1815. Melbourne at once fell in love with the benevolent sage, who, in turn, was delighted by the Negro's intellectual attainments. He dined at Jefferson's table in the company of eminent men including so Melbourne recalled, John Marshall! When the conversation finally came around to slavery, Jefferson asserted that the institution would "soon be ab lished in all the states." If the Negroes were given freedom and education, he predicted they would themselves explode the myth of inferiority. Some of his guests dissented. Jefferson pointed to the light-colored Melbourne, whose race they had not suspected in their admiration for his talents. Whether fictitious or not, Melbourne's recollection pointedly showed that Jefferson could be regarded as the Apostle of Liberty by Negroes struggling for their rights as well as by whites intent on their preservation.*

Viewing the whole record of Jefferson's opinions, most abolitionists were unwilling to associate him with slavery's modern advocates; but they repeatedly deplored Query XIV of the *Notes*. Their estimate of its damaging influence was not exceptional. George Tucker, although he had little to say on the subject in his biography, refuted Jefferson's position in his *Letters from Virginia*. Throughout thirty pages of the text, Jefferson's argument was held up to ridicule. It was not only frivolous and absurd, Tucker thought, but also inconsistent with Jefferson's fundamental beliefs in the unity of mankind and in progress through environmental change, beliefs which were amply demonstrated in other parts of the *Notes*. Jefferson's statement on the inferiority of the blacks, Tucker said from personal knowledge, was very popular in Virginia. It was periodically called up for public reconsideration after the Civil War. On one such occasion, in 1880, a Negro writer reviewed the history of Query XIV and concluded, "Few passages of any book have been more widely commented upon or used more extensively as texts for pro-slavery sermons and anti-abolition harangues than portions of the *Notes on Virginia*."

Jefferson's "strong suspicion" of Negro inferiority was a primary consideration underlying his adherence to the plan of colonization. Colonization was another of Jefferson's apostasies from principle, according to some abolitionists. J. Q. Adams, the "Old Man Eloquent" of congressional anti-slavery struggles, even called Jefferson "the father of the Janus-faced Colonization society." Jefferson's paternity

* The recollection in *Life and Opinions of Julius Melbourne* (1847) has had a curious public history. It was reprinted in J. J. Pipkin, *The Negro in Revelation, in History, and in Citizenship* (1902). When Southern congressmen assailed President Roosevelt for inviting Booker T. Washington, the Negro leader, to dine at the White House in 1904, Representative Bartholdt, of Missouri, informed his colleagues of Jefferson's hospitality to Melbourne in 1815. John Sharp Williams, of Mississippi, was incredulous: "Would anybody of common sense in this country believe that an old Virginia planter and slaveholder ate dinner with a negro at his table?" In April 1957, the Virginia State Chamber of Commerce withdrew the invitations it had inadvertently sent to several eminent Negroes to attend an important state function. Benjamin Muse, of the *Washington Post and Times Herald*, thought the Virginians might be interested in the passage he had found in Melbourne's obscure work. "Thomas Jefferson," he wrote derisively, "did not withdraw the invitation."

of the Colonization Society, though often imputed, was extremely remote; and most abolitionists were reluctant to credit it with so illustrious an ancestry.

When James G. Birney, the future leader of the Liberty party, renounced the Colonization Society in 1834, he published a reasoned defense of his action, *Letter on Colonization*. The "Jeffersonian solution," he insisted was not colonization but abolition almost to the limits of its present advocates. As early as 1777, in Virginia, Jefferson proposed emancipation except of the slaves then living and left colonization "entirely to the option of the colored man." Beyond question, Birney said, "the *primordia* of colonization originated in charitable feelings toward those who were suffering before his eyes." *The African Repository,* journal of the Colonization Society, answered Birney with an analysis of Jefferson's proposals and opinions that left little doubt of his adherence to the deportation principle at all times. Right down to the Emancipation Proclamation, leaders of both political parties advocated the "Jeffersonian solution" to the Negro dilemma. "His plan must be taken as a whole," they said. The root and branch abolitionists took his diagnosis of the evil but rejected his remedy, colonization, which was further evidence of the fragmentation of Jefferson's anti-slavery design in the course of the slavery controversy.

The abolitionists appeared before the public not solely as friends of the poor slaves but also as antagonists of the Slave Power. The concept of the Slave Power became prominent in abolitionist ideology around 1840. Although it eludes close definition, at its core was the idea that the slaveholding aristocracy dominated the Union by its political alliance with Northern free labor. Anti-slavery men as far apart in their beliefs as the New York abolitionist, William Goodell, and the aged Boston Federalist, Josiah Quincy, agreed that Jefferson had fixed this treacherous alliance on the nation.

Richard Hildreth's *Despotism in America,* in 1840, offered one of the earliest statements on the historical origins of the Slave Power. American history since the Revolution, Hildreth began, represented a conflict between two ideas: Democracy and Despotism. Democracy was the distinctive American idea, and it had enjoyed sixty years of progress without serious resistance from or injury to the despotism of slavery. But the peaceful era had passed. "Democracy and Despotism face to face, like Gabriel and the Archenemy, make ready for a desperate and dreadful struggle."

History gave the reason. In the early decades, Hildreth wrote, an oligarchy of priests and lawyers suppressed the spirit of democracy in the free states, while the liberal party gained power in the slaveholding states. It was the irony of American history that the Apostle of Democracy, Thomas Jefferson, was a Southern aristocrat and despot. Justly revered as "the earliest, ablest, boldest, and most far-going" of the democratic leaders, Jefferson could not preach the full extent of his principles in Virginia without coming into collision with the slaveholding interest. He preached at home the popular doctrine of all aristocracies: "democracy among all the aristocrats . . . the perfect equality of all the members of the privileged order." With his triumph over the old Virginia oligarchy and the ascendancy of his followers in neighboring states, this Jeffersonian compromise "became the settled and established creed of Southern politics." Striking for federal supremacy, the Virginian gave his hand to the struggling democrats of the North. And thus was cemented under an imposing array of popular slogans the alliance of slavery and democracy against the Northern oligarchy. The Southern despots ruled the nation. However, as the liberal Virginia leadership faded and as the Northern democracy demanded the full return on Jeffersonian principles, Southern supremacy was put in danger. Desperate efforts were made to restore the old alliance. But the power that had raised the spirit of democracy could no longer control it. "The alliance is broken; and conscious of superior power and higher claims, Democracy demands homage and submission, where hitherto she has paid them." Unfettered at last, Hildreth concluded, Democracy was ready for its inescapable struggle with Despotism.

William Goodell made an important addition to this far-fetched analysis. Speaking before the New York Anti-Slavery Society soon after the publication of *Despotism in America*, Goodell argued that the economic policy of the country was also "moulded by the slave power, for the benefit of slavery, and in consequent hostility to the interests of free labor." The slave system must either adroitly cripple its rival or be defeated by its superior power. "With this simple key,"

Goodell said, "the historian may unlock the otherwise inexplainable labyrinths of American politics, for the last forty years." The century opened with a golden opportunity for the economic advancement of the entire nation; but the Slave Power correctly saw in the growth of capitalism, of cities and free labor, its own destruction. Jefferson evolved an economic policy to meet the crisis. "The slave power, enthroned in the high places of the republic, read to us homilies upon the corrupting influence of commerce. . . . The fiat went forth in due form, that America must not be a commercial nation, lest commerce should corrupt the spirit of liberty." And the crowning achievement of Jefferson's policy:

Who has not heard of the embargo of 1807-8? . . . I sin not against the democracy of Thomas Jefferson, when I speak of the embargo as a measure of the Slave Power. There was none of Mr. Jefferson's democracy in the embargo. . . . Mr. Jefferson's democracy, like his abolitionism, was commendably accurate in the abstract; but unfortunately, his measures of national as well as of plantation economy were moulded at the bidding of the Slave Power, which proved itself too strong for Mr. Jefferson, and the nation over whom he presided.

The South's later attack on the American System, Goodell went on to argue, merely continued Jefferson's policy of sabotage of the Northern economy.

The Slave Power concept, in its countless forms and uses, became a fixture of the Northern agitation. Better than anything else it seemed to explain the baffling contradictions between the nation's democratic ideal and the reality of slavery. The Father of Democracy was also the architect of the Slave Power. This was, according to Hildreth, the supreme irony of American history; and the discovery on so many levels of the hidden relations between them, of democracy's complicity in slavery, seemed a necessary step in the dissolution of the incongruity.

These views had an enduring place in the history of the Jefferson image. They were easily assimilated to orthodox Federalist opinion, as Josiah Quincy, the last survivor of the Essex Junto, demonstrated on the eve of the Civil War. They left their imprint, decades later, on the pages of Henry Adams's great historical narrative, and thus strongly influenced much historical writing on Jefferson. The vaguely Federalist associations of the idea made it more creditable in the eyes of some abolitionists, less creditable in the eyes of others. It did not destroy the admiration they felt for Jefferson, but it certainly complicated their feelings.

It was an adage among abolitionists that "the best blood of Virginia flows in the veins of slaves." "Yes," Angelina Grimké added, "even the blood of Jefferson." In the slender annals of personal legend inspired by Jefferson's life, the legend of miscegenation has a conspicuous place. It lives to this day, though the crucial role of the abolitionists in its history seems to have been forgotten.

The .abolitionists etched on the American mind Jefferson's bleak picture of plantation life in Query XVIII of the *Notes on Virginia.* "It has been published a thousand times and will live forever." They constantly entered it in their own defense. Repeatedly inserting the passage in the *Liberator,* Garrison would exclaim "Jefferson a Fanatic!" and rest his case. Not to offend the South, Adams would say during his fight in Congress for the reception of abolition petitions, he refrained from stating his own opinion of slavery and deferred to that of Jefferson, "a slaveholder himself, and the acknowledged oracle of democracy throughout the Union." Reuben Crandall, brought before a Washington court on the charge of publishing malicious libels with intent to incite free Negroes to revolt, exhibited Jefferson's work in his defense. If his remarks were libelous, so was Jefferson's book. For all that, Reuben went to jail. The passage appeared in countless anti-slavery addresses, pamphlets, and convention proceedings. Its image of slavery, its solemn warning of God's justice, the words and phrases—these were so stereotyped in the lexicon of agitation that men fell to repeating them as if by habit.

But, alas, the Virginian's hatred of the evil appeared to many the hatred of one who had been personally contaminated by it. The fall of the Jeremiah was the surest proof of the system's crime against humanity. This part of Jefferson's life might be ignored, it was said, but for the fact "that like the faithful delineations of our sacred pages, of the sins of David, and other eminently great men, it should descend on record, as a solemn beacon ... to awaken the lovers of our country, of morality, honesty, and religion, to see the natural results connected with the *practical operation*" of slavery.

The beginnings of the tale are obscure. Federalists whispered it in the bitter campaign of 1800; but it did not become public knowledge until 1802, when James T. Callender included it among his libels of the President. According to Callender, Jefferson kept a slave mistress, Sally, who had borne him several children. "There is not an individual in the neighborhood of Charlottesville who does not believe the story, and not a few who know it." The malicious barbs of political satirists were thrown at Jefferson, and some were remembered. The indiscreet verses of J. Q. Adams were resurrected by his opponents in 1828; the youthful production of the poet William Cullen Bryant, "The Embargo," could never be entirely forgotten; and the story was preserved as well in the volumes of the admired English poet, Thomas Moore.

After the partisan uses of the story vanished, it was revived and retold by the abolitionists. Unlike the Federalists, the abolitionists were smearing the South's peculiar institution, not Jefferson or democracy. They dwelled less on Jefferson's "African brothel" than on his alleged mulatto offspring. The most common version of the story in anti-slavery circles was the one related in 1838 by Dr. Levi Gaylord, of New York. He had heard, he said, from the lips of a Southern gentleman: " 'I saw for myself, the DAUGHTER OF THOMAS JEFFERSON sold in New Orleans, for one thousand dollars.' " Gaylord wanted this "sounded longer and louder through the length and breadth of the land" until a virtuous indignation should wipe out slavery. Goodell's *Friend of Man* printed Gaylord's story, whence it spread to other newspapers.

Some years later the Negro writer and abolitionist, William Wells Brown, came across in the pages of the *Liberator* an anonymous poem, "Jefferson's Daughter." It had appeared originally in a Scottish journal, soon after the publication of the Gaylord report. Brown put the poem in an anti-slavery song book he was then compiling. Presumably the abolitionist flock chorused such verses as the following:

Can the blood that, at Lexington, poured o'er the plain,
When the sons warred with tyrants their rights to uphold,
Can the tide of Niagara wipe out the stain?
  No! Jefferson's child has been bartered for gold!

The daughter of Jefferson sold for a slave!
  The child of a freeman for dollars and francs!
The roar of applause, when your orators rave,
  Is lost in the sound of her chain, as it clanks.

Brown was fascinated by the mulatto theme. His most important work, *Clotel; or the President's Daughter,* opened on the sensational scene of a slave auction at which the alleged mistress and two daughters of Jefferson were going under the hammer. Frederick Douglass, the great Negro leader, added another generation to Jefferson's progeny: a granddaughter was among the colonists of Liberia!

Upon the flimsy basis of oral tradition, anecdote, and satire, the most intelligent and upright abolitionists avowed their belief in Jefferson's miscegenation. Theodore Parker stated in his historical portrait of Jefferson: "I think the charge that he was father of his own slaves too well founded." It was, so Richard Hildreth observed, "the voice of common report." In the campaign of 1860, enemy newspapers charged that Lincoln had told the Gaylord story. Lincoln denied this, and also called the story "a base forgery."

One other group, the British commentators on America, contributed to the revival of the legend in the second quarter of the nineteenth century. Insolent aristocrats many of them, they found in Jefferson—the idol of democracy—a convenient target for their criticism. Being also extremely credulous, they were almost unerringly drawn to this particular "tall tale," so scandalous, so wildly embellished, as a sure deflation of democratic pretensions. Mrs. Trollope led the list with her stinging *The Domestic Manners of the Americans* in 1832. That Jefferson was the venerable father of "unnumbered generations of slaves" was a fact "spoken openly by all, not whispered privately by a few." Wasn't this a "glorious commentary" on that mischievous sophistry: "all men are created equal"? It was the master's special pleasure, the sober Mrs. Trollope reported, to be waited upon at table by his slave-children, "and the hospitable orgies for which Monticello was so celebrated were incomplete,

unless the goblets he quaffed were tendered by the trembling hand of his own slavish offspring." Among the travelers who embroidered the legend and vouched for its accuracy were Captain Marryat, Thomas Hamilton, Mrs. Felton, and E. S. Abdy. Always the intent was to exhibit the hollowness of democratic virtue or, with the abolitionists, the horrors of slavery.

While there was not much evidence tending to prove the legend, neither was there positive disproof. Jefferson himself had never made a denial, although it was later alleged he had once repudiated the claim of a mulatto to his paternity. In none of his published papers, in none of the reports of his numerous auditors, in no documents whatsoever was there the slightest suggestion of miscegenation. Nor did any of his early biographers, not even his severest critics, take notice of this "common report." The first to do so was James Parton in his biography of 1874. It *was* known all along that a family of light mulattoes, the Hemings, had labored at Monticello, and that three of this name were among the five slaves Jefferson had freed by his will. From this it was inferred that the Hemings (and perhaps untold others left in slavery) were the children of Jefferson and Sally. The inference was rejected by Edmund Bacon, Jefferson's overseer for many years, in a volume of reminiscence made public in 1862. "Folks said that these Hemings'es was old Mr. Wayles' children," the Monticello slave, Isaac Jefferson, reported in some recollections set down, but not published, in the eighteen-forties. Recent scholarship tends to support this verdict. John Wayles was Jefferson's father-in-law. "Black Sal," described by Isaac as "very handsome: long straight hair down her back," was one of Wayles's children, brought to Monticello as part of the Wayles legacy. The historians Hildreth and H. W. Bartlett both recognized her true ancestry in 1856. "Black Sal," the latter wrote, "was Jefferson's concubine-by-compulsion, having also his own wife's blood in her veins." In this arch way, the very fact which might have helped to explain Jefferson's undue deference to some of his slaves and the brood of mulattoes at Monticello was used instead to reinforce the legend.

Numerous Negroes, especially in Albemarle, were named after Jefferson, some boasted descent from him, and a few publicly declared it in the course of time. In 1882 one Robert Jefferson died in

Oberlin, Ohio. A carpenter well known in Indianapolis, where he had gone to live after purchasing freedom for himself and his family, he held that he was the son of Jefferson and a house-slave belonging to a Mr. Christian of Charlestown, Virginia. He was born in 1803, he reported, and as a boy many times saw Jefferson visiting his master in Charlestown. "My mother and all her people always told me he was my father, and I have no reason to doubt their word. My mother was married when I was born and my master has often told me who my father was, and it was he who named me Robert Jefferson." The story is utterly incredible.

More credible than anything that survives are the recollections of Madison Hemings, of Pee Pee, Ohio, published in the local *Pike County Republican*, March 13, 1873.* Madison's story of his life, as related to the newspaper's editor, could only have come through family tradition. His grandmother, he said, was Elizabeth Hemings, the daughter of an English sea captain and the slave of John Wayles of Williamsburg. After his wife's death, Wayles took the grown Elizabeth as his concubine, and she bore him six children. On Wayles's death, mother and children went to Monticello as Jefferson's slaves. Sally, who was apparently the fifth child and second daughter of Elizabeth, accompanied Jefferson's younger daughter, Polly, to France in 1787. Madison thought she was then about the age of Jefferson's elder daughter, Martha, which was fifteen. In Paris Sally became Jefferson's concubine. Not wishing to return to the United States with him, she relented on the promise of extraordinary privileges and freedom for her children at the age of twenty-one. After their return she bore Jefferson five children, of whom four lived to

---

* It was in anticipation of this disclosure that Parton entered his rebuttal in the *Life of Jefferson*, 1874. He made inquiry of Henry S. Randall, who recalled in a personal letter, first, the determination he had reached after investigation of all the pertinent records on the Monticello slaves, that the father of the Hemings children was a near relative of Jefferson's; and, second, T. J. Randolph's report of an investigation made at the request of his mother, not long before her death, on the birth of one of the Hemings who claimed Jefferson's paternity. Randolph concluded from his investigation that the slave's mother, Sally, and Jefferson could not possibly have seen each other for a period of fifteen months prior to the birth. Randall appreciated the feelings and fully accepted the position of Jefferson's grandchildren on this subject. He made no reference to the miscegenation legend in his *Life*.

maturity: Beverly, Harriet, Madison, and Eston. All were freed, Madison supposed, by provision in Jefferson's will. Beverly and Harriet (who actually were not mentioned in the will) passed for white, married white men, and raised white families in Washington. Eston married a colored girl and migrated first to Ohio and then to Wisconsin. Madison himself, born in 1805, was put to the carpenter trade at fourteen, and many years later went to Pike County, Ohio, where he raised a large family and practiced his trade. Madison's memories of Jefferson at Monticello were vivid and accurate. Of his mother, he said, "It was her duty, all her life which I can remember, up to the time of father's death, to take care of his chamber and wardrobe, look after us children and do such light work as sewing, &c."

The recollection checks remarkably well with the data accumulated by scholars on Jefferson's domestic life and the Monticello slaves. But it does not prove that Sally was Jefferson's concubine or Madison his son. Paternity, of course, is one of the most difficult things in the world to prove. It will probably never be proven in this case. The legend survives, although no serious student of Jefferson has ever declared his belief in it. It is recorded as true or probably true in Arthur Calhoun's *Social History of the American Family*, in W. E. B. DuBois's *Black Reconstruction*, in J. C. Furnas's *Goodbye to Uncle Tom*, and in other important books. In 1954 the Negro analogue of *Life* magazine, *Ebony*, did a photographic essay on a handful of elderly Negroes who trace their ancestry to the illustrious Jefferson. "In four generations, these proud Negro descendants ... have made the long and improbable journey from the white marbled splendor of Monticello to the 'Negro ghetto' in the democracy their forebear helped to found." These are the great-grandchildren of Joseph Fossett (one of the five slaves freed by Jefferson's will) and, allegedly, the great-great-grandchildren of Jefferson and Sally. They are proud and sure of their distinguished ancestry. "My grandmother, rocking in her favorite chair, used to tell me about him [Jefferson] all the time," one of them recalled. "She called him 'Grandpa.'"

Three factors were chiefly responsible for the rise and progress of the miscegenation legend. The first was political: the hatred of the Federalists, the hope of his enemies inspired by Callender that

the African harem revelations would destroy him, and later the campaign of British critics to lower the prestige of American democracy
by toppling its hero from his pedestal. The second was the institution of slavery: the Negroes' pathetic wish for a little pride and their
subtle ways of confounding the white folks, the cunning of the slave
trader and the auctioneer who might expect a better price for a
Jefferson than for a Jones, the social fact of miscegenation and its
fascination as a moral theme, and, above all, the logic of abolitionism
by which Jefferson alone of the Founding Fathers was a worthy
exhibit of the crime. The third revolves around the personal habits
and history of Jefferson himself: his wife's early death, his brief
affair with Mrs. Walker (the wife of an Albemarle neighbor), his
great interest in Negroes generally along with his particular kindness to some of his slaves, and items of a similar nature, with which
some imaginations could piece together the intriguing "Black Sal"
relationship. Although the overwhelming evidence of Jefferson's domestic life refuted the legend, this side of his life was not well known
before the Civil War. The legend would not have been born but
for the Federalists; it would not have been revived but for the abolitionists or, conceivably, the British commentators; and when there
was little but Jefferson's own history and the memories of a few
Negroes to sustain it, it faded into the obscure recesses of the
Jefferson image.

Emancipation, Jefferson had said, was his legacy to the younger
generation. But those who sought guidance in this "dealer in oracles"
were disappointed. "Although the commands of conscience are essentially absolute, they are historically limitary." Jefferson shared this
wisdom with Emerson, and he knew what agony it entailed. His final
wish that an age of "persuasion, perseverance, and patience" would
end slavery was not to be realized. His own internal struggle between the moral imperatives of the democratic faith and the utilitarian interests of nation and society dissolved into an intransigent
conflict of opposites within the Union. As the "commands of conscience" ripened into the abolitionist crusade in the North, the sense
of "historical limitations" hardened in the South. This, not emancipa-

tion, was the legacy disclosed in the unfolding history of the slavery controversy.

Jefferson was the crucial figure in American history both for slavery and for abolition. Partisans on both sides sought justification in him, while they also indicted him for their distresses. Jefferson, the Virginia planter, who had written the Kentucky Resolutions and established the Republican party under Southern leadership, had also penned the Declaration of Independence, raised up the democratic spirit, and opposed slavery all his life. Behind the façade of Jeffersonian politics, the abolitionists discovered the Slave Power. And the republican slavocracy discovered that Jefferson's visionary ideas had produced a democratic giant. The *real* Jefferson, if he ever existed, was lost from sight as the fragments of his mind were parceled out among bitter antagonists and as legacies of discord were laid to him.

Beginning with the Mexican War, the slavery controversy developed increasingly at the center of American politics. The passage from agitation to politics led to further changes in the Jefferson image. Politics is a great simplifier. Jefferson remained an ambivalent figure, a confusion of opposite policies; but as the ranks formed on the slavery issue in the 'fifties, advocates on either side seemed to find in him more uniformity of opinion and singleness of purpose than had the earlier agitators. More and more Southern spokesmen came to regard him as the evil genius of democracy. "Never," George Fitzhugh wrote in 1860, "was a political party so fairly and fully entitled to be called by the name of a man as the Black-republicans by the name of Jefferson." Hinton Helper, himself a Southerner, had an actual case in mind when he wrote in his famous indictment of the slavocracy, *The Impending Crisis:* "Were Jefferson now employed as a professor in a Southern college, he would be dismissed and driven from the State, perhaps murdered before he reached the border." The most complete statement from the anti-slavery side was Andrew Dixon White's article, "Jefferson and Slavery," published in the *Atlantic Monthly* soon after the War began. Young White, who was to become the first president of Cornell University, had studied Jefferson closely and taken him as his political model. What was remarkable, White thought, was the marvelous consistency of his opinions. Always willing to face up to the logic of his own creed,

Jefferson was forced "from an attack on aristocracy to an attack on slavery." He was "fierce in opposition" to slavery; it violated every principle he held. His opinions were fixed; his tactics were flexible. When innovations in the Southern economy entrenched the slave institution, Jefferson found it advisable to restrain his youthful ardor and to attack by indirection, as in the choice of texts for the students at the University of Virginia. The remarks on the capabilities of the Negro, thrown off in a speculative moment, and the criticisms of federal intervention written in the depressions of old age, should not, in White's opinion, be allowed to spoil the faith and the work of a lifetime.

But how was it possible to reconcile the Jefferson of 1784 with the Jefferson of 1820? In 1784 he proposed to exclude slavery from the territories, and thus to stop its expansion. In 1820 he denounced the Missouri Compromise restriction: "a fire-bell in the night" sounding "the knell of the Union." "There is a wonderful harmony & consistency in his life generally, & I would fain find it in this case, *if it exists*," Henry S. Randall wrote to Martin Van Buren. The consistency eluded Randall. He finally concluded, in the *Life*, that the true Jeffersonian policy on the power of the federal government to restrict the spread of slavery was "a matter of opinion." It was thus that Jefferson was swept into the political debate that led to the Civil War.

2. *The Republican Jefferson*

In the summer of 1846, a Democratic congressman from Pennsylvania, David Wilmot, made the fateful proposal to exclude slavery from the Mexican conquest. After several years' intensive debate the Wilmot Proviso failed; but not until it had forged a link between the cardinal doctrine of anti-slavery politics—"no slavery in the territories"—and the Jeffersonian heritage.

The Wilmot Proviso was framed in the language of the Northwest Ordinance and announced in the name of Jefferson. Actually, Jefferson had no direct connection with the famous law of 1787. He had incorporated a slavery ban in the earlier Ordinance of 1784 drafted by him. Congress rejected the ban, but in modified form it was inserted three years later in the ordinance which replaced Jefferson's and became the fundamental law for the entire Northwest. On this tenuous thread the idea was hung that Jefferson was the author of slavery exclusion in the territories. " 'The Wilmot Proviso.' Well!" exclaimed "Old Bullion" Benton on the stump, "I think it is the Jefferson Proviso—the same that Mr. Jefferson drew up for the northwestern Territory, in 1784.... I think Mr. Jefferson, and not Davy Wilmot, was the author of the Proviso, and that it should bear his name, and not Davy's." The historic proviso became the "Jefferson Proviso," and its fame increased.

The "Jefferson Proviso" was the aegis, the banner, the old landmark of the cause of slavery restriction. Accustomed to regard Jefferson as the standard by which all disputes of political power should be tried, politicians might conclude that the principle in this case was settled beyond the need for further debate. How sublime the lineage! "The author of the Declaration of Independence and the author of the slavery restriction in the Ordinance of 1787, are the same person." Salmon P. Chase, the Ohio anti-slavery leader, was the high priest of this particular cult. Chase wrote one of the earliest eulogies of the Northwest Ordinance in 1833, when Jefferson was no part of his thought. During the debate on the Compromise of 1850, however, Chase called the restriction policy of the Wilmot Proviso "a revival after the lapse of sixty-two years, of the territorial policy of Jefferson." He paused to inquire in reverent tones what marked the hero's grave. William H. Seward, who had visited Monticello some years before, recited the inscription on the simple monument. Neither the monument nor the great works it named declared Jefferson's true fame, Chase went on. It lay beyond the Alleghenies. The cities and villages, the millions of free and happy homes, the churches and schools—these were Jefferson's monuments, all over the western land.

The "Jefferson Proviso" was the heart of the Free Soil platform of 1848. The party's Buffalo Convention called for the establishment in every Northern town and ward of "Jefferson Leagues of free soil and free principle." The next year, 1849, the Free Soilers staged at Cleveland the first public commemoration of the Northwest Ordinance. Winding up the celebration in a series of resolutions, the assemblage pledged itself to "the great principles of Human Rights" promulgated by Jefferson in the Declaration and the First Inaugural, and to "the Jeffersonian Ordinance of 1787." From 1846 to 1861, first Free Soilers and then Republicans lauded the resurrected principle of 1787 as the "Jefferson Proviso." Political opponents, however, called the idea a sham, and historical inquirers cast serious doubts on the Jeffersonian lineage. Behind the exaltation of Jefferson as the father of free soil is one of the most bewildering chapters in America's attempt to discover the true chronicle of its past.

The first important account of the Northwest Ordinance was given in 1824 by the Massachusetts Federalist, Nathan Dane, who also first claimed to be its author. In the Webster-Hayne debate six years later, the Massachusetts Senator disinterred Dane's account from a law digest, and cited it as evidence of the friendship of the states of the Northeast for the West. Dane was the genius of the Ordinance and Northern votes alone carried it through Congress, Webster said. To this Hayne replied that the South knew Dane only as a member of the Hartford Convention. Speaking for the West, Benton assailed the pretensions of New England to the Westerners' gratitude, and then turned his attention to this "rubbish" Webster had put in the way of historical truth. Dane had no more to do with the great charter of freedom than Benton himself: "That Ordinance, and especially the non-slavery clause, was not the work of Nathan Dane, of Massachusetts, but of Thomas Jefferson, of Virginia." The law of 1787, Benton said, simply re-enacted Jefferson's plan of 1784 for the government of the territories. In the face of this opinion Dane renewed his claim to authorship. Jefferson's plan, he argued, was so faulty "that it could not be mended to answer any purpose, nor could materials in it be found to form a thirteenth part of the Ordinance of July 13, 1787." The slavery proviso did indeed originate with Jefferson, but even it was radically altered. Dane felt that he was as much the author of the Northwest Ordinance as Jefferson was of the Declaration of Independence.

Here the matter rested until the Wilmot Proviso gave it fresh importance in national politics. In 1847 the American archivist, Peter Force, wrote what purported to be a true history of the Ordinance. Force had discovered a draft of the measure, as it stood five days before its passage, in Dane's handwriting. While this tended to support Dane's title, the draft did not contain the glorious provisions of the finished work—those on slavery, civil and religious liberty, education, and so on. The plan of government was there, but not the "charter of liberties" believed to be the great merit of the Ordinance. Whoever was its author, it certainly was not Jefferson. He was out of the country in 1787, and his earlier plan had only minor resemblances to its successor. The effect of Force's analysis was to deprive Jefferson of any significant influence on the Ordinance of 1787.

But of course the character of the Ordinance, for all practical purposes after 1846, lodged in its single provision against slavery; and thus the notion of Jefferson's authorship would not down. His proposal on slavery in 1784 applied to *all* the territory of the United States and was to take effect *in 1800*. The claim that this made Jefferson the father of free-soil ran in the face of two manifest facts: first, the Southern states in Congress defeated the proposal; and second, the slavery ban in the Ordinance of 1787 took effect at once, applied only to the Northwest, and was conditional on the return of fugitives to the slave states below the Ohio River. Two of these changes were proposed, unsuccessfully, by Rufus King in 1785; only the limitation to the Northwest was added in 1787. Charles King maintained that his father was, therefore, the rightful author of the proviso. Still others, in addition to Dane, had their champions. It seemed apparent, in any event, that the proscription was the result of a compromise devised over a three-year period, and that Jefferson had no part in this accomplishment.

This did not penetrate the Jeffersonian armor of most anti-slavery politicians, though. The encomium Chase gave to Dane in 1833 he gave to Jefferson in 1850. In 1856 Edward Coles offered his *History of the Ordinance of 1787*. Coles's name figured prominently in the history of Jefferson's opinions. A native of Virginia, a youthful disciple of Jefferson and convert to his anti-slavery opinions, Coles freed his own slaves and journeyed with them to the free soil of the Northwest. Jefferson's letter to him in 1814 was a significant anti-slavery document. An early governor of Illinois, Coles not only defeated a powerful movement to open the state to slavery, but also made valiant efforts to introduce Jefferson's plan of public education.

He worshipped Jefferson's memory, and repeatedly claimed to speak for him. Nathan Dane, in his eyes, was an insolent pretender. The charter of liberty could not have been born of Federalist hatred of the West! Coles's alleged "history" in 1856 was little more than a cursory comparison of the two laws, from which he determined that, a few minor provisions aside, Jefferson was properly regarded the author of the Northwest Ordinance.

Benton's views were fixed beyond the power of anyone to change but God or Andrew Jackson; one was dead the other had not spoken. Unlike Coles, Benton saw the radical difference between the slavery provisions of the two laws. Indeed, he based his moderate anti-slavery policy on the compromise contained in the latter: the exclusion of slavery *and* the return of fugitives. Nevertheless, he kept on saying the Ordinance of 1787 was Jefferson's "passed over again." The sublimity of Jefferson's work called his oratorical powers into full play.

It was one of the most perfect pieces of legislation that ever came from the human mind. . . . Plato had his imaginary Republic, and Sir Thomas More his mythical Utopia, for which they framed imaginary governments, founded on theories of human perfectibility; but Jefferson had a real field to work in—a vast domain, fertile and beautiful . . . in which to plot real communities, and to build up real republics; and nobly did he do his work —how nobly the States attest which have grown up upon it.

Meanwhile, as the historical inquiry proceeded under the tortuous influence of anti-slavery, the South took a second look at the Northwest Ordinance. Southern spokesmen in 1830 had proudly acclaimed its Jeffersonian ancestry; now they classified it with Jefferson's "fatal legacies." If the Union should perish, Calhoun declared in 1848, the future historian of the calamity "will devote his first chapter to the ordinance of 1787." Jefferson would never, in Calhoun's opinion, have countenanced the formation of a purely sectional party on the principle of slavery restriction. His mature opinion as expressed in opposition to the Missouri Compromise marked him a prophet. But when Jefferson heard the "death knell of the Union" in 1820, it was, Calhoun insisted, a reverberation of the very principle he himself had sounded in the Ordinance of 1784. "It was the first blow—the first essay 'to draw a geographical line coinciding with a marked principle, moral and political.' " Jefferson's paradoxical relation to the slavery controversy was here epitomized. The very words he had chosen to condemn the Missouri restriction were applied to his own "first blow." How to explain this paradox was a besetting problem of Southern statesmen. For Calhoun the explanation lay in the fact that the Virginia Republican was also the philanthropical democrat who had proclaimed in 1776 "all men are created equal."

Jefferson's armor proved the worthiest defense against Jefferson's missiles. In addition to his "mature" opinion ("superannuated" opinion, Free Soilers said), there was, first, the evidence suggesting that Jefferson's aim in 1784 was the abatement of the African traffic by narrowing the territory open to slavery. The interdict would not have been proposed had there been any prospect at that time of outlawing the trade. Madison had said as much; and Jefferson's apparently unbroken silence on the subject of restriction from 1784 to 1820 led some to infer that he lost interest in the policy when, by provision of the Constitution, the early outlawry of the slave trade was assured. Jefferson, others argued, was a slavery expansionist. He sought not to prevent the spread of slavery, but to encourage its diffusion. The true Jeffersonian policy on slavery in the territories, Southerners repeatedly said, was contained in the Louisiana treaty with France and the basic laws for the government of the Louisiana (Orleans) Territory. The former charged the United States with the protection of slave property in the cession, and the latter threw Louisiana open to settlement by slaveholders.*

* This, of course, had been the Federalist view. In 1853 Professor E. B. Andrews of Marietta College, Ohio, delivered the funeral eulogy on Ephraim Cutler. The son of Manasseh Cutler, whose large speculative holdings in western lands made him an interested party to the passage of the Northwest Ordinance, Ephraim Cutler was an early settler in Ohio and a leading Federalist in the convention that framed the state's first constitution. According to Andrews, who was privy to Cutler's journal, Cutler had helped to defeat a proposal made by the Southern members in the convention to open the state to slavery for a limited period. Jefferson, Cutler later learned, had backed the proposal and regretted its defeat, allegedly because of his belief in diffusion as an aid to emancipation but actually, Cutler thought, because of his attachment to the Southern interest. The Cutler-Andrews story attracted little attention at the time. Some later historians, notably B. A. Hinsdale in The Old Northwest, credited it. It appears to have no foundation in fact.

So while Southern leaders tended to view Jefferson as the father of the restriction principle, most of them denied that it represented his settled policy. The invocation of his name for the cause of free-soil seemed but another example of how his democratic errors were sifted from his politics, deposited in the Northern mind, and made to serve purposes his mature judgment never approved. Whatever his theories, Georgia's Senator Toombs declared in 1856, Jefferson never took the laboring oar against slavery. Why the Northern agitators rang a halo about Jefferson's head was a mystery. Turn to the Statute-Books: there was Jefferson's signature to the territorial law of Louisiana. Turn to his writings: there were his letters protesting against the Missouri Compromise. And look to Monticello, Toombs challenged. "He owned slaves. . . . He kept them as long as he lived; he consumed their labor without wages . . . and for aught I know, they and their posterity are owned by his descendants now. This is the model held up to the American people."

As there were three cardinal policies on slavery in the territories—restriction, expansion, and popular sovereignty—so there were three main political perspectives on the historic ordinances. Popular sovereignty remains to be considered. Broached by Lewis Cass in 1847, personified by the Illinois Democrat Stephen A. Douglas, and embodied in the Kansas-Nebraska Act of 1854, the popular sovereignty doctrine avoided the Scylla and Charybdis of congressional restriction and congressional protection by authorizing the citizens of the territories alone to decide for or against slavery. Although it was not originally advocated in Jefferson's name, its associations were unfailingly Jeffersonian: frontier autonomy, social contract, self-government, and home rule. Not surprisingly, therefore, when Douglas finally gave the doctrine systematic statement, he traced its origins to the Apostle of Democracy.

In an article in *Harper's Magazine* for September 1859, Douglas expounded his policy as "the Jeffersonian plan of government for the Territories." The great issue of the American Revolution, he said, was the inalienable right of each colony to self-government. This was the meaning of the Declaration of Independence. When the new nation acquired territories (colonies) of its own, it resolved in the Ordinance of 1784 to extend the rights of self-government to them.

The first plan of territorial government was drafted by the author of the Declaration and framed in its spirit, Douglas said.

It was not intended to be either local or temporary in its character, but was designed to apply to all "territory ceded or to be ceded," and to be universal in its application and eternal in its duration. . . . It ignored the right of Congress to legislate for the people of the Territories without their consent, and recognized the inalienable right of the people of the Territories, when organized into political communities, to govern themselves in respect to their local concerns and internal polity.

By striking the one impurity in Jefferson's plan—the mandatory slavery exclusion—Douglas continued, Congress gave consistency to the author's intention. At the time of the Constitutional Convention the dividing line between federal and local authority in the territories was clearly marked, and the delegates conferred upon Congress no power to legislate the internal polity of the territories. Had they acted otherwise, they would have repudiated the fundamental law founded by Jefferson upon the principles of the Revolution.

For a man who essayed a true history of territorial law, Douglas made some blatant falsifications of the record, as his opponents were to show. He said the law of 1784 was irrepealable; actually, Congress replaced it with the Northwest Ordinance at the very time the Constitutional Convention was in session. It was this act, whatever its relation to its predecessor, that was the fundamental law. The Convention was informed of it; the slavery proviso was part of the act; it was given effect in legislation for the Ohio Territory in 1789. And how could the Ordinance of 1784, minus the proviso, justly be called Jeffersonian? "This, indeed, is the play of Hamlet with the character of Hamlet omitted," Carl Schurz remarked. The second law restored the provision closest to Jefferson's heart; accordingly it was the *true* Jeffersonian plan. The Wisconsin Republican, Schurz, charged that Douglas mutilated both the Declaration and the Northwest Ordinance in order to sanction his doctrine historically. He transformed Jefferson's idea of individual freedom into the idea of corporate self-government, making human slavery one of the prerogatives of a "democratic" community. "While Mr. Jefferson excluded slavery in order to make room for true popular sovereignty, Mr. Douglas invents his false popular sovereignty in order to make room for slavery." Lincoln said the same thing.

Douglas was unmoved by these criticisms. Throughout the campaign of 1860 he maintained that popular sovereignty was "the Jeffersonian plan of government for the territories." At Syracuse, New York, a Republican heckler tossed him this question: "You refer to Jefferson as authority; will you please explain his views of the Ordinance of 1787?" Jefferson had no view of this law, the candidate replied, since he was in Paris at the time of its passage; but his law of 1784 authorized the people of each territory to frame their constitution "just as they pleased, and regulate all their affairs to suit themselves." There were, of course, in Jefferson's plan several propositions, including one on slavery, which were to be submitted to the people of each territory to accept or reject. "Thus you find," Douglas hurriedly concluded, "that Jefferson held to the doctrine of popular sovereignty even on the slavery question." Republican editors viewed this campaign humbuggery with some alarm. Douglas, they said, willfully distorted history in order to convince the people "that Jefferson had nothing to do with the Ordinance of 1787."

Having broken with the Buchanan administration and its Southern supporters on the Kansas question, Douglas had to face attack from the opposite flank as well. Attorney General Jeremiah S. Black's answer for the administration to the *Harper's* article was equally bad as history. In an acid retort, the "Little Giant" accused the Attorney General of a brazen attempt to destroy the authority of Jefferson's liberal measure in connection with the administration's policy of forcing slavery on the Kansas settlers. Southern Democrats joined in the attack on Douglas. His history of territorial law, one wrote in *DeBow's Review*, exhibited the farce habitual to American politics, the old mumbo-jumbo of the Jefferson name. "In other words, as there are some foemen against whom no other's steel is worthy, it is proposed to fight Thomas Jefferson *with* Thomas Jefferson."

Fort Sumter mercifully silenced the politicians, but not for long the historians. The authorship controversy was renewed in 1876, when the claims of Manasseh Cutler were urged with striking effect. The idea that Jefferson was the author or the father of the Northwest

Ordinance lived on, however, supported by the historical writings of
John Bach McMaster, Hannis Taylor, Edward Channing, Claude
Bowers, and others. Gradually, as the cloud of slavery lifted, the
grand features of the two ordinances as plans of territorial government came into view. The slavery clause, which was paramount in
the eighteen-fifties, fell to its proper and subordinate place. Jefferson's great title to fame lay, not in the slavery proviso, but in the
design of democratic self-government for the new western communities. The Ordinance of 1787, in some respects, carried his plan toward
fulfillment, but more by accident than by design. For that law
lengthened the tutelary period, expanded federal control, and, in
general, served the interests of eastern land speculators, who feared
and distrusted the men of the frontier. This is the verdict of the
most recent scholarship. Francis S. Philbrick goes so far as to say
that the Ordinance of 1787—largely Dane's work—was "utterly reactionary" when set beside the genuinely democratic measure it
replaced.

From this point of view, all the effort of pundits and politicians
to connect Jefferson with the Northwest Ordinance was based upon
an erroneous understanding of the two laws. The error was possible
because of the democratic reputation enjoyed by the second and the
single most compelling reason for its fame, "the Jefferson Proviso."
The surface of error and confusion spread across the Northwest
Ordinance has scarcely been scratched in the foregoing discussion;
but it is clear that the political considerations which gave importance
to Jefferson's relation to the Ordinance had much to do with the
historical disaster.*

When free-soil Whigs and Democrats deserted their brethren after
the passage of Douglas's Kansas-Nebraska Act in 1854, it was as if

* The so-called "Jefferson-Lemen Compact" further illustrates the belief that
Jefferson was deeply involved in the anti-slavery history of the Northwest.
Joseph B. Lemen, in a paper read before the Illinois Historical Society in 1908,
told how Jefferson, disappointed by the defeat of the slavery proviso in 1784,
entered into a secret compact with James Lemen (the author's grandfather)
under which Lemen would migrate to Illinois with his family and there serve
as Jefferson's agent to prevent the introduction of slavery. Willard C. MacNaul's
scholarly inquiry in 1915, *The Relations of Thomas Jefferson and James Lemen*

the fates had decreed the name of the new movement, the *Republican* party. It alone could compete with the Democratic name—and it bore the imprimatur of Jefferson. The name came spontaneously and surely, "instinctively, with obvious fitness," as Horace Greeley said. At the first state conventions, several held on the sixty-seventh anniversary of the Northwest Ordinance, the Jeffersonian designation was enthusiastically adopted.

In accordance with the conventions of ante-bellum politics, the Republicans formulated their own "history of the parties." Every party needed a forefather, and Jefferson was the best. He led the party loyal to the principles of the Revolution in the battle to overthrow the "monocratic doctrines and measures of the Federalists," a typical statement began. Raised to the Presidency, he spread democracy through the whole society, extended civil rights, enlarged the nation, and established a territorial policy based on the equality of mankind. When he retired to Monticello, "the ordeal of the Republican theory of our government had passed," and every idea in Jefferson's platform was stamped on the public policies of the United States. The Jackson party of 1828 adhered to many of the old landmarks; but neither of the new parties, Democratic or Whig, stood in the Republican tradition. Both fell before the Slave Power; both discarded the legacy of Jefferson. The new party of 1854 was a rebirth of Jefferson's principles and policies. "The Republican party of the United States is a reformation and continuation of the political association which exalted Thomas Jefferson to the Presidency, in the morning of the century, and exists for similar purposes."

"Apostasy of the Democracy," as Greeley termed it, was a sustained theme in the Republican discourse. Perhaps nowhere was it

---

in the Exclusion of Slavery from Illinois and the Northwest Territory, vouched for the truthfulness of the family tradition. MacNaul cited several letters from Jefferson, entries in James Lemen's diary, even the "compact" itself. These, however, were transcripts, certified as true copies of the originals by James Lemen, Jr. half a century or more after they had allegedly been written. The remaining evidence was inconclusive. Although the "Jefferson-Lemen Compact" initially won the support of some historians, the best authorities on the Old Northwest have for some time regarded it as false or unproven. According to Julian P. Boyd, present editor of *The Papers of Thomas Jefferson,* there is no record whatsoever of Jefferson's relationship to James Lemen.

developed through so many variations as in the pages of Greeley's widely read *New York Tribune*. The canon of Jefferson, like a litmus paper, was the unfailing test of the soundness of party creeds and measures. It showed, Greeley said, that "the Republican party has taken the place once occupied by the Democratic party, while mod-ern Democracy has fallen far behind ancient Federalism." Jefferson was the friend of state rights and the foe of judicial tyranny; modern Democracy, on the other hand, was known by the Dred Scott de-cision, the federal protection of slavery in the Territories, and the federal enforcement of the Fugitive Slave Law in the free states. The party of Jefferson placed the natural rights of man above the rights of property; modern Democracy rode roughshod over human rights in defense of slave-holders' privileges. Jefferson—and Jackson too— were bold radicals, heroes of the people; modern Democrats, like the Federalists of old, talked of nothing but law and order and shied away from strong leaders. "The doctrines of Jefferson, the teachings of his example, the prestige of his name," the *Tribune* accurately observed in 1860, "are far more often cited and applauded in Repub-lican than in Democratic assemblies. Nay, he and his principles are beginning to be scouted by the latter, while they are finding their home in the former."

The rising Republicans staked out their own claim to the great tradition. It became an axiom with many of them that they were "the very same sort of Republicans with Jefferson and Madison sixty years ago." They spoke of the "plighted faith" of the Founding Fathers in respect to slavery; and none of these luminaries had raised his voice as early, as piercingly, for so long, and with greater effect than Jefferson. In the several anti-slavery manuals that collected the wisdom of the Fathers, and in Republican tracts, Jefferson was nearly always the chief witness. George W. Julian, on the hustings in Indiana and in Congress, carried pocket notebooks filled with quot-able passages from the Sage's writings on slavery and freedom. "There is not a school boy," it was said in Congress, "who is not posted in his A B C's in our political history, but who can demon-strate that the Republican party stands upon the same platform that Thomas Jefferson stood upon, in reference to this question of slavery."

There were, of course, many Republicans whose heritage was

Federalist and whose opinions embarrassed the party's effort to capture the Jefferson symbol. The *Cincinnati Daily Gazette* praised the anti-slavery Jefferson but warned against the agrarian and infidel Jefferson. "Perhaps some of our readers so reverence the name of Jefferson that they admire his philosophy as well as his politics. We hope not. ... The idolatry of great men is one into which the popular mind is very apt to run." Run it did, but the sturdy conservatism of the Republican party on social and economic questions gave assurance that the idolatry would not spread beyond the penumbra of slavery. In Democratic eyes the living link between Old Federalism and Black Republicanism was Josiah Quincy of Massachusetts. Quincy became a Republican out of hatred for the Slave Power, which he charged was the creation of Jefferson. The editors of the compendious *Republican Scrap Book* of 1860 printed one of Quincy's speeches, but only after they had deleted that portion in which Jefferson was assailed.

The Jeffersonian platform of the Republicans was constructed of three great planks: the human rights asserted in the Declaration of Independence, the principle of "no slavery in the territories" grounded in the Ordinance of 1787, the doctrines of State Rights laid down in the Virginia and Kentucky Resolutions. The second of these has already been examined, for the Republicans merely continued the Free Soilers' preachments in this matter.

Rufus Choate wrote a public letter in 1856 which, in one electrifying phrase, has given Americans some reason to remember him. The noted Massachusetts advocate and Whig, in announcing his support for the Democratic ticket, scolded the Republican party for building its platform on "the glittering and sounding generalities of natural rights which make up the Declaration of Independence." ("Glittering generalities!—say, rather, Blazing ubiquities!" was Emerson's rejoinder.) Choate's unforgettable phrase summed up a growing reaction against the Declaration, and suggested an earnest train of reflections. To what end had American politics come, one editor wondered, that a man could declare himself a Democrat by repudiating the faith of the party's long-heralded founder! Charles Francis Adams branded the glitter idea a monstrous heresy, subversive of every political principle free Americans had been taught from childhood. "It is repeated, commented upon, justified and expounded before crowds of listening freemen. . . . Wherever it may go it carries with it poison to freedom." This was because it deprived the Revolution of its moral character, lowered the bars against oppression, and sneered at the idea of freedom itself. Adams was convinced that Jefferson had said exactly what he meant in the Declaration of Independence and that he had meant the principles of inalienable rights to apply to Negroes. The Republican party, by pledging itself to these principles in 1856 and 1860, resolved that they should have genuine force in society.

The Republican appeal to Jefferson was immeasurably strengthened by the party's stand on state rights. Part of the Compromise of 1850 was a new Fugitive Slave Law, which transferred power to enforce the constitutional guarantee on the return of fugitives from state to federal authorities. The law was a thorn in the flesh of anti-slavery men, goading them to renewed agitation, for many reasons. They attacked its constitutionality chiefly on the ground of exclusive state jurisdiction over slavery. The correct theory of the Constitution, Charles Sumner said in the Senate, was that of divided sovereignty. The central government possessed no power over slavery in the states. It could neither abolish slavery where it existed nor interfere with the sovereign right of each state to protect its citizens or inhabitants, white or black, from abuse. If the federal authorities intervened, said Sumner, who was not normally given to such views, the states were duty bound to resist. Arguing from the same premises, Sumner's Republican colleagues compared the odious statute to the Alien and Sedition Laws, which had called forth the Resolutions of '98. Since the Democratic party had renewed its loyalty to these historic Resolutions in the Baltimore Platform of 1852, Senator Wade did not understand how Douglas and others could uphold the centralizing Fugitive Slave Law. Douglas insisted he was, as always, "a State-Rights man," and he was surprised to hear the Senator from Ohio "resorting to the resolutions of 1798 . . . which he has been in the habit of ridiculing during his whole life."

The controversy came to dramatic climax in Wisconsin. Sherman M. Booth, a leader of the new party, was charged in 1854 with aiding a fugitive escape from custody, in violation of the law of 1850. In a *habeas corpus* proceeding, Booth's counsel, Byron Paine, pleaded the unconstitutionality of the law. The case rested, he said, on the principle of the Resolutions of '98: that a state could interpose its authority to unconstitutional acts of the central government and determine the mode and measure of redress. Booth won his case; the lower court's decision was upheld, on appeal, by the Wisconsin Supreme Court; and the same court annulled the Federal District Court's reversal of its ruling. Finally, in 1859, the United States Supreme Court overturned the actions of the Wisconsin judiciary.

Republicans throughout the North condemned Chief Justice Taney's decision in the Booth case. The reserved rights of the states are gone, declared the *Madison Free Democrat*. The Court's usurpation of authority in matters of personal liberty made the Constitution "a mere thing of wax in its hands," said Wisconsin Senator James R. Doolittle. It was precisely against this Federalist doctrine that Jefferson had protested in 1798 and again not long before his death. Yet, Doolittle cried, the party which claims Jefferson as its founder, and in the face of its own platform, bows down to "worship at the feet of an imperial court"! Two years earlier, when the Republicans took control of the state government, they adopted the "doctrines of '98" as part of their creed. The Wisconsin legislature in 1859 formally honored the pledge in a series of resolutions declaring, in the very words of Jefferson, the decision of the Taney Court void.

"The Resolutions of '98 Bearing Fresh Fruit" ran the headline of the politically moderate *National Intelligencer*. These hoary Resolutions, expelled from the house of Jefferson, were taken as a "family heirloom" under the new roof of the opposition party. The fact might well excite ominous forebodings among all "Jeffersonian Democrats," the Washington newspaper said, "tending to create the disagreeable impression that the gods of the olden faith have very handsomely changed sides in the pending conflict." Most Democrats, of course, continued to acknowledge the old gods even as they lauded the Supreme Court. The Democrats of 1798, they now argued, never thought of denying the Court's authority. For the first time in history, "Jeffersonian Democracy" and "judicial supremacy" were joined together.

Reactions to the Wisconsin controversy were highly colored by
the feelings generated in the wake of the Dred Scott decision of
1857. When the Court struck down with one blow the policy of
slavery restriction, the Republicans raised the old alarm, "Judicial
Tyranny," and put in circulation once again Jefferson's denunciations
of the Marshall Court. Illustrative of their response to these judicial
decrees on slavery was the oration of George Sumner from the
eminently respectable rostrum of Boston's Fourth of July observance
in 1859. Like most educated men, Sumner confessed, he had always
agreed with Hamilton and Story on the wisdom of a firm and
independent judiciary. But the "demagogical Mr. Taney" shocked
him into recognition of the validity of Jefferson's opinions and fears.
Sumner's *Oration*, with its calculated appeal to reasonable men,
quickly went through three editions. In direct answer to his Democratic critics, Sumner begged them to listen to the plea Jefferson had
made, in a letter to Edward Livingston, for popular vigilance in
"'restraining judges from usurping legislation.'" The *Boston Atlas*
came to Sumner's support. If Jefferson had been gifted with prophetic vision, the editor said, "he could not have more aptly hit the
case of Judge Taney and some of his associates."

All the Jeffersonian themes—state rights, human rights, slavery
restriction, and others of less moment—were gathered into the observances of April 1859. In Washington, politics had temporarily
yielded in interest to the sensational murder trial of the New York
congressman, Daniel Sickles. Capital reporters, nevertheless, grasped
the significance of a celebration of Jefferson staged by the Republican Association of the city. Over five hundred persons reportedly
attended the meeting in the Odd Fellows Hall, where they were
entertained by the Marine Band and instructed in the principles and
policies of Jefferson by Francis P. Blair and Daniel R. Goodloe. The
elder Blair, a veteran of Democratic politics who, with his two sons,
had joined the Republican crusade, assailed the "counterfeit presentment" of the modern Democratic party. Goodloe, a North Carolina
publicist who had compiled a manual of Southern sentiment against
slavery, read the Declaration of Independence and reviewed Jefferson's anti-slavery record. Every one of the new party's proposals in

respect to slavery, he said, "is only treading in the footsteps of Thomas Jefferson, only endeavoring to realize the dream of his life."

While Jefferson was being thus acclaimed in the national capital, nearly three hundred Republicans feasted at the banquet table of Boston's famed Parker House. The Boston affair had two practical objects: the consolidation of the party on the state rights issue, and the rescue of the Massachusetts Republicans from the predicament they had made for themselves, and for the party nationally, by helping to pass the "two years amendment" for the restriction of the immigrant vote. Jefferson was a suitable vehicle. The opening address of George S. Boutwell, Democrat turned Republican, set the tone for all the toasts and speeches to follow. Jefferson stood on the one hundred and sixteenth anniversary of his birth "as the chosen leader of a majority of the people of the nation." Jefferson led the first two American revolutions, in 1776 and 1800; Jackson led the third against the Money Power; and the Republicans were leading the fourth, without which all the others were meaningless, against the Slave Power.

The Boston proceedings were characterized by spectacular, and often bungling, panegyric; but the letters dispatched by Chase and Lincoln showed masterful command of the factors binding Republicans to Jefferson. Both viewed this "sign of the times" as a marvelous testament of Jefferson's livingness. Lincoln's statement of the Jeffersonian geometry of the American polity has already been noticed. Just as it was possible to convince a normal child of the simple propositions of Euclid, he said, it was impossible to succeed with anyone who denied the definitions and axioms. This was the anguish of the American Union, the house divided, the "definitions and axioms" against those who believed them to be "glittering generalities" and "self-evident lies." Chase thought the slavery problem would present no difficulty if Americans would study the teachings of Jefferson. Seven years after he wrote the Declaration, Jefferson proposed gradual emancipation in Virginia. Unfortunately, the remedy was never applied in the Southern states. But one year later, the Ohio lands became the domain of the Union. "The grand idea that with the New Century should be inaugurated a new era for Virginia, just sorrowfully relinquished, revived in the statesman's mind in respect to the new territory." The Jefferson Proviso became part of the organic law of the Northwest, Chase continued.

How simple, and yet how effectual this plan of Jefferson for the solution of the slavery question! Prevent its extension into territories by the legitimate action of the Federal government: stay its increase, mitigate its evils, and finally get rid of it altogether within the States by State action. . . . Who can doubt that, had the policy, then recommended, been adopted, and perseveringly pursued, the question of slavery would long since have found its peaceful and satisfactory solution in general amelioration and enfranchisement.

The suffering of the nation for over half a century could only be remedied, Chase said, by a return to Jefferson's policy.

Whether, as had been predicted in some quarters, the ghost of Thomas Jefferson appeared at the Parker House to rebuke these "mischievous agitators" was not reported; but shouts of fraud and deception were soon heard from all sides. The *Boston Courier,* an old-line Whig newspaper, sternly admonished that a political party had no right to "stoop to false pretenses" to advance its cause. Of course there were passages in Jefferson's writings which seemed to support the Republicans, but his approach to slavery was as moderate as theirs was radical. This party stratagem, the editor said, "is one of the boldest experiments on the ignorance and credulity of the community, that this age of political quackery can show." Democratic reactions were predictable. The *New Hampshire Patriot* thought the meeting resembled a celebration of Tom Paine by a party of professed Christians; the *Washington Constitution* compared this brazen thievery of Jefferson's name to similar tactics by the previous successors of Federalism; the *Boston Post* said it was all "bare-faced humbuggery." To the delight of the Democrats, Republicans were also heard to complain. The *Boston Atlas,* hard pressed by these conservative criticisms, stood its ground in a post-mortem editorial. Jefferson did not always think wisely, the editor conceded; but he was a much better man than the New England leaders of sixty years ago had supposed, and he certainly thought wisely about slavery and the Supreme Court. The *Atlas,* having once helped to democratize the Whig party with spectacular success, hoped that the Jefferson dinner had at least dramatized the altered position of the parties in relation to Jeffersonian principles.

New England supporters of the Buchanan administration managed the Democratic festival at Salem, in 1859, with the express purpose of refurbishing the Jefferson symbol in the ruling party. The great issue before the country, the speakers said, was the preservation of the Union, not the extinction of slavery. The Democrats celebrated Jefferson the Unionist, the constitutionalist, the expansionist, the enemy of sectional parties. More significant than the celebrants' silence on Jefferson's anti-slavery opinions was their silence on the Resolutions of '98. The Democratic party alone was national in its membership and in its policy. The Republicans were condemned out of Jefferson's own mouth, for they, like their Federalist predecessors, " 'are taking advantage of the virtuous feelings of the people, to effect a division of parties by a geographical line. . . . They are wasting Jeremiads on the miseries of slavery, as if we are advocates for it.' "

The case was carefully presented in a long letter addressed to the assemblage by Benjamin F. Hallett, perhaps the most powerful Democratic leader in New England. The one enduring line between the American parties, Hallett asserted, was made by the Jeffersonian policy for the expansion of territory and the multiplication of states. Other policies Jefferson had in common with other men; he alone dreamed and achieved an American empire. The policy required absolute equality of the new with the old states, and absolute equality of the citizenry of all the states in newly acquired territory. "This was the comprehensive policy of Jefferson from the beginning. This is the comprehensive policy of the Democratic party now," Hallett said. Louisiana, Florida, Texas, Oregon, California—these were its fruits. In 1803 the Federalists opposed the Louisiana Purchase; in 1859 the same opposition under a new name fought the acquisition of Cuba. Josiah Quincy was the living bond between the two oppositions. "And thus we trace the dividing line between Jefferson and sectionalism," the line which, when first imposed in 1820, led Jefferson to doubt the survival of the Union. Hallett ended with an urgent reminder that Jefferson was "the apostle of Freedom *under* Government, of Liberty *within* Law."

This was a remarkably candid attempt to reinterpret Jefferson in the light of Democratic policy in 1859. A new partisan image of Jefferson in these Unionist, even imperial, terms did not emerge, however. Events moved too rapidly and the debris of traditional ideology was too great. But there was no mistaking the policy considerations that formed the background of Hallett's unrealized conception. Backed by the Buchanan administration and the Taney Court, Southern Democrats discovered in the vigor of the federal government their best hope of liberty and security, traced their territorial policy to the Louisiana precedent, and searched the record for justification of current imperial ambitions. The slave oligarchists, F. P. Blair noticed in his Jefferson birthday address, "are now attempting to assimilate their designs against Cuba to Mr. Jefferson's acquisition of Louisiana." *

Although Democrats thus tried to reshape the Jefferson symbol, the new image remained vague and inchoate. The stamp of conviction was gone from the traditional rhetoric and imagery of the party; yet their revision was hopelessly complicated because, as to the great issue upon which events turned, the party seemed opposed to what most Americans had been taught to believe was Jeffersonian. Freed from their bondage to a divided and decadent party, Jeffersonian

---

* In March 1859 the *New York Times* disclosed that Commodore Charles Stewart, the oldest commissioned officer in the United States Navy, had informed President Buchanan that the secret object of Jefferson's famed gunboat navy was the conquest of Cuba. Stewart then made his views public. The tiny gunboats proved their effectiveness as offensive weapons in the Barbary campaign, according to Stewart, who had served under Commodore Preble in the Mediterranean. Jefferson stepped up their production under the guise of coastal defense, stationed the boats along the southern coastline inconspicuous to foreign powers but poised, Stewart said, to attack Cuba. There was nothing in the record to support Stewart's tale, and it was directly at odds with the tradition of ridicule surrounding Jefferson's gunboat armada. The tale was manufactured, a Republican editor charged, "in order to give the air of authenticity and respectability to Mr. Buchanan's designs on Cuba." Democratic spokesmen, while they paid little attention to Stewart's disclosure, seemed intent on crowning Jefferson "king of the filibusterers." They cited private letters in which he expressed a desire to see Cuba annexed to the United States, and discovered in his secret moves to wrest Florida from Spain precedent for Buchanan's Cuban policy.

ideas were transmitted to the Republican party. "Human Rights," "Anti-Slavery," "State Rights," were inscribed on the Jefferson image. Nothing was more predictable than the Republican appeal to Jefferson. No more than most politicians were the Republicans concerned to maintain the integrity of the historical Jefferson. They used him for political effect, carefully separating out what they liked and discarding what they did not like, as if his principles and opinions, manipulated in this way, were good for so much prestige and so many votes. It happened, however, in the political crisis of the eighteen-fifties that what the Republicans liked, what they stood for, corresponded remarkably well with what men imagined to be Jeffersonian and, in the essentials, with what had in fact been Jeffersonian. The Republican illusion was more convincing than the Democratic.

Given this, the main symbolic meaning of the 1859 celebrations must be re-emphasized. Jefferson was not the *true* father of one party or the other, but the imagined father of both, the declared saint of two giant sectional parties on the eve of conflict. This little quarrel over the Jefferson lineage and name, though relatively unimportant in the movement of events, was important as a reflection of the curiously divided Jeffersonian architecture in American politics. If there was any logic in this condition, if there was any hidden corridor connecting the divided house of Jefferson, the Civil War might be expected to reveal it.

3. *War, the Nemesis*

The dark shadow of the War fell across the Jefferson image like a great and furious Nemesis. The illusion of the fabled republic, in which Jefferson had figured so prominently from the crowning moment of his death, lay shattered. A people whose patriotism had been defined by beliefs that the American destiny was fixed and guided by a benevolent Providence, that the age-old riddles of liberty and authority were solved in its political system, that every divisive question found answer in the principles and ideals of the Fathers—this people faced the wreckage of the dream, and reflective men inquired how it had come to pass and with what profit. Jefferson was usually involved in their explanations, not always to the disadvantage of his reputation of course, but the testimony that the war was a judgment on him and on the nation caught in the charmed circle of his ideas stood in imposing contrast to the previous political idolatry. The revolution in the American Union accomplished a virtual revolution in political symbols as well. Jefferson's eternally saving grace of humanity alone preserved his reputation from total eclipse in a new age lighted more by Hamilton's sun than by Jefferson's. As the political past was reconstructed from the perspective of Fort Sumter or Appomattox, the classic dialogue of American politics, the dialogue of Jefferson and Hamilton, which in the past three decades had been smothered by the Jeffersonian monologue, was restored with Hamilton temporarily foremost.

Formulations differed, but the general sense conveyed by the literature of revision was that of an irreconcilable conflict, ending in civil disaster, between two major traditions of politics fostered by Jefferson. From the eulogies forward, two conceptions of liberty were associated with Jefferson: individual freedom under the rule of law, and the right of the people to rule. The former was sometimes called Whig and English; the latter democratic and French. The democratic idea occupied the foreground in the Jefferson image. However, its opposite was always present in, above all, the general theory of state rights. For in American politics the federal division of powers became the chief means of checking the exaggeration of the democratic principle, and of thus securing an equilibrium of majority power and constitutional guarantees. So the dilemma was still in Jefferson, only its terms had been altered: the dilemma of *democracy* and state rights or *republicanism*, to use a larger symbol for the same thing. "How was it possible," Richard Hildreth had asked in 1852, "to reconcile with the democratic theory of the sovereign power of numerical majorities that doctrine of state rights of which, as leader of the Republican party, Jefferson was the especial champion?"

Hildreth's question cried for answer in 1861, when the Jeffersonian scheme of politics exploded because of the "double pressure of tendencies" within it. The republican tradition transmitted the American passion for constitutionality, the state sovereignty theory of the Union, strict construction and local liberties, the agrarian order, and minority rights. Its Bible was the Virginia and Kentucky Resolutions of 1798-99.

Through the democratic tradition surged the ideas of natural rights and equality, sovereignty of the people, and majority rule. Its sacred text was the Preamble of the Declaration of Independence. During Jefferson's time, and certainly in his own mind, these two great ganglions of Jeffersonian politics seemed to work in unison. Experience proved (Hamiltonian Federalism, the American System) that consolidated power was class power, as hostile to the people as it was to the states. Jefferson envisioned the operations of democracy in local, individualistic terms, and never anticipated the mass popular will becoming a national power. But about 1830 the two streams diverged sharply. Tocqueville then predicted "that in the democratic ages ... individual independence and local liberties will ever be the produce of artificial contrivance; that centralization will be the natural form of government." The theory of popular sovereignty to which Jefferson's ideas gave birth was inherently centralizing, for once the people (or most of them) conceived of themselves as a nation and of the government as their instrument, they naturally wished to remove particularist obstructions to their will. Lord Acton, the brilliant student of modern nationalism, observed at the commencement of the American war: "The necessity for social equality and national unity has been felt in all democracies where the mass as a unit governs itself. . . . A democracy in abolishing classes renders national unity imperative." The assertion on the part of the Northern people that slavery was a national interest, subject to democratic processes, forced the Southern minority to the ultimate recourse of secession. The history of the Jefferson symbol charted the development. In the South, state rights was developed to the severe injury of democracy, while in the North, democracy went to the brink of destroying state rights. The integral Jeffersonian theory was split and replaced by two sectional interpretations of it. This was, as E. S. Corwin has aptly named it, "the Jeffersonian dilemma."

The Confederacy was a monument to the political prescience of John C. Calhoun, eleven years dead in 1861. No statesman better understood the centralizing tendency of democracy and its consequences for the South. The root error of Northern politics, he told the Senate in 1849, was the idea of the sinfulness of slavery. Though

Jefferson had contributed to this fatal error, it created no problem for the South so long as slavery was regarded in the Jeffersonian light as a local institution. "But," Calhoun continued,

with the growth of the power and influence of the Government, and its tendency to consolidation,—when it became usual to call the people of these States a nation, and this Government national, the States came to be regarded by a large portion of the North, as bearing the same relation to it, as the counties do to the States. . . . The increase of this belief was accompanied by a corresponding increase of the feeling of responsibility for the continuance of slavery, on the part of those in the North.

Calhoun considered the Proclamation of President Jackson in 1832 the point of juncture between national consolidation and anti-slavery, from which all the oppressions of the South logically flowed. The underlying issue of the Wilmot Proviso, as he saw it, was between a government given over to the democratic rule of the majority and a government constitutionally ordered to protect minority interests. He professed the state rights theory, but he consistently preached, as the only salvation, a united South and the principle of the concurrent majority. The original creed of the Republican party was crippled soon after its birth, he felt, when Jefferson, elevated to the Presidency upon it, did practically nothing to assure its ascendancy in the Union.

A small group of Southern spokesmen in the 'fifties openly rebelled against the sway of state rights dogma. Although this reflected to some degree the exigencies of Democratic policy in the federal administration, it was part and parcel of the incipient movement of Southern nationalism with its political lexicon of "organic" terms to replace the "mechanical" legalism of the Jeffersonian lexicon. The outcry reached its crescendo in the fall of 1860. The *Charleston Mercury*, a long-time spokesman of secession, emphatically rejected Jeffersonian counsels of caution. "We have practiced upon this advice of Mr. Jefferson for forty years without avail, while wreck and ruin have been growing around us." Constitutions, Fitzhugh announced, are "mere idle figments of the brain." And James Hammond, in recommending the secession of South Carolina, tartly observed, "State Rights have been all along a humbug."

Why it now seemed "humbug" was perhaps best explained in the tract *A Glance at State Rights,* by W. M. McCarty, a Virginia "State Rights Republican." The Resolutions of '98 were correct in theory, but Jefferson was content with the assertion of the theory lest action upon it injure his political ambitions. National power was won at the expense of state rights. The opportunity to restore the Union to original principles was defeated at the threshold, and from this disaster republican principle never recovered. For the next sixty years politicians and parties pledged allegiance to the doctrine but, under the blandishments of national power and prestige, they always found ways to evade its discipline. The Proclamation of Jackson, the treachery of Madison and Rives in supporting the Force Bill against South Carolina, the hollow professions of Northern Democrats and Republicans in 1860—the bottle was thus emptied, McCarty believed, and only the label, "doctrines of '98," was visible.

These views were fairly widespread, though not dominant, when the secession crisis forced the Southern states back upon traditional principles. A new edition of the historic Resolutions had been published at Richmond in 1859. The Democratic party was still pledged "to carry them out in their obvious meaning and import." Their meaning and import was no more obvious in 1860 than in 1798 or in 1832; yet Southern leaders in number professed to find in them the whole theory of state sovereignty, as developed by Calhoun, with the attendant right of peaceable secession. State rights might be humbug in fact, but it was a very convenient theory. The people were sovereign, not collectively as "one people," but separately as several states; therefore, they could by the exercise of their sovereignty in state conventions secede from the Union. South Carolina scrupulously observed the theory in December 1860. Others took considerable liberties with it. Generally, however, the secession movement was a remarkable testament to the compact theory of government, which Jefferson, more than anyone, had fixed upon the American political mind.

The point gained force from the secessionists' association of the constitutional doctrine with the theory of the Declaration of Independence. Jefferson Davis, in assuming the Presidency of the Confederacy, appealed to "the American idea that governments rest on

the consent of the governed, and that it is the right of the people
to alter or abolish them at will whenever they become destructive
to the ends for which they were established." The Confederate states,
he said, had "merely asserted the rights which the Declaration . . .
defined as 'inalienable.'" What was inalienable? Not the rights of
man, but the rights of the people as members of sovereign polities
called states to secede from the Union. In this ironic way, one great
Jeffersonian text was rolled into the other, after being cleared of
the moral doctrine that had brought down on Jefferson's head accusations from all over the South of first broaching in 1776 "the wild
pretensions of a wild democracy."

Southern ambivalence toward Jefferson did not end at Appomattox.
George Fitzhugh was still condemning in 1867 Jefferson's "powder-
cask abstractions" as the cause of the devastation around him. Albert
T. Bledsoe expressed similar sentiments in the reborn *Southern Review* under his editorship. The War stemmed from the spurious
democracy of the French Revolution, he argued. Jefferson's triumph
in 1800 converted the republic of 1787 into a pure democracy. "He
was the Rousseau, not the Montesquieu of the New World . . . the
eloquent advocate, or mouthpiece, of an unreasoning radicalism, and
consequently one of its greatest idols." The War proved Tocqueville
right in his prediction that the "sovereignty of the people," whose
most powerful champion was Jefferson, would issue into the "tyranny
of the majority." The great error of the eighteenth century—the power
of the people to secure the perfectibility of man—when taken up and
agitated by the anti-slavery party of the North, produced the recent
fruits of death and desolation. "It was," Bledsoe thought, "precisely
the same virus which convulsed and devoured France in 1789 and
America in 1861."

But the Jeffersonian law of compensation was still working. Bledsoe
himself, while he implicated Jefferson in the war-guilt of the North,
justified the South on the "doctrines of '98." Alexander H. Stephens,
Vice-President of the Confederacy, brought out his massive lawyer's
brief in the South's defense, his *Constitutional View of the Late War
Between the States,* in 1867. Moderate though he was, Stephens said
he had never questioned the right of a state to secede. "The first
lessons of my political creed from my earliest youth were the Virginia

and Kentucky resolutions of 1798 and 1799." Not long before the
Confederacy capitulated, Stephens had proposed to Union authorities that these long esteemed Resolutions be accepted as a constitutional basis of re-union. His *Constitutional View* interpreted the War
as the final outcome of the prolonged conflict between the opposite
principles of Jefferson and Hamilton: state rights versus national
consolidation. Jefferson himself was proof against those Northern
interpreters who accented the slavery issue; for he, despite his moral
position on slavery, "headed the great party in opposition to this
[federal] mode of effecting the great object of those who desired its
Abolition, as he had led the same party to success over the Centralists
on other questions in 1801." These views informed Stephens's popular *History of the United States,* which went through numerous
editions before and after it was assailed in Congress, in 1884, as a
compendium of the treasonous doctrine being fed to Southern youth.
    Stephens was actually too moderate to please a good many South-
erners. A stronger dose of the same medicine was administered by
Rushmore D. Horton's *Youth's History of the Great Civil War,* still
being published in 1925. The book featured long extracts from Jefferson's writings on the monarchical designs of the Federalists. It
attributed the War to the undying enmity of the Federalists and
their children for Jefferson and the party of the South. "After they
could no longer make headway against the democracy of Jefferson,
the old Hamilton party hunted round for some new issue on which
they could rally and keep alive their waning party strength. They
hit upon the negro." The Northern conspiracy, begun in 1798, was
consummated in 1860. "Hamilton was the true prophet," as Bledsoe
bitterly noted.
    Uprooted from a past entwined in their emotions, Southerners
contracted long political memories. Devastated by war, dispossessed
in Reconstruction, they were then victimized by the Lost Cause.
State rights was part of the Lost Cause which many cherished in
their hearts and not a few bent their efforts to regain. "State Rights
was the most marked peculiarity of the politics of the Southern
people," Edward A. Pollard wrote in his influential *Lost Cause* of
1866. Not a year passed that some spokesman did not call the South
back to its political destiny, back to the ancestral wisdom of the

Republican fathers, back to Jefferson, in order to repel the forces of consolidation. The picture of the Union worshipped by the South was, as Pollard recognized, imaginary; yet it never lost its appeal. It has recently been evoked in strong colors by the "nullification" resolutions of Southern states against the Supreme Court's mandate on segregation in the public schools. Rising and falling with the times, the conflict between State Rights and Human Rights, for which Jefferson was historically the ambivalent symbol, has always been peculiarly pungent in the Southern mind.

In the immediate secession crisis, Northerners defended Jefferson from the principles of the disunionists. Secession, they said, was the bastard offspring of the fortuitous union between the Essex Junto and the Calhoun Nullifiers. Soon, however, many were finding "the germ of the fatal heresy" in the Resolutions of '98 and charging to Jefferson "the first stab to the Union and the Constitution." From this recognition ensued a revolt against all things Jeffersonian. It was Jefferson's legerdemain that made the Union "a string of juggler's rings" seeming to charm while it pleased the operator but just as easily broken into separate rings again. It was Jefferson and his loose popular notions on the limits of authority and the right of rebellion that sapped the strength of free government to maintain itself. It was Jefferson's condemnation of manufactures which, perhaps as much as anything, fastened upon the South a plantation economy with its aristocratic impedimenta. State rights was nearly always the crucial complaint. Recantation followed revaluation. Andrew Dixon White, the young convert who had placed Jefferson at the top of the calendar of great Americans and lauded his anti-slavery record, laid aside the biography he was writing of the fallen idol. "Perhaps no doctrine ever cost any other country so dear," White later explained, "as Jefferson's pet theory of State rights cost the United States: Nearly a million of lives lost on battlefields, in prisons, and in hospitals; nearly ten thousand millions of dollars poured into the gulfs of hatred."

The first gun fired at Fort Sumter smashed the old Union and with it the political design of Thomas Jefferson. The War seemed suddenly to have rendered the fabled age of the republic unusable.

"For the control of rebellious States, the fathers left no rules; for the conduct of our treasury in civil war, they laid down no system of finance; for diplomatic dealings with foreign powers, while our government was threatened with disruption, they provided no precedent." Jefferson's political vocabulary, along with the party war-cries fashioned from it, were anachronistic. When Martin Van Buren's *Inquiry into the Origin & Course of Political Parties in the United States* appeared posthumously in 1867, it was like a voice from another age. "We have outgrown—or rather we have overleaped—all the party truisms," a reviewer declared. Had it been published in 1857, it would have been received, like Randall's *Life of Jefferson*, as a valuable addition to literature. In 1867 it was no more than a "distinterred fossil fragment."

The passage of the Jeffersonian polity was the subject of a brilliant essay by Samuel Fowler, of Massachusetts, in the *North American Review* at the close of the War. Because the War "changed the current of our ideas," Fowler thought it was at last possible to take an impartial backward glance over the preceding field dominated by Jefferson's ideas and the party he founded. That party first comprehended and expressed the mind of the American people. Jefferson was not only its founder but its spiritual leader for more than a generation after his death, during which "his lightest opinions were studied and regarded with a religious veneration singularly at variance with our national tendencies, as well as with the sturdy independence of his own character." His ideas, stamped upon the mind of the country, unfortunately led to "that political habitude and that incapacity to escape beyond their charmed circle of which we of this generation have seen such striking manifestations."

The foundation of Jefferson's system, Fowler continued, was the idea of state rights and local self-government. In the beginning it was no less liberal than it was necessary. Jefferson erred in mistaking the peculiar circumstances which made the idea appropriate in his time for fixed and universal conditions. Its fatal consequence could not fairly be charged against him; still disunion held no terrors for him, and this led to a certain slackness, if not irresponsibility, where the interests of the Union were concerned. The great and lamentable flaw in the system, Fowler thought, was that, like its Lockean model, it did not go beyond individuals. The laws of society were determined by the supposedly universal laws of the human mind, and the community was derived solely from the consent of its members. All higher bonds and obligations were omitted. "The theory of social compact by which political rights were regulated, places men like grains of sand in juxtaposition, but without affinity. For the deeper law of duty and of unity which ... is still the basis of all human intercourse, there is hardly a place in the system." Given this philosophy, it was axiomatic that government should be limited to protecting natural rights. Individuals were the sole source and object of authority; therefore, the nearer government approached to them the more perfectly it functioned. Whence came, Fowler thought, Jefferson's cardinal political beliefs: a simple agrarian society, broad diffusion of power, the sovereignty of the living generation.

But how remote was Jefferson's Elysium from the America of 1865! Now, Fowler observed, the progress of the people, the conditions of civilization itself, required an elaborate industrial and financial apparatus. Ever increasing concentration gave rise to a giant complex of dependent relationships. The dominant movements of philosophical speculation also ran counter to the atomistic and empirical canons of Jefferson's thought. Of primary importance was the centripetal force of nationalism, which had overcome the particularistic tendencies of Jefferson's system. "Beginning in darkness and doubt, national interests and policy have insensibly conquered the first place in the estimation of the people." The Virginian never contemplated this development; his philosophy excluded it. If this change relegated Jefferson to history at last, Fowler concluded, it in no way diminished the greatness of the man and his achievement. "His was the policy of his time." Since nationalism had triumphed without injury to the freedoms he prized, his name could never be rightfully invoked in support of doctrines "no longer vitalized by the popular breath, and only retained as a shackle on the movements of a free and progressive people."

Viewing the War as the fiery ordeal of the Union and the fulfillment of America's long neglected promise of nationality, many reflective Northerners welcomed it with a sense of relief, even of exaltation. Americans had not known, James Russell Lowell said, "that uncon-

scious feeling of nationality, the ideal abstract of history and tradition, which belongs to older countries, compacted by frequent war
and united by memories of common danger and common triumph. . . .
But what splendid possibilities has not our trial revealed even to
ourselves! What costly stuff whereof to make a nation!" It was a
serious question which the War must decide, others said, whether
the American people had a government at all. "The essence of government is that it command obedience." But the fatal spirit of the
Jeffersonian polity was to weaken the bonds of authority until dis-
obedience and rebellion seemed its natural condition.

On the Sunday after the disaster at Bull Run, the famed Hartford
theologian, Horace Bushnell, delivered a notable sermon, "Reverses
Needed." Two distinct elements entered into the formation of American political institutions, Bushnell began. First, the historical and
religious element, represented especially by the New England people.
Second, the speculative and infidel element, "represented in the life
and immense public influence of Mr. Jefferson." Going never higher
than man, lacking any conception of government as a divine ordinance, Jefferson supposed "that a machine could be got up by the
consent of the governed that would really oblige, or bind their consent; not staying even to observe that the moment anything binds . . .
it rules by the force of a moral idea, and teaches, by the supposition,
some throne of order and law above the range of mere humanity."
The worst practical mischief of this godless philosophy, Bushnell
thought, was state rights, its logical analogue in the federal sphere.
"Where nothing exists but a consent, what can be needed to end it
but a dissent? And if the states are formed by the consent of individuals, was not the general government formed by the consent of
the states?" Under the Jeffersonian delusions, the American people
dissolved all the higher-than-human supports of government until
nothing remained but "to fight out the question whether we shall
have a nationality or not." The true meaning of the struggle was,
therefore, the purgation of the Jeffersonian heresy and the resurrection of the religious element rooted in the Puritan tradition. Dwelling
on this favorite theme later in the War, Bushnell found encouraging
signs of return to a government sanctified by God in the movement
for a religious amendment to the Constitution and in Secretary of

the Treasury Chase's decision to inscribe the motto "In God We Trust" on the nation's coins.

The new nationalist philosophy incorporated many of the ideas conservatives of both sections had preached for years. That law is force, not consent; that true liberty is founded, not in abstract right, but in institutional arrangements backed by the authority of God or tradition; that government is an object of loyalty transcendent over individual or popular will; that sovereignty is in its very nature unitary and cannot be divided—these ideas had often been associated with the attack on centralized power and with the defense of slavery. Whatever Jeffersonian alloy they had had in the philosophy of such men as Calhoun was removed when they were put to the service of strident nationalism. Orestes Brownson, the outstanding intellectual champion of Calhoun's ideas in the North before the War, became one of the most influential theorists of the new nationalism without changing a single major premise of his thought. Fed by German metaphysics, as well as the Marshall-Story-Webster stream of constitutional theory, the movement to establish a unitary national theory of sovereignty claimed the energies of American political scientists for forty years to come. Jefferson held almost no status with these scholars, not only because his theory of federal relations was antagonistic to the theory of "national existence," but also because his theory of the relations of rulers to the ruled did not permit the requisite degree of organic unity, allegiance, and permanence in the polity. Numerous popular histories of the Civil War from Northern pens expressed similar ideas in vulgar terms. The image of the "great heretic" or "great conspirator" was prominent in their pages.

It is a wonder, then, that Jefferson's reputation was not totally eclipsed in the eyes of most Unionists. It was not, chiefly because of Abraham Lincoln and the love of humanity, founded in the faith of Jefferson, he came to symbolize. Part of the greatness of Lincoln, as men came to appreciate it, lay in the fact "that he did the work of Alexander Hamilton, on the basis of the principles of Thomas Jefferson; and thus united, in his leadership and career, the two strands of political philosophy that had divided our country." The democratic *basis* of the new national life was, or might appear to be, the vital achievement. Insofar as this held true, continuity with the

Jeffersonian faith was maintained. No one tried harder than Lincoln himself to secure this result.

Lincoln admired Jefferson for many things, but most of all for the Declaration of Independence. In the famous debates with Douglas, he stripped the democratic mask from the face of "popular sovereignty." It had nothing to do with the old and honorable principles of Jefferson, but was the naked assertion of "the right of the whiteman to breed and flog niggers in Nebraska." Slavery, as Lincoln saw it, was an interest not alone of a few settlers in Nebraska but of the whole nation; for the definition of American nationality itself, the Declaration of 1776, was involved. Although he never exceeded the flight of eloquence in the letter to the Jefferson Birthday celebration in Boston, that was only one of his many tributes to the Declaration. Speaking at Independence Hall on the eve of his Inauguration, he took direct issue with the Confederate appeal to the Declaration. The Revolution, he said, was "not a mere matter of separation . . . from the motherland, but that something in the Declaration giving liberty, not alone to the people of this country, but hope to the world for all future time. It was that which gave promise that in due time the weights should be lifted from the shoulders of *all* men, and that *all* should have an equal chance." The Declaration was the great creative myth of the American people. Superficially at stake in 1861 was the Union. Fundamentally at stake, Lincoln knew, was the moral proposition that gave it life, along with the democratic processes by which the goal could be realized. In one of the most precious Lincoln fragments, usually dated 1860, he reflected that the primary cause of American progress was neither the Union nor the Constitution, but "something back of these, entwining itself more closely about the human heart . . . the principle of 'Liberty to All.'" Without the assertion of this principle in 1776, independence would not have been won, the Union established, prosperity advanced. Lincoln then took a line from the fifth chapter of Proverbs—"a word fitly spoken is like apples of gold in pictures of silver"—and with this imaged his conception of America.

The assertion of that *principle, at that time,* was *the* word, "fitly spoken" which has proved an "apple of gold" to us. The *Union,* and the *Constitution,* are the *picture* of *silver,* subsequently framed around it. The picture was made, not to *conceal,* or *destroy* the apple; but to *adorn,* and *preserve* it. The picture was made *for* the apple—*not* the apple for the picture.

So let us act, that neither *picture,* or *apple,* shall ever be blurred, or bruised or broken.

Lincoln became a symbol of American Democracy more inspiring to most people than Jefferson; but the two symbols—Great Emancipator and Father of Democracy—often blended into each other, in part because of Lincoln's testament to the belief that the spiritual springs of national life were cemented in the principles Jefferson had declared self-evident. George Bancroft, in his eulogy of the martyred President, saw the two great figures as co-partners in the progress of human liberty. Far into the future, politicians of a progressive stripe would speak of the "Jefferson-Lincoln tradition." Jefferson portraiture in words and in bronze suggested, in many instances, Lincolnesque qualities—the homespun manner, the gangling frame, the meditative posture. The most moving pages of Moses Coit Tyler's great *Literary History of the United States,* in 1897, were devoted to the Declaration of Independence, whose "prodigious service" in the crisis of the Union was still fresh in the author's memory. Tyler described the document, not as a reasoned statement of political philosophy, but as "a kind of war-song . . . a stately and passionate chant of human freedom . . . a prose lyric of civil and military heroism," bound to go on and on spreading its influence so long as the world had ears to listen. And because The Word could not be separated from "the character and genius of its author," Jefferson's fame and influence were bound to spread with it.

Alexander Hamilton's place at any period on the imaginary scale that charts American reputations is always a good index to Jefferson's. Jefferson's reputation merely survived the War; Hamilton's was remade by it. "Who is Hamilton?" Englishmen were said to have asked bewilderedly when his name suddenly appeared in dispatches from the United States. Largely without honor in his own country, how was the world to know this man now widely acclaimed "the real genius" of the American republic?

Although Hamilton was not lost to history before the War, no skilled hand wrote his biography, and politicians seldom invoked his

name save as a curse. Eloquent lines were written and uttered about
him. The French historian, Guizot, described him as "the master
spirit" of the Constitution. Daniel Webster struck the vivid image:
"He smote the rock of the national resources, and abundant streams
of revenue gushed forth. He touched the dead corpse of the Public
Credit, and it sprung upon its feet." These tributes were destined to
become stereotyped, but few men of Webster's generation were
moved by them. Hamilton was best remembered where he lay entombed, in the very commercial and industrial heart of the land.
His portrait hung in the Chamber of Commerce of New York City,
and the city's merchants erected a statue to him, Roman toga and
all, before the Merchants Exchange. Hamilton went to posterity with
many advantages not possessed by his arch rival: stately Caesarean
features, military glory, the friendship of Washington, romantic
bravado in life and gallantry in death, a devoted wife and several
sons blessed with long lives. But these things could never entirely
compensate for the aristocratic, the faintly alien, odor of his character
and politics. This hung over him like a pall in the ante-bellum years,
when only his widow Elizabeth, his sons, and a few loyal Federalists
pleaded his cause and cherished his fame.

Then came the War. "Have you thought what a vindication this
war is of Alexander Hamilton?" George W. Curtis queried a Boston
friend. Surely, Curtis thought, "he was one of our truly great men,
as Jefferson was the least of the truly great." The new school of
nationalist thinkers pronounced him prophet, and many Republicans
called him father. "The civil war was his conflict. Chickamauga and
Chancellorsville were his anguish, and Appomattox was his triumph."
Confederate apologists unhappily agreed. How many Republicans
there were who, like James A. Garfield of Ohio, began to study
Hamilton's writings in 1861, it is impossible to say. But the act was
symbolic; and few would have disputed Garfield's assertion in Congress four years later "that the fame of Jefferson is waning, and the
fame of Hamilton is waxing, in the estimation of the American
people." Republicans of the Garfield sort emphasized the first half
of the War's nationality-democracy equation, running the new orthodox tradition from Hamilton through Lincoln.

One of the first books to herald the Hamilton revival came from

England, C. J. Riethmüller's *Alexander Hamilton and His Contemporaries; or, The Rise of the American Constitution,* in 1864. Riethmüller wrote from the conviction that Hamilton had foreseen the dangers of the Jeffersonian polity to the Union and had labored incessantly to overcome them. He felt, however, that nothing Hamilton did to prop up the Constitution remedied its fatal defects. When the Convention of 1787 rejected his plan of government, which called for absolute national sovereignty and firm aristocratic checks on the people, it invited the mad career of Jeffersonian democracy. American nationalists welcomed Riethmüller's book. Reviewing it in the *Atlantic Monthly,* C. C. Hazewell called Hamilton's "the greatest name in American history." Hamilton divined Europe, Talleyrand had said; but 1861 proved that he had divined America as well. Had he been allowed to shape our polity, Hazewell said, the bloody ordeal of the nation would never have been necessary. Few nationalists shared Riethmüller's opinion of the Constitution or proposed a return to Hamilton's plan of government. They tended rather to make Hamilton the architect of the Constitution itself, to read into it all those elements of force and unity the Fathers had rejected but Appomattox affirmed, to hail the triumph of arms the triumph of the *true* Hamiltonian Constitution. From this revaluation of Hamilton's work came the image of the "nation-builder," which had its opposite in the "nation-destroyer" image of Jefferson.

The most pretentious product of the Hamilton revival was the seven-volume *History of the Republic of the United States* by John C. Hamilton, the son whose most urgent mission in life was to restore his father's fame. In 1834 he brought out a volume of biography that carried Hamilton down to 1788; in 1880 he presented to New York City a statue of Hamilton to be erected in Central Park. In between, he edited the Congress Edition of Hamilton's work, wrote several wartime tracts on the Jefferson-Hamilton theme, prepared a highly controversial edition of *The Federalist,* piled up the volumes of the *History,* and acted as special pleader of Hamilton's cause in several public quarrels. It is no extravagance to say that this faithful son was the keeper of his father's fame through thirty years. By the time the *History* was completed in 1865, many others were ready to share the burden.

The *History*—a rambling and argumentative work—made the preposterous assumption that Hamilton's career and the early life of the republic were practically identical. It was the great repository of Hamilton lore for the next forty years; but the range of its influence was limited because of the absurd claims its author made for Hamilton's omnipresent genius. It belonged, as one reviewer said, in "the department of comic biography." Written from within the Federalist tradition, Hamilton's *History* was an unintentional travesty upon it. He, like his brother James and his nephew Allan McLane Hamilton in their more modest efforts, gave as one of the compelling reasons for the work the need to vindicate his father—"and, indeed ... the sacred patrimony of our national honor"—against Jefferson's lies and heresies. The heresy of heresies was Jefferson's demagogical contempt for the Constitution and the Union. The disastrous consequence was the Great Rebellion. "Stern realities are now uttering themselves aloud," Hamilton concluded his last volume, "and one voice is heard—'had Hamilton's views prevailed the crisis could not have taken place.' "

The Hamilton revival never fulfilled its early promise, largely because of its narrow ideological framework of historic Federalism. It made Hamilton's name politically respectable; it set Republican policy in a classic tradition; it resulted in a few monuments, a great many orations, and a number of Republican clubs devoted to his memory. On its literary side, the revival was summed up, its limits were reached, in Hermann Von Holst's *Constitutional and Political History of the United States* and in the work of the young nationalist historians, some of them inspired by the German scholar, who formed around John T. Morse and wrote the volumes of his "American Statesmen" series more than a decade after Appomattox. Morse, a Boston lawyer, published his two-volume life of Hamilton in 1876. It was based upon the simple proposition: Hamilton *or* Jefferson, America must choose. The viewpoint, both conservative and nationalist, informed the biographical series Morse then undertook to edit. "Let the Jeffersonian and the Jacksonian beware! I will poison the popular mind!!" he candidly wrote to his friend and colleague, Henry Cabot Lodge.

Lodge wrote the "American Statesman" *Hamilton,* went on to edit

Hamilton's writings in 1885, and over many years, during which he gave his main energies to the Republican party, was the irrepressible champion of Hamilton and the Federalism of his ancestors. Lodge showed admirable candor toward his hero. He conceded Hamilton's aristocratic bias, his devotion to the wealthy class, his support of the Alien and Sedition Laws, his part in the wrecking of the Federalist party. Despite these failings, or even because of them, Lodge felt that Hamilton gave the new nation the strength it needed to survive in freedom. In all personal qualities Jefferson was just the reverse of Hamilton—supple, feminine, visionary—not the stuff with which to build a nation. "The Federalists hated Jefferson with no common political hatred," the gritty Lodge wrote, "but rather with the vindictiveness of men toward a deadly foe who, as they firmly believed, sought the ruin of all they most prized and cherished." Nevertheless, Lodge held, contrary to Federalist expectations, the revolution of 1800 did not destroy the national foundations, partly because of Jefferson's timidity in action, partly because of Marshall and the Supreme Court, ultimately because of the Civil War. The Federalist system proved stronger than its strongest foe, and the Constitution vindicated its energy in the course of American history. This conclusion, Lodge and others of his school believed, set doubts at rest and made Hamilton a triumphant American figure.

"We balance one man with his opposite," said the Sage of Concord, "and the health of the state depends on the see-saw." The Civil War raised Hamilton and lowered Jefferson, which was natural enough given the leverage of Hamiltonian ideas and policies in the reformed nation. But the see-saw was not likely to remain still. For Jefferson, unlike Hamilton, was protean, capable of infinite reinterpretation within the shared faith of the American people. The same Jefferson who was implicated in the Union's tragedy survived as the symbol of its irreversible ideals and its democratic processes. The *picture* had changed, but so long as it was remembered with Lincoln that "the picture was made *for* the apple—*not* the apple for the picture," men would continue to renew their faith in Jefferson and seek guidance in his teachings.

BOOK TWO

* *Five* *

REDIVIVUS

If all the dust and bones of every Philip, Ferdinand and Charles of Spain and Portugal, of every Louis, Henry and Charles of France, and of all the Plantagenets, Tudors, Stuarts and Hanovers of England, were concentrated in one mighty urn, a single relic from Jefferson's remains, as they lie moldering on the slopes of the Blue Ridge in Virginia, would be more precious than them all in the sight of a just God, and the eyes of every lover of the human race.*

THE LONG ECLIPSE of the reputation was over, the luminous power of the Jefferson image restored, as the twentieth century dawned. One hundred years after his inauguration as President, seventy-five years after his death, Jefferson stood higher in public esteem than at any time since the Civil War. Jefferson's life was responding to fresh ideas and interests. The political symbol was as green as ever. In 1900 a mammoth *Jeffersonian Cyclopedia* made its appearance. Here, conveniently arranged from "Abilities" to "Zeal," and cross-indexed for ready reference, were Jefferson's opinions on any subject likely to arise in public discussion. In 1901 the first permanent outdoor memorial to Jefferson was dedicated in Louisville, Kentucky. There were four new biographies between 1900 and 1903. The Jefferson Bible, first published at St. Louis in 1902, was issued by Congress in full facsimile two years later. A Bible got up by Jefferson circulated by congressmen under the imprint of the United States government! Democrats, and not only Democrats, from all over were making pilgrimages to Monticello. This sacred spot, some said, should be

* Daniel W. Voorhees, "Thomas Jefferson," in *Forty Years of American Oratory,* 1898.

purchased by the government and made a national shrine. A group of prominent citizens, meeting in Washington in 1903, launched with much fanfare a movement to erect a fitting memorial to Jefferson in the nation's capital. Although the movement was premature, it resulted in the second new edition of Jefferson's writings within a decade. St. Louis was readying her great fair, the Louisiana Purchase Exposition, which opened one year behind schedule in 1904 and closed in 1913 with the dedication of the Jefferson Memorial Building in Forrest Park.

National politics of course fed this renewed interest in Jefferson. The single issue which, more than any other, catapulted Jefferson to the center of public controversy was American imperialism. Nothing cut so deeply to the heart of Jeffersonian principle since the slavery issue of forty years before. William Jennings Bryan, who often talked as if he had just had a spiritual visitation from Jefferson, pressed his contest with President McKinley in 1900 back upon the old landmarks. Mr. Dooley, the nation's political humorist, was heard complaining to his friend Hennessy that the "Boy Orator of the Platte" had lost his punch:

But nowadays he has tin wurruds f'r Thomas Jefferson an' th' rest iv th' sage crop to wan f'r hissilf. . . . 'Tisn't Bryan alone, Mack's th' same way. They're both ancestor worshippers, like th' Chinese, Hinnissy. An' what I'd like to know is what Thomas Jefferson knew about th' troubles iv ye an' me? Divule a wurrud have I to say again' Thomas. He was a good man in his day, though I don't know that his battin' av'rage'd be high again' th' pitchin' iv these times. I have a gr-reat rayspict f'r th' sages an' I believe in namin' sthreets an' public schools afther thim.

The philosopher of Chicago's Archy Road suggested the difficulties Jefferson might expect to encounter in the contemporary world by imagining him astride his horse in the city streets, startled and forced from the right-of-way by a clanging trolley. Jefferson and the rest of the "sage crop" "larned their thrade befure the days iv open plumbin'"; they had no working card for this century. But they were mighty level-headed fellows, Hennessy demurred. "'Thrue f'r ye,' said Mr. Dooley. 'But undher th' new iliction laws ye can't vote th' cimitries.'"

Despite plumbing, trolley lines, skyscrapers, and all the fixtures
of a life that had made Monticello a museum piece, and despite the
adverse winds of opinion and doctrine blown up by the Civil War,
Olympus was beckoning to Jefferson again in 1900. How far he was
even yet from the upper reaches, however, was indicated by the first
ballot for the newly established Hall of Fame. Jefferson ranked sixth,
behind Washington, Lincoln, Webster, Franklin, Grant, and Marshall. Since the jury was drawn from the politically conservative
segments of the population, the result was perhaps more encouraging
than otherwise.

The recovery of Jefferson's reputation proceeded along two main
lines. The first carried forward the curiosity Henry S. Randall's pages
had awakened in Jefferson's private and domestic life. The second
ran through politics, chiefly the renascent Democratic party. While
Democrats refurbished the political hero, others discovered in Jefferson ingratiating personal traits and civilized values that had little
to do with politics. Taken together, blended as they often were, these
two lines of interest led to the remarkable display of Jefferson's
vitality in American life at the turn of the century.

1. Who Was Thomas Jefferson?

Posterity exacts a heavy price in dehumanization from the great
man. "Every hero becomes a bore at last," as Emerson said. But
greatness, once it has been exhibited in works and ideas, invites
approach, however inadequate, to the human being. In the case of
Jefferson, this approach, barely begun before the War, became one
of the most edifying avenues of his modern reputation. A major
advance was recorded by two books within a few years of Appomattox: Sarah Nicholas Randolph's *Domestic Life of Thomas Jefferson*,
in 1871, and James Parton's *Life*, in 1874. Reviewers in *The Nation*
magazine felt some astonishment that their authors should have
chosen to praise Jefferson while the nation was still mourning the
bloody costs of his work. Nevertheless, they could not wholly resist
the captivating portraiture of these books. Edmund Quincy, as good
a Jefferson-hater as his father, confessed that for all of Jefferson's
political sins, he appeared in Miss Randolph's pages "entirely amiable

and charming" and would certainly be "more mildly judged because of her pious tribute to his memory."

Sarah Randolph grew up at Edgehill in sight of Monticello and in the presence of family relics and memories cherished by her father, Thomas Jefferson Randolph. "I do not," the great-granddaughter began, "write of Jefferson either as of the great man or as of the statesman. My object is only to give a faithful picture of him as he was in private life—to show that he was, as I have been taught to think of him by those who knew and loved him best, a beautiful domestic character." Scarcely a trace of vexation or controversy marred the narrative's mellow surface. Politics intruded only as an annoyance and a curse, for that, in the author's judgment, was the only part they had played in Jefferson's family circle.

The story was not really Miss Randolph's. Her main task was to knit it together from Jefferson's writings and the recollections by his children and grandchildren and intimate friends. Much that she published was taken from Randall's *Life*, for the New Yorker had drawn from the same bundles of family papers and the same wells of family remembrance. She was able to publish many things for the first time, however, partly because after twenty-three years the State Department had finally separated the "private" papers from the "public" papers sold to the government in 1848, and returned the former to their owner, T. J. Randolph. More than an engaging family portrait, the *Domestic Life* was a valuable aid to the serious student of Jefferson.

The outstanding traits of the "beautiful domestic character" created in Miss Randolph's pages were his enormous capacity for love, his scrupulous observance of duty in every personal relationship, his openness to all the windows of nature, his self-catechizing habits both moral and intellectual. Wherever he was, his heart was always at Monticello. Public office had no charms for him. On the testimony of this book, Jefferson's instincts were not those of a politician but those of a Virginia gentleman, who was quite incapable of posturing or demagoguery and who knew no happiness outside the bosom of his family.

Hamilton had once called Jefferson "womanish"; William Graham Sumner and Henry Cabot Lodge thought no single word better characterized him. Miss Randolph, of course, said he was "manly" in everything, from horsemanship to female companionship. Her narrative suggested, nevertheless, there was something to be said for the other view, with no disparagement intended. His unfailing joy in household cares, the raising of children, the arrangements of the house, the cuisine and the garden; his disgust for combat in any form and abstinence from most of the manly sports and habits of the Virginians of his day; most of all, the sweetness of his temper, seldom ruffled and almost never broken by anger—these traits would commonly be counted more effeminate than masculine. They were, on the whole, the traits that had made Jefferson the beloved head of the Monticello family.

The *Domestic Life* was liberally sprinkled with family tradition and reminiscence later writers found irresistible. The story of the young Jefferson's love for Dabney Carr, for instance, was to be told countless times. The boys, Tom and Dabney, studied and played together under the shade of a great oak on the side of the "Little Mountain." Here they made a pact: the one who lived the longer would see that the other was buried under the oak. Young Carr died in 1773, and was buried at his home while Jefferson was in Williamsburg. No sooner had he returned than he had the body moved to the sacred spot on his mountain. Here he also would lie; for the pact was the origin of the family graveyard at Monticello.

Numerous instances of Jefferson's honor and kindness conveyed the book's dominant message. Although his property greatly depreciated during the Revolution, he declined the protection of Virginia statutes furnishing relief from British creditors. Every spring for thirty years, he sent his carriage to rescue a married sister of slender means from the sickly climate of the Lower James, and when she was widowed he took her into his household, as he had done with the Carr family. In every turmoil and affliction of the members of his family, Miss Randolph said, Jefferson was present with sympathy and counsel.

James Parton, America's first professional biographer, acquainted a much larger audience with "the beautiful domestic character." Jefferson's great art was love, Parton thought:

In every other quality and grace of human nature he has often been equalled, sometimes excelled; but where has there ever been a *lover* so tender, so warm, so constant, as he? Love was his life. Few men have had so many sources of pleasure, so many agreeable tastes and pursuits; but he knew no satisfying joy, at any period of his life, except through his affections.

Jefferson was a political hero to Parton. "I think," he avowed at the start, "that the best chance of republican America is adherence to the general line of politics of which he was the embodiment." His views of early political history were virtually identical with Randall's. Still, there were important differences between the two works. Parton wrote from a viewpoint commonly called *liberal* in his time. The liberal was a nationalist who retained the Jeffersonian distrust of government, an advocate of maximum individual liberty who had no zeal for equality, a friend of "good government" rather than of popular government. Parton thus associated Jefferson with political principles not adequately comprehended in the tradition of the Democratic party. Moreover, his Jefferson was not in essence a political character at all. Judging from the letters, Parton said, "the more furiously the storm of politics raged about him, the more attentive he was to philosophy." No one cared to remember just what Parton said about Jefferson's political career—it had been said many times over—but no one seemed able to forget his description of Jefferson as "a gentleman of thirty-two who could calculate an eclipse, survey an estate, tie an artery, plan an edifice, try a cause, break a horse, dance a minuet, and play a violin." Nothing written before so clearly foreshadowed the emergence of Jefferson as a hero of American culture.

As well remembered was the flat proposition to which Parton dedicated the *Life:* "If Jefferson was wrong, America is wrong. If America is right, Jefferson was right." The proposition raised Jefferson above partisanship. Parton did not say Jefferson *was* right, but rather, right or wrong, Jefferson *is* America. As a New Yorker of the liberal persuasion writing just after the scandals of the Tweed Ring and the Grant administration, Parton had grave doubts about the American future. Reviewers were struck by the apparent anomaly of the author's attacking universal suffrage while nevertheless finding in Jefferson "the glory and hope of America." The trouble lay, Parton felt, in the perversion of Jeffersonian principles by non-Jeffersonian

methods—state rights perverted into rebellion, popular sovereignty
into statism, party organization into boss rule. The first error had
already been corrected, and the other two might be corrected by
better understanding of Jefferson's political methods.

Parton believed, as he had said in the *Life of Jackson*, that Jefferson's philosophy attained its highest statement in Herbert Spencer's
Social Statics. He regretted Jefferson had not lived to read it, "such
keen delight would he have had in seeing his cherished opinions
stated with the clearness of light." Joining Jefferson to the Darwinian
philosopher of "survival of the fittest" in the jungle of American
capitalism, Parton touched a vital theme of the next several decades.
Edward Sheldon, writing in the *North American Review*, contradicted Parton's estimate on this as on most points. Jefferson, he said,
was a smart party manager and sentimental philanthropist, with an
aversion to everything modern industry represented and a fatal
weakness for every scheme of popular reform. Were he alive today,
Sheldon thought, "he would advocate total abstinence and women's
rights, talk with Mill on the 'unearned increment of land,' harangue
against capitalists and in favor of the eight-hour law, and insist upon
the justice of paying United States bonds in greenbacks." These
contrasting liberal and radical conceptions pointed to a new Jeffersonian dilemma.

But the more immediate and enduring effect of Parton's popular
book was neither to make Jefferson, so soon, a cultural hero, nor
to make him, so narrowly, a Spencerian liberal; it was, rather, to
emphasize the virtues and the charms of the human being. With his
unique talent for characterization, Parton brought the figure into
relief from his political history. His biography was a great source,
as was the *Domestic Life*, of Jefferson legend. An example of how
it fostered legend, and also of the gradual shift of attention from the
public to the private life, was Parton's account of Jefferson's bridal
journey in January 1772. In the recollections which she furnished
George Tucker, Martha Jefferson Randolph told of the couple's one-
hundred-mile journey from the Wayles estate, through a heavy snowstorm, to the "horrible dreariness" of the little cottage ("Honeymoon
Lodge") atop Monticello. Tucker ignored this picturesque episode;
he was satisfied to record in a line that Jefferson got married. Randall

quoted Mrs. Randolph's account in passing. Her granddaughter, Sarah, added one or two picturesque details passed down to her.

Parton, however, wrote an entire chapter on Jefferson's marriage. The wedding journey became a delightful divertissement. The arrival on the bleak uninhabited mountain was not dreary at all but cheered by the warmth of young lovers, nestling in the cottage and reading the verses of Ossian. In one of his best-sellers, *Achievements of Celebrated Men,* Parton had the bride and groom leaving The Forest (the Wayles estate) after the wedding breakfast and arriving at Monticello sometime after nightfall—and he added a bottle of wine to the honeymoon picture! This fantastic tale—a one-hundred-mile journey in phaeton and on horseback over the Virginia roads of 1772, through a blinding snowstorm part of the way, all on the day of the wedding, and the final merriment at Monticello—was repeated by nearly every writer for the next seventy-five years. By 1943, when Sidney Kingsley recreated the "wedding night" in his Broadway play, *The Patriots,* the bride is playing the pianoforte and Jefferson the violin! "Was there ever such a wedding night?" Jefferson's daughter Martha asks after the flashback. No, Martha, there never was. The meticulous scholarship of Jefferson's present-day biographer, Dumas Malone, shows how far the plain facts were from the picturesque story. Jefferson and his bride, it appears, stayed at The Forest for two weeks, dallied a while at Tuckahoe (his mother's old home), and finally arrived at Monticello late one snowy night near the end of the month. Malone does not say whether the lovers read Ossian or uncorked a bottle of wine or played a duet.

By 1900 the image of the "beautiful domestic character" was well formed. Jefferson's public conduct came to be treated more generously in the process, although the public and the private images remained wide apart and apparently irreconcilable. The "beautiful soul" of Monticello did not fit the author of the Anas. If historical and juvenile fiction, two genres which had an amazing growth in this period, may be taken as indicative of the characterization filtered into the popular mind, then much importance must be assigned to the incidents and traits of Jefferson's Albemarle life—his wilderness boyhood and companionship with Dabney Carr, his love of the fiddle and his mellifluous temperament, his marriage and solicitude for his motherless girls. The editor of a newly opened hoard of Jefferson letters in 1886 thought them of interest primarily in showing "the character of the man, upright, earnest, sincere, with a tenderness of affection, a certain friendly and personal devotion which . . . is not usually attributed to Mr. Jefferson."

Sentiments surrounding home and family helped to lift Jefferson back into public affection. Perhaps the most striking instance concerned his resting place on the Monticello slope. He had directed the monument over his grave to be "a plain die or cube of 3f, without any moldings, surmounted by an obelisk of 6f," which was "to be made of the coarse stone of which my columns are made, that no one might be tempted hereafter to destroy it for the value of the materials." His faithful grandson saw to the details. But the sentimental value of the stone was greater than Jefferson had reckoned. The granite shaft, no longer the original, had been chipped away, Miss Randolph wrote, until it stood an ugly misshapen column, and the marble tablet bearing the epitaph had disappeared from the base. (Monticello's owner, many years before, had safely secured it to a wall inside the house.) The graveyard had grown up in weeds. The whole place was in a state of abandon and disorder—"a standing monument to the ingratitude of a great republic."

Hearing such things in 1878 from a Mississippi colleague who had just come from Monticello, Representative S. S. Cox, a New York City Democrat, introduced in Congress a joint resolution authorizing the government to acquire the property and build a new monument over Jefferson's grave. It was scandalous, Cox pleaded, that the nation had not lifted a finger to preserve and cherish the resting place of this "avatar of progress," this "incarnation of American Democratic Republicanism." After scattered protests, the Cox Resolution passed, only then to be caught in a legal snarl over title to the graveyard property. The title was held by the heirs (forty-seven persons, seven of whom were minors) of Martha Jefferson Randolph. They enjoyed the privilege of burial there, and wished to hold possession. Moreover, though they had access to the graveyard, the owner of the Monticello estate, Jefferson M. Levy, would not bestow the right on the American public. In 1882, Congress deferred to these conditions, doubled the original appropriation, and built a monument nearly

twice the size of the one Jefferson had specified. The descendants
undertook to maintain the graveyard, though not very diligently
until, under public criticism, they organized the Monticello Association in 1913.

The monument inevitably suggested other possibilities. If the state
of Virginia cared so little for Jefferson's memory, let the United
States raise a monument in Washington, some congressmen exhorted.
A Jefferson Monumental Association formally met and organized in
Washington in 1882. But nothing more was ever heard of it. It was
also proposed to remove Jefferson's remains to a pantheon in the
capital. In 1882, Mrs. Septima Meikleham, Jefferson's oldest (and
within a few months, sole) living grandchild, petitioned Congress
for this purpose. Mrs. Meikleham, then a needy widow residing in
Washington, had been born at Monticello and present at Jefferson's
deathbed. She pleaded that the monument to be erected there would
suffer the fate of its predecessor. The great-grandchildren opposed
her, however; and that ended the movement which, apparently, the
Glenwood Cemetery Company was behind from the start. Repetition
of a scandal such as had raged over Washington's remains several
decades before was thus averted.

Jefferson's last grandchild was in the news for two more years.
Moved by the plight of this lady—"the pet and solace of Jefferson's
old age," "the grandest link that connects the infancy of the republic
with its maturity"—Representative William E. Robinson, of New
York, made it his mission to obtain a pension for her as a token of
the nation's gratitude to Jefferson. Many flowery things were said
about Jefferson in the course of debate. In the end, Robinson's
resolution was defeated, mainly by Southerners and Democrats, who
charged that this proffered honor to Jefferson desecrated the principles of his immortal name.

"It somehow happens that now and then a man lives who seems
to have in his head every important idea that all his countrymen
together get into theirs for a century after he is dead." The editor
of the *Chicago Tribune* thus referred in 1880 to the discovery that
almost any new project of human welfare was anticipated, "and
likely enough the whole identical plan worked out in detail, some-

where in Jefferson's writings." This was conspicuously true, he
thought, of the plan of public education Jefferson presented to the
Virginia Assembly in 1778. No biographer had comprehended Jefferson's supreme interest in education. Parton, with his feeling for the
ubiquitous genius and Americanism of his subject, had come the
closest; even so, Parton supposed that Jefferson's educational work
was derivative of New England. Of course he was always remembered, though not as well as he had wished, as Father of the University of Virginia. But he did not come into fame as the philosopher
and progenitor of the American system of public education until the
latter part of the nineteenth century. This was the first clear sign of
the political hero's evolution into the multitudinous hero of American
culture. Nothing else he ever did, his present-day biographer be-
lieves, "showed him more clearly to be a major American prophet."

How did the Virginian's name come to be associated with an educational system that had always been one of New England's titles of
renown? The habit of thinking of the public school in essentially
political terms, as an auxiliary of free government, naturally suggested a common father of both; and this was strengthened by
greater acquaintance with Jefferson's writings, which contained plans
generously interpreted as prophetic and epigrammatic utterances
that seemed the distilled essence of American educational ideals.
His statement of 1818 on the six objects of primary education was the
most widely quoted.* It ought to be emblazoned in letters of gold
in every schoolroom of the land, James Coolidge Carter declared.

John C. Henderson, in 1890, first culled Jefferson's educational
views into a single volume. Here, and in most of the literature on

* The objects as stated by Jefferson in 1818:
"To give every citizen the information he needs for the transaction of his own
business;
To enable him to calculate for himself, and to express and preserve his ideas,
his contracts and accounts, in writing;
To improve, by reading, his morals and faculties;
To understand his duties to his neighbors and country, and to discharge with
competence the functions confided to him by either;
To know his rights; to exercize with order and justice those he retains; to
choose with discretion the fiduciary of those he delegates; and to notice their
conduct with diligence, with candor, and judgment;
And, in general, to observe with intelligence and faithfulness all the social
relations under which he shall be placed."

this subject, Jefferson was credited with three leading ideas. First, that it is the duty of the state to educate its citizens, both for their own and the republic's well-being. "Jefferson's plan for public schools was an inherent part of his political system." Second, that the system should be unified from the grammar school at the bottom to the university at the top, with as much care given to the selection and encouragement up the ladder of the best talent as to the general diffusion of rudimentary knowledge among the mass of citizens on the lower rungs. "Jefferson's ideas, if they should ever be realized throughout the country, will deliver us on the one hand from the over-education of mediocrity, and on the other hand from the under-education of genius." Third, that education should be in harmony with American principles. It should be, therefore, secular and practical, a matter of local initiative and responsibility, and as free as possible of any coercive discipline. These Jeffersonian ideals, many thought, had proved their superiority over the narrow religious and ethical ideals of the New England system. Because so much of Jefferson's educational work seemed right up to date, it was easy to overlook certain antiquated features: the limitation for all but a chosen few of *free* public education to three years of grammar school, the absence of any compulsory principle, the decided emphasis on higher education, and the assumption throughout that the mass of people are not truly educable.

The canonization of Jefferson the Educator was closely tied in with the Southern "education revival" toward the end of the nineteenth century. The Southern reformers, aided by Northern philanthropy, made Jefferson a fixture of their agitation. If only Jefferson's educational ideas had prevailed, they said, the melancholy history of the South might have been different. Instead, these ideas, like Jefferson's abolition m, took root in the Northern states, while the South continued the aristocratic system of old England. It was time the prophet was honored in his own country.

The Jeffersonian tissues of the Southern campaign were perhaps best exposed in the writings of Charles W. Dabney, President of the University of Tennessee. In numerous tracts and addresses, and finally in a comprehensive history, *Universal Education in the South*, Dabney instilled the key idea:

The fact is, that Thomas Jefferson was the first conspicuous advocate in this country of free education in common schools supported by local taxation as well as of state aid to higher institutions of learning. To him the schoolhouse was the fountainhead of happiness, prosperity and good government, and education was the "holy cause" to which he devoted the best thought and efforts of his life.

Jefferson's success with the University of Virginia, Dabney thought, had magnified the importance given to higher education in his philosophy. He really believed the common school was much more important, because, as he said, it was "safer to have the whole people respectfully enlightened than a few in a high state of science and many in ignorance" as in Europe. The task of the New South was the same as in Jefferson's time—"educating all the people"—only made more urgent by universal suffrage and modern industry.

Jefferson the Seer was the title of Dabney's glowing tribute before the triumphant Southern Educational Conference, meeting at the University of Virginia in 1903. All the speakers, as he said, sooner or later came around to eulogies of Jefferson. Recalling Emerson's aphorism—"an institution is the lengthened shadow of one man"— Dabney concluded with this peroration: "The ever-lengthening shadow of that colossal figure, standing on yonder height to the east, watching the upbuilding of this institution, watching the growth of his beloved State, watching the expansion and development of this nation, enwraps us completely across the valley of fourscore years in the folds of its inspiring influence." The aphorism had been applied to the University before, but never with such dramatic effect.

The University of Virginia, just then entering upon its most prosperous period under President Edwin A. Alderman, was more alive to its heritage than at any time since it was founded. There had been a time when the friends of that institution might have wished some other founder than Jefferson, a time when a clergyman would have preferred following a young man to his grave than to see him enter "Mr. Jefferson's University." But as these feelings diminished, the University linked its name with Jefferson's in the Emersonian motto, in annual Founder's Day observances held on April 13, and in literature and monuments. Many a student, like David Culbreth, who entered the University in 1872 and forty years later lovingly set down his memories, daily exposed to the train of reminiscence and the congealed wizardly of brick and mortar, fell irresistibly under Jefferson's spell. "You cannot speak of Mr. Jefferson around Charlottesville without feeling that he is about to turn the nearest corner," President Alderman remarked. "It is a pungent form of immortality that now and then almost gives one a turn."

Jefferson's fame as a far-sighted planner of higher education spread out from the University of Virginia. His heroic labors in the founding of the University had been documented in the correspondence with his chief partner in this enterprise, Joseph C. Cabell, published in 1856. The first influential history of this "greatest project of his life," however, was the work of the Johns Hopkins scholar, Herbert Baxter Adams, in 1888. His *Thomas Jefferson and the University of Virginia* was timely, for several of Jefferson's innovations were then being adopted by major universities. The substitution of the elective system for a prescribed course of study, the dissolution of the ties between church and academy, the switch from a predominantly classical curriculum to one embracing technical and utilitarian branches, the liberalization of disciplinary codes, the development of specific studies, such as Anglo-Saxon and political science, for which Jefferson had prepared the way—these tendencies of the "new education" were traced back, in whole or in part, to Jefferson's plans for the University of Virginia. He was chiefly responsible, Adams pointed out, for "the idea of *centralization in the higher education*," which was at the heart of the educational system of the younger states; and also for the idea of "the importance of moral and political education under our American system of government," which was already a commonplace. As educators and laymen together discovered "Jefferson's University," they gained fresh impressions of the man and formed some extravagant opinions of his influence. The University, a Northern observer wrote in 1900, was America's first "democratic" and "first real university." The influence of his ideas on the University of Michigan, another said, had saved the West for democracy.

Jefferson's connection with the state university idea was especially significant in the South, where the universities were, like the common schools, waging an uphill fight for public support. In North Carolina the campaign was unusually bitter because of sectarian opposition spearheaded by Dr. John C. Kilgo, President of Trinity College, a Methodist institution which had the powerful backing of the Duke family, whose name it now bears. Against the public institutions, Kilgo raised the old specter of infidelity. He denounced Jefferson up and down the state as an atheistical monster and warned every Methodist son to stay away from the University of North Carolina. "He was a deist, an infidel, agnostic and materialist," Kilgo said in his *Study of Thomas Jefferson's Religious Belief*. Jefferson's long-range plan for the subversion of Christianity was revealed in the University of Virginia, "a bold enterprise and a deistic daring of enormous proportions." The counterattack of the churches, in the establishment of colleges of their own, had heretofore saved the nation from infidelity. But disaster threatened, Kilgo warned, in the recrudescence of secular instruction in state universities. Another North Carolinian, Francis Lister Hawks, had said much the same thing seventy years before, only now, in 1900, the anti-Jeffersonian stood at the portals of the academy instead of the church.

Kilgo's slanders on Jefferson made a hot campaign even hotter. Under the "educational governor," Charles B. Aycock, North Carolina's reformers won their battle. In no other instance did Jefferson become an effigy for the opposition. Critics of the "new education" often vaguely noted its Jeffersonian ancestry. But the overwhelming effect of the educational revival, nationally and in the South, was to enhance Jefferson's fame as the prolific genius of American institutions. More significant for his reputation at this time than any attack made upon him was the division in attitude of those who united in praising him.

The division arose from the twofold objective of Jefferson's system: universal schooling to produce a mass of good citizens and intensive cultivation of the select few for public leadership and the advancement of learning. Depending on how the emphasis was distributed between these goals, Jefferson's intention was understood as either entirely democratic or somewhat aristocratic. His "elimination system," under which only the best talents would be annually "raked from the rubble" and sent on to secondary and higher education at public expense, was often likened to the Darwinian idea of "survival of the fittest." But John Sharp Williams, the Mississippi congressman, reduced the whole of Jefferson's philosophy to equalitarianism. He seemed to think that universities were truly Jeffersonian when they threw their doors open to everyone and let the students proceed pell-mell. When the Father of Democracy attained new eminence as an educator the aristocratic features of his system tended to be blotted out, as they had before been blotted out of his politics. Not entirely, however. In the recurrent educational warfare of the next several decades between "progressives" and "humanists," Jefferson would normally be associated with the former (John Dewey, Horace Kallen), but the latter (Robert Maynard Hutchins, Albert Jay Nock) could argue that the democratic heresy had no basis in his philosophy of education.

Who Was Thomas Jefferson? the Virginia professor William M. Thornton asked in an acclaimed address of that title in 1909. It was a good question. Despite the approaches to intimacy with the human being that lay in the hero's shadow, men seemed no more able to agree on such elementary things as Jefferson's personal appearance, manners, and tastes than they had for so long been able to agree on his political opinions. Had Jefferson suddenly appeared in full human scale among them, who would have recognized him? Lincoln, certainly, would have been known to everyone by his physical presence. Washington perhaps not, though his dominant features were, at least, stereotyped in the mind. This was not true as to Jefferson.

What, for instance, did Jefferson look like? "He had huge hands and feet, red hair, a reddish skin, a freckled face, high cheek-bones and a projecting chin," Thornton said. "In youth ugly, at maturity he had acquired a pleasing person and in old age he became a handsome man." But some who observed Jefferson in old age, and notably Daniel Webster, whose description found much favor, gave an impression the opposite of handsome. A Virginia congressman in 1882 said that Jefferson, "from his red hair to his homespun socks and red waist-coat, was a democratic republican pure and simple"; but others said he was a fastidious person, "a man of the greatest refinement; graceful, striking and refined in appearance and manners." Hair was always a problem. Was it red—"red as a fox"—or sandy? Did it always have a "sandy tinge" or was it white as early as 1809? Had it ever been powdered and delicately rolled or tied in a queue? And were Jefferson's eyes blue-gray or hazel or green or just hopelessly nondescript? "Six feet two & a half inches high, well proportioned & straight as a gun-barrel," Edmund Bacon, his overseer, described his stature; and those who knew him best agreed. But the historian William E. Dodd wrote, "His gait was a kind of shamble . . . his right shoulder was somewhat ["decidedly," other said] higher than the left; he stooped slightly and seemed constantly to be engaged in thought." This agreed with the description by Senator Maclay in 1790, which Henry Adams made famous. Portraits were not much help. There was no "standard likeness." The portraits ranged from Trumbull's towering red-head of 1776 to Bass Otis's gray-haired old man. Moreover, there was a world of difference between the Trumbull and the dignified Mather Brown, though both were painted at the same time, as there was too between the Otis and its near contemporary by Thomas Sully. Given any portrait, Goldwin Smith thought, there was something enigmatic about Jefferson's combination of "a body large and strong, fitted for horsemanship and athletic exercize, with a face somewhat feminine not to say feline."

Jefferson was generally supposed to have had a warm and expressive countenance, one that, in Parton's words, "gave assurance of a gentle heart and a sympathetic, inquisitive mind." This was his great personal attraction, it was believed, to friends and strangers, young and old, gentry and commoners. Searchers after Jeffersonia around 1900 went to its fount, the Charlottesville neighborhood, where they heard many stories illustrating his sympathy and kindness. The son of a worker on the first University buildings recalled that when Jefferson was making his frequent trips on horseback to inspect the work in Charlottesville, he used to jump up behind, plunge his boy's hands into Jefferson's capacious pockets, and pull out apples and nuts, the two of them chatting all the while. Despite these endearing touches, the notion survived of a cold and forbidding Jefferson, utterly humorless, and completely lacking in his personal demeanor those qualities that made him, as philosopher and statesman, a friend of the people.

In his letters, account books, and other memoranda, Jefferson left ample records of his personal tastes and habits; yet, as with his public record, it was possible to draw from these almost any picture the writer wished. "No man is a hero to his valet." And in the case of Jefferson, Paul L. Ford thought, the minutiae of his papers served as well as a valet to reveal a figure the public had scarcely imagined. Ford's "Jefferson in Undress" had a full measure of human faults and vices: a gambler in youth, a fastidious dresser, a lavish spender beyond his income, a connoisseur of wines with a fabulous cellar. A sojourner in Albemarle heard and reported that Jefferson had been one of "the most notorious and unlucky gamblers of his day." Another heard from an old Negro woman, who had labored for a neighborhood planter, how Jefferson in his spry old age would come for a visit, romp with the children, pour out a stream of talk such as she had never heard, eat a hearty meal, and then draw out a foot-long cherry stem pipe and smoke it. Most of the sports and vices of the Virginia gentry of his day were ascribed to him in one place or another. His grandchildren denied everything, even the smoking. Their views, as Randall and Sarah Randolph had presented them, were more often heeded than not. "Through all the fourscore and three years of his life," Thornton declared, "no vulgar amour, no vinous debauch, no fever of the card table ever smirched the fair fame of Thomas Jefferson." This was the measure of Jefferson's moral superiority.

"Democratic simplicity," as a characterization of Jefferson's politics, had long shown a tendency to escape from that restricted field and to attach itself to Jefferson's person. The picturesque image of the trait was always Jefferson's riding horseback to his inauguration, hitching his horse to the paling, and walking unceremoniously into the Capitol. Actually, as the historian John Bach McMaster discovered from an eyewitness report of the inaugural ceremonies, Jefferson walked the short distance from his boarding house to the Capitol, accompanied by members of Congress and local citizens, while cannon boomed and militia paraded. McMaster's disclosure proved timely for the Democrats, who in 1885 gave Cleveland an inauguration that was anything but simple. Anticipating partisan jibes at this betrayal of "Jeffersonian simplicity," the *New York World* ran a front

page spread on the history of presidential inaugurals and refuted
the legend of 1801. Its rival, the *Tribune*, could scarcely believe its
eyes. An icon sacred to Democracy had fallen! When one of Jefferson's great-grandchildren, two years later, described Jefferson as a
"swell," the *Tribune's* editor exploded,

The Jefferson who has been known to the majority, the essential Jefferson,
the characteristic Jefferson, the plain, simple Jefferson who ate pie with a
knife, picked his teeth with a fork and had his dining-room decorated with
an unostentatious tidy bearing the legend, "Get economy, get parsimony,
and with all thy getting, get penuriousness"—that Jefferson has been
smashed to pieces like a potter's vessel.

Smashed or not, the legend of the plain and simple Jefferson continued in service, minus its grotesque parts. Democrats constantly
boasted the simplicity of their progenitor, except of course on the
rare occasions when they were inaugurating one of their own President. Jefferson's critics, like the Federalists of old, said that his
simplicity was ostentation, a demagogic mask put on after he returned from France and dropped as soon as he retired to Monticello.
Whether simplicity or elegance was his true personal style could
not be conclusively established. According to Sarah Randolph, Jefferson actually had a fancy coach in Washington at the time of his
inauguration. It only lacked the horses to draw it. Soon he ordered
from Virginia four full-blooded bays costing him sixteen hundred
dollars; yet he seldom used this gallant equipage, preferring to roam
the city and the countryside on horseback. In 1899, one of Hamilton's
champions in Congress, Henry S. Boutell of Illinois, called attention to Jefferson's letter of 1771 requesting that a search be made
in England for the family arms. "What a picture! The founder of
Democracy looking for his lost coat of arms." Unbelievable! John
Sharp Williams retorted. Jefferson was of "common Welsh stock"
and a lifelong enemy of aristocratic trappings. Whatever the reason
for this mingling of the elegant and the simple in his life, "the essential Jefferson" clearly embraced not one or the other set of traits but,
in some subtle way, both.

Who was Thomas Jefferson? Here was Thornton's answer to the
riddle:

He was a man in whose veins mingled the two strains of blood which united have in all ages given to humanity its prophets and its priests and its kings, the plebian red of Peter and the aristocratic blue of Jane; the progeny of manly force and womanly sweetness, of virile energy and feminine refinement. . . . He was a man trained in both the great gymnasia of modern civilization—the country and the town.

The idea that Jefferson, both by birth and early environment, was formed in the confluence of two great streams—patrician and plebeian —was such a convenient, and at the same time poetic, solution to the problems posed by the dualities of his character that it grew to become by 1900 a convention of Jefferson portraiture. Parton seems to have been the first significant interpreter to make Jefferson's dual heritage vivid to the imagination. Writing of Jefferson's parents— Jane, the daughter of the lordly Randolphs on the James River, and Peter, the commoner of the Virginia frontier—Parton turned them into symbols of "ancient culture and unlettered force." Jefferson was both "tuckahoe and cohee," a later writer said, borrowing the Indian words which even in Jefferson's Virginia had signified the lowlands and the uplands, the plantation and the frontier.

As the idea was unfolded, Jefferson could be reduced to some blend of a number of opposites: father-mother, power-love, frontier-culture, simplicity-elegance, utilitarian-humanist, horsemanship-scholarship, homespun rustic-cosmopolitan gentleman. The dominant tendency was to regard Peter an unlettered backwoodsman, Albemarle a primitive clearing overrun with Indians, and Jefferson "the child of the wilderness." He grew up a "mountaineer," Elbert Hubbard said in his fantastically popular *Little Journeys to the Homes of American Statesmen,* but upon the early death of his father, his mother and sisters cultivated in him "a gentle sense of chivalry," and then Williamsburg polished him into a gentleman. Communing with nature in his youth, Philip Bruce wrote, Jefferson drank in "the spirit of liberty which lurked in its wild recesses," whence he came to believe that natural rights took priority over the prescriptions of civilization. From his father, Bruce added, Jefferson inherited his stout physique and liberal politics; from his mother, his refined tastes. Raised to man's estate with two contrasting ideals of citizenship before him, Jefferson followed the democratic ideal; but its opposite always gripped his mind and emotions.

Of the several factors which contributed to the Western characterization of Jefferson at the turn of the century, the "frontier thesis" of Frederick Jackson Turner had particular significance. If, as Turner postulated, "American democracy came from the forest," Jefferson must have come from the same place. "Jefferson was the first prophet of American democracy, and when we analyze the essential features of his gospel, it is clear that the Western influence was the dominant element." All his leading principles, from agrarianism to abolitionism, Turner said, were "eminently characteristic of the Western democracy into which he was born." Turner's influence on American historiography is well known. It became fashionable to attribute Jefferson's early Virginia reforms, the Republican party of 1800, and the Louisiana Purchase to his affinities with the West. The idea that he was a "backwoods statesman" colored conceptions of his personality. Turner himself, along with many of his followers, denied that Jefferson was truly a "western man," however. "Thomas Jefferson was the John the Baptist of democracy, not its Moses." The Moses was Andrew Jackson. The first prophet, Jefferson was too cultivated, too theoretical, too much an eighteenth-century man to personify the West. In the main, the Turner school of historians kept the sense of Jefferson's ambivalent or partial relationship to American character and democratic development, as these were reinterpreted on the "frontier thesis."

The "tuckahoe-cohee" convention was a way of making sense of Jefferson in terms thoroughly familiar to the American imagination. It was a simple device for explaining apparent incongruities in the man, but of course its effect was also to heighten these incongruities. Their origin was explained, in the vernacular at least, but they were not resolved. Allen Tate's beguiling poem, "On the Father of Liberty," in 1930, evoked once again the irresoluble riddle and gave it a capricious twist:

> Jefferson had many charms;
> Was democratic; still—and yet
> What should one do? The family arms
> On coach and spoon he wisely set

> Against historical alarms:
> For quality not being loath,
> Nor quantity, nor the fame of both.

Jefferson's *was* the fame of both. The convention, fairly started by
Parton and developed at a time when Jefferson's domestic life came
into view, was waning by 1930. But the riddles it was intended to
answer remained, and new ones equally puzzling caused it to be
revived in somewhat different terms.[*]

2. Touch the Bones of Jefferson

The cords of political memory, savagely cut by the Civil War,
were sewn painfully together again in the last quarter of the century.
An English observer in 1912 was "struck by the persistence of old
issues, old ways of looking at things, old shibboleths, in an age
newest of the new." There was something siren-like about American
political history that lured men and events out of time and context.
The lure of the past, the sorcery of heroic names and doctrines, was
especially marked in the Democratic party. As the party of long
memory renewed its strength on the national scene, it again took up
the Jefferson fetish. Let the crippled party "but touch the dead bones

---

[*] It is perhaps fortunate that the later fashion of psychological biography
never caught up with Jefferson. Yet this is surprising in view of the dual-heritage
profile, with its suggestions of a schizoid personality. Harry Elmer Barnes, an
early champion of Freudian interpretation in historical writing, indicated what
might be done with Jefferson as a case in the nineteen-twenties. In a paper read
before the New Jersey Psychiatric Society and published in *The Psychoanalytic
Review*, Barnes diagnosed Jefferson as an introvert with an anti-authority complex. His father was "a gruff giant with a tremendous temper," the worst pioneer
type, from whom Thomas, "a slight and pallid youth," recoiled in horror. Since
his father died when the son was fourteen, he never had the chance to bring
the father-image to the adult level. Brought up by his exceedingly feminine
mother and sisters, he retained the child's hatred of authority and acquired an
inordinate passion for love, combined with feelings of inferiority in the manly
encounters of the real world. And so, Barnes said, Jefferson's passionate attack
on rulers of every description was a "psychic release" from his subconscious
hatred of his father; his "living generation" theory was a symbolic escape from
reality; Jeffersonian Democracy was "an elaborate disguise and secondary
rationalization of his innate revolt against authority." Barnes presented Hamilton
as just the opposite case.

The *New York Times* accurately described Barnes's arm-chair analysis as
"half-baked." It had no discernible influence on later interpreters of Jefferson.

of its prophet Jefferson" and, like the man let down into the sepulcher to touch the bones of Elisha, it would stand upon its feet! The Republican sepulcher, if indeed one existed, had no such power over the party faithful. Even as Jefferson grew to become a hero of American culture, he remained in the minds of many the hero of a party, the historical symbol of a political creed.

The Civil War did not fundamentally alter the ideology of the Democratic party. Such leaders as the party had in the Reconstruction era, Horace Seymour and Samuel Tilden of New York primarily, preached the return to Jeffersonian principles. An extensive survey of the party literature nevertheless makes clear that Jefferson did not again attain a prominent place in the party's armory of rhetoric and symbol until the eighteen-eighties. The national platform of 1880 pledged the party to the doctrines and traditions of "a long line of Democratic statesmen and patriots," and as the decade advanced the standard lexicon of Jeffersonian and Hamiltonian returned to common usage. Then, in 1892, the platform reaffirmed for the first time in more than a generation Democratic "allegiance to the principles of the party as formulated by Jefferson." The phantom of Jefferson reappears in the party counsels, James G. Blaine warned, and Democrats "seize every occasion to assure that modern Democracy was founded by Jefferson at the beginning of the century, and that all the defeats they have since received are mere interruptions of the century's flow of Jeffersonian principles, which they are especially deputed to uphold."

The chief agency in this development seems to have been the National Association of Democratic Clubs, formed in 1888 after several years mushrooming growth of local societies of young Democrats. The constitution of the federated organization stated as its first object the dissemination of Jeffersonian principles of government. President Chauncey F. Black sought, through the Association, first, to heal factional divisions by gathering all Democrats under "the name and authority of Jefferson," and second, to separate truth from error by the submission of all current questions to "the infallible touchstone of the Jeffersonian test." Needing a Jeffersonian ancestry for the clubs themselves, Black recalled the Democratic Clubs of 1793, sometimes said to have been the nucleus of the party Jefferson organized. Ideally, Black thought, the clubs would function as surrogates of Jefferson:

Every proposition of whatever kind would be instantly brought to the decisive test of the Jeffersonian touchstone. The writings of that matchless sage would lie open upon the desk of every Democratic Society as the very scripture of Democratic faith. That which agreed with the Scripture would be received, and that which disagreed would be rejected as the device of the evil one. There is no other standard of authority to which all Democrats accede; no other which can be invoked as beyond dispute.

An infallible Jeffersonian thinking machine would apparently solve any and every problem.

The mission of the National Association was, at best, but partially fulfilled. Some of the local clubs, however, became awesome political powers in their own right, as well as important agents of Jefferson's reputation. For instance, The Jefferson Club of St. Louis, which billed itself "the most consistently Jeffersonian association" in the country, rose under the leadership of Henry B. Hawes to take control of the city's Democratic party and then, in 1901, of its government. Claiming a membership of six thousand, counting among its leaders Senator George G. Vest and the reform attorney Joseph W. Folk, the Club installed Jefferson's bust in its headquarters building, started the first of many movements to erect a fitting monument to Jefferson in St. Louis, and in the year of its great triumph performed a dramatic pilgrimage to Monticello. There two hundred and fifty persons, brought by special train nearly nine hundred miles, remained for three days, and dedicated a monument in commemoration of the Louisiana Purchase.

Republican reactions to the fresh stirrings of Jefferson's ghost in the opposition ranks ranged from boredom to indignation, from ridicule of Democratic pretensions to denunciation of Jefferson. Lacking an ancient forefather of their own, the Republicans could not decide whether to drape themselves in Jefferson's mantle or to drag it through the mud. The former course was in line with the "history of the parties" enunciated in Republican ideology before the War; the latter was a response to the more recent Hamiltonian enthusiasm. Not long ago, the *New York Tribune* scoffed in 1882, Tammany Hall was "about the only organization in the country that made a specialty of the Jefferson business," but now "Jefferson Clubs have sprung up all over the country, and the alleged 'birthday of Jefferson' has been spread, like the vernal equinox, all over the early spring." Some Republican organizations countered with anti-Jefferson Day addresses that denounced the "American Robespierre" and railed at the so-called "Jeffersonian principles" which seemed to answer for the Democratic party "the varied purposes of a pillar of cloud by day, a gauge, a confession of faith, a flank movement, a base of supplies, and a haven of refuge."

From its faint beginnings around 1880, the Democratic revival of Jefferson rolled to a climax in 1900, leaving the record of its progress in campaign buttons and banners and medallions, in party magazines, in pilgrimages to Monticello, even in verse and song. The National Association of Democratic Clubs sponsored a great Monticello celebration on April 13, 1896. One year later it held the first of the modern national Jefferson Day Dinners in Washington, on exactly the same spot as the ill-fated affair of 1830. Responding to the toast "Thomas Jefferson," William Jennings Bryan made one of his many silver-throated declarations of faith. After a long round of toasts and speeches, the assembled throng sang a new hymn, "The Jeffersonian Banner":

> Mid the crash of revolution and the wreck of constitutions
> We have borne that banner bravely in the van,
> As the symbol of the nation
> And the grand old Declaration
> And the Universal Brotherhood of Man

And so on for several more stanzas and chorus.

The spectacle of this party worship at the shrine of Saint Thomas was enough to sicken some of Jefferson's political admirers. A man could be smothered in too much praise. Indiana Senator Voorhees's Lyceum masterpiece on Jefferson (from which the quotation at the head of this chapter is taken) was a fair specimen of the dizzy heights scaled by Democratic oratory. The question was insistently raised whether "touching the bones of Jefferson" did not imply a treacherous mental servility to the wisdom of a bygone era. "We

have become a nation of hero-worshippers," one Jeffersonian announced in disgust. The "Jeffersonian touchstone" might clarify,
unite, arouse, of course; but it might also muddle the understanding
of actual problems. And its authenticity could never be taken for
granted. "There have been more crimes committed in the name
of Thomas Jefferson than there have been in the name of liberty."
Into the Senate chamber, it was observed, Jefferson was regularly
"trotted out . . . like a trick mule at a circus and made to perform
all kinds of tricks for the entertainment of those present." Although
the entertainment or fun value of "the Jefferson business" must not
be discounted, it had other, more serious, values as well. Perhaps,
as Woodrow Wilson later said of the party's long climb back into
public favor, not many Democrats knew much about the legendary
founder. Nevertheless, "they swore by the name and conjured with
the name of Thomas Jefferson" in the conviction "that he had something that would knock those fellows [the Republicans] out if the
people of the United States only believed it."

The style was set by a class of Democrats, code-Jeffersonians, who
retained the traditional ethos of the party in relatively pure form
and believed that Jefferson, like the Messiah, would rise again. Jefferson was the Christ of American government; they were his latter-day
apostles. The mildest jest at Jefferson they regarded as blasphemous;
the gentlest criticism they took as a personal insult. There were only
two ways in American politics: Jeffersonian and Hamiltonian. Although they knew that 1900 was not 1800, between their minds and
the realities hung the captivating veil of "Jeffersonian principles."
They shared a fundamentalist habit of mind, though differing somewhat among themselves on the application of the fundamentals. In
general, however, the code was "the sum of good government" Jefferson had described in the First Inaugural.*

---

* The poet Edgar Lee Masters, who was one of them, recaptured the spirit
decades later in his "Jefferson."

> By commerce and corruption still maligned,
> By steel and ship of every slander fouled
> He shines aloft no less, magnanimous souled,
> A fixed star of the mind.

In an age that felt the Darwinian shock to all the natural pieties, the Jeffersonians still derived government from the Creator's laws and still believed in natural rights. In an age marked by tremendous industrial and urban concentration, they kept the vision of a simple society, predominantly agrarian, individualized, decentralized, free-moving, and free-trading. Against the evidence that popular sovereignty had ended in the rule of the political machine, they advocated more popular sovereignty. Against the evidence that individualism had ended in the tyranny of the corporation, they advocated the return to individualism. Consent of the governed, equal rights, state rights, strict construction—novel and varied interpretations might be given to these principles but they formed a circle around the code-Jeffersonians from which any escape to the realities beyond was fraught with peril.

Who were the exemplars of this political style toward the end of the nineteenth century? Nearly all were Southerners and Westerners. The North Carolina editor, Josephus Daniels, was one. Old-fashioned in his morals and dress as in his politics, Daniels truly believed Jefferson was "the foremost man the world has ever known." When you die, his wife would say to him, "you will not want to go to Abraham's bosom as do most of the faithful, but you will ask St. Peter to take you to Jefferson's wisdom." In times of high political excitement, it was always Jefferson Day on Daniels's *Raleigh News and Observer*. There would be, perhaps, an editorial series ("Jefferson Said"), historical vignettes on the man and his times, comparisons of the current hero of Democracy, whether Bryan or Wilson or Franklin Roosevelt—Daniels served and loved them all—to the Sage of Monticello. "There can arise no problem of government," Daniels wrote in 1899, "that cannot be solved wisely by an appeal to Jeffer-

---

All our woe has come from disregard
Of what he taught: the city's poverty,
The loss of honor and state sovereignty,
And freedom, battle scarred.

He would have kept America on the land
Free of the levies of scheming privilege,
The Hercules that wrecks his sacrilege
On Earth's son with a strangling hand.

son." Himself a monument to Jefferson, it was peculiarly fitting that his last public appointment, from President Roosevelt in 1944, was to the Thomas Jefferson Memorial Commission.

Missouri Senator George G. Vest and Representative John Sharp Williams of Mississippi spirited Jefferson's awful majesty over the two houses of Congress. There is nothing to remember Vest by now except his county court *Eulogy on the Dog*. But in his day he was a dreaded foe of the Republicans and a mighty orator. His oration on Jefferson (one of several) at the University of Missouri in 1885 was greatly admired by the faithful. (Franklin D. Roosevelt had a copy in his personal library.) Daniels called Vest "the truest disciple of Jefferson living." The protective tariff was his special enemy. The present parties began, he said, when Hamilton submitted his *Report on Manufactures* in 1791, and Jefferson opposed it. Vest conscientiously tried to govern by Jefferson's code. When, for example, a bill to regulate futures trading in grain under the authority of the tax power was before the Senate in 1892, he confessed that as a Jeffersonian friend of the farmer he had searched for some principle on which he could support the bill. In vain. It was the very same kind of proposal that had led Jefferson to found the Democratic party. "It proposes, under the fraudulent pretext of collecting revenue, to police every State in the Union." He would rather go into every township of Missouri to defend his vote than go on the record for a Hamiltonian measure.

Vest's career as a Jeffersonian bulldog was drawing to a close when Williams was beginning his. The Mississippian's outbursts against the "slanders" still visited upon his hero must have been something to behold. "Oh, this hatred, this old federalistic relic of hatred of Thomas Jefferson would be pathetic if it were not amusing!" A planter-statesman nourished in the traditions of the Old South, educated at the University of Virginia, Williams fancied himself the Democratic party's historical authority on Jefferson. He was generally so recognized in Congress. At a time when most of the scholars-in-politics, like Henry Cabot Lodge and Albert J. Beveridge, were strongly Hamiltonian, Williams was the best the Jeffersonians could show. In 1912 he delivered a series of lectures at Columbia

University, later published as *Thomas Jefferson, His Permanent Influence on American Institutions*. This rambling commentary on a few major phases of Jefferson's public career was chiefly interesting for the pointed answers it gave to the Federalist historians. Williams combatted the prevalent idea that Jefferson's permanent influence was an abstract faith in the people, whereas Hamilton's was in the actual institutions of government. The "system of neutrality" in foreign affairs, local self-government, "Jeffersonian simplicity" in the federal administration, religious freedom, public education—these were a few of the constructive and permanent influences which furnished Jefferson's modern disciples with more than a vague spirit to guide their footsteps. Williams retired to his Cedar Grove plantation in 1921. Sitting in a rocking chair on the porch of his family's ante-bellum house, he mused about Jefferson and damned the Hamiltonian restoration for several years more.

While Vest and Williams were party men first, last, and always, other Democrats who took their politics from Monticello went into the Populist party in the eighteen-nineties. Jeffersonianism was for them, as for the others, a yardstick for viable political remedies, but they emphasized particularly the radical and agrarian side of the tradition. They were leading the embattled farmers in the third great revolt against the plutocracy. The lanky Texas spellbinder, James H. "Cyclone" Davis, stumped for the Populists from Oregon to North Carolina with the works of Jefferson locked under his arms. "On this question," Davis would say, "let us turn to vol. 3, page 103, Jefferson's works, and read what he says, viz: 'The question whether one generation of men has a right to bind another . . .'" Expounding Jefferson in this way, drawing from his works all the Populist answers to the new plutocracy, from government ownership of railroads to free silver, Davis wrote and spoke like a rural Moses of the faith:

Let us now bow in adoration of the sainted sire of American liberty, pull off our shoes while we tread the holy ground around the sods where he lies in the caverns of the dead, or with the hand of faith pull away the mystic curtains, that swing twixt us and the spirit land, or on the winged winds let us waft a message to Mr. Jefferson and tell him that there is another hereditary high-handed aristocracy in our land.

The pathological possibilities of this political style were revealed
in the career of the Populist leader, Tom Watson of Georgia. Disillusioned with the Democratic party, Watson labored mightily to
restore the intersectional agrarian alliance of Jefferson and Jackson
in the Populist party. Through it he hoped to mobilize the federal
government against the privileged money class, which was, in his
view, choking the farmers to death. But the Populist fusion with the
Democrats, followed by Bryan's disastrous defeat in 1896, wrecked
Watson's hopes. He retired to his Hickory Hill plantation, wrote
(among other books) a desultory biography of Jefferson which
debunked the Federalist historians and exhibited Jefferson as a
Southern prophet of his own gloom, and through his magazine, *The
Jeffersonian,* transmuted his class hatred into sectional and racial
hatred of the most vicious sort. He was brought to this pathetic
end—the John Randolph of this century—in part because of the
impoverishment of old Jeffersonian solutions in the industrial age.

Henry George, the Single Tax philosopher and reformer, furnishes
still another projection of the Jeffersonian political mind. George
was firmly planted in Jeffersonianism. He entered California politics
in 1869 as a Democratic candidate for the Assembly; he died in 1897
while leading the Bryan Democracy of New York City under the
banner "The Party of Thomas Jefferson" in a mayoralty campaign.
George's social philosophy could only have arisen in a mental climate suffused with Jeffersonian principles and ideals. He received,
more or less via Herbert Spencer, Jefferson's faith in the beneficent
natural order, his belief in natural economic abundance and in equal
access to natural resources, and his firm distrust of concentrated
power, economic and political. George and the Single Taxers, who
often celebrated Jefferson's birthday and constantly spread his word,
had several favorite Jeffersonian texts: the praises of husbandry, the
idea that "the earth belongs in usufruct to the living," and the advice
that in societies where great inequality of property has become the
rule legislators "cannot invent too many devices for subdividing
landholdings."

George regarded Jefferson as a radical who had "allied himself
absolutely, unreservedly, actively, permanently with the wronged
masses." The problem of his age had been political freedom and

equality. He had been able to assume social equality as a virtual guarantee of American nature. Now, George argued, Jefferson's political axiom must be logically extended into the economic axiom: "that men have equal rights to natural opportunities, to land." The Single Tax was "the Jeffersonian solution." Holding that under modern conditions of life the realization of the Jeffersonian dream logically involved "the dream of socialism" as well, George's philosophy opened new vistas to traditional Jeffersonian aspirations.

Perhaps no American political leader ever loved Jefferson more or cherished his memory more dutifully than William Jennings Bryan. Certainly none since Bryan has worked more consciously under the regimen of Jeffersonian ideas. He often said that all he knew of the science of government he had learned from Jefferson. In the library of his simple Nebraska home, he looked up from his desk to a big portrait of Jefferson, flanked by smaller portraits of Washington and Lincoln. His favorite reading, according to his wife, was in the works of Demosthenes and Jefferson; add the Bible, which was surely preferred reading too, and Bryan's approach to politics, along with the ambit of his mind, is fairly well defined. Intellectually, he was nearly Jefferson's opposite. Bryan, however, regarded Jefferson not from an intellectual but from an essentially religious standpoint. "Greater than his intellect was his love for all mankind." The people loved Jefferson because, like the Christian Savior, he first loved them. The "Boy Orator's" most eloquent tribute to Jefferson was first voiced before the Jefferson Club of Lincoln in 1895:

Alexander "wept for other worlds to conquer" after he had carried his victorious banner throughout the then known world; Napoleon "rearranged the map of Europe with his sword" amid the lamentations of those by whose blood he was exalted; but when these and other military heroes are forgotten and their achievements disappear in the cycle's sweep of years, children will still lisp the name of Jefferson, and freemen will ascribe due praise to him who filled the kneeling subject's heart with hope and bade him stand erect—a sovereign among his peers.

Progress, Bryan believed, "is measured not so much by the discovery of new principles as by the more perfect assimilation of old principles." The articles of the creed were fully stated in the First

Inaugural Address. Bryan devoted whole speeches to expounding it line by line. Let the government return to the "comprehensive rule," "equal rights for all, special privileges for none," and the mass of farmers, workers, and small propertied men would rise to their feet. Calling the Democracy to pursue "Jeffersonian principles with Jacksonian courage," Bryan's radicalism lay more in the Jacksonian political temper and tactics than in the policies and the principles. Except in the East, the Democracy responded. Bryan was hailed as "Democracy incarnate," "the Jefferson of today," "the embodied spirit of Jefferson." Josephus Daniels fondly remembered Virginia Senator John W. Daniel's introduction of Bryan at Richmond during the 1896 campaign. The platform was the balcony of the Jefferson Hotel, and as the light fell upon a marble statue of Jefferson in the interior rotunda, Daniel said he felt the statue come to life to speak through the Nebraskan.

No public figure did more to revitalize the statue than Bryan. This was one of the missions of his life. He loved the Sage of Monticello as well as the Father of the Democracy, and was the first person of prominence to urge the claim of the American people to Jefferson's home. The superintendent of Monticello well remembered Bryan's last pilgrimage there just before he went off to Dayton, Tennessee, to defend the old-time religion of simple country folk against the revelations of the intellect Jefferson had helped to make free. " 'To my mind,' Bryan said on parting, 'Thomas Jefferson was the greatest statesman our country produced—then or since.' Then he rose and went to the edge of the lawn and looked out over the valley and down at Jefferson's birthplace, and in the twilight went away. In two months he was dead." He was the last Jeffersonian.

Democrats accustomed "to measure all systems, to try all causes, to determine all policies, by the rules laid down in Jefferson's philosophy" met with the usual difficulties. The philosophy had never been codified. It evoked a familiar picture of American government. It was a fixed standard of judgment on the ruling order. It built up Democratic morale. But it was not a rigid code. The rules were often ambiguous and were made increasingly so by the altered social framework to which they had to be referred.

On such questions as the tariff Democrats achieved a fair degree of unity, thereby helping to maintain the illusion of Jeffersonian regularity. Other questions sharply fractured that illusion by forcing choices between conflicting Jeffersonian values. An instance was the much debated proposal for federal aid to public schools, with the proviso barring aid to those states whose schools discriminated on account of color. "An act to erect a monument to the memory of Alexander Hamilton, and to encourage mendicancy in the Southern States," Vest vociferated in 1888. If so, a Florida Senator replied, "the first stone in that monument was placed by the hands of Thomas Jefferson." For, leaving the Negro question aside, Jefferson had repeatedly declared the advancement of education to be a national interest, and in 1806 had recommended appropriations for this purpose. He had thought a constitutional amendment necessary; but times had changed. Was the enterprise that lay nearest Jefferson's heart to be neglected by the federal government when lesser measures of public improvement, such as rivers and harbors bills, were freely passed, often with the votes of self-appointed guardians of the faith? Why, Republicans exasperated, "a stranger to our institutions would conclude that our Constitution was framed for the express purpose of perpetuating the woes of mankind."

The obvious need for civil service reform brought into collision the precepts of "Jeffersonian simplicity," from which the Jacksonians had constructed the spoils system, and the rigorous standards of official appointment enunciated by Jefferson. The Federalist critics, it will be recalled, had generally placed the odium of the spoils system on Jefferson's head. John T. Morse, in 1883, handsomely retracted the charge and praised Jefferson for his "painstaking conscientiousness" in patronage matters. The liberal leaders of the reform cause, though their background was anything but Jeffersonian, tended to agree with James Parton in tracing the practice to the Burrite politicians in New York, whence it came to the Albany Regency, and finally to the Jackson administration. Jefferson, they said, introduced the partisan theory of public office, though for reasons of expediency, not the practice; and so, according to George W. Curtis, "when Jackson came in the spoils carnival was simply the bursting of the gates from which Jefferson had drawn the bolts, and which he held by main force." Some Democrats paraded Jefferson as the original civil service reformer, the true precursor of Grover Cleveland. (His sentiments on public office as a public trust were among the first "Jeffersonisms" to be included in Bartlett's *Familiar Quotations*.) Other Democrats, however, and Republicans too, who did not welcome the loss of patronage power, described Jefferson's policy as a "guillotine," "radical and revolutionary," "a clean sweep," and so on.

The blurred and refracted light Democrats got from Jefferson was further illustrated in the currency and banking controversy which gripped national politics between 1893 and 1898. The issue between hard and soft money, between private note issue and government issue, had been building up ever since "the crime of 1873," when the federal government demonetized silver and made gold the single monetary standard. Monetary expansionists, from the greenbackers to the free-silverites, repeatedly quoted from a series of letters (actually a small treatise on money and banking) Jefferson had written in 1813 to his son-in-law, John W. Eppes, then Chairman of the Finance Committee in Congress. Jefferson called for the suppression of private note circulation by state-chartered banks and, in its place, the emission of Treasury bills under the authority of Congress on a specific tax appropriated for their redemption. This would, he said, restore control over the circulating medium "to the nation, to whom it belongs," and the bills would "take the place of so much gold and silver." The letters not only put Jefferson in opposition to the present national bank system, expansionists said, but also put him on the side of government-issued currency irredeemable in coin.

Actually, as Garfield and other "hard money" men pointed out on numerous occasions, Jefferson's letters, whatever their purport as to banks, were a powerful indictment of paper money, which he seemed willing to risk in the wartime emergency *provided* specie was speedily restored. Jefferson's authority proved just as slippery for the bimetallists. Although there was some basis for tying Jefferson to the "dollar of the daddies"—the silver dollar and bimetallic coinage— he had demonetized the silver dollar in 1806, and he had always supposed that the coinage ratio must be determined by prices in the world market. Of the three major financial proposals of the Bryan

Democracy in 1896—suppression of private bank issue in favor of government control of the circulating medium, regular government issue of paper money as legal tender, free coinage of silver at the legally fixed ratio of 16 to 1—only the first had clear warrant in the Eppes letters, though not in anything Jefferson ever did as President.

The currency controversy ripped wide the sectional seams of the Democratic party, and fully exposed for the first time the profound internal conflict on the meaning of Jefferson. Caught between old principles and new exigencies, Democrats came to interpret their tradition in two sharply contrasted ways. The radical way, identified with Bryan, the West, and silver, emphasized the populistic and equalitarian side of Jefferson's thought. The conservative way, identified with Cleveland, the East, and gold, emphasized the individualistic and libertarian side. Both were traditionalist. Both pretended to "unlock the future's portal with the past's blood-rusted key." Both preached endlessly against tariff, monopoly, and centralization. Yet Jeffersonian principles that were armed by Bryan's "Jacksonian courage" and Jeffersonian principles that were linked to Cleveland's "safe and sane Democracy" were not really the same.

It made some difference whether Jefferson's democracy was conceived as "a code of restraints upon sovereignty . . . a system of limitations upon public power" or, on the other hand, as a system designed "not so much to restrain the popular will as to *express* it, not to obstruct, but to *execute* it." From the conservative viewpoint, Jefferson was "the chief exponent of the individualism of our republic, as opposed to centralism and statism." "He would probably now agree with Herbert Spencer." From the radical viewpoint, Jefferson's enduring greatness lay in his belief in the collective wisdom of the people. Strict construction, state rights, least governmentism—all the repressive and negative features of the code—these, it was said,

were not the causes of that great attachment to his name and memory . . . but it was his sympathy with popular rights, with free government, his profound conviction that all civil power should be so created and so exercized that the interest and happiness of the great mass of the people would be secured and provided for; it was this sympathy with humanity that gave, and still gives, to his name its prestige, and draws to it the affections of the oppressed people of the world.

Democrats who were thus early drawn, in response to imperative
public needs, to emphasize the spirit over the form of Jefferson's
teachings pointed toward the radical revision of Jeffersonian symbol
and tradition under Franklin D. Roosevelt.

To use the terms *radical* and *conservative* to characterize the two
versions of tradition in the Democratic party may suggest a sharper
ideological conflict than was actually present. Antipathy to government and government by the people were, fundamentally, always the
polar points in the Jeffersonian field. A conscientious Jeffersonian
was drawn to one without ever escaping the other. The conflict was
within Democrats as well as between them. Bryan, for instance,
advocated government ownership of the railroads because no private monopoly was defensible; but his Jeffersonian fears of centralization led him to the utterly impractical "dual plan," wherein the
trunk lines would be nationalized and local option would prevail
as to the intrastate lines. The exigencies of party unity and time's
blurring effect on Jefferson's principles further moderated the Democratic split. Nevertheless, an aura of radicalism, of class politics,
demagoguery, and socialism, hung over Bryan, just as the stigma of
Wall Street clung to Cleveland.

The attempt, observed the *New York Post* in 1905, "to make Jefferson at once the great individualist and the great socialist is pretty
clear evidence of the hesitation in which the Democratic party finds
itself." From a Republican point of view, the two Democracies were
"an opposition of straw" and "an opposition of blood and bone."
"Conservative Democracy" was a paradox, another Republican voice
declared. "Jefferson's state rights and weak government doctrines
were the mere creatures of circumstance. His social philosophy took
that practical form at the moment, but as the champion of the common people under different conditions he would now practically
apply it in the direction of national control of railroads and the
populistic program in general." Not many Jeffersonians had arrived
at this conception. Yet it was the sense of harmony between "the
radicalism of 1800 and the radicalism of 1900" that tied Jefferson
to men like Bryan, Watson, and George.

The Jefferson Birthday Dinners were often striking testimonials
to the "hesitation in which the Democratic party finds itself." Illinois's

radical Governor, John P. Altgeld, declined an invitation to address
the birthday dinner of Chicago's conservative Iroquois Club in 1895,
because he believed its real purpose was to celebrate Grover Cleveland. "To laud Clevelandism on Jefferson's birthday is to sing a
Te Deum in honor of Judas Iscariot on a Christmas morning." Jefferson was trapped in "the battle of the standards" when gold and silver
Democrats alike lauded him at the Monticello celebration of 1896.
Bryan's indignant refusal to join with New York's gold forces in a
rally of all the party faithful under Jefferson's battered banner in
1899 caused a commotion that split the Democratic celebrants of
the metropolis half a dozen ways. Bryan himself went east to address
two of the "one dollar a plate" Jeffersonian dinners that had been
arranged in answer to the gilt-edged banquet of the Wall Street-
Tammany Hall coalition at the Metropolitan Opera House. Three
thousand were reported at one of the dinners, where "Jeffersonian
simplicity" reigned all the way down to granite-ware coffee pots and
bunches of celery as table decor.

When Jefferson was parcelled out among so many different types
of Democrats (as well as non-Democrats), "the Jeffersonian touchstone" seemed no more than a rhetorical device, Jefferson's message
to the present was shrouded in deeper doubt than ever, and the idea
of a partisan Jefferson became patently absurd. But the Democrats
were undaunted. The tradition served them either as a brake or a
goad, and usually as both at once. The logic of the situation seemed
to call for those who were most critical of the present order to be
the least given to Jefferson conjuration and the least inclined toward
the ancestral code. Just the opposite tended to be the case. They
were radical not because of the novelty of their ideas but because,
like the Jacksonians before them, they revitalized a tradition that
still had a somewhat Jacobinical character. Reimposing the Jefferson-
Hamilton conflict, they approached the struggles of their own time
with the same feeling that the things they fought for were fundamental. Subsuming the problems of 1900 under the political categories of 1800, they could not succeed. But they could, with the
Jeffersonian principles, erect defenses against imperious Hamiltonian
forces.

3. Republic or Empire

The United States went to war in 1898 on the declared principle that the Cuban people "are and of right ought to be free and independent." The Spanish-American War, its purpose thus restricted to wiping out one of the last vestiges of European colonialism in the Western Hemisphere, resulted in an American protectorate over Cuba, and acquisition of Puerto Rico, Guam, and the Philippines. The nation's fundamental principles were again called up for debate. Bryan, upon leaving his command in the liberation army, warned his countrymen that they were in greater danger, from the prospect of abandoning these principles, than the people whose oppression they had just lifted. A nation, he said recalling Lincoln, "cannot endure half republic and half colony." "We may believe that governments come up from the people or we may believe that governments come down to the people from those who possess the heaviest cannons and the largest ships, but we cannot advocate both doctrines." The great debate reached its peak in the campaign of 1900 and then reverberated down the years.

Jefferson's name figured prominently in the debate, for the Declaration of Independence and the Louisiana Purchase were the historic symbols of the two lines of policy, self-government and imperial expansion, drawn up on opposite sides. "The mighty figure of Thomas Jefferson comes down in history with the Declaration of Independence in one hand, and the title deed of Louisiana in the other," George F. Hoar declared, adding the cogent question, "Do you think his left hand knew not what his right hand did?" Here was the old dilemma of word and deed mounted on an issue of principle as inescapable as any since the slavery crisis.

The issue was clearly drawn by Senator Vest on his resolution introduced in December 1898, simultaneous with the signing of the treaty with Spain but before its ratification by the Senate. Disavowing the power of the United States to acquire and govern colonies, the Vest resolution stipulated that any territory "must be acquired and governed with the purpose of ultimately organizing such territory into States suitable for admission into the Union." (Later anti-imperialist resolutions affirmed this position, sometimes with the explicit injunctions of freedom and self-government stated in the Declaration.) The idea that the United States could "govern millions, without their consent, as mere chattels," Vest said, was the essence of the European system thrown off by the Declaration. Nor did it have any support in the most authoritative expositions of the Constitution, or in any act of government for the territories from the Northwest Ordinance to the present. Colonialism, Vest argued, assails "the basis of all republican institutions, that governments derive their just powers from the consent of the governed."

Vest was answered, for the administration, by Senator Platt of Connecticut. Voicing the extreme nationalist ideas brought to maturity in the aftermath of civil conflict, Platt urged that the nation's— any nation's—right to acquire and govern territory was an inherent and essential attribute of its nationality. Senator Hoar had a question: Did governments, in Platt's opinion, derive their just powers from the consent of the governed? "From the consent of some of the governed," he was answered. The question had been definitely settled in America by Jefferson's acquisition and government of the Louisiana Territory, Platt said. The Massachusetts Senator was shocked. After thirty years of loyal service to the Republican party, he broke with the administration, became the acknowledged leader of the anti-imperialists and a keen admirer of Jefferson. Jefferson, Hoar told the Thomas Jefferson Memorial Association in 1903, "stands in human history as the foremost man who ever lived, whose influence has led men to govern themselves in the conduct of States by spiritual laws." America must, lest her moral fiber weaken, remain true to Jefferson's faith, as the world must in due time come around to it. The imperial adventure inaugurated a revolution in the nation's fundamental law. "We have had so far some fundamental doctrine, some ideals to which the people have been devoted. Have you anything to give us in their place?" Hoar asked his antagonists. "You are trying to knock out the corner-stones." Jefferson was an expansionist, Hoar conceded, but an expansionist of freedom, not of empire. "I ask you," the old Senator pleaded with the young apostles of the New Evangel, "to keep in the old channels, and to keep off the old rocks laid down in the old charts, and to follow the old sailing orders that all the old captains of other days have obeyed, to take your bearings, as of old . . . and not from this meteoric light of empire."

Quite aside from the leading principle—consent of the governed—the common conception of Jefferson gave little support to the imperialists. He stood, it was generally thought, for an aloof, pacific, and humanitarian policy in world affairs. War, he had denounced "the greatest of human evils." Pacifists praised his name, and internationalists found the key to his statesmanship in Henry Adams's felicitous sentence: "Jefferson aspired beyond the ambition of a nationality and embraced in his view the whole future of man." "Peace, commerce, and honest friendship with all nations—entangling alliances with none" was the American standard raised in the First Inaugural, from which the invasion of the Orient could only be judged a "great aberration."

But there stood Jefferson, the title deed to Louisiana in his hand! Jefferson bought Louisiana from Napoleon believing the acquisition itself and the promise to incorporate the new land with its inhabitants into the Union to be unconstitutional. Then, having acquiesced in making the Constitution, as he said, "a blank paper by construction," he governed the Territory of Orleans under laws to which its people gave no consent, under officials of his own appointment, and in a manner, overall, which even staunch Republicans in Congress had denounced as despotic and colonial. Not until March 1805 were the fifty thousand-odd citizens, mostly of French extraction, authorized to elect a representative assembly, and assured of eventual admission to the Union. These were the relevant facts.

Most anti-imperialists, nevertheless, denied that principle had been flouted in the case of Louisiana or that it constituted a precedent for 1898. First, they said Louisiana (and every subsequent acquisition except Alaska) was geographically contiguous with American settlement, thinly populated, racially homogeneous, and capable, after a tutelary period, of being admitted into the Union. Second, the Louisiana Treaty, unlike the Treaty of 1898, guaranteed statehood, and the first laws for the Orleans Territory were closely limited in time. Moreover, as John Sharp Williams pointed out, "the practical operation of the Jefferson Act [of 1803] was merely to invest in the Executive . . . the power to carry on the government there as it then existed. Mr. Jefferson never made a law for Louisiana. He never construed a law for Louisiana." It was "almost blasphemous" to compare the two cases. The laws for the government of the Philippines invested the President with full authority civil and military. Third, Louisiana was acquired in order to disentangle the United States from foreign affairs; it was a measure of internal expansion for the peace and well-being of American citizens; and it required no increase in the nation's military establishment. Finally, Jefferson, if he went beyond the Constitution, did so in the conviction that he was wrong. The present-day rulers, it seemed, were not similarly chastened by principle.

The cornerstones were dealt some hard blows by the imperialists. "'Consent of the governed,' indeed! . . . War is the great civilizer." So many complaints were made in Congress about the "exaggerated respect for the past," about the "fatality of submissive acquiescence in the traditions of the fathers," and about the impracticality of governing "by strict abstract rights," that Senator Tillman of South Carolina felt bound to conclude, "there is no longer any pretense that the Declaration of Independence is a governing force in our affairs." "The consent of the governed!" Henry Cabot Lodge exclaimed. It was one of those eloquent generalizations Jefferson got from Rousseau, Lodge thought. "To pull a sentence out of a revolutionary manifesto and deal with it as if it was one of the labored and chiseled clauses of the Constitution shows a sad confusion of thought." Lyman Abbott, editor of the militant *Outlook,* assailed the idea as a relic of the exploded philosophy of the French Revolution.

But the burden of the imperialists' argument was that the cornerstones, if they had been knocked out, had been knocked out not by them, but by Jefferson in 1803-04. "The first man in our history to disregard Jefferson's aphorism as to 'the consent of the governed' was the versatile genius who can be quoted on both sides of almost every question which has agitated the public mind of the country—Thomas Jefferson himself." Nor was that all. By a sort of lightning change, Jefferson, the strict constructionist, became in 1803 "the annihilator of the Constitution." Surmounting his own principles in the acquisition and government of Louisiana, Jefferson brought about a revolution in the American polity from which there was no retreat.

Tradition did not chain the eagle of empire, its advocates exulted, but plumed her for flight.

This was the eternal glory of Jefferson. In circumstances promising greatness for his country, "he did not for a moment allow his well-known philosophy of the right of self-government to obscure his practical judgment as to the immediate work in hand." Democrats in 1900 invited their opponents to "listen to Thomas Jefferson." But this talk of Jefferson's liberalism and humanity was laughable, the Republicans answered, to anyone who bothered to look at the Louisiana record—the statute books, the petitions of oppressed citizens, the histories of Francis X. Martin, Henry Adams, and others. "Jefferson's practices were better than his principles. His deeds were more beneficent than his theories." The *New York Times* expressed the view that

Jefferson was the great opportunist of his time and of all our history. Nor is it ill for the country that he was so. His marvellous strength with the people lay in the fact that he was in close sympathy with their ideas, hopes, and aspirations, and his pliable mind, coupled with unflagging energy and patient persistence, enabled him to carry forward the real purposes of the Nation quite regardless of minute consistency.

Tying up with Jefferson, the imperialists searched his letters and found in them numerous assertions that education and fitness were conditions precedent to the application of the consent principle; they recalled his thoughts on Cuba, freely interpreted as an ambition to annex the island; they said his Ordinance of 1784 provided an oligarchical form of territorial government. Essential parts of the Philippines Government Bill of 1900 were in the very words of the act which authorized Jefferson to govern Louisiana. "We may safely tread in the footsteps of the author of the Declaration of Independence," Lodge remarked. And Theodore Roosevelt, in formally accepting the vice-presidential nomination of his party, wrote from Oyster Bay: "The parallel between what Jefferson did with Louisiana and what is now being done in the Philippines is exact." In sum, the Jefferson set forth by the Republicans was a militant nationalist, a ruler over colonies, an opportunist statesman of empire—"the first imperialist of the Republic."

How long will the American Republic endure? a famous Frenchman had asked years ago. "So long as the ideas of its founders
continue dominant," James Russell Lowell had answered. The anti-
imperialists remembered the question and the answer. When the
Declaration was called "a living lie" and its leading principle "the
relic of an exploded philosophy," the nation's soul was again
imperiled.

In the ultimate outcome, however, the nation remained truer to
itself than had seemed possible in 1900. It backed away from an
imperial destiny almost as soon as that destiny was opened. It made
and carried out a broad commitment to self-government in its over-
seas possessions, spectacularly completed in the Philippines in 1946.
The reason for this, it has been said, was the "bad conscience" left
by the derelictions of 1898-1900. The reassertion of traditional principles forced the debate back into "the old channels," where the
heresy of imperialist policy and ideology could be exposed. The
moral sanctions of American government, which administration
leaders threw out the front door, were brought in again at the back
door, as in the official acknowledgment that the United States could
not govern dependent peoples except "under moral obligations and
restraints" and "in the hope that they may be finally fitted for independent self-government." The ambiguity of the Jefferson symbol
in this "time of national hesitation" reflected the ambiguity of the
nation's character and purpose. But it was too late to convert the
paramount symbol of the nation's political ideals into a symbol of
empire. What Jefferson did in the Louisiana Purchase was historically relevant; what he said in the Declaration of Independence
entered into the spirit of American institutions. This was the key to
the vitality of the symbol. If the left hand that clutched the Purchase
Treaty was to be put in harmony with the right hand that held the
Declaration, it would have to be on the latter's terms.

As the imperialism debate faded away, the nation commemorated
the one hundredth anniversary of the Louisiana Purchase. The two
events in quick succession focused attention on Jefferson's signal
contribution to the nation's growth. On April 30, 1903, the Louisiana
Purchase Exposition was dedicated at St. Louis. Millions of visitors

gazed upon the Jefferson statue at the Fair, bought souvenirs of every description bearing his likeness, and learned of his part in the founding of the West.

In the nineteenth century, the Louisiana Purchase had not been one of the major titles of Jefferson's fame. He had modestly refrained from crowing over his conquest. He let his agency in it, as Randall observed, "go unexplained to the day of his death." He made no mention of it in the epitaph he inscribed for his tombstone—one of the strangest omissions in all history, Champ Clark thought. The Louisiana Purchase was usually a glowing chapter in the accounts of Jefferson's administration, and such ardent westward expansionists as Thomas Hart Benton called him father and prophet. But the achievement was suspect on several grounds—constitutional, sectional, and diplomatic—which had not been entirely obliterated at the end of the century. Henry Adams, after his exhaustive study of the diplomacy of the Louisiana Purchase, assigned the major share of the credit to Robert Livingston, Jefferson's minister to France. Thomas M. Cooley, the distinguished jurist and foe of "paternalism," charged that Jefferson "offered to demagogues who should come after him a corrupting and dangerous precedent, when he proposed to violate the Constitution in order to accomplish an object of immediate desire." Josiah P. Quincy, grandson of the Federalist who had condemned the Purchase from 1803 until his death in 1864, chose the centennial year to restate the old position and to praise the foresight of his ancestors "who perceived the disaster that must come from an unconstitutional concession to the slave power."

However, these were definitely minority opinions by 1900. The most respected historians and statesmen, without the faintest aura of Jefferson about them, glorified his triumph. In the 'eighties, James G. Blaine marveled at Jefferson's "master-stroke of policy which advanced the United States from a comparatively feeble nation, lying between the Atlantic and the Mississippi, to a continental power of assured strength and boundless promise." Even John T. Morse, in his "American Statesman" biography, awarded "the entire credit of the achievement" to Jefferson. Hamiltonians of the Lodge and Roosevelt caliber, finding so little else to admire in Jefferson, praised the Louisiana Purchase.

As Jefferson's name was chanted "the greatest of American expansionists" and the Louisiana Purchase "his noblest service to posterity," two important tendencies could be observed in his reputation. First, the association of Jefferson with expansion eased the weight of ancient state rights heresy and niggardly constitutionalism. The really decisive thing about the Louisiana Treaty, it was said in 1903, was that Jefferson had to place himself "on national grounds and appeal to the principle of nationality," and from this step neither he nor America could ever retreat. Second, Jefferson's association with the Great West further accentuated the rustic-pioneer side of his character. Like Daniel Boone, wrote H. A. Bruce, "he felt the frontiersman's longing to press on and on through the cool green spaces of the mountains, and beyond the mountains to the mysterious depths in which each night the sun sank in respose." Expansionist and Westerner—both added enormously to Jefferson's stature as an *American* hero.

Citizens in the Purchase lands made their gratitude evident from time to time. "But for Jefferson and this one act," Missouri's Champ Clark declared, "people could not live where I live and be American citizens." No American state has paid as many honors to Jefferson as Missouri. The pioneers gave his name to counties, townships, schools, streets, hotels, and so on. There are today eighteen Jefferson townships in Missouri. In 1820 the City of Jefferson was the name given to the state's capital. A towering statue of Jefferson, by James E. Frazer, commands the principal entrance to the new capitol dedicated in 1918. The federal army post, Jefferson Barracks, was established at St. Louis in 1826. In 1885 the University of Missouri dedicated on its campus the battered granite obelisk that had marked Jefferson's grave before its replacement by the present monument. (His descendants, holding council at Monticello, awarded the relic to the first state university west of the Mississippi.) Over two thousand people witnessed the ceremonies at Columbia and heard Senator George G. Vest deliver his most famous oration on Jefferson. For a quarter century, patriotic societies laid wreaths at the monument on Jefferson's birthday; more recently, the School of Journalism has held annual exercises on April 13. In 1931 Jefferson's birthday was made a legal holiday in Missouri, the second state, Alabama having been the first, so to honor him.

The idea of erecting a fitting monument to the Father of the West was planted in the minds of Missourians by James G. Blaine. Addressing the St. Louis Merchants' Exchange in 1887, Blaine declared, "My reproach to this section, to every inhabitant of the Territory of Louisiana is that on its surface, which represents a third part of the United States, there is not a statue raised to Thomas Jefferson." Blaine's reproach rang down the years in Missouri. David R. Francis remembered it in 1899 when he spoke to the planning convention of the Louisiana Purchase Exposition, of which he became president. In the fanfare of the Exposition, Jefferson's admirers in St. Louis started several memorial campaigns. The Jefferson Club sponsored one of them, but this resulted instead in the pilgrimage to Monticello and the monument dedicated there in 1901. Nothing matured until 1909, when the Exposition closed its books with a one-half million dollar surplus. Congress waived its claim on one third of this money in favor of a permanent memorial to Jefferson in the "capital city" of the Louisiana Territory. It would be, some thought, a counterpart to the Lincoln Memorial then rising in Washington. The officials discarded suggestions ranging from a replica of Monticello to a modest version of the Arc de Triomphe, finally deciding on the plan of a "living memorial": a grand arch sheltering the statue of Jefferson, on either side a combined library and depositary of the Fair and a historical museum of the Louisiana Territory.

The Jefferson Memorial, with the noble statue by Karl Bitter, was dedicated on April 30, 1913. William M. Thornton, the orator of the day, said that in the retrospect of more than a century the Louisiana Purchase, not the Declaration or the Constitution, "marked the true beginning of the national phase of our history." Jefferson transformed the tiny confederation into a great union of indestructible States. "The man who bought Louisiana was the man who created this great Republic of the West."

St. Louis, and America, could take pride in this Jefferson Memorial. Yet the old reproach lingered. The lack of a fitting monument to Jefferson's pioneer spirit, Alben Barkley complained in 1935, was "a national disgrace." He was speaking for the Jefferson National

Expansion Memorial Commission, recently established by Congress to plan and build on the St. Louis riverfront "the most pretentious memorial ever erected to man." But this is another story.

"All reputations each age revises." Beginning prominently around 1880, Jefferson's fame revived until it burst in remarkable efflorescence at the turn of the century. This was, above all, a period of growing Americanization of the Jefferson image. The recognition of the "beautiful domestic character" helped to dispel the legends of the man of bronze and the political monster. The sympathy Americans came to feel with the private man affected by a kind of reciprocity their feelings toward the political hero. The susceptibility was the greater because the strongest basis of opposition to his politics, which lay in the principles of nationality, gradually shrank with the association of his name with the epic expansion of the nation. Paradoxically or not, the first notable memorial erected to Jefferson was in honor of the most nationalizing act of his life. The American people concluded, for the most part, that Jefferson's two hands had worked in unison. The Declaration and the Louisiana Purchase were viewed as promise and fulfillment, the abstract idea and the thing itself, the dream of freedom and the awakening to national destiny. The idea defined, as it had for Lincoln, the moral character of American nationality.

Jefferson's fame in American political life was still largely bound up with the fate of the Democratic party and the unresolved conflict between its conservative and radical wings. It only remained to be seen whether the Democrats could unite on a version of the Jeffersonian tradition serviceable to the nation's needs and agreeable to its reason. But with the enhanced appreciation of Jefferson's "Americanism," the fortunes of parties were likely to have less effect than in the past on the course of his reputation. The figure began to multiply itself in every reach of the culture. The vivid recognition of his part in the American enterprise of public education pointed to more and richer appreciations of the cultural heritage from Jefferson. Finally, the beginnings of patriotic commemoration implied the recession of the partisan Jefferson. A man to whom monuments could be erected had a substantial margin of fame secure from the uncertainties of events. Monuments, moreover, commemorate the past. History was imperceptibly catching up with Jefferson at last.

The appeal of Jefferson's private and domestic life, the association of his fame with nationality and expansion, the diffusion of his political principles, the awakening to his cultural legacy, the commemorative impulse—these factors, in sum, contributed to the revival of Jefferson's reputation and assured its American character. But perhaps in nothing was the subjective feeling of Jefferson's Americanness imaged as strikingly as in the figure who fruitfully, if somewhat incongruously, united the heritages of civilization and nature, nobility and simplicity, tuckahoe and cohee. As Jefferson's was "the fame of both," so too, men began to perceive, was America's.

* Six *

HISTORY II

It is obvious that the weak point of what may be called the Jeffersonian system lay in its rigidity of rule. That system was, it must be confessed, a system of doctrinaires, and had the virtues and faults of *a priori* reasoning.

His idealism and the actualities of American politics had continuing points of contact.*

THE PENALTY which Jefferson, like other great men, exacted from posterity was to compel it to understand him. Prejudice and error, the rage surrounding the Jefferson symbol, the elusiveness of the *real* man, all added to the burden of historical understanding. Increasingly, from the late nineteenth century forward, the responsibility fell to men who were especially equipped for it. History, once the province of any man, became a profession. It had its schools of instruction, its guild, its code of disinterested scholarship. The labors of collectors, archivists, and editors constantly enriched the historians' resources. The historical document gained in respect: the Kentucky Resolutions presented problems for investigation rather than texts for political sermons. The American story itself gained in richness, as historians gradually broke the political, or essentially constitutional, mold in which most of their interpretations had been cast. The progress of historical science was unmistakable; and Jefferson was sure to be better understood because of it.

Yet, as one of the guild conceded in 1918, "Jefferson seems far less willing than any of his illustrious compeers to fall into his definitive

---

* Henry Adams, *The Life of Albert Gallatin* (1879); Edward Channing, *A History of the United States* (1917).

place of honor." Why was this? There was, for one thing, the persistence of vendettas against Jefferson by the blood descendants and
self-appointed avengers of men whose fame he had allegedly injured
or destroyed. All the old complaints on the score of character were
heard again. Added to the standard list of the defamed were the
names of Patrick Henry (Jefferson "attempted to stab his character
to death" in a biographical sketch not published until 1867); Edmund
Randolph (Jefferson was one of the enemies who hung up his "black-
ened effigy . . . in a moment of partisan passion"); Citizen Genêt
(Jefferson posed as the emissary's friend and then betrayed him to
save his own face). The vendettas had been fairly well played out
by 1900. Ancestral piety ceased to be an important motive in historical writing.

Political partisanship, however, defied time itself. The scholar was
an exotic whose treatment of the American past, especially the early
national period, was not conditioned by the great American political
myth built around the antagonism of Jefferson and Hamilton. "Indeed," David Muzzey wrote, "no more astonishingly persistent prejudice can be found in our American historiography than the treatment
of these two great men like two buckets in a well, alternately elevated
or depressed according as an historian of the Federalist or the Republican school manipulates the chain." Historians would never arrive
at "a true appreciation of the father of American Democracy," Muzzey
thought, until they overcame the habit of "praising, exculpating, or
berating him, according to their own political bias," and instead
became "satisfied with the sufficiently absorbing task of appreciating
the intrinsic qualities of the man." Muzzey was right, of course; but
American politics, which American historiography tended to reflect,
would have to change before Jefferson could be studied for himself.

The historians could not fairly plead the lack of information on
Jefferson. If still fragmentary, it was constantly on the increase. The
difficulty was less one of the scholars' knowledge than of the uses
they made of it. The image of Jefferson shattered when they came
through the doors of partisan, and perhaps hereditary, prejudice to
the interpretation of the facts. Surely no work packed more information than John Bach McMaster's influential *History of the People of
the United States,* commenced in 1883. Behind the imposing façade,

the historian announced opinions that had little foundation other than Federalist prejudice. This was crude; discerning readers detected, and some exposed, the bias and the errors. More often Jefferson's scholarly judges let sneer and innuendo, under the guise of balance and objectivity, replace the cruder forms of belittlement and abuse.

Jefferson mirrored, despite the cautions of objectivity, the different minds of the historians; but the cause lay in the object perceived as well as in the subjects doing the perceiving. The chameleon quality of the Jefferson image could not have been wholly a fiction of the historians' imagination. The protean shapes of Jefferson's life not only enabled but practically compelled every observer, quite apart from his political bias, to become his own Jeffersonian. There were facts enough to accommodate almost any theory. It was plainly not enough, in the interest of "a true appreciation," to ask historians to be satisfied with the study of the man himself when, as they had already discovered, he was many men.

Three major cycles of Jefferson historiography have occurred since the last quarter of the nineteenth century. The first had its prominent beginnings in Hermann von Holst's *Constitutional and Political History of the United States* and in John T. Morse's American Statesmen series; it ran its course early in the twentieth century in Albert J. Beveridge's *Life of John Marshall*. The dominant theme of these historians was the *Union*. Most of them were New Englanders, many were influenced by Germans such as Holst, nearly all were Republicans. With marked exceptions, such as Henry Adams and the lesser known James Schouler, whose seven-volume political history was nationalistic without enmity to Jefferson, their works were vehemently anti-Jeffersonian. The second cycle was already well begun by 1900. Among its outstanding figures, the Westerners Charles A. Beard and Vernon L. Parrington and the Southerner William E. Dodd were keenly interested in Jefferson. Associated with progressive currents in American social and political thought, these scholars helped to break New England's intellectual supremacy, brought a refreshing realism into American historiography, and centered the theme of *democracy*. For the first time a substantial segment of the historical fraternity wrote from a viewpoint favorable to the democratic tradition. But not until the appearance in 1925 of Claude Bowers's *Jefferson and Hamilton: The Struggle for Democracy in America*, could it be said that American scholarship had at last been converted to Jefferson. The third cycle was just then beginning and is still in progress. Although it falls outside the limits of this chapter, it has been characterized by the intensive study of Jefferson's varied and complex *culture*.

Since nothing is more tedious than detailed discussions of "what historians said," no attempt at comprehensive coverage or systematic treatment of the major cycles is made in the following pages. Instead, the discussion centers on four areas of Jefferson study in which there were paramount achievements over a forty-year span: Jefferson's administration, Jeffersonian documents, the history of parties, and the Jeffersonian tradition. A strong undercurrent of criticism runs through most of this historical writing. Its tenor is suggested by the paired quotations that head this chapter. Historians on either side of the partisan line inclined to agree with Henry Adams that Jefferson's system of politics, far in advance as it was of its time, "made too little allowance for human passions and vices" and "relied too absolutely on the power of interest and reason as opposed to prejudice and habit." His idealism, they repeatedly said with Channing, overreached his, and America's, powers of constructive action. On the strictest historical accounting, Jefferson was a failure; yet his doctrines and ideals survived. "Jefferson's influence," James Bryce pointedly observed, "has been on the spirit of the people and their attitude toward their institutions rather than on the formation of institutions themselves." Small minds were incapable of appreciating these imponderables of Jefferson's influence. To them, as Muzzey said, "Jefferson seems like a dreamer dwelling in a fool's paradise of optimism or blocking the path of efficient government with exasperating political scruples." The great historians, however, perceived the complexity of the problem and dealt with it as if they were dealing with the very soul of America.

1. *Henry Adams*

Nothing ever written about Jefferson rivals in serious interest, if not in popular influence, the first half of Henry Adams's nine-volume

History of the United States During the Administrations of Jefferson and Madison. Why an Adams three generations removed from the nation's second President and two generations from its sixth should have made his great subject the interregnum "Jeffersonian period" was as perplexing as anything in the perplexing annals of his family. No first-rate history of the period existed. Study of the early republic had always centered on the Federalist administrations, from 1789 to 1801. This was considered the formative era of American politics, always more absorbing even to Jeffersonian historians than the years just beyond, which they were inclined to view as "a miniature golden age of American history." National history was dominated by the conception of "the history of the parties." With the triumph of Jefferson and the disintegration of the Federalist party, the drama of conflict was gone, and partisans on neither side could find in the sequel enough to sustain prolonged attention. By beginning his narrative at the point of the triumph, Jefferson's inauguration, Adams threw the party conflict into the background, found his dramatic center in Republican statecraft, and conceived the Jeffersonian era as the matrix of democratic nationality.

The field as a whole was virtually untouched; but this fact does not adequately explain Adams's attraction to it. It was a unified period, and one in which he could shun the ancestral thicket. The defeat of John Adams lay in the past; the major phase of J. Q. Adams's career lay in the future. Henry Adams had a profound distaste for the filial-pietistic history that had for so long engaged New Englanders and was still represented, to his regret, in the work of his favorite student, Henry Cabot Lodge. He seemed determined not to be tempted in this direction, even if it meant perversely writing up the objects of family distaste and Federalist hatred. In two biographies, of Albert Gallatin and John Randolph, much more than in the later *History*, he dealt with subjects that formed important chapters in the family history. The *Life of Gallatin* gave Adams an opportunity to sketch in the indispensable Federalist background for the *History*. In writing of Randolph, the scourge of all Presidents but most particularly of J. Q. Adams, the historian projected his view far beyond 1817 to the rise of the "slave power." Adams thus encompassed the long career of Jeffersonian Republicanism—its rise, triumph, and decline.

The Jeffersonian period had a still more forcible attraction for Adams. He was convinced that the destiny of the nation was bound up with the resources and capabilities—political, social, moral, intellectual—of democracy. Experience was the only test of their efficiency. The brilliant inquiry on "The State of the Nation in 1800," with which the *History* opened, was not one to encourage the hope that America marked a new era in human history. Everywhere Adams looked he was impressed by "the immensity of the task and the paucity of the means." The country was poor, the mind was sluggish, the states spread out over half a continent with only the most primitive facilities of communication and with no resistance to dispersion except that provided by a jealously guarded central government. The United States had thus far made a single great advance over the Old World: the experiment in republican government over a vast territory. But this was as yet far from success, and many, including Jefferson, thought it "not very important." Bolder and far more dubious was the democratic commitment "to lift the average man upon an intellectual and social level with the most favored."

In 1800, by a political decision that reflected their social conditions and registered their ideals, the American people risked their fortunes on the new experiment. Could their vivid social and political imagination be given tangible shape? Could they succeed, "by mere process of growth," without benefit of old world institutions and safeguards? Could their raw instincts for industry and use, their boundless ambitions in a land free of the age-old barriers to progress, be directed toward the higher forms of human achievement? These questions of 1800, Adams felt, could be answered reassuringly by 1815. "Probably no great people ever grew more rapidly and became more mature in so short a time." Physical obstacles and popular inertia were being overcome. The unity of the nation was established; the political system was everywhere accepted. The mind was redirecting its energies into literature and science. American character was formed and its divergence from Europe assured.

The *History* was, therefore, in its larger outlines, a chronicle of the rise of democratic nationality. The place of Jefferson and his administration in this story was bound to be complex in the extreme. Adams undertook to show that at the end of the Jeffersonian era America was a success, or at least well on its way to success; but his narrative was a crowded record of failures—loss of principle, political ineptitude, administrative bungling, cowardice, treason, and deceit. He necessarily made Jefferson a hero of sorts. Like his leading predecessor, Richard Hildreth, Adams was able to enter sympathetically into the Jeffersonian world of ideas, though not, any more than Hildreth, into the feelings of the agrarian party. He repeatedly called Jefferson a great man and his political creed the only workable starting point for American nationality. Yet he showed Jefferson casually abandoning his principles, creating none in their place, suffering the most humiliating defeats, drifting helplessly on the tide of circumstance. As one reviewer observed, "the reader is justly provoked that the showman will not make his monkey perform his boasted tricks." The curve of his narrative was downward, a story less of rise and triumph than of decline and fall. No wonder, then, that the admirers of the *History* from the day of its appearance to the present have been unable to agree whether it is Jeffersonian or anti-Jeffersonian. In truth, it is neither and both at once, which is the secret of its endless fascination and the mark of its distinction in American historiography.

The interest attached to Jefferson's administration, Adams wrote, was "an interest at all times singularly personal." During eight years, Jefferson's personality "appeared to be the Government, and impressed itself, like that of Bonaparte, by a different process, on the mind of the nation." Unlike almost every other American statesman, Adams thought, "Jefferson could be painted only touch by touch, with a fine pencil, and the perfection of the likeness depended upon the shifting and uncertain flicker of its semi-transparent shadows." Whether because of the model or the painter or the light, perhaps because of all three, the image was constantly shifting. Jefferson was the Virginian, possessing the virtues with the faults of the type, believing the Union was "a question of expediency," somewhat provincial in his manner and Arcadian in his outlook for America. His ambition was colored, if not set, by the highest aim of the Virginia

school, which was "to fix upon the National Government the stamp
of their own idyllic conservatism." Jefferson was also the cosmopolitan eighteenth-century philosopher, who "seemed during his entire
life to breathe with perfect satisfaction nowhere except in the liberal,
literary, and scientific air of Paris in 1789," and who in his political
philosophy "aspired beyond the ambition of a nationality, and embraced in his view the whole future of man." Jefferson was the
American democrat, not only in his beliefs and system of government, but also in his supple leadership and love of popularity above
commitment to doctrine. Virginian, philosopher, democrat: the Jefferson depicted by Adams was constantly changing masks.

The historian seemed uncertain whether to treat Jefferson seriously
or comically. As an intellectual who sought to put his theories to
work, Jefferson merited respectful study. His idealistic system represented "all that was most philanthropic and all that most boldly
appealed to the best instincts of mankind." Only trivial men could
treat it trivially. The party conflict that brought him to power was
a desperately serious business. "Mr. Jefferson meant that the American system should be a democracy, and he would rather have let the
world perish than that this principle, which to him represented all
that man was worth, should fail. Mr. Hamilton considered democracy
a fatal curse, and meant to stop its progress." But Jefferson in power,
Adams sometimes felt, was "a character of comedy." He recalled
Washington Irving's thinly disguised portrait of Jefferson, William
the Testy, in *Knickerbocker's History of New York:* a bustling little
man whose statesmanship was mired in the slough of futile learning.
He tried to match Irving's light touch. Federalist criticism had been
spoiled by its heavy-handed malignity. Adams preferred irony, paradox, satire. His portrait of Jefferson as a practicing statesman was
quite obviously meant to evoke ridicule. Jefferson appeared on the
scene, at his inauguration, very much as Senator Maclay of Pennsylvania had described him a decade earlier: a loose and shackling
figure, eyes rambling and vacant, clothes too small for him, with
nothing to dignify his personal presence. Yet this man was "unable
to see himself in any but a heroic light." He left the scene in 1809,
a modern Don Quixote in flight. "On horseback, over roads impass-
able to wheels, through snow and storm, he hurried back to Monti-

cello to recover in the quiet of home the peace of mind he had lost in the disappointments of his statesmanship."

The portrait gained in precision by contrast with Gallatin and Randolph. Adams described Gallatin in terms he might have liked applied to himself: force of ability and character without the tricks of popularity, more of a scientific than a political mind, a balanced approach to every political question with entire disregard of the emotions. Gallatin epitomized Pennsylvania's prosaic efficiency, and Pennsylvania epitomized America. He too was an idealist wishing to reduce the powers of government to a minimum; but, unlike the Virginia Republicans, he hoped thereby to free democracy in its true moral, intellectual, and industrial strength. As Jefferson's Secretary of the Treasury, Gallatin appeared a model of "practical statesman-ship" equaled in America only by Hamilton. If Gallatin represented for Adams the constructive and progressive side of Jeffersonian Democracy, Randolph stood for just the opposite. Rancorous, ego-tistical, obstinate, Randolph adhered to his convictions with a vehemence bordering on insanity. As Jefferson's congressional gadfly, he seemed bent on no higher aim than the embarrassment of the administration by holding it accountable to Virginia principles. Adams suggested the crucial tension in Jefferson's personality and politics by placing him between these opposite types of Republican leadership.

The partnership Jefferson formed between the Northern and Southern Republicans, Adams said, "was from the first that of a business firm." The Northerners, like Gallatin, did not share Jeffer-son's antipathy to banks and cities or his fears of the central government. "Such theories were republican in the Virginian sense, but not democratic; they had nothing in common with the democracy of Pennsylvania and New England, except their love of freedom; and Virginia freedom was not the same conception as the democratic freedom of the North." Adams's usage of the terms *republican* and *democratic* was neither precise nor consistent. *Republican*, however, was usually associated with the "Virginia dogmas," while *democratic* was associated with the general social ideals of the nation. The Northern democrats "understood the practical forces of society." They sought to improve its moral, economical, and intellectual capabilities. The Southern Republicans feared the progress of the North, and sought to check it by their superiority in the arts of law and politics. The bearings of the term *democratic* were social, national, practical, progressive; the opposite *republican* bearings were political, provincial, doctrinaire, and archaic. The key to Jefferson's political character and leadership lay in his representation of all that was involved in both terms—"the hopes of science as well as the prejudices of Virginia." By common consent, Adams said, Jefferson was the leader and philosopher of the Virginia school. Its creed was stated in the Virginia and Kentucky Resolutions, wherein the art of politics was reduced to an enumeration of powers reserved from exercise. Yet nothing was so little suited to Jefferson's intellectual temper.

If Jefferson appeared ill at ease in the position of a popular leader, he seemed equally awkward in the intellectual restraints of his own political principles. His mind shared little in common with the provincialism on which the Virginia and Kentucky Resolutions were founded. His instincts led him to widen rather than narrow the bounds of every intellectual excercize; and if vested with political authority, he could no more resist the temptation to stretch his powers than he could abstain from using his mind on any object merely because he might be drawn upon ground supposed to be dangerous.

The history of Jefferson's administration, so largely an extension of his personality, bore out this view. The awkward Virginia principles were dropped, powers were stretched beyond the limits of Federalism, nationalism went forward. Adams fixed the turning-point away from the Republican landmarks and along the path of democracy at Jefferson's second inauguration. Although it lacked the flourishes that had made the First Inaugural Address the quintessential expression of Virginia ideals, the creed of a powerful political party, and the standard by which future movements were measured, the Second Inaugural was no less interesting and far more promising for the American future. Jefferson broached the idea, and Gallatin soon developed it into a comprehensive plan, of a federal system of internal improvements ranging from roads and canals to arts and education. Jefferson's proposal put to naught every principle of the

Republican party, Adams declared. "At no time since the Declaration of Independence had the prospects of nationality seemed so promising as in the spring of 1805." They were doomed in Jefferson's administration, as the sequel showed, and Jefferson still later reverted to his Virginia principles; but America's *democratic* direction was fixed.

This ascending theme of the narrative was hopelessly snarled in the tangle of Jefferson's personality. Fascinated by the play of events on that personality, Adams could not resolve the clash within it, as he alleged, between the "idyllic conservatism" of Virginia Republicanism and the "intellectual instincts of liberality and innovation" which he associated with democracy. On one page, for instance, Adams said that Jefferson believed his task in 1800 was "to establish a democratic republic, with the sciences for an intellectual field, and physical and moral advancement keeping pace with their advance." Then, a few pages later: "The Republic which Jefferson believed himself to be founding or securing in 1801 was an enlarged Virginia." Ultimately, the historian was unable to solve the enigma of Jefferson.

The moral drama of the *History* revolved around the eternal problem of ideals and realities in the conduct of government. The ideals and doctrines of the Jeffersonians were defeated, deflected, diluted by realities of power—its responsibilities with its temptations—and forces of circumstance. The moral had been drawn before, but never with such skill. Adams's outstanding contribution to the factual knowledge of Jefferson's administration was his exhaustive study of its foreign relations. The first student of the period to use the material in the archives of major foreign capitals, he substantially reconstructed the history of Jeffersonian statesmanship. The story within the story, the action that objectified the moral, the thread that held the whole sweeping narrative together, unfolded from the fundamental commitment of Jefferson's administration, so Adams believed, to keep the United States at peace. "The essence and genius of Jefferson's statesmanship lay in peace. Through difficulties, trials, and temptations of every kind he held fast to this idea, which was the clue to whatever seemed inconsistent, feeble, or deceptive in his Administration."

Overwhelmed by this insight, Adams made the "peace policy" the key to Jefferson's entire administration and the fairest standard by which to measure its success. What he called "the Jeffersonian system" was based upon the theory that reason and interest rather than force and violence could rule the world. Policies were determined, the nation's fortunes were staked, on the prospects of this visionary idea. Jefferson, with doctrinaire enthusiasm, carried the pacific theory too far; yet in no part of his statesmanship did he more accurately reflect popular convictions. In Adams's conceptual scheme, *peace* meant much more than the opposite of war. It was loaded with meanings that had little to do with foreign relations. It stood for the rule of reason and interest in all human affairs, for hostility to "any system organized with military energy," for government based upon consent, for the idea that the strength of nations lay not in what the world had always counted as strength—arms, organization, loyalty and command, splendor of state—but in the simple, efficient pursuits of a democratic society. The real difference between Jefferson and the bulk of Federalists, Adams wrote, "lay in the question how far a government could safely dispense with the use of force as an element in politics." The term *force* in such a statement was a symbol of the whole problem of politics, embracing questions of individual freedom as well as of national security.

Jefferson was determined to prevent war not only because he believed passionately in peace among nations but also, Adams said, because peace was essential to the Republican system. Internal taxes must be abolished, the Hamiltonian debt extinguished, the military establishment reduced, the central government converted, in sum, into "simply a judicature and a police." The success of the system was thus largely a question of economy and diplomacy. Diplomacy would have to function within the rigid limits set by Republican doctrine; the true principles of government could not be fixed beyond peradventure except under the conditions of peace. Jefferson's calculation was twofold. First, that if the Americans could rid themselves of the common burdens of other peoples, they must in time outstrip every rival and prove the strength of the simple republican order. Second, believing the interests of the warring European powers required peace and commerce with America, Jefferson calculated

HISTORY II

that he could "enforce against foreign nations such principles as national objects required, not by war, but by 'peaceable coercion' through commercial restrictions." He was as steady as a magnet in his aim to prevent war, Adams thought. Ironically, however, the more he pursued that aim the farther he drifted from Republican principles and the nearer he came to the rule of force he abhorred. He had not been in office three months before the system of peace and economy was deranged by the Mediterranean campaign against the Barbary pirates. The Louisiana Purchase was the great triumph of Jefferson's pacific diplomacy; but the acquisition cost him dearly in principle, required a military system to organize it, and a far-flung network of internal improvements to secure it to the Union.

The theory of "peaceable coercion" was put fully to the test in the Embargo of 1807-09. Jefferson's attempt to win concessions from England and France by playing them off against each other had failed, for the two powers combined to drive neutral commerce from the seas. It remained to be seen if Jefferson's ultimate recourse would succeed. Adams devoted his fourth volume to the experiment. Like J. Q. Adams and Richard Hildreth before him, he assailed the persistent Federalist dogma that the Embargo was motivated by friendship for France. The hardshell Federalists—"fit inmates for an asylum"—invented the doctrine of Jefferson's subservience to France in order "to cover and justify their own devotion to England," which went to the limits of treason. "The embargo was an experiment in politics well worth making," Adams declared.

In the scheme of President Jefferson's statesmanship, non-intervention was the substitute for war—the weapon of defense and coercion which saved the cost and danger of supporting army or navy and spared America the brutalities of the Old World. Failure of the embargo meant in his mind not only the recourse to the practice of war, but to every political and social evil that war had always brought in its train. In such a case the crimes and corruptions of Europe, which had been the object of his political fears, must, as he believed, sooner or later teem in the fat soil of America. To avert a disaster so vast was a proper motive for statesmanship and justified disregard for smaller interests.

But like all noble experiments, the Embargo must be judged by the standard of practical efficiency. In his brilliant chapter, "The Cost of the Embargo," Adams attempted to show that it not only failed to coerce England and France but also that it rapidly produced the same effects in America Jefferson had feared from war. Adams added up the costs. Economic hardships were everywhere felt, more in the agricultural than in the commercial sections, most of all in Jefferson's Virginia. Politically, the measure drained off what was left of Jeffersonian principles, revived Old Federalism, and stirred up disunionism in New England. Morally, lacking any of war's heroic compensations, the Embargo "opened up the sluice-gates of social corruption" and "turned every citizen into an enemy of the laws." The sum was this: that the Jeffersonian system "which made peace a passion could lead to no better result than had been reached by the barbarous system which made war a duty."

Swept up in the drama, Adams gave free rein to his imagination in the denouement. "Under the shock of these discoveries," he wrote, "Jefferson's vast popularity vanished, and the labored fabric of his reputation fell in sudden and general ruin." Repeal of the Embargo was forced on him three days before the end of his term. No President was ever more deeply humiliated; no administration, with the exception of Buchanan's in 1861, ever left the nation in a more calamitous state. "Facts, not theories, were all that survived the wreck of Mr. Jefferson's administration." The spectacle was appalling, as Adams painted it, because of the heroic heights from which Jefferson started and the glitter of his progress during the first seven years.

The disaster that ended Jefferson's administration engulfed Madison's in the second war with England. Jeffersonian statesmanship could only be adjudged a failure. Adams, who once confessed a greater interest in the limitations than in the powers of men, had plainly written a history which taught the impossibility of human reason and will to order the destiny of a nation. The hero had vanished from the scene of American history. Adams, in summing up, agreed with his admired Tocqueville: in the American democracy the hero counted for much less than in Europe, the vast trudging society for much more. But the Americans, "without kings, nobles, or armies; without church, traditions, and prejudices," felt the need for the heroic element in history even more than other nations,

Adams wrote, "and in unconscious protest against their own social conditions they adorned with imaginary qualities scores of supposed leaders, whose only merit was their faculty of reflecting a popular trait." In the end, this was true of Jefferson. The last philosopher-statesman, his fall demonstrated not alone the deterioration of Jeffersonian Democracy, as had been said many times before, but also the disintegration of the eighteenth-century hope of a society, even a world, ordered to philosophical design. This was the historian's excuse for tiresome reiteration, chapter after chapter, of Jefferson's deviations from theory. At the end of the Jeffersonian era, facts had triumphed over theories, circumstances over men, experience over dogma. Vast new social energies, impersonal and industrial, had taken over; the statesmen and their theories no longer counted for much.

"I never yet heard of ten men who had ever read my history," Henry Adams remarked fifteen years after its publication. The work had few readers. In the small fraternity of scholars, however, it was soon recognized as a masterpiece. None who thereafter ventured across the boundaries of the Jeffersonian period could escape "the great *History.*" Paradoxically, the work which established the crucial importance of Jefferson's administration in American history had the effect of impoverishing it so far as American historiography was concerned. Whether because of the work's inherent merit, or because of its power to catch at the imagination, or because of the exaggerated respect it obtained in scholarly circles, no one has attempted to rewrite the history of the period and few, apparently, have felt the need to do so. For all its faults, the *History* remains, as the historians say, definitive.

2. *Quest for the Document*

Fresh stirrings of concern for the preservation of Jefferson's personal papers were in evidence around the end of the century. This legacy was first divided, its dispersal commenced, in 1848, when Thomas Jefferson Randolph sold the so-called "public" papers to the United States government. After his death, the "private" papers passed to Sarah Randolph. She worked with the collection, actually began to edit it, made various items available to interested scholars (Herbert Baxter Adams for one), and attempted to sell it to the government. Congress was interested, but Sarah Randolph's death closed this avenue. Not long after, in 1898, the Boston cousin Thomas Jefferson Coolidge purchased the larger part of the private papers (over three thousand items) from Sarah's sister and heir, Carolina Randolph. Coolidge gave the papers to the Massachusetts Historical Society as a sign, he said, "that the two states of Virginia and Massachusetts, where Jefferson's blood intermingled, treasured alike his memory." The Coolidge branch of the family, as Jonathan Daniels later remarked, "kept Jefferson's relics and cherished Hamilton's philosophy." In the long run, this too could serve Jefferson's memory.

Also indicative of the rising interest in the Jefferson corpus at the turn of the century was the publication within a few years of each other of two new editions of his writings. The second of these, a work in twenty volumes under the auspices of the Thomas Jefferson Memorial Association in 1903-04, although a valuable addition to knowledge, belongs as well to the history of Jefferson commemoration. The object of the Association was to create a memorial in the national capital. Impressively inaugurated at a Jefferson birthday banquet in Washington, April 14, 1903, at which William Jennings Bryan and George F. Hoar were the main speakers, the Association was forced to abandon its original plan because of technical difficulties and insufficient funds. Instead, it published within the next year a big and gaudy edition of Jefferson's writings.

Albert E. Bergh, who directed the work, though experienced in editing, lacked the skills necessary for a scholarly performance. The bulk of the Memorial Edition was simply a reprinting, without alteration of plan or correction of errors, of the Congress Edition of fifty years before. Four main additions were made to this more or less standard repertory: one, a block of heretofore unpublished letters in the government collection, which had only recently been calendared; two, a block of letters relating to Jefferson's governorship, taken from an unpublished file in the Virginia State Library; three, the cycle of two hundred letters from the family papers which the Massachusetts Historical Society had published in 1900; four, several obscure and surprising items, such as Jefferson's *Thoughts on English Prosody* and *Essay on Anglo-Saxon Grammar*. Numerous pictures, interpretive essays, and political speeches by Jefferson's admirers cluttered the volumes. Conceived as a memorial to Jefferson, the Lipscomb and Bergh edition was a faulty tool of historical scholarship. But as the most nearly complete edition of Jefferson's writings, widely circulated and frequently reprinted, it remains to this day the one most generally used.

Much higher standards were set by Paul L. Ford in an earlier ten-volume work published between 1892-99. Ford was only twenty-five years old when he took this assignment from the house of G. P. Putnam, which was then bringing out in superb editions the writings of eminent American statesmen. Ford was not a professionally trained scholar, but rather a bibliophile and collector, who practically grew up within the confines of the incomparable library of Americana his father had assembled in an enormous room of the family's Brooklyn, New York, home. With several novels on historical and political themes to his credit, Ford was a literary celebrity before his early death in 1902. His enduring reputation rests, however, on numerous editorial and bibliographical labors, of which the most important was *The Writings of Jefferson*.

Ford's work was scarcely less important than Henry Adams's *History*. Many parallels to Adams suggest themselves. Ford's background was antipathetic to Jefferson. His parents and ancestors were New Englanders. Except for the *Jefferson*, most of his scholarly work was on the Federalist side of the great divide—a bibliography of Hamilton, a life of Washington, collected pamphlets and essays on the Constitution. (His older brother Worthington C. Ford, a no less skillful and in the course of time a more eminent scholar and archivist, probably expressed the family opinion of Jefferson in several monographs which seldom let pass an opportunity to disparage the man and his work.) Although the *Writings* showed traces of Federalist cant, it showed more significantly that Ford, like Adams, felt the fascination of the historical figure. The problem that allured him, "the Jeffersonian puzzle," he wrote in the Introduction to the *Writings*, was how it had happened that Jefferson alone of his contemporaries, and despite serious flaws, became a "man of the people" for his time and all time. This could not be explained upon any "limited view," such as particular sects and parties had projected back into history. Taking a broader view, Ford said that Jefferson's high and unvarying purpose was to expand the area of individual liberty. He interpreted the Constitution strictly or loosely according as in his judgment the fundamental purpose was well-served. His political conduct was often bad, but the people understood him and knew that he stood for them. Eventually, Ford said, this popular judgment—"that he fought for the ever enduring privilege of personal freedom"—must universally obtain.

Not the eternal debate on Jefferson but the refinement of its subject matter was Ford's major contribution. He was the first editor of Jefferson, one of the first editors of any American's papers, to be guided by procedures that would now be taken for granted. At the outset, he made an extensive search for new and unpublished manuscripts. In addition to the main barely exploited source, the family papers, Ford sought out autograph collectors and dealers, obscure publications, and descendants of men who had had correspondence with Jefferson. The search was fairly productive, though of course the larger part of the ten volumes came from the government collection then held in the State Department. Refused permission to enter its Library and copy from the Jefferson manuscripts, Ford was fortunate in making arrangements with a Department archivist, S. M. Hamilton, who satisfied his exacting standards. The process of establishing verified texts did not end until the printer's proof was checked against the original manuscripts. This was a great advance over anything previous, and over the later Memorial Edition. As with the correspondence, so too with Jefferson's only book, the *Notes on Virginia*. Ford labored to publish a variorum edition of this work, which was already a puzzle and a challenge to bibliophiles.

Ford's awareness of the editor's responsibilities could also be seen in his handling of the problems of arrangement, selection, and editorial guidance. His simple chronological arrangement, maintaining the continuity of Jefferson's life in its written record, was superior to the usual practice of establishing separate series for laws, addresses, correspondence, miscellaneous writings, and so on. Attempting to stay above the battle, he sometimes yielded to an irrepressible impulse to disparage Jefferson. He collected and arranged as a single series all Jefferson's letters concerned with finding a sinecure for his old friend John Page, because, Ford explained, it was a clear illustration of "the use of public offices for private benefit." Similarly, the printing of all Jefferson's letters to the federal prosecutor, George Hay, in the Burr Trial was a covert slap at Jefferson. But there were not many such lapses. Although actually less complete than the Congress Edition of forty years earlier, Ford's *Writings of Jefferson* was by far the most reliable and useful edition. Discerning historians accepted it as standard, and some of them, Charles Beard for instance, saw no need to use any other.

Ford's work helped to focus certain phases of Jefferson's career through the unprecedented opportunity it gave for the study of key documents. This attention to documents, as distinguished from letters and writings, was another differentia of the Ford Edition. It was the first to publish any considerable portion of Jefferson's work in the revision of the Virginia laws. When he came to the Kentucky Resolutions, Ford printed in parallel columns Jefferson's rough and final drafts, and also a photofacsimile of the text adopted by the Kentucky legislature.

The most important items in the entire ten volumes were two drafts of a constitution for Virginia in 1776. It had long been known that Jefferson sent the draft of a constitution to the Virginia Assembly in June 1776, that it arrived too late for consideration, and that only the preamble was incorporated in the finished Constitution. But every trace of this manuscript had vanished; no account of it had ever been given. Then, in 1890, *two* copies came to light in Lexington, Virginia. Worthington C. Ford made the discovery the subject of an article, "Jefferson's Constitution for Virginia," in the *Nation*, August 1890. Paul Ford first published the two drafts, one a rough and the other a finished bill. As to the significance of these documents, he followed his brother in the belief that the proposed constitution was far more conservative than would have been expected and, in fact, "less democratic than the instrument adopted by this convention." This was an astounding interpretation. Jefferson assailed the Virginia Constitution for fifty years chiefly because it was *not* democratic; it seemed incredible that he could have proposed in 1776 a *less* democratic instrument than the one he assailed. Yet the Fords' interpretation was very influential.

In 1916, D. R. Anderson refuted the new interpretation in the *American Historical Review*. The Fords, observing that Jefferson's plan called for direct election only of the lower house of the Assembly, had argued that this was too narrow a foundation for popular government. Anderson, however, focused attention on the "radically democratic character" of Jefferson's other provisions. He would have made every man a landowner and a voter, equalized representation, put slavery on the way to extinction, abolished entail and primogeniture, and established religious freedom. The newly discovered documents did not upset but actually supported the tradition of Jefferson's relation to the Virginia Constitution, Anderson thought. His plan was too democratic for Virginia in 1776, and this, not alone its late arrival at the convention, prevented its adoption. "The wonder is not that he was so conservative . . . in 1776, but that he was so democratic and farseeing."

The next important, and the only detailed, study of these documents was made by Julian P. Boyd in the first volume of *The Papers of Thomas Jefferson* (1950). In the interim, a third manuscript draft-constitution of 1776 had been found. Boyd identified it as the original and gave it paramount importance. Between the two views of Jefferson's proposed constitution, Boyd definitely favored the democratic. But whereas scholars had supposed that Jefferson's plan was solely of theoretical interest, Boyd showed that it was, in fact, considered by the convention and adopted in some of its parts. The seam of inquiry opened in 1890 by the discovery of a lost Jefferson document thus culminated in the remarkable textual analysis by Boyd, who argued that the Virginia Constitution of 1776 was, in some sense, "a Jeffersonian document." This was the ultimate in complexity! Undoubtedly Boyd was right. But Jefferson must become unintelligible if the fascination with the document led to many such revelations as this one, in which he had to be understood both as an author of the Virginia government and as its worst enemy.

Few texts in American history had been more diligently studied than the Kentucky Resolutions; yet nothing seemed to present greater problems to the historian. The Resolutions were hopelessly entangled in the strands of thought and emotion knotted in the Civil War. It was important, therefore, to cut the knot, bring the documents nakedly into view, and write the true history of the Resolutions. In a paper presented to the American Historical Association in 1888, James C. Welling listed seven points still in controversy. These fell, in general, into two classifications—first, the strictly historical questions: what was their inception? who drafted them, when, and where? And second, the subjective questions of meaning and intent; most pertinently, how far did they go toward proposing nullification in the South Carolina sense?

The history of the Resolutions was reopened in 1886-87 by the writings of two men based upon information newly discovered in the papers of the Breckinridge family of Lexington, Kentucky. R. T. Durrett, in a series of articles in *The Southern Bivouac,* and Ethelbert D. Warfield, in a scholarly monograph, *The Kentucky Resolutions,* both attempted to show that the true author of the Resolutions, as well as their mover in the Kentucky legislature, was John Breckinridge. From 1798 to 1821, long after his death, the honor or the odium of authorship had belonged to Breckinridge. Then, it will be recalled, the *Richmond Enquirer* trumpeted the news that Jefferson was their author. Startled by this disclosure, J. Cabell Breckinridge wrote to Jefferson for confirmation of his father's title to fame. Jefferson, in reply on December 11, 1821, confessed "the naked truth." He wrote the Resolutions and delivered them to Breckinridge for action in Kentucky. This was a bitter blow, according to Warfield, to the Breckinridge clan. As if it were not enough, Jefferson's letter appeared in the *Memoirs* eight years later under the heading "To----Nicholas." Presumably the name of Jefferson's correspondent was indecipherable on the press-copy, and Randolph, well aware of the part George Nicholas had played in the Kentucky agitation against the Alien and Sedition Laws, supposed the letter had been addressed to one of his sons. So the Nicholas family, into which Randolphs had married, was able to claim that George Nicholas had moved the famous Resolutions. This was demonstrably false: Nicholas had not been in the legislature in 1798. But Randolph's error tripped many historians into the false position. It was finally corrected in 1886 by Durrett, who reproduced from the Breckinridge papers the letter of December 11, 1821. It was plainly addressed to J. Cabell Breckinridge. Sarah N. Randolph, finding some of her Nicholas kin unshaken by Durrett's disclosure, searched and found among the Jefferson papers in Washington the corroborating evidence. John Breckinridge, then, had carried the Resolutions to Kentucky and moved their adoption.

Durrett and Warfield were not content with this victory. They built up a theory of the Kentuckian's intimate association with the Resolutions. Breckinridge, the theory ran, was visiting his old home near Charlottesville in the summer of 1798, when Jefferson took up the question of state protest against the Federalist laws. He brought two men to Monticello for consultation, W. C. Nicholas (the Virginia brother of George Nicholas) and Breckinridge. Here, at their request, Jefferson sketched out a rough draft of the Resolutions, and also decided upon their origination, not in North Carolina as he had first planned, but in Kentucky, where Breckinridge could shepherd them through the legislature. Breckinridge carried the draft across the mountains, made a "searching revision" of it, and independently managed the fight for the Resolutions. Much more than Jefferson's errand boy, he was, as his friends had always insisted, "the responsible author of the Kentucky Resolutions of 1798."

This was sheer fantasy. The "radical difference" which Breckinridge's advocates professed to find between Jefferson's draft and the text adopted consisted of two rather minor points in two of the nine resolves. Even if the changes were important, there was no proof Breckinridge had made them. The notion of his part in the inception of the Resolutions hinged on the occurrence, hinted by Jefferson, of a meeting at Monticello. Miss Randolph, writing in the *Nation*, flatly denied that Breckinridge ever met or talked with Jefferson in 1798. He simply received the draft from an intermediary, W. C. Nicholas, who in a letter to Breckinridge on October 10 spoke of Jefferson's regret that he had not seen his Kentucky friend. Many years later the Harvard historian, Edward Channing, came up with a letter from Nicholas to Jefferson at about the same date. It reported Breckinridge's disappointment that he had been unable to see Jefferson because of the latter's desire to wrap in secrecy his connection with the Kentucky Resolutions. The authorship controversy raised by Durrett and Warfield in behalf of John Breckinridge actually led, in the course of time, to the magnification of Jefferson's responsibility for the Kentucky Resolutions.

With the first class of questions clarified, a few historians began a needed revaluation of the theory and purpose of the Kentucky Resolutions. Neither Warfield nor Durrett defended the theory, as it was then commonly understood. But they believed the Jefferson draft was alone heretical, needing only, in Warfield's words, "to be acted on by bold and uncompromising men to be all that the advocates of nullification in South Carolina held that it was." Scholars noted numerous differences between the theories of Jefferson and Calhoun; in the end, however, the two ran together in their minds. So long as men viewed 1798 from the perspectives of 1832 and 1861, they were bound to interpret the Virginia and Kentucky Resolutions almost exclusively as state rights documents.

One of the first signs of a new perspective was James Schouler's discussion of the Resolutions in the first volume of his *History*. Schouler, a Union veteran and Boston lawyer, could not approve of the "doctrines of '98." But he begged men to see Jefferson's Resolutions in context.

Acts probably unconstitutional had passed, and personal liberty was in jeopardy. Jefferson, on the present occasion, did not preach disunion, but decentralization. He meant, and he pursued, a political resistance for political effect. . . . It was because Jefferson's name was found long after to honor this method of State remonstrance, that the Kentucky and Virginia protests were brought at length from their dusty archives, not for nullifying Federal supremacy alone, not for obstructing a tyrannous Congress, but to resist the enforcement of legitimate legislation, to rupture and break the whole Union.

If Jefferson had only preached "decentralization," then he had done no more than many good Unionists ever since. Frank M. Anderson went beyond this still essentially legalistic interpretation in several articles published between 1899 and 1912. Unquestionably, Anderson said, the fundamental aim of the Adams administration was the suppression of political liberty. "The Virginia and Kentucky Resolutions of 1798, whatever their whole purpose, were designed primarily

as a protest against the infringement of this principle by the Alien
and Sedition Laws." What the Resolutions actually *were*, as distinguished from what they became, could best be ascertained, Anderson
thought, by the study of contemporary opinion about them. And this
showed, first, that the Resolutions were endorsed by Republicans as
a solemn protest against infringements of liberty; and, second, that
the verdict of 1800 was neither much influenced by the Resolutions
nor an endorsement of their constitutional theory.

Both conclusions were novel in 1900. The latter led to a redistribu-
tion of emphasis among the factors at work in the election of 1800.
Channing, for example, said there was no connection between the
Resolutions (or the infamous laws) and the Republican victory.
William E. Dodd, in his influential *Statesmen of the Old South*,
made no mention of the Kentucky Resolutions in discussing Jefferson, and he treated the South Carolina theory as if it were entirely
de novo. More important were the new insights obtained when the
Resolutions were wrested from constitutional history and relocated
within the history of freedom. Reviewing the current tendency to
reinterpret the American past in the light of the idea of democracy,
Andrew C. McLaughlin, in his presidential address before the American Historical Association in 1914, singled out the fresh reading of
the Resolutions of '98 "as embodying in a new way the principles
upon which the Revolution—not the Civil War—was fought." Jefferson's purpose in 1798 was to buttress a union dedicated to freedom.
If this viewpoint should be adopted, the Kentucky Resolutions would
once again become, though for a different reason, one of the assets
of Jefferson's reputation.

The collection of Jefferson muniments and manuscripts—an enterprise that rarely received the attention it deserved—proceeded more
by accident than by design. A case in point was the Jefferson Bible,
the primary exhibit in the ultimately successful defense of Jefferson
in the eyes of a Christian community.

In order to reveal the "pure principles" of Christianity, Jefferson
wrote to John Adams in 1813, "we should have to strip off the
artificial vestments in which they have been muffled by priests,"
and carefully select from the four evangelists "the very words only

of Jesus." He went on to say that he had "performed this operation for my own use," reassembling the verses so as to present a connected narrative of Jesus' life and teachings. He later improved on this "Philosophy of Jesus." The same verses were cut from Greek, Latin, French, and English texts, pasted neatly in parallel columns on the pages of an octavo volume, bound in red morocco, and named on the title page in his own hand, "The Life and Morals of Jesus of Nazareth." This, he said, "is a document in proof that I am a *real Christian,* that is to say, a disciple of the doctrines of Jesus." He kept it to himself, as was his custom in religious matters. Randall, who saw the book at Edgehill and buried his description of it in an appendix, stated that Jefferson's grandchildren had not known of its existence until after his death; they then learned from a family friend that Jefferson had been in the habit of reading from it nightly before bed.

Nothing more was heard of the Jefferson Bible until 1890, when it was described in the report of the Senate Library Committee on a bill for the purchase of the papers belonging to Sarah N. Randolph. The bill failed; but Dr. Cyrus Adler, Librarian of the Smithsonian Institution, who had earlier been on the book's trail, determined to obtain it for the museum. In 1895 he persuaded Carolina Randolph to part with the volume for four hundred dollars. For five years it rested, seldom disturbed apparently, in Adler's office safe. In 1900 an inquiring congressman, John F. Lacey of Iowa, got a look at the rarity, and wrote a short article which was printed in many newspapers. He was instrumental in the private publication of the book in St. Louis two years later. At the same time, having aroused considerable public interest, he sponsored a resolution for its publication, in full facsimile, by Congress. Congress quickly agreed, as the government had published most of Jefferson's other works and as nine thousand copies of this one were to be placed at the disposal of the congressmen. There were scattered protests that the circulation of Jefferson's infidel opinions under the imprimatur of the United States government constituted "a direct, public and powerful attack upon the religion of Christians everywhere." But the legislators stood by their decision.

The Life and Morals of Jesus of Nazareth was published by the

government in 1904, reproduced the same year in Volume XX of the
Memorial Edition, and it has since appeared in many different
versions. While it presented some fascinating technical problems for
bibliophiles and New Testament scholars, the work was chiefly interesting for the light it cast on Jefferson's religion. Expurgating from
the New Testament everything that failed to satisfy his own reason,
presenting Jesus solely as a human being and teacher of morals,
Jefferson's Bible could not on any strict accounting be considered
the work of a Christian. Yet it had obviously been prepared in a
reverent spirit, and it accorded exactly with the tendency of liberal
Protestantism to focus the person and the morals of Jesus. As Leonardo, in his famous portrait, had removed the unreal halo from
above Jesus' head and put the radiance in His face, Henry E. Jackson
observed, so Jefferson removed the extraneous elements from Jesus'
literary portrait to let his own words express his spirit. Believing
that no true religion was possible except on the terms of absolute
freedom of mind and conscience, Jefferson's "system of morals" along
with his assaults on ecclesiastical power, it could be said, actually
testified to the depth of his religious devotion. Despite the views
expressed by clerics like John C. Kilgo and freethinkers like Robert
G. Ingersoll, Jefferson was clearly no "Virginia Voltaire."

Whether or not Jefferson's Bible satisfied his claim to being "a
real Christian" became a somewhat academic question. By certain
progressive criteria it did. Among the orthodox it was enough to
erase all but the faintest traces of the infidel tradition. The radical
gloss on Jefferson's religious opinions had worn thin; if the mass of
Christians could not condone his deistic faith, they had ceased to
believe he was a dangerous heretic and were increasingly ready to
acknowledge their religious, as well as political, debt to him. But
what church could embrace Jefferson? Certainly not the Episcopal,
though Jefferson died a member of that church.* Another, the Bap-

* The Episcopal clergy in Virginia had not altogether forgiven Jefferson for
his work in the disestablishment. In 1908 there was erected at Cumberland
Parish, Lewisburg County, a tablet to the memory of Dr. John Cameron, deceased 1815, inscribed with these lines: "Selected by the Church as Chairman
of its Committee to cope with Mr. Thomas Jefferson against the Act for the
Despoliation of the Church." (The allegedly despoiling acts were those of 1799
and 1802, with which Jefferson had no direct connection.) Possibly indicative

tist, remembered him for his services to religious freedom, but it made no spiritual claim on him.

The only Protestant denomination to have shown the slightest interest in Jefferson's religious remains was the Unitarian. In the twentieth century, Jefferson became one of the saints of this "free religious faith." Although never formally a convert, he adhered, Unitarians believed, to their three cardinal principles: freedom of mind and spirit, tolerance of religious difference, trust in reason and science. He was a prophet of *this* Christian faith. "I trust," he had written, "that there is not a young man now living who will not die a Unitarian." Some argued that Jefferson had directly influenced William Ellery Channing and other precursors, chiefly New Englanders, of American Unitarianism. There was slight basis for this. The Jefferson Bible, with its disbelief in revelation and the miracles, would have appeared radical to the Unitarians of Channing's generation and for decades after. In the twentieth century, however, the book could be accepted as, in effect, a Unitarian Bible. The Unitarian apotheosis of Jefferson occurred on Sunday, April 13, 1947, in a service at the Jefferson Memorial in Washington. Passages from his writings were sung as hymns, the Jefferson Bible was read as Scripture, and Frederick May Eliot, President of the American Unitarian Association, preached a sermon, "What Kind of Christian Was Thomas Jefferson?" Should Christianity ever be revolutionized on Unitarian principles, Eliot said, "it will owe a great debt to the free religious faith of Thomas Jefferson."

By 1947, though, or even two or three decades earlier, rabbis, priests, and ministers of various denominations were acclaiming the reality of Jefferson's faith and drawing lessons from it. In the twentieth century, Jefferson's religion has been the subject of more articles, many of them scholarly, than any other topic except politics; and the great majority have attempted to demonstrate that he was *some kind* of Christian. His conversion to Christianity at the hands of posterity was due to many factors. By far the most important was organized

---

of changing opinion at about this time, however, was the fact that the famous Bruton Parish Church in Williamsburg named one of its best pews in Jefferson's honor.

religion's growing appreciation of its debt to Jefferson for the blessings of freedom. "He made America a cathedral where all men may
worship God according to the dictates of their conscience." But the
authentic and positive evidence that Jefferson's liberal faith was
entwined with Christ's teachings was afforded by the Jefferson Bible,
an almost forgotten relic which, when brought to life, exerted a
profound influence on his reputation.

Whatever else the Declaration of Independence had been to Americans—a charter, a philosophy, an anthem—it had also been a document of surpassing interest in itself. The original embossed copy was
displayed at the Centennial Exhibition in Philadelphia, and before
and after 1876 in Washington. As early as 1817, facsimile or near-
facsimile reproductions were published and sold commercially. Anything associated with the birth of the Declaration was interesting.
The little writing desk upon which it had been written was made a
gift to the United States in 1880 from the late Joseph Coolidge, who
had received it from Jefferson in 1825. The house where Jefferson
wrote the Declaration was a matter of controversy even in Jefferson's
lifetime. Thomas C. Donaldson definitely established its location at
the southwest corner of 7th and Market Streets. When it was de-
molished to make room for a bank in 1883, Donaldson fondly gathered up its remains and, some years later, wrote a book about it.
    The document was cherished and sometimes debated in the nine-
teenth century, but not much studied. John H. Hazelton inaugurated
the scholarly inquiry with *The Declaration of Independence—Its
History* in 1906. Hazelton was not alone; but his book, a massive
compilation and careful winnowing of everything related to the
history of the document from the First Continental Congress to its
proclamation, laid the basis from which further study could proceed.
This study took two general directions: first, the evolution of the
text, which involved the identification of several drafts and copies,
the comparative analysis and interpretation of the changes made at
different stages of composition, and the determination of direct influences upon it. The quest for understanding through the record of
the document itself approached the point of perfection in Julian
Boyd's Jefferson Bicentennial brochure on the Declaration. Intellec-

tual historians pursued the other line of investigation. Where did
the draftsman, Jefferson, get his ideas? What was the philosophy of
the Declaration? What were the relations between ideas and events
in its history? Scholars seeking answers to these questions could not
properly ignore the evolution of the text, which as Carl Becker,
the outstanding interpreter of the Declaration's philosophy, was to
show furnished indispensable keys to its meaning. Becker's *The
Declaration of Independence*, in 1922, knit the two lines of inquiry
together to form a small masterpiece.

The degree of merit fairly belonging to Jefferson on account of
the Declaration had long been in dispute; and so it becomes a question of some interest how well his fame fared in the new research.
Few men credited the fantastic claim advanced by William H. Burr
around 1880, and elaborated by a string of Thomas Paine's disciples
down to the present day, that Paine was the author, or the ghost-
writer, of the Declaration. The Mecklenburg Declaration of Independence had numerous supporters until two scholarly works in the
first decade of this century demonstrated to the satisfaction of all
sensible men that the North Carolina document was a good deal less
than its title implied and of no discernible influence. Careful study
of the Declaration seemed to increase rather than lessen the impression of Jefferson's personal responsibility. It had been said that he
merely acted as one of a committee; but analysis did not bear out
this view. It had been said that he merely copied other men's thoughts
and writings; but the discovery, for instance, of Jefferson's Virginia
draft-constitution, with its long preamble arraigning the King, demonstrated that the major written source of the Declaration was another Jeffersonian document.

Although several students questioned the literal accuracy of Jefferson's statement that he had turned to nothing in writing the Declaration, they saw no merit in the long-standing criticism on the grounds
of unoriginality. "But it was not the object of the Declaration to
produce anything new," Daniel Webster had protested in his famous
eulogy of Jefferson and Adams. The new interpreters made the point
again, and in doing so invariably recalled Jefferson's own view of his
task: "Not to find out new principles, or new arguments, never before
thought of . . . but to place before mankind the common sense of the

subject, in terms so plain as to command their assent." The Declaration's lack of originality, in this narrow sense, thus came to be regarded one of its greatest merits. All the old attempts to detract from Jefferson's fame as the author of the Declaration were destined for oblivion.

In a different category were the attempts to assign certain intellectual antecedents to the Declaration and its author. If the problem was not to explain the originality of the philosophy, then it must be to determine the key sources of Jefferson's "common sense." In the past, the philosophy was prominently associated with French ideas. The new studies usually traced it to seventeenth-century England. It was Lockean, not Rousseauistic. The old tradition hung on, of course; but the separation of the Declaration from the French philosophy helped to mark the deterioration of the Gallicized image of Jefferson.

Surely the most curious, in some respects the most significant, notion of Jefferson's intellectual debt was set forth by Catholic scholars. In 1917, Gaillard Hunt, of the Library of Congress, published an article in the *Catholic Historical Review* suggesting that Jefferson (and George Mason, author of the Virginia Declaration of Rights) got his ideas on political equality and consent of the governed from the sixteenth-century Jesuit, Cardinal Bellarmine. There was not a shred of evidence that Jefferson had ever read Bellarmine; but, Hunt said, he had in his library, and presumably had read, Robert Filmer's *Patriarcha*, a defense of the divine right theory which quoted for refutation a key passage from Bellarmine. This passage, Hunt supposed, must have lodged in Jefferson's mind to reappear when he took up his pen to write the Declaration. "Did the Americans," Hunt asked, "realize that they were staking their lives, their fortunes, and their sacred honor in support of a theory of government which had come down to them as announced by a Catholic priest?" A number of Catholic scholars and publicists rode Hunt's thesis much harder and farther than he had intended. The Declaration was "a Catholic document," democracy "a Popish innovation," they exulted. Early attacked by non-Catholic scholars, the "Bellarmine-Jefferson legend" was challenged by a Capuchin Father,

John M. Lenhart, in 1931-32. He renewed the attack a decade later. By then most Catholic scholars seemed ready to agree with Father Lenhart that the religious sources of the Declaration were Protestant rather than Catholic. From the early Orestes Brownson, Catholic scholars had branded the Declaration, mildly, as Puritan and Lockean; stringently, as Jacobin and Rousseauistic. Perhaps the effort to link Jefferson and Bellarmine reflected the desire in certain quarters of the Church for an accommodation between Catholic theology and American democracy. But there was little basis for the connection in Jefferson's thought or, for that matter, in Bellarmine's.

The search for the intellectual roots of the Declaration proved a frustrating experience. "Where Jefferson got his ideas," Carl Becker announced, "is hardly so much a question as where he could have got away from them." What, then, was his peculiar merit as author of the Declaration? It was essentially a literary merit, Becker thought, "the peculiar felicity of expression" which John Adams praised in him and which was the main reason he was chosen to draft the document. Not the ideas but the style made the Declaration Jefferson's. Going from the style to the man, Becker reached a surprising estimate of Jefferson's character and genius. The Declaration had been commonly described as "manly," "aggressive," "throbbing with life in each of its nervous sentences." Moses Tyler had called it a "war-song." And of course the most quoted criticism, that of Rufus Choate, had referred to "the glittering and sounding generalities" of a "passionate" manifesto. Becker described it in terms just the reverse of these.

Taking the Declaration as a whole, this is indeed its conspicuous quality: it states clearly, reasons lucidly, exposes felicitously; its high virtue is in this, that it makes a strong bid for the reader's assent. But it was beyond the power of Jefferson to impregnate the Declaration with qualities that would give to the reader's assent the moving force of profound conviction. With all its precision, concise rapidity, its clarity, its subtle implications and engaging felicities, one misses a certain unsophisticated directness, a certain sense of impregnable solidity and massive strength, a certain effect of passion restrained and deep convictions held in reserve, which would have given to it that accent of perfect sincerity and that emotional content which belong to the grand manner.

The thought, like the style, was a little too precious, too bland, too abstract, too fragile, ready to fall apart at the merest brush with real life. Jefferson's true intellectual home, Becker said, was the Paris of the Encyclopedists, "those generous souls who loved mankind by virtue of not knowing too much about men." Returning to his theme twenty years later, Becker rephrased it in terms of a recognizable dualism in Jefferson's character. "Jefferson was a democrat by intellectual conviction," Becker said, "but by training and temperament a Virginia aristocrat—a man of cultivated tastes and preferences, with an aversion from all that is crude and boisterous, vulgar and passionate, in human intercourse." Democracy, in sum, was an idea for Jefferson; he had not sufficiently experienced, and he did not sufficiently comprehend, "the harsh, brute facts of the world" in which it must be realized.

The realities of the modern world, in Becker's view, had undermined the "humane and engaging faith" stated in the second paragraph of the Declaration. Few thinking men any longer supposed that "natural rights" furnished an adequate foundation for government. The Declaration's truths were not "self-evident"—that notion was part of its naïveté. "To ask whether the natural rights philosophy of the Declaration of Independence is true or false is essentially a meaningless question." It was meaningless to the historian since it had no bearing on the actual purpose of the Declaration: the justification of American independence to the world. Recognition that the Declaration belonged to a particular historical milieu did not detract from its magnificent virtues. Yet, Becker thought, the very felicity with which it stated and Jefferson represented "the common sense of the matter" in 1776 also demonstrated, in retrospect, its and Jefferson's limitations in the forward campaign of history.

Primary documents are the beginning of historical understanding, but it was not until the end of the nineteenth century that American scholars made significant progress in the accumulation, verification, and analysis of the documentary record of the national life. The varied evidences of the movement in Jefferson historiography, almost without exception, proved beneficial to his reputation. Jefferson's papers had been so badly managed—broken up, passed out as souvenirs, abandoned in private cabinets or entirely lost, and botched in editing—that the recovery and purification of the record was one of the principal tasks of American scholarship.

No one fully appreciated this in the period under study. Those who appreciated it best were motivated, like the two Fords, not by personal or political adulation but by the conviction that a man such as Jefferson was worthy of knowledge. Most men continued to observe the figure through the lenses of partisan prejudice or preconceived theory; accordingly, the primary writings and documents, when they were encountered at all, were glossed or misunderstood or recklessly used. Gradually, however, a more prudent and respectful approach was asserting itself. The benefits that might be expected from it were suggested by the Massachusetts Historical Society's acquisition of Jefferson's private papers, by Ford's careful edition, by the fresh inquiry into the history of the Kentucky Resolutions, by the discovery and publication of the Jefferson Bible, and by the new researches of the Declaration of Independence. The scholarly quest for the document was far from its destination; but a continuous line of progress runs to Jefferson's present-day editor, who knows that Jefferson's altar, like the altar of the Puritans' God, "needs not our pollishings."

3. Beard and the Parties

The British scholar and M.P., James Bryce, commencing his study of American institutions in 1883, was puzzled by the absence of any account of the organization and functioning of political parties. "In America the great moving forces are the parties," he was to write in The American Commonwealth; yet citizens had described their government as if "the vast and intricate political machine" which lay outside the Constitution and furnished its motive power did not exist. "The historical action of the parties, their principles or tenets, their local distribution, the social influence that pervaded them, and the character of the men who led them—these were the matters on which attention had been fixed, to the neglect of the less attractive and less conspicuous questions connected with the machinery by which they worked." The judgment was singularly correct. The conception of "the history of the parties" ruled the mind. In Washington's first administration, the distinguished popularizer John Fiske said, "the seeds of all party differences hereafter to bear fruit in America were sown and sedulously nurtured." The inevitable corollary followed. As in philosophy all men must be Aristotelians or Platonists, Fiske thought, "So it may be said that in American politics all men must be disciples either of Jefferson or of Hamilton." Bryce himself paid homage to this historical convention. But he saw that it was no longer a viable one. A new era had dawned, the nation faced grave problems calling for new principles and policies; yet neither the parties nor their interpreters seemed able to throw off the past. "The American parties now continue to exist, because they have existed," was Bryce's harsh judgment. "The mill has been constructed, and its machinery goes on turning, even when there is no grist to grind."

According to the convention, the parties originated in the natural duality of political life. The controlling dispositions of men are such that in every community there are those who trust the people and wish to enlarge their sphere of competence, while others fear the people and wish to check or control them. Jefferson had repeatedly stated the idea. Paul Ford considered it one of the four core ideas of Jefferson's philosophy. In the political tradition it was primarily, but not exclusively, a Jeffersonian idea. Liberty and order, the masses and the classes, idealism and realism—polar terms of this sort, as well as "Jeffersonian" and "Hamiltonian," were commonly employed to characterize the "grand division" of parties. The abstract conflict crystallized in the United States, thereby strengthening its influence, around opposing doctrines on the Constitution: strict versus loose construction and state rights versus national supremacy. This theory of the parties was as old as the parties themselves. It was restated to the fullest extent in the influential writings, both scholarly and popular, of the Princeton professor, Alexander Johnston, in the eighteen-eighties.

Parties originated and had their enduring basis, therefore, in contradictory political temperaments under the formal arrangements of the United States Constitution. This was the convention. Jefferson, in organizing an opposition party, was moved by democratic principles which were as natural to him as aristocratic principles were to Hamilton. When he said the Republicans "cherished the people," he spoke the truth, and this generous, if somewhat demagogical, faith was the secret of his power. Few of Jefferson's critics any longer cared to dispute the point. After they had said all that was to be said against Jefferson's party leadership—his inscrutable cunning and supple management, his monomania with "monarchical conspiracy," his visionary and particularistic ideas—they conceded as his heroic compensation what the multitude remembered as the essence of his greatness: "trust the people." "His abiding faith in the multitude . . ." Edward Elliott declared, "was the secret of his success as the greatest political leader this country has produced." But Jefferson's importance, as Bryce said in his rendering of the old theme, also lay in the fact "that he became the representative not merely of democracy, but of local democracy." The democratic ideal, in short, was associated with local self-government, the maintenance of which required a strict view of the federal Constitution.

This grand conception of the parties had completely lost touch with realities. It failed of course to take sufficient account of the centralizing action of democracy. Moreover, scholarly inquiry gradually undermined the fundamental premise of political duality. Mosei Ostrogorski's ground-breaking *Democracy and the Organization of Political Parties,* in 1902, traced in detail the evolution of democratic parties from an original collision of principle, through successive improvements in organizational force, ending in purely mechanical contrivances by which two sets of politicians struggled "to get out of politics 'what there was in it' for the benefit of the Organization or of the allied special interests." The conception of "the history of the parties," cultivating as it did the idea of radical, uniform, and continuous party division from the origin of the government, was part of a diseased system. Although they ceased to be agents of principle and became powers in their own right, the parties nevertheless maintained the illusion of continuity with the fundamental cleavage from which they sprang. All that had been said about "the enduring basis of parties" was, from Ostrogorski's standpoint, dangerously misleading.

This realistic approach, as it was applied by other students to the formative period, led to the realization that parties had furnished, not principles primarily, but the machinery necessary to make the

Constitution a going concern. Why was it that a Constitution intended
by its framers to operate without parties so soon gave rise to them?
The new answers to this riddle pointed up several *institutional* factors: first, the separation of powers, which called party organization
into being in order to secure the harmonious action of the government's several branches; second, the nominating system, since in the
absence of constitutional provision for the screening of candidates
to elective office, parties assumed this crucial job; third, the need for
some means of facilitating orderly change of administration in response to changing public opinion.

Jefferson's place in party history was especially significant in connection with the third development. The studies of Anson D. Morse,
Jesse Macy, and Henry Jones Ford at the turn of the century, of
O. G. Libby, Edgar E. Robinson, and others sometime later, all
agreed that Jefferson organized the first party in the electorate,
aroused the citizenry, and carried through a peaceful revolution in
the government. While the Federalist ideal was the rule of a united
governing class, the Republicans, according to Robinson, "saw in
the organization of the voters themselves the vital power that made
possible an organization of public opinion."

Conceived in this way, democratic party organization was a substitute for revolution. Hamilton and the Federalists, whatever might
be said for the efficiency with which they organized the new government, had no idea of how it might be perpetuated in conformity with
"the consent of the governed." Circumstances forced Jefferson to go
outside the government, into the electorate, in order to defeat the
ruling power. Succeeding in this, the principle established was revolutionary. "It was the great unconscious achievement of Thomas
Jefferson," Henry Jones Ford declared, "to open constitutional channels of political agitation, to start the processes by which the development of our constitution is carried on." The birth of an opposition
party was the salvation of the government, the Federalist-minded
Ford argued, for change became possible without destruction. Jefferson's "trust the people" was, therefore, something more than an abstract principle or faith. His proud boast—"the revolution of 1800"—
had some basis after all, though perhaps not the one he had supposed.
Walter Lippmann described it as a "revolution in the mind." "For it

was Jefferson," Lippmann thought, "who first taught the American people to regard the Constitution as an instrument of democracy, and he stereotyped the images, the ideas, and even many of the phrases, in which Americans ever since have described politics to each other." The Constitution was in spirit rewritten.

Only recently, Andrew C. McLaughlin said to the assemblage of historians in 1914, has the political party been seen in its true light as a vital institution of government.

We have commonly studied parties as if the main thing was the doctrines which they professed; we now see that we must study them with the knowledge that principles were often only *impedimenta,* and we wish to know how . . . they advanced or hindered the activities and qualities of a people who would be and thought they were self-governing and were win- -ing and using opportunity for self-realization.

Although the new viewpoint, brought to bear on Jefferson, focused once again the character and influence of his party leadership, it led to estimates quite different from those that had prevailed in the past. The principles and doctrines habitually associated with the party he founded were transient; they became useless shadows. The institution of the party itself permanently revolutionized the system of the Founding Fathers. Parties might degenerate in the course of their development, but it was impossible to conceive of democracy without them.

Historians thus came to take a more sympathetic view of certain actions incident to Jefferson's party leadership. The Kentucky Resolutions, as previously noticed, came to be regarded less as a statement of creed than as a maneuver to keep open the channels of political agitation. New studies of Jefferson's executive management of the patronage concluded that his policy was as proscriptive as the Federalists had charged and as Jackson's had always been supposed. "Technically," Carl Russell Fish wrote in his authoritative *Civil Service and the Patronage,* "one must assign to Jefferson the introduction of the spoils system into the national service, for party service was recognized as a reason for appointment to office, and party dissent as a cause for removal." The historian did not condemn Jefferson on this account, since he appreciated the democratic and organizational merits of the spoils system. Through it, for the first time in history, a widely scattered people came into possession of its government.

Despite the scholarly attention given to the origins and workings of the early parties, Jefferson as party leader remained vague and elusive. It was simply not possible to draw from the facts a picture of Jefferson mustering the scattered ranks of the opposition, breathing principle and discipline into this army, and leading it successfully against the fortress of Federalism; yet this was the picture the interpretive framework demanded. Even among serious scholars, traditions have a way of filling the void of facts. In the political tradition, Jefferson was the enterprising leader of the Republican party. The new viewpoint made his leadership respectable. Not for some time would scholars question the accuracy of a tradition which they found meagerly supported in Jefferson's history. They tended to solve the riddle by resort to timeworn opinions of Jefferson's personality. He was "cool, subtle, persevering, and insinuating, laying his deepest plans with the most profound secrecy," they said. "Almost never," Channing wrote, "has a political party been so efficiently and so secretly marshalled and led." If Jefferson was the genius of the Republican party, the innovator of party organization in the political system, his actual performance in this role was a major mystery.

In the twentieth century, the scholars' emphasis shifted from the political to the economic sources and functions of the parties. The first type of study pulled parties down from the clouds of principle; the second type sank them into the economic foundations of society. The former found the key to Jefferson's achievement in his substitution for the narrow class unity of the Federalists a system of organizing government through party; the latter called attention to the class basis of the Jeffersonian party itself.

Charles A. Beard's *Economic Origins of Jeffersonian Democracy* applied the economic interpretation with impressive effect in 1915. The book was a sequel to Beard's highly controversial work on the Constitution, published two years earlier, and the acids of time have treated it more gently. Many strands of thought were gathered into Beard's analysis of Jeffersonian Democracy. First, of course, the revaluation of parties as functioning institutions. The conventional explanation of party history was absurd; it might, Beard thought, be summed up in the proposition, "God made Democrats and Republicans, and that is all there is to it." Second, the interest group theory of the political process, one of the products of the new research. Beard admired Arthur Bentley's *The Process of Government*, the first systematic study of politics in terms of group behavior. The economic interpretation in Beard's hands was less a class than an interest group interpretation; and he found its classic American statement in Madison's tenth paper of *The Federalist*. The character and distribution of property, according to Madison, substantially determined party divisions and public policy. Third, the sectional viewpoint in American historiography, centered in the writings and immense influence of F. J. Turner. Turner's frontier theory led to renewed emphasis on the agrarian and Western characteristics of Jeffersonian Democracy. Beard took a single sentence from Turner as the motto of his book: "We may trace the contest between the capitalist and the democratic pioneer from the earliest colonial days." Fourth, the critical study of the United States Constitution. According to these studies, including Beard's own, the Constitution was framed in the interests of certain capitalist groups and in hostility to democracy. J. Allen Smith's *The Spirit of American Government*, in 1907, expanded the idea into a comprehensive theory of American history. Finally, the general intellectual orientation of what was called the "New History." The domain of the past ought to be wrested from the conservatives, who used it to buttress the status quo, and made an instrument of progress along liberal lines. History might liberate the mind from the tyrannies of the past; it might demonstrate—what social science was only beginning to understand—the power of economic forces in effecting political changes; it might even become the veritable science of progress.

Beard approached Jeffersonian Democracy with a keen awareness of the obstacles to progress in that "joyous season" of reform and enlightenment just before the First World War. Each of his historical monographs over a four-year period, 1912-15, was addressed to a single mighty obstruction. *The Supreme Court and the Constitution*, the first, demonstrated the organic relation of the institution of judicial review to the system of the Founding Fathers, and its success, as they intended, in checking popular legislation harmful to capitalist power. The book on the Constitution correlated the political design with the property interests of the men who conceived, framed, and ratified it. The current obstacles to social and economic reform were, therefore, built into the Constitution; but Beard seemed to say that the obstacles might be overcome by an attack as imaginative, as well organized and deeply founded in economic interest, as the Federalist attack in 1787. Why had the twentieth-century Progressives faltered? Beard gave part of the answer in *The Economic Origins of Jeffersonian Democracy.*

The greatest obstacle of all was within the American democratic mind: its commitment to an outworn Jeffersonian ideology, its idealization of the democratic tradition, its failure to understand the economic basis of political power, its moralistic reading of Jefferson in terms, to borrow the contemporaneous phrases of Van Wyck Brooks, of "high ideals" instead of "catchpenny realities." Viewed in this light, Beard's *Jeffersonian Democracy* was, as Max Lerner has said, "the meatiest and richest" of all his books. It was, moreover, equally as radical in its implications as the book on the Constitution, which raised such a fuss. The one, aimed at conservatives, exploded the myth of the Constitution. The other, aimed at liberals like himself, dispelled in the same methodical way the aura that surrounded Jefferson and the democratic tradition. Having removed the Constitution "from the realm of pure political ethics" and set it "in the dusty way of earthy strife and common economic endeavor," as Beard said, he undertook the same operation on the movement that rose against the Constitution—the movement of Jeffersonian Democracy.

Beard opened his inquiry with a careful argument on the conformity of the Federalist-Republican division with the conflict over the adoption of the Constitution. The friends and enemies of the Constitution were the friends and enemies of the Federalist administrations. This position was generally assumed, he said, until the publication of O. G. Libby's investigations. Libby held that the Constitution ceased to be a devisive issue once the new government went into operation, that the fluid factionalism of Washington's administration did not congeal into firm party alignments until 1798, that only then did Jefferson launch the Republican party on the

ample platform of freedom and expansion. Beard denied Libby's
entire thesis. The first administration merely gathered the fruits of
the victory on the Constitution; the Hamiltonian system actually
intensified the capitalist-agrarian conflict on which the history of the
new nation had turned; and Jefferson formed the Republican party
on the agrarian base of Anti-Federalism in 1792.

Beard had the better of the argument with Libby. His thesis was,
nevertheless, vulnerable. As was his habit, he softened the shock of
his own opinion by an impressive show of higher authority. The
older historians close to the events in question, Beard said, supported
his position. What historians? In the main, the Federalist historians
of the first half of the nineteenth century. The standard works most
often cited by Beard were those of Marshall, Hildreth, and Gibbs.
In the 467 pages of his book Beard never cited Randall or any other
Jeffersonian historian of the period under study. In truth, the underlying idea of continuity was a Federalist idea. It was as if Beard had
taken one of the myths of Federalism—that the Federalists were the
friends of the Constitution and the Jeffersonians its enemies—drained
off its grosser content, added some fresh ingredients, and then presented the result as a true history of the original parties. Republican
arguments to the contrary by Jefferson, Madison, and John Taylor,
Beard laid to the "extraordinary cleverness" with which these partisans "claimed the Constitution for themselves." Beard was committed
to the Federalist position by his earlier book. If the Constitution
was framed in hostility to democracy and for the benefit of capitalist
groups, then it naturally followed that the Hamiltonian system conformed to the Constitution.

In the last sentence of his book, Beard offered this summary definition of Jeffersonian Democracy:

Jeffersonian Democracy simply meant the possession of the federal government by the agrarian masses led by an aristocracy of slave-owning planters,
and the theoretical repudiation of the right to use the Government for the
benefit of any capitalistic groups, fiscal, banking, or manufacturing.

Jeffersonian Democracy did *not* involve, in any fundamental way, an
attack on property or the political privileges it conferred, a revision
of the Constitution upon either state rights or equalitarian principles,

or a triumph of democracy over aristocracy. The government simply
passed from one class to another. The planter leadership was even
more of a gentry than the Northern leadership it replaced. Anti-
capitalist in theory, Jeffersonian Democracy did not, in fact, weaken
the political foundations of capitalist power.

The key term in the definition was *agrarian*, which Beard used
in the confusing double sense of agricultural and anti-capitalist.
Hamilton's fiscal policy was "the recognized source of substantially
all of the partisan opposition to the government." Men opposed
Hamilton's system principally because it was designed to stimulate
capitalist enterprise at the expense of agriculture. Although other
administration measures evoked strong opposition, they were accessory to the financial system, Beard thought. Hamilton's justification
to posterity for his indulgence of class interests was founded in the
conviction that he thereby secured the ascendancy of the national
authority. Beard, of course, recognized this genius of Hamilton's
statesmanship, but he considered it a genius rooted in capitalism
rather than in nationalism. Reciprocally, state rights was merely a
weapon of the agrarian interest, whose leader seemed to ascribe to
capitalism "the doctrine of innate depravity." Nothing in Adams's
administration altered the fundamental basis of party division. The
polemics as well as the distribution of the vote in the election of
1800 showed the persistent "alignment of agrarian mass against the
capitalistic class."

The historian's major concern was not Jefferson's party leadership
but rather, as Beard defined it, "whether underlying all his general
doctrines there was not in Jefferson's political science a reasonably
clear recognition of economic forces as the basis of party divisions."
Jefferson could not be considered a great statesman unless it could
be shown that he, like Hamilton and all truly great statesmen,
rooted his politics in economic realities. The Virginia Republican's
praises of husbandry, his fears of cities, his hostility to capitalist
methods, his adherence to policies clearly in the interest of the farming population—all this made it difficult for Beard to believe that
Jefferson did not represent the agrarian class. "He was not dealing
in the fustian of a demagogue when he pressed his deep and firm
faith in the virtues of the farmer and in the fitness of the farming

class to maintain a stable republican government. His faith was a class faith and his appeal was a class appeal."

The agrarian image fell apart as Beard worked at it, however. His chief exhibit of agrarian political science was not Jefferson but John Taylor of Caroline. Jefferson, to be sure, had commended Taylor's *magnum opus* published in 1814; but he had also, at an earlier time, commended John Adams's *Defense of the American Constitutions,* which Taylor's work answered. By presenting Taylor as the outstanding philosopher of Jeffersonian Democracy, Beard associated Jefferson with the views of a radical and doctrinaire agrarian. He conceded, nevertheless, many things in Jefferson's politics not easily reconciled with Taylor's philosophy. And he could only account for Jefferson's strength among the urban workers in 1800 on the ground that they were "more stirred by denunciation of the rich and mighty than by constructive proposals on their own behalf." But this kind of motivation obviously did not fit the economic interpretation. It indicated rather that Jefferson's appeal transcended class interests.

Jefferson's administration offered equally difficult problems. Beard felt, on the whole, that the Republican President consciously directed public policy toward the satisfaction of agrarian demands. He noted especially the repeal of internal taxes and the determined effort to retire the debt; but he failed to note, as Henry Adams had with studied irony, the measures which increased the debt, the plan of 1806 for internal improvements, and similar deviations from agrarian principle. There were certain Jeffersonian policies which Beard, too, could only interpret as appeasement of capitalism. Thus, he said, Jefferson took a leaf from Hamilton's book when he undertook "to detach the banking interests from the Federalists and to fasten them to the Republican party." Whatever the reasons, Jefferson "decided that the country could not be ruled without the active support, or at least the passive acquiescence, of the capitalistic interests." Jefferson's administration evinced the breakdown of class politics and the introduction of methods of moderation and compromise. And if Jefferson was capable of accommodating his party and his administration to these methods, then Beard's conception of Jeffersonian Democracy was seriously at fault.

The Economic Origins of Jeffersonian Democracy has usually been placed, with nearly all of Beard's work, on the Jeffersonian side of the perennial debate. On what grounds it is difficult to see. At later times, during the Roosevelt New Deal, Beard wrote admiringly of Jefferson and linked his philosophy to progressive tendencies. Still later he saw in Jefferson the best American symbol of the highest values of civilization. In 1915, however, Jefferson was for Beard, as he was for many Progressives, a symbol of defeat. "What message has the Sage of Monticello for us?" he asked in a magazine article at this time. The answer was implicit in the discussion: none. For Jefferson was convinced, Beard thought, the republic would endure only so long as the mass of Americans were farmers. A political science formed in this conviction made no contact with an America half of whose citizens belonged to "the mobs of great cities." Jefferson qualified his democratic doctrines "by making them inapplicable to an industrial population."

As critical as he was of twentieth-century capitalism, Beard nevertheless believed the Federalist regime, which gave the spur to capitalism, had been good for the country. The Jeffersonians had cried privilege and corruption. They were right, of course; but it was, Beard thought, merely a question of whose ox was gored. "It was a clear case of a collision of economic interests: fluid capital versus agrarianism. The representation of one interest was as legitimate as the other." The only standard Beard could apply to the parties was that of capacity for constructive work, which in turn depended upon the ability to organize politics around economic want and need. Unquestionably, in Beard's judgment, Hamilton and the Federalists were superior to Jefferson and the Republicans in this crucial task of statesmanship. A refrain of innuendo ran through the book to the effect that the new government would have suffered irreparable injury had the decision on such momentous issues as Hamilton's "been left to those highly etherealized persons who 'cherished the people'—and nothing more." Hamilton's understanding of the economic basis of politics caused Beard to rank him "with the great statesmen of all time." No such encomium was passed on Jefferson.

The cycle of revisionist thinking on "the history of the parties" that began with Bryce, then passed through a phase of political interpretation, ended in the economic interpretation. After Beard's work no serious student could ignore the class, or agrarian, aspect of Jefferson's politics, and some gave it the same importance Beard did. Yet, as his own work demonstrated, the economic interpretation proved of limited value when applied to Jefferson, his party, and his administration. Other historians, like the Socialist A. M. Simons, more deeply committed to a class analysis than Beard, also found Jefferson a singularly unsatisfactory case, a casualty of the Federalists' superb mastery of predestined economic forces. When the votaries of the economic interpretation had so much difficulty encompassing Jefferson, it could not be expected to make a major impression on the modern image.

The quality of idealism had always been uppermost in Jefferson's reputation. And despite the tendency toward more realistic views, it remained uppermost. His fame hung largely on the belief that he, beyond any other American of his age, put his faith and his hope in democratic principle. He was, the Harvard historian Mellen Chamberlain said, "the first statesman who had faith in the sufficiency of ideas not merely as tests of the validity of political institutions but as a power to subvert arbitrary government, and to overthrow errors however strongly intrenched in ancient wrong." But it was hard for the modern scholar addicted to more materialistic views of the historical process to share this somewhat ahistorical faith of the Enlightenment in "the sufficiency of ideas." In the instance of a scholar who was emotionally committed to this faith but intellectually attracted to the more down-to-earth approach Beard represented, the result was apt to be poignant. Such was the case of Vernon Louis Parrington.

4. Parrington and the Jeffersonian Tradition

The story of Vernon Parrington is the story of a book, his three-volume *Main Currents in American Thought*. Begun in 1913, the peak year of the "democratic renaissance" which furnished the critical spirit of the work, it was not published until well over a decade later. Between the two sides of his personality—the Kansas-born Populist and the Harvard-educated Professor of English—it was hard for the author, as well as his audience, to decide precisely what kind of history *Main Currents* was. It dealt largely with American literature, but it was not a literary history. Nor was the book, despite its title, a general history of American thought. Parrington treated the ideas that interested him, fit them into preconceived patterns, and judged them as a partisan. *Main Currents* is best understood as a history of American thought and expression within the limited ideological framework of Jeffersonian "liberalism." This is its peculiar character, the source of its strength and of its weakness.

At the very beginning, Parrington frankly stated his point of view: "liberal rather than conservative, Jeffersonian rather than Federalistic." And near the end of the tragically uncompleted third volume, he further defined the ideological underpinning when he said that American history was "largely a struggle between the spirit of the Declaration of Independence and the spirit of the Constitution, the one primarily concerned with the rights of man, the other more practically concerned with the rights of property." Parrington wrote only fifteen pages directly on Jefferson, but all 1300 pages were inferentially about Jefferson. He was concerned with the rise and the fortunes of a native stream of "liberalism," which he believed Jefferson best represented. His portrait of Jefferson was of no special significance. His attempt to map out "the Jeffersonian tradition" was remarkably fruitful. The general concept became one of the most used and abused in American historical discourse.

Parrington assigned three stages to the movement of American liberalism. First was the stage of naturalization: the disintegration of Old World tyrannies under the pressure of a free environment, and the emergence of a liberal philosophy in harmony with native conditions and ideals. The second was the stage of romanticization. In the vibrant, confident young America of the early nineteenth century, liberalism neglected the cautions of experience and reached for Utopia. The third stage, from the Civil War into the twentieth century, saw the collapse of the classic eighteenth-century creed, and the effort to build a new liberalism on the postulates of modern science. The chief interest the historical experience held for the present centered in the question: How far had the tradition succeeded in integrating liberal values and ideals with the realities and techniques of power? The question had been insistently raised as to Jefferson. The answers of Adams, Becker, Beard, and others were not encouraging. Was the Jeffersonian tradition, Parrington wondered, fatally handicapped by its idealism? This was the critical problem, as Parrington saw it, running through all the stages of liberal experience.

In his first volume, *The Colonial Mind*, Parrington pushed the Jefferson-Hamilton dichotomy backwards to the beginnings of American civilization. The line of liberalism ran through Roger Williams, Benjamin Franklin, and Jefferson; the line of conservatism through John Cotton, Jonathan Edwards, and Hamilton. During the revolutionary era these fluid streams of thought were fixed in their courses by the two liberal philosophies, "English Whiggery" and "French Romantic Democracy," which struggled for mastery of the new nation.

The Whig philosophy, though it had liberal parts, harked back to the Old World patterns of Calvin and Hobbes. Its theory of history was deterministic, its view of man was pessimistic, its politics coercive and elitist. The Whig model formed the mind of the rising middle class of the Eastern towns in the eighteenth century. "Realistic and material rather than romantic and Utopian, it was implicity hostile to all the major premises and ideals of the French school." Reluctant rebels in 1776, the Whig merchants, lawyers, and planters successfully countered the young democratic movement by the new government under the Constitution.

The rival democratic force was the natural offspring of the American environment, Parrington thought. But its intellectual sanctions were provided by the revolutionary thinkers of the French Enlightenment. Their humanitarian theories ordered and clarified emerging American ideals: human dignity, equality, and progress, the decentralized agrarian society and popular rule. The philosophy seemed ready-made for the American situation. It was easily appropriated by the great body of yeomanry who won the nation's independence; and so great was the impact of the French Revolution, in Parrington's judgment, that its chief American exponent, Jefferson, was able to divert the Whig movement and lead the agrarian masses to power in 1800.

The anatomy of these rival philosophies, as they came to be

embodied in the figures of Hamilton and Jefferson, needs further examination. Of fundamental importance was Parrington's distinction between the "realism" (or "materialism") of the Hamiltonians and the "romanticism" (or "idealism") of the Jeffersonians. When Parrington wrote, "the Hamiltonian principles lie at the core of the problem which has proved so difficult of solution by modern liberalism," he suggested his deep respect for the Hamiltonians' proficiency in laying their hands on the economic levers of power. That self-interest is the mainspring of ambition, that power follows property and government exists for its protection, that the state should use its authority to extend the field of profitable operations and safeguard exploitation, that it should therefore be so constituted as to check popular rule and assure the ascendancy of the propertied class— these were the enduring axioms of Whig politics from which the Founding Fathers erected a centralizing constitution hostile to democracy. Hamilton extracted every ounce of the original liberalism contained in the Whig theory. Devoid of sentiment, contemptuous of theorists, unmoved by liberal ideals, Hamilton was, in Parrington's view, "the creative organizer of a political state answering the needs of a capitalistic order."

Jefferson appeared to Parrington as the first American leader to break consciously with the past and to erect a political philosophy consonant with American experience.

Back of the figure of Jefferson, with his aristocratic head set on a plebeian frame, was the philosophy of a new age and a new people—an age and a people not yet come to the consistency of maturity, but feeling a way through experiment to solid achievement. Far more completely than any other American of his generation he embodied the idealisms of the great revolution—its faith in human nature, its economic individualism, its conviction that here in America, through the instrumentality of political democracy the lot of the common man should somehow be made better.

Whence came Jefferson's philosophy? It was, Parrington answered, "an amalgam of English and French liberalisms, supplemented by the conscious influence of the American frontier." The frontier, with its simple freedoms, was bred into Jefferson. This was only "the plebeian frame"; "the aristocratic head" of the student and philosopher felt the influence of both the European traditions. But in the Declaration of Independence, by substituting the humanitarian goal of "the pursuit of happiness" for the Whig "protection of property," Jefferson broke completely with the English theory and opened the road to idealism in America.

Jefferson's idealism was much needed, Parrington said, "to leaven the materialistic realism of the times." His glowing tribute—"a perennial inspiration," "one to whom later generations may return most hopefully"—sprang from the belief that Jefferson almost alone of American liberals harnessed his ideals to social realities. He was, to be sure, a visionary, which was his permanent glory; but his theories and dreams were rooted in American fact. Old World doctrine was always judged in the light of native conditions. Physiocratic agrarian theory, for example, appealed to Jefferson "as little other than a deduction from the open facts of American life."

There had been created here the psychology and institutions of a decentralized society, with a corresponding exaltation of the individual and the breakdown of caste. In the broad spaces of America the old-world coercive state had dwindled to a mere police arrangement for parochial duties; the free citizen refused to be regimented; the several communities insisted on managing their affairs by their own agents. Such was the natural consequence of free economics; but with the turning of the tide would not the drift toward centralization nullify the results of earlier American experience and repeat here the unhappy experience of European peoples?

This was the haunting question. The Constitution, its gears of exploitation meshed and turned by the Hamiltonian system, artificially stimulated the movement toward Leviathan. Government was strengthened at the expense of society. The state became less an instrument of justice and good will than of class privilege and national power. The more it was centralized, the better it was able "to override and nullify the democratic will." "To preserve government in America from such degradation, to keep the natural resources open to all, were the prime desire and object of his life."

Parrington closed his first volume on the Jeffersonian triumph of 1800. "The new liberalism was in the saddle." Jefferson might have looked back over the first two hundred years of New World experi-

ence with satisfaction, forward with optimism. Yet Parrington, from
his darker perspective, saw that the materialist Hamilton, not Jefferson, owned the future. "He blazed the path America has since
followed." The Great Democrat's noble work was "foredoomed to
failure." So long as its ideals ran parallel with common experience,
Jeffersonian theory was fortified by social facts, liberal values were
sustained by the environment without much regard to the techniques
of power. This, however, soon ceased to be the case. While capitalism crushed the agrarian society, a fog of romanticism enveloped
the liberal tradition. The scattered fragments of Jeffersonian philosophy were blown into ecstatic and nebulous idealisms. An overreaching Utopianism in the liberal tradition made it heedless of the
power of property, caused it to forget that the Constitution was a
Whig frame of government, and drowned it in the honeyed rhetoric
of equalitarianism, which, all together, left liberalism ill-equipped
to battle plutocracy.

Inspiring, hopeful, and humane, liberalism was foredoomed by
its innocence of the realities of power. In his third volume, writing
of the new adventure of liberalism in his own time, Parrington
sharpened his point. The conception of the state as determined by
economic forces, he wrote, underlay the thinking of the English
school and was accepted as axiomatic by the Founding Fathers. "It
was the main-traveled road of political thought until a new highway
was laid out by the French engineers, who, disliking the bog of
economics, surveyed another route by way of romantic equalitarianism.... In divorcing political theory from contact with sobering
reality it gave it over to a treacherous romanticism. In seeking to
avoid the bog of economics it ran into an arid desert." Parrington
insisted that Jefferson, firmly planted on agrarian economics, "was
not so foolish as many of his disciples have been"; but, alas, there
was an inherent tendency in liberalism toward "profitless romanti-
cisms." The predicament of the modern liberal was that he could not
be, like Jefferson, both pragmatist and Utopian.

In the Middle Period (1815-61), the subject of *The Romantic
Revolution in America*, Parrington charted the fortunes of liberalism
in several strategic culture centers. In the South, the slaveholders'
white-porticoed dream of a Greek Democracy replaced the Jeffer-

sonian vision of an agrarian democracy. On the Western frontier, where nature had seemed its best guaranty, Jeffersonianism fell victim to the acquisitive spirit; Jacksonian Democracy, in its haste to capitalize the West, forgot "the humanitarian spirit that underlay the earlier democratic program." Parrington found in New England the finest expression of the liberal faith during these years; but against the gigantic dehumanizing forces of industrialism, the outraged conscience of the New England moralists and mystics and Utopians was ineffectual. The romanticizations of Jeffersonian liberalism, under separate sectional influences, were all delusory.

The complete triumph of capitalism and the advance of mechanistic science after the Civil War left the Jeffersonian tradition a shambles. This, and the formation of a new liberalism answerable to modern conditions, were the concerns of Parrington's final volume, *The Beginnings of Critical Realism in America.* The old faith lingered in a few men of greatness. There was Walt Whitman, rhapsodist of fraternity, the magnificent ideal of the Enlightenment all but forgotten in America. There was Henry George, Jeffersonian idealist, who closed his mind to all the lessons of economic determinism and labored with reason and compassion to restore the "old-fashioned agrarian democracy." These were not prophets of new dawns but "afterglows." All the liberals of Jeffersonian vintage were, Parrington concluded, "fighting the battles of capitalism with weapons as antiquated as the old cap-and-ball musket." But Critical Realism, originating in the agrarian revolt and the post-Darwinian science of the late nineteenth century, stripped away the excessive idealism of the liberal heritage and came to grips with "sobering reality." "After a hundred years political romanticism was slowly dying in America."

Critical Realism offered, Parrington thought, a method that might rescue liberalism from the arid desert into which the French engineers had driven it. He had repeatedly emphasized the crucial dilemma of liberalism: because it was a *faith,* based on premises assumed to be self-evident and dedicated to humanistic ends, it shied away from disagreeable realities and declined to yield its high truths to terrestrial authorities, whether of natural science or of political economy. Thus there was a kind of genteel tradition within liberalism, a great separation of value from fact, of higher goals from lower processes. With the foundations of the old faith crumbling under their feet, liberals took their bearings anew, substituted investigation for speculation, studied techniques, and left values alone.

This was the work of that "great stock-taking adventure," the Progressive Movement. Although productive of far-reaching reforms, Progressivism's outstanding result, Parrington thought, "was the instruction it afforded in the close kinship between business and politics—a lesson greatly needed by a people too long fed on romantic unrealities." There could be no true democracy until the economy was made responsible to the common good, a task not of sentiment or of ideals but of practical organization and technique. Beard's *Economic Interpretation of the Constitution* was the chief educator. If, as it taught, political principles are but fictions of all-controlling economic interests, Hamilton had been more right than Jefferson and liberalism had to get into "the bog of economics." If the Constitution had been framed in hostility to democracy, then the rule of plutocracy was but an unfolding from its premises, which no amount of Jeffersonian idealism could counteract. A tough-minded liberal politics, on the other hand, converting the centuries old theory of economic determinism into an instrument of democracy, promised the marriage of Jeffersonian ends to effectual Hamiltonian means.

The Progressive harvest was never reaped in full. For, as Parrington recalled, "the war intervened and the green fields shriveled in an afternoon. With the cynicism that came with post-war days the democratic liberalism of 1917 was thrown away like an empty whiskey flask." The War gave currency to the results of psychological inquiry—"the moron emerged as a singular commentary on our American democracy"—and then followed the theories of Freud and others. If the people never rise much above "sex appeals and belly needs," what prospect for democracy? All realism, all scientific knowledge seemed against the dream of Jefferson. Parrington, the elder liberal, who had warmed to the rich afterglow of the Enlightenment, joined in the agrarian revolt, and shared the green hopes of Progressivism, at last found himself with his liberal contemporaries in "the unhappy predicament of being treated as mourners at their own funerals." At the end of his voyage in the Jeffersonian tradition, he noted sadly, "It is a discouraging essay."

So Parrington's carefully structured monument to the Jeffersonian tradition ended on the note of disaster. Jefferson's tragic failure in the presence of imperious forces to save America from Old World degradations did not "detract from the nobility of his ideal or the inspiration of his life." He remained for Parrington the vivid symbol of democratic ideals, but because they had no continuing contact with the movement of real life, the symbol grew more and more obsolete. The dilemma of the twentieth-century Jeffersonian, torn between visionary ideals and the corrupting pragmatics of economic power, represented the historic tension at its most acute stage. There seemed to be no way to effect Jefferson's larger humanitarian aims except by resort to the tactics of the enemy. If so, it behooved the Jeffersonian to know the price he was paying and the risks he ran, to keep the sense of contradiction between the Jeffersonian and the Hamiltonian visions, to convert ideals not into realities, which was impossible, but into platforms of criticism. The adherent of the Jeffersonian faith would always in practical affairs be encumbered by idealism. But the promise of democracy belonged, Parrington felt, "to those who like Merlin pursue the light of their hopes where it flickers above the treacherous marshlands."

How central *Main Currents* was to the Jeffersonian predicaments of American democracy in the twentieth century becomes clearer in the following chapter; for the moment it is enough to note that the problem it focused had repeatedly appeared in some of the most important historical writing on Jefferson during the preceding decades. It was, in a sense, *the* Jeffersonian problem in American history, though seldom as keenly felt as by Parrington, since Jefferson was the hero of principles and ideals which history was supposed to affirm, but instead eroded or rejected. One of the tasks of democratic thought and politics was to find some way out of the dilemma.

* Seven *

DEMOCRACY II

Jefferson's objects have not fallen out of date. They are our own objects, if we be faithful to any ideals whatever; and the question we ask ourselves is not, How would Jefferson have pursued them in his day? but How shall we pursue them in ours? It is the spirit, not the tenets of the man by which he rules us from his urn.*

THE CRISIS of American democracy in the twentieth century has been at heart a crisis in the Jeffersonian philosophy. Its economic base in a simple agrarian order of small property owners was gone. Some of its ruling principles—private property, economic freedom, limited government—were appropriated by the corporate powers of industrial capitalism. The Jeffersonian philosophy defined liberty largely in terms of the absence of governmental restraint. The conception seemed not only useless but positively harmful in a society where the aggressions against the individual were economic rather than political, begging to be met by more rather than less government. Other Jeffersonian ideas were similarly turned upside down: for example, "trust the people." Experience seemed to prove that the more power was diffused among the people, the more oligarchical and irresponsible the governing authority became. In this topsy-turvy political universe, the inherited philosophy could not readily clarify the great issues of the time or serve democratic progress.

Traditional concepts were thus called up for review and revision, first in the Progressive Movement at the beginning of the century and later in the New Deal. Progressivism, although it lacked unity

* Woodrow Wilson, Jefferson Day Address, New York City, April 16, 1906.

of theory or of program, possessed an underlying critical spirit which justified Parrington's characterization, "a great stock-taking adventure." Walter Weyl captured this spirit in the opening sentences of *The New Democracy*, in 1912. "America today is in a somber, soul-questioning mood. We are in a period of clamor, of bewilderment, of an almost tremulous unrest. We are hastily revising all our social conceptions. We are hastily testing all our political ideals. We are profoundly disenchanted with the fruits of a century of independence." Disenchantment with "our old time democracy" involved for Progressives like Weyl a large measure of disenchantment with Jefferson. To hasten the advance toward the New Democracy, wherein the state would become the overlord of many rights previously held to be private, Americans must escape from the thralldom of the individualistic tradition. "Our hand is stayed by ancient political ideas which still cumber our modern brains; by political heirlooms of revered—but dead—ancestors," Weyl said.

The political idiom of these advanced Progressives was distinctly Hamiltonian. Many of them were, in fact, admirers of the impetuous adventurer whose administrative exploits at another time of crisis they hoped to see duplicated. But other Progressives spoke in the Jeffersonian idiom without, however, suffering the constraints of inherited doctrine. The difference between Bryan, who epitomized the code-Jeffersonian, and Woodrow Wilson, the new evangel of the Democratic party, was in this respect the difference between the leader for whom Jefferson was the father of a set creed and the leader for whom Jefferson represented the "spirit of democracy." The two idioms of Progressive thought clashed most significantly in the presidential contest of 1912. The debate between Wilsonian New Freedom and Theodore Roosevelt's New Nationalism carried the traditional dialogue of Jefferson and Hamilton to the crossroads of American democracy in this century.

For reasons that are generally well known, the nation retreated from Progressivism after the First World War. The extent of the retreat, so far as it affected public policy, is usually exaggerated; but the fact that during the nineteen-twenties Hamilton was a saint of Republican reaction and Jefferson was torn between agrarian and urban Democrats suggests the reversion to an earlier ideological configuration. The Democratic party, crushed and broken, once again commenced the search for a "new Jefferson," and seemed to find him at last in the person of Franklin D. Roosevelt. The Roosevelt New Deal replaced the party's tradition of individualistic democracy, which had ended in its own negation, with a shapeless Progressive synthesis accenting a pragmatic approach to grave national problems. The New Deal's importance for Jefferson's reputation was twofold. First, the voice of its opposition was Jeffersonian. The alternate Hamiltonian road to progressive democracy was not reopened; conservatives on the right and, to a lesser degree, radicals on the left, sought the support of the Jefferson symbol the New Deal claimed as its own. Second, the New Deal killed the Jeffersonian philosophy as a recognizable and usable tradition in American government and politics. As if in acknowledgment of the act, some said in requital for it, the Roosevelt administration built a great national temple to Jefferson's memory. In the death of the political tradition, the *American* hero was full-born at last.

Every society needs a sense of continuity with its history, a set of commonly diffused symbols rooted out of the past to manifest its modes of action and evoke its ideals. But the symbols, unless they are constantly revised to meet the tests of an ever changing national life, may drag the society down to disaster. The proposition of Alfred North Whitehead may be taken as self-evident:

The art of free society consists in the maintenance of the symbolic code; and secondly in fearlessness of revision, to secure that the code serves those purposes which satisfy an enlightened reason. Those societies which cannot combine reverence to their symbols with freedom of revision, must ultimately decay either from anarchy, or from the slow atrophy of a life stifled by useless shadows.

In the American polity, Jefferson and Jeffersonian philosophy consistently furnished important elements of the "symbolic code." They survived the great ordeal of the nineteenth century. Would they survive the ordeal of the twentieth century? They would not unless made serviceable to a society far different from the one Jefferson knew. Despite the restored prestige of Jefferson symbol and precept in 1900, there were alarming signs of that atrophy Whitehead mentions and, partly because of it, general uneasiness with Jeffersonian concepts. The possibility presented itself of a social and political reconstruction under Hamilton's star rather than Jefferson's. But this was not destined to be. The process of revision, although it was more than political, was completed during the Roosevelt era. It was fearless; much that had always passed as Jeffersonian dropped out of the symbolic code. Whether the progressive synthesis of the New Deal satisfied "an enlightened reason" is a question about which men may still differ. But it is irreversible. And the fact that the Jefferson Memorial rose from the Potomac in 1943 testifies to the artistry with which the New Deal combined reverence for the symbol and freedom of revision.

1. *The New Hamiltonians*

The Hamilton revival started by the Civil War was reorganized during the Progressive era into a Bismarckian cult of strenuous statesmanship. The Federalist trammels loosened, men of a new generation associated Hamilton with advanced political ideas and measured him on a revised scale of political values. The strongest appeal of Hamilton and Hamiltonian tradition to a small but significant segment of the Progressive mind lay in his bold use of the powers of government for constructive national purposes. The New Hamiltonians differed from the old in their redirection of nationalist principles to Progressive ends. It was the difference between the Hamiltonianism of President McKinley and the Hamiltonianism of President Roosevelt, the one triangulated by the sound dollar, the protective tariff, and the inalienable rights of corporations, the other aiming to make the government an engine for the control of capitalism and the achievement of social justice.

Although the garments of the new Hamilton were cut from the old cloth, the styling was quite different. He symbolized political "mastery" against Jeffersonian "drift," the positive state against *laissez faire*, socially useful privileges against equal rights for all, aristocratic distinction against leveling democracy, world power against isolation. The cult had its romancer in Gertrude Atherton, its philosopher in Herbert Croly, its exemplary statesman in Theodore Roosevelt. Remarkably influential was the Englishman Frederick Scott Oliver, whose *Alexander Hamilton: An Essay on American Union* brilliantly presented the new image in terms the whole world might be expected to understand. A serious scholar could write in 1920: "Hamilton was in advance of his time in comprehension of democratic principles of government and in knowledge of the proper application of them." The estimate would have been as incomprehensible in 1900 as it would again be in 1940.

Before Hamilton could take hold of the imagination of a new generation, he had to be brought to life. Gertrude Atherton's historical romance, *The Conqueror*, in 1902, succeeded in making Hamilton not only a vivid but a vivacious figure. Earlier, while writing a political novel, Mrs. Atherton turned to Bryce's *American Commonwealth* for background. There she came upon Bryce's brief eulogy of Hamilton. To Europeans, he wrote, Hamilton was the most interesting of the early figures of the republic, and yet "his countrymen seem to have never, either in his lifetime or afterward, duly recognized his splendid gifts." These words were "letters of fire to me," Mrs. Atherton recalled. She determined then and there to give Hamilton back to the American people, viewing her whole career as nothing but a preparation for this "peculiar destiny." She wrote *The Conqueror* with unabashed feminine passion, "as if I had stood beside Hamilton throughout his life, discarding only those wearisome details we all turn to books to forget." This was the romancer's privilege. It assured her and Hamilton a wider audience than either had ever enjoyed. But it betrayed her advertisement of *The Conqueror* as a "true story."

Mrs. Atherton's Hamilton was a composite of Chesterfieldian aristocrat, Faustian genius, Nietzschean superman—and "Alexander the Great." He was youth, invincible youth. He was the first American patriot, the first to call for arms against Britain when a mere lad of seventeen but two years on the mainland in 1774. He was the moving spirit of the Constitutional Convention. Having obtained the ratification of the Constitution, he breathed into it the vigor of life. At the close of his career, he was "the first of the 'Imperialists.'" More than the "nation builder," Mrs. Atherton's Hamilton was "the genius of the American race." He typified all that was greatest in the national character: power and extravagance, honor and integrity, unquenchable optimism and progress, nimbleness of mind and high spirits, remorseless industry and inventiveness, bravery in war and intrepidity in peace, youth and adventure. Jefferson typified the reverse side of the national character.

The romancer's chief complaint against Jefferson was that he "plebeianized the country." She had discovered a patrician ancestry for Hamilton, from which, she supposed, he took naturally to aristocracy. Jefferson was a more complicated psychological case. The extremes, patrician and plebeian, met in his blood:

The plebeianism of his father showed itself in the ungainly shell, in the indifference to personal cleanliness, and in the mongrel spirit which drove him to acts of physical cowardice for which his apologists blush. But his mother had belonged to the aristocracy of Virginia, and this knowledge induced a sullen resentment that he should be so unlike her kind, so different in appearance from the courtly men of his state.

Thus cruelly misshapen by his dual heritage, the novelist continued, Jefferson saw in the rampant democracy of France and America the opportunity to revenge his fate, "to level his country to a plane upon which with his natural gifts he easily could loom as being of a superior mould." Probably no previous portrayal made so much of Jefferson's alleged cowardice. Mrs. Atherton painted Hamilton in the red hues of courage; but Jefferson's character was "the most despicable in history," soiled like his linen and frayed like his threadbare coat. Congealing this vaguely familiar pattern, the New Hamiltonians objectified in the tradition the kind of political leadership they valued.

Theodore Roosevelt, who seemed to possess many of the attributes of Mrs. Atherton's Hamilton, never disguised his contempt for "the scholarly, timid, and shifting doctrinaire." Like Admiral Mahan and countless others, Roosevelt charged to Jefferson's softness and vacillation the national humiliation of the War of 1812. He thought "the worship of Jefferson a discredit to my country." Pondering these well-known views of the President, and hearing them echoed in the

House of Representatives by Henry S. Boutell in 1904, John Sharp
Williams rose to a pitch of anger:

They talk about Thomas Jefferson! . . . They have my hobby now. . . .
A coward! A man who dared to confess a disbelief in the divinity of Christ
and be a candidate for the Presidency in the eighteenth century? A coward!
The man who dared to drag up by the roots primogeniture and entail
against the opposition of all the old Virginia aristocracy. . . . A coward!
The American President who threw down the gauntlet to Napoleon the
Great and informed him of the fact that if the Mississippi River fell into
the hands of France it would be a cause of unending conflict between the
two nations. . . . A coward! The man who dared—why, he was morally one
of the most courageous men who ever lived.

Some Democrats traced the new Hamilton cult of heroic vitalism
to the imperialist adventure of 1898. But Hamilton's name had
scarcely figured in the arguments of the imperialists. The picture of
Jefferson as Louisiana's conqueror and iron ruler was, in part, the
creation of the imperialists. It endured. With the passage of the
special circumstances that called it forth, however, it was offset by
more conventional views of Jefferson's soft and timid nature, much
magnified by the New Hamiltonians in their enthusiasm for the
masterful leadership of the great state. Jefferson, they thought, obviously lacked the fighting mettle. "Where is Jefferson?" Washington
wrote from Valley Forge in America's darkest hour. Albert J. Beveridge repeated the question, violently wrenched from context, in
his *Life of Marshall*. That Marshall suffered at Valley Forge, while
Jefferson reposed at Monticello and Richmond, seemed to Beveridge
the perfect characterization of the two men and the basis of their
long conflict. He conceded that Jefferson was not to be blamed
(fantastically supposing everyone at Valley Forge *did* blame him).
"He was a philosopher, not a warrior."

The Conqueror centered the character type; F. S. Oliver's essay
of 1906 centered Hamilton's ideas and statecraft. The two books
might be considered companion pieces. Oliver began on the assumption that Mrs. Atherton had achieved "a most serious and truthful
portrait." She, in turn, enthusiastically recommended his study to
the American audience. A London business executive with no more

than the average enlightened Britisher's knowledge of American affairs, Oliver undertook the *Hamilton*, he said, to satisfy his own curiosity. All the existing accounts of Hamilton's career were "too 'American.'" His life, viewed from another standpoint, addressed itself to the world. In the great work of his life, "the vigorous union of the states," Oliver saw the principles, the skills, and the dedication needed to consolidate the British Empire.

Hamilton, Oliver supposed, had something to say to the subjects of King Edward. But many Americans, concerned to lift their government to new levels of service and responsibility, discovered in Oliver's book an opportunity to test their motives and ideals in the traditions of American politics. President Roosevelt at once extolled Oliver's *Essay*, ordering copies sent to Lodge and Whitelaw Reid. One Roosevelt Progressive, Frank Vrooman, called it "perhaps the most intelligent piece of writing on American politics published in this generation," and another, Walter Lippmann, hailed it as "one of the noblest biographies in our language." The fascination of the book lay not in the realm of historical scholarship, for it was based on the skimpiest kind of research, but in the realm of political science or, specifically, the art of statesmanship. Oliver reconstructed the Hamilton-Jefferson conflict in terms of opposed ideals and types of statesmanship: the one instinct with reality, the other duped by illusion; the one masterful, the other adrift on the tides of circumstance; the one positive in its methods and nationalist in its aim, the other negative and individualistic.

Oliver draped Hamilton in the garb of New Toryism. He drew one of his mottoes of political wisdom from Disraeli: "The divine right of kings may have been a plea for feeble tyrants, but the divine right of government is the keystone of human progress." So believing, Hamilton's enmity to Jefferson was as "fundamental as that of fire and water." To Hamilton the state was everything; the true goal of politics was "an aggregate of self-sacrificing men." To Jefferson the divine nature of man was all, and "he would have rejoiced to see the state a dismasted hulk, so confident was he that by the action of beneficent and eternal currents, she would drift for ever upon a smiling sea, within bow-shot of the delectable islands, without the aid of sails or rudder." The passion of Hamilton was order, efficiency, a corporate national life. The passion of Jefferson was freedom, orthodoxy, and conformity to the popular voice. "It is the old battle of the moralists against the evangelists," Oliver wrote, "of salvation by works or by grace."

The vital core of Hamilton's statecraft, Oliver thought, was commercial policy. His *Report on Manufactures* envisioned a "composite and self-contained state," in which the welfare of the whole would be increased through scientific division of labor under the guidance of the central government. He rejected *laissez faire*, a "pessimist's creed," because it enslaved men to their fears of authority. With reason and with hope, Hamilton believed the state could "create the industrial conditions it desires, precisely as the landowner goes about his forestry." Inequality and privilege, he knew, were the inevitable corollaries of state intervention; but he had nothing but contempt for the little doctrinaires who thought they had refuted the policy by pointing to these effects. Jefferson offered no constructive alternative to Hamilton's system, only a politics of drift, negation, convenience, and easy faith.

Oliver recognized that Hamilton lacked the art of governing a democracy under the conditions then imposed; but under new conditions, which dispelled the vapors of revolutionary idealism, his statecraft might be accommodated to democracy. How this could be done, Oliver did not explain; he was only sure that nothing could be gained from continuation of the Jeffersonian practice. The people owed nothing to Jefferson but untold grief and a few ungraceful fashions. "His legacy was a lexicon of phrases, a dramatic reputation of homespun equality, and a tangle for posterity to unwind." His great fame in America, so disproportionate to his deserts, was owing to the simple fact that the mass of men wanted not a master but a friend. "Fidelity to ideas rather than success in action was their concern." He enjoyed an immense reward from his sympathy with humanity, though he gave nothing but sympathy and astute party management in return. The last of the giants of the American epic, he enjoyed the last word and unrivaled adulation. "He was the grand keeper of the Touchstone of Democracy." And in the end he died, Oliver wrote in his most stinging phrase, "died, as he had lived, in the odour of phrases."

The new rage for Hamilton was, of course, continuous with the old. It manifested the historic Federalist concern for the discipline of the citizenry, the order of the economy, the immitigable sovereignty of the nation-state. Its complaint against Jefferson was the old complaint against the shapelessness, the indignities, the caprices of the democratic system. Admiration of Hamilton ran strong in the Republican party early in this century, and nowhere stronger than among its conservative leaders—Lodge, Elihu Root, Nicholas Murray Butler, Whitelaw Reid, and others. Reid, in his official capacity as Ambassador to England in 1912, delivered an address on Jefferson before an audience in Wales that was such a shocking piece of Federalist cant he was called to account for it in Congress. Hamiltonians of this older type patronized Chicago's famed Hamilton Club, blessed the statues raised in Paterson, New Jersey and elsewhere, lent their support to the movement for the preservation of the statesman's home, The Grange, in Manhattan, and hymned the name on the centennial of Hamilton's death. Their intention was thoroughly conservative.

But, as Oliver's book intimated, the Hamiltonian categories might be adapted to modern reform. The New Hamiltonians were Tories, according to the Jeffersonian lexicon, but Tories with a reform mission. With remarkable prescience, David Wasson had pointed out in 1874 how modern industrial society reversed the historical roles of Jefferson and Hamilton. Jefferson became the conservative; Hamilton the radical. Obsessed with liberty, Wasson wrote in the *North American Review,* Jefferson never understood that oppression could spring from liberty. By giving unqualified supremacy to private interest and inclination, he created the conditions under which the brute selfishness and oppressions of the new industrial order arose and flourished. The situation called for the replacement of Jeffersonian "weathercock rule" by the stiffer regimen of men who were not afraid to govern. The modern Jeffersonian, Wasson said, "spinning out his little store of maxims borrowed from the century past . . . seems the saddest anachronism the time has to show." The living, pregnant reality, on the other hand, might be grasped by men with Hamiltonian clarity and daring. This became the conviction of the New Hamiltonians.

The tradition was most brilliantly mustered into Progressive thought by Herbert Croly's *The Promise of American Life* in 1909. The book's influence on modern reform ideology is well established. "It became a reservoir for all political writing," as Felix Frankfurter said in 1930. One of the most literate men of the new generation, Harvard educated, indoctrinated by his public-spirited parents in the Positivist social science of Auguste Comte, Croly believed that the old promise of a democratic national life could be fulfilled only if Americans were prepared to sacrifice the traditional way of seeking it. Croly identified the standard democratic way—"a mixture of optimism, fatalism, and conservatism"—with Jefferson. Americans were enslaved not so much by new social conditions, Croly thought, as by Jeffersonian habits of mind. From Croly's reconstruction of the political past, Hamilton emerged as the true, Jefferson the false, idol of Progressive Democracy.

A double perversion, Croly argued in his most famous chapter, was inflicted on the American dream at the outset. Hamilton perverted the national ideal by associating it with aristocracy; Jefferson perverted the democratic ideal by associating it with fears of the national government. Jefferson's error was by far the more serious, Croly thought. For Hamilton's error could be redeemed merely by shifting his model of the positive state to the democratic base. The Jeffersonian model was congenitally unsound. Jefferson disbelieved in enterprising leadership, raised the ghosts of monarchy, and introduced the career of lethargy and confusion that ever after characterized American politics. Unable to discern the natural antagonism between the principles of liberty and equality, believing that individual liberty was the fruit of equality and equality the fruit of individual liberty, Jefferson supposed that energetic government was the only danger the people had to fear. Hamilton saw that liberty must be continuously organized by government, that it must consist in something more than free economic opportunity and legally constituted rights, that it must issue in fruitful social, economic, and intellectual inequalities. He failed because the great majority of

Americans wanted deliverance from government. They found it in
the Jeffersonian system of "individual aggrandizement and collective
irresponsibility."

Chief among the benefits of modern progress, Croly thought,
was the growth of combination and specialized talent, especially
in industry; but could these great forces, which had aroused so
much dread in the populace, be brought under the discipline of
the national-democratic ideal? Not on the Jeffersonian principles
of most reformers, in Croly's judgment. It was impossible to remedy
the ills of the economic order by attempting to restore the individualistic system from which they came. Reformers of the Bryan
type were incapable of embracing the means essential to democratic
progress. Calling for the return to equal rights, they overlooked
the fact that just insofar as equal rights had been freely exercised,
inequality had grown. Nor was it possible to secure more efficient
and responsible government by resort to the timeworn Jeffersonian
shibboleth, "trust the people." The "direct democracy" movement,
with all its devices for increasing the direct and constant exercise
of the popular will, stemmed from "the old and baleful democratic
tendency of always seeking the reason for failure of a democratic
enterprise in some betrayal of trust." Political democracy, in an age
of organization, could not be improved simply by more democracy.

And so Croly came to his radical solution: "the rejection of a
large part of the Jeffersonian creed, and a renewed attempt to
establish in its place the popularity of its Hamiltonian rival." Gradually, as intelligent men dared to question the traditional premises,
Croly predicted, Progressivism would split in two, divided between
those who stuck to "the spirit of the true Jeffersonian faith" and
those who attempted to "unite the Hamiltonian principles of national
political responsibility and efficiency with a frank democratic purpose." To make democracy a force for national achievement rather
than national distraction, for collective responsibility in place of
individual selfishness, for mastery instead of drift, Croly proposed
a comprehensive agendum of reform. Economic centralization necessitated a corresponding shift of political power from the states to
the national government. The benefits of modern industrial organization must be kept; therefore the Sherman Anti-Trust Law and similar

efforts to restore free competition should give way to policies of regulation and control. Privileges should be fearlessly granted to special interests, such as trade unions, provided they contribute to human and national welfare. Devices should be invented to reduce the inequalities of wealth. The role of executive decision-making should be enlarged, the number of elective officials lowered and their terms of service lengthened, specialized administrative talent encouraged. Finally, the nation should assume more active leadership in world affairs. All policies, Croly warned, should be kept fluid, readily adaptable to the changing needs and wants of a progressive society, practical and creative in the Hamiltonian mode.

Croly's intellectual alchemy turned the Jeffersonian ideal into conservatism, the Hamiltonian into progressivism. Perhaps nothing more radical had ever been attempted within the tradition of American political thought. The book was written, of course, as a contribution to Progressive thought; yet its profile of Hamilton accorded with that of the Tory-minded interpreters. Other Progressives reached reform conclusions similar to Croly's via the Jeffersonian route. But Croly, approaching contemporary problems from a unique intellectual background, sharing the cultivated man's distaste for what usually passed as Jeffersonian in American politics, and seeing at the end of its illusions disaster, found in the New Hamilton an ideal that appealed to his almost mystical sense of nationality, and a model of statesmanship that combined the elan of a great adventure with the modern passion for scientific organization.

Progressives in the Hamiltonian vein found their leader in Theodore Roosevelt. The whole tendency of his leadership, Croly said, was "to emancipate American democracy from its Jeffersonian bondage," and "to give a democratic meaning and purpose to the Hamiltonian tradition and method." Roosevelt reciprocated the compliment, declaring Croly's *Promise of American Life* "the most profound and illuminating study of our national condition which has appeared for many years." Its philosophy informed the New Nationalism, which Roosevelt announced in 1910 and which became the creed of the Bull Moose party in 1912.

The division of the reform ranks along the Hamilton-Jefferson line, foreseen by Croly, occurred in the presidential election of 1912. Roosevelt advocated a large role for the national government in the correction of social evils, in the husbandry of the nation's resources, and in the control of great economic power. The Wilsonian creed was avowedly Jeffersonian. It represented, as Croly observed, "an attempt to do away with privilege rather than an attempt to make privilege socially useful." The ideas of Wilson and Roosevelt thus suggested two sharply contrasted approaches to the modern problems of democracy: one attempting through the rule of law to revitalize the traditional values of equal rights, the other attempting through novel administrative methods to turn the values of industrial organization and scientific intelligence to humane social use. The polemics of the conflict, therefore, carried forward the historical dialogue of American politics.

Woodrow Wilson, at first glance, was an unlikely candidate for the Jefferson mantle. As a scholar he had advanced opinions of Jefferson which, in 1912, rejoiced his enemies and embarrassed his friends. Jefferson was an aristocrat, he had said, a clever party manager, and a statesman of the French type who let preconceived theories, rather than facts, govern his actions. And so Wilson judged him, in 1894, "though a great man, not a great American." According to Newton D. Baker, Wilson read Oliver's *Hamilton* with great admiration. An admirer of most things British, Wilson was one of the first scholars to advocate raising American congressional government toward the levels of unity and efficiency attained in the parliamentary system—a singularly un-Jeffersonian idea. His opinions of Jefferson reflected, in the main, the thinking of the class of scholars to which he belonged.

The subtle change in Wilson's political views in the several years before 1912 involved as well a shift in his opinion of Jefferson. Invited to address the Jefferson Day dinner of the Democratic Club of New York, in April 1906, Wilson took as his subject "The Spirit of Jefferson." Why did Democrats still celebrate Jefferson's memory and still learn from his teachings? Not, Wilson answered, because "we seek to be governed by Jefferson's opinions or search among his policies for measures to suit our own times." His opinions were meant to express two main ideals: "the right of the individual to

a free opportunity and . . . the right of the people to the unmonop-
olized benefits of the nation's development." While it was true that
the practical policies he pursued did not always square with his
abstract theories, Wilson observed, "they did always square with
what he conceived to be the interest of the individual and of the
people." The great ends were fixed, the means were flexible. The
present-day Jeffersonian, Wilson declared, should be guided in the
same way. The question to ask was not how Jefferson pursued his
ideals in his day, "but How shall we pursue them in ours? It is the
spirit, not the tenets of the man by which he rules us from his urn."

In the Jefferson Day address, in others to follow, and most of all
in the campaign speeches of 1912, Wilson sought to interpret the
Jeffersonian spirit for the new America. The economic order must be
"freed from the spirit of monopoly," but Wilson also warned against
the political "danger of centralized and corruptible control." "The
history of liberty is the history of the limitation of governmental
power," the Democratic candidate said, "not the increase of it."
Unquestionably, however, Jefferson would now see at once that "law
in our day must come to the assistance of the individual." His belief
in the natural processes of a "spontaneous and self-sufficient democracy" was antiquated; and yet the nation's life could be kept "full
of vigor and promise only if free and natural." Wilson thus reaffirmed
Jeffersonian ideals—equal rights, limited government, trust the people
—while at the same time calling for new methods to implement them.
Leadership must come, Wilson repeatedly stated, from men who felt
in their hearts and knew in their minds "the instincts and impressions
of the common average man." Jefferson was the type. Wilson the
scholar had emphasized Jefferson's aristocratic and visionary qualities. Wilson the Democrat emphasized his frontier background, his
popular sense, and his practical idealism. In 1912, it was Hamilton
whom Wilson judged "not a great American," primarily because
Hamilton, like Roosevelt in his plans for state guardianship and
control, did not "trust the people."

The spirit of Jefferson hovered in the background of Wilson's administration. The President-elect, it was reported, had wanted to
walk to the Capitol for his inauguration in emulation of "Jeffersonian
simplicity," but was satisfied to have his reviewing stand before the

White House designed as a replica of the portico of Monticello. The return of the Democrats revived the movement for a Jefferson memorial. The first big administration measure, the tariff reform bill of an old-style Jeffersonian, Oscar Underwood of Alabama, was a fillip to "the Jefferson business." Democrats sat "at his feet in historic memory," kept alive his principles "in the hearts of the American people," returned to "the old landmarks."

By 1916, however, the plan for a Jeffersonian Progressivism was in serious trouble. Perhaps the trouble was foreshadowed in 1913, when Wilson decided to deliver his annual address to Congress in person. This dramatic departure from a fixed Jeffersonian precedent implied a Hamiltonian, or British, type of executive leadership. More alarming was the tendency of the administration to abandon the fight for free competition in industry and to support legislation of the New Nationalism type. "Oh, shades of Jefferson!" the cry went up on April 13, 1916, "Jeffersonian Democracy is but a hollow name."

The great war in Europe presented a formidable new challenge to government in the Jeffersonian spirit. Much to the disgust of Roosevelt and his diminished ranks, Wilson seemed to be retracing the dishonorable course of Jefferson in the international crisis of his time. "The Plutarchian parallel between Jefferson and Wilson . . ." his Ambassador to England, Walter Hines Page, reflected. "It was Jefferson all over again." Then, as one critic interpreted Wilson's shift in 1917, finding that "no sage-like retreat to Monticello was possible," he "leaped upon the war horse"; but, still in the Jeffersonian posture, he attempted to reconstruct the world along the lines of peace and democracy. Wilson did not, like some of his followers, directly link Jefferson's name with the World War. But his justification of intervention and his program of reconstruction were bathed in the lambent rhetoric of Jeffersonian ideals. He became, as John H. Latané said, "the spokesman for humanity the world over," alone with Jefferson of American statesmen to hold a "world vision" of democracy. Most Democrats, indeed most Americans, followed Wilson along the spiritual bridge he erected between Jeffersonian ideals and world leadership, just as they had followed his Jeffersonian version of reform. The bridge collapsed, sending the Democratic party adrift once again and leaving unanswered the question of whether or not Jefferson was a viable symbol of American democracy in the twentieth century.

If, in the final calamity of Wilsonian idealism, the question remained in doubt as to Jefferson, it was soon settled as to Hamilton. The attempt to build him into an American, even a democratic, hero was as exotic as the man himself. After the War, Hamilton was returned to the conservative Republicans whence he came. In 1921 Arthur H. Vandenberg, the Michigan publisher and later United States Senator, produced the first of three books in praise of Hamilton. The Hamilton of these books was a constitutionalist, a republican (not a democrat), a capitalist, an isolationist—the epitome of "one-hundred percent Americanism." What would he do today? Maintain the independence of the courts; abolish strikes, the closed shop, and similar industrial abuses; defend the protective tariff, fight the hyphenated Americans, insist upon full payment of debts, and uphold the American tradition of "self-sufficient nationalism" in foreign affairs. In 1923 President Harding and Secretary of the Treasury Mellon dedicated the statue of Hamilton (the gift of an anonymous New York woman) before the Treasury Building in Washington. Both eulogized Hamilton's constitutionalism, his financial integrity, and his sturdy patriotism. The President had orated on Hamilton before Chatauqua audiences. But no man in public life during this Republican decade was more often linked with Hamilton than Andrew Mellon. His funding of the war debt and tax program to instill business confidence drew from President Coolidge the ultimate encomium: Mellon had handled the country's finances with "a genius and success unmatched since Hamilton."

Hamilton's reputation fell disastrously during the decade of the Great Depression. The Hamilton Club of Chicago went bankrupt. Nicholas Murray Butler and many others long accustomed to Hamilton worship now saw a better symbol of conservative policy in Jefferson. The decline hit bottom in 1936 when, so far as can be discovered, nowhere in the land was the anniversary of Hamilton's birth observed, not even in Manhattan's Trinity Church graveyard where he lay entombed. William Guggenheim and a handful of prominent Republicans tried to revive the Hamilton symbol in 1939.

What stood out, however, was the defeat of the Hamilton symbol in any significant political context. The contrast between the spacious grandeur of Monticello and the shabby disrepair and virtual anonymity of Hamilton Grange on crowded Manhattan Heights is a true reflection of the two rivals' contemporary reputations.

2. Claude Bowers and the "New Jefferson"

The publication late in 1925 of Claude G. Bowers's *Jefferson and Hamilton: The Struggle for Democracy in America* was a major event in Jefferson's posthumous history, unlike anything in the literary way since Henry S. Randall's biography in 1858. Politicians joined scholars, Republicans joined Democrats, in showering praise upon the book. All agreed that Bowers had succeeded in making a serious study of the foundations of American democracy as readable as a good novel, and many welcomed the book as an antidote to "the one-sided productions of Hamiltonian hero-worshippers" in recent years. Fame and honors came swiftly to Bowers. At the dedication of Monticello as a national shrine in 1926, President Alderman of the University of Virginia presented a Jefferson medal to the man who had destroyed the monstrous creation of Federalist passion and prejudice, and restored to the vision of his countrymen the true Jefferson. Week after week, Alderman said, he was asked to recommend some single great book on Jefferson. "I used to reply, 'There is no such book.' Now I say, 'Read Bowers's *Jefferson and Hamilton.*'" And it has probably been read by more living Americans (not to mention Englishmen, Germans, and Italians) than any other single volume on Jefferson or on the formative era of American politics.

Claude Bowers discovered his hero, and simultaneously his party, when as a boy at Shortridge High School, Indianapolis, he represented his school in a state oratorical contest. His parents' political allegiance was divided; but the boy was a great admirer of Alexander Hamilton, and his local idol was the young Republican orator of Federalist loyalties, Albert J. Beveridge, so he chose Hamilton as his subject. Plunging into the literature, he was soon disillusioned. Since it was too late to change his subject, he built the oration around the most creditable part of Hamilton's career (his leadership in New

York's ratification of the Constitution), and won the contest. Finding himself in "no-man's land politically," as he later recalled, he turned to the Ford Edition of Jefferson's writings, read it, and thus became a lifelong Jeffersonian. In 1899, at the age of twenty-one, Bowers was writing articles on the Jefferson-Hamilton theme for the national magazine of the Democratic party, *The Jeffersonian Democrat.* "Understand, therefore, Hamilton and his principles," the young man instructed, "and we become familiar with the deep undercurrent of the Republican party. Familiarizing ourselves with the writings of Thomas Jefferson, and the fundamental principles of Democracy stand forth illuminated by his clear, forcible expression." The viewpoint was fixed.

In 1901, still in Indiana, Bowers began his distinguished career as an editorial writer on several Democratic newspapers. Three years later he ran for Congress in the Terre Haute district, and lost. He briefly interrupted his journalistic career in 1911 to become the personal secretary of Indiana Senator John Worth Kern, a Bryan Democrat and the subject of Bowers's first venture in biography. A book on Jacksonian politics in 1922 brought him to the attention of Frank I. Cobb, editor of the *New York World,* the Democratic newspaper with a long habit of conjuring with Jefferson's name. Cobb was in search of "an unterrified Democrat" to write national editorials for the evening paper. Bowers met the test. It was from the *Evening World's* editorial desk that he wrote *Jefferson and Hamilton.*

The book got its impact not primarily from the originality of materials, still less of ideas, but from the dramatic power of its literary style. Bowers was a superb historical dramatist. Politics in his hands became as important, as exciting, as colorful and heroic as war; he used the military lexicon to described its men and movements. His conception of the epic party struggle was, in the main, the traditional Democratic conception, tracing back through Bryan, Randall, Van Buren, and others. The two giant antagonists, Jefferson and Hamilton, personified "elemental differences that reach back into the ages, and will continue to divide mankind far into the future." Their struggle, which shaped up on the issue of democracy versus aristocracy, must always, in one form or another, be fundamental in human affairs; and every American, at least, must be a disciple of Jefferson or of Hamilton.

Bowers's principal advance over his Jeffersonian predecessors lay in the boldness with which he imaged Jefferson as "the master politician." The very traits of character and methods of leadership which had generally been put on the debit side of Jefferson's account with posterity, Bowers shifted to the opposite side of the ledger. He gloried in Jefferson's stealthy maneuvers, his mastery of men, his understanding of mass psychology, his ability to tack and trim his sails. As a politician—"the original 'Easy Boss'"—Bowers exulted, Jefferson mobilized a mass party, successfully led it against the entrenched army of Federalism, and thus commenced the epoch of popular government.

The conception said more for Bowers's powers of imagination than for his abilities as a historian. He read back into the first fumbling stage of party organization the practices and techniques of a later period. His Jefferson was modeled on the modern political boss! Once the gloss was stripped away, Jefferson's party leadership was as dim an abstraction as before. Bowers was vaguely aware of the problem. Jefferson writing letters to his Republican friends from atop Monticello did not, after all, fit the character of "the master politician" or justify the imagery of a general directing his troops in the field. At times he pictured Jefferson "keenly enjoying the turmoil"; at other times he saw him anxiously withdrawing to his mountain or into the sanctuary of the American Philosophical Society.

Since *Jefferson and Hamilton* covered only the crucial decade of party conflict, it was perhaps inevitable that Jefferson's party leadership should stand in sharp relief. Later, as Bowers found time during and between ambassadorial appointments to Spain and Chile, he filled out the image in two volumes, *Jefferson in Power* (1936) and *The Young Jefferson* (1945). So his first volume undesignedly became the center-piece of a full-length biography. But the later volumes, even more thinly researched than the first, were also primarily concerned with Jefferson as a political man. *Jefferson in Power,* which was really less about Jefferson's "brilliant" administration than about the violent Federalist opposition, appeared, whether coin-

cidentally or not, just before the presidential campaign of 1936.
The final volume spread a broader canvas than either of its predecessors. But it too focused Jefferson's political accomplishments,
notably the Virginia reforms, which Bowers called "a new deal in
the social set-up." Jefferson, the child of the frontier, was always
a democrat, in Bowers's view, and he traced through the life of the
young Virginian the emergence of American democratic ideals.

Jefferson and Hamilton was an eventful book because it directly
related itself to conditions. In the postwar reaction against hyper-
bolic nationalism, both foreign and domestic, many Americans of a
liberal persuasion found in Jefferson just that range of ideas that
most needed re-emphasis. The intellectual wind was strongly blowing in Jefferson's favor; and Bowers's book, even though its premises
were more democratic than liberal, was propelled by it.

Furthermore, the year 1926 represented the high point thus far
in the patriotic commemoration of Jefferson. Under a commission
established by Congress, the sesquicentennial of American independence and the centennial of Jefferson's death were observed
throughout the land. President Coolidge appointed Bowers to the
Sesquicentennial Commission. As its Secretary, he was chiefly responsible for the climactic Independence Week program. At about
the same time he became associated with the Thomas Jefferson
Memorial Foundation, whose spirited campaign to purchase Monticello was closely tied in with the patriotic celebration. Trying with
indifferent success to start a Jefferson revival in order to further
its mission, the Foundation latched on to *Jefferson and Hamilton*
as the "answer to its prayer." Bowers became one of the Foundation's
most valued workers. The two movements, Sesquicentennial and
Monticello, swiftly raised Jefferson's stature on the scale of patriotic
veneration. Although Bowers's book made little sense measured on
this scale, it naturally benefited from the association.

It was to still another condition—the morbid condition of the
Democratic party—that *Jefferson and Hamilton* most notably addressed itself. After the collapse of Wilsonian Democracy, the party
was thrown back into the factional strife of the Bryan era. The
country faction, while still moderately progressive on economic issues,

was prey to the forces of bigotry and xenophobia released by the War. Bryan at Dayton, defending the Tennessee law against the teaching of biological evolution in the schools, symbolized the old-fashioned agrarian democracy at the end of its journey. The city faction was both more liberal and more responsive to the needs of modern life. The reform impulse was gravitating from the country to the city, with the power of the census returns behind it. Nevertheless, as in the earlier period, the Eastern Democracy was tied hand-and-foot to the city machines and the big money. The two great factions, identified with the candidacies of William G. McAdoo and Alfred E. Smith, slugged it out in the Madison Square Garden Convention of 1924. After this fiasco, the humiliating defeat at the hands of the Republicans in November was a dull anticlimax.

In this alarming state of affairs, good Democrats began to pray for "another Thomas Jefferson" to put Humpty Dumpty together again. Many of them read the book of their fellow Democrat, Claude Bowers. They did not find in its pages ready-made prescriptions for their ills or the country's ills, but rather the myth of the Democratic party masterfully recreated, a fresh awareness of the elemental differences between the parties, an ideology with which they might make sense of the too often senseless conflicts of the present, and a feeling for the importance of dynamic leadership. The book was a mirror for Democrats. Although they might lose themselves in admiring the image conjured up from the past, they might also be inspired to revitalize it.

Franklin D. Roosevelt had never reviewed a book before in his life, and he would never review another, but he heeded Bowers's personal request to review *Jefferson and Hamilton* in the *Evening World*. One year before, in December 1924, Roosevelt had addressed a circular letter to two thousand leaders of the Democratic party, asking what should be done to put the party back on its feet. The response was enough to crush anyone but a Roosevelt. Nearly all Democrats, it seemed, could agree on the Jeffersonian creed, but every Democrat was his own Jeffersonian. Roosevelt was undismayed. Believing the Democratic party should be the progressive party, and impressed by the all-inclusiveness of the traditional creed, he concluded from the response that, in his words, "the clear line of demarkation which differentiated the political thought of Jefferson on the one side and Hamilton on the other, must be restored." This age-old counsel caused sneers and jeers in some quarters. "The Great Jefferson Joke," Herbert Croly called it in *The New Republic*. "A political party which, when asked to deal with difficult and novel political and economic problems, always answers by shouting, 'Hurrah for Jefferson,' belongs to musical comedy rather than to the sinister and tragic drama of politics." But Roosevelt's conviction was strengthened by Bowers's book; and he took the opportunity in his review to answer those "smug writers" who saw nothing in the party's attachment to Jefferson but the substitution of vaguely exciting steretoypes for the realistic use of intelligence.

Jefferson and Hamilton came as a revelation to the Hyde Park patrician. Although a Democrat, he had not experienced, in any intimate way, either the pride or the passion, the fear or the hope, of men who wore their Jeffersonianism as a badge. As a fair-minded history of the Federalist decade, Roosevelt said, the book dispelled the "romantic cult" that had surrounded Hamilton since the publication of *The Conqueror*, and returned Jefferson to the esteem of the American people. "I felt like saying 'At last.'" Its principal importance was not historical, however, "but the constantly recurring thought of parallel or at least analogous situations existing in our own generation." The "moneyed class" still lorded over the "working masses." And so Roosevelt concluded:

I have a breathless feeling as I lay down this book—a picture of escape after escape which this nation passed through in those first ten years; a picture of what might have been if the Republic had been finally organized as Alexander Hamilton sought. But I have a breathless feeling, too, as I wonder if, a century and a quarter later, the same contending forces are not again mobilizing. Hamiltons we have today. Is a Jefferson on the horizon?

Perhaps Roosevelt himself was "the new Jefferson," as some Democrats, like Josephus Daniels, already believed. It was indeed a "breathless" thought.

Your review, Bowers wrote as soon as he saw it in the *World* office, "hits the nail on the head with a resounding whack in its application of the lessons of the Jeffersonian period to the problems of today." In retrospect, Bowers denied any thought of party politics when he wrote *Jefferson and Hamilton*. "I was writing of Jefferson the democrat, not the Democrat." But the two terms blended in Bowers's mind; in any event, he felt grateful to Roosevelt in 1925 for making absolutely clear his partisan intention. "I wrote the book," he frankly stated, "really to recall the party of Jefferson to the real meaning of Jeffersonian Democracy and you have brought it out." *Jefferson and Hamilton* was more than a history; it was a party manifesto. Democrats soon got the point. Almost overnight Bowers became the party's unofficial Jeffersonian philosopher, from the platform as well as from the printed page.

Bowers's oratorical reputation among Democrats had gone before his literary reputation. On the party's banquet and luncheon circuit, he instilled the lessons of *Jefferson and Hamilton*. "Let the word go forth," he exhorted the Democratic women of Philadelphia in 1927, "that we fight solely for the fundamentals and the response of the people will be as hearty as when crashing over the barricades of centralization and privilege they bore the red-headed philosopher of Monticello to the seat of power." Bowers's greatest oratorical triumph was the Keynote Address at the Democratic National Convention in 1928. Back in January of this presidential year, he had made the principal address at the quadrennial Jackson Day banquet in Washington, where it was the custom for the party's hopefuls to prime their respective candidacies. Recalling the examples of Jefferson and Jackson, Bowers attacked internal factionalism and feudism with such commanding eloquence that the candidates ditched their prepared speeches and turned the affair into a love feast. The address was a sensation. He was at once boomed for the Keynote spot, and at length unanimously chosen by the faction-ridden National Committee.

A little wizened man, youngish-looking, with straggling hair, a sallow complexion, and a great booming voice, Bowers treated the Democrats at Houston (and Americans at radios across the country) to a masterpiece of old-style political oratory, which invited comparison with Bryan's "Cross of Gold" in 1896. The delegates were moved back and forth from spellbound silence to wild enthusiasm;

and when the orator's voice died away, the demonstration was the noisiest in memory. Bowers sounded "a vibrant and clarion keynote for Jeffersonians"—straight from the pages of *Jefferson and Hamilton*. The issues, he said, were as fundamental as when Jefferson and Hamilton crossed swords. The "black horse cavalry of privilege and pillage" again rode roughshod over the rights of states and individuals, again picked the pockets of farmers, workers, and small businessmen. "The dreams of the Hamiltonians have literally come true while the people slept." The Republicans had lulled them with the myth of prosperity. Jefferson, when told in Paris of the prosperity of the French nation, went into the country and looked into the pots and fireplaces of the common people. "That is our answer now," Bowers thundered. He invoked Jefferson against every heresy without, however, pointing the road ahead for orthodoxy. The Keynote was a battlecry in the oldest tradition of the party to go forward to democracy by going backward to Jefferson. "We are going back— back to the old landmarks of liberty and equality"—this was Bowers's shrill peroration.

"I have heard so much at this convention," the newspaper humorist Will Rogers quipped from Houston, "about 'getting back to the old Jeffersonian principles' that being an amateur, I am in doubt as to why they *left them* in the first place." The party's historic pledge to Jefferson was returned to the platform, after its mysterious disappearance in 1920. But if the Democrats had been resold on Jeffersonian principles, neither the remainder of the platform nor the ensuing campaign gave much evidence of the transaction. The "new Jefferson" did not arrive in 1928. It was doubtful that he would so long as the Democrats crowded the Republicans on the political right rather than set up a new basis of politics on the left. The principles to which the country was asked to return, the threadbare formulas offered as adequate to the solution of every problem, were usually ambiguous, and more than likely conservative, when brought to bear in vital situations. In association with the patriotic demonstration of 1926 and the post-war intellectual reaction against exaggerated nationalism, the "new Jefferson" movement, which Bowers best articulated, succeeded in popularizing Jefferson anew. It *revived* the party's root tradition; it did not sufficiently *revise* it.

"Certain traditions have great powers of prepossession, even if they are not followed," Albert J. Nock acutely observed; "indeed much of the usefulness of a tradition is in the fact that it need only be possessed, not followed." The Jeffersonian tradition was no longer useful as a code to be followed; the crisis of the next decade would make that absolutely clear. But the fact that the most radical political regime in American history was preoccupied with its relation to Jefferson pointed up the peculiar value of the tradition.

3. Jefferson and the New Deal

The New Deal lacked a consistent philosophy, but it possessed a sense of tradition, a faith in democratic ideals, a set of symbols and conventions, which served some of the purposes of a philosophy. Addressing the Jefferson Day dinner at St. Paul, Minnesota during his pre-convention campaign in 1932, Franklin D. Roosevelt called for the renewal of the old social contract on the new terms of American life. The "long and splendid" day of Jeffersonian individualism was over, Roosevelt announced. Americans who shared Jefferson's faith in the ability of free men to work out their own destiny might safely undertake to plan and direct their social and economic life. "Government with him was a means to an end, not an end in itself; it might be either a refuge and a help or a threat and a danger, depending on the circumstances." To make the national government "a refuge and help," in the present circumstances, was not to negate but to affirm the tradition. "If Jefferson could return to our councils," Roosevelt thought, "he would find that while economic changes of a century have changed the necessary methods of government action, the principles of that action are still wholly his own." The Roosevelt Revolution, as it has been called, went forward within a fixed structure of "principles" to which the changed methods of action were *not* answerable, except in the pragmatic sense of justifying the traditional faith by its works for human welfare.

In speeches and writings, in party ritual and in commemorative acts, the New Dealers consciously sought to give a Jeffersonian face to the revolution. The Jefferson symbol was one device by which the New Deal satisfied what Thurman Arnold defined as the crucial need of intelligent statesmanship: "a formula which is capable of dramatizing our ideals, and at the same time of giving us freedom to progress along the road of experiment and discovery."

The New Deal was to be, in Henry Wallace's words, "a twentieth century model of Jefferson's principles of government." If nearly all that had been known for over a century as Jeffersonian principles was missing from the new model, it could still be argued that new-modeling itself—"the earth belongs to the living"—was the one sacred principle in the philosophy. Jefferson, an administration spokesman said in 1934, "was fixed in adherence to the principle that the administration of government at any given time should be controlled by conditions then existing, so as to promote the interests and opportunities of the people." *Administration* was not a matter of fundamental principle. The ideal was to be realized by radiant cooperation with reality. While this could be said to have saved the ideal it also killed the political philosophy. State rights: it could not be taken seriously after the Prohibition repeal, and the Roosevelt administration was the most centralizing in American history. Free trade: the Democratic platform of 1928 abandoned the "tariff for revenue only" doctrine and, despite the reciprocal tariffs program of a Jeffersonian Secretary of State, New Deal trade policy was nationalistic. The "least government" principle: New Dealers even denied that Jefferson ever uttered the familiar axiom attributed to him. Equal rights: the deliberate policy was no longer to abolish but to spread and balance privileges. Public economy: Roosevelt soon retreated from his Jeffersonian position of 1932. The primacy of the legislative branch: the President became "chief legislator," and old fears of executive tyranny were pushed aside. And so on, down the page, the list of principles pushed aside could be stated. The effect of the New Deal on the Jeffersonian philosophy of government was not changed by calling the principles *methods*.

Nevertheless, it was deceptively easy to see in Roosevelt a "new Jefferson" and in his administration a "new model" of the old Democracy. Democrats were prepared to witness the new evangel. The search was fulfilled in Roosevelt. Some were quickly disillusioned. But with the mass of Democrats the illusion remained convincing. If, as the scholar Dumas Malone said in 1933, the New Deal could not possibly be Jeffersonian, if Jefferson's armory was strong in defensive weapons and weak in offensive ones, if his own Presidency proved the disastrous consequences of negativism, it was still likely, Malone thought, that his flexible mind would devise new methods to combat today's tyrannies and that "he would bestow his apostolic blessing on Franklin D. Roosevelt, as the new President buckles on his Hamiltonian sword." Tying up to Jefferson—what could be simpler? Jefferson, the aristocratic champion of the common man; Roosevelt, the patrician champion of the underprivileged. Jefferson who drove the "paper and stock interest" from the government; Roosevelt who drove "the money-changers from the temple." Jefferson assailed the Supreme Court; so did Roosevelt. Jefferson distinguished between "human rights," which were natural, and "property rights," which were civil; the New Deal interfered with the latter in order to strengthen the former. The essence of Jeffersonian Democracy was hostility to every form of oppression; the New Deal's attack on the "economic royalists" was in the spirit of Jefferson's attack on the "corrupt monarchists." Whenever in any country there are unemployed lands and unemployed poor, Jefferson had said, "legislators cannot invent too many devices for subdividing property." Was not social welfare legislation a modern application of Jefferson's teaching? The political scientist, Charles E. Merriam, labored to prove that Jefferson preceded Roosevelt as a "national planner." Deliberately and systematically, he wrote, Jefferson "planned to put a floor under equality and liberty" by a free public land system, a broadly conceived transportation network, and a democratic educational system. "Jefferson planned not only liberty *from* evils but also liberty *for* something—for the pursuit of happiness."

The pragmatic element in Jefferson's statesmanship, so often obscured in the past, established another link between the historic symbol and the New Deal. He was no reverential worshipper of constitutions, it was said, and his administration was notably free of dogma. The Embargo represented a greater interference with individual liberties than the National Recovery Administration. The Louisiana Purchase mocked every Jeffersonian of niggardly constitutional views. Speaking at Little Rock, Arkansas in 1936, Roosevelt interpreted the Louisiana Purchase so as to make Jefferson appear to be the author of the constitutional theory it assumed. Not Jefferson but his advisers, according to Roosevelt, thought the acquisition unconstitutional. (He was equally ingenious in 1940, when he cited the Louisiana Purchase as a precedent for the executive agreement on the exchange of destroyers for bases with Great Britain, conveniently ignoring the Senate's advice and consent to Jefferson's treaty with France.) Perhaps as journalist-historian Irving Brant thought, a workable Jeffersonian theory of the New Deal might be built on Jefferson's practice, but not on his theory.

The universal solvent of every difficulty encountered in the translation of Jefferson into a symbol congruous with the New Deal was his faith—"the cardinal element bequeathed by Jefferson to the American tradition," according to philosopher John Dewey—in the right and ability of the people, the *living* generation, to govern themselves. This faith, Dewey wrote in 1940, "was stronger than his faith in any article of his own political creed—except this one." The various articles were thus dissolved in the conviction that democracy constantly vindicates itself in its working. "Democracy is not a goal," said another philosopher, T. V. Smith, with the New Deal's pragmatic slant; "it is a going. Democracy is whatever can be arrived at democratically." He associated this view with Jefferson. So too, with more thoroughness, did Charles M. Wiltse in arguing for the "essentially Jeffersonian" groundwork of the New Deal in *The Jeffersonian Tradition in American Democracy,* in 1935. Jefferson's legacy, this young scholar said, "is not his solution to the political problem, but his realization that the problem must be solved anew in each succeeding era." The residual core of Jefferson's faith was preserved by lopping off the "principles" that inhibited its working.

When the individualistic references of Jefferson's creed were frustrated by the inability to locate the individual in the intricate social maze, when society no longer and largely of itself supported the individual in his inalienable rights, when even the primary value of political freedom must now be maintained, not in the old way as freedom from government, but as freedom to use government intelligently to solve social problems—when these new conditions and assumptions pertained, then Jefferson ceased to represent a particular political design and came to represent instead the going democratic process. Even socialism, reached and maintained democratically, would affirm Jefferson's faith. For socialism was not, according to this logic, a separate *ism* opposed to Jeffersonianism. The latter was infinitely expansible in regard to the relations between government and property, since it conceived of property as an auxiliary value, a civil or legal right, rather than an indefeasible moral right. "Nothing," Jefferson had said, "is unchangeable but the inherent and inalienable rights of man." Viewing the problem in this spirit, Dewey asserted, "it is sheer perversion to hold that there is anything in Jeffersonian democracy that forbids political action to bring about the equalization of economic conditions in order that the equal rights of all to free choice and free action be maintained."

Although the Jefferson symbol was thus radically revised, its essential *moral* basis was unchanged. The belief in inalienable rights, in "trust the people," in consent rather than coercion—the vocabulary Jefferson had used to express these truths was outmoded, as Dewey said, but it was doubtful if democracy could survive unless men unreservedly took "the position Jefferson took about its moral basis and purpose." And, leaving aside for the moment the massive partisan predisposition to apostolic succession in the Jeffersonian line, perhaps the felt need to renew this faith furnishes an important key to why the Roosevelt Revolution occurred under Jefferson's sign instead of Hamilton's. In many respects, the New Deal's prophet was Herbert Croly. Its administrative theory and practice, its fiscal apparatus, its political economy were Hamiltonian. Observing this in 1934, Broadus Mitchell, a Johns Hopkins economist just beginning a life's work on Hamilton, thought it ironical that Jefferson's fancies should have been laid away in lavender by a Democratic administration. "Have our major tendencies been centrifugal or centripetal?" Mitchell asked. "The world over, has the separate citizen preserved his autonomy, economic and political, or has he yielded it up to the central authority?" The answers were self-evident. Hamilton pointed the way to the work of the New Deal in mastering an unruly economy, Mitchell asserted. But in this opinion he had little company; for, like Hamiltonians before him, Mitchell seemed blind to the intransigent ideal, the faith in democratic government, for which the American people remembered Jefferson and, because he lacked it, forgot Hamilton.

The clue of the New Deal's Jefferson image leads finally to the President's desk. Whether or not Roosevelt imagined himself a "new Jefferson," the role was thrust upon him and he seemed to enjoy it. People were constantly trying to interest him in Jefferson mementoes —a letter, a portrait, a silver cup, a gold toothpick. Would the President like to see them? No, the answers came back, he was too busy putting Jefferson's ideas to work to treasure his relics. One portrait in particular, the crayon drawing by the Polish patriot and American revolutionist, Thaddeus Kosciusko, kept turning up at the White House. Admirers, including the Polish Ambassador, were struck by the resemblance to Roosevelt. He was flattered and amused. Finally, the owner of the original portrait offered to sell it to Roosevelt. He, as usual, declined.

The incident ties another Jeffersonian thread into the Roosevelt story. The portrait's owner was Mrs. Martin W. Littleton, who had inspired the campaign several decades earlier for the government's acquisition of Monticello. Her pamphlets were in Roosevelt's collection of Jefferson literature, for he had enlisted in the Monticello movement at the start. From 1930 until his death, he served on the Board of Governors of the Thomas Jefferson Memorial Foundation. Stuart Gibboney, its President, was a warm personal friend. Roosevelt did everything he could to help the Foundation improve Monticello. Annually, from 1934 to 1938, he personally saw to the assignment of a Civilian Conservation Corps detail to clean up the woods and fields on the property. Since the Foundation was a private association, the government's assistance had no legal warrant. The President gave the Independence Day address at Monticello in 1936. Monticello showed that Jefferson was a "great gentleman" and a "great commoner." "The two are not incompatible." The statement said as much about Roosevelt as about Jefferson. The President often expressed the hope that Monticello might yet become the property of the United States, entrusted to the care of the National Park Service, like his own Hyde Park estate. Every April 13 of his Presidency, a personal aid placed a wreath at Jefferson's tomb. The last was laid there on April 13, 1945, as his funeral train moved up through Virginia.

Monticello was only one of Roosevelt's works for Jefferson. The Democrats were determined to build Jefferson a memorial in the nation's capital as splendid as Washington's and Lincoln's. The President constantly had his hand in this project. Without his personal intervention, the gigantic National Expansion Memorial in St. Louis would probably never have got off the drawing boards. Beginning in 1938, by authorization of Congress, the President annually proclaimed April 13 in commemoration of Jefferson. In January 1939, the President inquired of the Corps of Engineers if there was any record of a Jefferson memorial tree on the White House grounds. The record showed nothing. So he had the Corps plant a grove of twenty tulip poplars (his favorite tree, though the Lombardy poplar was, in the way of trees, an original Jeffersonian symbol) on Jefferson's next birthday.

There were many ways to work "the Jefferson angle" into the New Deal, and few escaped the President or his subordinates. He named Claude Bowers and William E. Dodd, perhaps the nation's two best known Jeffersonian historians, ambassadors to Spain and Germany respectively. Every executive department or office seemed to have its own Jefferson specialist and project. In Agriculture, Everett Edwards, M. L. Wilson, and others wrote pamphlets on Jefferson as Farmer. In Interior, Saul Padover produced a major study, *Thomas Jefferson and the National Capital.* The Patent Office dedicated a bust to its first superintendent. And the Library of Congress, under Archibald MacLeish, installed an impressive series of Thomas Jefferson Murals in its new annex. The national Democratic boss, James A. Farley, was an avid Jefferson Day speaker; and nearly every high administration official sooner or later came around to the Jefferson theme.

Roosevelt put Jefferson into many of his speeches. His aids compiled huge files of Jefferson quotations arranged under subject headings. Friends and advisers sent him copies of Jefferson letters, which they hoped he might find useful. Occasionally he directed some subordinate to run down a Jefferson text suited to buttress his position on a delicate question. One instance in which the Jefferson research entered into a major address concerned the diplomatic recognition of the Soviet Union on November 16, 1933. Two weeks before, the Executive Office asked the State Department's historical adviser to make and forward photo-duplicates of certain Jefferson manuscripts relating to United States policy toward Imperial Russia. This was done the following day. In one of the manuscripts, a letter addressed to his Russian friend, M. Dashkoff, on August 12, 1809, Jefferson said: "Russia and the United States being in character and practice essentially pacific, a common interest in the rights of peaceable nations gives us a common cause in their maintenance." The passage was marked, perhaps by Roosevelt, with three red lines. Some days later it was incorporated in a speech memorandum. It appeared in Roosevelt's address at Savannah, Georgia on November 18, 1933, as a justification of the recognition and an illustration of the spirit in which it was tendered.

If Hamilton was the true father of the New Deal, the administration certainly made valiant efforts to redeem its error by increasing Jefferson's fame. In 1938 both the Jefferson nickel and the Jefferson three-cent postage stamp made their appearance. Jefferson's visage had been on the nation's postage for several decades, but never on the most generally used denominations. The philatelist President decided in 1937 upon a general revision of the postage designs, the first in twenty-five years. The new standard designs should compose a "presidential series," correlating the sequence of American Presidents with the postage denominations. In accordance with this directive, the Post Office Department drew up the specifications and submitted them to the President. Seeing that strict adherence to his original plan would put Jefferson on the scarce one and one-half-cent stamp, Roosevelt picked up a pencil, assigned Benjamin Franklin to the lowest denomination, Washington to the next, inserted Martha Washington in Jefferson's inconspicuous place, added Adams, and thus brought Jefferson out on the three-cent stamp—the carrier of nearly every letter in the first class mail. The Department adopted this amended presidential series. Its publication caused a mild political hassle. Lincoln, after all, had been stricken from the three-cent stamp in favor of Jefferson. A New York congressman charged that the new series was "a scheme to make sure that all Republicans are forgotten." But then the Republicans, in 1929, had relegated Jefferson to the scarce two-dollar bill. The Jefferson nickle replaced the "buffalo nickel" after the expiration of the latter's normal twenty-five-year term. While a no less deliberate maneuver to put Jefferson's name and visage in circulation, it did not receive the same personal attention from the President, nor did it annoy many Republicans.

Roosevelt of course regarded Jefferson as the founder of the Democratic party, and a playful kind of partisanship entered into his decision to put Jefferson on the three-cent stamp and to quote him against the opposition. But he had also come to believe that Jefferson ought to be celebrated nationally, like Washington and Lincoln, as an American hero. So he soft-pedaled the conventional partisan use of the Jefferson symbol, seeming to prefer Andrew Jackson for this purpose. As much as we love Jefferson, he wrote to E. M. House in advance of the Jefferson Day dinners in 1934, we should celebrate him not as the founder and philosopher of the Democratic party but as the supreme spirit of American liberalism and progress. And the accumulated effect of the varied Jefferson enterprise of the New Deal, over which Roosevelt presided, was to enhance Jefferson's reputation in reference to a larger constellation of civilized values than the political tradition comprehended. The partisan symbol was dying even in the house of Democracy.

"This is a very prosperous time for Thomas Jefferson," the newspaper columnist Simeon Strunsky wrote in 1936. "Everybody has a kind word for him. Nearly everybody writes a book about him. Every political party and faction in the end calls him father." The situation was not unprecedented in Jefferson's posthumous history. All American history, it sometimes seemed, represented the effort to discover Jeffersonian answers to the problems encountered in the nation's progress. During the depression decade, Jefferson shaded the entire political spectrum from the American Liberty League on the far right to the Communist party on the far left. "Sacerdotal cults" arose, it was observed, "differing among themselves, but each professing the exclusive validity of its own interpretation of the American scripture according to Thomas Jefferson."

Of these cults, the one called Southern Agrarianism had the most

earnest affair with Jefferson. Usually dated from the Twelve Southerners' manifesto of 1930, *I'll Take My Stand,* the agrarian movement
of thought came to reflect during the succeeding decade several
diverse influences: the aesthetic and cultural ideas of the Fugitive
group of Southern writers, first centered at Nashville and then at
Louisiana State University; the Southern Regionalism of Howard
Odum and his group at the University of North Carolina; the English
Distributist school of Hilaire Belloc and others, which especially
influenced the work of the National Catholic Rural Life Conference;
and the agrarian current in American historiography. All agrarians
advocated retreat from the rootless materialism of industrial society
and restoration of an integral way of life, the economic basis of
which was landed property, with individual ownership and control
sufficient for personal independence and family livelihood. The
movement arose in the South as an alternative solution to the Southern problem. The liberal evangels of the New South, with their faith
in education and industrialism, stood condemned. They had, it was
said, betrayed the true Southern heritage of classical thought, Christian religion, and rural life to the Northern ideal.

The agrarians were, on the whole, predisposed to see Jefferson
as the father of their faith. Monticello—the Palladian villa of a cultivated country gentleman—in a sense symbolized the best part of the
heritage they wished to regain. John Gould Fletcher, one of the
Twelve Southerners, attacked the liberals' association of Jefferson's
name with their idea of universal education, and called for a return
to his, as Fletcher believed, selective system. Jefferson's democratic
ideal, another of the twelve wrote, was an "unmixed agrarian society,"
with local and region autonomy, just enough government to prevent
disaster, and—"the keystone of the arch"—broadly diffused ownership of land. Not only was Jefferson a symbol of the agrarian tradition; he was himself a traditionalist, whose ideas and habits of life
antedated the modern age not by accident but by choice. But the
agrarians, least of all the Southerners, could not embrace Jefferson
without serious qualms and reservations. Allen Tate, for example,
convicted him of the root American heresy against culture and
religion: the idea that the ends of man are sufficiently contained in
his political destiny. Nevertheless, the agrarian movement's general

effect was a grotesque exaggeration of Jefferson's traditional, Southern, and agrarian features. It made Jefferson into a symbol of ideas and policies which were, under the circumstances, at once futile and reactionary.

As the movement spread beyond the South during the depression, the provincial analysis was shaped into a key to the American problem. By far the most illuminating of Jefferson were the popular historical writings of Herbert Agar. This poet, man of letters, and journalist, New York born of Southern parentage, gradually outgrew the intense conservatism of the Southern Agrarians and, as he did, came to write with more discrimination of Jefferson. But, in the gross, his books on American history, commencing in 1933 with the Pulitzer prize-winning *The People's Choice*, a study of the Presidency, pitched upon a dominant idea: Jefferson dreamed the American dream, betrayed it, and America has been damned ever since.

The dream was an agrarian utopia. A political democracy, a free economy, a native culture, all based upon and infused with the common values and habits of a people living on the land—this was the dream. Why was it, then, that when the opportunity for realization came to him, Jefferson "betrayed the America of his dream"? Why did Jefferson the President fail permanently to secure his principles, broaden the base in landed property, raise up legal bulwarks for its protection, and divert, while there was still time, the industrial revolution into salutary channels? Though Agar's several reports did not always agree with each other, the main points of the diagnosis were clear. First, Jefferson's unfortunate personality: "exaggerated charm," "softness of character," "easy hopefulness," most of all "an alarming wooly mindedness." Second, Jefferson built the Democratic party upon an untenable farmer-labor, rural-urban, combination. Having already, through his Virginia reforms, degraded and impoverished the landed gentry from which the agrarians should have drawn their leaders, Jefferson "then gave a vested interest in the party to the carefree demagogues of New York City," who cared not for principle but for the powers of office. Third, Jefferson, gave up the game by clinging, in the face of invasion, to his principle of the least possible government. "This was a poor principle with which to fight the most dynamic forces in Western history, forces which had just begun to invade our shores from Britain and which Hamilton had been welcoming with open arms." Finally, as Jefferson lost the economic battle in this way, he lost the constitutional battle as well by lowering the defenses against Federalist tactics: liberal construction, centralization, bank and debt. America was thus doomed to become a mere "money-based democracy." Jefferson's democratic ideas grew more and more popular as the actual environment became less and less Jeffersonian. "Democratic, egalitarian principles suitable to the rural world of Jefferson's dream were grafted on a greedy, middle class Hamiltonian capitalism."

But there was still a way out, Agar thought. Jefferson understood the heart's desire of the American people. They held him in affection, a kind of tragic hero, despite his historical defeat; they constantly returned to "that lost fight." What was required was not merely the restoration of Jeffersonian principles but the restoration of Jeffersonian society. Agar called, with other agrarians, for federal action to break down corporate power, to build up the small property-holders' democracy and the family-type farming of the Jeffersonian ideal. But lest the means employed to this end become too Hamiltonian, Agar voiced the old Jeffersonian fear of a government empowered to achieve the ideal. Reflecting the teachings of the arch-conservative economist Friedrick Hayek, he denounced government planning and Keynesian fiscal policy. Agar, with the other agrarians, clung to "the noble dream" but could not, any more than the man he arraigned as its betrayer, will the means of realization.

Everybody else was claiming Jefferson, columnist Heywood Broun noted in 1938, so there was "no reason why the Communists should not make the attempt to press a red card upon the sage of Monticello." The claim was as absurd as it was spectacular; yet it was congenial with the New Deal's stress on Jefferson's progressiveness and with the intellectuals' discovery during the decade of a revolutionary past inviting leaps into the future. American radical sects, from the early Owenite Socialists to Marxists Socialists and Communists, had never been strongly attracted to Jefferson. Of course, he was something of a free-thinker, a pacifist, a revolutionist, and an equalitarian. This was good for inspiration; but his crucial role in history was to break the trail for an individualistic capitalism to which there was no return and beyond which his philosophy of government promised nothing. A. M. Simons enunciated this modern Socialist view in his pioneering work of 1911, *Social Forces in American History*, and it was still being repeated in the early 'thirties. "Today . . . it is the struggle of the proletariat which is important and not the struggle of the petty bourgeoisie," V. F. Calverton declared; "the Jeffersonian challenge as a result has become anachronistic."

As the decade advanced, however, the leftists tried to deduce Marx from Jefferson. First the Socialists and then, after 1935, the Communists moved to furnish their creeds with heroes from the American past. "Communism is Twentieth Century Americanism" the party cried. Serious scholars, such as Charles M. Wiltse, had traced the Jeffersonian tradition into democratic socialism, so why should the Communists not take the next step? "We Communists today are continuing the heritage of Jefferson and Lincoln. . . . Jefferson's theory of democracy realized fully that political power can be maintained and extended only when given a solid economic foundation. The essential features of Jefferson's program must be brought up to date." Furthermore, as Jefferson fought the reactionary nations of his day in alliance with revolutionary France, so present-day American foreign policy ought to support revolutionary Russia against the fascist nations. The party's chief, Earl Browder, acknowledged that Jefferson was not Marx; but the Father of Democracy stood at the portal of the mighty torrent of revolution destined to sweep through the world. Jefferson was a "bourgeois democrat" and "the architect of American capitalism"; yet he might serve, it seemed, as a symbol of the proletarian revolution against the order he founded.

Jefferson quite obviously could not be imaged as a proletarian. Using him as a heroic symbol of revolution, the Communists still did not idolize the man or his principles. In the Jefferson Bicentennial of 1943, the weekly *New Masses* paid him handsome tribute; but Howard Fast's historical novel, *Citizen Tom Paine*, published in the same year, furnished a truer reflection of Communist feelings. Jefferson merely played, and rather fearfully, Fast thought, at adoring the common man. Paine *was* the common man, his ideas "closer to those of the average working man than Jefferson's ever could be." Jefferson enjoyed a certain éclat among the Communists; and, of course, there was no comparison between the propaganda value of the two symbols, Jefferson and Paine. As Fast's book indicated, however, the Communists retained the historic preference of radical sects for the Founding Father America rejected.

The much more serious, indeed the only significant, challenge to the New Deal's Jefferson image came from the motley assemblage on the political right: the reactionaries of the millionaire-financed American Liberty League, Old Guard Republicans, liberal intellectuals of the nineteenth-century vintage, and insurgent "Jeffersonian Democrats." From the New Deal standpoint, all these people were *conservative*, though they rallied under Jeffersonian colors. The tactics implied the wholesale transference of conservative allegiance from Hamilton to Jefferson. Hamilton was nearly forgotten as the conservatives hurled Jeffersonian missiles at the Roosevelt administration:

In questions of power, then, let no more be heard of confidence in man, but bind him down from mischief by the chains of the Constitution.

When we must wait for Washington to tell us when to sow and when to reap, we shall soon want bread.

Such were the texts of Liberty League sermons. The titles of a few scattered editorials in Colonel Robert R. McCormick's *Chicago Tribune* suggest the frame of mind: "Jefferson or Marx" (this is the issue), "The Discarded Founder" (the Democrats have repudiated their patron saint), "State Rights and the Constitution" (hurrah for the doctrines of '98), "The Man of Prophesy" (Jefferson predicted the "third term" peril), "Maxims of Jefferson" (isolation, frugality, constitutionalism, and so on). Jefferson was quoted in the letter again.t the finer distillations of his spirit. What he had said in 1800, he would have repeated were he present in the flesh in 1936.

The Republican trend is Jeffersonian, William Allen White wrote from the National Convention at Cleveland in 1936: "we may easily have the Democrats defending Hamiltonian principles in the campaign of '36 and the Republicans presenting a program calling for Jeffersonian home rule." The Republicans rediscovered the party's lost Jeffersonian origins in the slavery crisis. Party Chairman John D. M. Hamilton kept up the "back to Jefferson" cry several years after the terrible defeat in 1936. At a Lincoln Day dinner in 1938, he raised his glass to Jefferson and Lincoln, entwined in the party's history and memory. "Jefferson was the hero of the Lincoln Republicans. The Republican party is more Jeffersonian today than those who pay mere lip service to his name." On July Fourth 1938, both Hamilton and New Deal Senator Claude Pepper acclaimed Jefferson as the father of their respective parties before a record audience at the University of Virginia's Institute of Public Affairs. "This afternoon," newspapers reported, "a wreath, sent by President Roosevelt, was laid on Jefferson's tomb at Monticello by Senator Pepper, at 2:30 o'clock and at 3:30 o'clock another was placed there by Mr. Hamilton."

Whatever may be said of the logic of the Republican appeal to Jefferson, it had certain practical values, not the least of which was to sever dissident "Jeffersonian Democrats," mostly Southerners, from their party allegiance. Roosevelt's "court packing" plan in 1937 and his later decision to seek a third term helped to make the self-styled Jeffersonians a formidable faction in 1940. Fighting the "nine old men," the administration drew upon Jefferson's well-furnished armory of "anti-judicialism," which had seen service in every major offensive mounted against the Supreme Court from the last years of Jefferson's life down to Robert LaFollette's valiant campaign in 1924. Distinguished authority supported the New Deal contention that Jefferson had denied the Court's ultimate power and gone to great lengths to control it. Neither Jefferson's theory nor his practice, Charles Beard reported, yielded any comfort to conservatives who regarded the Court as the sacrosanct palladium of American liberty. Indeed, conservative elements had always deplored Jefferson's "anti-judicialism." But now the stage revolved and Jefferson the Constitutionalist held their attention. The "Jeffersonian Democrats," unlike the Republicans, could at least make a case for their consistency in this matter. Constitutionalism had always been an article of Democratic orthodoxy. No less an authority than Claude Bowers had recently pronounced the idea of Jefferson's hostility to the judiciary a myth. Concededly, as Virginia's Senator Carter Glass said, Jefferson hated Marshall and feared *his* Court; his complaint, however, was that the Court was too liberal, too centralizing, too casual in regard to constitutional limitations. Even then, alarmed as he was, Glass said, Jefferson never proposed to remedy the condition by *packing* the Court.

Jefferson's position on the "third term" was seemingly less equivocal than his position on the judiciary. As far back as 1880, when Grant threatened to upset the two-term tradition, prominent Democrats had appealed to Jeffersonian opinion and precedent. Grant Republicans had then answered that Jefferson's real reason for declining a third term had nothing to do with the high principle he stated, but rested on the certain knowledge he could not be re-elected. No Jeffersonian could ever believe that canard! Yet Harold Ickes had to be satisfied with it in his attack on "The Third Term Bugaboo." As Fred Rodell showed in his careful analysis, "Thomas Jefferson had plenty to say about perpetual presidential reeligibility, and all of it was decidedly unfavorable." For historical witness, the Democrats in 1940 were forced to rely almost entirely on Hamilton's seventy-first *Federalist* paper, while Republicans were amply supplied with Jefferson texts, all "the reasoned result of deeply felt political principles." Here, if anywhere, in the Roosevelt years was a conclusive Jeffersonian principle. It did not admit of exception on the plea of changing circumstances, since the circumstances in this instance were essentially those that had caused Jefferson to declare against re-eligibility. In fact, the new capabilities of the Presidency would seem to have made Jefferson's principle more urgent in 1940 than in 1800. New Dealers might say re-eligibility was merely a question of mechanics. "Jeffersonian Democrats" were not put off by this ruse. There must be fundamental principles somewhere! Of course there were; but not in the old sense of unchanging Jeffersonian principles of government. The new model Jeffersonian Democracy not only discarded old methods; it discarded old principles as the need arose.

James M. Beck, a long-time worshipper at Hamilton's shrine and peerless exemplar of constitutional fetishism in the decade or so prior to the New Deal, struck one of the keynotes of the conservative discourse in a dramatic speech in Congress on April 18, 1934. The administration, he declared, "is realizing beyond any dream of Alexander Hamilton his ideas as to the nature of our government and what its desired form should be." The principles of Jefferson?—"they are virtually non-existent for any practical purpose." The future?—"a unitary socialistic state." The nation should, by all means, build a towering monument to Jefferson; nevertheless, the portentous reality, Beck insisted, was that Jefferson is "the 'forgotten man' in the philosophy of American politics."

Is Jefferson the Forgotten Man? Nicholas Murray Butler asked in a widely publicized address in 1935. That Butler could even raise the question, let alone answer it in the affirmative, was a revelation. He grew up in Paterson, New Jersey, which traced its beginnings to Hamilton's Society for the Establishment of Useful Manufactures; he was a delegate, often a very influential one, to every Republican Convention from 1880 to 1932; and as President of Columbia University from 1902, Butler did as much as any man of his time to perpetuate Hamilton's fame, locally, nationally, and internationally. Butler admired Hamilton as "the nation-builder," yet he described himself as a liberal in respect to the limits of political authority. As the tension between his nationalism and his liberalism built up in the nineteen-twenties, Butler began to talk about the soundness of Jefferson's principles. These principles which, had they prevailed at any time during the last century would have done irreparable harm, were now needed to maintain a free society at home and peace in the world. Although Butler loved Hamilton too much ever to abandon him completely, he clearly enlisted under Jefferson's standard in 1935. He condemned the decline of individual and local liberties, the use of the tax power to force social and political changes, the growth of warlike nationalism and oppressive collectivism. "All these considerations enforce the conviction that Thomas Jefferson was right; that Government must be carefully restricted in its powers and functions; that it must be held closely to them; and that every attempt on the part of Government to invade the reserved field of Liberty, no matter on what pretense, must be stoutly and stubbornly resisted." Was it argued that conditions had changed since Jefferson's day? Yes, Butler replied, but "Fundamental principles do not change." The urgent task of the time was to restore The Forgotten Man, and thus to redress the true liberal balance of Jefferson and Hamilton. These two great leaders were not antagonistic but complementary, Butler said. He liked to think the statues of the two rivals, as they stood on the Columbia campus, facing the observer on the right and on the left, symbolized the idea of American government.

The Indiana congressman, Samuel B. Pettingill, was a "Jeffersonian Democrat" who had looked upon Roosevelt as a returned Jefferson. Gradually disillusioned, he broke with the administration on the Court Bill. Speaking in the House a year later, Pettingill recalled to American memory July Fourth 1826. Millions of Americans for over a century had rejected the proofs of Jefferson's passing; a great political party had dedicated itself to the perpetuation of his teachings. Now, after five years of the dictatorial New Deal, the congressman solemnly announced, "the most serious of all questions facing America and the masses of mankind everywhere is whether Thomas Jefferson is dead." Pettingill's *Jefferson, The Forgotten Man,* in 1938, was the most elaborate attack on the New Deal written in Jeffersonian chapter and verse. Disclaiming any quarrel with Roosevelt's broad objectives, Pettingill said they were spoiled by non-Jeffersonian methods. Jefferson, he wrote, "did not believe liberal ends could be attained by illiberal means." Like Walter Lippmann, whose *The Good Society* was a much more sophisticated statement of the position, Pettingill thought the foundation stone of liberalism was the "free market" economy. Just insofar as the New Deal, in its action on the economy, substituted for the freedom of the marketplace centralized planning and control, it was Hamiltonian and a throwback to the authoritarian mercantilist state. Assuming that the ills of the economy arose from the business community, the New Deal invoked the powers of the state against business. In fact, Pettingill asserted, the root of the trouble was political, as always; the root was government intervention of any sort, for any purpose, in the economy. The privileges the Republicans had used in a Hamiltonian way, the New Dealers tried to use in a Jeffersonian way, not stopping to realize that the enemy was privilege itself. The task of liberalism, the Hoosier congressman concluded, must always be liberation. No better guide existed than Jefferson's First Inaugural Address. The Jeffersonian, Pettingill, and the Hamiltonian, Butler, thus ended up on the same side.

A few, though not many, intellectuals joined the attack from the right on the New Deal. The historian James Truslow Adams, in the previous decade, was a typical liberal intellectual: a debunker of patriotic myths, a denouncer of Puritanism and Babbittry, a somewhat supercilious observer of the political scene. Politics made no sense, he said in 1929, because the Americans had illogically built a Hamiltonian economic machine within their Jeffersonian house of faith. "We practice Hamilton from January 1 to July 3 every year. On July 4 we hurrah like mad for Jefferson. The next day we quietly take up Hamilton again for the rest of the year as we go about our business." Adams's fantastically popular *Epic of America*, in 1931, explained how America had been brought to this soulless condition. Jefferson represented "the American dream"—the dream of the common man in constant quest of freedom and opportunity—which Adams unfolded in five great forward movements: the Revolution, Jeffersonian Democracy, Jacksonian Democracy. Lincoln Republicanism, and Wilsonian Progressivism. But the dream, betrayed by the Hamiltonian Mammon, gradually retreated into the lost world behind the city and the corporation. The question for Adams, as for other Jeffersonians of "the noble dream," was whether America could reconcile the Jeffersonian philosophy with social realities more and more distant from its fundamental postulates. Mammon had displaced God in 1931, but Adams hesitated to announce the end of the epic. He looked at the problem again in 1936. *The Living Jefferson* applied Jefferson's philosophy to the present crisis. Roosevelt had preached "sound Jeffersonian doctrine" in 1932; his administration plunged America deeper into the Hamiltonian abyss. "What we need is not a Hamilton, but a Jefferson, to persuade the masses . . . that the 'more abundant life,' if thought of only in terms of economics and state planning, will be ashes in our mouths if we cannot at the same time retain those personal liberties of action . . . which alone make life worthy."

"Beating the Living with the Bones of the Dead," Texas congressman Maury Maverick entitled a scathing review of Adams's book. Maverick unfairly accused Adams of gross ignorance of Jefferson and subservience to the Liberty League crowd. The title of the book should have been, "Jefferson Repainted: Pigments by Du Pont, Oils by Standard Oil, Canvas by Hoosac Mills, Scenery by Schecter Bros." Maverick also registered his complaint in Congress. The thin film of scholarship on *The Living Jefferson* must not be allowed to conceal the author's true purpose, he warned, which was to dig up the dead Jefferson and exhibit him as a live model reactionary. "Thomas Jefferson specifically warned future generations against beating the living with the bones of the dead.' But the Liberty Leaguers have stolen him for their hero, and have publicly paraded him before the American people in garments he never wore."

The last word on Jefferson and the New Deal was uttered by Godfrey D. Gloom, "the well-known pawpaw planter and old-fashioned Jeffersonian Democrat from Amity, Indiana," as he expired, struck down by a passing auto, on a busy Philadelphia street corner in June 1936. Gloom, the fictional creation of newsman Elmer Davis in 1920, was a figure as real as life to many readers of the *New York Times*. His grandfather, it appeared from Gloom's obituary, had always boasted to the fame of having held Jefferson's horse at his inauguration. His father had come from Virginia to Indiana, where young Gloom trained briefly in the law office of Daniel Voorhees, a peerless Jeffersonian, and then entered the bear-skinning trade. At a ripe age (he had cast his first vote for James Buchanan), Gloom developed the habit of attending national political conventions, where Davis found him in 1920 and quadrennially (except for 1928) thereafter. Surprised to discover Gloom at the Republican convention in 1936 wearing a Landon sunflower in his lapel, the reporter asked an explanation. "The modern streamlined Democrats have got no more use for Jeffersonians than they have for a Model T, to say nothing of the horse and buggy," Gloom replied. The Republicans had become the grand old party of Jefferson. But the Democratic habit was too strong; two weeks later, Gloom set aside his Jeffersonian fears and meekly endorsed Roosevelt. Then death nipped him. It was time, the "last Jeffersonian" told the crowd that gathered around to hear his dying words:

Jefferson has now been endorsed by both parties, and there seems as little prospect that the endorsement will ever be repudiated as that either party will ever put Jeffersonian doctrine into practice. And maybe . . . that is just as well. For the principles of Thomas Jefferson I have unshaken respect;

but when he translated those principles into concrete policies he did so according to the peculiar conditions of his time, as any man of sense would have done.

It was impossible to return. Gloom was convinced that Jefferson, were he alive, "would stick to his principles of standing up for the rights of ordinary people by whatever means might seem most advantageously adapted to that end." When the self-styled Jeffersonians put a halo around the words uttered by the prophet in 1800, then, Gloom said, "the best place for a genuine Jeffersonian is in the tomb."

It may still be too early to say how well the New Deal, tackling the severest crisis since the Civil War, combined "maintenance of the symbolic code" with "fearlessness of revision"—the art of free society, as Whitehead thought—but in the case of the Jefferson symbol a good report may be given. Although the administration treated Jeffersonian canons with remarkable abandon, it appealed for justification to Jefferson's progressive spirit. "Not by ancestors, but by practical considerations, the modern problems of liberty are to be disentangled," wrote the prize-winning essayist of *Harpers Magazine's* contest in 1937 on the redefinition of "The American Way." This Benthamite wisdom colored the New Deal far more brilliantly than the Jeffersonian wisdom about government. It was, however, the kind of wisdom about means which a people resolutely committed to ancestral ideals of democracy could well afford. The hazards of the voyage away from the old landmarks were reduced by the fact that the compass pointed unwaveringly to freedom. "If we think that Jefferson created a free democracy," Gilbert Seldes remarked, "we miss the essence of democracy which is that every moment the people must create it for themselves." Democracy was not something Jefferson had dreamed once and for all, and which could be had by the simple expedient of returning to his principles. Nor was it a theory of government or a code of action valid for all time. The old complaints on the score of "rigidity of rule" were beside the point. Jefferson was not doctrines but ideals. He symbolized the faith that an informed people secure in their inalienable rights are always capable of saving themselves.

This was the end of the political tradition. After the Roosevelt Revolution, serious men stopped yearning for the agrarian utopia, politicians (and most historians too) laid aside the Jefferson-Hamilton dialogue, and almost no one any longer maintained the fiction that American government was run, or ought to be run, on the Jeffersonian model. What mattered was the faith in the power of free men constantly to rediscover their heritage and to work out their destiny in its spirit. The New Deal consummated the process by which Jefferson came to stand, above any other American, the hero of this faith, and for great clusters of civilized values as well. Paradoxically, the ultimate disintegration of the Jeffersonian philosophy of government heralded the ultimate canonization of Jefferson.

* *Eight* *

CULTURE

Leader in the philosophy of government, in education, in the arts, in efforts to lighten the toil of mankind—exponent of planning for the future, he led the steps of America into the paths of the permanent integrity of the Republic.*

"TODAY, in the midst of a great war for freedom, we dedicate a shrine to freedom." The day was April 13, 1943, gray and gusty like the state of freedom two hundred years after the birth of Thomas Jefferson. The place was the Jefferson Memorial, Washington, D.C., being officially dedicated on this day by the President of the United States. The President, as he stood with his back to the gleaming white portico rising from the Tidal Basin, and briefly addressed an audience of five thousand on the plaza below, must have felt a great sense of satisfaction. Far off to his right stood the Capitol, ahead of him like a sword thrust to the sky was the Washington Monument, on the northern point beyond, the White House, and appearing through the spring bloom to the left the Lincoln Memorial. Something had been completed: the central cruciform design of the national capital, three of whose cardinal points were fixed by noble monuments to the nation's great. Roosevelt knew the meaning of the design and of its completion in the Jefferson Memorial. Jefferson had conquered the American Olympus. "To Thomas Jefferson, Apostle of Freedom, we are paying a debt long overdue." We of this generation, he said,

* Franklin D. Roosevelt, Dedication Address, The Jefferson Memorial, April 13, 1943.

understand what other generations could not understand so well: "that men who will not fight for freedom will lose it; that free conscience and mind were battles constantly to be rewon." Living Americans were united to Jefferson across the distances of history by a common experience and a common cause. "His cause was a cause to which we also are committed, not by our words alone but by our sacrifice." Roosevelt noted without attempting to describe the many items in posterity's account with Jefferson. He chose to dedicate the Memorial to the oldest, the surest, and the truest conception, Apostle of Freedom, closing his address on the ringing note of the oath that girdled the Memorial room: "I have sworn upon the altar of God eternal hostility against every form of tyranny over the mind of man."

Although the Jefferson Memorial would certainly not have been dedicated in Jefferson's bicentennial year had it not been for Roosevelt and the Democratic New Deal, its existence implied a fundamental change in Jefferson's reputation for which political developments provide only part of the answer. The man glorified in the monument had transcended politics to become the hero of civilization. He had come to stand for ideals of beauty, science, learning, and conduct, for a way of life enriched by the heritage of the ages yet distinctly American in outline. The range of his appeal, if not its intensity, increased with the disclosure of his varied and ubiquitous genius. Many who balked at the political hero laureled "the civilized man." And thus it is not too much to say that Jefferson, having found his century-long climb up Olympus trammeled by political agonies and ordeals, at last reached the summit along a somewhat circuitous route. The Great Democrat was exalted, but exalted in large part because he had been disenthralled of a political tradition.

The development of the Culture Hero, previously obscured, may be traced clearly and surely from the time of the Sesquicentennial in terms of three main agents, suggestively figured as the Shrine, the Academy, and the Temple. The Shrine was Monticello, dedicated as such in 1926. Monticello was the place sanctified by the presence of Jefferson's physical remains, the relics of his hand and brain, the congealed expression of his inmost life. Monticello, which said so much, occupied the foreground of the new image. The Academy stood as a symbol both of Jefferson's own voluminous learning and of the enterprise of scholars and professionals in various fields who investigated its many parts. Jefferson, who had belonged primarily to public men, came increasingly into the possession of academic men wishing more to understand than to use him. Their researches gradually gave shape to the configuration of "the civilized man." The Jeffersonian Memorial was the Temple—literally a temple in terms of its architectural prototype and symbolically in the context of American patriotism. As the Monticello memorial consummated the long but subordinate interest in Jefferson's private life, the monument on the Potomac was the supreme achievement of the commemorative impulse. A mere glance suggests its relation to Monticello, as well as its air of high culture and academic respectability. Monuments of this majestic pomp are not built to the living, only to the dead; and thus the Jefferson Memorial was the most important thing to happen to Jefferson since July Fourth 1826.

On the two hundredth anniversary of his birth the nation was locked in a desperate world struggle for the rights he had declared inalienable. The nation, the world, were so distressingly different from anything Jefferson had envisioned; yet, fundamentally, his faith was the American faith, reaching out now to the world from which he had reluctantly withdrawn. And so during the Bicentennial nearly every celebrant saluted Jefferson's livingness. "Probably no great American of the past still seems so thoroughly alive," *Life* magazine said; symposia ventured to "present Thomas Jefferson as a burning issue today"; the advertisement of a popular cigarette put the issue bluntly, "Thomas Jefferson versus Adolf Schicklegruber." What was living was, in general, the idea of the rights of man. The world might still need instruction in this idea; but among Americans it was generally accepted as the definition of national character and purpose. Largely framed by this idea, Jefferson was a patriotic symbol. The old rage of controversy receded from the image. Viewed as a patriotic rite, the Bicentennial marks Jefferson's passage into the American pantheon.

1. *Monticello: The Shrine*

Of Jefferson more than of any other famed American it might be said that the history of the inner man was the history of his house. Before he came of age he was making plans for a mansion atop the little mountain where he romped as a boy. He took up residence in the first completed building (the one-room brick cottage on the west lawn) soon after fire destroyed his Shadwell birthplace. Here he brought his bride in January 1772. During the greater part of the next forty years, he was putting up and tearing down, determined to express in his home the essence of his heart and mind. His fame was always, in some part, the fame of Monticello. He was the Sage of Monticello almost from the moment he left the Presidency, and many counties and towns honored him by adopting the Italian name. Yet the Monticello image of Jefferson was distinctly a creation of this century. The obsession with his political career, the physical remoteness of Monticello, the slowness to recognize that it was, more than Jefferson's home, an artistic achievement of the first order— these factors combined until recent times to confer upon Monticello a history of neglect very different from the posthumous history of its master.

Jefferson's shrunken estate passed from the family in 1831 to James T. Barclay, a Charlottesville druggist who had ideas of silk worm culture on the mountain. He had no interest in the mansion itself, treated it shabbily, and reportedly vowed in vengeance on Jefferson's infidelity to leave "not a stone . . . upon a stone." But Barclay's project soon collapsed. Monticello was again on the market. The prize—house, outbuildings, and over two hundred acres—went to Lieutenant Uriah P. Levy, U.S.N., for twenty-five hundred dollars. He revered Jefferson, commissioned the first statue of him, which he presented to Congress in 1834, and appreciated Monticello. Unfortunately, Levy had little time for the management of the place. Busily accumulating a fortune in the North and engaged, most tempestuously, in naval affairs, he was never more than a part-time resident. Newly married in 1858, he permanently settled in New York, leaving Monticello to the beggarly custody of his tenant, Joel Wheeler. Wheeler scraped a living from the run-down lands, installed pig pens on the front lawn and stored grain on the parquet floors of the interior rooms. He discouraged visitors. Still they came, pilgrims and scavengers, as many as ten thousand a year. "Dilapidation and ruin" was the common report, as it had been almost from the hour of Jefferson's death; but the nadir of gloom was sounded during the two decades after Commodore Levy's death in 1862.

Levy willed Monticello to the United States for use as an agricultural school to train children, ages twelve to sixteen, of deceased warrant officers of the Navy. Alternate dispositions were provided should the United States refuse this eccentric bequest. There was no reason for urgency, however, since the Confederacy at once confiscated the property. It was broken up and sold under decree of a Confederate court in 1864. The next year it reverted to the United States; but after long drawn out litigation, Levy's executors broke the will. Finally, in 1882, Jefferson M. Levy, the Commodore's nephew, became the sole owner of Monticello.

A New Yorker, sometime later a Democratic congressman, Jefferson M. Levy lavished money and love on Monticello, his bachelor's hall and summer estate. He regained several hundred acres of the original estate, hired an expert superintendent, Thomas L. Rhodes, and put house and grounds in good shape again. Photographs taken before and years after his tenure testify to the great improvement, though at some expense to the original design, Levy made in the property. Despite the periodic grumblings of visitors against his regulations, Levy proved to be an accommodating host. Most observers around 1900 felt that he was as good a steward of Monticello as any the government might furnish. Still, it was not Jefferson's home but Levy's; he owned it, even the access road to Jefferson's grave. The caprices of private ownership must in time prove intolerable.

In the first decade of the century, as Monticello became better known and more accessible, the number of visitors doubled to forty or fifty thousand annually. Indicative of the rising interest was the organization in Virginia of a Jefferson Memorial Association for the purpose of building a well-engineered road up Jefferson's mountain. The Jefferson Memorial and Interstate Good Roads Convention, meeting in Charlottesville in 1902, endorsed the project and enlisted congressional support. Nothing matured, but it was clear that conditions were ripe for the first concerted campaign to make Monticello a national shrine.

The first personage to set his heart on this object was William Jennings Bryan. On April 3, 1897, Bryan wrote to Levy asking the value he placed on Monticello and urging him to make some conveyance of it, preferably to the United States, as a public memorial. Levy replied that all the money in the United States Treasury could not buy Monticello. Bryan awaited a more favorable opportunity.

It came in 1912 in the person of Mrs. Martin W. Littleton and her Monticello Memorial Association. The effervescent wife of a prominent New York Democrat then in Congress, Maud Littleton first laid eyes on Monticello in 1909. To see Monticello had been a cherished dream of her childhood. Seeing it at last as Levy's guest, she said, "I did not get the feeling of being in the house Thomas Jefferson built and loved and made sacred, and of paying tribute to him. . . . My heart sunk. My dream was spoiled." In Washington two years later, Maud Littleton heard of the plans then circulating to erect a Jefferson memorial in the capital. She thought Congress would be better advised to acquire Monticello. Digging up the forgotten will of Commodore Levy, she begged the United States to take back his gift. Her attractive brochure, *One Wish*, made a bid for generous public support. Taking as her motto Jefferson's moving line, "All my wishes end where I hope my days will end, at Monticello," she sketched a melancholy history of Jefferson's home and enlisted every patriotic emotion in her cause. "I read it with my heart in my throat and tears in my eyes," "Marse Henry" Watterson wrote from Louisville. "I am a Federalist by inheritance and belief, and I should not probably agree with you about Jefferson as a politician," Senator Lodge wrote to Mrs. Littleton. But there was a side of Jefferson too often overlooked: "his love of art and architecture in a country where they were hardly known." Because Monticello stood for this side of Jefferson, Mrs. Littleton's wish commended itself even to the Senator from Massachusetts.

The Monticello Memorial Association was launched under Mrs. Littleton's direction. Although its Executive Committee was overwhelmingly Democratic in composition, the support of numerous patriotic societies, along with prominent Republicans, evinced the movement's non-partisan character. The Association memorialized Congress in 1912 for the purchase of Monticello. Levy, then in the House of Representatives, was adamant. "My answer to any proposition seeking the property of Monticello is: 'When the White House is for sale, then I will consider an offer for Monticello.'" (He had reportedly declined private offers of as high as one million dollars.) The committee hearings turned into verbal duels between Levy and Mrs. Littleton. She charged that he had stood in the way of every right the American people had to Monticello—the Commodore's bequest, access to the grave, and now ownership of the historic site. While many men of lesser fame than Jefferson had been honored with public memorials, "his remains have lain unhonored and his home left to the fate of private property" because of the selfishness of one man. She denied that Levy was a good custodian or a fit host. He guarded it like an Oriental palace; he had replaced Jefferson's portraits and mementoes with his own; he had commercialized Monticello; the place was in a state of ruin. Levy was indignant at these "slanders." He alone had preserved Monticello during all the years when Americans slumbered with indifference. He had spent several thousand dollars every year to maintain it, and a small fortune to restore its character. Some thought the house was now exactly as Jefferson had left it, which would certainly not be the case, Levy observed, if it were converted into a public museum. He had kept Monticello not for "selfish and sordid purposes," as Mrs. Littleton charged, but "by an unceasing flow of the fountain of a heart filled with love for Thomas Jefferson."

In the absence of the owner's consent to sell, the efforts of the Association seemed pointless, unless the ground was being prepared to seize Monticello by eminent domain. The Association never admitted this intention, but Levy's brief anticipated it and the suspicion caused some of the Association's original supporters to withdraw. A concurrent resolution calling for a joint committee of inquiry on Monticello hastily passed the Senate in July 1912, after, it should be noted, a preamble eulogizing Jefferson was stricken at the behest of a few Republicans. By the time the resolution reached the floor of the House in December, many congressmen were convinced that its "ulterior purpose" was to deprive their colleague Levy of his private property by legislative fiat. This, of course, was abhorrent to Jeffersonian principles. The resolution lost on a record vote, 141 to 101.

"The Lady of Monticello" continued the fight. The Association stepped up its agitation of public opinion. More and more patriotic societies fell into line, hundreds of thousands of citizens petitioned Congress, several state legislatures sent memorials in favor of public ownership. In March 1914, after the Virginia Assembly endorsed the Association's aim, the Senate Lands Committee reported resolutions to establish a joint congressional committee authorized to acquire Monticello either by purchase or by condemnation. Levy was beginning to see the light. An eloquent appeal from Secretary of State Bryan in October ended his opposition. Bryan suggested that the government's acquisition at this time "would commemorate the great Democratic administration of President Wilson, which is being conducted on Jeffersonian principles, and would be more opportune because the President is by birth a Virginian." Touched by this thought, his defenses crumbling, Levy replied, "I must put aside my feelings and yield to the national demand." He agreed to sell Monticello for five hundred thousand dollars, half its market value, provided only that the place be made the Virginia home of the Presidents as well as a national shrine. The next three years were wasted in quibbling over the price and details of managing the property. Congress took no firm action. Public interest lagged during the World War. Mrs. Littleton's Association vanished. Levy still wished to sell, but in the default of the memorial movement he turned to private buyers. In 1921, a Washington real estate firm advertised "a dignified country home" overlooking Charlottesville.

The pioneer association found a more than worthy successor in the Thomas Jefferson Memorial Foundation, incorporated at Albany on April 13, 1923. The Foundation consolidated three groups interested in Monticello: an association of Richmond women formed in 1921 by, among others, Ruth Reed Cunningham, one of whose ancestors had founded the Mount Vernon Ladies Association over half a century before; a similar association started in Washington by

Marietta Minnigerode Andrews, artist and society leader; and, in February 1923, a New York group headed by Stuart Gibboney and Henry Alan Johnston, both Virginians practicing law in New York. The Foundation was a non-profit corporation organized for the primary purpose of acquiring, restoring, and maintaining Monticello as a patriotic shrine under its trusteeship. It also had an educational purpose: the revival and promotion of Jefferson's political philosophy. Perhaps this was its major object in the long run, with Monticello an incident to its accomplishment. But the Foundation was to find that the two objects, one patriotic and the other political, were not easily joined; and to the disappointment of some of its early leaders the former steadily eclipsed the latter. With Gibboney as Chairman, Johnston as Secretary, and Theodore F. Kuper as Director, the Foundation at once inaugurated a national campaign to raise one million dollars. Half of this was the purchase price, of which one-fifth was to be paid before the end of 1923 and the remainder over four successive years. The initial campaign failed miserably. The Foundation had to call New York bankers to its rescue in December, in order to obtain legal title to the property.

"Save Jefferson's old home from the sheriff" became the cry in 1924—a curious echo across a hundred years. With the co-operation of Governors and Mayors, churches, schools, and patriotic societies, "Jefferson Week," April 6–13, was proclaimed and celebrated in several states and three hundred cities. "The people of this country look upon Jefferson as they do on Washington," Charles Evans Hughes declared for the New York Jefferson Week Committee. "The Republicans are just as enthusiastic as the Democrats." "Jefferson's gig," a two-wheel chaise falsely advertised as the one in which Jefferson rode to the Continental Congress in 1776, was brought from Monticello and exhibited in New York. During the next two years the gig, sometimes escorted by a crack Virginia military outfit, probably made more mileage than ever it did in Jefferson's lifetime. The Foundation circulated the idea that Monticello was to be a "Patriotic Shrine for the Children of America." It collected their pennies by the millions. In 1926, children in thousands of schools across the land took a "Pledge of Faith" to Jefferson and invested in the ideals of the Declaration.

In 1925–26, as previously noted, the Monticello campaign was associated with the Sesquicentennial. Indeed, the patriotic observance was a case of the tail wagging the dog. The Thomas Jefferson Memorial Foundation had a reported one thousand Jefferson Centennial Committees formed more than a year before the two-million-dollar federal Commission started to work. Gibboney was the Commission's chairman, Bowers its Secretary, and Kuper wrote its Pledge. Of course, the Sesquicentennial was a godsend to the Foundation. The publication of Bowers's *Jefferson and Hamilton*, along with Paul Wilstach's *Jefferson and Monticello*, and several other books; the circulation of the Foundation's literature, especially an attractive series of brochures, *The Monticello Papers;* the numerous centennial observances in cities and towns, radio addresses, exhibits, essay contests, the gig pilgrimage, balls, and pageants (at Baltimore's Lyric Theatre, the *Thomas Jefferson Memorial Pageant* by Marietta Minnigerode Andrews)—the sun shone on Jefferson, a bit sticky in its warmth, and blessed the Foundation's work.

The day after the climactic observance of the one hundred and fiftieth anniversary of the Declaration of Independence and the one hundredth anniversary of Jefferson's death, the Foundation formally dedicated Monticello. Financially, it was over the hump. It had raised more than the purchase price, the great bulk of it in small donations. But much of this had gone into the campaign and needed repairs and improvements at Monticello. The mortgage would not be retired for many years yet. Except for the briefly renewed threat of foreclosure in 1932, however, Monticello was secure. The Foundation did not let up, nor did it confine its activities to Monticello. For several years to come the Foundation, not the government, was the chief agent of Jefferson commemoration. The enormous searchlight, said to have been the largest in the world, it turned on Monticello in 1927 was a fair symbol of its illumination of Jefferson.

All was not sunny and warm where Jefferson lived in fond memory, however. *What* Jefferson was being celebrated? *Which* teachings were being revived? One of the Foundation's officers, a Republican and businessman, announced in 1924 that the object was to make Monticello "an active agency of relentless war against the dangerous radicalisms of our time." Colonel Robert R. McCormick, publisher

of the *Chicago Tribune*, actively supported the Monticello movement (he was Chairman of its Freedom of the Press Day in 1931)
in the belief it would help to revive the vanishing Jeffersonian ideal
of government. But others of his persuasion felt that any celebration
of Jefferson would aid radical causes. The American Rights League,
for instance, said the movement stirred up sentiment for the Jeffersonian assailants of the Supreme Court. More serious than the coolness of Old Guard Republicans to a Jefferson revival were the winds
of religious bigotry blowing around Monticello. At the height of the
campaign in 1926, Governor Alfred E. Smith withdrew as speaker
at Monticello on July Fourth after the Foundation's generous invitation to him had aroused Ku Klux Klan slanders and threats. The
Foundation's leadership, though oriented in the main to the McAdoo
element of the Democratic party, was guiltless either of political
radicalism or of religious bigotry. To erase any impression that Monticello was a shrine of bigots, the Foundation focused its searchlight
for the next several years on the Father of Religious Liberty, and
simultaneously pressed its search for common Jeffersonian appeals
to the patriotic feelings of all Americans.

After 1930 the Foundation steadily withdrew into its glorious
museum. Whether this was because the public goals it sought were
being realized, and indeed realized beyond expectations, by a Democratic administration in Washington, or because the business side of
this Virginia tourist attraction became uppermost, or because the
American people were coming to feel that Jefferson, after all, was
a museum-piece—perhaps all these factors were involved. In any
event, the general tendency was to feature Monticello rather than
Jefferson, the relics of his domestic life and aesthetic vision rather
than the political philosophy.

The Foundation commenced its restoration work in 1924. By 1941,
when the mortgage was burned, over two hundred thousand dollars
had been spent to preserve, restore, and, where necessary, reconstruct
the house and its furnishings, the outbuildings and the grounds.
Even then the work was far from complete. Rotted beams were
replaced, the original furniture was reassembled or likely facsimiles
introduced, the interior was redecorated so far as possible in accordance with original specifications, Jefferson's own garden plans were

discovered and the gardens faithfully restored with the help of the Garden Club of Virginia. All of this was done, with absolute integrity to the historical conception, under the supervision of Fiske Kimball, Director of the Philadelphia Museum of Art. The ingenious machinery of Monticello was set in motion. In 1927 the visiting Governor of Indiana discovered the secret of the large clock over the hall door, which marks the days of the week by the descent of cannon ball weights. Still for half a century, it was set running again.

Monticello! Jefferson's life rendered visible. Not an American with a shiny new nickel in the last twenty years is without some image of the place. In the contemporary imagination Jefferson and Monticello are two sides of the same coin. Before the last war 125,000 annually stopped to visit; in recent years twice that number. What they have seen is not Monticello as it was in Jefferson's time, overrun with children and slaves (though the visitors were there then too), battered from daily use and showing the ravages of debt; but Monticello expertly restored as an architectural masterpiece, a fascinating museum, a shrine to Jefferson's memory.

Monticello was meant to commemorate Jefferson's services to the nation, above all his political philosophy. It was meant to solemnize his place in history and to celebrate his ideas anew. It was to be a "mecca of democracy" or a symbol of "the American ideal of government," however that was understood. Few of those who initiated the memorial movement and carried it forward saw anything incongruous between their object and the chosen shrine. Monticello was Jefferson, and Jefferson was democracy, so of course Monticello was sacred to democracy. But one had only to stand at Monticello and doubts rubbed the margins of the mind. Where was Jefferson's equalitarianism, his love of the people, his "democratic simplicity" at Monticello? "I had somehow gotten the idea that as a landed gentleman Jefferson was only playing the aristocrat," Republican Speaker Thomas B. Reed remarked when he was a guest of Jefferson M. Levy. "But look at this!—this is inherent. He was an aristocrat." The serenity, the beauty, the exquisite personal touch in every detail —Monticello was, above everything else, the poetic statement of a spiritual nobleman. If few had been cold to the charms of the domestic Jefferson, almost none could resist the spell of Monticello. The last hatreds faded from the mind; but this did not make the task of understanding easier. For at Monticello the dualities of Jefferson's life—private and public, patrician and plebeian, scholar and politician —were powerfully extended and reinforced, with the emphasis shifted to the first set of terms. The image of the man of culture, a symbol of the nation's civilized values, struck the mind; and reflective men tried to make sense of it in relation to the ineffaceable democratic image.

Compared to Mount Vernon, Monticello was studiously aristo- cratic in its planning. Unlike everyone else, Jefferson built his man- sion on a mountain's summit. Perhaps it implied a natural desire, as Kenneth Umbreit thought, "to live in an ivory tower." Whatever the reason, it evoked the Olympian. The impression was strengthened by Jefferson's arrangement of the plantation's outbuildings (kitchen, dairy, servants' quarters, and so on) in two long arcaded terraces sunk into the sides of the mountain and stretching to the west on either side of the house. At Mount Vernon all these adjuncts of labor and industry were grouped closely around the mansion, plainly in view. If Jefferson's "catacombs" gave an unparalleled aesthetic ad- vantage to the mansion, they certainly were not functional in the modern sense. Perhaps, as Lewis Mumford thought, Jefferson could find no place for the utilitarian in his aesthetic, so he hid these lower activities from view. But most observers simply filed the item with the first impression got from ascending the mountain. "Great nobles and kings have been more open to the human touch, more accessible to their familiars" than Jefferson at Monticello.

The mansion looked rather smaller than expected from the out- side; but this was the illusion Jefferson had created, in part, by ingeniously blending the windows of the first and second stories. Entering through the brilliant white columned portico of the east front, the illusion was at once dispelled. Here was a great spacious hall. Some thought it "baronial." The absence of a grand staircase was a puzzle, until Fiske Kimball explained that Jefferson ripped out the original staircase during remodeling because it invited an inti- macy he shunned. Off to the left of the hall lay Jefferson's bedroom. Everyone had heard of Jefferson's ingenious bed that could be raised to the ceiling in the daytime—the original Pullman berth! But, alas, according to the renovators, the bed had never left the floor. "Here his extreme fastidiousness crops out in amazing fashion," O. C. Sherlock wrote. "It is hard to reconcile oneself to the bed as the place of repose of a strong and active man." Jefferson's revolving chair ("the whirligig chair" which, satirists had said, enabled Jefferson to see in all directions at once) was in this room. Other furniture and gadgets of his inventive brain appeared in the library denuded of his books. But the Parisian furnishings and decor of the saloon and dining room added again to the image of Old World elegance and taste. It was difficult to associate the stateliness of the house with the man who, as legend had it, rode to his inauguration on horseback and received the envoys of foreign nations in shabby slippers and dressing gown. "Jeffersonian simplicity" was merely absurd.

Going out of the house along one of the pavilions above the terraces and stepping down to the beautiful west lawn, one remembered Jefferson's passion for landscape gardening. Were there ever really peacocks with full-fledged tails strutting these walks, as an old print showed and some students still believed? Probably not; but on the north side of the mountain overlooking his University, Jefferson had planned a rustic park of English design, picturesquely decorated with grottoes, cascades, and Chinese temples, and stocked with peacocks, partridges, deer—even a buffalo! His taste was decidedly eclectic. More baffling was the contrast between the romanticism of the gardens and the classicism of the architecture. From the west lawn, the octagonal dome at last came into view. The house appeared larger, more majestic, than before. The circular windows and plinths of the dome, the delicately carved cornice, the Palladian correctness of the two pediments, the columns, and the orders—the house in all its proportions registered the mathematical precision of Jefferson's mind and his love of the ancients.

Before descending the mountain, one took in the panorama. It was a prospect, as William Wirt had said in 1826, "in which you see and feel at once, that nothing mean or little could live." Down across the Rivanna, not far away, lay Shadwell, his birthplace. "He spent the eighty-three years he dwelled upon earth as close as possible to the spot where his cradle had stood and where some day his grave was to be dug," Hendrik Van Loon observed. "For there he could be himself and to be one's self seemed to him the highest form of human happiness." He cultivated his own garden, to be sure, but had it really been possible for the architect of Monticello to be himself in this rugged environment? And there was not one but many selves, even at Monticello. Half-way down the road was the graveyard—memories of Dabney Carr, clerical pontifications, the battered obelisk. The ground seemed hallowed now; the desecrators were fenced out; and if the Government's monument was not exactly what Jefferson had ordered, it still conveyed the right message.

Here Was Buried

THOMAS JEFFERSON

Author of the

Declaration

of

American Independence

of the

Statute of Virginia

For

Religious Freedom

And Father of the

University of Virginia

Everyone now recognized both the justice and the simple dignity of that epitaph. If the style of the man was aristocratic, the things for which he chose to be remembered were not. It was commonly said that Jefferson chose these three because he asked no fame for the things the people had done for him, only for the things he had done for the people. David Muzzey was impressed by the sequence, in which "the political motive is progressively eclipsed by the humanitarian." Perhaps; but on the way from Monticello it was about as hard to think of Jefferson as a humanitarian as it was to think of him as a politician.

Under the charms of Monticello, the traditional political symbol broke down. Whatever importance political ideas, activities, and ambitions had in his life, they must have been integrated in some subtle way with a grand design of culture. So the student tried to knit the pieces together again in a new image with Monticello in the foreground.

Searching for the clue, John Dos Passos, the novelist who announced his rediscovery of the American tradition in *The Ground We Stand On* (1941), was moved to write one of the most sensitive chapters in the Jefferson literature: "A Portico Facing the Wilderness." Dos Passos saw nothing strange in the fact that Monticello and the Declaration of Independence were the cardinal achievements of the same man; indeed, the first was father to the second. Jefferson, like "a free nobleman with the sky over his head ... takes it for granted other men must be as good as he." Planned full scale to the human figure, manifesting not only self-respect but respect for mankind, Monticello was "a house where a free man could live in a society of equals." As for the gleaming portico seemingly so incongruous with the surrounding wilderness, it acted as a spiritual frame for the American task otherwise formless and materialistic. It served Jefferson, and he meant it to serve America, as an ideal of beauty, conduct, and workmanship in the great republic of which he was one of the founders. Monticello, Dos Passos affirmed, "would make manifest in brick and stucco his own adaptation to the Virginia frontier of an antique Roman sense of the dignity of free men."

Monticello was the poetry of Jefferson's democracy. With this recognition the poets, who had unanimously shunned Jefferson before, were attracted to the subject. Lawrence Lee found in Monticello's classic lines the fundamental purity and simplicity of the democratic ideal:

> Mute marble or the word
> Both are clean will expressed.
> The line unblurred,
> Proportioned stone,
> Sang that the simple just
> Had found their own.

To Karl Shapiro, Monticello was radiant with vision at a dark time:

> I see the tender gradient of your will;
> Virginia is the Florence of your soul.
> Yes, ours. The architecture of your hands
> Quiets ambition and revives our skill
> And buys our faithlessness.

Perhaps President Alderman summed it up: "Jefferson gave a winged soul to democracy." Democracy yes; but not as Americans had been accustomed to imagine it, ill-proportioned, common, starved for beauty, perhaps even the offspring of the frontier. Democracy, rather, framed, made light and just, by the classic ideal, the sense of which Robert Penn Warren conveyed in his evocation of Jefferson's response to the ancient form:

> Here is a shape that shines, and here is
> A rooftree so wrought and innocent of imprecision
> That a man who hoped to be a man, and be free,
> Might enter in, and all his mind would glow
> Like a coal under the breath, in that precinct
> Where the correctness of our human aspiration
> Has body and abides and bespeaks the charmed space.

If this was Jefferson's true monument, then it put men in touch with a native ideal redolent of ancient, and perhaps Renaissance, humanism, and referable to American culture as a whole.

This was poetry, of course. It called up a "world picture," as Dos Passos said, "heartbreakingly different from our own," and thus seemed to throw Jefferson farther into the past. Viewing Monticello from the plebeian side of Jefferson's heritage, others found there the vivid proof of his modernity and Americanism. Gerald W. Johnson argued in a provocative essay, "The Changelings," that recent history had forced a modification of the stereotyped images of Hamilton and Jefferson. The hardheaded realist and the visionary dreamer had changed places. Monticello demonstrated as nothing else could, Johnson thought, that the man called the visionary had a firmer grip on American realities. "The place is filled with a practical man's highly practical devices for eliminating small nuisances; and if there is anything characteristic of the poetic temperament, that thing is its incapacity to deal with the trivial disturbances of ordinary life." The swivel chair, the dumb-waiter, the "double-acting street car doors" between the hall and the saloon, the wind-vane on the eastern portico that enabled Jefferson to see which way the wind was blowing without getting his feet wet—what was antique or poetic about these things? Monticello, Johnson said, and others agreed, was "an amazing palace of gadgets."

Monticello cleanly exposed Jefferson's fundamental ambiguity. "He was of the old order and he was not." The mind fluctuated between its antithetical meanings, those that were past and reminiscent of the Old World, those that were new in the American vernacular. Jefferson inherited a double tradition, Lewis Mumford said, that of the Renaissance man who sought to transcend provinciality through the universal forms of the ancients, and that of the American pioneer whose bent was mechanical and utilitarian. He did not in Monticello, could not in his own mind, Mumford thought, harmonize his formal tastes with his love of vital American things. The locale, the gadgets, the American curiosities that hung from the walls had no organic relation to the building itself. Monticello suggested, even in Jefferson's time, the museum of Americana it has indubitably become.

Because it made these ambiguous impressions on the mind, no uniform Monticello image of Jefferson emerged. Monticello predicated culture, but in what precise sense it was difficult to say. The dominant recognition, however, was the one which shocked political preconceptions the most. The poetry of Monticello, in landscape, architecture, and interior decor, was more persuasive than its practical mechanism; the sense of the archaic more powerful than the sense of the modern; the impression of Old World order and refinement more compelling than the impression of New World life. But the portico, after all, faced the wilderness. There was the riddle.

2. *The Civilized Man: The Academy*

Monticello graphically presented Jefferson's prodigious genius. Here were his music stand and his architect's table, the furniture and gardens of his own design, the numerous mementoes of his work in science and invention. The library, the dining room, the old man's lookout over the rising University, the stables and the nailery —the imagination could hardly keep up. Was Jefferson the American Leonardo?

> The big hands clever
> With pen and fiddle
> And ready, ever,
> For any riddle.

> From buying empires
> To planting 'taters,
> From Declarations
> To dumb-waiters.

The recognition, which Stephen Vincent Benét thus caught up in rhyme, was first clearly foreshadowed in James Parton's famous description of "a gentleman of thirty-two." "Posterity," the *Springfield* (Mass.) *Republican* correctly observed in 1902, "is apt to remember Jefferson only as a statesman and politician." The appreciation of "how much else he was" besides "the father of democracy" came gradually, first in education, next in law and religion and science, then in the arts and letters. Finally, by 1943, in almost everything from "planting 'taters . . . to dumb-waiters." The varied tributaries of this research fed into the conception of "the civilized man."

Although Jefferson was the recognized architect of Monticello, the importance of that achievement, and of his architectural work generally, both from a professional and an artistic standpoint, went comparatively unnoticed until the second decade of this century. For a century or more, practicing architects in this country worked in a tradition of classical design, especially in public buildings, without realizing Jefferson's seminal role. That he had some connection with such eminent architects in this tradition as Robert Mills was noted by William Dunlap in his pioneer history of American art in 1834. That he conceived the Capitol at Richmond from the Maison Carrée, the Roman temple at Nîmes on which he had gazed whole hours, as he said, "like a lover at his mistress," was known because of his autobiographical account of this enterprise. That he was the architectural, as well as the educational, father of the University of Virginia was usually taken for granted. All of this vaguely suggested Jefferson's importance without fixing his architectural responsibility.

The architects remained, for the most part, ignorant of Jefferson's pretensions in their domain for years to come. In the few instances where they did not ignore, they were skeptical and inclined to attribute the buildings to practicing architects with whom Jefferson consulted. Thus a member of the firm that restored the Virginia

Capitol spoke of "Jefferson and his architect," the Frenchman
Clérisseau; and Montgomery Schuyler voiced the same opinion even
more strongly in an article which traced the classical revival in
America to Benjamin H. Latrobe. Glenn Brown, who had earlier
associated Mills with Monticello, argued in 1913 that William Thornton was the true architect of the University. Comparing Thornton's
drawings for the United States Capitol with unsigned drawings for
the University, a number of which Herbert Baxter Adams had published in his 1888 monograph, Brown concluded that they came
from the same hand and that hand was Thornton's. Jefferson thus
acted, architectural historian Norman M. Isham wrote, "with Thornton's sketches in his hands and Thornton's advice in his mind." These
deprecatory opinions were not surprising in view of prevalent ideas
about Jefferson. It seemed reasonable to pass off the political hero
as a dilettante or dabbler in other fields, one associated with household gadgets, serpentine walls, and impractical plows. Moreover, in
the absence of respectable evidence bearing on Jefferson's architectural work, incredulity seemed warranted.

The corner was turned in 1913 with the publication of *Thomas
Jefferson as an Architect and Designer of Landscape,* the collaboration of two professionals, William A. Lambeth and Warren H. Manning. The part by Manning on landscape was superficial. The major
part, by Lambeth, though far from comprehensive or definitive,
anticipated the later canonization of Jefferson as "the father [Lam-
beth was satisfied with "godfather"] of American architecture." He
found no evidence that Thornton contributed anything but possibly
a few rough suggestions to Jefferson's plans for the University. Unquestionably, Jefferson was "the real and only architect of Monticello." Lambeth called attention to the crucial influence of the
sixteenth-century Italian, Palladio. In England and elsewhere in
America, the Palladian became Georgian. Jefferson, on the other
hand, worked back from Palladio to the pure Roman types, such as
the Pantheon. Every form by Jefferson, Lambeth said, "became increasingly refined and classical." But he made daring innovations,
especially at Monticello, neither degrading the classic form nor
forgetting, in his buildings, "the abiding integrity" that resides in
harmony with time, setting, and function. Lambeth observed the

influence of Monticello on other famous Virginia mansions, but he was unable to assign them to Jefferson.

Jefferson's twentieth-century reputation as an architect is very largely due to the talent and energy of one man, the architect, art historian, museum director, and restorer of historic buildings, Fiske Kimball. The richest unsearched treasure of Jefferson manuscripts then in existence opened to Kimball just before the World War, when he was a student at Harvard and the University of Michigan. This was the collection of over three hundred sheets of drawings in the possession of Mrs. Thomas Jefferson Coolidge, Jr.* In 1915 Kimball published with the appropriate drawings his initial study, *Thomas Jefferson and the First Monument of the Classical Revival in America*. The Virginia Capitol, mentioned only in passing by Lambeth and generally attributed to Clerisseau, was not only Jefferson's work but also the beginning of the classical revival, Kimball argued. The implications of this position were truly startling. The reign of the classical in the public architecture of the United States, and by virtue of association in American taste generally, was inaugurated by Jefferson. Indeed, the more Kimball, along with Talbot Hamlin and others, studied the matter, the more convinced they became that Jefferson's Capitol prefigured the classical revival everywhere. And since this adaptation of ancient forms to the service of the new nation's republican ideals represented the first departure from the mindless copybook carpentry of early American building, Jefferson was "the father of our national architecture."

Kimball reached this conclusion in the text he wrote to accompany the magnificent folio volume of Jefferson's drawings, *Thomas Jefferson Architect*, which Mrs. Coolidge published as a memorial to her husband in 1916. Here for the first time was massive documentation

---

* The Coolidge branch of the family was especially interested in Monticello. Young Archibald Cary Coolidge attempted to buy his great-great-grandfather's estate in 1889, and he later opposed the successive efforts to make Monticello a national shrine. His cousin, Thomas Jefferson Coolidge, Jr., built a near replica of Monticello as his home on Boston's fashionable North Shore. Collecting in the Jefferson neighborhood in 1911, he and his wife came upon a great number of well-nigh forgotten architectural drawings in the keeping of two descendants in the Randolph line. These formed the bulk of the collection to which Kimball, with the help of Worthington C. Ford, gained access.

of Jefferson's architectural work from as early as 1769. He must have got his ideas and skills almost entirely from books, chiefly Palladio's, Kimball thought. But no explanation in terms of intellectual influence really sufficed. Why Palladio? Kimball asked. Because Jefferson saw in Palladio's codification of the laws and proportions of classical design the architectural statement of his own philosophy. It confirmed his Newtonian faith in a rational and ordered universe. Palladio appealed to his scientific precision of mind, and also to his love of the ancients. "Jefferson's art was the art of retrospection and of science." His influence, as Kimball showed, was not limited to a few model buildings. Quietly, almost imperceptibly, he worked to encourage a profession of architecture with schools of instruction, and public appreciation and patronage of this most useful of the fine arts.

Many students, lay and professional, followed in Kimball's track; but, as Talbot Hamlin said in his authoritative study, *The Greek Revival in American Architecture* (1944), Kimball had so accurately appraised Jefferson's position "that any further statement is unnecessary." Hamlin, it is worth noting, did not discount Jefferson's importance because his Roman style was soon superseded by the Grecian. The decisive fact was Jefferson's innovation of the distinctive American style, classic but modern in the circumstances of the time, from which the history and profession of architecture in this country took their rise. On the trail of Jefferson's influence, students discovered his contribution to the National Capitol and to numerous Southern mansions. And his name came to be so closely identified with the monumental style in public architecture that it seemed only fitting to enthusiasts like Kimball that a Roman temple should be his memorial in Washington.

The architectural inquiry gradually opened into other branches of the fine arts. The documentary record, illustrated with a few monuments, was most abundant in the instance of landscape gardening. He planned his gardens as carefully as he planned his buildings, yet in a radically different style. One was classical, the other rococco; one straight and purely proportioned, the other serpentine and ornamental to excess. One evoked the humanist, the other the romantic naturalist. None of the explanations advanced for this mingling of styles proved satisfactory. The personality which the architect revealed to Kimball was contradicted by the personality of the landscape gardener. A revealing instance was Jefferson's serpentine garden wall on the grounds of the University. The philosopher Horace Kallen thought the idea must have come from William Hogarth, the English champion of the serpentine line, the line of nature, as he thought, against the artificial lines of the regnant Palladian style. But there was no record of Jefferson's knowledge of Hogarth; Kimball and other scholars explained the design of the famous wall on practical and economical grounds. Then, in 1943, a Jefferson memorandum of 1771 came to light: he was familiar with Hogarth after all. Jefferson's artistic originality, the overjoyed Kallen wrote, lay precisely in his orchestration of the two styles, the austere formalism of the Palladian and the lambent freedom of the Hogarthian. Kallen's student, Eleanor D. Berman, in her *Thomas Jefferson Among the Arts*, flatly stated that Jefferson's serpentine wall was "harmonious with the spirit of American democracy," "a directive toward liberty," because it "goes with both the wilderness and the simple virtuous life of the American countryside." Here again, then, the search for plausible answers to new riddles tempted the student to focus Jefferson's role in providing aesthetic forms agreeable to the native culture.

Of the other arts, only music seriously engaged Jefferson. Stories of Jefferson and his violin were commonplace in the nineteenth century. Their intent was not so much to show his musical forte as it was to illustrate certain personal habits and add amusing or rustic touches to the image. In these stories it was not a violin but a "fiddle"; Jefferson was a "fiddler," and whether the best or the worst in Virginia did not really matter. Then, as Jefferson acquired titles of firstness in so many areas of talent, his reputation in music grew until he was called "America's first great amateur violinist." Jefferson bought a good violin in 1775 (there was an amusing story about this too), generally believed to have been a Cremona by Amati. If so, it was one of the finest in the colonies. Albert Hildebrandt, a cellist and collector of rare violins, while in Charlottesville to play a concert in 1899, asked his barber if he knew of any old violins in the vicinity. The barber sent him to a ninety-three year old Negro who claimed to own a violin bequeathed to his father by Jefferson.

Although its authenticity has never been established, the violin Hildebrandt thus bought for a farthing has since been valued at a price that silences doubt.

Beginning with the legend of the violin, students explored the range of Jefferson's musical interests: the music he knew, the compositions he owned and played in Virginia; the operas and concerts he attended in Paris and, while there, his romantic affair with the talented painter and musician, Maria Cosway; his alertness to technical improvements in musical instruments; and his concern for American musical production. The gift of Jefferson's music library to the Thomas Jefferson Memorial Foundation by Fanny Maury Burke, a descendant, led two scholars, Carlton Sprague Smith and Helen Duprey Bullock, to commence a study of his musical life. Although the project never matured, an important by-product was the latter's editing of the Jefferson-Cosway correspondence. During the Bicentennial, Jefferson's love of music—"the favorite passion of my soul"—was commemorated in concerts devoted to the music he knew.

Jefferson embraced in some fashion all the arts; but how should his aesthetic ideas and interests be characterized? Some thought he was, at heart, an "artist spirit," perhaps "the father of the arts in America" as well. No contemporary ranged as widely or with more proficiency and enthusiasm. He sought with some success to break down provincialism, to elevate tastes, and to inspire the young nation with ideals of beauty the world could respect. But despite porticoes, opera, and cuisine, some scholars denied that Jefferson was really so far removed from the commonplace life of Americans. A memorandum of 1788, "Traveling Notes for Mr. Rutledge and Mr. Shippen," which Gilbert Chinard uncovered and labeled "a most damning document," seemed to anticipate Mark Twain in the Philistinism and Puritanism it displayed toward European civilization. Jefferson advised the touring Americans to fix their minds on agriculture, the mechanical arts, and politics. Painting and statuary were "worth seeing, but not studying." Two arts were recommended as *useful* to the Americans: gardening, because the noblest gardens might be made at least expense in America; and architecture, because the Americans had to have houses and, besides, "it is desirable to introduce taste into an art which shows so much." Enraptured by the simple virtues of his own country, Jefferson could not surrender to the aesthetic charms of Europe. From this it might be concluded that he, like the bourgeois gentleman, found art amusing but unworthy of serious pursuit. And yet, there was Monticello. Perhaps, as Albert J. Nock thought, it was necessary to distinguish between the *contemplation* of art, which never touched Jefferson deeply, and the *cultivation* of those arts in which he and the mass of practical-minded Americans could participate. Even in music, Kallen observed, Jefferson was "much more articulate about the processes of musical production than about the enjoyment of the musical product; his delight was more in the how than in the what of music."

The marked dualities of Jefferson's aesthetic could not be organized into a uniform pattern, such as would authorize sweeping generalizations about his mind and thought. But like the dualities of Monticello, they tended to fall naturally into the categories of the dual heritage. Thus, Kallen said, Jefferson united in his person Virginia's divided culture: the elegance of the Cavalier and the workmanship of the Pioneer. "Fundamentally, Jefferson's aesthetic involved a dissolution of classical attitudes in spontaneously pioneer sentiments and practices." In this dissolution, it would seem, the classical ideals of order and decorum acquired a distinctive American practicality, spaciousness, and freedom. Puzzled by the apparent dichotomies in Jefferson's artistic life, students might make sense of them in the generalized image of one who synthesized two contrasting cultural ideals.

The earlier and continuing appreciation of Jefferson the Scientist helped to check the exaggeration of his "artistic spirit." The scientific side had been evident ever since the publication of the *Notes on Virginia,* called by a leading scientist one hundred years later the most influential scientific work published in America up to that time. One of its purposes was to refute the theory of certain European savants on the degeneration of animal species in the New World. An often repeated story concerned the trouble and expense Jefferson incurred to have the bones of a great moose shipped to Paris in order to vindicate American nature. Jefferson was President of the Ameri-

can Philosophical Society for many years. He sent Lewis and Clark
into the Northern wilderness partly with a view to satisfying the
scientific curiosity of the world. He even laid the foundations of the
Republican party, some would believe, while on a "botanizing excursion" in New York. Because his scientific ideas and activities had a
broad public character, they entered into the image of the political
man. Satirists worked them into their portrait of the impractical
visionary, while admirers eulogized him for uniting in his life "the
retired love of science with the practical energy of the world."

Well known as something of a scientist (or natural philosopher)
during his lifetime, Jefferson was pretty much forgotten by working
scientists for several generations after his death. In the general
literature, his scientific aspect was, at best, a subsidiary aid in the
characterization of the political leader. It helped Henry S. Randall,
for instance, to refute the idea of the visionary. Jefferson's experiments in agriculture, which most interested Randall, showed the
same bent toward discovery, the same traits of practicality, he displayed in politics. Henry Adams, on the other hand, though be-
wildered by the clash between Jefferson's scientific temperament and
doctrinaire politics, finally left the impression of "a theorist, prepared
to risk the fate of mankind on the chance of reasoning far from
certain of its details." Emphasis on one side led to the idea of the
gadgeteer, with the American's vaunted practicality. Emphasis on
the other side continued the legend of the speculator, with the
eighteenth-century philosopher's love of abstraction and treacherous
omniscience. On either side, it was hard to take Jefferson seriously
as a scientist.

The faint beginnings of the scientists' appreciation appeared in
the eighteen-eighties. Frederic N. Luther's article on "Jefferson as
a Naturalist," in 1885, first illuminated the subject. The following
year, G. Brown Goode of the Smithsonian Institution bracketed Jefferson with Louis Agassiz as the two men who had done most for
the advancement of science in America, "not so much by their direct
contributions to knowledge, as by the immense weight which they
gave to scientific interests by their advocacy." At about the same time
the earliest special studies appeared, for example, Henry A. Martin's
paper, "Jefferson as a Vaccinator," in the *North Carolina Medical*

Journal. Studies of this type, however, would not appear in number for another thirty or forty years. Curious about the American beginnings of their work, scientists were to find Jefferson's writings suggestive and sometimes instructive. By 1943 a sizable literature, ranging from horticulture to astronomy, from entomology to mathematics, had accumulated on Jefferson the Scientist. To his many titles of renown, the scientists added "Pioneer Soil Conservationist," "Pioneer Botanist," "Pioneer Student of American Geography," "Father of American Paleontology," and so on.

While some of this literature added to the stock of the "wild and visionary" conception, the preponderant weight of it fell into the practical scale. Jefferson always sought to turn his investigations to tangible use, it was commonly said. His scientific spirit, as some thought his artistic spirit, looked toward clearly defined social and moral purposes. Especially significant in this connection was his devotion to agriculture: the moldboard of the plow, crop rotation, animal breeding, control of pests, improvement of seeds, and so on. "It was Jefferson more than any other man of his time who foresaw the fruitfulness of the application of science to agriculture." Just as he was more interested in personal and public health than in the science of medicine, he was particularly interested in the economic branches of entomology, botany, chemistry, and geology. He was the kind of man who in the later years of his life, as Albert J. Nock recalled, could seriously ask himself, "Whether my country is the better for my having lived at all"; then seriously name among his best services the removal of obstructions to navigation on the Rivanna River, the importation of olive trees from France and of heavy upland rice from Africa.

Paleontology was Jefferson's one passion in pure science. Frederic A. Lucas named him "the Father of Paleontology" in 1926; such eminent authorities as Henry Fairfield Osborn concurred. Jefferson laid the foundations of the science, it was said, with his systematic refutation of Buffon's degeneracy theory, and with his subsequent work on the "Great Claw," an extinct species which he named Megalonyx and which became known as *Megalonyx jeffersoni.* He constantly interested himself in paleontology. Specimens that passed through his hands are still exhibited in American museums. After

Jefferson, according to Osborn, the science slept for several decades
in the United States. Jefferson's reputation became well established
among paleontologists. How well, and upon what slight basis, is suggested by the statement of George G. Simpson, of the American
Museum of Natural History, in his paper on "The Beginnings of
Vertebrate Paleontology in the United States," read before the
American Philosophical Society in 1942:

Thomas Jefferson has become a fabulous figure to paleontologists, few of
whom know what he really did but most of whom consider him as the
father or founder of vertebrate paleontology in America. . . . It should not
be considered iconoclastic (although I have already learned that it seems
so to my colleagues) to state that he was not a vertebrate paleontologist
in any reasonable sense of the words, that he never collected a fossil or
gave one a technical name, and that his scientific contributions were
negligible or retrogressive.

Jefferson's only importance, Simpson said, was in helping to make
paleontology respectable and to bring together the materials necessary for its advancement. The entire basis of his natural philosophy
was retrogressive, since he denied that animal species could ever
become extinct. The science of paleontology could not begin until
exactly the opposite premise was established. Having no claim to
scientific eminence in the field, Jefferson would have been the first,
Simpson thought, to repudiate the legend of the paleontologists.

The true understanding of Jefferson's scientific work could begin
only after the investigators realized that Jefferson, and the intellectual species Jeffersoni, was extinct. Too many of his scientific interpreters had interpolated his ideas into their own worlds of thought.
The result was distortion of Jefferson's natural philosophy and exaggeration of his importance as the common father, midwife, and nurse,
along with Benjamin Franklin, of the American sciences. The first
significant study to go on the assumption of an extinct species of
thinkers, of which Jefferson was the pre-eminent type, was Daniel J.
Boorstin's The Lost World of Thomas Jefferson in 1948. The Jeffersonian world of ideas was lost, in science as well as in morals and
politics.

Boorstin's book emphasized as never before the activistic and utilitarian bent of Jefferson's mind. While this was the major impression left by the study of Jefferson's science, it could not be forgotten that he cultivated the sensible and useful with a transcendental aim. Just as he believed the useful in architecture would beautify the American landscape and elevate the American character, he regarded science as an instrument in the pursuit of humanitarian goals. Science with the technology derived from it, rather than institutions of government, some came to feel, was the engine of his faith. "It was always his opinion that whoever could make two ears of corn, or even two blades of grass grow upon a plot of ground where only one grew before would deserve better of mankind, and do more essential service to his country than the whole race of politicians put together."

The praise of Jefferson by the votaries of science was not mistaken, though it was often given for the wrong reasons. More important than anything or everything Jefferson did as a scientist was his creation as a statesman of a favorable climate for scientific progress. The connection he made between knowledge and humanitarian purpose, the freedom of inquiry gained by his works for freedom, the encouragement and prestige he gave to scientific endeavor as a private citizen (the American Philosophical Society), public official (the Patents Office, the Coastal Survey, the Naval Observatory), and educator (the curriculum of the University of Virginia)—this statesmanship of science addressed the distant future and assured his fame, if not as a scientist, then as the sciences' best servant and advocate.

Still another side of Jefferson, the Man of Letters, came increasingly into view in the twentieth century. "As a political leader, he was literally a man of letters; and his letters are masterpieces, if viewed as illustrations of the arts by which political leadership may be attained," the critic Edwin P. Whipple wrote in a centennial essay on the nation's literature. He thought Jefferson "the greatest, or, at least the most generally known, of American authors." The view was eccentric, though shared in part by Moses Coit Tyler and a few others. The American people had felt "the magic persuasiveness" of Jefferson's pen in documents (the Declaration of Independ-

ence, the Kentucky Resolutions) and in the private letters by which
he built and still inspired the Democratic party. But this, of course,
was a masterful literary talent in the service of politics. Except for
the Declaration, little if anything in the Jefferson canon commended
his admission to the world of letters, and he certainly never asked
entrance. He was a superb rhetorician, in the ancient usage of that
term, interested in the communication of ideas rather than in the
beauties of expression. He never wrote a book in the literary sense.
Even the *Notes on Virginia* showed scarcely a trace of literary effort.
"It is a book of statistics, without pretense of being anything else,
and," A. J. Nock added, "it is probably the most interesting statistical
work ever produced." Although the response to Jefferson's artistic
side led to numerous appreciations of his writings as literature, his
growing reputation in the world of letters hinged more securely on
two things: his devotion to literature, especially the classics, and his
scholarly interest in language.

The attention of philologists was first pointedly drawn to Jefferson
in 1882. Henry E. Shepherd, writing in the *American Journal of
Philology*, scrutinized Jefferson's advocacy of neologism, his belief
in the dynamic growth of language from everyday usage, and his
detection of the historical process of dialectic regeneration of languages. In these things, Shepherd said, he anticipated the work of
the most eminent English philologists. Jefferson's *Essay on Anglo-
Saxon Grammar,* though published for instructional use at the University of Virginia in 1851, was first made generally accessible in
the Memorial Edition, as were several other literary curios. Before
1920 the scholars were calling Jefferson a "linguistic liberal," "an
astute scientific philologist," and "the real pioneer in historical English work in America."

In this field, as in others, Jefferson swept a wide arc. Classicists
applied his methods to the analysis of ancient verse, and found them
fruitful. Anthropologists discovered in his speculations on language
anticipations of the importance of linguistics for the study of primitive cultures. And students of the *American* language hailed him as
a pioneer.

One of the major tasks of recent Jefferson scholarship has been
the establishment of his literary calendar. The knowledge of the

books he owned, and more than likely read, at various intervals of his life gradually came to be regarded as the desideratum of authentic study of his thought. The definitive reconstruction of Jefferson's mind as revealed through his books was manifestly impossible, chiefly because, as Randolph G. Adams observed, "it almost seems as though some ghostly pyromaniac had pursued Mr. Jefferson all of his days." Still there were fragmentary sources: the internal evidence of his letters, the account books where he often enumerated his acquisitions, book lists he prepared at the invitation of friends, the commonplace books into which he copied favorite passages, and, most of all, the more than two thousand volumes saved from the Library of Congress fire of 1851, supplemented by the Library's catalogue of 1815 and subsequent years. The Library, conscious of the scholars' need and eager to repay its debt to Jefferson (not only did his collection become the nucleus of one of the great libraries of the world, but the Library also employed his classification system for the better part of a century), engaged the British scholar and bibliophile, E. Millicent Sowerby, to compile an annotated catalogue of every item in the original Jefferson collection. The project was announced on April 13, 1943.

The calendar, painstakingly assembled, documented a mind too prodigious in its learning and too varied in its wellsprings to permit easy classification. One of the dominant impressions was that of Jefferson's "constant commerce with the ancients." Of course, every educated man in the eighteenth century was a classical scholar of sorts. But Jefferson's knowledge of the histories and languages, the schools of science, ethics, and aesthetics, of the ancient world gave him claim to a higher order of accomplishment, and invited reconsideration of the man's personal style and ideal of civilization. The ideal, like its vivid presentment Monticello, was seen to involve the transplantation of the humanistic heritage from its fountainhead in the ancient world to the western vastnesses of America. An uncompromising innovator, a radical and defiant foe of mere tradition, Jefferson nevertheless, Thomas Fitzhugh warned, "recognized the original and primal leadership of Greece and Rome in human civilization, and saw that the continuity of human ideals and achievement depended upon a continuous maintenance of touch between the ancient and modern leaders of our race."

Jefferson's likes and dislikes in belles-lettres furnished another clue to his well-guarded inner life. Ranging from Homer to Ossian, Jefferson's taste was not markedly different from the taste of his time. He matured in the neo-classic age, but felt the pull of the romantic age, fully arrived when he died. A Virginia scholar, John W. Wayland, argued in 1910 "that Jefferson had the poetical spirit and feeling in considerable measure, and that his poetical tastes were not only keen but also in some degree cultivated." But the evidence was not convincing. Several poems were attributed to him from time to time, but with one or two exceptions all of these have since been traced to other writers, from whom Jefferson copied them. Gilbert Chinard, in the introduction he wrote to *The Literary Bible of Thomas Jefferson*, the commonplace book of philosophers and poets kept by the young Jefferson, came to the opposite conclusion from Wayland's. "In spite of the quotations from ancient and modern poets his was not a poetical mind." Jefferson, it seemed, had at one time the moralist's taste *in* poetry, but never an aesthetic taste *for* poetry. He also had, as *Thoughs on English Prosody* showed, the technician's interest in verse. How a poem was constructed engaged his mind; what a poem was did not seriously engage his emotions.

Of Jefferson as a Man of Letters, Max Herzberg wrote in 1914, he "had in him two powerful tendencies: one that of the idealist and dreamer, one that of the practical man of affairs." Here again, then, was the fundamental duality: Jefferson magnetically gathering to himself the poles of human experience. Wherever in any particular field the revolving needle of his mind turned, as in this field it turned chiefly to the "profit" aspect, it was never possible to forget that it campassed the "pleasure" aspect as well.

The Arts, the Sciences, and Letters: most of the talents of the cultivated man—the Culture Hero—are embraced in these categories, though not every one has been noticed. Jefferson the Lawyer, for example. "It is the fate of great men to devour themselves; the earlier man is swallowed up in the later." Such had been the fate, John W. Davis thought, of "Thomas Jefferson: Attorney at Law."

William Wirt's famous eulogy had reminded Americans of the brilliance of Jefferson's early career at the bar and of its influence on the later statesman. But this was quickly forgotten. He could not have been a successful advocate, many believed, because of a temperament indisposed to personal combat and a voice that seldom rose above a whisper. Randall, in 1858, found it necessary to reestablish ·Jefferson's reputation as a lawyer; lawyers and scholars half a century later took up the task again. By 1943 there could be no question of Jefferson's success at the bar. (He was employed in as many as four hundred and thirty cases in a single year.) His lawyer's knowledge, moreover, was by then widely regarded as the foundation of his political philosophy.

Perhaps the most amazing curiosity gathered from the profusion of talents was *Thomas Jefferson's Cook Book*. Marie Kimball, wife of Fiske Kimball and Curator of Monticello, published this volume of recipes, with an account of Jefferson's Lucullan appetite and culinary arts, in 1941. The recipes were taken from the cookbook kept by a granddaughter at Monticello, Virginia Randolph Trist, and presented to the Memorial Foundation by a descendant. With the help of this book it was at last possible to have a real Jeffersonian dinner! It would be anything but simple. The French cuisine predominated. Jefferson, as Patrick Henry had said, "abjured his native vittels." Although Mrs. Kimball hesitated to acclaim him "Father of Cooking," she pointed out that he introduced Americans to such foods as vanilla and macaroni, and wrote in his own hand the first American recipe for ice cream. "He penned a rule for *Nouilly à macaroni* with the gravity that he signed a treaty." The *Cook Book* belonged to Monticello along with the gardens, the wedgewood, the gilt mirrors, and the wine cellar—relics of the epicure whose great art was "the art of living."

In his life and in his vision, Jefferson transcended politics. He stood for a cultural heritage Americans could admire, cherish, perhaps be elevated by, but could not hope to possess in its fullness. Its remnants lay everywhere—in what Americans thought, in how they were educated and governed, in the way they worshipped, in the sciences they professed, in the houses they built, the words they used, the foods they ate. Jefferson stood for a life planned and executed in full human scale, for thought down to the last detail, for a mind that related every fact to every other fact in the universe, for a life "not split into bits," as Ezra Pound said, but given "wholeness and mental order." Being part of a culture so painfully "split into bits," compartmentalized and intellectually disordered, this century's American has been astounded by the full felicitous sweep of Jefferson's genius. Generously exposed to view, Jefferson's attainments were naturally exaggerated. Men tended to forget that it was not just Jefferson who was different but also the age in which he lived, an age populated with versatile gentlemen, although none, unless the older Franklin, as eminent and brilliant as he.

"Under what formula," Charles Beard asked in 1943, "may the multitudinous events, the intellectual strivings, and the moral interests of Mr. Jefferson's life be ordered for comprehension?" It was no longer permissible, he thought, for particular classes or parties engaged in current controversies to take possession of Jefferson. "To do this would be to take possession of him for our purposes instead of allowing the richness of his character, thought and spirit to take possession of us." The ideas commonly identified with him—democracy, agrarianism, constitutionalism—were much too narrow. Jefferson, like the American spirit itself, Beard thought, could only be defined by the idea of *civilization*. In his belief in the processes of freedom and enlightenment, in his commanding sense of order and form, in the whole pattern of his thought, action, and aspiration, Jefferson embodied "the world view known as civilization."

Although the idea encompassed the figure, he was lost in its vastness. Scholars had for several years been searching for a formula to describe with some exactitude Jefferson's "overreaching view of the universe and humanity." One found it in "Americanism," another in "liberalism," still another in the vision of a world community; in time "naturalism" and "humanism" would be tried. No doubt these, and not only these, were all parts of Jefferson's *weltanschauung*, neither consistent with each other nor complete in sum; yet it could be hoped that by a kind of dialectical process a synthesis—the whole man—would gradually emerge. It had never been easy to comprehend the man. In the past, however, students could presume to

infer completeness from partial or partisan views. Engaged primarily
with the political figure, they had stereotyped formulas, such as the
Jefferson-Hamilton one, close at hand. Now the whole character of
Jefferson study had changed. The old presumptions were condemned
as unscholarly and unhistorical. And yet few, if any, scholars could
presume to master the expanding Jefferson corpus or attain competence in all the varied realms of his genius.

In these conditions, the new and more humbling attitude of letting
Jefferson "take possession of us" arose. Historians gradually curbed
their manipulations of the Jefferson-Hamilton bucket and chain. They
backed away from the older type of biographical narrative, and
tended to isolate for study those parts of Jefferson that fell within
their different fields of competence. Some of them, however, once
launched in these restricted channels, virtually made the larger study
of Jefferson a career in itself. A small group of dedicated Jefferson
scholars thus appeared in the second quarter of this century. It numbered as its most important members Gilbert Chinard, Professor of
French Literature at Johns Hopkins and Princeton University for
many years; the late Fiske and Marie Kimball; Dumas Malone, historian, who has recently returned to the University of Virginia; and
Julian Boyd, formerly Librarian of Princeton University, currently
editor of *The Papers of Thomas Jefferson*. Their work was aided by
librarians specializing in Jefferson materials, at the University of
Virginia and the Library of Congress in particular, and of course
complemented by the studies of many scholars on Jefferson and his
times. The Jefferson scholars were a varied group. Some were historians by profession, others were not. Some were Jeffersonians in
the political sense, others were indifferent or adverse to the political
tradition. Though some might have wished otherwise, no cult or
coterie or school formed around Jefferson, as it had around Lincoln.
Jefferson scholarship has been as unbridled as its subject.

From these scholars came four types of distinguished Jefferson
study. The monograph in all dimensions: Kimball's early study of
the Virginia Capitol; Edward Dumbauld's *Thomas Jefferson: American Tourist;* Adrienne Koch's *The Philosophy of Thomas Jefferson*.
Jefferson, as Hamilton Basso observed, has become "a happy hunting
ground for those in search of their doctorate"; but the intensive study

of single phases and aspects of his life has not been limited to budding Ph.D.'s The comprehensive historical biography: the two major attempts have been made by Marie Kimball and Dumas Malone, but the former died after completing three volumes which carried her subject to 1789, and the latter's work is still in progress. The monumental approach accorded with Randall's precedent and with a current fashion in professional historiography; it was also a response to the need, obvious but now almost beyond any man's reach, to embrace the accumulated knowledge of Jefferson within a single narrative pattern. Studies of mind and character: Chinard's *Thomas Jefferson, the Apostle of Americanism,* and more recently the books by Daniel Boorstin and Karl Lehmann. Highly interpretive works of this type, while neither exhaustive nor definitive, have added enormously to the understanding of Jefferson's personal style and mental outlook. Finally, as the foundation of everything else, the authentication, cataloguing, and analysis of Jefferson's papers, books, relics, life portraits, and so on. The range of activity is barely suggested by mention of Boyd's work, Marie Kimball's study of the furnishings of Monticello, and Fiske Kimball's diggings at Shadwell. The new scholarship rose to a peak of productivity at the time of, and just after, the Bicentennial. Jefferson became both a favorite of the American historians and their most spacious subject. The *Dictionary of American Biography,* completed in 1937, awarded him more pages than any other individual, whereas in the fifty-year-old *Appleton's Cyclopedia of American Biography,* he ranked, in this respect, behind Washington and Lincoln. This is a fair index to his growing fame in the academy of historians.

The dividing line between the old and the new Jefferson study coincided roughly with the Sesquicentennial of 1926. On the one side, at the end of the century-long tradition, stood Claude Bowers's *Jefferson and Hamilton.* It gave a final influential thrust to that tradition; but, unknown to Bowers, it was being displaced at the moment of his triumph. Francis Hirst's *Life and Letters of Thomas Jefferson,* representing the Jeffersonian side of the great American debate which F. S. Oliver had transferred to England twenty years before, also belonged to the past. It was, moreover, the last one-volume biography of Jefferson to attract significant notice in this country.

On the other side, Paul Wilstach's *Jefferson and Monticello*, though of minor importance to future scholars, drew attention away from politics to culture, as the writings of Fiske Kimball and others had already done. Chinard, in 1926, edited Jefferson's *Commonplace Book*, the most valuable of the additions to scholarly knowledge he was making from discoveries in Jefferson's papers.

If there was any nexus between the old and the new it was Albert Jay Nock's *Jefferson*. He described his book as "a study in conduct and character." A supremely literate man, a connoisseur of taste and intellect, a brilliant essayist, Nock regarded Jefferson as his ideal because he had "the ability to act like a democrat while practicing the manners of a highly civilized being." Viewing the democrat, somewhat astigmatically through the two lenses of Herbert Spencer and Henry George, Nock argued that he was eternally right in his perception of the political problem: that the natural process is for liberty to yield and government to gain ground; that the greater the government the stronger the exploiter and the weaker the producer; that as a rule, therefore, the hope of republican liberty depends upon local self-government and the vigilance of the producer class. But Nock felt, even more than the early Beard, that Jefferson was incredibly naïve about economics and thus let the contest against the Hamiltonian enemy go by default. He could not be counted either a great radical or a great statesman, in Nock's judgment. America had paid a heavy price for his political failure, though it still had much to learn from his political philosophy.

Jefferson's true greatness lay elsewhere, Nock thought. He perceived and exemplified the realities of civilization: "A dominant sense of form and order, a commanding instinct for measure, harmony and balance, unfailingly maintained for fourscore years toward the primary facts of human life—towards discipline and training, towards love, parenthood, domesticity, art, science, religion, friendship, business, social and communal relations. . . ." Here he was not only right in his perception, but also a consummate model of civilized conduct and philosophy. He was a man disillusioned about politics. He knew the real business of life was neither the governing of men nor the piling up of treasure but the discipline of self and the study of man. Writing with the essayist's freedom, Nock subtly penetrated the

man's public disguises to his well-hidden "inner springs of sentiment." The inner man thus revealed was essentially conservative in
social outlook, austere in his conduct and systematic to the last
degree, studious, empirical, and upright "towards the primary facts
of human life," which always invited his mind for the improvement
of self and humanity. It was this characterization that lent permanent
distinction to Nock's *Jefferson,* and prefigured a "new Jefferson" far
different from Democratic imaginings in 1926.

More crucial for the new scholarship, which he as much as anyone
shaped, was the ripe fruit of Chinard's labors in 1929. This French
scholar, teaching at Johns Hopkins, had given many years to the
study of the intellectual relations between the United States and
France in the eighteenth century. It had led him into Jefferson's
correspondence with Volney, Destutt de Tracy, Lafayette, and other
Frenchmen, some of which he edited, and finally into the center of
Jefferson's thought. By the time he came to write his major book
on Jefferson, Chinard had thus shown two dominant concerns. One,
in respect to subject, the concern for Jefferson's ideas, particularly
in their formative stage about which little was known and later in
relation to French thinkers about which there was only a legend.
Two, in respect to method, the determination to discover Jefferson
afresh in the mass of unpublished papers few scholars had ever
troubled themselves to explore.

Tracing the unifying design in the varied carpet of Jefferson's
mind, Chinard could find no better word to describe it than Americanism. The point had been made before, most notably by Parton;
and Americans had often used Jefferson as a mirror of national
character. At the same time, however, and especially in academic
circles, there was "the legend of a denationalized Jefferson": a
Frenchman in his ideas, a Virginian in his party leadership, a uni-
versalist in his ultimate vision. Chinard's own investigation had
begun in the shadow of this legend. But having set out to determine
the French influence on Jefferson, having then experienced the cultural shock incident to the transplantation from Europe to America,
and, as his fascination led him more deeply into Jefferson's papers,
having found the same cultural contrasts in the eighteenth century,

Chinard came to realize that Jefferson was "the most integrally and truly American among his contemporaries."

The gradual mergence of Jefferson's personality in a philosophy which ought, in Chinard's judgment, to be known as Americanism instead of Jeffersonian Democracy, began with his education in English law. "His was eminently the mind of the lawyer." Converted by his youthful legal studies to the Anglo-Saxon conception of English history, this became the true foundation of his political system. (John Fiske had broached the key idea decades before: that Jefferson was "simply the earnest but cool-headed representative of the rural English freeholders that won Magna Charta and overthrew the usurpations of the Stuarts.") Jefferson's position was racial not philosophical, historical and legal not abstract, conservative not radical. The two faces he proposed in 1776 for the shield of the new nation—the children of Israel in the Wilderness and the Saxon chiefs Hengist and Horsa—expressed his conviction the Americans were a people chosen to reclaim the Saxon birthright. "The Jeffersonian Democracy was born under the sign of Hengist and Horsa, not the Goddess of Reason." Viewed in this light, Jefferson's radicalism was, like so much of American radicalism, retrospective. He ruled, as Henry Adams had said, with a Golden Age in view; but it was set in the past. Chinard made his point with the extravagance of a discoverer.

"We are led to a very unexpected conclusion," Chinard said of Jefferson's years abroad, 1785–90. "There is little doubt that Jefferson's democratic theories were confirmed and clarified by his prolonged stay in Europe. But this was not due to the lessons he received from the French philosophers." Recent historians of the French influence (the American, Charles Hazen, and Chinard's French contemporary, Bernard Faÿ, for example) had not really changed the underlying idea of the European experience as a form of intellectual expatriation for Jefferson, who thus became, upon his return, the advance agent of radical democracy in the United States. Chinard thought the effect of Jefferson's immersion in European, particularly French, civilization just the reverse. His mental horizon and his manner of life were unchanged. But Europe strengthened his sense of nationality. As an American minister abroad, Jefferson was compelled to subordinate his provincial attachment to Virginia and to think of the United States as "one nation." Europe swelled Jefferson's pride in the simple virtues of American life and the superiority of American character. At first dazzled by the splendors of the Old World, he soon concluded "that the game was not worth the candle." In letters to American friends, he warned against the aesthetic temptations of Europe; and he denounced the moral corruptions of European civilization, Chinard said, "as vehemently as any Puritan preacher and with the same frankness of expression." His political principles, which laws and social conditions made practicable in America, merely beat the air in Europe. Seeing this, Jefferson, reluctantly but decisively, curtailed the universal references of his political philosophy and made it into the creed of Americanism.

Europe, the world, being what they were, Chinard went on, isolation seemed to Jefferson the wisest policy for the United States. His ideal did indeed transcend the limits of nationality—he dreamed of "a family of nations." But since, as Jefferson learned, the European powers were not prepared for his liberal system, and since no real co-operation appeared possible except among free nations, he advocated a realistic foreign policy while at the same time holding intact his ideal of a universe of freedom. Here, Chinard thought, was perhaps the most striking instance of Jefferson's happy faculty of maintaining his ideals apart from, but in constant tension with, political realities. "Far from being a single-track mind, his was decidedly a double-track intellect with two lines of thought running parallel without any apparent contradiction, for theory never seemed to have interfered with his practice." Much of the confusion about Jefferson centered in this trait. So often condemned either as a visionary philosopher or as a hardheaded politician, even as both at once and therefore a hypocrite and deceiver, Jefferson in fact, Chinard said, combined idealism and practicality in a creative outlook all the world has since taken to be the characteristically American outlook of "Practical Idealism." Its expression in American foreign policy was "an equal balance between national selfishness and philosophical idealism," the maintenance of which was beset with the greatest difficulties in Jefferson's time and was now unworkable.

Jefferson, like American civilization itself, could not be reduced to formula. Such polarities as idealism and practicality, universalism and isolationism, the agrarian dream and scientific progress, which observers found in American life, Chinard found in Jefferson. The roots of his thought spread into many traditions, chiefly the classical, the Christian, and English law. But Jefferson took from these only the ingredients America needed, synthesized them, and thus helped to make America the heir of all without being the heir of any one. The political creed he espoused in 1800 owed nothing to Europe. It was a national, not a partisan, creed: the first complete definition of Americanism in government, Chinard thought. Contrary to Bowers, Jefferson had not been a party leader during the previous decade of party warfare, and the little "Quarrel with Hamilton" had no significant influence on the destiny of the nation. Contrary to Beard, Jefferson never conceived of his party as agrarian, his faith as a class faith, or sought to favor agriculture at the expense of industry. Contrary to Henry Adams, he no longer (if he ever had) regarded himself as "a world prophet of the democratic faith"; and thus most of Adams's arraignment of Jefferson fell to the ground.

Coming to the study of Jefferson from outside the provincial setting of American scholarship, Chinard broke the molds of partisan interpretation and comprehended what others had only vaguely glimpsed—the Americanism of Jefferson. Later Jefferson scholarship proved the fruitfulness, though not the definitiveness, of Chinard's conception. Much of it consisted in following up his leads: the revaluation of Jefferson's intellectual genesis, the elaboration of the conservative-legalistic-utilitarian viewpoint, the reinterpretation of his political theory and party leadership.

A different type of scholarly inquiry, leading to conclusions as unexpected as Chinard's, is identified with the work of Marie Kimball. Those who followed Chinard's bent attempted to map out Jefferson's intellectual terrain and establish its concentric character. Mrs. Kimball's work, on the other hand, evinced an essentially antiquarian interest in the paraphernalia of Jefferson's life, a fondness for external detail with a corresponding neglect of inner meaning and pattern, an uncritical devotion to the man and to all he had touched. Mrs. Kimball attempted to do in biography what she had already done as Curator of Monticello: turn Jefferson into a museum and a shrine.

Marie Kimball's most important revision of traditional ideas belonged to her first volume, *The Road to Glory, 1743–1776*, which opened with the question, "Aristocrat or Backwoodsman?" Jefferson was very casual about his ancestry, and biographers had happily followed his example. For reasons already examined, the convention of a double heritage grew up. The tendency around 1900 was to emphasize the "backwoodsman" side of the heritage; then, with the recognition of Monticello a quarter century later, the emphasis shifted to the "aristocrat." Mrs. Kimball methodically explored Jefferson's ancestry in county records, patent books, diaries, and every musty source. The Jeffersons, she discovered, were a well-furnished and respected family almost from the commencement of the colony. Jefferson's father, like Washington, was a prosperous planter, land speculator, and surveyor. There was nothing out of the ordinary in his marriage to Jane Randolph, for he too was "upper class"; or in his migration westward, for this was the pattern of the Tidewater gentry. The Albemarle in which he settled was one hundred miles east of the true frontier. When Thomas was two years old, it was populated with one hundred and six whites, one hundred and seventy-seven Negroes, and one Indian. Shadwell, which was generally imagined from Randall's description as a rude pioneer dwelling, was in fact "a gentleman's seat." (The remains of the buildings had long since vanished; but in 1941 Fiske Kimball's excavations located the ruins, some distance from the monument supposed to mark the site.) Jefferson grew to man's estate rich in worldly goods, educated in the best manner of his time, gay and elegant according to the Virginia type, a servant of the people by reason of intellectual convictions and feelings of noblesse. He was all Tuckahoe!

This was an authentic report, as most historians at once recognized. It strengthened the scholarly tendency already well advanced by 1943 to soften the radical tones of the Jefferson image. And since the Academy increasingly assumed the custody of Jefferson's reputation, the scholarly tendency was of first importance. In this instance, however, it was not controlling. The idea that democracy was in Jefferson's heritage had powers of prepossession against which the curator's evidences were unavailing. Peter Jefferson, Claude Bowers wrote in *The Young Jefferson* (1945), was in every sense "a lusty pioneer," and his son bore the stamp. Bowers was concerned to maintain the integrity of a political tradition; Mrs. Kimball wished to establish the historical integrity of the man. The dual heritage idea repeatedly occurred in the musings on Monticello. It was a commonplace of popular and juvenile biography. Its presence could be detected in the only two dramas worthy of notice which centered the character of Jefferson, Sidney Kingsley's *The Patriots*, in 1943, and Paul Green's *The Common Glory*, in 1947.

But the outstanding expression of this theme in literature was Elizabeth Page's whopping historical novel, *The Tree of Liberty*, in 1939. The author, an elderly Southern lady with a revolutionary Virginia pedigree, sought through the life of Jefferson "to make vivid the processes by which modern America has developed out of the colonial conditions of the eighteenth century." Although Jefferson is the hero of her novel, Mrs. Page evidently despaired of telling the story primarily in the movement of his life. So the story is carried, from 1754 to 1806, through the fictional characters of Matthew Howard and his family. Matt is a pioneer with all the rough, impetuous traits of the type. He grows up in Albemarle, and becomes the schoolboy chum of Tom Jefferson and Dabney Carr. When he first meets Tom at Shadwell, another world opens before him. Colonel Jefferson is plain and friendly, but over there is "the great lady," covered with lace, sitting grandly in her chair. A harpsichord is somewhere in the background. Tom, Matt at once noticed, "wore shoes on his feet and a well-cut suit of clothes." Grown to manhood, Matt courts and weds Jane Peyton of Williamsburg. She is Tuckahoe with all the frills and features of the type. She hates Jefferson for deserting the Randolph side of his heritage, while her huband loves him for his democracy. Matt and Jane have two sons. Peyton, who takes after his father, becomes Jefferson's trusted lieutenant in the party warfare of the Federalist decade. James, who takes after his mother, early falls under the influence of Alexander Hamilton, intermarries with the Anglified Humphreys family of New York City, and there becomes a prosperous merchant. Thus the division within the Howard family images the division between two ways of life in

Virginia and, as this is extended through the generations, images as well the great conflict of political ideals that threatens the tree of liberty planted in 1776.

Jefferson, as imaged by Mrs. Page, unites in his person the best of the two worlds. His principles are on one side, but he is able to appreciate and conserve the values on the other side. When young Peyton brings his problem of divided family loyalty to Jefferson, he is told, " 'Peyton, my mother was a Randolph; my father was a man of the frontier. For men like us there are always two roads to follow. It makes action difficult and understanding easy. Perhaps our first object, then, should be to understand.' " Peyton nods and says, " 'My father's ideas seem to me to make more sense; but then, my mother's—.' " " 'Exactly!' Jefferson spoke quickly. 'Cherish that "but," Peyton. It may very well be that the most important thing you can bring to the side of liberty is your knowledge of your mother's point of view.' " In the end, after Jefferson has calmed the storm and rallied "all Federalists, all Republicans" around the tree of liberty, Matt is converted to his moderate politics, and even Jane, though she still fears his principles, concedes that Jefferson is "oh, well, noble."

Uniting the two worlds of America to form a stronger and richer heritage, Jefferson emerged from Mrs. Page's novel the supreme American hero. Freedom was guarded with restraints, democracy was fused with nationality, the frontier consorted with civilization. Whether or not this was a valid conception of the processes of American development, it was an imaginative projection of the actual reconciliation that had occurred in the history of Jefferson's reputation. His, as Allen Tate noted, was "the fame of both." The Howards and the Peytons could worship together at his shrine.

3. *The Jefferson Memorial: The Temple*

No monument raised by a grateful posterity was necessary to Jefferson's memory or fame, it was said for generations after his death. Americans professed to believe with the ancients that monuments to the nation's great image what is most revered in the past and most aspired to in the future. Yet Jefferson's was the case of a man remembered without the benefit of the monument's image.

Several statues were executed before 1900, but only the David d'Angers bronze figure of the Author of the Declaration of Independence, which Lieutenant Levy presented to Congress in 1834, left any kind of impression. After forty years' weathering on the White House grounds, it was, at last, formally received by Congress and placed in the National Statuary Hall of the Capitol. In 1901 the first permanent outdoor monument was dedicated—the Sir Moses Ezekial "Liberty Bell" statue, in Louisville, Kentucky. From this date, Jefferson monuments, large and small—tablets, busts, statues—rapidly multiplied. The University of Virginia raised two statues on its grounds just before the First World War. In 1914 the benefaction of Joseph Pulitzer placed Jefferson's figure in the inner court of Columbia University. The great Karl Bitter bronzes in St. Louis in 1913 and the next year, 1914, in Cleveland; James Frazer's towering statue before the Missouri State Capitol in 1919; tablets at his birthplace (1926), at his places of residence in Paris and New York City (1919, 1929), and in Wales, the country from which the Jeffersons came, in 1933; busts in numerous colleges and public buildings; the gigantic head carved at Mt. Rushmore, dedicated in 1927—the list is already long enough to suggest that the movement for a truly national memorial to Jefferson did not arise in a void.

The original impetus was the Thomas Jefferson Memorial Association (not to be confused with the later Foundation) in 1903. It hoped, with some assistance from Congress, to erect a suitable memorial in Washington. "I want it to stand as high as the monuments erected to warriors," Bryan declared at the Association's inaugural banquet. "I want this monument to testify that a man can live for his country as well as die for his country." The plan failed; but the Association planted the memorial idea in public consciousness and aroused the interest, in particular, of Georgia's Senator Augustus O. Bacon. In 1904, as an "antidote" to a proposed statue of Frederick the Great in the capital, Bacon called for a commission to plan a memorial statue of Jefferson. The commission was duly authorized and appointed, but its authority lapsed before anything could be accomplished. In 1911 Bacon agreed to join his bill with an analogous one sponsored by Senator Lodge on behalf of the recently organized

Alexander Hamilton Memorial Association. Both bills, with their one hundred thousand-dollar appropriations, won unanimous consent in the Senate, then went astray in the House. They were stalled again in the House two years later. And that was the last heard of the project for many years.

The movement for a national memorial was revived in 1926 in connection with the Sesquicentennial observance, the Monticello campaign, and the general resurgence of Jefferson's reputation at that time. The principal memorial project before then Congress had been initiated several years back by the Theodore Roosevelt Memorial Association. In February 1925, Congress authorized this Association to procure at its own expense plans for a great Roosevelt memorial on a site between the Washington Monument and the Potomac River. Approximately fourteen months later, the Association submitted architect John Russell Pope's design to the House Library Committee with the hope of obtaining the go ahead signal from Congress. But during the preceding months Jefferson's stock had soared upward. It was blasphemous, some said, to build an ostentatious monument to a late President when Jefferson was "uncommemorated in bronze or stone in the capital." Representative John J. Boylan, a Tammany Democrat, old-fashioned Jeffersonian, and ardent patriot, made himself the congressional voice of this indignation. Through speeches, public letters, and committee testimony, he forced Roosevelt's admirers to abandon their efforts and the House Library Committee to support his resolution for a Jefferson memorial. Although the idea was widely endorsed, and although the Sesquicentennial Commission called for a "memorial building" in its final report, it was eight years before Congress passed the Boylan resolution.

Several considerations finally moved Congress to act. A Democratic administration had come to power under a leader dedicated to the memorial idea. Old-time Democrats, like Josephus Daniels, envisioned the Jeffersonian memorial as a fitting testament to the spirit of the New Deal. Action would not have come at this time, however, had it not been for Congress's creation in June 1934 of the United States Territorial Expansion Commission to build on the

St. Louis riverfront the Jefferson National Expansion Memorial—
a stupendous project, still incomplete a quarter century later.*

If St. Louis was to have another Jefferson Memorial, Boylan and
his supporters pleaded, it was criminal to neglect the national capital.
Congress heeded the plea a few days after it authorized the Territorial Commission. The Boylan resolution called for the creation of
a twelve-member Thomas Jefferson Memorial Commission. It was to
select the site, determine the design, and oversee the construction of
the memorial. Organized a few months later, the Commission named
Boylan its chairman. The Executive Committee, upon which the
larger burden fell, was composed of Joseph Tumulty, Hollins N.
Randolph, Fiske Kimball, and Stuart Gibboney. The latter succeeded
to the chairmanship after Boylan's death. Building a memorial to
Jefferson, it soon became evident, was no sunshine task. The Commission was villified and obstructed at every turn. The appropriation
for the work was stalled in Congress for two years. Not until the
Commission broke ground in December 1938 could it feel reasonably
confident of accomplishing its mission.

The battle of the Jefferson Memorial raged verbally on issues of
site and design, especially the latter; but these issues were significantly shaped by antagonistic conceptions of Jefferson and of his
place in American history. In February 1936, after discarding several
possible sites, the Commission tentatively approved the Tidal Basin
location earlier coveted by Theodore Roosevelt's admirers. The

* The brainchild of a group of St. Louis businessmen headed by Mayor
Bernard Dickman, the project called for the demolition of thirty-seven blocks
of dilapidated waterfront buildings, and the conversion of the eighty-two acres
of cleared land into a vast memorial park with suitable accompaniments. Uncle
Sam was to pay all or, as it turned out, a sizable part of the estimated thirty
million-dollar bill. The motivation seemed to be something less than patriotic,
particularly in view of the fact that Mayor Dickman was the former head of the
local real estate exchange. But Missourians loved to commemorate Jefferson—
once again Blaine's old reproach was heard—and the memorial recommended
itself in 1934 as a relief project. In any event, it won the enthusiastic support
of many leading citizens in the Mississippi Valley and elsewhere. President
Roosevelt, not Congress, really put the Commission in business eighteen months
after it was constituted by declaring the St. Louis waterfront to be a historic site
(he even said the Santa Fe and Oregon Trails originated there!), thereby making
it eligible for nearly seven million dollars of Public Works Administration funds.

famous McMillan Plan of 1901 for the recomposition and beautifica-
tion of the capital's central area had contemplated a "Memorial to
the Constitution Makers" on this site, which was the southern
terminus of the cross-axis running from the White House and inter-
secting the main axis from the Capitol to the Lincoln Memorial at
the focal point, the Washington Monument. The Tidal Basin, a large
inlet opening into the river on the south and surrounded by Potomac
Park, thus represented, once the Lincoln Memorial occupied the
western terminus, the one cardinal point as yet unexploited in the
central composition of the capital.

A Jefferson memorial on this "fifth point" would splendidly close
the composition around the Washington Monument and, in effect,
bring Jefferson into the choice circle of American heroes. The Fine
Arts Commission, the capital's artistic conscience, was agreeable to
letting the Jeffersonians have the site, but other influential groups
objected to the defacement of the natural beauties of Potomac Park
and the increase of automobile traffic in this area. After extensive
hearings in April 1937, the House Library Committee reported a
resolution to block the construction of the memorial on the Tidal
Basin site. But the Memorial Commission, backed by President
Roosevelt, refused to budge from its final unanimous decision of two
months before.

The question of site was inseparable from the question of design.
For instance, the engineering risk of piling tons of marble atop this
strip of land at the water's edge might be overcome if the Commission would agree to a somewhat less grandiloquent monument. Its
original plan called for a monument twice the bulk and twenty-one
feet higher than the Lincoln Memorial. It finally agreed to a one-
third reduction in scale, along with other alterations, thereby win-
ning certain agencies, such as the National Park Service, to its side.
But here, in the determination of the memorial's character and design, the Boylan body came into collision with the Fine Arts Commission and the most vocal elements of the architectural profession
of the United States. According to some reports, the memorialists'
first thoughts were along the lines of Gibboney's recommendation
as Chairman of the Sesquicentennial Commission in 1928: a building,
perhaps of colonial design, to house Jefferson literature and relics.

But early in 1936, the Commission, without the formalities of open competition, retained John Russell Pope to draw up plans for a memorial that dispensed with any utilitarian object. Pope, the last exponent of American classicism, was currently engaged on Andrew Mellon's National Gallery of Art. (Some progressive architects derisively called him "the greatest architect since Alexander Hamilton.") As most of the Commission's critics surmised, the decisive voice of classicism in its councils was Fiske Kimball's. At its meeting on February 18, 1936, Kimball held forth at length on the death of classicism in American architecture, on the appropriateness of a Roman memorial to the father of American classicism, and on Pope's solitary eminence in this traditional mode. Ten months later, Pope submitted alternative plans, both classical. One was a cruciform design; the other was circular after the Pantheon, the Roman temple built by Agrippa and rebuilt by the Emperor Hadrian in the second century. In February 1937 the Commission voted to accept the circular plan. Boylan announced the decision and released Pope's sketches to the press.

A storm of protest greeted the announcement. The advisory Fine Arts Commission, charged with maintaining the artistic integrity of the capital, had not been consulted by the high-handed Boylan body. The Commission was classical, in conformity with the McMillan Plan, but apparently not as classical as Pope and Kimball. It wished a simpler and more original design, one better suited to the site, and one which preserved a historical balance in regard to Jefferson as well as an artistic balance in the capital. It therefore rejected the Pope plan.

The plan had modest support from the battered fortress of conservatism in American art, but the progressives were loud in protest. Of course, in their view, Washington was already a "wilderness of temples," so it was pointless to mourn the addition of another to the landscape. But they, like many of their countrymen who were relatively indifferent to the professional issue at stake, considered the proposed temple an insult to Jefferson's memory. The temper of professional indignation is conveyed in the following excerpts selected at random from the numerous letters and manifestoes of protest:

Milton Horn, President, American Sculptors Society: "To Jefferson, to whom simplicity and truth were a motive of life, they have now elected to erect an empty shell which possesses not even the kernel of these; a hollow mockery of a spirit which embodies an ideal; a useless structure to symbolize a useful life; a pretentiousness and falsehood to symbolize the search for truth, a high-handed method of award in place of an equal chance for all.... Its growth is not natural to our soil; its derivation is from the dead. Like a cadaver, it cannot function."

Talbot Hamlin, Joseph Hudnut, Lewis Mumford, and others of The League for Progress in Architecture: "This pompous pile," barren and joyless, unknown to Jefferson's spirit, "could equally well serve, by a single change in the inscription, as a memorial to Theodore Roosevelt, Edgar Allen Poe, or the Supreme Court. In fact, one rather suspects it has."

Frank Lloyd Wright, for himself: "Thomas Jefferson? Were that gentleman alive today he would be the first to condemn the stupid erudition mistaken in his honor.... I imagine I see the sarcastic smile with which his shade must receive this fashionable design proposing to drag his mortal remains to the surface of the present ... in terms of the feudal art and thought that clung to him then, deliberately to make of him now, a fashionable effigy of reaction instead of a character appreciated by his own people as a noble spirit of progress and freedom.

Chiefly because of the fuss kicked up by the progressive architects in the spring of 1938, Congress blocked the appropriation of construction funds, and the Memorial Commission beat a fast retreat. Although the questions of site and competitive award were still in controversy, the overriding issue was that of design.

And what this plainly involved was the question whether the memorial to Jefferson should be retrospective or prospective, whether it should conform closely to the historical figure as he had revealed himself in the work of his own hands or to the democratic "spirit of Jefferson." Many opponents of the Commission's plan called for a "living memorial." This would not be on the order of a museum, such as Gibboney and Boylan had once favored, but rather a building named in Jefferson's honor and assigned a useful purpose consonant with his spirit. A chance remark by President Roosevelt just after the rainswept inaugural ceremonies on January 20, 1937 started a movement in Congress for a national auditorium as Jefferson's memorial. This would fill a long felt need, and might be dedicated, as Interior Secretary Ickes suggested, to the Jeffersonian principles of free speech and free assembly. Administration officials and congressmen made a dozen alternative proposals: a national health center (Jefferson "idealized good health," Maury Maverick observed), a scientific laboratory, an academy of political science, a national highway, a national university (such as he had once advocated), a great stadium, and so on. One congressman wanted to rededicate the new Supreme Court Building in Jefferson's name. Another proposed a planetarium, to which there was an obvious rejoinder: "Why not just adopt the stars as a memorial to Thomas Jefferson?"

Boylan, who fought off these maneuvers in the House, believed their intent was to kill the memorial altogether. This was true, in part. The old excuses—Jefferson's true memorial lay in the hearts of the people or in adherence to his principles of government—were still heard. A New Deal memorial to Jefferson was blasphemous, some Republicans charged, unless possibly he was imaged within "with tears streaming down his cheeks." Many felt too that the three million-dollar temple was a ridiculous extravagance during the depression. How much better, then, to give Jefferson's name to some useful establishment—it hardly mattered what, for Jefferson touched everything. But as the Commission recognized, and also President Roosevelt when he endorsed the Pope plan in February 1937, the experience of "living memorials" showed that the utilitarian side rapidly effaced the commemorative side. Even on the unlikely assumption that Americans could agree on *which* utilitarian side of Jefferson to exploit in his memorial, they would not by that act be rendering honor to Jefferson but to themselves.

The question of Jefferson's livingness had another aspect. The Commission favored the pantheon design in the conviction that it was true to Jefferson's character and artistic preferences. "When you choose a symbol," Kimball declared, "the symbol is only of value if it has some suggestive character." Pope's marble symbol unmistakably suggested Jefferson. If Lincoln's memory had been well served by a Greek temple, which superficially suggested nothing about him, how much more suited was the Roman style to Jefferson, who introduced it in America. But it was still a question whether this symbol evoked the *intrinsic* Jefferson. Many critics, lay and professional, thought the Commission was unduly influenced by one aspect of Jefferson: his taste in architecture. The Pope design, they said, expressed neither the simple democratic traits dear to American memory nor the progressive spirit of the forever "living Jefferson." "I think a modern in antique dress is just an object of ridicule," he had written in 1786 in regard to a proposed sculpture of Washington. The Commission's critics believed the memorial should be executed in this spirit lest Jefferson should himself become "forever ridiculous." Even in architecture, he was a modern, a radical, an innovator. The Roman style was the modern of his time, as Kimball himself had said. *Then* it elevated American taste and clarified national ideals. *Now* it insulted his progressive mind, pompously mocked his ideals, and mortified him with "the gangrene of sentimentality." This symbol of Imperial Rome appeared equally senile from the standpoint of the New Deal, which celebrated Jefferson's progressiveness. "A design indefensibly pedantic," Gilmore Clarke, the new Chairman of the Fine Arts Commission, appealed to the President, "cannot represent the modern social feelings and character of your administration and our time and suitably honor Jefferson." Roosevelt was unmoved. The progressive administration backed the retrospective memorial to its patron saint.

The controversy led back finally to the old question, "Who was Thomas Jefferson?" The nation was choosing the manner of his monument. It should, of course, blend into the Washington landscape, but it should also make Jefferson and his ideals vivid to the senses. Despite his borrowings and his antique Romanness, Jefferson in a pantheon, "like a canary in a cage of peristyles," strained the imagination. Critics recalled the simple directions he gave for his own tombstone, and marveled at "the academic mind" that could deduce from these words a pantheon. The memorial could attempt to recapture Jeffersonian form or to revitalize Jeffersonian spirit. How long could Jefferson's spirit survive in a marble temple? The universality of Jefferson's vision bespoke the form; but even the scholars were beginning to recognize his Americanness, and he would certainly be more approachable in a memorial that seemed to belong on the Potomac rather than on the Tiber.

Regardless of Jefferson's true character, there was the larger question of American character; for a memorial to Jefferson must necessarily reflect the American self-image. The monuments to the great are symbolic acts. In them the nation celebrates itself. What especially alarmed some critics of the Commission was that it, and inferentially the nation, could find no better artistic expression of American accomplishments and ideals than this "senile sham" from the drawing-boards of John Russell Pope.

Although this little controversy agitated the architectural profession, some segments of the press, and enough congressmen to stall appropriations, the only opposition to the Boylan Commission that was ever likely to affect the end result came from the Fine Arts Commission. On February 17, 1938, nearly a year after its rejection of the Pope plan, the advisory body finally persuaded the Jeffersonians to adopt another plan. This called for a large, open, semicircular colonnade centering a statue of Jefferson. The undoubted originality of the conception, its appropriateness to the flat elevation of the site, the light, free, and daringly horizontal impression it gave to Jefferson—these were the features praised by the Fine Arts Commission. The design was classical without senility or sham. But the new-found harmony between the two commissions lasted just one month. At its next meeting the Memorial Commission abruptly reversed itself. It had discovered in the interim that the supposedly original colonnade plan was a rehash of Pope's conception for the Theodore Roosevelt memorial in 1926. Moreover, it could not be modified to suit the Commission's tastes, since Pope had died a few months before and his widow barred any tampering with his work. On March 30, 1938, the Commission, with Roosevelt's approval, went ahead with the pantheon, three times rejected by the Clarke group. Congress soon voted the first installment on an authorized three million-dollar appropriation. Although the fight between the two Commissions continued for several months, the design of the Jefferson memorial was set.

The last phase of the memorial battle—"the cherry tree rebellion"— occurred in November, when workmen and bulldozers invaded the Tidal Basin. The early agitation against the site had been stirred, in part, by the desire to preserve the scenic beauties of Potomac

Park. The Commission gave assurances on this point, and the opposition abated. Not for long, however. The annual spring bloom of the Japanese cherry trees and other plants that covered the Park was dear to the local citizenry, dear to the businesses catering to tourists, dear to everyone who valued trees above memorials. So when the workmen came with their shovels and machines, many citizens flew into a rage. Hysterical estimates of the number of cherry trees to be sacrificed at Jefferson's altar ran as high as seven hundred. Hotel associations, women's clubs, and civic groups vigorously protested the desecration. Eleanor Patterson's Washington *Times* and *Herald* denounced the planners of this project with the same invective these Republican newspapers habitually used on the New Deal. The destruction of the cherry trees, some predicted, would precipitate a diplomatic crisis with Japan! Crowds of women gathered at the memorial site; some chained themselves to the trees, others attacked the workmen, wresting the shovels from their hands. Parading women before the White House sang Joyce Kilmer's *Trees*.

The President, who had so far avoided public involvement in the memorial controversy, now made his position absolutely clear. At his press conference on November 18, he said his personal interest, and the interest of most Democrats, in a national memorial to Jefferson went back to Wilson's administration. "When the Democratic Administration came back in 1933, we all decided to have a memorial to Thomas Jefferson." Everybody seemed to favor the idea, but no sooner was it agreed upon than there commenced "the worst case of flim flamming this dear old capital of ours has been subjected to for a long time." The half-hearted seized on every excuse and tried every trick to obstruct the Memorial Commission. Roosevelt reviewed the stages of the controversy down to the current comic opera finale. "Well," he said, "I don't suppose there is anybody in the world who loves trees quite as much as I do but I recognize that a cherry tree does not live forever." Jefferson did live forever. Let the enchained ladies be forewarned: they would be shoveled up bodily with the trees!

One year later, November 1939, Roosevelt laid the cornerstone. The Commission, now under Gibboney's chairmanship, appointed a distinguished art jury to select the sculptor in an open competition, but then, in combination with Roosevelt, overrode the jury's choice in favor of Rudulph Evans's brilliant, though conventional, conception. Strong and serene, plain yet dignified, accenting thought and vision, the encircled statue commemorated the republican citizen and philosopher. A committee of three Commissioners, headed by Senator Elbert Thomas of Utah, selected the inscriptions for the four panels of the Memorial Room. The Declaration of Independence was the source of the first panel; the Virginia Statute of Religious Freedom of the second; the third combined two famous passages on slavery and education from the *Notes on Virginia;* and the New Dealers' favorite lines, from the 1816 letter to Kercheval, on the need for institutions to keep step with the progress of thought, were placed in the fourth panel. Surrounding the frieze of the dome high above was the noblest inscription of all: "I have sworn upon the altar of God eternal hostility against every form of tyranny over the mind of man."

As the harried Commissioners made these decisions and countless others of less moment, the workmen raised the pediment, the walls, the gleaming columns, and the dome to the full ninety-six feet above the bulky stylobate that rested, somewhat uncertainly, on the foundations sunk into the south shore of the Tidal Basin. Not long ago men were calling it "Boylan's Folly." But Boylan, who died before his vision could be realized, had then reminded his critics of the other "follies": the Washington Monument, which had consumed the labor of a generation and when completed been mourned by architects as "the ugliest monument in the world"; and the Lincoln Memorial, which some had predicted "would shake itself down with loneliness and ague." The Jefferson Memorial might yet prove to be a success.

Lustrously mirrored in the waters below, offering vistas from its portico of the Washington Monument and the Lincoln Memorial, commanding reverence in its form, declaring the highest ideals in its inscriptions, presenting the hero in strong and clear lines—the Jefferson Memorial *was* a success. After all allowance is made for their critics, President Roosevelt and the Commission better understood not only the requisites of a fitting monument to Jefferson in the national capital, but also and more significantly the meanings which it ought to carry two centuries after his death. It should make manifest the ascendancy of historical consciousness over the vivid sense of presentness, of idealization over use, of patriotic veneration over partisan rancor. It should evoke a range of meanings wider than the democratic tradition, deeper than Americanism, older and surer than progressive styles. The artistically reactionary monument was, nevertheless, a brilliant symbol of the Culture Hero: the creator of Monticello, the spiritual heir of the Western tradition, "the civilized man." The Jefferson Memorial reported the past, as it must. It could not frame the future; but the lengthening shadow of its caged figure might inspire and enlighten the future if Americans, in the spirit of the Memorial itself, let "the richness of his character, thought and spirit take possession of us."

4. *The Thomas Jefferson Bicentennial*

The dedication of the Jefferson Memorial on April 13, 1943 was the high point of the Bicentennial celebration that continued to the end of the year. The day was proclaimed in Jefferson's honor nationally, in most of the states, and in thousands of cities. On this and the few days before and after, pulpit, press, platform, and radio intoned the theme: "Thomas Jefferson Still Lives."

Washington was the hub of the commemoration. The parchment text of the Declaration of Independence, having two decades before at last found a secure public resting place on a bronze altar in the Library of Congress, only to be put in hiding at the commencement of the War, was placed on exhibit at the base of the statue in the Jefferson Memorial. The National Gallery of Art offered an exhibit of jefferson's architectural drawings, and brought together for the first time all the known life-portraits of him. The Library of Congress displayed the remains of the library Jefferson sold to Congress in 1815. Under its Roosevelt-appointed chief, Archibald MacLeish, the Library gave its father belated recognition—in murals, drama, symposia, addresses, and scholarly undertakings—on his two hundredth anniversary.

This anniversary, as Charles Beard remarked, was "no sunshine celebration." Against the darkening horizon Jefferson appeared rather like the man against the sky of E. A. Robinson's poem, like "a dome / Against the glory of a world on fire," whose "vision answering a faith unshaken" was as ours. But if Jefferson's faith thus burned more luminously, the War sharply curtailed the celebration. The usual federal commission was created by act of Congress in 1940. Slow to organize, it then lumbered under the chairmanship of Carter Glass, United States Senator from Virginia, until Edward Boykin was brought in as Executive Secretary in March 1943. Boykin, a retired advertising executive experienced in radio history production and a Jefferson popularizer, sized up the job as "a piece of promotion business," and went to work. Boykin tried, so far as his meager wartime budget would allow, to copy the promotion devices congressman Sol Bloom had used so effectively in the Washington Bicentennial. An official portrait was selected: the gentle and dignified Stuart, called the Bowdoin portrait, of Jefferson the President. A forty-minute color film, *Thomas Jefferson and Monticello*, was produced and widely shown. The Commission encouraged and supplemented the work of local commemorative bodies, and endeavored, with only modest success, to interest museums and like institutions in the Bicentennial.

If the commemorative bodies needed any special incentive to press the campaign in the schools, one was furnished by a widely publicized report in the *New York Times*, April 4, 1943. Benjamin Fine, the newspaper's educational editor, announced the shocking results of a survey of the knowledge of American history possessed by seven thousand freshmen in thirty-six colleges and universities. In this anniversary year, only sixteen per cent of the young scholars could satisfactorily identify Jefferson. To the old question, "Who was Thomas Jefferson?" students gave some baffling answers. "He was . . . president of the Confederacy, founder of the Saturday Evening Post, a Salvation Army worker, and the originator of the Monroe Doctrine. . . . Thirty or more thought that Jefferson earned his right to immortal fame by discovering electricity." In charity to the students, Jefferson's many selves made difficult any clear sense of identity. Still, the results of the survey were distressing. Let the Bicentennial, some urged, be dedicated to "a rebirth in the teaching of American history

and Americanism," as well as to "a regeneration of the Jeffersonian
principles of government and democracy."

The Bicentennial had Democratic overtones. Roosevelt made certain the eight men he appointed to the otherwise bipartisan Bicentennial Commission were *his* kind of Democrat. The observance at
every level, from the children's play to the scholar's discourse, underscored the New Deal's revised image of Jefferson. Some Republicans
and "Jeffersonian Democrats" were genuinely irritated. Mississippi
congressman John E. Rankin repeatedly took the floor of the House
to denounce "the hideous attempts of this Commission to distort
American history." And a Strasburg, Virginia newspaper accused
the Commission of wishing "to change Jefferson's democracy into a
socialistic, totalitarian state." Recognition of the Bicentennial's partisan features should not, however, be allowed to obscure its large and
fundamental area of agreement on Jefferson.

Turning Jefferson into the furrows of the mind, the anniversary
produced sheaves of books, essays, learned discourses, and pious
reflections. Nearly every popular magazine and learned journal had
something to say about Jefferson. Among the books were several
anthologies (one ran to six hundred thousand words) of Jefferson's
writings, the first volume of Marie Kimball's work, Adrienne Koch's
monograph on Jefferson's philosophy, Hendrik Van Loon's curious
and suggestive *Thomas Jefferson,* and a symposium which presented
the views of prominent Americans on Jefferson's meaning in and for
the present. Taken together these books helped to characterize the
Bicentennial. In honoring Jefferson's memory, Americans were concerned with Jefferson's hope. The historical was mixed with the
inspirational, Jefferson *was* with Jefferson *is.* This last big harvest of
thought and feeling about Jefferson confirmed the old truth, as
William D. Grampp observed, that every man is his own Jeffersonian.
From the harvest, nevertheless, may be culled some of the distinctive
features of Jefferson's reputation two hundred years after his birth.

The large participation of the scholarly community in this commemoration was in marked contrast to anything that had gone before.
The meetings of the American Philosophical Society and similar
associations, entire numbers of *Ethics* and other learned journals,

exhibits at the Library of Congress—these made manifest the scholars' succession to Jefferson. The acclaim of the historians, in particular, closed at last the rift between them and the public in respect to Jefferson's claim to greatness.

At this juncture in Jefferson's posthumous history, the older attributes of the doctrinaire, the poltroon, and the politician almost vanished from the figure to be replaced by the attributes of "the civilized man." The civilized and civilizing attributes were, most of all, those of the manifold genius. These were described *ad nauseam* in the Bicentennial literature; Jefferson's versatile genius quickly became a hackneyed subject. Anthologist Saul Padover called Jefferson t most astonishingly brilliant figure since the Italian Renaissanc Men compared him to Leonardo. Farmer, Lawyer, Scientist, Artis Classicist—Jefferson was exhibited in his various roles until it seeme sheer audacity for Bernard Mayo, in a skillful reconstruction of Jef ferson's life through his writings, to present him as Himself.

The political man, "the political father of his country," was incorporated into the larger configuration. History's marching orders had smashed the older political castings of his fame. What was left was the Jefferson whose faith in the power of free men to work out their own salvation was greater than all his words and deeds. "Jefferson's legacy to us is not so much his solution to the problem of government," J. W. Studebaker said, "but rather his conviction that the problem must be solved anew by each generation." The pervasiveness of this opinion in 1943 testified to the influence of the New Deal revision of the Jefferson symbol. Jefferson represented in politics not a creed or a philosophy but an attitude of experimentation and progress within the general design of American ideals. The spirit had triumphed over the letter of Jefferson.

The image that dilated in the labyrinthian paths of civilization and fell apart under the constraints of political formulae concentrated itself again, as it had before, in the Apostle of Liberty. Why was it, historian Allan Nevins asked, that despite Jefferson's failures of statesmanship and foresight his influence steadily grew and surpassed every President after him? "In a sentence," Nevins suggested, "his influence lives because he was one of the great liberators of the human spirit." The liberation involved democracy, the people being the only true guardians of their liberty; but democracy was only the political instrument of a far vaster enterprise for the freedom and happiness of man. The conception of the Apostle of Liberty, to which President Roosevelt dedicated the Memorial, had acquired a new meaning: the liberation of the human spirit in every phase, through every channel of the nation's progress as a civilization. The President swept up the meaning in one flourish: "Leader in the philosophy of government, in education, in the arts, in efforts to lighten the toil of mankind—exponent of planning for the future, he led the steps of America into the paths of the permanent integrity of the Republic."

The war against Fascist barbarism made "Jefferson's children" better aware of their legacy and the toils of its custody. A few years ago, Nevins thought, Jefferson might have been depressed by American lethargy and faithlessness. "But today he would feel that the spiritual insurrection of which he was the principal American voice had again vindicated his power." An eloquent testament of the vindication under the cloud of totalitarianism was Sidney Kingsley's drama *The Patriots*. Asked by a congressman why he had written a play about Jefferson, Kingsley explained that he, like many of his generation, had grown up in an intellectual void so far as the American tradition was concerned; but that after returning in 1939 from Europe, where he had seen freedom and democracy spit upon, he determined "to rediscover in its purity the American faith." Cleaving through the morass of skepticism, Kingsley found in Jefferson the best representation of the faith. The result was *The Patriots*, a Broadway hit which also had a "command performance" in the capital. As editor Norman Cousins observed, it "carried over the entire gear and tackle of the present ideological struggle and dumped it squarely in the laps of the Founding Fathers." Randall Thompson's composition for chorus and orchestra, *The Testament of Freedom*, structured largely on passages declaring America's revolutionary birth, rose to crescendo on a more far-reaching note: "The flames kindled on the 4th of July, 1776, have spread over too much of the globe to be extinguished by the feeble engines of despotism; on the contrary, they will consume these engines and all who work them." Jefferson, "most serious of our poets," passed as a word-god of freedom, buying back our faithlessness, in Karl Shapiro's moving poem:

> So temperate, so remote, so sure of phrase
> Your music sweeps a continent, a sphere,
> Fashions a modern language for a war
> And by its cadence makes responsible
> Our million names to you.

But was it possible to extend Jefferson's libertarian spirit to the world? The global war for freedom pointed up a dilemma never satisfactorily resolved in American consciousness or in its frequent counterpart, the Jefferson image. Liberty must eventually encircle the globe, Americans had said with Jefferson; but in the meantime they heeded one of his most memorable counsels: "no entangling alliances." As Gilbert Chinard suggested, America had followed contradictory ideals in world affairs, and Jefferson was involved with both of them. In the interval between the two wars, the insular ideal was uppermost and isolationists conjured with Jefferson's name. But the dominant voice of the Bicentennial was internationalist. Neither national nor hemispheric isolationism, though both were advocated in Jefferson's name, could assure American survival or, ultimately, the survival of the Apostle of Liberty. In tomorrow's world, Justice Wiley Rutledge declared, "we must find a way to work out in a society so knit and bound together Jefferson's basic ideal of the dignity, individuality and independence of each citizen." The principal realm of Jefferson's vision, it now seemed, was no longer America, where he was elevated above political strife, but the troubled world outside.

Startling, naive, messianic, the idea of Jefferson's significance for an emerging world order was the theme of Senator Elbert Thomas's *Thomas Jefferson, World Citizen*. Long a student of the Orient and advocate of international co-operation, Thomas made a searching study of Jefferson's philosophy in connection with his duties on the Thomas Jefferson Memorial Commission. "Jefferson became, in everything I read, a world citizen." The Americanist and isolationist misconceptions, he said, had tended to deprive the nation of one of its richest heritages in the present crisis. No figure in world history better represented the "united nations" philosophy for which America was contending than Jefferson. His true spirit was hard to define, the Senator conceded, but underlying everything was a theory of human nature: the natural unity of mankind, the universal morality and innate goodness of man, the inalienable rights and the supreme value of each individual. Whether in art, science, religion, or government, Jefferson worked on this theory. In religion, for instance, it caused him to reject the traditional Western test of revelation, which was partial and subjective, and to adopt instead the universal and socially objective standard of religion's consequences in the conduct of life. By virtue, therefore, of "a universal morality in man," men of diverse creeds and conditions could reach agreement on an ethical code binding them together in peace and friendship. Founding his political theory on the natural goodness of man, Thomas went on, Jefferson sought to secure human rights in the American polity by the fullest application of the principle of federation. He realized its inescapable conclusion in world federation. As in a great ascending chain, the same rules of conduct that held for all individuals, and in the relations of man and state, ought to hold among states. Jefferson implemented his world vision by the means then available to him—free trade, the right of expatriation, peaceable coercion, and so on. Such policies, the Senator thought, "grew out of a sense, not of nationalistic isolation, but of the moral bonds between nations." If the promises of the present struggle were to be fulfilled, Thomas said, "it is essential that we view Jefferson as a great world citizen," for only with the furthest application of his principles could freedom be established in the world. And should it be established, through some federation of nations, Jefferson would rightly be reckoned among its "spiritual founders."

Thomas thus sought to open a new path to Jefferson's living fame along the only way mankind could freely and safely travel in tomorrow's world. Whether or not his conception was historically sound, it was morally sound. "In this historic year," President Roosevelt was to have said on April 13, 1945, "more than ever before, we do well to consider the character of Thomas Jefferson as an American citizen of the world." Jefferson's meaning, in other words, must be determined, as it had always been, by "Jefferson's children," endlessly relating itself to the changing tasks of freedom. In hindsight, however, it is distressingly apparent that the "world citizen" idea failed to give a new face to Jefferson. His spirit continued to occupy America, though strangely remote and silent in its majesty; but the prospect of it ever occupying the world grew dim beyond all recollection. In the Bicentennial, one hundred and seventeen years after his death, Jefferson's apotheosis was achieved at last.

The fitting culmination of the Bicentennial was the announcement in December of a monumental edition of Jefferson's papers. The federal Commission had originally been authorized to provide some appropriate monument of the celebration. Mindful of the precedent set by the Washington Bicentennial, and heeding the pleas of the historical profession, the Commission decided to memorialize Jefferson in his writings.

Since Gilbert Chinard, in 1929, first raised the "pious hope" for a substantially complete and accurate redaction of Jefferson's papers —"the richest treasure house of information ever left by a single man"—many scholars had voiced their concern. Seventy per cent of Jefferson's letters remained unpublished, to say nothing of the letters written to him, which were often indispensable to establish the context of his thought. They were scattered in numerous private and public collections. The ink was beginning to fade, the paper to crumble; soon the loss would be irretrievable. Of the four editions of Jefferson's writings, all long since out of print, only Ford's was reliable. The deplorable neglect and mismanagement of Jefferson's papers, A. J. Nock asserted, brought "the literary and social character of this country into contempt."

Cost alone was a major obstacle to the Commission's plan. "It would take many lives and a fortune to edit them properly," Chinard had said. The Commission's Enabling Act of July 1942 allotted only fifteen thousand dollars of the total appropriation for the memorial. A pittance; but all that Congress deemed warranted in wartime. In March 1943 the Commission appointed, on Kimball's recommendation, Julian P. Boyd, Princeton University Librarian, as its Historian. Seven months later, Boyd submitted his report on the editing and publication of Jefferson's papers. The proposed work would run to forty-four volumes and cost an estimated three hundred thousand dollars. Boyd had attempted to interest several universities and foundations in the mammoth project, but without success. Finally, in desperation, he went to Arthur Hays Sulzberger, publisher of the *New York Times,* which had earlier subsidized the *Dictionary of American Biography.* The *Times* agreed to meet two thirds of the estimated cost, on the conditions that Princeton University assume the remainder and that the work be dedicated to the memory of Sulzberger's predecessor, Adolph S. Ochs. Princeton agreed to sponsor and publish the edition on these terms. The plan met with the approval of the Commission and President Roosevelt. Boyd assumed the direction of the project. In the spring of 1944, the Jefferson mill at Princeton began to grind, slowly but exceedingly fine.

The task proved more gigantic than even Boyd had imagined. Photo-duplicates of Jefferson manuscripts poured into Princeton from over four hundred sources, from nearly extinct Indian tribes, from Parisian archives, from Australia and Japan. Sixty thousand separate items—letters written and letters received, documents, memoranda, and miscellany—piled up the shelves. "There are," Associate Editor Lyman Butterfield wrote, "mathematical calculations, designs for machines and furniture and landscape details; recipes for macaroni and other dishes; itineraries; agricultural and meteorological data; tables of useful information; book lists, and notes and memoranda on an incredible variety of subjects, from the use of Archimedes' screw at Kew to snuff, Sophocles, and specific gravity." Estimates of size and cost were continually revised upward. Not until 1970, at the earliest, will the fifty or more-volume edition be completed.

The finest tools of historical research and the printer's art went into making *The Papers of Thomas Jefferson* the largest and perhaps the most distinguished work of editorial scholarship ever produced. The editors aimed to include "everything legitimately Jeffersonian by reason of authorship or relationship." Every care was taken to assure the authenticity and accuracy of each item; to each was appended a note giving the informative details; variant copies or drafts were collated; and for major documents Boyd wrote what amounted to definitive historical essays. The work was a triumph of the scholar's craft; but blessed with an incomparable grace and felicity in handling the documents and muniments of the past, Boyd made it an artistic triumph as well. The Princeton University Press added other fine touches. A special type-face, called Monticello, was struck, a special paper manufactured, in order to lend a Jeffersonian character to every last detail of the edition. Boyd and his capable staff resolved that their work would never have to be done again.

Volume I was formally presented to the nation at ceremonies in the national capital on May 17, 1950. "Is it possible for Princeton scholars, well furnished though they are, to make grist for the American mind from the vast phantom Thomas Jefferson cultivated?" Douglas Southall Freeman pointedly asked on this occasion. When the last letter was filed away and all the accumulated reflections of decades put in focus, would the editors be able to assert, Freeman wondered, " 'Here is Jefferson; this is the image of his soul; see in these words, the kernels of his creed?' " If so it would be an unprecedented achievement. Without presuming to omniscience, Editor Boyd set the theme in his Introduction. This and the succeeding volumes, he said, were most specifically "the record of a man's career," more generally "a record of the origin, formation, and early growth of the Republic," but above all they "should be regarded as the embodiment of an idea." It would be unfortunate, Boyd thought, if the range and ubiquity of Jefferson's genius was allowed to obscure the single great idea that guided and informed it: the idea of freedom and self-government for all humanity, as stated in the Declaration of Independence. "This, perhaps the most potent idea of modern history, as valid for the twentieth century as for the eighteenth, was the idea that gave meaning to Jefferson's versatile inquiry and selfless industry." The monument inspired by the Bicentennial was thus dedicated, in the sense of Jefferson's significance, to its dominant theme.

Despite these clear affirmations, echoed and re-echoed in the public reception of *The Jefferson Papers,* Freeman's question tugged at the mind. Would the millions of Jefferson's words embody as in a uniform design the fundamental idea? What was to be done with the kernels of his thought on the Negro, on the proper government for the people of Louisiana, on the enforcement of the Embargo?

The state rights republican and the majoritarian democrat, the man of Monticello and the party leader, the American and the world-citizen—could these be brought within the frame of a single image? This, indeed, would be a rare achievement, and one which Boyd must leave to other scholars to puzzle out of the rich treasure laid before them. It is a work for connoisseurs, the consummation of the scholars' affair with Jefferson. It may furnish the impetus to the prophesied "new era of Jefferson historiography," but it is very doubtful that it will make "grist for the American mind" in the public sense. In this, the contrast between the Boyd Edition and the Randolph Edition a century and a quarter before is no less striking than are their differences in size, method, and format. The *Memoirs* agitated the public mind, at once became a canon of political orthodoxy, and thrust Jefferson's shadow over the next several decades. The Boyd Edition has a different address, and must grind in a different way. While it testifies to a living faith in freedom, it opens the way to authentic historical understanding of freedom's most inspiring American voice.

THE LENGTHENING SHADOW

I have sworn upon the altar of God, eternal hostility against every
form of tyranny over the mind of man.

Thomas Jefferson

THE GREAT MAN makes history—and is consumed by it. He swiftly
becomes a symbol, perhaps many symbols, through which men of
different persuasions and at different times seek to comprehend their
experiences and state their purposes. Confusion and error, legend
and myth, wish and aspiration transform the life that has thus been
imaginatively extended in posterity. The process is never the same
with any two individuals. George Washington, for example, was a
demigod before he died, and forever after, with barely a shade of
turning, the lonely and immutable monument of American glory.
"He created his own silence whilst the others were obliged to await
the hand of time." Andrew Jackson, to take another American
instance, witnessed the creation of his own legend years before he
became President. "The symbol for an age," as John William Ward
has shown, Jackson was also encompassed by it. Thomas Jefferson
presents a case altogether different from either of these, perhaps
from any other known to history. When he died, Americans thought
to shape his life and work into a symbol of the fabled republic. But
Jefferson was not of an age, not limpid, not stereotyped, not a demigod. An ill-arranged cluster of meanings, rancorous, mercurial, fertile, the Jefferson Image was constantly evolving. Crudely unfinished
at his death, his contract untransacted, Jefferson was fulfilled in the
procession of the American mind. The templed god of an American

faith in 1943 was, therefore, a different Jefferson from the one who lived in the remote spaces behind 1826.

The chronicle of his progress calls, in retrospect, for some final accounting of Jefferson's prodigious vigor and kaleidoscopic change-ability. At the beginning was the man. He lived eighty-three years, helped to found a nation, reflected deeply, wrote voluminously, and plied himself at countless tasks. The image mirrored Jefferson's prodigality. In the vast corpus of his mind anyone could find things to arouse anger or sympathy, invite ridicule or admiration. He was a great rhetorician, one who lived on the spiritual capital of his words even more than on the tangible rewards of his work. "He walked through life pencil in hand." The written record of a life such as his could not be consistent in every detail. He willingly risked the hobgoblin "consistency," and risked too the vicious constructions which his regard for the amenities of human intercourse enabled his enemies to put on his thoughts. Their shifting contexts were easily ignored; Jefferson seemed to exist in a historical void. Men called him a philosopher, and demanded of him more thorough and timeless wisdom than he could supply. He never had the occasion, probably never the desire, to work out a systematic statement of his philosophy. So he appeared before posterity with his rich intellectual garments dangling and disarrayed. This was relatively inconsequential except in the main arena of his life and reputation, politics. His failure to codify political ideas and doctrines confused his followers, enabled fractional and pseudo Jeffersonians of various descriptions to cut his creed into pieces, and contributed, some thought disastrously, to the rule of expediency in American politics and the general collapse of the Jeffersonian polity. Whether or not this lack of a firm political code seriously weakened Jefferson's powers of resistance, there did seem to be a wide gap between his theories and his actions. His reputation suffered accordingly, but chiefly in quarters where it did not amount to much anyway. The loss was far more than offset by the gain. For just as Jefferson multiplied himself through the range and variety of his interests, he doubled, quite unconsciously of course, his political usefulness to the generations, simultaneously posing in himself the dilemmas they must face, by seeming to recommend one thing in theory and another thing in practice. The Louisiana

Purchase offered the most striking instance of this curious doubling of Jefferson's significance, though numerous others may be recalled. *Which Jefferson Do You Quote?* Clinton Rossiter asked in a recent magazine article. He counted seven different Jeffersons still being "batted around the political arena": Anti-Statist, States'-Righter, Isolationist, Agrarian, Rationalist, Civil Libertarian, Constitutional Democrat. And there had been, still were, several others. Of course, Rossiter had his own opinion as to the *real* Jefferson, and he decried the presence of Jefferson's flag on any craft other than his own. Jefferson had been so indiscriminately parceled out, Rossiter thought, "he may yet be classed as a long-winded trimmer and be allowed to sink into disuse." And so he had been classed many times, but without sinking into disuse. "If he goes on belonging to everyone, he may end up belonging to no one." And yet it was precisely because Jefferson lent himself to everyone that he had been so useful, that he had been for generations after his death a political watchword, that his reputation was carried forward until, indeed, he belonged to everyone and no one.

While the man explains much, it cannot explain why posterity felt the need constantly to recall Jefferson to its experience. He could be quoted on every side of every question, it was often said; but why did men quote him? First, because among the nation's founders Jefferson was the most eloquent exponent of political ideals which were to be called democratic and which were to become virtually synonymous with the American ideal. Had his life not been enough, the circumstances of his death and the subsequent course of events assured his pre-eminence as a democratic symbol. As such, he was vociferously hated by some; but the symbol and the ideal were fortified by the massive power of public opinion. Second, because of the compelling sense of tradition in American politics. Politicians were the main carriers of Jefferson's reputation. Its history was determined to a very large extent by political events, and particularly by the fortunes of the Democratic party. The strange fascination with the nation's classic age, combined with the stereotyped images of the American conflict, kept alive the historical debate in which Jefferson figured as protagonist of democracy. Third, because Jefferson was implicated in the successive crises of the democratic experiment.

American history sometimes seemed a protracted litigation, negotiations and hearings, trials and appeals in endless number, on Jefferson. The major trial during the first period of his posthumous reputation turned on the ideological conflict between republicanism and democracy. It was practically decided, so far as it concerned the Union, by the Civil War. In the second period it turned more precisely on the conflict between the individualistic and anti-statist clauses of the Jeffersonian creed, on the one side, and the humanitarian and progressivist clauses, on the other side. The verdict in this case called for the subordination of the formal elements of doctrine and principle to the "spirit of Jefferson"—the New Deal solution to the dilemma. Finally, Jefferson summoned the imagination because he prefigured a civilization and furnished important clues to its ethos. When Americans outgrew the political hero, their interest quickened in the cultural hero. Difficult as it was to form Jefferson's varied qualities and activities into a single design, the cultural image best presented itself at Monticello, "portico facing the wilderness." Here was luminously preserved for the inspiration of men in search of their own cultural identity the two heritages discovered in Jefferson—pioneer and aristocrat, American and world-citizen, the values of nature and of civilization—which, fruitfully joined in him, signified the common heritage of America.

It is impossible to say with assurance whether the evolution of the Jefferson image in all its loosely structured parts carried the generations toward or away from the elusive *himself*. Perhaps the question is purely academic anyway: Jefferson *was* what he seemed to be. Still this shocks our sense of historical truth; the obligation persists to reward greatness in its authentic, unimpaired state. The desire and the means of doing so have grown enormously in the past several decades. The knowledge of Jefferson possessed by some recent scholars surpasses that of his most intimate contemporaries (if there were any who were genuinely intimate with that reserved man). Their works have achieved a more richly textured and, as the candid observer must feel, a truer image of the man in his time.

Only recently have the emotions surrounding the Jefferson symbol receded far enough into the background to permit the historian to keep his eye trained on Jefferson. Still the historian's vision must be impaired. To say that he works within a frame of reference that is not Jefferson's is merely to recognize the elementary problem of all written history. Where the object is Jefferson, however, the historian's obligation to historical truth is compromised, in some degree, by his sense of obligation to the Jefferson symbol. Jefferson occupies such an important place in the symbolical architecture of this nation that the search for the elusive *himself* from the vaunted summit, Objectivity, must not be allowed to empty the symbol of meaning for "Jefferson's children." Not only does the historian in common with other enlightened men feel this, but he also approaches Jefferson with some knowledge of what has gone before: the hysteria of denunciation and the hysteria of exaltation, the errors and legends and myths, the shapes Jefferson has assumed and the strategies he has served through the generations. Knowing some of this, no matter how clear his vision, he must see Jefferson in the light of this knowing. He must shift his glance to redress some error, must offset some partial view of a matter with a more comprehensive view, must, in short, take account of Jefferson's bewildering career in American thought and imagination. So many problems of Jefferson interpretation have stemmed, not from the actualities of his own history, but from the needs he filled and the uses he served after his death that the historian, addressing these problems, is, in some sense, addressing not Jefferson himself but the Jefferson image.

The creation of the national hero was a long and tortuous process. Along the way, the serpentine recesses of Jefferson's reputation were to be straightened; hereditary hatred, political rancor, most of the memories and fears that had troubled the hero's progress, were to be overcome in a more temperate climate of common veneration; the Rousseauistic Frenchman was to be changed into the American Democrat, the infidel into the Christian, the Virginian into the nationalist, the visionary into the father of everything practical, the odious character into a model of good, the party leader into "the civilized man." Jefferson's road to Olympus was turbulent and tortuous, but he would never have reached the destination by any less exacting route. Looking back from Olympus, what stood clear as if in a rising straight line was the indomitable faith in human freedom that, in Roosevelt's words, "led the steps of America into the paths of the permanent integrity of the Republic."

The post-Bicentennial history of Jefferson's reputation will certainly be of a very different character from the one charted in these pages. No doubt Jefferson, after adapting to changes of a century and a quarter, possesses reserves for still others to come. Nor are Americans likely suddenly to drop the old habit of imagination that has served his survival. The scattered indicia of the Jefferson image in the nineteen-fifties suggest its continued currency and appeal. But deeper reflection on contemporary developments points to the realization that the pantheoned hero is not likely to perform the same role in the generations ahead that Jefferson performed in the generations past.

The American mind has encountered during the last quarter century a new political world. Under the threat of Communist totalitarianism, the near revolutionary changes in American government and politics in the Roosevelt era reached staggering new dimensions. The thrust of world problems and responsibilities severed many political traditions, obliterated the conventional lines between peace and war, domestic policy and foreign policy, and put an end to the distinctly national phase of American history. It becomes increasingly difficult to understand our politics in a Jeffersonian frame of reference. The old-style Jeffersonians have passed from the ranks of the Democratic party. With them have gone the apprehension of a social and political environment tractable by Jeffersonian ideology, the prepossessions, the feelings, the aspirations that made "tying up with Jefferson" a significant act. Jefferson now seems destined to serve the Democrats as Lincoln has for decades served the Republicans: the formal symbol of the party's legendary beginnings, whose uses were largely dissipated when the founder outgrew the party and the party outgrew his principles of government. The New Deal undermined the historical integrity of the party. After Roosevelt there was no "return to Jefferson," though there might arise at some future time the wish to return to Roosevelt. The party was furnished with a new tradition. And this was only somewhat less true of American politics as a whole.

Partly because the traditional cast of politics has been shattered, a tendency has developed in American historiography to reinterpret the political past in terms of solidarity. The first influential work of this revisionist school was Richard Hofstadter's *The American Political Tradition* in 1948. There was only *one* tradition operative in a "common climate of American opinion," Hofstadter said; but this truth had been "obscured by the tendency to place political conflict in the foreground of history," a tendency in which the historians abetted the politicians. "While the conflicts of Jefferson's day are constantly reactivated and thus constantly brought to mind, the commonly shared convictions are neglected." The latter, "the central faith" in the strivings of a free capitalist society, was the more important historically. The key to American political history was furnished, not by the clash between Jefferson and Hamilton, but rather, Hofstadter thought, by the record of Jefferson's administration, which set the pattern for the ongoing assimilation of Jeffersonian democracy into Hamiltonian capitalism. Louis Hartz, in *The Liberal Tradition in America* (1955), went several steps further. Because their society was liberal, the Americans had not needed a genuine revolution in 1776, had not needed and did not develop political philosophy or parties expressive of class and ideological conflicts. The American democrats, thunderously proclaiming their Jeffersonian slogans and raising Hamiltonian phantoms of oppression, were all, or nearly all, "actors in the drama of a liberal society none of them understood."

Paradoxical though it may seem, it is mainly because the great world rushes in on American consciousness that the unique features of the American political experience now come into startling relief. Historically separated, physically and emotionally, from other nations, unable to escape from the provincial frame of reference, Americans had exaggerated the themes of revolution, democracy, and social conflict in their history. But now, as Hartz said, "A hunger has finally appeared for getting outside the national experience." And once outside, viewed from the contemporary angle of America's involvement with the world, the political tradition entirely changes its character. The world is a turbulent and revolutionary place; America, by contrast, clearly is not. Whether or not this interpretation is valid, it represents a conscious attempt to understand the political tradition in the light of America's international position. As the light falls on Jefferson, he appears less radical and more conservative, less theoretical and more practical, less universal and more national. The revisionists do not consign Jefferson to political oblivion. But by smashing the old categories of interpretation and by deflating the revolutionary pretensions of American democracy, the revisionists leave to Jefferson little opportunity to act on the contemporary mind.

Understood in this way, American democracy is not for export. Part of "the genius of American politics," Daniel Boorstein argued in his book of that title, consists in the fact that its institutions developed under a unique set of national conditions and, therefore, cannot be appropriated by other peoples. The long cherished idea of America as a revolutionary nation with a mission of freedom and self-government to all mankind has suffered some hard blows since the Second World War. Communism, not democracy, unfortunately appears to be the world's revolutionary ideology. The faith that men are not born "with saddles on their backs" recedes everywhere. The hope of a world community is, if anything, more distant than ever. The Progressive party of Henry Wallace, in 1948, called for a renewal of Jefferson's policies of peace and friendship with all nations, and defended its conciliatory approach to the Communist revolution on the historical ground of Jefferson's friendship for the revolutionary nation of his time. But this sounded vaguely like the Moscow line. Indeed, the Moscow radio occasionally blared the same message. There were other men, like Yale historian Ralph H. Gabriel in 1950, who reiterated Elbert Thomas's belief that the dedication of the Jefferson Memorial was a symbolic act of world significance. The Jefferson idea was crumbling the walls of nationality, Gabriel said. "The idea of fundamental human rights everywhere had begun to take form." But in actuality it was an old idea, more formless than ever, rapidly falling into muddle and disuse. Admittedly, the traditional power and use of the Jefferson symbol could only be renewed in an international context; but events did not encourage the prospect, and strong currents of American thought denied the possibility.

If America could not export Jefferson, was he likely to be imported by foreign nations? Struggling democrats in South America and elsewhere had, at former times, appropriated his ideas and found strength in his vision. On May 20, 1956, President Sukarno of Indonesia, on a state visit in the United States, made a pilgrimage to Monticello to honor "my great teacher." The Moslem chief and father of one of the world's newest republics placed a wreath at Jefferson's tomb, then with eyes closed and hands upraised in solemn invocation, he prayed that God would "give Jefferson the best place in Heaven." Jefferson, Sukarno said in what was a truly remarkable testament, had set "a big fire burning in Indonesia." Within a year, however, Sukarno laid down for Indonesia the bogus doctrine of "guided democracy" and, in the judgment of some observers, opened the gates to Communism. The discrepancy between the faith professed in 1956 and the course of action in 1957 suggests the difficulty of a Sukarno assuming the mantle of Jefferson in this age. Indeed, the picture is a grotesque caricature of the incongruity of Jefferson in the present world.

The acute sense of this incongruity led the Protestant theologian Reinhold Niebuhr, in 1952, to place Jefferson in the matrix of what he called "the irony of American history." America was the prime bearer of the liberal dreams of modern Western culture, Niebuhr said, the dream of managing history by the simple correlation of reason and desire, the dream of fulfilling in history the highest hopes of human dignity and brotherhood. The Messianic consciousness of America compassed the world in its sight. It was thus that Jefferson declared "the pursuit of happiness" the goal of humanity, and saw in the physical circumstances and social conditions of his native land the promise of reaching it. But recent history had refuted the dream: first, internally, by the growth of industry, class conflict, and consolidated political power; now, externally, by America's involvement in world responsibilities that negate its moral pretensions. "The same strength which has extended our power beyond a continent" Niebuhr said, "has also interwoven our destiny with the destiny of many peoples and brought us into a vast web of history in which other wills, running in oblique or contrasting directions to our own, inevitably hinder or contradict what we most fervently desire." The historical faith, of which Jefferson was the influential voice, would have to be transcended if Americans were to accomplish their own and the free world's survival. Only by attaining a dimension of meaning—the Christian dimension of sin, contrition, and humility—above the optimistic rationalism of the Jeffersonian faith, Niebuhr argued, could America attain the wisdom needed for the struggle.

This was not the first time Jefferson was locked in the jaws of an ironic predicament. Always before—the Civil War, the New Deal—the dilemma he personified was overcome, his complicity in untoward, even tragic, developments was dissolved, the image reformed and its power reclaimed. In the present international crisis, the conviction that Jefferson was a man of dangerous illusions spread along a wide intellectual front. No one was angry at the American hero. No debate took shape. But among Christian pessimists like Niebuhr, "national interest" theorists like Hans Morgenthau, and some of the "new conservatives," there was an ill-defined feeling, faintly reminiscent of the prevalent criticism several decades before, that the Jeffersonian faith had lost contact with the vital realities upon which it was supposed to act. The gloomy climate of the mind did not hurt Jefferson's reputation so far as it was keyed to memory; only so far as it was keyed to hope. For probably no revision of the Jefferson symbol answerable to the pessimistic diagnosis of the national condition was possible. Could the moral innocent become contrite? The champion of human pretensions their critic? The master of history its humble slave? The man of illusions a man of sorrows? Nothing in Jefferson's history suggested this possibility. But a poet, deeply aware of the tragic miscarriage of the Jeffersonian ideal in our time, might imagine the spiritual father of America being brought to terms with the unpleasant facts divulged to his children.

The poet, in this instance, was Kentucky-born Robert Penn Warren. At first he had a story, a legend of the Kentucky wilderness, a tale of human brutality preserved in dusty court records, obscure abolitionist tracts, and the folk memory. On the night of December 15, 1811, in the meathouse of the Lewis plantation above the Ohio River, Lilburn Lewis, assisted by his brother Isham, murderously butchered a slave named George, whose crime it was to have broken a pitcher cherished by the brothers' dead mother, Lucy Lewis, sister

of Thomas Jefferson. Wishing to make this shocker speak meaning-
fully of the human condition to Americans, Warren discovered the
appropriate theme in Jefferson, "the prophet of human perfectibility"
and the "true-blood kin" of the actors of the old horror. The story
finally took the form of a long dramatic dialogue, *Brother to Dragons*
(1953). Jefferson is the real protagonist, his heart split, his dream
shattered, by the terrible knowledge of "the immitigable ferocity of
self" discovered in the betrayal of his own blood. Yes, he had known
man's capacity for evil, Warren's Jefferson avows; but in the absolute
ecstasy of his vision, he had believed a form could be contrived
"fit to hold the purity of man's hope." Now he knows the heartbreak
of his lie, and seeks redemption by facing the ignoble truth. "There
is no forgiveness for our being human," he comforts Lucy:

> It is the inexpungeable error. It is,
> Dear Sister, the one thing we have overlooked
> In our outrageous dreams and cunningest contrivances.
> And I who once contrived should know that now.

The anguish of George under the axe evokes in Jefferson the anguish
of a nation that can neither live with the Noble Lie nor live without
it. The voice is, of course, the poet's, not Jefferson's. He, so far as
is known, never made mention of the disaster that befell his family
in Kentucky. Warren granted this. Irony, he said, "is always, and
only, a trick of light on the late landscape." Whether or not Jefferson's
moral universe crumbled under the shock of discovering what his
own blood was capable of, the poet wrote, "subsequent events in
the history of America, of which Jefferson is the spiritual father,
might still do the job."

On the basis of precedent these reconsiderations of Jefferson and
the democratic tradition could be expected to influence Jefferson
scholarship; however, there were reasons to believe precedent was
not controlling. The point was approaching where the study of the
historical Jefferson need not reflect the fortunes of the Jefferson
symbol. The scholarly wish to possess Jefferson for *himself* might
never be realized; but a Jefferson about whom politicians cease to
contend, whose ideas suffer drastic erosion from all sides, and whose
own history proves to be a rewarding field of study in itself—this

figure invites the true scholar and begs the true historical discovery.

The most authentic contemporary witness to the scholarly tendency is Dumas Malone's *Jefferson and His Time*. The monumental project began to form in the historian's mind when he was teaching at the University of Virginia in the nineteen-twenties; but not until the bicentennial year was he able to make rapid progress with it. Two volumes of a scheduled five appeared in 1948 and 1951. Drawing on the specialized or partial illuminations of other students, Malone endeavored to bring within a single broad-gauged biography "the whole of a many-sided man." The work may thus be considered the capstone of the most fruitful era of Jefferson historiography, as Randall's *Life* was, in its own way, the capstone of an earlier era. Unlike Randall's work, Malone's is not marred by polemicism, either of the political or of the literary type. It manifests the attitude, and achieves some of the timelessness, of true scholarship. How recently this attitude has been assumed may be suggested by the comparison to Claude Bowers. It was simply no longer important for Malone to maintain many of the legends of Jefferson's political democracy. Only fourteen years Malone's senior, Bowers was spiritually closer to Randall two generations removed. As the Bowers type of advocacy was missing, so also was the different type represented by Marie Kimball. His young Jefferson, like hers, was one of the Virginia gentry, distinguished from the Tidewater aristocrats only in degree, "a sensitive and fastidious gentleman," "an enthusiast for the arts," a man who was most truly himself in Paris. But Malone avoided her extravagances. He wrote in the firm conviction that Jefferson did not need an advocate.

Malone's volumes immediately won the assent of the scholarly community. Malone portrayed Jefferson without acrimony or hyperbole, without one-sidedness or the exaggeration of single-minded interpretations, without concealment of faults or loss of historical perspective, without obtrusive scholarly vendettas, and without the aimless antiquarianism that risked the loss of the subject in the vastness of the record. The work was full, reasonable, and honest. The consistency of Jefferson's life, which had given so much trouble to students who looked for it in the pattern of ideas and politics, became clear in the growing pattern of the man's experience. Nothing in Malone's *Jefferson* jarred the understanding or invited contention. His literary style added enormously to the impression he wished to convey, and was a further index to his spiritual distance from Bowers. Gracious, low-keyed, and smoothly polished, it was, as Douglass Adair noted, "not a call to battle but an invitation to understand the history that Jefferson made." Others thought this was the clue to the work's limitations. Malone's Jefferson was too bland. He blunted the sharp edges of Jefferson's mind, quieted his democratic passions, and smoothed out the ironies and paradoxes that had given his life a special fascination. The work won the assent of the mind without exciting it. But it was precisely in this character that Malone's work, along with Boyd's and Sowerby's, made manifest the triumph of scholarship over controversy. It invited the quiet of historical understanding rather than the rage of contemporaneous debate.

There is, of course, still tremendous room for divided opinions on Jefferson. Without division and debate the historians' industry would perish; for this reason, if no other were available, Jefferson must continue to be one of its inexhaustible subjects. But other reasons are available. Students must feel, for instance, the inherent limitation, perhaps inseparable from the virtue, of "a larger synthesis" such as Malone's. The quintessential character of the man vanishes in "the whole man." The scholar who hungers for the marrow of Jefferson, confident it must exist somewhere, is apt to feel rather like the disenchanted "well-rounded man" of a Scott Fitzgerald novel, that "life is much more successfully looked at from a single window, after all." Continuing to view Jefferson from their separate windows, the scholars help to maintain essentially antithetical images of Jefferson. While Daniel Boorstin sees the naturalistic philosopher, Karl Lehmann, in his *Thomas Jefferson, American Humanist,* accents the opposite essence of his mind. Malone's fair and comprehensive view was pointedly challenged in 1951 by Nathan Schachner's admiring but more critical two-volume biography. Schachner, a skillful free-lance historian who came to Jefferson after having written sympathetic biographies of Burr and Hamilton, heightened the very qualities Malone subdued. His Jefferson was a democratic firebrand, a slippery politician, a very erratic scientist and thinker, a cold and forbidding person, and one of strong but repressed passions.

But it is, after all, misleading to let the emphasis fall on controversy. Within the walls of the academy, a quiet, almost subterranean, research goes forward, its issue usually no more than notes and articles in learned journals, its justification the belief that every nook and crevice of Jefferson's life merits study. The informed scholar now realizes how little is *really* known about Jefferson. For the first time, it becomes feasible systematically to explore Jefferson's intellectual terrain through his books and writings. What *was* Jeffersonian Democracy? The older definitions are patently inadequate. Jefferson the President has not been comprehensively studied since Henry Adams; and the prodigy who manages to study it as if Adams had never written is sure to offer many surprises. Jefferson is an old, old subject; but the quest for the historical Jefferson, under the formal discipline of scholarly inquiry, is young.

Into whatever remote niches the historians pursue Jefferson, they help to illuminate the American faith in freedom. Of freedom, Jefferson speaks to the present with the same urgency as to his own time, and with a voice as affirmative as it is authentic. "Liberty was his chief concern," Dumas Malone wrote in setting the motif of his book, "and his major emphasis was on the freedom of the spirit and the mind." This was fundamental, both to the individual's "pursuit of happiness" and to the collective enterprise of democratic government. Nothing irreparable was lost so long as "freedom of the mind," with the accessory "consent of the governed," survived.

But this too was sorely strained in the decade following the Second World War. Confronted within and without by the menace of world Communism, many Americans grew afraid of the freedom they presumed to defend. Fear weakened the nerve of freedom, and they proposed to combat tyranny with tyranny's proven devices. Jefferson's voice was heard with most impressive effect during these years in the denunciation of the hysteria that proscribed heretical opinions, demanded oaths of loyalty, clogged the channels of public information, restricted political debate, and impaired the sovereign guarantees of personal liberty. Sometimes the voice was heard in strange quarters. When the Internal Revenue Service padlocked the office of the Communist *Daily Worker* in 1956, an agent remarked to the newspaper's editor, "now I suppose you will start quoting Thomas Jefferson." The editor, John Gates, promptly obliged. While no one would give a Jefferson nickel for the future of freedom under a Communist regime, it was equally certain that Jefferson's faith could not endure the fear that incited repression. "To be afraid of ideas," Alexander Meiklejohn declared, "any idea, is to be afraid of self-government." Perhaps, as Julian Boyd argued in several public addresses, the root of the trouble lay in the new pessimism about man's nature and his capacity for self-government. Distrusting the people, freedom's cowards could not accept Jefferson's fundamental proposition—his most quoted line in these times—that "error of opinion may be tolerated where reason is left free to combat it." Even if the trouble did not go this deep, the attack on freedom of thought and expression sapped the wellsprings of democratic government. Such had been Jefferson's conviction in the "terror of '98," and the underlying motivation of the Virginia and Kentucky Resolutions. Although these Resolutions served the reactionary cause of Southern segregationists, they performed a greater service, one authenticated by the latest historical judgment, in directly connecting Jefferson to the champions of freedom in an analogous situation a century and a half later. The ironic fact that the latter now found their best support in the federal courts illustrates once again how the accidents of time have turned Jefferson's political doctrines all around without, however, disturbing the axis of his faith.

Americans, it has been said, venerate Washington, love Lincoln, and remember Jefferson. The long and myriad chain of memory has passed to this generation with its most vital links worn and abused, but still intact. "Nothing, then, is unchangeable but the inherent and inalienable rights of man." When so many of Jefferson's values have slipped away, he may yet go on vindicating his power in the national life as the heroic voice of imperishable freedoms. It is this Jefferson who stands at the radiant center of his own history, and who makes for the present a symbol that unites the nation's birth with its inexorable ideal. But whether this and later generations will be able to repeat with earlier generations John Adams's deathbed deliverance, "Thomas Jefferson still survives," must depend on a power greater than Jefferson's historical momentum. It must depend, in the final analysis, on the conscious knowledge of Jefferson's faith and the responsible commitment to its survival.

GUIDE TO SOURCES

No even remotely complete bibliography of writings about Jefferson is in existence. The problem is discussed by William H. Peden, *Some Aspects of Jefferson Bibliography* (Lexington, Va., 1941). Three useful guides are Hamilton B. Tompkins, *Bibliotheca Jeffersoniana* (N.Y., 1887); Richard H. Johnston, "A Contribution to a Bibliography of Thomas Jefferson," in *The Writings of Thomas Jefferson*, XX (Washington, 1903); W. Harvey Wise, Jr. and John W. Cronin, *A Bibliography of Thomas Jefferson* (Wash., 1935). The best brief listing is in *The Literary History of the United States*, III (N.Y., 1948), to which a supplement is forthcoming. Francis Coleman Rosenberger, ed., *The Jefferson Reader* (N.Y., 1953) culls many of the best things written and said about Jefferson, and its introduction gives a conspectus of the literature.

The following Guide has two purposes. First, to acquaint the reader with the sources used in this study. Second, to make a modest contribution to Jefferson bibliography. In neither respect does the Guide approach completeness. Except where it was clearly inappropriate not to do so, I have rigorously excluded secondary sources. As to primary sources, I have omitted many things of routine interest and have often let a few titles serve as samples of a larger literature. I have tried to minimize the repetition, with more exact citations, of titles sufficiently indicated and described in the text. The Guide is intended to supplement as well as support the text.

Something should be said about newspaper sources. Sixty-nine separate newspapers were consulted for Book I, the extent of the use ranging from a few selected issues to continuous coverage for periods upwards to twenty-five years. Twenty-eight newspapers were consulted for Book II, with less continuous coverage. There are several reasons for the greater newspaper coverage of the earlier period. These newspapers are smaller and thus more convenient to use in a study of this type. They are more concerned with politics and therefore more concerned with Jefferson. The revolution that occurred in the dimensions and scope of American newspapers in the fourth quarter of the last century reduces the feasibility and importance of tracking Jefferson through this medium. The major compensations are, first, the abundance of writing on Jefferson in other media, particularly periodicals, and second, excellent indexes to a number of outstanding newspapers, most notably the *New York Times*, which have proved useful as well by furnishing leads into newspapers that are not indexed. The geographical concentration of the newspapers consulted is the Northeast and, more generally, the Atlantic Coast. Although the greater number, along with the accessibility, of these newspapers had something to do with the choice, it soon became evident to me that Jefferson was nearly always a livelier topic of discussion in the East than in the West.

As to manuscript sources, very few have been consulted for this study, partly because the subject is the *public* image of Jefferson and partly because adequate coverage of manuscript collections would have entailed years more labor in research than the subject warrants.

PROLOGUE

The best account of the last days, death, and burial of Jefferson is in Henry S. Randall, *The Life of Jefferson*, III (N.Y., 1858). The report of Jefferson's son-in-law, Thomas Mann Randolph, appears in the *N.Y. Eve. Post*, August 2, 1826. There are numerous recollections by his grandchildren, that of Septima Randolph Meikleham, for example, in Thomas Donaldson, *The House in which Jefferson wrote the Declaration of Independence* (Phila., 1898). David M. R. Culbreth, *The University of Virginia* (N.Y., 1908) reprints an interesting but probably inaccurate account of the funeral. Valuable on the funeral is the letter of Henry R. Worthington to R. B. Hicks, July 5, 1826 (MS, Alderman Library, University of Virginia). The history of the lottery and subscription funds may be reconstructed from the newspapers, especially the *Richmond Enquirer*, though Randall is helpful as always.

The leading Eastern newspapers carry the reports of the Jubilee, the deaths of Jefferson and Adams, and the public observances. Lyman Butterfield, "The Jubilee of Independence, July 4, 1826," *Va. Mag. of Hist. and Biog.*, LXI (April 1953) re-creates the occasion. For interesting reactions and reflections: Alexander H. Everett, *America* (Phila., 1827); John P. Kennedy, ed., *Memoirs of the Life of William Wirt* (Phila., 1849); Charles Chauncey Binney, *Life of Horace Binney* (Phila., 1903); "A Yankee," *A Glance at the Times* . . . (Phila., 1827). George Lippard rhapsodizes the Jubilee in *Washington and His Generals, or Legends of the Revolution* (Phila., 1847). The event is later recalled by Robert C. Winthrop, *A Century of Self-Government* (Boston, 1876), and still later by Francis N. Thorpe, "Adams and Jefferson: 1826-1926," *No. Amer. Rev.*, CCXXIII (June 1926). Eighteen of the eulogies are included in *A Selection of Eulogies, pronounced in the Several States, in Honor of those Illustrious Patriots and Statesmen, John Adams and Thomas Jefferson* (Hartford, 1826). The volume offers a good cross section of a vast literature, but it omits four of the best eulogies: Nicholas Biddle's before the American Philosophical Society, Samuel L. Mitchill's before the N.Y. Lyceum of Natural History, Samuel Harrison Smith's before the Columbian Institute of Washington, and Edward Everett's in Charlestown, Massachusetts. T. P. H. Lyman's *Life of Thomas*

Jefferson (Phila., 1826) suggests the range of public knowledge. On Jefferson's assets and liabilities as a hero, see Dixon Wecter's chapter in *The Hero in America: A Chronicle of Hero-Worship* (N.Y., 1941).

Randall covers the settlement of Jefferson's estate. The Edgehill-Randolph Papers at the Univ. of Va. contain useful information, as does the *Register of Debates in Congress* for several years after Jefferson's death. Paul Wilstach's *Jefferson and Monticello* (Garden City, 1925) is the standard but far from definitive account. There are numerous reports on Monticello and its deterioration: Anne Royall, *Southern Tour* ... (Phila., 1830); George Leiper in the *National Gazette* (Philadelphia), September 6, 1833, with a Virginian's rejoinder, September 25, 1833; J. S. Buckingham, *The Slave States of America* (London, 1842); Benson J. Lossing, "Monticello," *Harper's New Monthly Mag.*, VII (July 1853). An intimate view of Martha Jefferson Randolph and her father is in the reminiscences of Margaret Bayard Smith, *The First Forty Years of Washington Society*, Gaillard Hunt, ed. (London, 1906). See also the brief sketch by a granddaughter, Sarah N. Randolph, in Sarah Butler and Agnes Irwin, eds., *Worthy Women of Our First Century* (Phila., 1877), and a biography by Mildred Criss, *Jefferson's Daughter* (N.Y., 1948). On the David d'Angers statue, see *Réception de la Statue de Thomas Jefferson* ... (Mesnil, 1905). For the debate in Congress on Levy's gift, *Register of Debates*, 23 Cong., 1 Sess.; and for the final acceptance, *Report of the Senate Committee on Buildings and Grounds*, 43 Cong., 1 Sess., February 25, 1874 (Number 138).

I. RESURRECTION

George Dangerfield, *The Era of Good Feelings* (N.Y., 1952) provides the best single background against which to understand Jefferson's reaction to political events before his death. *Niles' Register* is particularly valuable as a depositary of National Republican thinking. Henry Clay's speeches have the same usefulness for this study. See his collected *Works*, Calvin Colton, ed., 7 v. (N.Y., 1897). Joseph Dorfman treats the American System political economists and their foes in *The Economic Mind in American Civilization*, II (N.Y., 1946). Leading theoretical statements for the opposition: Thomas Cooper, *Lectures on the Elements of Political Economy* (Columbia, S.C., 1826) and Thomas R. Dew, *Lectures on the Restrictive System* (Richmond, 1829). See also the collected writings of William B. Giles, *Political Miscellanies* (Richmond, 1829). Niles's counterpoise is Condy Raguet's *Free Trade Advocate*.

Martin Van Buren recalls his visit to Monticello in his *Autobiography*, J. C. Fitzpatrick, ed., *Annual Report of the American Historical Association for the Year 1918*, II (Wash., 1920). It is valuable for his views of political parties, but see in addition *Inquiry into the Origin & Course of Political Parties in the United States*, Edited by his Sons (N.Y., 1867). An abridged version of his Senate speech of 1828, "On the Powers of the Vice-Presidency," is in William M. Holland, *The Life and Political Opinions of Martin Van Buren* (Hartford, 1836). The Old Republicanism, which Van Buren typified, is evoked and analyzed in Charles Grier Sellers, Jr., *James K. Polk, Jacksonian* (Princeton, 1957). The *Proceedings and Address of the New Hampshire Republican State Convention* ... (Concord, 1828) points up the Jeffersonian ideology of the Jackson party. But the newspapers furnish a rich source. In the way of congressional debates, particularly revealing of attitudes toward Jefferson is the retrenchment debate, January-February 1828, in *Register of Debates*, 20 Cong., 1 Sess.

J. Q. Adams's "On the Discoveries of Captain Lewis" originally appeared in *The Monthly Anthology*, IV (March 1807). Sam Houston read it in the House of Representatives, February 1827, and it was later printed in several pro-Jackson newspapers. See also Evert and George L. Duyckinck, eds., *Cyclopedia of American Literature*, I (N.Y., 1856). The more damaging "Song Supposed to have been written by the Sage of Monticello," although attributed to Adams, was probably not his. It will be found in the *Port-Folio*, II (October 2, 1802) and in the *Albany Argus*, June 10, 1828. For Adams's complaint on the use of these verses against him, and for many comments on Jefferson, see his *Memoirs*, Charles Francis Adams, ed. (Phila., 1874-77).

Samuel L. Southard's address before the Columbian Institute will be found in the *National Gazette*, May 2, 1828. The best brief account of Jefferson's attitude on science and government, along with the history of the Coastal Survey, is A. Hunter Dupree, *Science in the Federal Government* (Cambridge, 1957). Henry Adams, *Life of Albert Gallatin* (Phila., 1879) is still indispensable for understanding the scientific and nationalistic aspects of Jeffersonian Republicanism. Jefferson's letter to Benjamin Austin, January 9, 1816, was repeatedly printed and widely discussed. Examples are Friedrich List, *Outlines of American Political Economy* ... (Phila., 1827); [Mathew Carey], *Examination of the Report* ... (Phila., 1828); *Niles' Register*, April 4, 1829. Several of Jefferson's letters in the same vein, none of them included in the *Memoirs* of 1829, were published in *Niles' Register*: August 2, 1828, March 7 and April 4, 1829, May 15, 1830. The career of the "Southworth forgery" may be followed in the *Richmond Enquirer*, particularly July-August 1830 and July 1838. See also the *National Intelligencer* (Washington), August 13, 1830; the *Cleveland Herald*, August 19, 1830; and Henry Clay's letters to Francis Brooke, August 17, 1830, June 23, 1831, in *The Private Correspondence of Henry Clay*, Calvin Colton, ed. (Boston, 1856). Interesting for Jefferson's position on internal improvements is the running debate between the *National Intelligencer* and the *Richmond Enquirer*, October-December 1826. There is a vast literature on Jefferson's political economy. Suggestive of the contrasting attitudes of recent scholars are the discussions in A. Whitney Griswold, *Farming and Democracy* (N.Y., 1948), Dorfman, *Economic Mind*, I, and William D. Grampp, "A Re-examination of Jeffersonian Economics," *Southern Economics Journal*, XII (January, 1946).

On Jefferson's opinion of Jackson: Edward Coles to a group of citizens of Illinois, (Edwardsville) *Illinois Intelligencer*, November 23, 1827; T. W. Gilmer's letter to Coles, *Richmond Enquirer*, December 25, 1827; Peter Minor to Garret Minor, August 1, 1826, as published in the *Richmond Enquirer*, January 3, 1828, confirms Coles's report; *Niles' Register*, December 29, 1827, reports Gilmer's disavowal; Thomas Mann Randolph's letter of August 18, 1827, is in the *Virginia Advocate* of that date and in other newspapers; D. C. Terrell's testimony favorable to Jackson is printed in the *National Gazette*, January 9, 1828; Daniel Webster's "Memorandum" of conversations with Jefferson is in Fletcher Webster, *Private Correspondence of Daniel Webster* (Boston, 1857). For William B. Giles's part in the controversy, see his *Political Miscellanies*. For Adams, see Henry Adams, ed., *Documents Relating to New England Federalism* (Boston, 1877). Thomas Jefferson Randolph tries to set the record straight in *To the Public* (Richmond, 1828). Jackson is viewed as a new Jefferson in John Warren James, *An Oration Delivered on the Occasion of the Inauguration of Andrew Jackson as President of the United States* (Boston, 1829).

Information bearing on the editing and publication of Jefferson's *Memoirs* may be found in the Edgehill-Randolph Papers (Univ. of Va.); the Lee Papers (Va. State Library); *Letters and Other Writings of James Madison*, Congress Edition (Phila., 1865); and George Tucker, *Life of Thomas Jefferson* (Phila., 1837). Martha Randolph's report on the editing is quoted from the Preface of "The Jefferson Papers," *Colls. of the Hist. Soc. of Mass.*, 7th Series, I, 1900. An obituary of T. J. Randolph appears in the *Charlottesville Chronicle*, October 22, 1875; see also Culbreth's recollection in *The University of Virginia*. One who knew Randolph well describes his feelings about his grandfather: Richard Thomas Walker Duke, Jr., "The Private Life of Thomas Jefferson," *Al. Bul. of the Univ. of Va.*, XIV (July, 1921). Very valuable is Randolph's long letter to Henry S. Randall in the latter's *Life*, Appendix XXVI. Joseph Vance's doctoral dissertation on Thomas Jefferson Randolph, Univ. of Va., was not available for this study. Helen D. Bullock, "The Papers of Thomas Jefferson," *American Archivist*, IV (October, 1941) is a description and historical account.

The temper of the reception may be gauged from the reviews in *The Southern Review*, V (February 1830), London's *Westminster Review*, XIII (October 1830), and the *No. Amer. Rev.*, XXX (April 1830). J. Q. Adams's protest against the latter is a letter to Alexander H. Everett, September 18, 1831, printed in the *Amer. Hist. Rev.*, XI (January 1906). See also Joseph B. Cobb, "Review of Jefferson's Memoirs," in his *Miscellanies, Historical, Literary and Political* (N.Y., 1858). Interesting sidelights: *N.Y. American*, February 6, 1830; *Niles' Register*, April 3, 1830; *Washington Globe*, June 18, 1831; Frances Trollope, *The Domestic Manners of the Americans* (London, 1832); William W. Story, ed., *Life and Letters of Joseph Story* (Boston, 1851). Nearly everything written or said on Jefferson for the next several decades is relevant for estimating the impact of the *Memoirs*.

On the Bayard vindication: *Register of Debates*, 21 Cong., 1 Sess.; Richard H. and James A. Bayard, *Documents Relating to the Presidential Election of the*

Year 1801 . . . (Phila., 1831); *Congressional Globe,* 33 Cong., 2 Sess. Early biographies of Jefferson and Burr discuss the episode. Madison's defense of Jefferson, first published in the *National Gazette,* is included in Tucker's *Life,* Appendix C. Other reactions unfavorable to Jefferson are reported in J. Q. Adams, *Memoirs,* VIII, and *Niles' Register,* February 6, 1830.

The Virginia background is treated in Maude H. Woodfin, "Contemporary Opinion in Virginia of Thomas Jefferson," in *Essays in Honor of William E. Dodd,* Avery Craven, ed. (Chicago, 1935). The state rights revival may be followed through the pages of the *Richmond Enquirer.* Charles Sydnor, *The Development of Southern Sectionalism, 1819-43* (Baton Rouge, 1953) is a superb historical study. There are numerous editions of the Virginia and Kentucky Resolutions: Richmond, 1826; Charleston, 1828; Boston, 1831; Richmond, 1832; Washington, 1832; Baltimore (*Niles' Register* Supplement), 1833; Richmond, 1835; Richmond, 1850; Alexandria, 1851; Richmond, 1859. The list does not purport to be complete. The Resolutions were repeatedly printed in newspapers, books, and political tracts. Spencer Roane's "Hampden" and "Sidney" essays are included in the *John P. Branch Historical Papers of Randolph Macon College,* I and II (1905, 1906). All of John Taylor's turgid works are pertinent, for example, *New Views of the Constitution* (Wash., 1823). Giles, *Political Miscellanies,* is important for Jefferson's role. Charles H. Ambler, *Thomas Ritchie: A Study in Virginia Politics* (Richmond, 1913) is a standard biography. Jefferson praises the *Enquirer* in a letter to William Short, September 8, 1823; but he indicates a different attitude in a letter to Nathaniel Macon, January 12, 1819, which was joyfully seized upon by the *Richmond Whig* when first published in 1837. John Marshall's feelings on the state rights idolatry are best summed up in a letter to Joseph Story, July 31, 1833, in John E. Oster, *The Political and Economic Doctrines of John Marshall* (N.Y., 1914). Albert J. Beveridge analyzes the Virginia developments from Marshall's viewpoint in *The Life of John Marshall,* IV (Boston, 1919). Joseph G. Baldwin, *The Flush Times of Alabama and Mississippi* (Americus, Ga., 1853) suggests the prestige of the "doctrines of '98" in the South.

Charles H. Ambler, *Sectionalism in Virginia from 1776 to 1860* (Chicago, 1910) and Fletcher M. Green, *Constitutional Development in the South Atlantic States, 1776-1860* (Chapel Hill, 1930) furnish backgrounds and foregrounds of the Virginia Convention. Very perceptive of Jefferson's importance are Hugh Blair Grigsby's discourses: *The Virginia Convention of 1829-30* (Richmond, 1854) and *The Virginia Convention of 1776* (Richmond, 1855). But nothing is as good as the source itself: *Proceedings and Debates of the Virginia Convention of 1829-30* (Richmond, 1830). On Randolph and Jefferson, see Hugh A. Garland, *Life of John Randolph* (N.Y., 1850) and a series of "Randolphiana," *Niles' Register,* September 13, 1834. Jefferson's letter to Kercheval was also used in the constitutional conventions of other states, for instance, *Proceedings and*

Debates of the Convention of the Commonwealth of Pennsylvania ... (Harrisburg, 1838), IV.

The best study of the Virginia slavery debate is Joseph Clark Robert, *The Road from Monticello*, a monograph in the *Historical Papers of the Trinity College Historical Society*, Series XXIV (Durham, N.C., 1941). Included are maps to show the density of the colored population and the sectional distribution of the vote on a test question. Its generous extracts from the debates must be supplemented by the reports in the Richmond newspapers. William Lloyd Garrison's *The Liberator*, in Boston, shows great interest in the debate and in Jefferson's relation to it. Benjamin Watkins Leigh assails Jefferson and the reformers in the "Appomattox" letters, *Richmond Enquirer*, February 4, 28, 1832. Thomas R. Dew's *Review* may be found in *The Pro-Slavery Argument* (Phila., 1853). For the opposite side: [Jesse B. Harrison], *Review of the Slave Question, extracted from the American Quarterly Review, December 1832* ... (Richmond, 1833). [Henry Ruffner], *Address to the People of West Virginia* (Lexington, Va., 1847) shows the survival of Jefferson's anti-slavery ideas; and F. L. Olmsted, *Journey in the Seaboard Slave States* (N.Y., 1854) recalls the fate of Jefferson's plan. Herbert E. Wilgis, Jr., "State Rights in Virginia, 1829-1833" (Senior Thesis, Princeton University, 1957), analyzes by sections the crucial votes in the constitutional convention, the slavery debate, and the nullification debate of the following year. It provides convincing documentation of the ideological conflict between democracy and state rights.

Historians grew thoroughly tired of the nullification controversy a long time ago; a fresh look is badly needed. Valuable studies on or around the subject are Frederic Bancroft, *Calhoun and the South Carolina Nullification Movement* (Baltimore, 1928); Charles M. Wiltse, *John C. Calhoun, Nullifier, 1829-1839* (Indianapolis, 1949); Jesse T. Carpenter, *The South as a Conscious Minority, 1789-1861* (N.Y., 1930), Louis M. Hartz, "South Carolina vs. the United States," in Daniel Aaron, ed., *America in Crisis* (N.Y., 1952). Several scholarly articles establish the basis for distinguishing the Virginia case in 1798 from the South Carolina case in 1832, for instance, P. G. Davisson, "Virginia and the Alien and Sedition Laws," *Amer. Hist. Rev.*, XXXVI (January 1931) and Adrienne Koch and Harry Ammon, "The Virginia and Kentucky Resolutions: An Episode in Jefferson's and Madison's Defense of Civil Liberties," *Wm. and Mary Qtly.*, 3rd Series, V (April 1948).

The story about John Randolph and James Hamilton, Jr., is reported in [Lewis Cuger], *Sovereign Rights of the States* (Wash., n.d.). Hamilton's Walterborough address is *The Operation of the Tariff on the Interests of the South, and the Constitutional Means of Redressing Its Evils* (Charleston, 1828). He tells of the effect of the Resolutions of '98 on him in a public letter, *Columbia Telescope*, September 3, 1830. On William Smith's Jeffersonianism, see J. B. O'Neall, *Biographical Sketches of the Bench and Bar in South Carolina*, 2 v. (Charleston, 1859), and Benjamin F. Perry, *Reminiscences of Public Men* (Phila., 1833).

Dumas Malone, *The Public Life of Thomas Cooper* (N.Y., 1926), points up Cooper's relations with Jefferson. Cooper's tract *Consolidation* ... (Columbia, S.C., 1824) was scarcely less important than [Robert J. Turnbull's] *The Crisis: or Essays on the Usurpations of the Federal Government* (Charleston, 1827) in alerting South Carolina. Nothing should be overlooked in Calhoun's *Works,* Richard K. Crallé, ed., 6 v. (N.Y., 1851-56). The Nullifiers' use of Jefferson may be seen in the following: Robert J. Turnbull, *An Oration Delivered in Charleston* ... *on the 4th of July, 1832* (Charleston, 1832); Robert Y. Hayne, *An Oration* ... *4th of July, 1831* (Charleston, 1831); William Harper, *The Remedy by State Interposition, or Nullification* ... (Charleston, 1830); A. P. Butler and others in *The Debate in the South Carolina Legislature, in December, 1830* ... (Columbia, S.C., 1831). The conjuring is satirized in [A. S. Johnson], *Memoirs of a Nullifier* (Columbia, 1832) and in C. G. Memminger's "The Book of Nullification," which is appended to Henry D. Capers, *The Life and Times of C. G. Memminger* (Richmond, 1893).

The famous debate on Foot's Resolution consumes most of the *Register of Debates,* 21 Cong., 1 Sess. Jefferson is much in evidence throughout. The proceedings and address of the Jefferson Birthday Dinner may be found in the *Richmond Enquirer,* April 23, 1830. For the view, generally held at the time, that the affair was engineered by Calhoun and his followers to christen nullification in Jefferson's name: Van Buren, *Autobiography;* Thomas Hart Benton, *Thirty Years View* ... 2 v. (N.Y., 1854); *Niles' Register,* April 24, 1830. This view is rejected by Richard R. Sternberg, "The Jefferson Birthday Dinner, 1830," *Journal of Southern History,* IV (August 1938) and Wiltse, *Calhoun, Nullifier.*

The *Richmond Enquirer,* March 13, 1832, makes the first publication of Jefferson's manuscript draft of the Kentucky Resolutions of 1798. Jonathan Elliot includes it in his edition of the Virginia and Kentucky Resolutions (Wash., 1832). For Madison's discovery of the draft, see his letters to Edward Everett, September 10, 1830, and Nicholas P. Trist, September 23, 1830, *Writings of James Madison,* Gaillard Hunt, ed. (N.Y., 1910). The startling effect of the discovery is recalled in the *Life of John C. Calhoun* (N.Y., 1843), a work authoritatively attributed to Calhoun himself. From 1830 until his death Madison was preoccupied with the constitutional and political questions raised by nullification. His letters and writings offer the best critical analysis. Unionist arguments that distinguish the historic and the Carolina doctrines: Langdon Cheeves, "Occasional Reviews," *Richmond Enquirer,* October 9, 1832; William Smith, "To the Good People of South Carolina," *Columbia Telescope,* November 12, 1830; William Drayton, *An Oration* ... *July 4, 1831* (Charleston, 1831). Hugh S. Legaré's invective against "St. Thomas of *Canting*-bury" is scattered through his *Writings,* Mary S. Legaré Bullen, ed., 2 v. (N.Y., 1846).

State Papers on Nullification (Boston, 1834) collects the important documents. *An Imaginary Conversation between President Jackson and the Ghost of Jefferson* (Columbia, 1831) anticipates the Nullifiers' reaction to Jackson's proclamation. Littleton W. Tazewell, *A Review of the Proclamation* . . . (Norfolk, 1888), which originally appeared in a Virginia newspaper in 1833, shows the extreme reaction of some Virginia state-rightists. There is no published study of the debate in the House of Delegates. Wilgis, "State Rights in Virginia," already cited, treats the subject. Jackson's little noticed "authorized exposition" appears in the *Washington Globe*, September 21, 1833. Condy Raguet's *Examiner and Journal of Political Economy* stated one month later that not a single Northern newspaper had published the exposition. Ritchie reports his conversation with Jackson in the *Enquirer*, March 9, 1837. Frederick W. Seward, *Autobiography of William H. Seward* (N.Y., 1877) highlights the importance of the New York report on nullification. One of the South Carolina developments subsequent to the proclamation is covered in *The Book of Allegiance; or, A Report of the Arguments of Counsel, and Opinions of the Court of Appeals of South Carolina on the Oath of Allegiance* . . . (Columbia, 1834).

II. DEMOCRACY

The newspapers and biographies, especially Randall's, are the best source of Jefferson anecdote and legend. John Davis's famous tale first appeared in his *Travels of Four Years and a Half in the United States of America* . . . (London, 1803). Several stories of the two types described, as told by the court and legislative stenographer, Arthur J. Stansbury, are reprinted in John Frost, *The Presidents of the United States* (Boston, 1855). *The Yankee in London; or A Short Trip to America* (Phila., 1826) and *The Philosophical Emperor: A Political Experiment; or, The Progress of a False Position* (N.Y., 1841) continue the Federalist tradition of satire.

The roles of symbol and myth, ideology, and tradition in American government and politics have not been systematically studied. Several conceptual formulations that have proven helpful: Alfred North Whitehead, *Symbolism, Its Meaning and Effect* (Cambridge, 1928); Karl Mannheim, *Ideology and Utopia*, Louis Wirth and Edward A. Shils, tr. (N.Y., n.d.); Lyman Bryson and others, eds., *Symbols and Values: An Initial Study* (N.Y., 1954); Walter Lippmann, *Public Opinion* (N.Y., 1922); George Woodcock, *The Writer and Politics* (London, 1948); Kenneth Burke, *Permanence and Change; An Anatomy of Purpose* (N.Y., 1936) and *The Philosophy of Literary Form; Studies in Symbolic Action* (Baton Rouge, 1941); William A. Dunning, "Truth in History," *Amer. Hist. Rev.*, XIX (1914). Of the writings on American history, the following may be singled out as particularly suggestive: A. V. Dicey, "An English View of American Conservatism," in Gustav Pollok, ed., *Fifty Years of American Idealism: The New York Nation, 1865-1915* (Boston, 1915); Henry Jones Ford, *The Rise and Growth of American Politics* (N.Y., 1898); M. Ostrogorski, *Democracy and the Organization of Parties*, II (N.Y., 1902); Max Lerner, "The Constitution and Court as Symbols," in *Ideas for the Ice Age* (N.Y., 1941); William Y. Elliott, "The Constitution as the American Social Myth," in Conyers Read, ed., *The Constitution Reconsidered* (New Haven, 1938); Gunnar Myrdal,

"American Ideals," in *An American Dilemma,* I (N.Y., 1944); A. M. Schlesinger, Jr., *The Age of Jackson* (Boston, 1945), Chapter XXXVII; Richard Hofstadter, *The American Political Tradition* ... (N.Y., 1948); Louis Hartz, *Economic Policy and Democratic Thought: Pennsylvania 1776-1860* (Cambridge, 1948) and *The Liberal Tradition in America* (Cambridge, 1955); Henry Nash Smith, *Virgin Land: The American West as Symbol and Myth* (Cambridge, 1950); Daniel Boorstin, *The Genius of American Politics* (Chicago, 1953); John William Ward, *Andrew Jackson, Symbol for an Age* (N.Y., 1955); Marvin Meyers, "The Jacksonian Persuasion," *The American Qtly.,* V (Spring 1953). Mr. Meyers's book of the same title, along with Bray Hammond, *Banks and Politics in America* (Princeton, 1957) appeared too late to be of use to the present study.

Specific recognitions in the Jackson era of Jefferson's importance as a political symbol associated with the Democratic party may be found in the following: *The Examiner and Journal of Political Economy,* November 13, 1834; *Washington Globe,* August 27, 1832; Robert Rantoul, "Fourth of July Oration, at Scituate, Massachusetts, 1836," in his *Memoirs,* Luther Hamilton, ed. (Boston, 1854); George M. Dallas, *Oration on the Centennial Anniversary of the Birth of Thomas Jefferson* ... (Phila., 1843); Abel P. Upshur, "Mr. Jefferson," *Southern Literary Messenger,* VI (September 1838); Alexander H. Everett, *The Conduct of the Administration* (Boston, 1832); William Cost Johnson, in *Register of Debates,* 25 Cong., 1 Sess. Usage of the axiom "words [or names] are things" will be found in H. M. Brackenridge, "To the Democratic Party," *National Intelligencer,* January 23, 1840; John P. Kennedy, *Quodlibet* (Phila., 1840); Daniel Webster, Speech at Patchogue, New York, 1840, *The Writings and Speeches* ... National Edition (Boston, 1903). On "democracy" as a talisman, see especially Calvin Colton, ed., in *Works of Clay,* I. On "Federalism" as a pejorative: *Washington Globe,* November 28, December 28, 1837, January 2, 1838; *N.Y. Advertiser,* August 18, 1830; *National Intelligencer,* August 11, 1847. Two Jacksonian formulations of "the history of the parties" are "A Committee," *A Compilation of Political Historic Sketches* (Carrollton, Ohio, 1838), and Benjamin F. Hallett, *An Oration Delivered July 4th, 1836* (Boston, 1836). John Quincy Adams's posthumously published *Parties in the United States* (N.Y., 1941) is valuable for the Whig side. Benton's *Thirty Years View* is the most convenient compendium of the citation and use of Jefferson in political discussion. The currency of Jefferson's letter to Albert Gallatin, December 13, 1803, is suggested by the fact that it was printed at least once a year for five consecutive years in the *Frankfort* (Ky.) *Argus:* June 29, 1830, March 15, 1831, September 12, 1832, September 11, 1833, January 22, 1834. The *Richmond Enquirer,* July 15, 1831, and the *Boston Post,* September 25, 1838, discover in it "the germ" of the sub-treasury system. See also William M. Meigs, *The Life of Charles Jared Ingersoll* (Phila., 1897). The *Albany Argus,* October 10, 1829, revived Jefferson's report on the unconstitutionality of the first United States Bank. N. P. Tallmadge's speech in the New York Senate, printed in the *Argus*, April 3, 1832, suggests how the report was used.

Joseph Blau, ed., *Social Theories of Jacksonian Democracy* (N.Y., 1947) is a useful collection of Jacksonian writings of a more or less theoretical character. For the concept of "Nature," Ward's *Andrew Jackson* is especially good. Richard Hofstadter, "William Leggett, Spokesman of Jacksonian Democracy," *Political Science Qtly.*, XLVIII (December 1943) is a key article. George Bancroft's extended parallel on John Locke and William Penn in his *History of the United States*, II, 11th ed. rev. (Boston, 1860) touches a vital theme. See also Edwin Forrest, *Oration . . . in the City of New York, Fourth July, 1838* (N.Y., 1838); John L. O'Sullivan, "Introduction: The Democratic Principle . . ." *United States Mag. and Democratic Review*, I (October-December 1837); "Declaration of Principles of the Locofoco Party," in Fitzwilliam Byrdsall, *History of the Loco Foco or Equal Rights Party* (N.Y., 1842). The concept of "popular sovereignty" is superbly analyzed, though with doctrinaire enthusiasm, in Edwin Mims, Jr., *The Majority of the People* (N.Y., 1941). Henry S. Commager, *Majority Rule and Minority Rights* (N.Y., 1943) treats the problem with respect to constitutional law. Several of the works by European commentators are penetrating: Alexis de Tocqueville, *Democracy in America*, 2 v., Henry Reeve, tr. (N.Y., 1899); Harriet Martineau, *Society in America*, 2 v. (N.Y., 1837); Francis J. Grund, *Aristocracy in America*, 2 v. (London, 1839). The best statement of George Bancroft's majoritarianism is "The Progress of Mankind," *Literary and Historical Miscellanies* (N.Y., 1953). Schlesinger, *The Age of Jackson*, Chapter XXXI, treats a significant debate on the majority rule principle. *Speech of Mr. Rathbun of New York . . . Delivered in the House of Representatives* (Wash., 1844) illustrates the uses of Jefferson in reference to the Door Rebellion. Benjamin F. Hallett's argument before the Supreme Court in the crucial case that grew out of the Rhode Island controversy, *The Right of the People to Establish Forms of Government* (Boston, 1848), brilliantly states the radical Jeffersonian position. The agrarian conception of "the people" is indicated in Jackson's third and fourth annual messages to Congress, in Van Buren's *Inquiry*, and many other places. It is vigorously attacked by J. Q. Adams (and Lewis Condict), "Minority Report of the Committee on Manufactures . . ." *Register of Debates*, 22 Cong., 2 Sess. Alexander H. Everett, having earlier reviewed Victor Cousin's *Lectures on the History of Philosophy*, applied his definition of the "Great Man" to Jefferson in "Origin and Character of the Old Parties," *No. Amer. Rev.*, XXXIX (July 1834). For Bancroft's conception of democratic "genius" see the following: *Oration Delivered before the Democracy of Springfield . . . July 4, 1836* (Springfield, Mass., 1836); *Address at Hartford . . . February 18, 1840* (Boston, 1840); Review of George Ripley's *Philosophical Miscellanies*, in the *Washington Globe*, March 9, 1838; and the famous chapter on Jefferson and the Declaration in the *History*, VIII. William Holland, *Life of Van Buren* also elaborates the conception. Ralph Waldo Emerson's *Representative Men*, along with several of his essays, is a fruitful source for the character and role of great men.

The synthesis of conservative ideas and attitudes in respect to Jefferson has been drawn from a wide variety of sources. Perhaps the best brief statement is the article, "Our Political Errors," *Amer. Qtly. Rev.*, XXII (September 1837). Often cited and quoted, it was usually attributed to the journal's editor, Robert Walsh. For Francis Lister Hawks, see especially the *New York Review and Quarterly Church Journal*, I-IV (1837-39), which he edited. Orestes Brownson, *Works*, Henry F. Brownson, ed., 20 v. (Detroit, 1887) is of first importance for the distinction between "republic" and "democracy." The classicist and theologian, Taylor Lewis, conducted the "Editor's Table" in *Harper's Magazine* for several years; see also his *Discourse on the True Idea of the State as a Religious Institution* . . . (Andover, Mass., 1843). Less systematic but illuminating are the following: Stephen Simpson, *The Life of Thomas Jefferson, with Parallel comprising Washington and Jefferson* (Phila., 1844); Rufus Griswold, *The Prose Writers of America* (Phila., 1846); [Charles Fenton Mercer], *An Exposition of the Weakness and Inefficiency of the Government of the United States of North America* (n.p., 1945); [Calvin Colton], *Democracy* (N.Y., 1844) and *A Voice from America to England* (London, 1839); Joseph Seawell Jones, *A Defense of the Revolutionary History of the State of North Carolina from the Aspersions of Mr. Jefferson* (Boston, 1834). Some of the works listed under Chapter III below are equally pertinent to conservative thought. Several newspapers expressed their hatred of Jefferson with considerable vehemence, for example, the *Boston Courier*, the *N. Y. American*, the *N. Y. Advertiser*, and the *Cincinnati Daily Gazette*.

The conservative view of the proper relationship between religion and government is expressed in the works of Hawks, Lewis, Colton, and Brownson, already cited, and also in the following: Joseph Story, *Commentaries on the Constitution of the United States*, 3 v. (Boston, 1833); Floyd S. Mines, *The Church the Pillar and Ground of the Truth* (N.Y., 1838); Jaspar Adams, *The Relations of Christianity to Civil Government in the United States* (Charleston, 1833); and [Henry W. Warner], *An Inquiry into the Moral and Religious Character of American Government* (N.Y., 1838). The last named work has also been attributed to Theodore Frelinghuysen. Jefferson is nearly always depicted as an infidel or atheist in this literature. John Trumbull, the painter and youthful friend of Jefferson, reports his own tilt with the infidel in his *Autobiography* (New Haven, 1841); it is included in Rufus Griswold's nostalgic *The Republican Court, or American Society in the Days of Washington* (N.Y., 1855). Justus E. Moore, *The Warning of Thomas Jefferson* . . . (Phila., 1844) is answered by *The Pope and the Presbyterians: A Review of the Warning of Jefferson* (Phila., 1845). The *Register of Debates*, 22 Cong., 1 Sess., supplemented by *Correspondence of Andrew Jackson*, J. S. Bassett, ed. (Wash., 1926-33), gives the facts on the fast day controversy in the federal government, as does the *Albany*

Argus, June-November 1832, on the New York controversy at the same time. The movement for a religious amendment to the Constitution was born at Xenia, Ohio, February 4, 1863. A very interesting document is the *Proceedings of the National Convention to secure the Religious Amendment of the Constitution* ... (Phila., 1874).

Courtney Kenney traces "The Evolution of the Law of Blasphemy," with special reference to England, *Cambridge Law Journal,* I (1922). W. S. Holsworth, *A History of English Law,* VIII (Boston, 1926) presents a somewhat different view and one which gives less importance to Jefferson's alleged discovery. For that discovery, see Jefferson's essay, "Whether Christianity is part of the Common Law?" appended to *Report of Cases determined in the General Court of Virginia, from 1730 to 1740, and from 1768 to 1772* (Charlottesville, 1829). Johnson Brigham first brought this essay to public notice in the law magazine, *Green Bag,* XII (August 1900). Jefferson enclosed an abbreviated copy of the essay in a letter to Thomas Cooper, February 10, 1814; Cooper takes Jefferson's opinion in his *Treatise on the Law of Libel and Liberty of the Press* ... (N.Y., 1830). Joseph Story's main criticism of Jefferson's well-known letter to John Cartwright appears in *The American Jurist and Law Magazine,* XVIII (April, 1833). See also the answer to the query, "Is Christianity a Part of the Common Law of England?" *American Qtly. Christian Spectator,* VIII (March 1836). Jefferson's argument had several uses for liberals: Thomas Herttell, for example, used it in his brilliant brief, *The Demurrer* (N.Y., 1828), against the common law basis for determining the credibility of witnesses. Of the several treatments of the Abner Kneeland case, the best is Leonard W. Levy, "Satan's Last Apostle in Massachusetts," *American Qtly,* V (Spring 1953). The prosecution and defense arguments: Samuel D. Parker, *Arguments of the Attorney for the Commonwealth in the Trials of Abner Kneeland, for Blasphemy* (Boston, 1834) and Andrew Dunlap, *A Speech* ... *in Defense of Abner Kneeland* ... (Boston, 1834). The United States Supreme Court's recent adherence to Jefferson's conception of the First Amendment ("a wall of separation between Church and State") is shown most clearly in Illinois *ex rel* McCollum *v.* Board of Education of Champaign, Illinois, 333 U.S. 203 (1948).

On the origins of the Whig name for the opposition party, see E. Malcolm Carroll, *Origins of the Whig Party* (Durham, N.C., 1925). The *N.Y. Courier and Enquirer,* April 1 and May 1, 1834, takes credit for the christening. The Jacksonian defense of the administration's removal policy, by analogy to Jefferson's, may be seen in the *Argus of Western America,* May 10, 1829 and June 24, 1829; *Washington Globe,* October 8, 1831, and October 29, 1835; Isaac Hill's speech in the House, *Register of Debates,* 23 Cong., 2 Sess.; Benton, *Thirty Years View,* I. The Old Federalist arraignment of Jackson, by analogy to Jefferson: *Boston Courier,* September 30, 1834; William Sullivan, *Familiar Letters on Public Characters and Public Events* (Boston, 1834). The Whig position is best stated by Henry Clay, Speech at Lexington, Ky., 1829, *Works,* V.

An interesting exchange between John Bell and J. Q. Adams is reported in the *Cong. Globe*, 26 Cong., 1 Sess. On William C. Rives's experience with the bill to prohibit electioneering by federal officials: *Cong. Globe*, 25 Cong., 3 Sess., and his speech at Louisa Court House, Va., September 7, 1839 (*Richmond Enquirer*, October 29 and November 1, 1839). Old Federalist regrets on the strong executive are expressed in Sullivan, *Letters*, and also in the *Boston Atlas*, May 28, 1836. Wilfred Binkley has a penetrating analysis of this aspect of Whig ideology in *President and Congress* (N.Y., 1947). The insurgency of a stalwart Old Republican is treated in Raymond Dingledean, "The Political Career of William Cabell Rives," Doctoral Dissertation, University of Virginia, 1947.

Noah Webster's "Sidney" letter originally appeared in the *N.Y. Commercial Advertiser*, November 20, 1837; a Democratic version is *Appeal to Americans* (n.p., n.d.) Two similar letters, "Marcellus" and "To the Honorable Daniel Webster," are in Noah Webster, *A Collection of Papers on Political, Literary, and Moral Subjects* (N.Y., 1843). The reactions of two liberal Whig newspapers: *Albany Journal*, December 1, 1837, and the *N.Y. Courier and Enquirer*, December 16, 1837. The Address of the Whig Young Men's Convention in 1838 will be found in the *N.Y. American*, July 24, 1838. Most of the newspapers in the state apparently had something to say about it. The *Boston Atlas*, July-December 1838, espouses democratic realism while its rival, the *Daily Advertiser and Patriot*, denounces the strategy. The flavor of the Whig campaign of 1840, together with several of Harrison's speeches, is preserved in A. B. Norton, *The Great Revolution of 1840: Reminiscences of the Log Cabin and Hard Cider Campaign* (Mount Vernon, Ohio, 1888). Webster's log cabin lament is in his Speech at Saratoga, N.Y., August 19, 1840, *Speeches and Writings*, III. His later speeches in Virginia draw the wrath of the *Richmond Enquirer*, September 29, October 6, 1840. Philosophical reflections which heighten the significance of the election for the Jefferson symbol are furnished by Benjamin F. Butler in *The Rough Hewer* (Albany), October 22, 1840; Horace Greeley in *The Log Cabin* (Albany), December 26, 1840; and Charles G. Greene in the *Boston Post*, November 7, 18, 1840.

III. HISTORY I

The *Southern Literary Messenger*, I-XXXVI, 1834-66, is a principal source for Virginia attitudes toward Jefferson and the history he made. The image of the "mighty reformer" dominates its pages. Always respectful of Jefferson, the magazine indicates a good deal of dissatisfaction with his revolutionary reforms in Virginia, his supposedly French philosophy and irreligion, and his educational projects. Hugh Blair Grigsby, *The Virginia Convention of 1776*, previously cited, and *Oration . . . in Norfolk on the 4th July, 1831* (Norfolk, 1831) point up the exaggerated view of Jefferson's abolition of entail and primogeniture in Virginia. Clarence R. Keim, "Influence of Primogeniture and Entail in the Development of Virginia," *Univ. of Chicago Abstracts of Theses, Humanistic Series*, V (1926) corrects a historic misconception. Several magazines published at the University of Virginia, along with the periodic anniversary orations of its Jefferson Society, are suggestive, particularly with respect to education and religion. *The Jefferson Monument Magazine* (1849-51) promoted an unsuccessful student campaign for a Jefferson statue in the University. But the House of Delegates (*Journal*, February 21, 1854) provided for a statue to be sculptored by Alexander Galt, which was later installed in the Rotunda.

Burton J. Hendrick, *The Lees of Virginia: Biography of a Family* (Boston, 1935) sketches the checkered career of Henry Lee, the younger. Henry A. Wise, *Seven Decades of the Union* (Phila., 1876) gives a revealing glimpse of Lee's exile. Other details are in the Lee Papers, Va. State Library, Richmond. Madison's reaction will be found in the Congress Edition of his *Writings*. The *N.Y. American* praises the *Observations*, April 5, 1832, and prints extracts, May 10, 1832. But the work was not generally noticed in the press. Randall's Appendix XXXII, *Life*, is important for understanding Lee's character and motives. Randall discusses the governorship crisis in the context of historical controversy about it. Other Virginia criticisms contemporary with Lee's *Observations*: Robert R. Howison, *A History of Virginia* (Richmond, 1848); Henry A. Morgan, *A Description of the Peaks of Otter, with Sketches and Anecdotes of Patrick Henry, John Randolph and Thomas Jefferson* (Lynchburg, Va., 1853); "History of Richmond," *So. Lit. Mes.*, XVII (December 1851). H. J. Eckenrode, *Revolution in Virginia* (Boston, 1916) continues this tradition, while its reversal in recent years may be seen in Marie Kimball, *Jefferson: War and Peace* (N.Y., 1947) and Paul Green, *The Common Glory, A Symphonic Drama of American History* (Chapel Hill, 1948).

Howard R. Marraro scrutinizes "The Four Versions of Jefferson's Letter to Mazzei," *Wm. and Mary Qtly.*, 2nd Series, XXII (January 1942). Jefferson's late defense is his letter to Martin Van Buren, June 28, 1824; Randall reprints it with his own analysis as Appendix XVI of his *Life*. The letter was called forth by Timothy Pickering's *Review of the Correspondence between the Hon. John Adams . . . and the late William Cunningham, Esq.* (Salem, 1824). John Marshall reaches conclusions similar to Lee's in the revised edition of the *Life of George Washington* (Phila., 1832). Two articles by Philip M. Marsh are important for Freneau: "Freneau and Jefferson: The Poet-Editor Speaks for Himself about the *National Gazette* Episode," *American Literature*, VIII (1936) and "The Griswold Story of Freneau and Jefferson," *Amer. Hist. Rev.*, LI (1945). Pickering's *Review* first raised the question of a late correspondence between Jefferson and Washington, but it was rumored in Virginia before that. On this and the "Langhorne letter," see Randall, *Life*.

George Tucker's manuscript "Autobiography" is in the Alderman Library, University of Virginia. Also valuable for understanding his outlook are his *Essays on Various Subjects of Taste, Morals, and National Policy* (Georgetown, 1822); his novel, *The Valley of the Shenandoah, or Memoirs of the Graysons* (N.Y., 1824); and his *History of the United States*, 4 v. (Phila., 1856-57), which is probably the closest approximation of a Jeffersonian history of the republic to be written before the Civil War. See also, Leonard C. Helderman, "A Social Scientist of the Old South," *Journal of Southern History*, II (May 1936); Jessie Bernard, "George Tucker, Liberal Southern Social Scientist," *Social Forces*, XXV (December 1946 and May 1947); Dorfman, *Economic Mind*, II. Tucker's relationship with Madison is documented in both editions of the latter's works and also in unpublished letters in the Madison Papers, Library of Congress. Abel P. Upshur's review in the *So. Lit. Mes.*, VI (September 1840) and "A Voice of Virginia," *ibid.* VII (April 1841) indicate the biography's high stature in Virginia. It was not much noticed or read in the North. The *American Qtly. Review* pointedly refused to review it on the grounds of its dangerous political tendency. An edition in England proved a losing proposition, but it may have contributed to raising Jefferson's prestige with some Englishmen. See Lord Brougham's *Historical Sketches of Statesmen Who Flourished in the Times of George III*, 3rd Series (London, 1843).

Francis Lister Hawks's violent attack, "Character of Jefferson," appears in the *N.Y. Review and Qtly. Church Journal*, I (March 1837). It is answered in the *So. Lit. Mes.*, IV (April 1838) and, though anonymously, by Tucker himself: *Defense of the Character of Thomas Jefferson* ... (N.Y., 1838). Hawks's opinion of the disastrous effect of Jefferson's blows against the religious establishment in Virginia was widely shared: Robert Baird, *Religion in America* ... (N.Y., 1844), and Samuel Wilberforce, *A History of the Protestant Episcopal Church in America* (N.Y., 1849). The tradition, somewhat moderated, is continued in George M. Brydon, *Virginia's Mother Church*, 2 v. (Phila., 1952) and the author's subsequent articles. But many Virginians, including clerics, were to take a more generous view of Jefferson's work: William Meade, *Old Churches, Ministers and Families of Virginia* (Phila., 1857), and Howison, *History*. The same may be said of Virginia opinion of the University where, it was generally agreed, Jefferson's design to exclude religion had failed. See, for example, Howison's *History;* Anne Royall, *Southern Tour;* "University of Virginia," *So. Lit. Mes.*, VIII (January 1842); and William Hooper, *Fifty Years Since: An Address* ... (Raleigh, 1859). Dr. Stephen Higginson Tyng's letter appears in *The Episcopal Recorder*, June 13, 1840, and in the *Virginia Advocate*, July 4, 1840. The latter's high estimate of Jefferson's local reputation accords with that of several writers, for example, Henry D. Gilpin, "Thomas Jefferson," in John Sanderson, ed., *Biography of the Signers of the Declaration of Independence* (Phila., 1828). The Lee Papers, however, attest to violent feelings in some quarters. The *Virginia Advocate*, August 8, 1840, reports the resolutions of the Albemarle citizenry disavowing Dr. Tyng's statements. The affair is treated, with notice of Dr. Tyng's recantation, in Randall, *Life*, Appendix XXXVII.

On William Sullivan, see Samuel Eliot Morison, *Life and Letters of Harrison Gray Otis*, 2 v. (Boston, 1913); Peter O. Thacher's eulogy in the *National Gazette*, October 17, 1839; and the biographical sketch by John T. S. Sullivan, a son, in the edition he prepared of the *Letters* under the title, *The Public Men of the Revolution* (Phila., 1847). Alexander H. Everett's sixty-page "Origin and Character of the Old Parties" is in the *No. Amer. Rev.*, XXXIX (July 1834). Sullivan replies in *Remarks on Article IX* ... (July 1834). Everett counters with "Character of Jefferson," *No. Amer. Rev.*, XXXX (January 1835). Letters from both, and their partisans, appear in the *Boston Courier.* See also Everett's *Address* ... *in Commemoration of the Victory of New Orleans* (Boston, 1836) and *A Defense of the Character and Principles of Mr. Jefferson* ... *on the 4th of July, 1836* (Boston, 1836). Schlesinger, *Age of Jackson,* makes some interesting observations on Everett's politics.

Theodore Dwight, *The Character of Thomas Jefferson, as Exhibited in his own Writings* (Boston, 1839) is probably the best-known statement of the Federalist case. Dwight frequently refers to Jefferson in the *N.Y. Advertiser,* which he edited until 1835. Federalist arraignments of Jefferson on the law and the judiciary: Story, *Commentaries on the Constitution;* Nathan Dane, *A General Abridgment and Digest of American Law* (Boston, 1824, 1829); Nathaniel Chipman, *Principles of Government: A Treatise on Free Institutions* (Burlington, Vt., 1833). On immigration and naturalization: Alden Bradford, *History of the Federal Government* (Boston, 1840); Dwight, *Character of Jefferson.* On the naval and "peace policy": Theodore Dwight, *History of the Hartford Convention* ... (N.Y., 1833); Sullivan, *Letters;* Bradford, *History.* The Embargo had few defenders anywhere, though Jefferson's naval policy is viewed favorably in B. L. Rayner, *Sketches of the Life, Writings and Opinions of Thomas Jefferson* (N.Y., 1832) and in James Fenimore Cooper, *History of the Navy of the United States,* 2nd ed., corrected (Phila., 1840).

Alfred H. Kelly, in *The Marcus W. Jernegan Essays in American Historiography,* William T. Hutchinson, ed. (Chicago, 1937) treats Hildreth, the historian, as "the complete Federalist." The description is quite mistaken. Hildreth is better appreciated by Arthur M. Schlesinger, Jr., "The Problem of Richard Hildreth," *New England Qtly.,* XIII (June 1940). See also Donald E. Emerson, *Richard Hildreth* (Baltimore, 1947). Several generations of the Adams family were preoccupied with Jefferson. J. Q. Adams's deepest feelings are expressed in his *Memoirs.* Of his writings and speeches, see especially the following: *An Eulogy: On the Life and Character of James Madison* (Boston, 1836); *An Eulogy: On the Life and Character of James Monroe* (Boston, 1831); *An Oration Delivered before the Inhabitants of the Town of Newburyport* ... (Newburyport, Mass., 1837); *The Social Compact, Exemplified in the Constitution of the Commonwealth of Massachusetts* ... (Providence, 1842); *Parties in the United States,* and *Documents Relating to New England Federalism,* Henry Adams, ed., both previously cited. Charles Francis Adams settles several old scores in his *Life of John Adams* (Boston, 1856) and "Introductory Memoir" of the *Letters of Mrs. Adams,* 2nd ed. (Boston, 1840). Randall treats most of C. F. Adams's complaints; particularly interesting is his discussion of the controversial "Forrest letter," Appendix XV. Brooks Adams's Introduction to Henry

Adams, *The Degradation of the Democratic Dogma* (N.Y., 1920) is the best key to understanding J. Q. Adams's divergence from Jeffersonian Republicanism.

There is no need to cite works in praise of the Declaration. Rayner's discussion is one of the most thoughtful; Levi C. Judson, *A Biography of the Signers ...* (Phila., 1839) scales the peaks of eloquence. A touring pictorial exhibition adapted from Trumbull's "The Declaration of Independence" is described in the *Boston Advertiser*, May 8, 1837. For the early facsimile publications of the Declaration, see John C. Fitzpatrick, *The Spirit of the Revolution* (N.Y., 1924). Criticism by Timothy Pickering and others was well started before Jefferson's death. It is exemplified in Lee's *Observations;* Griswold's *Prose Writers;* Mercer's *An Exposition;* and with special attention to rhetoric in [Richard Ely Selden], *Criticism of the Declaration of Independence, as a Literary Document* (N.Y., 1846). On the Declaration in the slavery controversy, see the discussion under Chapter IV following. Leading advocates of the Mecklenburg Declaration indulged the penchant of anti-Jeffersonians for criticism of his Declaration.

William Henry Hoyt, *The Mecklenburg Declaration of Independence* (N.Y., 1907) is the best study. The official North Carolina defense in 1831 will be found in several places, for example, William A. Graham, *Address ... on the Mecklenburg Declaration of Independence of 20 May 1775* (N.Y., 1875). For the North Carolina background, see William K. Boyd, *History of North Carolina* (N.Y., 1919) and Charles C. Norton, *The Democratic Party in Ante-Bellum North Carolina* (Chapel Hill, 1930). The Charlotte celebration is reported in the *Raleigh Register and North Carolina Gazette,* June 2, 1835; additional information and comment in *Niles' Register* and the *Washington Globe* at about the same time. The question of the document's authenticity was involved in the larger controversy between Tucker and Hawks. See also the latter's *Revolutionary History of North Carolina, in Three Lectures* (Raleigh, 1853). The *National Intelligencer,* December 18, 1838, announces Peter Force's discovery of the May 31 resolutions. The episode involving Stevenson is described in Francis Fry Wayland, *Andrew Stevenson; Democrat and Diplomat, 1785-1857* (Phila., 1949); but see also Joseph Seawell Jones, *Memorials of North Carolina* (N.Y., 1838); Hoyt, *Mecklenburg Declaration;* and W. Noel Sainsbury to George Bancroft, March 19, 1852, MS, The Bancroft Papers, N.Y. Public Library. Sainsbury reported, as Sparks had earlier, that the newspaper clipping had been removed from Governor Martin's dispatch to the Colonial Secretary. S. Millington Miller, *pseud.,* publishes the alleged facsimile reproduction of the clipping in *Colliers Mag.,* July 1, 1905; A. S. Salley, Jr., *The True Mecklenburg "Declaration of Independence"* (Columbia, 1905) exposes the fraud. George W. and Alexander Graham, *Why North Carolinians Believe in the Mecklenburg Declaration of Independence of May 20th, 1775,* 2nd ed., rev. (Charlotte, 1895) expresses the conviction that Stevenson wantonly destroyed the positive proof of the existence of the May 20th document. Grigsby, *The Virginia Convention of 1776* is one index to the importance Virginians attached to refuting the North Carolina claim. Randall's judgment of the "real object" of the Mecklenburg advocates is in a letter to George Bancroft, February 4, 1858, MS, Massachusetts Historical Society. James C. Welling, "The Mecklenburg Declaration of Independence," *No. Amer. Rev.*, CXVIII (April 1874) marks the document's eclipse in American historiography.

Attacks on Jefferson's authority as a historical witness, more generally on his probity, were quite common. The Anas were thus constantly assailed by, among others, the leading advocates of the Mecklenburg Declaration. An article, probably from Hawks's pen, "The Congress of 1774," *N.Y. Review and Qtly. Church Journal*, IV (April 1839) refutes Jefferson's account of the events immediately preceding the American Revolution. Brantz Mayer, *Tah-gah-jute; or Logan and Captain Michael Cresap* (Baltimore, 1851) accuses Jefferson of wilfully distorting the truth for political purposes in his famous account, contained in the *Notes on Virginia*, of the massacre of the Indian Chief Logan and his family. Irving Brant, *James Madison, the Virginia Revolutionist* (Indianapolis, 1941) reviews this episode.

Nearly all the literature, Federalist and Jeffersonian, attests Aaron Burr's evil reputation. Samuel H. Wandell, *Aaron Burr in Literature* (London, 1936) offers an annotated bibliography. The response to James Parton's *Life and Times of Aaron Burr* (N.Y., 1858) shows what the biographer was up against: *New England Mag.*, XVI (May 1858); *So. Lit. Mes.* XXVI (May 1858); and the running comment in the *Albany Journal*, January-March 1858. On Matthew L. Davis's relations with Burr, see Nathan Schachner, *Aaron Burr* (N.Y., 1937). Two damning reviews of Davis's *Memoirs of Aaron Burr: N.Y. Review and Qtly. Church Journal*, II (January 1838), and the *United States Mag. and Democratic Review*, I (January 1838). The latter refutes Davis on the matter of the Georgia vote. There is no definitive appraisal of it. John Neal states his positive conviction in "Aaron Burr," *The Pioneer Mag.*, I (January 1841); W. H. Bartlett, *The History of the United States* (N.Y., 1956) credits the Davis report; George Gibbs, *Memoirs of the Administrations of Washington and John Adams* (N.Y., 1846) is more equivocal. The subject is reviewed in the Senate, January 1877; see the *Cong. Record*, 44 Cong., 2 Sess. The books of Sullivan and Dwight denounce Jefferson's conduct in the apprehension and trial of Burr. Most of Sullivan's account is embodied in Samuel L. Knapp's brief and friendly *Life of Colonel Burr* (N.Y., 1835).

Several writers make the Burr-Jefferson comparison to the latter's disadvantage. See the articles of Neal and Hawks, cited above, and the reviews of Davis's *Memoirs* in the *National Gazette*, November 14, 1837, and the *American Qtly. Review*, XXI (March 1837). For Francis P. Blair's blast: *Washington Globe*, November 22, 1837. Isaac Jenkinson champions Burr's cause anew in a paper, *Jefferson and Burr* ... (Richmond, Ind., 1898), and in *Aaron Burr*,

His Personal and Political Relations with Thomas Jefferson and Alexander Hamilton (Richmond, Ind., 1902).

The Henry A. Washington Papers, Institute of Early American History and Culture, Williamsburg, Virginia, throw a little light on the Congress Edition. J. Johns, *Memoir of Henry Augustine Washington* ... (Baltimore, 1859) makes clear Washington's distaste for Jefferson. It may also be inferred from some of Washington's writings, for example, "The Virginia Convention of 1776," *So. Lit. Mes.*, XVIII (November 1852). Randall, *Life*, III, calls attention to some of the Congress Edition's worst features.

Randall's papers are scattered. There are collections in the N.Y. State Library, the New York Historical Society, and the N.Y. Public Library. A number of his letters will be found in the Bancroft Papers (Mass. Historical Society) and the Van Buren Papers (Library of Congress). Frank J. and Frank W. Klingberg have edited *The Correspondence between Henry Stephens Randall and Hugh Blair Grigsby, 1856-1861* (Berkeley, 1952), which is very important for Randall's *Life of Jefferson*. See also George Green Shackelford, "New Letters of Hugh Blair Grigsby and Henry Stephens Randall, 1858-60," *Va. Mag. of Hist. and Biog.* LXIV (July 1956). Randall's politics are discussed in the *N.Y. Tribune*, August 14, 1860, and in the *N.Y. Eve. Post*, October 1, 1860. There is no biography of Randall, but see the sketch in the *Dictionary of American Biography*, Dumas Malone, ed. (N.Y., 1935).

John Esten Cooke's humanized image of Jefferson may be gathered from two novels and several minor essays: *The Youth of Jefferson, or, A Chronicle of College Scrapes at Williamsburg, in Virginia* ... (N.Y., 1854); *Henry St. John, Gentleman, of "Flower of Hundreds"* ... (N.Y., 1859), "Thomas Jefferson," *So. Lit. Mes.*, XXX (May 1860); "Jefferson as a Lover," *Appleton's Journal of Literature, Science, and Art*, XII (August 1874); and "Thomas Jefferson," *Harper's New Monthly Mag.*, LIII (July 1876).

The marked attention and respect accorded Randall's work make manifest its tremendous importance for Jefferson's reputation just before the Civil War. The following newspaper reviews are of interest: *Boston Courier*, February 11, 1858; *Charleston Mercury*, August 4, 1858; *N.Y. Times*, December 24, 1857; *Washington Union*, January 16, 1858; *Richmond Enquirer*, January 15, June 26, 1858 (by Grigsby, copied in several newspapers); *Boston Post*, March 10, May 19, June 28, 1858; *N.Y. Eve. Post*, June 24, 1858; *Richmond Whig and Public Advertiser*, April 13, 1858; *N.Y. Tribune*, January 2, July 31, August 14, 1858. Magazine reviews: *The National Mag.*, XIII (July 1858); *No. Amer. Rev.*, LXXXVII (October 1858); *Virginia University Mag.* (March 1859); *Harper's New Monthly Mag.*, XVI (March 1858) and XVII (September 1858); *So. Lit. Mes.*, XXVI (April 1858); *Russel's Mag.*, as reprinted in *DeBow's Review*, XXIV (June 1858); *The Knickerbocker Mag.*, LII (October 1858). William Dorsheimer's brilliant two part article appears in the *Atlantic Monthly*, II (November, December, 1858). E. O. Dunning's "Private Character of Thomas

Jefferson" in the *New Englander,* XIX (July 1861) was written in answer to
"Jefferson's Private Character," *No Amer. Rev.,* XCI (July 1860).

Parts of Randall's correspondence with Lord Macaulay were published in
the *So. Lit. Mes.,* XXX (March 1860) and XXXI (August 1860). The latter
was earlier printed in the *N.Y. Times,* June 3, 1860. The complete series of
four letters is in "Lord Macaulay on American Institutions," *Harper's New
Monthly Mag.,* LIV (February 1877). Several Englishmen either questioned
the authenticity of these letters or denounced Randall for publishing them.
See the *N.Y. Times,* April 27, June 3, 1860. Representative comment in the
American press: *Cincinnati Daily Gazette,* July 7, 1860; *Richmond Whig and
Public Advertiser,* April 5, 1860; *N.Y. Weekly Day Book,* May 5, 1860; *Springfield* (Mass.) *Republican,* April 14, 1860. Some of Macaulay's lines became
familiar quotations in the United States. Presidents Garfield (1878), Roosevelt
(1937), and Eisenhower (1957) have recalled and rejected Macaulay's criticism
of the American polity.

IV. UNION

W. S. Jenkins, *Pro-Slavery Thought in the Old South* (Chapel Hill, 1935)
is a sound study with considerable awareness of the Jeffersonian aspect. Two
related themes especially significant for Southern attitudes toward Jefferson
are centered in Clement Eaton, *Freedom of Thought in the Old South* (Durham,
N.C., 1940) and Rolin G. Osterweis, *Romanticism and Nationalism in the Old
South* (New Haven, 1949). W. G. Bean, "Anti-Jeffersonianism in the Ante-
Bellum South," *North Carolina Historical Review,* XII (April 1935) observes
the tendency. See also Joseph C. Robert's monograph on the Virginia slavery
debate, previously cited.

The Southern treatises on slavery by Thomas R. Dew, James H. Hammond,
William Harper, and William Gilmore Simms are collected in *The Pro-Slavery
Argument* (Phila., 1853). The preoccupation with the Declaration of Inde-
pendence is shown in the following: William Harper, *Anniversary Oration:
The South Carolina Society for the Advancement of Learning* (Columbia, 1836);
Daniel K. Whitaker, *Sidney's Letters to William E. Channing* ... 2nd ed.
(Charleston, 1839), *Reflections on Domestic Slavery elicited by Judge Harper's
Anniversary Oration* (Charleston, 1835), and "Channing's Duty of the Free
States," *Southern Qtly. Review,* II (July 1842); Hugh S. Legaré, "The Democ-
racy of Athens," in *Writings,* Mary S. Legaré Bullen, ed. (N.Y., 1846); William
Drayton, *The South Vindicated from the Treason and Fanaticism of Northern
Abolitionists* (Phila., 1836); W. S. Grayson, "Natural Equality of Man," *De
Bow's Review,* XXVI (January 1859) and "The Legation of Thomas Jefferson,"
ibid. XXXI (August 1861). For the racist argument, see in addition several
writings which cite Jefferson's authority: Richard H. Colfax, *Evidences against
the Views of the Abolitionists* ... (N.Y., 1833); John Campbell, *Negro-Mania:
Being an Examination of the Falsely Assumed Equality of the Various Races
of Man* (Phila., 1851). John H. Van Evrie's principal work is *Negroes and*

Negro Slavery: The First an Inferior Race; The Latter its Normal Condition
(N.Y., 1861). The *So. Lit. Mes.* is especially significant for the rejection of
the revolutionary legend: Henry A. Washington, "The Virginia Convention of
1776," XVIII (November 1852); "Early History of Richmond," XXII (February
1856); Review of Bancroft's *History*, XXXII (August 1860). On slavery as
the bulwark of republican institutions, see A. P. Upshur, "Domestic Slavery,"
So. Lit. Mes., V (October 1839); *Selections from the Letters and Speeches
of James H. Hammond* (N.Y., 1866); Robert B. Rhett, "Address to the People
of Beaufort and Colleton," in the *Liberator*, January 15, 1838; and, of course,
Calhoun's *Works.*

Harvey Wish, *George Fitzhugh, Propagandist of the Old South* (Baton
Rouge, 1943) is significant for the last phase of the pro-slavery argument.
In addition to his books, *Sociology for the South* (Richmond, 1854) and
Cannibals All! (Richmond, 1857), Fitzhugh wrote numerous articles in *De Bow's
Review,* several years before, during, and after the Civil War. Additional state-
ments of the radical viewpoint: "H.O.R.," *The Governing Race . . .* (Wash.,
1860); J. Quitman Moore, "Past and Present," *De Bow's Review,* XXX (Feb-
ruary 1861); John W. Dubose, *The Life and Times of William Lowndes
Yancey* (Birmingham, 1892); *Charleston Mercury,* March 29, 1858, and
passim. For Calhoun's melancholy musings on "democracy," see his letter to
R. B. Rhett, September 13, 1838, *Annual Report of the American Historical
Association, 1899,* II, *Correspondence of John C. Calhoun* (Wash., 1900), and
a conversation reported by Orestes Brownson, *Works,* XVI.

The abolitionist mind awaits a historian. Alice Felt Tyler surveys the reform
setting in the North in *Freedom's Ferment* (Minneapolis, 1944). Russel B. Nye,
Fettered Freedom (East Lansing, 1949) is very useful. No better study of
the temperament of the agitator has ever been written than John Jay Chapman's
brief *William Lloyd Garrison* (N.Y., 1913). There are, of course, numerous
biographies and letters of anti-slavery leaders.

B. L. Rayner lauds Jefferson's anti-slavery record in his biography of 1832.
For a fuller statement, see Andrew D. White, "Jefferson and Slavery," *Atlantic
Monthly,* IX (January 1862). Randall, *Life,* Appendix XXXIV is an incon-
clusive summary. Daniel P. Thompson, "A Talk with Jefferson," *Harper's New
Monthly Mag.,* XXVI (May 1863) purports to be an authentic report of Jeffer-
son's anti-slavery position in 1822; it should be treated with skepticism. Several
abolitionist recognitions of Jefferson's primacy in the cause: John Greenleaf
Whittier, "Democracy and Slavery," *Prose Works* (Boston, 1889); Thomas
Morris, *Cong. Globe,* 25 Cong., 1 Sess.; James Wilson, *ibid.* 30 Cong., 2 Sess.;
Theodore Parker, "Thomas Jefferson," *Historic Americans,* S. A. Eliot, ed.
(Boston, 1908). Garrison's ambivalent feelings are revealed in his editorials
in the *Liberator,* for example, February 25, 1832; see also the work of his
children, *William Lloyd Garrison,* 3 v. (N.Y., 1885-89). The accent on the
Declaration: *Proceedings of the Anti-Slavery Convention, Assembled at Phila-
delphia . . .* (N.Y., 1833); Theodore Parker, "The Anti-Slavery Convention,"

and "The Destination of America," *The Slave Power,* James K. Hosmer, ed. (Boston, n.d.); J. Q. Adams, *Report on the Massachusetts Resolutions, April 4, 1844,* 28 Cong., 1 Sess., and also "Letter to the Citizens of the United States," *Boston Courier,* June 6, 1839. William Ellery Channing, "Slavery," *Works* (Boston, 1841) is the most pointed defense of natural rights theory against the pro-slavery writers. Wendell Phillips, "Public Opinion," *Speeches, Lectures, and Letters* (Boston, 1863) expounds the principle of agitation. The criticism of Jefferson's failure to act on his theory: *The Emancipator* (N.Y.), July 18, 1839, July 16, 1840; J. Q. Adams, *Memoirs,* VIII; William Goodell, *Slavery and Anti-Slavery; A History* (N.Y., 1852). See also Erastus Brooks's observations, reported in the *United States Telegraph,* April 12, 1833. Uses of Jefferson's letter to Richard Price, August 7, 1785: *Qtly. Anti-Slavery Mag.,* II (January 1837); William Slade, *Cong. Globe,* 26 Cong., 1 Sess. The *Liberator,* January 12, 1834, describes Dorothy Ripley's project. The New Hampshire abolitionist congressman, M. W. Tappan, brought to light Jefferson's letter to James Heaton, May 20, 1826, his last on the subject of slavery; see the *Cong. Globe,* 36 Cong., 1 Sess.

Clement Eaton, "A Dangerous Pamphlet in the Old South," *Journal of Southern History,* II (August 1936) discusses the David Walker incident. The *Liberator* denounces Jefferson's "vulgar opinion," May 14, 1831, February 25, 1832; but a correspondent, November 16, 1831, cites Jefferson's letter to General Chastellux, June 7, 1785, in order to correct the false impression gained from the *Notes on Virginia.* George Livermore, *An Historical Research respecting the Opinions of the Founders of the Republic on Negroes...* (Boston, 1862) cites Jefferson to M. Gregoire, February 25, 1809. Also of interest are the discussions in [George Tucker], *Letters from Virginia* (Baltimore, 1816); James Parton, "Antipathy to the Negro," *No. Amer. Rev.,* CXXVII (December 1878); R. T. Greener, "The Intellectual Position of the Negro," *National Qtly. Review,* XLI (July 1880). J. Q. Adams pronounces Jefferson the father of the Colonization Society in "Speech at North Bridgewater, Mass., November 6, 1844" (included in vol. I of a collection of speeches by Adams, Widener Library, Harvard University). James G. Birney, *Letter on Colonization Addressed to the Reverend Thornton J. Mills* (N.Y., 1834) clears Jefferson of the colonization heresy. Supporters of the Society claim Jefferson's paternity: Review of Birney's *Letter, The African Repository and Colonial Journal,* X (November 1834); T. C. Thornton, *An Inquiry into the History of Slavery* (Wash., 1841); Philip Slaughter, *The Virginia History of African Colonization* (Richmond, 1853). For the later advocacy of colonization as "the Jeffersonian solution," see Francis P. Blair, Jr., *Colonizing Central America by the Colored People of the United States* (n.p., 1858), and the *Springfield* (Mass.) *Republican,* February 26, 1859. Hildreth's historical introduction to *Despotism in America* (Boston, 1840) is printed, with editorial comment, in the *Liberator,* February 14, 28, 1840. William Goodell's "Remarks... at the Annual Meeting of the N.Y. Anti-Slavery Society," *Emancipator,* December 24, 1840, are substantially reproduced in his *Slavery and Anti-Slavery*. The Federalist basis of the "slave power" idea may be discerned in J. Q. Adams's "Speech at North Bridgewater," and in Josiah Quincy, *Address Illustrative of the Nature and Power of the Slave States* . . . (Boston, 1856).

New editions of the *Notes on Virginia* (Boston, 1829, and Philadelphia, 1832) may have contributed to the popularity of Jefferson's Query XVIII. For the varied uses to which it was put: *Liberator*, January 22, November 19, 1831; J. Q. Adams, *Report on the Massachusetts Resolutions, April 4, 1844*, cited above, and *Cong. Globe*, 27 Cong., 2 Sess.; *The Trial of Reuben Crandall, M.D.* . . . (N.Y., 1836); Theodore D. Weld, *American Slavery as It Is: Testimony of a Thousand Witnesses* (N.Y., 1839); Benjamin Godwin, *Lectures on Slavery* (Boston, 1836); *Proceedings of the Rhode Island Anti-Slavery Convention* . . . (Providence, 1836).

Levi Gaylord's "Sale of a Daughter of Thomas Jefferson," after its original publication in *The Friend of Man*, appeared in the *Emancipator*, October 25, 1838. On the granddaughter in Liberia, see *The North Star*, March 25, 1852. Several abolitionist references crediting the legend: Angelina Grimké, *Letters to Catherine Beecher* (Boston, 1838); Theodore Parker, "Thomas Jefferson," *Historic Americans*, and also his essay on William Ellery Channing in *The American Scholar*, G. W. Cooke, ed. (Boston, 1907); William Goodell, *Slavery and Anti-Slavery*. On Lincoln, see Carl Sandburg, *Abraham Lincoln: The Prairie Years* (N.Y., 1925). William Wells Brown's "Jefferson's Daughter" appears in his *The Anti-Slavery Harp: A Collection of Songs for Anti-Slavery Meetings* (Boston, 1848). At least two bowdlerized American editions of *Clotel; or The President's Daughter* (London, 1853) struck all references to Jefferson and changed the President of the original into an unidentified Senator. W. Edward Farrison, "The Origin of Brown's *Clotel*," *Phylon*, XV (1954) is a careful article, which also makes use of the Monticello records on the Hemings family. The comment of British travelers: Mrs. Trollope, *The Domestic Manners of the Americans;* F. A. Cox, *The Baptists in America* (n.p., 1836); Captain [Frederick] Marryat, *A Diary in America* (Phila., 1839); E. S. Abdy, *Journal of a Residence and Tour in the United States* . . . (London, 1835); Thomas Hamilton, *Men and Manners in America* (Phila., 1833); Mrs. Felton, *Life in America* (London, 1838). Several works evince awareness of Sally Hemings's paternity: Hamilton W. Pierson's account of Edmund Bacon's recollections, *Jefferson at Monticello* (N.Y., 1862); Rayford W. Logan, ed., *Memoirs of a Monticello Slave, As dictated to Charles Campbell in the 1840s by Isaac, one of Thomas Jefferson's Slaves* (Charlottesville, 1951); W. H. Bartlett, *History of the United States;* Cornelis DeWitt, *Jefferson and American Democracy*, R.S.H. Church, tr. (London, 1862). Robert Jefferson's story is in the *N.Y. Times*, April 30, 1882. The recollections of Madison Hemings, as told to the editor of the *Pike County Republican*, are in that newspaper, March 13, 1873. (Credit for the discovery of this rare item belongs to James H. Rodabaugh, Head of the Division of History and Science, The Ohio Historical

Society.) The photographic story "Thomas Jefferson's Negro Grandchildren" appears in *Ebony* (November 1954).

Raymond A. Billington, "The Historians of the Northwest Ordinance," *Illinois State Historical Society Journal,* XXXX (December 1947) helps to put the historiography in perspective. The verdict of recent scholarship is stated in Merrill Jensen, *The New Nation* (N.Y., 1950); Herbert Philbrick, Introduction to *The Laws of the Illinois Territory,* in *Collections of the Illinois State Historical Library,* XXV (Springfield, 1950); and Julian P. Boyd, ed., *The Papers of Thomas Jefferson,* VI (Princeton, 1952).

The idea of Jefferson's authorship, in whole or in part, of the Northwest Ordinance is asserted in the following: *Speech of John A. Dix on the Three Million Bill, and the Wilmot Proviso* . . . (Wash., 1847); Enoch Hoag, *The Slave Power* (Boston, 1848); *Speech Delivered by Thomas Hart Benton at Jefferson* . . . (Jefferson City, Mo., 1849); Philip Snyder, *Issues of the Contest; Speech* . . . *in the Campaign of 1860* (n.p., n.d.); and George W. Julian, *Cong. Globe,* 31 Cong., 1 Sess. For Salmon P. Chase's view, see *ibid.* and J. W. Schuckers, *The Life and Public Opinion of Salmon P. Chase* (N.Y., 1874). Compare with Chase's *A Sketch of the History of Ohio* (Cincinnati, 1833). For Jefferson and the Free Soilers: O. C. Gardiner, *The Great Issue* . . . (N.Y., 1848), and the reports of the 1849 commemorations in the *Richmond Whig,* July 23, 1849, the *North Star,* August 3, 1849, and the *N.Y. Eve. Post,* July 20, 1849.

The authorship controversy may be traced through the following: *Register of Debates,* 21 Cong., 1 Sess.; Nathan Dane, *A General Abridgment and Digest of American Law,* VII, but more particularly the Appendix to IX of the 2nd ed. (Boston, 1829); Peter Force's article in the *National Intelligencer,* August 25, 1847; assertions of Rufus King's claim, *ibid.* August 6, 1845, and also the *Ohio State Journal,* July 9, 1849; George T. Curtis's reassertion of Dane's claim, *N.Y. Tribune,* January 29, 1855; Edward Coles, *History of the Ordinance of 1787* (Phila., 1856); T. H. Benton, *Historical and Legal Examination* . . . *of the Dred Scott Case* . . . (N.Y., 1857). See also William F. Poole, "Dr. Cutler and the Ordinance of '87," *No. Amer. Rev.,* CXXII (April 1876). E. B. Andrews, *A Funeral Discourse on the Occasion of the Death of the Hon. Ephraim Cutler* . . . *July 24, 1853* (Marietta, Ohio, 1854) was noticed in the *N.Y. Tribune,* February 28, 1854. Two recent scholarly views of the Cutler-Andrews story: Emilius O. Randall and Daniel J. Ryan, *History of Ohio* (N.Y., 1912); C. B. Galbreath, "Thomas Jefferson's Views on Slavery," *Ohio Archaeological and Historical Qtly.,* XXXIV (1925).

Calhoun's view of Jefferson and the restriction principle of the Northwest Ordinance is amply set forth in his speeches, *Works,* IV. A. H. Colquitt says the abolition of the slave trade was Jefferson's main concern: *Cong. Globe,* 33 Cong., 1 Sess. James M. Mason regards Jefferson as a slave expansionist: *ibid.* 35 Cong., 1 Sess. Robert Toombs develops the Louisiana precedent: *ibid.*

34 Cong., 1 Sess. Stephen A. Douglas's article "Popular Sovereignty in the Territories," *Harper's Mag.*, XIX (September 1859) was also published separately: An earlier controversy between Douglas and Coles on the no-slavery proviso is reported in the *National Intelligencer*, February 17, 18, 1854. Republican attacks on Douglas's position: "History Vindicated," *N.Y. Tribune*, October 13, 1859; George T. Curtis, *The Just Supremacy of Congress over the Territories* (Boston, 1859); Carl Schurz, Speech at Springfield, Mass., January 4, 1860, in *Speeches, Correspondence and Political Papers of Carl Schurz*, Frederic Bancroft, ed. (N.Y., 1913); Abraham Lincoln, Speech at Columbus, Ohio, September 16, 1859, *Complete Works*, John G. Nicolay and John Hay, eds. (N.Y., 1894); Salmon P. Chase, Speech at Covington, Ohio, *Cincinnati Daily Gazette*, November 2, 1860. [Jeremiah S. Black], *Observations on Senator Douglas's Views of Popular Sovereignty*...(Wash., 1859) speaks for the administration. Percy Roberts, "Popular Sovereignty—A Review of Mr. Douglas's Article," *De Bow's Review*, XXVII (December 1859) brings Jefferson to the support of the Southern Democracy. For Douglas's campaign humbug on the two ordinances, see the reports of his speeches, *Dubuque* (Iowa) *Herald*, October 3, 9, 1860; and also the editorial comment in the *N.Y. Tribune*, October 9, 1860 and the *N.Y. Eve. Post*, September 26, 27, 1860.

Benjamin F. Hall, *The Republican Party and its Presidential Candidates* (N.Y., 1856) offers a representative statement of "the history of the parties." The Republican appeal to Jefferson must be gathered from the newspapers, of which the *N.Y. Tribune* is the most useful, from the *Cong. Globe*, and from the campaign literature. Two manuals collecting the fathers' wisdom are Daniel R. Goodloe, *The Southern Platform: or, Manual of Southern Sentiment on*...*Slavery* (Boston, 1858); and *The Doctrines of the Fathers* (Indianapolis, 1860). The battle for the Jefferson standard in New Hampshire is recorded in the following: *Address of the Democratic State Convention* (n.p., [1856]); the *Independent Democrat* (Concord), 1858-59; and the *New Hampshire Patriot and State Gazette* (Portsmouth), 1858-59. An oddity is John M. Spear, *Twelve Discourses on Government*...*by Thomas Jefferson of the Spirit World* (Hopedale, Mass., 1853), the work of a Boston medium.

Rufus Choate's memorable indictment of the Declaration is in his Letter to the Whigs of Maine, August 9, 1856, *Works*, Samuel G. Brown, ed. (Boston, 1862). For C. F. Adams's defense of the Declaration: *An Oration*...*July 4, 1860* (Fall River, Mass., 1860), and *The Republican Party a Necessity*... *Delivered in the House of Representatives, May 31, 1860* (n.p., n.d.). Jefferson's name is much used in a Southern controversy involving freedom of speech against slavery: [Benjamin S. Hedrick], *Are North Carolinians Freemen?* (n.p., [1856]); Hinton R. Helper, *The Impending Crisis in the South* (N.Y., 1857); William M. Evarts, *Speeches in the Republican Campaign of 1856* (n.p., [1856]).

James L. Sellers, "Republicanism and State Rights in Wisconsin," *Miss.*

Valley Hist. Rev., XVII (September 1930) discusses the Booth case. Byron
Paine states his case: *Unconstitutionality of the Fugitive Act* (n.p., n.d.). The
National Intelligencer, April-June 1859, reacts sharply to the Republican adop-
tion of the "doctrines of '98." The revival of Jefferson's opinions on the federal
judiciary may be seen in the following: Philemon Bliss and Israel Washburn,
Cong. Globe, 35 Cong., 1 Sess.; "Jefferson and the Judiciary," *Cincinnati Daily
Gazette*, September 10, 1860; Daniel R. Goodloe, *Federalism Unmasked . . .
Being a Compilation of the Writings and Speeches of the Leaders of the Old
Jeffersonian Republican Party* (n.p., 1860); George Sumner, *An Oration . . .
July 4, 1859* (Boston, 1859). In his *Reminiscences* (N.Y., 1907-08), Carl
Schurz says that when he compiled his speeches for publication in 1865, he
omitted as "unsound" his political address in 1859 "for States' rights and
Byron Paine."

If there were, as reported in the *National Intelligencer*, April 18, 1859,
Republican celebrations of Jefferson's anniversary "in many of our cities,"
they left few traces except in Washington and Boston. For the proceedings of
the former: *Celebration of Jefferson's Birthday in Washington* (Wash., 1859).
The latter must be reconstructed from the newspapers, of which the *Boston
Atlas and Daily Bee* is the most useful. It publishes Chase's letter, April 15,
1859, and Lincoln's letter in full, June 29, 1860. The *National Intelligencer*,
April 18, 1859, along with other Unionist newspapers, emphasizes the celebration's demonstration of the Jeffersonian alikeness of the two major parties.

For the proceedings at Salem, Massachusetts: *Celebration of the Birth-Day
of Thomas Jefferson* (Salem, 1859). Jefferson is mustered to the support of
imperial ambitions in the following: "Democratic Policy—The Empire," *United
States Mag. and Democratic Review*, XLII (November 1858); *Boston Post*,
August 7, 1854, and January 21, 1859; "Report of the Senate Committee on
Foreign Relations," January 24, 1859, *Cong. Globe*, 35 Cong., 1 Sess. On
Commodore Charles Stewart, see especially *To the Democratic Party of the
United States on the Presidential Election, to which is appended a Biographical
Sketch of Commodore Charles Stewart* (Phila., 1844). His original letter first
appeared in the *National Intelligencer*, March 23, 1859; additional letters in
the same newspaper, March 31, 1859. Indicative of the Republican reaction
are the *N.Y. Eve. Post*, March 29, 1859; the *Springfield* (Mass.) *Republican*,
March 16, 1859; and the *Ohio State Journal* (Columbus), March 18, 1859.

Particularly suggestive for the interpretation of the Civil War as a crisis
of the Jeffersonian ideology are the following: Lord Acton, "Political Causes
of the American Revolution," *Essays on Freedom and Power*, Gertrude Himmel-
farb, ed. (Glencoe, Ill., 1948), and "The Civil War in America," *Historical
Essays and Studies*, John N. Figgis and R. V. Laurence, eds. (London, 1908);
H. H. Bellot, "Thomas Jefferson in American Historiography," *Transactions
of the Royal Historical Society*, 5th Series, IV (1954); Roy F. Nichols and
Edward S. Corwin, in Roscoe Pound and others, *Federalism as a Democratic*

Process (New Brunswick, 1942); Roy F. Nichols, "American Democracy and the Civil War," *Proc. of the Amer. Phil. Soc.*, XCI (April 1947).

Crucial for understanding Calhoun's position are his "Speech on Amendment of the Oregon Bill," August 12, 1849, *Works*, IV, and "Discourse on the Constitution and Government of the United States," *Works*, I. See also Charles M. Wiltse, *John C. Calhoun, Sectionalist* (Indianapolis, 1951). For the incipient Southern revolt against state rights: George Fitzhugh, "Small Nations," *De Bow's Review*, XXIX (November 1860); [John Scott], *The Lost Principle; or the Sectional Equilibrium* (Richmond, 1860); James H. Hammond, Speech at Columbia, South Carolina, November 8, 1860, MS, Hammond Papers, Library of Congress; *Charleston Mercury*, 1860; [W. M. McCarty], *A Glance at State Rights* . . . (Richmond, 1860). For the justification of secession: *Jefferson Davis, Constitutionalist: His Letters, Papers and Speeches*, Dunbar D. Rowland, ed. (Jackson, Miss., 1923); "The Address of the People of South Carolina . . ." *De Bow's Review*, XXX (March 1861). Southern reflections which emphasize the Jeffersonian causes of the War: Fitzhugh, "Revolutions of '76 and '61 Contrasted," *De Bow's Review*, New Series, IV (July-August 1866); George Lunt, *The Origins of the Late War* . . . (N.Y., 1866); A. T. Bledsoe, "The Origin of the Late War," "De Tocqueville on the Sovereignty of the People," *Southern Review*, I (April 1867), and "The Great Error of the Eighteenth Century," *ibid.* V (January 1869). Bledsoe, *Is Davis a Traitor?* (Baltimore, 1866) is a good statement on the constitutional right of secession and one which emphasizes, like the writings of Davis, Alexander H. Stephens, Edward A. Pollard, and others, the great prestige before the War of the "doctrines of '98." [Bernard J. Sage], *The Republic of Republics* (Boston, 1878) is a later Jeffersonian defense of the South. Edward A. Powell, *Nullification and Secession in the United States* (N.Y., 1897) makes some trenchant observations on the fate of state rights principles.

The Northern view in 1860-61 of Jefferson's relations to secession may be gleaned from the following: *National Intelligencer*, July 24, 1860; *Boston Post*, May 29, 1861; the speeches of Tom Corwin, Andrew Johnson, and others in the *Cong. Globe*, 36 Cong., 2 Sess.; Joel Parker, *The Right of Secession* (Cambridge, 1861); Edward Everett, Oration on July 4, 1861, in the *Boston Advertiser* of the same date. For the subsequent reaction against Jefferson and state rights: Peter H. Burnett, *The American Theory of Government considered with reference to the Present Crisis*, 2nd ed. (N.Y., 1863); J. Sheldon, "Thomas Jefferson, as Seen by the Light of 1863," *The Continental Monthly*, V (February 1863); James R. Lowell, "The Rebellion and Its Consequences," *No. Amer. Rev.*, XCIX (July 1864); Orville J. Victor, *History of American Conspiracies* (N.Y., 1863); C.C.S. Farrar, *The War, Its Causes and Consequences* (Phila., 1864); Joseph P. Thompson, *Revolution against Free Government not a Right but a Crime* (N.Y., 1864); Douglas Campbell, "Climactic Influences as bearing upon Secession and Reconstruction," *No. Amer. Rev.*, CII (January, 1866). Andrew D. White recalls his change of opinion in his *Autobiography* (London,

1905). See also Moses M. Granger, *Washington* vs. *Jefferson; The Case Tried by Battle in 1861-65* (Boston, 1898).

The passage of Jefferson's political world is emphasized in C. C. Hazewell's review of Van Buren's *Inquiry*, *No. Amer. Rev.*, CV (July 1867); Samuel Fowler, "The Political Opinions of Jefferson," *ibid.* CI (October 1865); George Loring, *Safe and Honorable Reconstruction: An Oration* ... (South Danvers, 1866). In addition to Horace Bushnell's *Reverses Needed* (Hartford, 1861) see his *Building Eras of Religion* (N.Y., 1881). The career of "In God We Trust" on the coinage is traced by Representative Sheppard, *Cong. Record*, 60 Cong., 1 Sess. Variant views of Jefferson in the popular Unionist histories of the Civil War will be found in Horace Greeley, *The American Conflict: A History of the Great Rebellion*, 2 v. (Hartford, 1864); John D. Chamberlain, *Young Folks History of the War for the Union* (N.Y., 1881); John A. Logan, *The Great Conspiracy: Its Origin and History* (N.Y., 1886). For the general subject, see Thomas J. Pressly, *Americans Interpret Their Civil War* (Princeton, 1954). A useful guide to the growth of nationalist political theory is Chapter XIV, with accompanying bibliography, of Herbert W. Schneider's *History of American Philosophy* (N.Y., 1946). On Lincoln, see Lyman C. Munson, "Comparative Study of Jefferson and Lincoln," *The Commonwealth Mag.* (September-October 1903); F. Lauriston Bullard, "Lincoln as a Jeffersonian," *More Books*, XXIII (October 1948); Edward H. Griggs, *American Statesmen* (Croton, N.Y., 1927). The Lincoln fragment on the Declaration and the Union is in Paul M. Angle, *New Letters and Papers of Lincoln* (Boston, 1930). George Bancroft, "The Place of Abraham Lincoln in History," *Atlantic Monthly*, XV (June 1865) gives a strong Unionist interpretation of Jefferson.

The turn to Hamilton is clearly indicated in the following: R. S. H. Church's Preface to Cornelis DeWitt, *Jefferson and the American Democracy;* Burnett, *Theory of American Government;* C. J. Riethmüller, *Alexander Hamilton and His Contemporaries* (London, 1864); and C. C. Hazewell's review of this work in the *No. Amer. Rev.*, XVI (November 1865). See also A. T. Bledsoe, "Alexander Hamilton," *Southern Review*, IV (October 1867) and VI (July 1869); Edward Carey, *George William Curtis* (Boston, 1894); B. A. Hinsdale, ed., *The Works of James A. Garfield*, 2 v. (Boston, 1882); Thomas Lee, *Presentation of the Statue of Alexander Hamilton to the City of Boston* (Boston, 1865). John Clark Ridpath, *Alexander Hamilton: A Study of the Revolution and the Union* (Cincinnati, 1881) is a particularly vivid statement. In addition to John C. Hamilton's *History of the Republic of the United States*, 7 v. (New York, 1857-65) see his Unionist writings, *Coercion completed, or Treason Triumphant* (N.Y., 1864) and *The Slave Power: Its Heresies and Injuries to the American People* (N.Y., 1864). Elizabeth Hamilton's devotion to her husband's fame is described in Alice Curtis Desmond, *Alexander Hamilton's Wife* (N.Y., 1952); see also James A. Hamilton, *Reminiscences* (N.Y., 1869). John T. Morse recalls "Incidents Connected with the American Statesmen Series," *Proc. of the Mass. Hist. Soc.*, LXIV (November 1931). His candid statement to Lodge of bias against Jefferson appears in John A. Garraty, *Henry Cabot Lodge, A Biography* (N.Y., 1953). Charles R. Wilson discusses Holst in *The Marcus W. Jernegan Essays in American Historiography*. The review of the crucial first volume by Lodge and Henry Adams appears in the *No. Amer. Rev.*, CXXIII (October 1876). Lodge wrote voluminously of the early history of the republic, but see especially his *Life and Letters of George Cabot* (Boston, 1877) and *Alexander Hamilton* (Boston, 1882).

V. REDIVIVUS

The reception of the books by Sarah N. Randolph and James Parton may be gleaned from the reviews by Edmund Quincy and Edward Sheldon respectively in the *Nation*, XIII (November 9, 1871), XVIII (April 30, 1874). The following shed a little light on Sarah Randolph: *N.Y. Tribune*, June 13, 1876; W. Stull Holt, ed., *Historical Scholarship in the United States, 1876-1900: As Revealed in the Correspondence of Herbert B. Adams* (Baltimore, 1938); Alexander McAdie, "Thomas Jefferson at Home," *American Antiquarian Society Proceedings*, New Series, XL (1930); and the Paul L. Ford Papers, New York Public Library. Julius H. Ward writes with intimate knowledge of James Parton in the *New England Magazine*, VII (January 1893); see also Milton E. Flower, *James Parton, the Father of Modern Biography* (Durham, N.C., 1951). Parton's *Life* was first serialized in the *Atlantic Monthly*. T. J. Randolph's blast against the biographer's use of Edmund Bacon's reminiscences, already cited, is *The Last Days of Jefferson* [Charlottesville, 1873]. *The Life of Andrew Jackson*, 3 v. (N.Y., 1860) shows Parton's Spencerian slant, and several of his brief popular treatments, for example, *Achievements of Celebrated Men* (N.Y., 1883), focus the domestic life. The latter emphasis may also be seen in Hezekiah Butterworth, *In the Days of Jefferson* (N.Y., 1900), *juvenilia;* Hallie Ermine Rives, *Hearts Courageous* (Indianapolis, 1902), a novel; Helen L. Campbell, *Thomas Jefferson* (Boston, 1899), in the Young Folks Library of Choice Literature; Edward S. Ellis, *Thomas Jefferson; A Character Sketch* (Milwaukee, 1898); Robert Stephens, *Famous Loves of Famous Americans* (n.p., 1914); Harriet Taylor Upton, *Our Early Presidents, their Wives and Children* . . . (Boston, 1890). It is carried forward, with some modifications, in Betty Elise Davis, *Monticello Scrapbook* (Charlottesville, 1939) and *Young Tom Jefferson's Adventure Chest* (N.Y., 1942); Sonia Daugherty, *The Way of the Eagle* (N.Y., 1941); Gene Stone, *The Story of Thomas Jefferson* (N.Y., 1922). See also a number of articles: A. H. Guernsey, "Thomas Jefferson and His Family," *Harper's Mag.*, XLVIII (July 1871); Cornelia Jefferson Taylor, "Gleanings from the Life of Thomas Jefferson," *American Monthly Mag.*, II (January 1893); "Jefferson's Early Life," *St. Louis Republic*, April 21, 1894; Frederick Daniel, "Virginian Reminiscences of Jefferson," *Harper's Weekly*, XLVIII (November 19, 1904); and the articles by R. T. W. Duke, Jr., and Alexander McAdie, both cited above.

A photograph of Jefferson's tombstone as it appeared a few years before the erection of the present monument is in David M. R. Culbreth, *The University of Virginia.* On the Cox Resolution, see the *Cong. Record,* 45 Cong., 2 Sess.; the *Washington Post,* March 23, 1878. *Senate Miscellaneous Document No. 88,* 46 Cong., 2 Sess., deals with the title problem. G. S. Weaver, *The Lives and Graves of Our Presidents* (Chicago, 1884) is a contemporary account. *Frank Leslie's Illustrated Newspaper,* June 17, 1882, reports the movement to transfer Jefferson's remains to Washington. See also T. W. Bartley, *Address ... before the Jefferson Monumental Association* (Washington, 1882). Mrs. Meikleham's petition on the removal: 47 Cong., 1 Sess. The pension resolution for her was introduced in this session, but debated more fully in 48 Cong., 1 Sess. William E. Curtis, *The True Thomas Jefferson* (Phila., 1901) upbraids Virginia for its neglect of Jefferson.

Roy J. Honeywell, *The Educational Work of Thomas Jefferson* (Cambridge, 1931) is the standard study. Jefferson's varied influence on education in an earlier period is recognized in the following: Paul E. Belting, "The Development of the Free Public High School in Illinois to 1860," *Journal of the Illinois State Historical Society,* IX (1918-19); Orie William Long, *Thomas Jefferson and George Ticknor: A Chapter in American Scholarship* (Williamstown, Mass., 1933); Thomas C. McCorvey, "Henry Tutwiler, and the Influence of the University of Virginia on Education in Alabama," *Univ. of Va. Al. Bul.,* New Series, X (July 1917). The key work for the later period is John C. Henderson, *Thomas Jefferson's Views on Public Education* (N.Y., 1890). See also "Thomas Jefferson," *American Journal of Education,* XXVII (1877). Jefferson in the Southern education movement: *Proceedings of the Trustees of the Peabody Educational Fund, 1874-1881* (Boston, 1881); Southern Education Board, *Thomas Jefferson on Public Education* (Knoxville, 1902); A. D. Mayo, *The New Education in the New South* (Boston, 1903), and "The Organization and Development of the American Common School in the Atlantic and Central States of the South, 1830 to 1860," *Report of the Commissioner of Education from 1899-1900* (Washington, 1901); Conference for Education in the South, *Proceedings of the Sixth Session* (N.Y., 1903). Charles W. Dabney was but one of many extollers of Jefferson at this Conference. For Dabney, see also *The Problem of Education in the South; An Address ...* (N.Y., 1902), and *Universal Education in the South,* 2 v. (Chapel Hill, 1936).

Herbert Baxter Adams, *Thomas Jefferson and the University of Virginia* (Wash., 1888) is the key work for higher education. This was the first of a series of monographs, under Adams's general editorship, written for the United States Bureau of Education. The letter of N. H. R. Dawson to the Secretary of Interior, December 9, 1887, *Report of the Commissioner of Education, 1887-8* (Wash., 1888), is an important statement of Jefferson's educational philosophy. Also significant are E. P. Powell, "Jefferson and Hamilton in Our Education," *New England Mag.,* XIV (August 1896); James Coolidge Carter, *The University of Virginia: Jefferson its Father, and his Political Philosophy* (Charlottesville, 1898); Hamilton Wright Mabie, "The Intellectual Movement in the West," *Atlantic Monthly,* LXXXII (November 1898); John Sharp Williams, *The Uni-*

versity of Virginia and the Development of Thomas Jefferson's Educational Ideas (Charlottesville, 1904). *A Study of Thomas Jefferson's Religious Belief* (Durham, N.C., 1900) is the main statement by John Carlisle Kilgo. *The Raleigh News and Observer* reports the controversy and publishes several answers (one by William E. Dodd) to Kilgo. See also Josephus Daniels, *Editor in Politics* (Chapel Hill, 1941); Paul N. Garber, *John Carlisle Kilgo, President of Trinity College, 1894-1910* (Durham, 1937); V. O. Key, Jr., *Southern Politics in State and Nation* (N.Y., 1949). The divided opinion on Jefferson as a philosopher of education is indicated in the following: John Dewey, *Freedom and Culture* (N.Y., 1939); James B. Conant, "Education for a Classless Society: The Jeffersonian Tradition," *Atlantic Monthly*, CLXV (May 1940); Horace Kallen, *The Education of Free Men* (N.Y., 1949); Albert Jay Nock, *Theory of Education in the United States* (Chicago, 1949); Robert M. Hutchins, Address at the University of Virginia, reported in the *N.Y. Times*, April 15, 1934.

Fiske Kimball, *The Life Portraits of Jefferson and their Replicas* (American Philosophical Society, 1944) is a definitive study. The great Browere life mask is discussed in Charles Henry Hart, "Unknown Life Masks of Great Americans," *McClure's* Mag., IX (October 1897). Interesting and vivid eye-witness accounts of Jefferson's physical appearance are in the recollections of Margaret Bayard Smith, Isaac Jefferson, and Edmund Bacon, all previously cited. And also in Sir Augustus Foster, *Jeffersonian America*, Richard B. Davis, ed. (San Marino, Calif., 1954); *Journal of William McClay, 1789-1791*, E. S. McClay, ed. (N.Y., 1890); Francis Calley Gray, *Thomas Jefferson in 1814, Being an Account of a Visit to Monticello*, Henry S. Rowe and T. J. Coolidge, Jr., eds. (Boston, 1924); and the *Private Correspondence of Daniel Webster*, Fletcher Webster, ed. (Boston, 1857). Randall and T. J. Randolph take exception to Webster's "notes" in the former's *Life*, III and Appendix XXXVI. Elegance is accented in Daniel W. Voorhees, "Thomas Jefferson," *Forty Years of Oratory* ... (Indianapolis, 1898); A. H. Lewis, "Thomas Jefferson's Great Day," *Everybody's Mag.*, VII (December 1902); Paul L. Ford, "Thomas Jefferson in Undress," *Scribner's Mag.*, XII (October 1892). The simplicity accent: John S. Wise, 47 Cong., 1 Sess.; William E. Dodd, "The Times of Jefferson," *Raleigh News and Observer*, January 14, 1900. On simplicity and the First Inaugural, see Randolph, *Domestic Life*; the editorial in the *Washington Post*, April 10, 1878, and Mrs. Meikleham's answer printed on the next day; John Bach McMaster, *A History of the People of the United States*, II (N.Y., 1883); the *N.Y. World*, March 3, 1885; the *N.Y. Tribune*, March 4, 1885, October 9, 1887; John W. Daniel, "Jefferson," *Speeches and Orations of* ... (Lynchburg, 1911); B. O. Flower, "Topics of the Time," *Arena*, XXV (May 1901); Samuel C. Busey, "The Centennial of the First Inauguration of a President at the Permanent Seat of the Government," *Records of the Columbia Historical Society*, V (Wash., 1902); William Bayard Hale, "Presidential Inaugurations at Four Crises," *World's Work*, XXV (March 1913); Edythe H. Browne, "The Great Simplicity of Jefferson," *Commonweal*, IV (July 14, 1926). Edward S. Ellis, *The Life of Thomas Jefferson* (Chicago, 1913) collects many anecdotes current at this time. See also John P. Foley, "Outdoor Life of the Presidents, Number 2," *Outing*, XIII (December 1889); Fred Eastman, *Men of Power*, 2 v. (Nashville, 1938); and several of the works already cited.

James K. Paulding, *Letters from the South*, new edition (N.Y., 1835) explains the terms "tuckahoe" and "cohee." Edward T. Booth, *Country Life in America* (N.Y., 1947) explicitly applies them to Jefferson. William M. Thornton, *Who Was Thomas Jefferson?* (Richmond, 1909) and *Who Bought Louisiana?* (Wash., 1913) are highly suggestive. Allen Tate's poem "On the Father of Liberty" originally appeared in *Sewanee Review*, XXXVIII (January 1930). F. J. Turner's most important statement on Jefferson belongs to "Contributions of the West to American Democracy," first published in the *Atlantic Monthly*, 1903, and included in *The Frontier in American History* (N.Y., 1920). See also William E. Dodd, *Statesmen of the Old South* (N.Y., 1911); Homer Hockett, *Western Influences on Political Parties to 1825* (Columbus, 1917); Arthur N. Holcombe, *The Political Parties of To-day* (N.Y., 1924); Frederic L. Paxson, *When the West is Gone* (N.Y., 1930). The "mountaineer" is accented in Elbert Hubbard, *Little Journeys to the Homes of American Statesmen* (N.Y., 1898) and Philip A. Bruce, *The Virginia Plutarch*, 2 v. (Chapel Hill, 1929). The dual heritage convention is carried forward in John S. Patton and Sallie J. Doswell, *Monticello and Its Master* (Charlottesville, 1925); Mary M. Elliott, *Colonial Days in Virginia* (Savannah, 1931); and Claude G. Bowers, *Making Democracy a Reality* ... (Memphis, 1954).

Representative Sibley, Pennsylvania, beseeches the Democrats to "touch the bones of Jefferson" in the *Cong. Record*, 53 Cong., 3 Sess. Frank R. Kent, *The Democratic Party: A History* (N.Y., 1928) is sensitive to the Jeffersonian strain. Its persistence in the years following the Civil War may be seen in Stewart Mitchell, *Horatio Seymour of New York* (Cambridge, 1938); John Bigelow, ed., *The Writings and Speeches of Samuel J. Tilden*, 2 v. (N.Y., 1885); Ransom H. Gillet, *Democracy in the United States* (N.Y., 1868). Democratic speeches, articles, and campaign polemics give an index to the Jefferson revival in the 1880's. Examples are Charles W. Jones, *Jeffersonian Democracy: Address* ... (Wash., [1881]); and Chauncey F. Black, *Jefferson and Hamilton* ... (N.Y., 1888). For recognition of the revival: *Washington Post*, July 2, September 11, 1880; *Chicago Tribune*, April 7, 17, 1881; *New York Tribune*, March-July 1882; James G. Blaine, "The Presidential Election of 1892," *No. Amer. Rev.*, CLV (November 1892). Charles Reemelin, *A Critical Review of American Politics* (Cincinnati, 1881) is perceptive of the political ordeal of Jefferson's reputation. Stephen M. Allen, *The Old and New Republican Parties* (Boston, 1880) shows Republicanism's lingering attachment to Jefferson, as does Francis Curtis, *The Republican Party: A History* ... , 2 v. (N.Y., 1904). The Republican attack on Jefferson may be seen in Jonathan Norcross, *History of the Democracy* ... (N.Y., 1883); J. Harris Patton, *The Democratic Party: Its Political History and*

Influence (N.Y., 1884), and also his *Political Parties in the United States* (N.Y., 1896); E. R. Kennedy, An Address, *N.Y. Tribune*, April 14, 1885; and the lavish campaign sheet, *Our Bandanna*, Thomas W. Lawson, ed. (Boston, 1888). Chauncey F. Black sketches the history and purpose of the National Association of Democratic Clubs in *The Jeffersonian Democrat*, II (January 1900); see also his Address at the Convention of Democratic Clubs, 1888, in *The Campaign Text Book of the Democratic Party* . . . (N.Y., 1888). The Association's celebration at Monticello in 1896 is reported in the *N.Y. Tribune*, April 14, 1896; a brochure, *Jefferson* (Wash., 1897) gives the full program of the birthday celebration in Washington. Volume I of William Rufus Jackson, *Missouri Democracy: A History* . . . (Chicago, 1935) contains a history of the St. Louis Jefferson Club. *The Pilgrimage to Monticello . . . by the Jefferson Club of St. Louis, Missouri, October 10 to 14, 1901* (St. Louis, 1902) should be supplemented by the reports in the St. Louis newspapers, for example, *Reedy's Mirror*, October 17, 1901. Another Democratic Club, the Iroquois Club of Chicago, issued several publications, including a magazine.

Edgar Lee Masters's "Jefferson" appears in *Poems of People* (N.Y., 1936). Masters's Jeffersonian style may be seen most clearly in *The New Star Chamber and Other Essays* (Chicago, 1904). Significantly, he dedicated his bitter *Lincoln the Man* (N.Y., 1931) to Jefferson. Henry Budd's address, *Thomas Jefferson*, delivered at several places, separately published, and collected in his *St. Mary's Hall Lectures, and Other Papers* (Phila., 1898), offers a moderate statement of the Jeffersonian code. Oscar W. Underwood's autobiography, *Drifting Sands of Party Politics* (N.Y., 1928) is a superb rendering of the old-fashioned Jeffersonian. On Josephus Daniels, in addition to the *Raleigh News and Observer*, see his *Editor in Politics* and his son Jonathan's *The End of Innocence* (Phila., 1954). On Vest, in addition to his speeches in the Senate, consult his two main addresses under the title *Thomas Jefferson*, the first delivered at the University of Missouri, June 4, 1885 (St. Louis, 1885), the second before the Jefferson Club of St. Louis, October 31, 1895 (St. Louis, 1895). John Sharp Williams's Columbia University lectures, *Thomas Jefferson, His Permanent Influence on American Institutions* (N.Y., 1913), throw more light on the author than on the subject. George C. Osborn, *John Sharp Williams: Planter Statesman of the Deep South* (Baton Rouge, 1943) is an able biography, but one must turn to the *Cong. Record* to appreciate Williams's ardent championing of Jefferson. James H. (Cyclone) Davis, *A Political Revelation* . . . (Dallas, 1894) and *Memoir* (Sherman, Texas, 1935) are fascinating. C. Vann Woodward, *Tom Watson, Agrarian Rebel* (N.Y., 1938) is a superb biography. Watson speaks for himself in *The Life and Times of Thomas Jefferson* (N.Y., 1903; revised, 1927), in his *Political and Economic Handbook*, 5th ed. (Thomson, Ga., 1916), and in various magazines, especially *The Jeffersonian*, I-V (1907-10) which invariably carried pictures of Jefferson and Monticello on the cover.

Of primary importance for George's Jeffersonianism are "Jefferson and the Land Question," included in *The Writings of Thomas Jefferson*, A. A. Lipscomb and A. E. Bergh, eds., XV (Wash., 1903), and also the report of his speech at the Jefferson Day celebration of the Democratic League of King's County, the *Brooklyn Eagle*, April 14, 1897. See too the following: Henry George, Jr., *The Life of Henry George* (Toronto, 1900) and *The Menace of Privilege* (N.Y., 1906); James G. Maguire, *Direct Taxation of Land Values* (Wash., 1894); Hamlin Garland, "A New Declaration of Rights," *The Arena*, III (January 1891); Frederic C. Howe, *Revolution and Democracy* (N.Y., 1921); Edmund J. Burke, *Thomas Jefferson, Apostle of Freedom and Equality of Opportunity* ... (Cambridge, 1934); Albert Jay Nock, *Henry George* (N.Y., 1939); and various Single Tax organs, especially *The Public*, I-XIII (1898-1913). Bryan is best approached through his *Speeches*, 2 v. (N.Y., 1909), *The First Battle: A Story of the Campaign of 1896* (Chicago, 1896), and his various news media, especially *The Commoner*, I-XIII (1901-13). The latter includes many speeches and writings relevant to Jefferson not collected elsewhere. Others of interest are in the *Raleigh News and Observer*, January 8, 1899, and the *New York World*, April 20, 1899. See also, "Jeffersonian Principles," *No. Amer. Rev.*, CLXVIII (June 1899). Bryan's parting words at Monticello are reported by James O. Bennett, *Chicago Tribune*, December 20, 1931.

The *Cong. Record* is the primary source for Jefferson's involvement in current public issues. The views of the civil service reformers may be gathered from the following: "A Look Before and After," *No. Amer. Rev.*, CVIII (January 1869); George T. Curtis, *Report of the Senate Committee on Civil Service and Retrenchment*, 47th Cong., 1 Sess., May 15, 1882; Dorman B. Eaton, *Term and Tenure of Office* (N.Y., 1882); E. C. Howland, "The Spoils System: Its Origin and Cure," in *Prize Essays on Civil Service Reform* (Boston, 1882). Jefferson's letters to Eppes on the currency were widely publicized and debated in Ohio, 1874-76; see the *Cincinnati Enquirer* and *Cleveland Leader*, and also James A. Garfield's analysis in his collected *Works*. The letters are repeatedly cited in Peter Cooper, *Ideas for a Science of Good Government* ... 2nd ed. (N.Y., 1883).

The Democratic bugbear, centralization, is sharply revealed in William A. Wallace, "The Mission of the Democratic Party," *No. Amer. Rev.*, CXXXII (January 1881). But the concern was widespread, as witnessed by Brooks Adams, "The Platform of the New Party," *No. Amer. Rev.*, CXIX (July 1874) and Charles Ingersoll, *Fears of Democracy* ... (Phila., 1875). Several expressions of the conservative view of the Jeffersonian tradition: Matthew Mark Trumbull, *Thomas Jefferson, A Lecture* ... *February 20, 1887* (n.p., n.d.) and *Thomas Jefferson, The Father of American Democracy* (Chicago, n.d.); William E. Russell, "Jefferson and His Party Today," *The Forum*, XXI (July 1896); John R. Dunlap, *Jeffersonian Democracy* (N.Y., 1903); John W. Wayland, *The Political Opinions of Thomas Jefferson* (N.Y., 1907); Judson Harmon, Address, in National Democratic Club, *Annual Dinner of Jefferson Day* ... (n.p., [1909]). Grover Cleveland's opinion of Jefferson may be found in his *Writings and Speeches*, G. F. Parker, ed. (N.Y., 1892); see also, Everett P. Wheeler, *Sixty Years of American Life* (N.Y., 1917). John Fiske's essays on Jefferson and Jackson in *Essays Historical and Literary*, I (Boston, 1902) make a valuable statement of the *laissez-faire* view. The opposite view is accented in Mary Platt Parmalee, "Jefferson and His Political Philosophy," *The Arena*, XVI (October 1897); and in the *Cong. Record*, 51 Cong., 1 Sess. (Representative Enloe, February 6, 1890), 52 Cong., 1 Sess. (Senator Call, July 22, 1892), and 55 Cong., 2 Sess. (Senator Butler, February 3, 1898). Clear recognition of the Democratic party's "hesitation": B. O. Flower, "Pure Democracy Versus Vicious Governmental Favoritism," *The Arena*, VIII (July 1893); *N.Y. Eve. Post*, April 14, 1905; *N.Y. Tribune*, July 8, 1905. The Jefferson Birthday squabble of 1899 in New York City is best followed in the metropolitan press; but see also Perry Belmont's account in *An American Democrat* (N.Y., 1940).

Several historical studies contribute to the understanding of the Jeffersonian aspect of the imperialism controversy: Albert K. Weinberg, *Manifest Destiny: A Study of Nationalist Expansion in American History* (Baltimore, 1935); Julius W. Pratt, *Expansionists of 1898* (Baltimore, 1935); Fred H. Harrington, "The Anti-Imperialist Movement," *Miss. Valley Hist. Rev.*, XXII (Sept. 1935); Frank Tannenbaum, *The American Tradition in Foreign Policy* (Norman, Okla., 1955). Jefferson's part in the debate is detailed in *Cong. Record*, 55 Cong., 3 Sess., primarily. George F. Hoar's great address on Jefferson appears as the "Special Introduction" to the Memorial Edition (Lipscomb and Bergh, eds.) of Jefferson's *Writings*. See also Hoar's *Autobiography of Seventy Years*, 2 v. (N.Y., 1903). David Starr Jordon, *Imperial Democracy . . .* (N.Y., 1899) illuminates the political doctrine of the anti-imperialists, as do John Clark Ridpath, "Three Epochs of Democracy and Three Men," *Arena*, XIX (April 1898) and *Official Proceedings of the Democratic National Convention . . . 1900* (Chicago, 1900). William E. Dodd, "The Times of Jefferson," *Raleigh News and Observer*, January 14, 1900, and E. P. Powell, "Struggle of Autocracy with Democracy at the Opening of the Twentieth Century," *Arena*, XXXIV (September 1905) link Hamilton's expansionist plans to the imperialism of 1898. Sidney Webster, *The Two Treaties of Paris and the Supreme Court* (N.Y., 1901) compares the treaties of 1803 and 1898; see also Williams, *Jefferson's Permanent Influence*. The *Springfield* (Mass.) *Republican*, 1899-1900, is probably the best newspaper source for Jefferson.

For the use of Jefferson by the imperialists: Albert J. Beveridge, "The March of the Flag," *Meaning of the Times and Other Speeches* (Indianapolis, 1908); Theodore Roosevelt, Letter of Acceptance, September 15, 1900, *Works* (N.Y., 1926); John B. Stanchfield, "The Meaning of Jefferson," *Writings*, Memorial Edition, XIV; Albert Shaw, *Address . . . Richmond, Virginia, April 13, 1904* (n.p., n.d.). Morris M. Estee, "Jeffersonian Principles," *Overland Monthly*, XXXIV (July 1899) answers Bryan's article of that title in the *No. Amer. Rev.* of the previous month. John B. McMaster, "Annexation and Universal Suffrage," *The Forum*, XXIV (December 1898), and Hannis Taylor, *The Origin and Growth of the American Constitution* (Boston, 1911) link imperialist principles to

Jefferson's Ordinance of 1784—and 1787. The *N.Y. Tribune*, 1899-1903, is particularly articulate on "Jefferson as a Despot." Lyman Abbott's editorials in *The Outlook* and lectures, *The Rights of Man* (Boston, 1901) attack the Jeffersonian political philosophy. *The Battle of 1900: An Official Handbook for Every American Citizen* (Haverhill, Mass., 1900) offers a convenient guide to Republican and Democratic arguments in the presidential campaign. Mr. Dooley's "Voices from the Tomb" is reprinted in *Mr. Dooley: Now and Forever*, Louis Filler, ed. (Palo Alto, 1954).

On the Louisiana Purchase and the government of the Orleans Territory, see particularly the accounts by Henry Adams, *History of the United States . . .* II (N.Y., 1889) and Alcée Fortier, *A History of Louisiana*, III (N.Y., 1904). Two interpretations highly critical of Jefferson are Thomas M. Cooley, "The Acquisition of Louisiana," *Indiana Historical Society Publications*, II (Indianapolis, 1887) and Josiah P. Quincy, "The Louisiana Purchase; and the Appeal to Posterity," *Proc. of the Mass. Hist. Society*, XVIII (November 1903). The imperialism controversy offers abundant illustration of the new prestige of the Louisiana Purchase. An earlier encomium is James G. Blaine's in *Twenty Years in Congress*, 2 v. (Norwich, Conn., 1884). See also E. M. Heim, "The Louisiana Purchase," *The Bucknell Mirror*, XXII (May 1903); H. Addington Bruce, *The Romance of American Expansion* (N.Y., 1909); William M. Thornton, *Who Bought Louisiana?*; Emerson Hough, *The Magnificent Adventure* (N.Y., 1916). Fortier, *Louisiana*, recalls that state's gift to Jefferson's daughter; Frederic L. Paxson, *The Territory of Jefferson: A Spontaneous Commonwealth*, in *University of Colorado Studies*, III (Boulder, 1905) treats a significant episode; the *St. Louis Globe-Democrat*, May 5, 1900, reports the proposal to give Jefferson's name to the Indian Territory. "In Honor of Jefferson," *Missouri Historical Review*, XXXVII (January 1943) is an index to Jefferson in Missouri. The *Weekly Missouri Statesman* (Columbia), June 12, 1885, reports the dedication of the monument at the University of Missouri. See also the *University of Missouri Bulletin*, May 1, 1930.

Blaine's reproach is quoted in Walter B. Stevens, *Centennial History of Missouri*, II (St. Louis, 1921). The *Al. Bul. of the Univ. of Va.*, New Series, I, 1901, reports on two abortive monument enterprises. See also, Jackson's *Missouri Democracy*, I. David R. Francis, *The Universal Exposition* (St. Louis, 1904) is self-explanatory. More valuable for Jefferson is Stevens's *Centennial History* and the "Scrapbook" on the Exposition and the Jefferson Memorial kept by him and deposited in the Missouri Historical Society. The dedication of the Memorial is fully described in the St. Louis newspapers. Karl Bitter is the subject of a biography by Ferdinand Schevill, Chicago, 1917.

VI. HISTORY II

Cardinal examples of family vengeance on Jefferson are the following: Henry Cabot Lodge, *Life and Letters of George Cabot;* George Clinton Genêt, *Washington, Jefferson, and "Citizen" Genêt, 1793* (N.Y., 1899); William Wirt Henry,

Patrick Henry: Life, Correspondence, and Speeches (N.Y., 1891). The same author wrote a detailed rebuttal of Jefferson's biographical sketch of Patrick Henry, which was first published in *The Age* (Philadelphia) in 1867, in *Character and Public Career of Patrick Henry* (Richmond, 1867). Jefferson's letter and other reactions to it are published in Dawson's *Historical Magazine*, 2nd Series, II (August 1867). The Randall-Grigsby correspondence, previously cited, contains interesting sidelights on the Henry-Jefferson relationship. Meade Minnigerode, *Jefferson, Friend of France, 1793* (N.Y., 1929) continues the defense of Genêt against his "betrayer." Other biographies of Jefferson's lesser contemporaries which manifest inherited animosity are Moncure Conway, *Omitted Chapters of History disclosed in the Life and Public Papers of Edmund Randolph* (N.Y., 1888); Edmund Quincy, *Life of Josiah Quincy of Massachusetts* (Boston, 1867); William Whitelock, *The Life and Times of John Jay* (N.Y., 1887). [Lloyd Simpson], *Notes on Thomas Jefferson* (Phila., 1885) is a compendium of old complaints.

David S. Muzzey's Preface to his *Thomas Jefferson* (N.Y., 1918) has some penetrating things to say about partisan historiography; see also his "Thomas Jefferson, Humanitarian," *The American Review*, IV (January 1926). Henry Budd, *Thomas Jefferson*, exposes some of McMaster's distortions. Perry Belmont, *Survival of the Democratic Principle* (N.Y., 1926) is substantially devoted to the examination of Federalist influence in the writing of political history. Champ Clark bewails the New England "literary conspiracy," *Cong. Record*, 53 Cong., 3 Sess. (December 10, 1894) and 60 Cong., 1 Sess. (February 13, 1908). In the latter session, March 25, 1908, Augustus O. Stanley dwells at length on the subject. J. F. Jameson, *The History of Historical Writing in America* (Boston, 1891) has some provocative observations. The "great man" emphasis is pointed up by Charles Warren, *The Trumpeters of the Constitution* (Rochester, 1927). The changed viewpoint around 1900 in American historiography is observed in Charles Grier Sellers, Jr., "Andrew Jackson Versus the Historians," *Miss. Valley Hist. Rev.*, XLIV (March 1958). See also Merle Curti, "The Democratic Theme in American Historical Literature," *ibid.* XXXIX (June 1952). A general treatment is Michael Kraus, *A History of American History* (N.Y., 1937).

J. C. Levenson, *The Mind and Art of Henry Adams* (Boston, 1957) is the best analysis of Adams's historical work from a literary angle. Valuable too are the following: William H. Jordy, *Henry Adams: Scientific Historian* (New Haven, 1952); Henry S. Commager, "Henry Adams," *The Marcus W. Jernegan Essays;* Herbert Agar, Introduction, *The Formative Years*, 2 v. (Boston, 1947), an abridgment of the *History;* E. C. Rozwenc, "Henry Adams and the Federalists," in H. Stuart Hughes and others, eds., *Teachers of History; Essays in Honor of Laurence Bradford Packard* (Ithaca, N.Y., 1954). Ernest Samuels's brilliant *Henry Adams, The Middle Years* (Cambridge, 1958) was unfortunately not available for my study. *The Letters of Henry Adams, 1858-1891*, Worthington C. Ford, ed. (Boston, 1930) is often illuminating. Lodge's review of the

Life of Albert Gallatin, included in his *Studies of History* (Boston, 1884), furnishes but one of many indexes to the difference between Adams and Lodge. Two reviews of the *History* which recognize Adams's ambivalent attitude toward Jefferson will be found in the *Nation,* XLIX (December 12, 19, 1889) and the *Atlantic Monthly,* LXV (February 1890).

Edward Channing's Preface to *The Jeffersonian System 1801-1811* (Boston, 1906) and his bibliographical notes in *A History of the People of the United States,* IV (N.Y., 1917) acknowledge his heavy indebtedness to Adams. Alfred T. Mahan, *Sea Power in Its Relation to the War of 1812,* 2 v. (Boston, 1905) reflects Adams's ideas but with more direct criticism of Jefferson's posture of weakness. The Unitarian and world peace advocate, Edwin D. Mead, shows the opposite influence of Adams's work; see, for example, *The Principles of the Founders* (Boston, 1903), *Washington, Jefferson, and Franklin on War* (Boston, 1913), and "Jefferson, Wilson, and the Democratic Party," *Unity,* CXII (December 3, 1928). The critical view of the Embargo prevalent when Adams wrote is evinced in William Cullen Bryant and Sidney Howard Gay, *A Popular History of the United States,* IV (N.Y., 1880). The beginnings of reappraisal may be seen in Francis W. Hirst, *Life and Letters of Thomas Jefferson* (N.Y., 1926); Louis M. Sears, *Jefferson and the Embargo* (Durham, N.C., 1927); Gilbert Chinard, *Thomas Jefferson: Apostle of Americanism* (Boston, 1929); Schuyler Dean Haslett, "Jefferson and England: The Embargo as a Measure of Coercion," *Americana* XXXIV (January 1940); Julius H. Macloed, "Jefferson and the Navy: A Defense," *Huntington Library Qtly.,* VIII (February 1945). Herbert Agar, *The Price of Union* (Boston, 1950), and indeed all of his writings on Jefferson, shows Adams's continuing influence. For a recent critical view: Irving Brant, "James Madison and His Times," *Amer. Hist. Rev.,* LVII (July 1952).

Helen D. Bullock briefly sketches the history of the Jefferson Papers in the nineteenth century in an essay contained in *The Jefferson Papers of the University of Virginia* (Charlottesville, 1950). The House Library Committee reports on the acquisition of the family papers, September 26, 1890, 51 Cong., 1 Sess. Thomas Jefferson Coolidge, "Remarks," *Proc. of the Mass. Hist. Soc.,* XII (June 1898) deals with his acquisition and bequest. Note also his *Autobiography* (Boston, 1923). For Jonathan Daniels's trenchant comment, see *The End of Innocence.* In addition to the volume of letters from the Coolidge bequest, which the Massachusetts Historical Society published in its *Proceedings* of 1900, the growing interest in Jefferson's Papers is marked by the following: Selections from the correspondence with William Short, *The Southern Bivouac,* New Series, II (December 1886, March, May 1887), John Bigelow, "Jefferson's Financial Diary," *Harper's Mag.,* LXX (March 1885), *Calendar of the Correspondence of Thomas Jefferson* (Wash., 1894). On the latter, which first revealed the largeness of the State Department collection, see the comment in the *Nation,* LXIII (September 3, 1896).

John P. Foley edited *The Jefferson Cyclopedia* (N.Y., 1900), a huge "Manual of Jeffersonian Doctrine." Several anthologies of Jefferson's writings, sometimes combined with biography, appeared around the turn of the century: Richard S. Poppen, *Thomas Jefferson; the Declaration of Independence and Letters, Addresses* . . . (St. Louis, 1898); S. E. Forman, *The Life and Writings of Thomas Jefferson* (Indianapolis, 1900); Benjamin S. Catchings, *Master Thoughts of Thomas Jefferson* (N.Y., 1907). The latter was compiled from the Memorial Edition. The inaugural banquet of the Thomas Jefferson Memorial Association is fully reported in the *Washington Post*, April 14, 1903. For the debate on federal aid to the movement, see the *Cong. Record*, 57 Cong., 2 Sess. Photographs of the medals struck for the Association, along with several others bearing Jefferson's likeness, will be found in Robert J. Eidlitz, "Medals Relating to Thomas Jefferson," *The Numismatist*, XXXVII (September 1924).

Lindsay Swift sketches Paul L. Ford in *The Critic* (November 1898); see also the *Dict. of Amer. Biog.* The Ford Papers in the N.Y. Public Library reveal him at work on his *Writings of Thomas Jefferson*, 10 v. (N.Y., 1892-99). Worthington C. Ford's decidedly hostile opinion of Jefferson may be found in *Thomas Jefferson and James Thompson Callendar, 1798-1802* (N.Y., 1897) and "Jefferson and the Newspaper," *Records of the Columbia Historical Society*, VIII (Wash., 1905). Paul Ford states his more generous opinion in the Introduction to the *Writings* and in the brochure, *Thomas Jefferson* (Boston, 1904). *The Dial*, XIV (February 16, 1893), XIX (August 1, 1895), and XXXVI (April 16, 1904), reviews Ford's work and finds it too friendly to Jefferson. His edition is compared favorably to the Memorial Edition by Harold Jefferson Coolidge, *Thoughts on Jefferson* (Boston, 1936), and Edward Channing, *History*, IV; compared unfavorably with the Congress Edition by Charles D. Hazen, *Contemporary American Opinion of the French Revolution* (Baltimore, 1897). For Jefferson and the Virginia Constitution: W. C. Ford, "Jefferson's Constitution for Virginia," *Nation*, LI (April 7, 1890); Paul Ford, *Writings*, II; Kate Mason Rowland, "A Lost Paper of Thomas Jefferson," *Wm. and Mary Qtly.*, I (July 1892); D. R. Anderson, "Jefferson and the Virginia Constitution," *Amer. Hist. Rev.*, XXI (July 1916); Julian P. Boyd, "The Virginia Constitution," *The Papers of Thomas Jefferson*, I (Princeton, 1950). For the controversy on the authorship of the Revolutionary document, the Declaration of the Causes and Necessity of Taking Up Arms, see George H. Moore's address, New-York Historical Society, 1882, conveniently included in Charles J. Stillé, *Life and Times of John Dickinson* (Phila., 1891). Stillé, of course, supports Moore; Muzzey's biography of Jefferson discusses the controversy; Boyd's definitive treatment is in *Papers*, I.

James C. Welling, "The State Rights Theory," *Papers of the Amer. Hist. Assn.* (N.Y., 1888) states the problem of the Virginia and Kentucky Resolutions. The relevant inquiries are as follows: R. T. Durrett, "The Resolutions of 1798 and 1799," *The Southern Bivouac*, New Series, I (March, April, May, 1886); Ethelbert D. Warfield, *The Kentucky Resolutions of 1798* (N.Y., 1887); Sarah N. Randolph, "The Kentucky Resolutions in a New Light," *Nation*, XLIV (May 5, 1887) and Warfield's reply, *ibid.* (May 24, 1887); Edward Channing, "The

Kentucky Resolutions of 1798," *Amer. Hist. Rev.*, XX (January 1915); Frank M. Anderson, "Contemporary Opinion of the Kentucky and Virginia Resolutions," *ibid.* V (October 1899, January 1900), and "The Enforcement of the Alien and Sedition Laws," *Annual Report of the Amer. Hist. Assn. for 1912.* Koch and Ammon, "The Virginia and Kentucky Resolutions," cited earlier, and James Morton Smith, *Freedom's Fetters; The Alien and Sedition Laws and American Civil Liberties* (Ithaca, N.Y., 1956) exemplify the current tendency.

Jefferson is viewed as an infidel or freethinker in the following: B. F. Underwood, *Jefferson, the Free-Thinking Philosopher and Statesman* (Seymour, Ind., n.d.); John E. Remsburg, *Six Historic Americans* (N.Y., 1906); Joseph Lewis, *Jefferson, the Freethinker* (N.Y., 1952). The pious agree: Simpson, *Notes on Jefferson;* J. S. C. Abbott, *Lives of the Presidents of the United States* (Boston, 1869); and editorial comment in the *Chicago Tribune*, April 18, 1881, on Robert G. Ingersoll's popular lecture, "The Great Infidels." Randall describes "The Life and Morals of Jesus of Nazareth," *Life*, Appendix XXX. Cyrus Adler's Introduction to the Congress Edition under that title provides further information on the document and explains his part in its discovery. John F. Lacey's promotion is reported in the *St. Louis Globe-Democrat*, May 20, 1900, and in the *Richmond Dispatch*, May 22, 1902. See the latter, May 27, 1902, and the *N.Y. Tribune*, May 21, 1902, for opposition to government publication.

The following is offered as a representative sample of the discussion of Jefferson's religion: W. J. Bryan, "The Statute for Establishing Religious Freedom," Memorial Edition, VIII; Edward N. Calisch, "Jefferson's Religion," *ibid.* VII; J. Leslie Hall, "The Religious Opinions of Thomas Jefferson," *Sewanee Review*, XXII (April 1913); John T. Christian, "The Religion of Thomas Jefferson," *The Review and Expositor*, XVI (July 1919); Henry E. Jackson, Introduction, *The Jefferson Bible* (N.Y., 1923); various sermons reported in the *N.Y. Times*, April 12-July 15, 1926; Joseph Fort Newton, "Thomas Jefferson and the Religion of America," *Forum*, LXXVIII (December 1927); Walter Lippmann, *American Inquisitors* (N.Y., 1928); Claude G. Bowers, *Civil and Religious Liberty* (Worcester, Mass., 1930); Christopher Hollis, *The American Heresy* (N.Y., 1930); Roydon J. Mott, "Sources of Jefferson's Ecclesiastical Views," *Church History*, III (December 1934); "Jefferson on Religion," *America*, LXIX (May 8, 1943); W. M. Plöchl, "Religious Freedom," *Catholic Digest*, VII (June 1943); George Harmon Knolles, "The Religious Ideas of Thomas Jefferson," *Miss. Valley Hist. Rev.*, XXX (September 1943); Arnold Peterson, *Theocracy or Democracy?* (N.Y., 1944); S. W. Baron, *Modern Nationalism and Religion* (N.Y., 1947); Edgar J. Goodspeed, "Thomas Jefferson and the Bible," *Harvard Theological Review*, XL (January 1947). Several of the above express sectarian viewpoints. Marguerite F. Melcher, *The Shaker Adventure* (Princeton, 1941) quotes a curious, and probably apochryphal, statement of Jefferson's endorsing the Shaker faith. On the Unitarians, see E. P. Powell, "Thomas Jefferson and Religion," *Open Court*, X (1896); Thomas R. Slicer, "Thomas Jefferson and the Influence of Democracy upon Religion," in *Pioneers of Religious Liberty in*

America (Boston, 1903); Samuel M. Crowthers, *The Religion of Thomas Jefferson* (Boston, 1926); A. Powell Davis, "The Religion of Thomas Jefferson" (Summit, N. J., May 2, 1943; mimeographed copy in the American Philosophical Society); Henry Wilder Foote, *Thomas Jefferson: Champion of Religious Freedom, Advocate of Christian Morals* (Boston, 1947); Frederick May Eliot, *What Kind of Christian was Thomas Jefferson?* (Boston, 1947). The *N.Y. Times*, April 4, 1947, reports the Unitarian services at the Jefferson Memorial.

John H. Hazelton, *The Declaration of Independence, Its History* (N.Y., 1906) is a great work of scholarship. Particularly important in the study of the document itself: Mellen Chamberlain, "The Authentication of the Declaration of Independence, July 4, 1776," *Proc. of the Mass. Hist. Soc.*, 2nd Series, I (November 1884); Sydney F. Fisher, "The Twenty-eight Charges against the King in the Declaration of Independence," *Pa. Mag. of Hist. and Biog.*, XXXI (July 1907); John C. Fitzpatrick, *The Spirit of the Revolution* (Boston, 1924); Julian P. Boyd, *The Declaration of Independence* (Wash., 1943) and "New Light on Jefferson and His Great Task," *N.Y. Times Mag.*, April 13, 1947. Fitzpatrick, in the book cited, treats several aspects of the document's history in the nineteenth century. Thomas Donaldson, *The House in Which Jefferson Wrote the Declaration of Independence* (Phila., 1898) is definitive. On the writing desk: *Proceedings had in the Senate and House of Representatives, April 23, 1880, on the Occasion of the Presentation of Thomas Jefferson's Writing Desk . . .* (Wash., 1882). See also the *N.Y. Tribune*, April 16, 1880. Moses Coit Tyler's discussion of the Declaration in his *Literary History* was very influential, as witnessed, in part, by Herbert Friedenwald, *The Declaration of Independence* (N.Y., 1904). William F. Dana, "The Declaration of Independence as Justification for Revolution," *Harvard Law Review*, XIII (January 1900) is an important article. Carl Becker's *The Declaration of Independence* (N.Y., 1922) is a classic; but for a different view, see Ralph Barton Perry, *Puritanism and Democracy* (N.Y., 1944). Edward Dumbauld, *The Declaration of Independence and What It Means Today* (Norman, Okla., 1950) is the best guide to the interpretation of the Declaration.

Discussions of Jefferson's borrowings (sometimes translated as thefts) are numerous. H. L. Ganter, "Jefferson's 'Pursuit of Happiness' and Some Forgotten Men," *Wm. and Mary Qtly.*, 2nd Series, XVI (July, October, 1936) sifts the evidence as to a key phrase. Three of Paine's advocates are represented as follows: William H. Burr, *The Declaration of Independence, A Masterpiece; But How It Got Mutilated!* (n.p., 1881); W. M. Van der Weyde, *Who Wrote the Declaration of Independence?* (N.Y., 1911); Joseph Lewis, *Thomas Paine, Author of the Declaration of Independence* (N.Y., 1947). The major citations for the Bellarmine-Jefferson legend: Gaillard Hunt, "The Virginia Declaration of Rights and Cardinal Bellarmine," *Catholic Historical Review*, III (October 1917); Alfred O'Rahilly, "The Catholic Origins of Democracy" and "The Sources of English and American Democracy," *Studies* (March, June, 1919); Joseph Husslein, "Democracy a 'Popish' Innovation," *America*, XXI (July 5,

1919); David S. Schaff, "The Bellarmine-Jefferson Legend and the Declaration of Independence," Paper read before the American Society of Church History, reported in the *N.Y. Times*, December 28, 1926; John C. Rager, "Catholic Sources of the Declaration of Independence," *Catholic Mind*, XXVIII (July 8, 1930); John M. Lenhart, "Genesis of the Political Principles of the American Declaration of Independence," *Central Blatt and Social Justice*, September, October, 1932; Frederick J. Zwierlein, "Jefferson, Jesuits, and the Declaration," *America*, XLIX (July 8, 1933); "Reviving a Controversy," *Extension*, XXXVII (January 1943); John F. Whealon, "The Great 'Preamble': Did Bellarmine Influence Jefferson? A Look at the Record," *Commonweal*, XLII (July 6, 1946). The last article indicates the demise of the legend; an index to changing views is provided by the two editions of John F. Ryan and Moorhouse F. X. Millar, *The State and the Church* (N.Y., 1924, 1950).

Several recent studies of political parties are full of insights for the historian. Particularly helpful for the present study were E. E. Schattschneider, *Party Government* (N.Y., 1942); Maurice Duverger, *Political Parties; Their Organization and Activity in the Modern State*, Barbara and Robert Worth, tr. (London, 1954); Austin Ranney and Willmore Kendall, *Democracy and the American Party System* (N.Y., 1956). For Bryce, in addition to Part III of *The American Commonwealth*, see his Preface to M. Ostrogorski, *Democracy and the Organization of Political Parties*, and also a not very candid address on Jefferson, *University and Historical Addresses* (N.Y., 1913). George T. Smart, *The Temper of the American People* (Boston, 1912) makes some penetrating observations on the sense of the political past in America. The conventional view of the "history of the parties" is stated, with slight variations, in the following: Alexander Johnston, *History of American Politics* (N.Y., 1879), *American Political History 1763-1876* (N.Y., 1905); J. P. Gordy, *A History of Political Parties in the United States*, 4 v., 2nd ed. (N.Y., 1900); James H. Hopkins, *A History of Political Parties in the United States* (N.Y., 1900); James A. Woodburn, *Political Parties and Party Problems in the United States* (N.Y., 1903). See also, Meville Weston Fuller, "Jefferson and Hamilton," *The Dial*, IV (May 1883) and William G. Brown, "A Defense of American Parties," *Atlantic Monthly*, LXXXVI (November 1900).

Of cardinal importance for the new viewpoint are the following: Anson D. Morse, *Parties and Party Leaders* (Boston, 1923); Henry Jones Ford, *The Rise and Growth of American Politics* (N.Y., 1898); Jesse Macy, *Political Parties in the United States, 1846-1861* (N.Y. 1900); O. G. Libby, *Geographical Distribution of the Vote* ... (Madison, Wis., 1894), "A Sketch of the Early Political Parties in the United States," *Qtly. Journal of the Univ. of North Dakota*, II (April 1912), "Partisan Scholarship" and "Political Factions in Washington's Administration," *ibid.* III (April, July, 1913); Edgar E. Robinson, *The Evolution of American Political Parties* (N.Y., 1924); Arthur N. Holcombe, *The Political Parties of Today* (N.Y., 1924). Andrew C. McLaughlin discusses the

tendency: "American History and American Democracy," *Amer. Hist. Rev.*, XX
(January 1915). New light is shed on a perennial problem in J. M. Merriam,
"Jefferson's Use of the Executive Patronage," *Papers of the Amer. Hist. Assn.*
(N.Y., 1888); Gaillard Hunt, "Office Seeking During Jefferson's Administration," *Amer. Hist. Rev.*, III (January 1898); Carl Russell Fish, *The Civil Service
and the Patronage* (Cambridge, 1904). Jefferson's role as party leader is emphasized in such older works as those of Schouler, Lodge, and Henry Adams, as
well as in such newer works as John Spencer Bassett, *The Federalist System*
(N.Y., 1906) and Edward Channing, *History*.

   Charles A. Beard: An Appraisal, Howard K. Beale, ed. (Lexington, Ky., 1954)
collects the opinions of a number of scholars and provides the best introduction
to the subject. In addition to Beard's writings cited in the text, the following
contribute to the understanding of his viewpoint: "Jefferson and the New Freedom," *New Republic*, I (November 14, 1914); *The Economic Basis of Politics*
(N.Y., 1922); *The American Party Battle* (N.Y., 1928); *The Republic* (N.Y.,
1943). Rather different impressions, however, are gathered from his *Jefferson,
Corporations, and the Constitution* (Wash., 1936); his report for the Educational
Policies Commission, *The Unique Function of Education in American Democracy* (Wash., 1937); and his Bicentennial address, "Thomas Jefferson: A Civilized Man," *Miss. Valley Hist. Rev.*, XXX (September 1943).

   E. H. Eby writes discerningly of Vernon L. Parrington in the commemorative
essay prefacing v. III of *Main Currents in American Thought*. J. Allen Smith,
The Spirit of American Government (N.Y., 1907) is particularly important for
understanding Parrington's angle of vision. Granville Hicks, "The Critical Principles of V. L. Parrington," *Science and Society*, III (Fall 1939) is an excellent
essay. See also, Richard Hofstadter, "Parrington and the Jeffersonian Tradition,"
Journal of the History of Ideas, II (October 1941) and Arthur A. Ekirch, Jr.,
"Parrington and the Decline of American Liberalism," *American Qtly.*, III
(Winter 1951). The criticisms of Parrington advanced by Yvor Winters in
The Anatomy of Nonsense (N.Y., 1943) and by Lionel Trilling in *The Liberal
Imagination* (N.Y., 1950), while often perceptive are also often mistaken.
Henry Steele Commager, *The American Mind* (New Haven, 1950) helps to
put Parrington in historical context.

VII. DEMOCRACY II

   The sense that the future, conceived not only nationally but also progressively,
belonged to Hamilton was forecast by D. A. Wasson, "The Modern Type of
Oppression," *No. Amer. Rev.*, CXIX (October 1874). Suggestive too are the
remarks in the following: Joseph Brucker, *The Chief Political Parties in the
United States* (Milwaukee, 1880); *Butler's Book; Autobiography and Personal
Reminiscences of Major General Benjamin F. Butler* (Boston, 1892); Homer
B. Sprague, "The Mayflower Compact and the Jeffersonian Heresy," *Our Day
and Altruistic Review*, XV (September 1895); John Beattie Crozier, *History*

of Intellectual Development: On the Lines of Modern Evolution, II (N.Y., 1901).

Gertrude Atherton describes her affair with Hamilton in *Adventures of a Novelist* (N.Y., 1932). Hamilton's ghost makes an appearance in her political novel, *Senator North* (N.Y., 1900). See also her article "The Hunt for Hamilton's Mother," *No. Amer. Rev.*, CLXXV (July 1902), and *A Few of Hamilton's Letters* (N.Y., 1902). Roosevelt's comments on Jefferson and Hamilton are scattered throughout his *Works* and in the letters edited by Joseph B. Bishop as *Theodore Roosevelt and His Time,* 2 v. (N.Y., 1920). John S. Williams's outburst will be found in *Cong. Record,* 58 Cong., 2 Sess., January 26, 1904. Albert J. Beveridge, *Life of John Marshall,* I (Boston, 1916) accentuates Jefferson's shortcomings as a man of action. Hamilton's illicit affair with Mrs. Reynolds had a curious fascination for his new admirers, as seen in George A. Townsend, *Mrs. Reynolds and Hamilton, A Romance* (N.Y., 1890); Mary P. Hamlin and George Arliss, *Hamilton, A Play in Four Acts* (Boston, 1918); Chard Powers Smith, *Hamilton, A Poetic Drama in Three Acts* (N.Y., 1930).

F. S. Oliver's general political outlook is set forth in *Ordeal by Battle* (N.Y., 1915) and *The Endless Adventure,* 2 v. (London, 1930), as well as in his book on Hamilton. Acclaim of the latter by American Hamiltonians: Bishop, *Theodore Roosevelt;* N. M. Butler, *Looking Forward* (N.Y., 1932) and *Across the Busy Years* (N.Y., 1940); Frank Buffington Vrooman, *The New Politics* (N.Y., 1911); Walter Lippmann, "Integral America," *New Republic,* February 19, 1916; Claude Bowers, *Beveridge and the Progressive Era* (N.Y., 1932). Augustus O. Stanley, *Character and Services of Thomas Jefferson and Alexander Hamilton . . .* (Wash., 1908) links Oliver's book to the revival of Hamilton's reputation and policies. Claude Bowers, *N.Y. Journal,* March 17, 1932, reports the work's influence on the Irish nationalist and poet, George Russell ("A.E."); David C. Somervell, *Critical Epochs in History* (London, 1923) suggests Oliver's influence on an English historian. Henry Jones Ford, *Alexander Hamilton* (N.Y., 1920) is consciously formed on Oliver's conception.

Older appreciations of Hamilton's greatness, and depreciations of Jefferson's, are preserved in M. W. Stryker, *Hamilton, Lincoln and Other Addresses* (Utica, N.Y., 1896); Chauncey M. Depew, *Orations, Addresses, and Speeches,* J. D. Champlin, ed. (N.Y., 1910), the first volume particularly; Rufus H. Choate, *Inaugural Address of . . . the American Ambassador, March 19th, 1904* (London, 1904); Joseph B. Simpson, *Hamiltonianism vs. Jeffersonianism* (Chester, Ill., 1904); Frank P. Stearns, *True Republicanism* (Phila., 1904); Alfred Neuberger, *Alexander Hamilton* (Paterson, N.J., 1907); *Gunton's Magazine,* editorials and articles, 1896-98. *One Welshman* (London, 1912) is the title of Whitelaw Reid's controversial address in Wales; Democrats in Congress protest, *Cong. Record,* 62 Cong., 3 Sess., December 5, 1912. The publications of the Hamilton Club of Chicago, for example, the magazine *The Hamiltonian* (1900-17), reflect conservative attitudes. Various honors (statues, anniversary commemorations, memorial associations, etc.) paid to Hamilton in and around

New York are reported in the *N.Y. Tribune:* November 23, 1880; February 23, 1892; March 25, 1900; October 13, 1900; November 18, 1903; July 10, 13, 1904. Henry Minor, *The Story of the Democratic Party* (N.Y., 1928) observes the currency of Hamilton symbol and doctrine in the Republican party.

For Herbert Croly, in addition to *The Promise of American Life* (N.Y., 1909), see his biography, *Marcus Alonzo Hanna* (N.Y., 1912) and *Progressive Democracy* (N.Y., 1914). Felix Frankfurter, "Herbert Croly and American Political Opinion," *New Republic,* LXIII, Part 2 (July 16, 1930) is one of several discerning essays in this memorial supplement of the magazine. Eric Goldman, *Rendezvous with Destiny* (N.Y., 1952) describes Croly's political outlook in the context of Progressivism. Vrooman, *The New Politics,* William S. Culbertson, *Alexander Hamilton: An Essay* (New Haven, 1911), and Franklin W. Collins, *The Constitution of the United States* (Wash., 1913) express similar views of Jefferson and Hamilton. The reaction against Jeffersonian concepts may be seen in much of the Progressive literature: Bernard Moses, *Democracy and Social Growth* (N.Y., 1898); Arthur George Sedgwick, *The Democratic Mistake* (N.Y., 1912); Edward Elliott, *American Government and Majority Rule* (Princeton, 1916); Frank J. Goodnow, *The American Conception of Liberty and Government* (Providence, 1916); Mary P. Follett, *The New State* (N.Y., 1912); William B. Munro, *The Invisible Government* (N.Y., 1928). Especially important for Walter Lippmann are *Preface to Politics* (N.Y., 1913), *Drift and Mastery* (N.Y., 1914), and *Public Opinion* (N.Y., 1922). Henry L. Stimson and McGeorge Bundy, *On Active Service in Peace and War* (N.Y., 1948) delineates the mind of a progressive-minded Hamiltonian.

Arthur Link charts Wilson's growth in *Wilson, The Road to the White House* (Princeton, 1947). His early views of Jefferson may be found in *Selected Literary and Political Papers and Addresses of Woodrow Wilson,* 3 v. (N.Y., 1925-27) and in *A History of the American People,* 5 v. (N.Y., 1902). These were much discussed in 1912-13; see, for example, *Cong. Record,* 62 Cong., 2 Sess.; Alfred Henry Lewis, "The Real Woodrow Wilson," *Hearst's Mag.,* XXI (May 1912); and "Jefferson-Wilson: A Record and A Forecast," *No. Amer. Rev.,* CXCVII (March 1913). Wilson's "The Spirit of Jefferson," appears in the *Princeton Alumni Weekly,* April 28, 1906; his Jefferson Day Address of 1912 in the *Cong. Record,* 62 Cong., 2 Sess. *The New Freedom* (N.Y., 1913) collects a number of the campaign speeches; it should be supplemented with John Wells Davidson, *A Crossroads of Freedom* (New Haven, 1956). The *Raleigh News and Observer,* January-March 1913, reports the inaugural's Jeffersonian hoopla; Arthur W. Dunn, *Gridiron Nights* (N.Y., 1915) recounts two Gridiron Club Dinners; William P. Borland, "Thomas Jefferson, the Great Progressive," *Cong. Record,* 63 Cong., 2 Sess., expresses the new Democratic conception. The first session of the same Congress, April 7, 1913, gives the debate on Wilson's departure from Jefferson's precedent of written messages. See also Charles Warren's article on the subject, *Proc. of the Mass. Hist. Soc.,* LVII (1924). Two opposed views of Jefferson, Wilson, and foreign policy are John Corbin, "From Jefferson to Wilson," *No. Amer. Rev.*, CCX (August 1919) and John H. Latané, "Jefferson's Influence on American Foreign Policy," *Al. Bul. of the Univ. of Va.*, XVII (July 1924). Josephus Daniels, "Jefferson's Philosophy and the Present Crisis," *ibid.* XI (July 1918) and Franklin P. Foster, *The World War, Jefferson and Democracy* (Anderson, Ind., 1917) link Jefferson to Wilsonian idealism. William K. Woolery, *The Relation of Thomas Jefferson to American Foreign Policy, 1783-1793* (Baltimore, 1927) is a standard work.

Arthur H. Vandenberg's three books are *Alexander Hamilton, The Greatest American* (N.Y., 1921), *If Hamilton Were Here Today* (N.Y., 1923), and *The Trail of a Tradition* (N.Y., 1926). Robert J. Warshow's *Alexander Hamilton, First American Business Man* (N.Y., 1931) was dedicated to Andrew Mellon. Several reports in the *N.Y. Times* are suggestive: January 12, 1922 (Vice-President Coolidge's address at the Hamilton Club, Chicago), May 18, 19, 1923 (dedication of the Treasury Building statue), November 18, 1924 (the conveyance of Hamilton Grange to the American Scenic and Historic Preservation Society), December 4, 5, 1924 (the Columbia University commemoration of the one hundred and fiftieth anniversary of Hamilton's matriculation), January 12, 13, 1928 (the National Republican Club's commencement of annual services at Hamilton's burial place), March 21, 1928 (the gift of one million dollars to the city of Chicago for a statue in Grant Park). The demise in the next decade may also be traced in the *Times;* see particularly, January 14, 1936; November 27, 28, 1929; January 15, 16, 1941.

Claude G. Bowers describes his early encounter with Jefferson and Hamilton, and how he came to write his famous book, in a personal letter to me, September 10, 1954. How he came to the *N.Y. Eve. World* is told by Arthur Krock in a letter to the Editor of the *N.Y. Times,* published therein January 26, 1958. Bowers's articles in the *Jeffersonian Democrat,* II (January, March, 1900) anticipate his book and emphasize his grounding in the Democratic tradition. The Bowers-Beveridge relationship is an intriguing one, as suggested by the following: James M. Cox, *Journey Through My Years* (N.Y., 1946); Bowers, *Beveridge and the Progressive Era;* Beveridge and David R. Barbee, *An Excursion in Southern History* ... (Richmond, 1928); Monroe F. Cockrell, *After Sundown* ... II (n.p., 1951); Beveridge's review of *Jefferson and Hamilton, Boston Evening Transcript,* December 12, 1925. A sheaf of reviews indicating the highly favorable opinion of the book: J. G. de R. Hamilton, *North Carolina Historical Review,* III (October 1926); William E. Borah, *New Republic,* XLV (December 23, 1925); William E. Dodd, *The N.Y. Herald Tribune,* December 5, 1925; Samuel F. Bemis, *Amer. Hist. Rev.,* XXX (April 1926); Arthur N. Holcombe, *Amer. Pol. Sci. Rev.,* XX (February 1926). T. P. Abernethy, in the *Va. Qtly. Rev.,* XXII (January 1946), critically reviews Bowers's three volume series on Jefferson. E. A. Alderman's address at the presentation ceremonies, Monticello, July 5, 1926, is included in the *Report of the Sesquicentennial of American Independence and Thomas Jefferson Centennial Commission* (Wash., 1928).

The revaluation of Jefferson from a *liberal* standpoint is highlighted by Edward Grigg's essay in *American Statesmen* and by Stuart P. Sherman's two pieces on Jefferson in *The Main Stream* (N.Y., 1927). Suggestive too of the changing opinion are William B. Swaney, *Safeguards of Liberty* (N.Y., 1920); Walter Lippmann, "Why I Shall Vote for Davis," *New Republic*, XL (October 29, 1924) and *American Inquisitors;* J. G. de R. Hamilton, "Mr. Jefferson Visits the Sesquicentennial," *Va. Qtly. Rev.*, III (Winter 1927); James T. Adams, *Our Business Civilization* (N.Y., 1929); Ludwig Lewisohn, *Expression in America* (N.Y., 1932). But note in contrast Irving Babbitt's reassertion of an old opinion in *Democracy and Leadership* (Boston, 1924). Bowers's connection with the Monticello movement is noted in Theodore F. Kuper, "Collecting Monticello," *Manuscripts*, VII (Summer 1955). His letter to the author, September 10, 1954, explains his role in the Sesquicentennial. The *N.Y. Times*, March 1, 1933, reports the Thomas Jefferson Memorial Foundation's testimonial dinner to Bowers.

Congressional debates and newspapers are the best sources for understanding the predicament of the Democratic party and the revival of Jefferson symbol and slogan among Democrats. There is biting criticism of the party and its ritual in the following: "The Sickness of American Politics," *New Republic*, XXXIX (July 23, 1924); Arthur Krock, "Jefferson's Stepchildren," *American Mercury*, VII (February 1926); Louis D. Jaffe, "The Democracy and Al Smith," *Va. Qtly. Rev.*, III (July 1927); *N.Y. Times* editorials, January 28, 1927, April 19, 1927, June 7, 1929, March 11, 1932. The National Committee of the Democratic party issued a series of pamphlet-lessons in the history and principles of the party in 1924. The Thomas Jefferson League, organized in 1926, was responsible for *Common Sense and State Rights—A Call to the People of the South in the Name of Thomas Jefferson;* it is reprinted in the *Cong. Record*, 69 Cong., 1 Sess. Bowers was a leading member of the League, as well as the main speaker at the testimonial dinner in honor of Harry B. Hawes, St. Louis, as reported in the *St. Louis Post-Dispatch*, April 14, 1926. Hawes's address in the House of Representatives, April 9, 1926, separately published as *Jeffersonian Democracy* (Wash., 1926), evinces Bowers's influence and expresses the "new Jefferson" movement. A number of revealing Jeffersonian speeches, by Finnis J. Garrett, Josephus Daniels, William G. McAdoo, and others appear in the *Cong. Record*, 69 Cong., 1 Sess. Mark Sullivan, "Seeing America with Jefferson's Eyes," *World's Work*, LII (July 1926) points up the impact of Bowers's book among Democrats.

Frank Friedel, *Franklin D. Roosevelt: The Ordeal* (Boston, 1954) treats Roosevelt and the search for a "New Jefferson." The Roosevelt Library, Hyde Park, N.Y., has two boxes of correspondence on his circular letter of December 1924. Also there are Bowers's letters to Roosevelt, November 18, December 2, 1925, and January 19, 1926, which concern the review in the *Eve. World*.

It is reprinted in the *American Mercury*, LXI (September 1945). "The Great Jefferson Joke," *New Republic*, XLVII (June 9, 1926) states the opinion of the "smug writers" Roosevelt criticized.

Bowers's addresses from Democratic platforms: "Principles of Jefferson Applied to the Problems of Today," *St. Louis Post-Dispatch*, April 14, 1926; *Thomas Jefferson: An Address before the Democratic Women's Luncheon Club of Philadelphia* (n.p., [1927]); Jackson Day Dinner Address, *The Ohio Review*, II (February 1928). See also "Jefferson, Master Politician," *Va. Qtly. Rev.*, II (July 1926), and "Democracy: Its Past and Future," in *Democracy at the Crossroads: A Symposium*, Ellis Meridith, ed. (N.Y., 1932). The keynote address of 1928 is reported, printed, and commented on in the *N.Y. Times*, June 27, 1928. Other editorial comments: *Chicago Tribune*, June 28, 29, 1928; *Louisville Courier Journal*, June 28, 1928; *St. Louis Post-Dispatch*, June 27, 1928. See also *The Campaign Book of the Democratic Party* (N.Y., 1928).

Considerations of Jefferson and the New Deal are numerous. Roosevelt's views are assembled in his *Public Papers and Addresses*, S. I. Rosenman, ed., 15 v. (N.Y., 1938-50). His address at St. Paul in 1932 was fashioned into the Introduction of *Looking Forward* (N.Y., 1933). Guy B. Park, *Address . . . before the Women's Jefferson Democratic Club, Kansas City, Missouri* (Kansas City, 1933) expresses the Jeffersonian anticipations of many Democrats. Administration officials advocate the "new modeling" of Jeffersonian Democracy in several addresses, as reported in the *N.Y. Times*: R. Walton Moore, July 5, 1934; Henry A. Wallace, April 14, 1935; James A. Farley, April 14, 1938. Perhaps the best statement of the administration's position is Claude Pepper's address at the University of Virginia's Institute of Public Affairs, July 4, 1938, *Cong. Record*, 75 Cong., 3 Sess. Other speeches either made in Congress or inserted in the *Record* are the following: Judge Glenn Terrell, Senator Lewis B. Schwellenbach, Representative Fred H. Hildebrandt, all in 74 Cong., 1 Sess; Representative Joseph B. Shannon, in 74 Cong., 2 Sess; and Senator Allen J. Ellender, 75 Cong., 1 Sess. The New Deal is defended as a modern adaptation of Jeffersonian principles in several books and numerous magazine articles. A representative listing: Dumas Malone, "Jefferson and the New Deal," *Scribner's Mag.*, XCIII (June 1933) and "Mr. Jefferson to Mr. Roosevelt: An Imaginary Letter," *Va. Qtly. Rev.*, XIX (September 1943); Robert K. Gooch, "Reconciling Jeffersonian Principles with the New Deal," *Southwestern Social Science Qtly.*, XVI (June 1935); Richard Carlyle, *The Earth Belongs to the Living* (Los Angeles, 1936); Irving Brant, *Storm Over the Constitution* (Indianapolis, 1936); Charles E. Merriam and F. P. Bourgin, "Jefferson as a Planner of National Resources," *Ethics*, LIII (1940); Thomas T. McAvoy, "Roosevelt: A Modern Jeffersonian," *Review of Politics*, VII (July 1945).

The outstanding expositions of the pragmatic approach to government and politics are the two books by Thurman Arnold: *The Symbols of Government* (New Haven, 1935) and *The Folklore of Capitalism* (New Haven, 1937). See also Raymond Moley, *After Seven Years* (N.Y., 1939). David Cushman Coyle and others, *The American Way* (N.Y., 1938) and Gilbert Seldes, *Mainland* (N.Y., 1936) help to relate the changed outlook to the Jeffersonian tradition. David Lilienthal, *TVA—Democracy on the March* (N.Y., 1944) emphasizes new administrative techniques within a Jeffersonian frame of values, as does A. Whitney Griswold, "Jefferson's Republic: The Rediscovery of Democratic Philosophy," *Fortune Mag.*, XLI (April 1950). The older Progressive belief that these new techniques are Hamiltonian is best stated by Broadus Mitchell, "Jefferson and Hamilton Today," *Va. Qtly. Rev.*, X (July 1934). The dissolution of Jeffersonian doctrine into the faith in democratic change is exemplified in the writings of T. V. Smith, particularly, *The Promise of American Politics*, 2nd ed. (Chicago, 1936) and "Thomas Jefferson and the Perfectibility of Mankind," *Ethics*, LIII (July 1943); also in John Dewey, particularly, *Freedom and Culture* (N.Y., 1939) and *The Living Thoughts of Thomas Jefferson* (Phila., 1940); and in Charles M. Wiltse's *The Jeffersonian Tradition in American Democracy* (Chapel Hill, 1935). Charles Beard's writings in the 'thirties suggest the difficulty of working out a satisfactory conception of American policy from within either the Jeffersonian or the Hamiltonian tradition; see especially *The Idea of a National Interest* (N.Y., 1934) and *The Open Door at Home* (N.Y., 1935).

The Jeffersonian threads in the Roosevelt story are drawn almost entirely from the magnificent collection of manuscripts, mementos, and miscellany in the Roosevelt Library. On the Kosciusko portrait, see also Arthur Krock's column, *N.Y. Times*, June 21, 1938. Roosevelt's patrician resemblances to Jefferson were often noted; but the best expression is Roosevelt's own in his address at Monticello, July 4, 1936, *Public Papers*, V. Republican dissatisfaction with the "presidential series" of stamps is reported in the *N.Y. Times*, March 9, 1938; see also Blair Bolles, "A Postage Stamp Makes a Debut—and a Stir," *ibid.* April 24, 1938. The files of the Fine Arts Commission (National Archives, Washington, D.C.) contain data on the Jefferson nickel. Complaints are aired in the *Washington Post*, April 21, 1938, and in the *Cleveland Plain Dealer*, September 8, 1938. The leading congressional champion of a national Jefferson birthday is Joseph B. Shannon; see especially his speech and resolution in the House, 72 Cong., 1 Sess. and *Thomas Jefferson, the Advocate of Truth, Freedom, and Equality*, 2nd ed. (Kansas City, 1931).

Pointed recognitions of Jefferson's presence all around the political spectrum are furnished by Simeon Strunsky, "Topics of the Times," *N.Y. Times*, April 14, 1936; Cary Johnson, Jr., "New Priests of Jefferson," *Va. Qtly. Rev.*, XII (July 1936); D. W. Brogan, "The Ghost of Jefferson," *Fortnightly*, CXCVI (July 1936); Charles A. Beard, "Jefferson in America Now," *Yale Review*, XXV (December 1935). The agrarian cult is discussed in Patrick F. Quinn, "Agrarianism and the Jeffersonian Philosophy," *Review of Politics*, II (January 1940). Quinn's assertion that the agrarian claim to the tradition is valid is not supported by his own analysis. *I'll Take My Stand: The South and the Agrarian Tradition* (N.Y., 1930) is the epitome of Southern agrarianism. See also the articles by Frank Owsley, "Two Agrarian Philosophers: Jefferson and Du Pont," *Hound and Horn*, VI (October 1932) and "The Foundations of Democracy," *The Southern Review*, I (Spring 1936), and the writings of Donald Davidson, "Expedients vs. Principles—Cross Purposes in the South," *Southern Review*, II (Spring 1937), *The Attack on Leviathan: Regionalism and Nationalism in the United States* (Chapel Hill, 1938). The variations on the agrarian theme are many, as illustrated by Nathaniel Wright Stephenson, *Lectures on Typical Americans and Their Problems* (Claremont, Calif., 1930); John McConaughy, *Who Rules America? A Century of Invisible Government* (N.Y., 1934); Russell A. Kirk, "Jefferson and the Faithless," *South Atlantic Qtly.*, XL (July 1941); Louis Bromfield, *A Few Brass Tacks* (N.Y., 1946). The major writings of Herbert Agar during his agrarian phase are *The People's Choice* (Boston, 1933), *Land of the Free* (Boston, 1935), *Who Owns America?* in collaboration with Allen Tate (Boston, 1936), *Pursuit of Happiness* (Boston, 1938). His ambivalent attitude toward Jefferson, common to most of the agrarians, is preserved in *The Price of Union* (Boston, 1950). Gilbert Seldes, *Mainland*, cited above, makes a pungent comment on "the dream theory of American history."

Heywood Broun lays "two to one that Jefferson would go stronger for Marx than for John D. M. Hamilton," in "Shades of Thomas Jefferson," *New Republic*, XCV (July 20, 1938). Oscar Ameringer's autobiography, *If You Don't Weaken* (N.Y., 1940) shows the positive appeal of Jefferson to a leading Socialist. The critical viewpoint of Marxist Socialists is stated in A. M. Simons, *Social Forces in American History* (N.Y., 1911) and V. F. Calverton, *The Liberation of American Literature* (N.Y., 1932). But McAlister Coleman, *Pioneers of Freedom* (N.Y., 1929) presents Jefferson as fighting "the ever rising tide of capitalism." Henry Bamford Parkes examines Jefferson and Marx in "Jeffersonian Democracy," *The Symposium*, III (July 1933), and then comes, surprisingly, to an agrarian conclusion in *Marxism: An Autopsy* (Boston, 1939). The insufficiency of Jefferson's philosophy, but its termination in Marxism, is the theme of Norman Thomas and Charles Soloman in *Karl Marx or Thomas Jefferson? A Debate . . .* (N.Y., 1931). Herbert M. Morais, *The Struggle for American Freedom* (N.Y., 1944) views Jefferson as a revolutionary but "bourgeois democrat." See also, S. Bernstein, "Jefferson and the French Revolution," *Science and Society*, X (1946). Earl Browder's position is best stated in the symposium, with Claude Bowers and Francis Franklin, sponsored by the Jefferson School of Social Science, April 9, 1943, and published as *The Heritage of Jefferson* (N.Y., 1945). The Jefferson Bicentennial number of the *New Masses*, XXXVII (April 13, 1943) is a good key to Communist attitudes and usage of the Jefferson symbol. A curiosity which associates Jefferson with Fascist ideology is Ezra Pound's *Jefferson and/or Mussolini* (N.Y., 1935).

One of the best sources for the Jeffersonian attack on the New Deal from the right is the *Chicago Tribune*. Jefferson's name is conspicuous in numerous Liberty League tracts, for instance, Fitzgerald Hall, *The Imperilment of Democracy* (Wash., 1935), William H. Stayton, *Today's Lessons for Tomorrow* (Wash., 1935), and Raoul E. Desvernine, *The Principles of Constitutional Democracy and the New Deal* (Wash., 1935). The latter's *Democratic Despotism* (N.Y., 1936) is a fuller statement. Alpheus T. Mason, "Business Organized As Power: The New Imperium in Imperio," *Amer. Pol. Sci. Rev.*, XLIV (June 1950) is a brilliant scholarly analysis of the Liberty League ideology. The conservative theme is developed in Richard Rothchild, *Three Gods Give an Evening to Politics* (N.Y., 1936); William M. Houghton, "An Open Letter to Mr. Jefferson," *American Mercury*, XXXVII (March 1936); Raymond Moley, "The Wisdom of a Ghost," *Newsweek*, XII (November 21, 1938); Herbert Brauff, *Today's Forgotten Man* (N.Y., 1940); and John de Meyer, *F.D.R. and the Patriots' Club* (N.Y., 1940). A. J. Nock once again relates Jefferson to Spencerian *laissez faire* in *Our Enemy, The State* (Caldwell, Idaho, 1935). Edwin B. Lindsay, *Toward a Political Philosophy . . .* (Davenport, Iowa, 1937) focuses the ends and means problem. Carl Wittke, *Jefferson Lives On: A Lecture . . .* (Columbus, Ohio, 1942) is a cogent reminder of the individualistic values of the Jeffersonian tradition, as is, in a somewhat different context, James B. Conant's "Wanted: American Radicals," *Atlantic Monthly*, CLXXI (May 1943).

Alfred M. Landon is presented with a bust of Jefferson, *N. Y. Times*, September 13, 1936; John D. M. Hamilton ties the party to Jefferson, *ibid*. February 13, July 5, 1938. The *Cong. Record* is full of Jeffersonian protests, by Republicans and Democrats alike, against the New Deal. Interesting glimpses of the traditional conservative opinion of Jefferson's "anti-judicialism" are provided by two controversies reported in the *N.Y. Times*: April 1, 11, 20, 1924, on the LaFollette Progressives' attack on the Supreme Court; April 27, 1930, on the battle over confirmation of Judge Alton Parker's nomination to the Supreme Court. Charles S. Thomas's excellent "Jefferson and the Judiciary," *Report of the Colorado Bar Association*, XXVIII (December 1925) deplores the Progressives' use of Jefferson and offers a reasoned statement of the contrary position. See also, Claude Bowers, "Thomas Jefferson and the Courts," *Proceedings of the North Carolina Bar Association*, May 1927. Burton J. Hendrick, *The Bulwark of the Constitution* (Boston, 1937) represents the traditional conservative view during the fight on Roosevelt's "court packing" plan. A radio address by Senator Carter Glass, *N.Y. Times*, March 30, 1937, represents a Jeffersonian defense of the Court. Henry S. Commager, *Majority Rule and Minority Rights*, and Edwin Mims, Jr., *The Majority of the People* set forth the radical Jeffersonian position against the Supreme Court. Morris L. Ernst, *The Ultimate Power* (Garden City, 1937) is wildly exaggerated. More sober, but also bringing Jefferson to Roosevelt's support are Beard's *Jefferson, Corporations, and the Constitution*, and Brant's *Storm over the Constitution*. An anticipation of the "third term" controversy occurred in 1880; see the debate between Timothy

O. Howe and Jeremiah S. Black, *No. Amer. Rev.* XXX (February, March, 1880). Fred Rodell, *Democracy and the Third Term* (N.Y., 1940) contains the most reasoned statement of Jefferson's position. Robert K. Gooch, "Jeffersonianism and the Third Term: A Retrospect," *Southern Review*, VI (Spring 1941) agrees with Rodell that the Republicans were right as to Jefferson's opinion, but then concludes that the issue is not *basic*.

The cast of James M. Beck's mind may best be measured in *The Constitution of the United States* (Garden City, 1924). His changing attitude toward and response to Jefferson may be traced through the following lectures and speeches: *The Scholar in Politics* (n.p. [1914]); *The Changed Conception of the Constitution* (Rochester, 1925); "The Triumph of Democracy," *Cong. Record*, 69 Cong., 1 Sess.; "Our Changing Constitution," *Bul. of the Col. of Wm. and Mary*, XXI (November 1927); and the "forgotten man" speech, *Cong. Record*, 73 Cong., 2 Sess., April 18, 1934. Several of Nicholas Murray Butler's works, including his autobiography, have been cited. His Hamiltonianism comes out clearly in various addresses collected in *Is America Worth Saving?* (N.Y., 1920) and *Building the American Nation* (N.Y., 1939). But the liberal, even the Jeffersonian, ambit of his faith is described in *The Faith of a Liberal* (N.Y., 1924) and *Looking Forward*. His address, *Is Thomas Jefferson the Forgotten Man?* was delivered at Southampton, Long Island, September 1, 1935. The *N.Y. Times*, September 2, 1935, considered it front-page news. For Butler's remarks on the two statues at Columbia University, see the *N.Y. Times*, December 24, 1927. Samuel B. Pettingill mourns Jefferson's death in the *Cong. Record*, 75 Cong., 1 Sess., June 16, 1938. Some of James Truslow Adams's writings in the 'twenties have been noticed. *The Epic of America* (Boston, 1931) is the key work. Adams edited *Jeffersonian Principles; Extracts from the Writings of Thomas Jefferson* (Boston, 1928). Maury Maverick's review, *New Republic*, May 13, 1936, is one of several severely critical notices of *The Living Jefferson*. The review is inserted, with additional comment, in the *Cong. Record*, 74 Cong., 2 Sess. Elmer Davis's interviews with Godfrey D. Gloom appear in the *N.Y. Times*, June 1920, June 1924, June-July 1932, June 1936. June 28, 1936, carries the report of Gloom's death and the obituary.

VIII. CULTURE

Several of the publications previously cited (Prologue and Chapter V, particularly) are relevant to the history of Monticello after Jefferson's death. Paul Wilstach's *Jefferson and Monticello* briefly sketches the history, but his subject is Jefferson's life there. The recent works by Marie Kimball and Dumas Malone, *Jefferson: The Road to Glory* and *Jefferson the Virginian*, respectively, are definitive on the beginnings of Monticello, while William H. Gaines, Jr., "From Desolation to Restoration," *Virginia Cavalcade*, I (Spring 1952) offers the best brief account of Monticello's history after 1826. James G. Randall, "When Jefferson's Home was Bequeathed to the United States," *South Atlantic Qtly.*, XXIII (January 1924) treats the litigation of Commodore Levy's will. The sale of Monticello by court order in 1864 is reported in the *N.Y. Times*, December 1, 1864. Jefferson M. Levy's superintendent, Thomas L. Rhodes, gives his account in *The Story of Monticello, as told . . . to Frank B. Lord* (Wash., 1928). Other writings, not cited heretofore, which throw some light and considerable confusion on that story are the following: "Miss Grundy," in the *Washington Post*, June 27, 1880; Maud Peterson, "The Home of Jefferson," *Munsey's Mag.*, XX (January 1899); Edward C. Mead, *Historic Homes of the South-West Mountains, Virginia* (Phila., 1899); George A. Townsend, *Monticello and Its Preservation since Jefferson's Death* (Wash., 1902); "National Monument to Jefferson," *The Independent*, XXVII (January 12, 1914); Dorothy Dix, "Monticello—Shrine or Bachelor's Hall," *Good Housekeeping*, LVIII (April, 1914). See also the brochures of Maud Littleton and the testimony in congressional hearings, both cited below. George A. Baer, Jr., *Old Pictures of Monticello, An Essay in Iconography* (Charlottesville, 1957) is excellent as a starter.

Bryan's early bid for Monticello is reported in the *Richmond Dispatch*, April 9, 15, 1897. The memorial road project is described in *Proceedings of the Jefferson Memorial and Interstate Good Roads Convention . . .* (Wash., 1902) and in C. P. Shaw, "The Jefferson Memorial Road," *Al. Bul. of the Univ. of Va.*, III (April 1903). For its consideration in Congress, see the *Cong. Record*, 57 Cong., 1 Sess., 58 Cong. 2 Sess., and 62 Cong., 2 Sess. Maud Littleton makes her appeal in *One Wish* (n.p., n.d.) and *Monticello* (n.p., 1912). The latter prints portions of her testimony before congressional committees and excerpts from many letters received from supporters. The relevant *Hearings* on public ownership of Monticello: House Library Committee and Senate Library Committee, 1912; House Rules Committee, 1915; Senate Committee on Public Buildings and Grounds, 1917. These constitute the primary source, but see as well the debates in 62 Cong., 2 Sess., 63 Cong., 1 Sess., and Appendix F of the *19th Annual Report of the American Scenic and Historic Preservation Society* (Albany, 1914).

The history of the Thomas Jefferson Memorial Foundation, its campaign and activities, must be reconstructed from the newspapers, particularly the *N.Y. Times*, which gave excellent coverage to the Monticello enterprise. The President's reports and minutes of the meetings of the Foundation, 165 Broadway, New York City, have been consulted. More useful are the Foundation's brochures, "The Monticello Papers," several of which are gathered in John S. Patton and Sallie J. Doswell, *Monticello and Its Master* (Charlottesville, 1925). Theodore F. Kuper's article, previously cited, represents the recollections of the Foundation's director. Marietta Minnigerode Andrews tells of her part in *My Studio Window* (N.Y., 1928). Her "Thomas Jefferson Memorial Pageant" is fully described in the *Baltimore Sun*, May 17, 1925. The *Cong. Record*, of course, contains much information on both the Monticello campaign and the Sesquicentennial. See also the *Report of the Sesquicentennial . . . Commission* (Wash., 1928). Roland Sawyer, "Jefferson Was Always Changing Monticello," *Christian Science Monitor*, March 9, 1954, describes the progress of the restoration. The *Annual Reports* of the Monticello Association are chiefly valuable for the genealogy of Jefferson's family, but they also bear on the care and restoration of Monticello.

The image of Monticello has been synthesized from the whole body of writing and reflection on the subject. This includes many things already cited and some things yet to be cited under, for example, Jefferson's art. Pertinent are the following: a number of editorials and features in the *N.Y. Times,* July 28, 31, 1921, April 15, 1923, October 19, 1924, May 31, 1925; Anniversary Address by Edwin A. Alderman, April 13, 1930, in *Cong. Record,* 71 Cong., 2 Sess.; James O. Bennett, "Vivid Stories Still Being Told of Thomas Jefferson," *Chicago Tribune,* December 20, 1931; Lawrence F. Abbott, "Thomas Jefferson, the Aristocrat," *Twelve Great Modernists* (N.Y., 1927); Kenneth Umbreit, "Thomas Jefferson," *Founding Fathers* (N.Y., 1941); O. C. Sherlock, "Thomas Jefferson and Abraham Lincoln," *Tall Timbers* (Boston, 1926); Paul Wilstach, "Jefferson out of Harness," *American Mercury,* IV (January 1925) and "Thomas Jefferson," in *Portraits off Their Pedestals* (Indianapolis, 1927); H. G. Dwight, "Jeffersonian Simplicity," *Harper's Mag,* CLXIX (June 1934); E. A. Powell, *A Virginia Pilgrimage* (n.p., n.d.); John R. Dos Passos, "Portico Facing the Wilderness," *The Ground We Stand On* (Boston, 1941); Gerald W. Johnson, "The Changelings," *Va. Qtly. Rev.,* XIX (Spring 1943); Hamilton Basso, "Farewell and Hail to Thomas Jefferson," *Mainstrean* (N.Y., 1943); Hendrik Willem Van Loon, *Thomas Jefferson* (N.Y., 1943) and also *Van Loon's Lives* (N.Y., 1942). Several articles in the Bicentennial number of *Hobbies,* April 1943, are relevant to Monticello as a museum. Outstanding poems are Lawrence Lee's in *Monticello and Other Poems* (N.Y., 1937), F. C. Rosenberger's "Jefferson at Monticello," *XII Poems,* Karl Shapiro's "Jefferson," *V-Letter and Other Poems* (N.Y., 1944), and Robert Penn Warren's *Brother to Dragons* (N.Y., 1953).

Benét's "Thomas Jefferson, 1743-1826" appears in Rosemary and Stephen Vincent Benét, *A Book of Americans* (N.Y., 1933). Eleanor D. Berman, *Thomas Jefferson among the Arts* (N.Y., 1947) is the best general study, but it has many deficiencies, which are partly offset by Karl Lehmann's *Thomas Jefferson, American Humanist* (N.Y., 1947). Fiske Kimball reviews the literature on Jefferson's architectural work in his initial study, *Thomas Jefferson and the First Monument of the Classical Revival in America* (n.p., 1915). Particularly significant are the following: John Keevan Peebles, "Thomas Jefferson, Architect," *Al. Bul. of the Univ. of Va.,* I (November 1894); Montgomery Schuyler, "The Old Greek Revival," *American Architect,* XCVIII (October 12, 1910); Glenn Brown, "Letters from Thomas Jefferson and William Thornton, Architect, Relating to the University of Virginia," *Journal of the American Institute of Architects,* I (January 1913). Norman M. Isham's review of Lambeth and Manning's work, under the title "Jefferson's Place in Our Architectural History," *ibid.* II (May 1914), states the skeptical opinion. Suggestive for the changing opinion are two articles by Mildred Stapley, "Thomas Jefferson, The Architect," *Architectural Record*, XXIX (February 1911) and "Monticello and the Jeffersonian Style," *Country Life in America*, XX (October 1911). Thomas Jefferson Coolidge discusses his son's collection of Jefferson's architectural drawings in his *Autobiography*. See also, Worthington C. Ford, "The Jefferson Papers," in Fiske Kimball, *Thomas Jefferson, Architect* (Boston, 1916).

Kimball's views may also be found in the following: "Jefferson as Architect," *Nation*, XCVIII (January 8, 1914); "Thomas Jefferson as Architect of Monticello and Shadwell," *Architectural Qtly. of Harvard University*, II (June 1914); "Thomas Jefferson and the Origins of the Classical Revival in America," *Art and Archeology*, I (May 1915); "A Church Designed by Jefferson," *Architectural Record*, LIII (February 1923); "The Genesis of Jefferson's Plans for the University of Virginia," *Architecture*, XLVIII (December 1923); "Monticello, the Home of Jefferson," *Journal of the American Institute of Architects*, XII (April 1924); *Jefferson's Grounds and Gardens at Monticello* (Charlottesville, 1926); "Jefferson the Architect," *Forum*, LXXV (June 1926); "Jefferson and the Arts," *Proc. of the Amer. Phil. Soc.* CXXXVII (1943); "Form and Function in the Architecture of Thomas Jefferson," *Mag. of Art*, XL (April 1947); "Jefferson and the Public Buildings of Virginia," *Huntington Library Qtly.*, XII (February 1949); "Jefferson's Designs for Two Kentucky Homes," *Journal of the Society of Architectural Historians*, IX (October 1950).

Significant for Jefferson's reputation as an architect are Ihna T. Frary, *Thomas Jefferson, Architect and Builder* (Richmond, 1931); Talbot Hamlin, *The Greek Revival in American Architecture* (N.Y., 1944); Thomas T. Waterman, *The Mansions of Virginia* (Chapel Hill, 1946); and Saul K. Padover, *Thomas Jefferson and the National Capital* (Wash., 1946). H. G. Dwight spoofs the reputation in "Jeffersonian Simplicity," cited above; Lewis Mumford offers a discriminating appraisal in *The South in Architecture* (N.Y., 1941); and Karl Lehmann discusses "Thomas Jefferson, Archeologist," in the *American Journal of Archeology*, XLVII (April 1943). Two interesting sidelights are Walter S. Rodman, "The Lighting Schemes of Thomas Jefferson," (n.p., 1916), a paper presented to the Illuminating Engineering Society; and Marie Kimball, "Jefferson's Furniture Comes Back to Monticello," *House Beautiful*, LXVI (August 1929). *Thomas Jefferson's Garden Book, 1766-1824*, Edwin M. Betts, ed. (Phila., 1944) is of major importance for landscape. Horace M. Kallen, "Jefferson's Garden Wall," *The American Bookman*, I (Winter 1944) describes an interesting episode.

Oscar Sonneck, *Suum Cuique; Essays in Music* (N.Y., 1916) includes an early appreciation of Jefferson's musical side. Randall discusses Jefferson and his fiddle, *Life*, I. See also Morgan Dix, ed., *Memoirs of John Adams Dix* (N.Y., 1883). Vachel Lindsay's "The Litany of Thomas Jefferson's Violin" in *The Litany of Washington Street* (N.Y., 1929) is particularly suggestive of the homespun associations of Jefferson's fiddle. Hildebrandt's story is retold in Louis Biancolli, "Thomas Jefferson, Fiddler," *Life Mag.*, XXII (April 7, 1947). Jane

C. H. Randolph, *Thomas Jefferson, Monticello Music, 1785* (St. Louis, 1941) prints the words and music of eight song favorites. Helen D. Bullock describes the acquisition of Jefferson's musical library and the projects which grew from it in *My Head and My Heart* (N.Y., 1945). Gilbert Chinard discusses Jefferson's "Travelling Notes," in *Thomas Jefferson, Apostle of Americanism;* James Truslow Adams begs to differ in *The Living Jefferson,* as does Elizabeth Cometi, "Mr. Jefferson Prepares an Itinerary," *Journal of Southern History,* XII (February 1946). Horace Kallen, "The Arts and Thomas Jefferson," *Ethics,* LIII (July 1943) emphasizes the dualities.

Edwin T. Martin, *Thomas Jefferson: Scientist* (May 1952) is an excellent general study. Gerald Johnson, "The Changelings," and Kenneth Umbreit, *Founding Fathers,* both cited above, carry forward the views of Jefferson's science as gadgeteering and as dilettantism. Frederic N. Luther's "Jefferson the Naturalist," appears in *Mag. of American History,* XIII (April 1885). The scientists' recognition is clearly indicated in G. Brown Goode's Presidential Address before the Biological Society of Washington, *The Beginnings of Natural History in America* (Wash., 1886), and in Cyrus Adler, "Jefferson as a Man of Science," Memorial Edition, XIX. Henry A. Martin's "Jefferson as a Vaccinator," *North Carolina Medical Journal,* VII (January 1881) should be supplemented by Robert H. Halsey, *How the President, Thomas Jefferson, and Doctor Benjamin Waterhouse established Vaccination as a Public Health Procedure* (N.Y., 1936). See also, Andrew De Jarnette Hart, "Thomas Jefferson's Influence on the Foundation of Medical Instruction at the University of Virginia," *Annals of Medical History,* New Series, X (1938).

A sampling of the articles on Jefferson's scientific work: A. W. Greeley, "Jefferson as Geographer," *National Geographic Magazine,* VII (1896); Alexander Chamberlain, "Thomas Jefferson's Ethnological Opinions and Activities," *American Anthropologist,* New Series, IX (1907); Rodney H. True, "Thomas Jefferson's Relation to Botany," *Scientific Monthly,* III (October 1916); C. D. Hellman, "Jefferson's Efforts toward the Decimalization of the United States Weights and Measures," *Isis,* XVI (November 1931); Henry Raphael, *Thomas Jefferson, Astronomer* (n.p., 1943); Charles A. Browne, "Thomas Jefferson's Relation to Chemistry," *Journal of Chemistry Education,* XX (1943); Harry B. Weiss, "Thomas Jefferson and Economic Entomology," *Journal of Economic Entomology,* XXXVII (December 1944). Jefferson and agriculture has been much noticed: Everett E. Edwards, ed., *Jefferson and Agriculture: A Sourcebook* (Wash., 1943); M. L. Wilson, "Thomas Jefferson, Farmer," *Proc. of the Amer. Phil. Soc.,* LXXVII (1943); Hugh H. Bennett, *Thomas Jefferson, Soil Conservationist* (Wash., 1944); C. A. Browne, "Thomas Jefferson and Agricultural Chemistry," *Scientific Monthly,* LX (January 1945); James E. Ward, "Thomas Jefferson's Contribution to Agriculture," *Cong. Record,* 79 Cong., 1 Sess.

Frederic A. Lucas names Jefferson "Father of Paleontology" in "Thomas

Jefferson, Paleontologist," *Natural History*, XXVI (May 1926). See also the articles on the same subject by Henry Fairfield Osborn, in *Science*, New Series, LXIX (April 19, 1929) and LXXXII (December 6, 1935). George Gaylord Simpson's attack on the legend is "The Beginnings of Vertebrate Paleontology in the United States," *Proc. of the Amer. Phil. Soc.*, LXXXVI (1942). Charles A. Browne, *Thomas Jefferson and the Scientific Trends of His Time* (Waltham, Mass., 1944) is a useful summary; and Austin H. Clark's paper on the occasion of Jefferson's Bicentennial, "Thomas Jefferson and Science," *Journal of the Washington Academy of Science*, XXXIII (1943) attempts an over-all appraisal. Isaiah Bowman, "Jefferson's 'Freedom of Speech' from the Standpoint of Science," *Science*, LXXXII (December 6, 1935) goes to the heart of the matter. A. Hunter Dupree, *Science in the Federal Government* (Cambridge, 1957) centers the dominant trend.

There is no major study of Jefferson as Man of Letters. Of first importance are Gilbert Chinard's Introductions to the two *Commonplace Books* (Baltimore, 1926, 1928) edited by him. Edwin P. Whipple's essay in *American Literature, and Other Papers* (Boston, 1887) represents an older view. Louis H. Boutell, *Thomas Jefferson, the Man of Letters* (Chicago, 1891) is disappointing; Max J. Herzberg, "Thomas Jefferson as a Man of Letters," *South Atlantic Qtly.*, XIII (October 1914) is very perceptive; Edd Winfield Parks, "Jefferson as a Man of Letters," *Georgia Review*, VI (1952) is a useful fresh look.

Edwin B. Setzler is the editor of *The Jefferson Anglo-Saxon Grammar and Reader* (N.Y., 1938), an attempt to apply the principles of Jefferson's essay. For Jefferson's interest in philology and linguistics, see especially Henry E. Shepherd, "Thomas Jefferson as a Philologist," *American Journal of Philology*, III (1882); Charles A. Smith, "Thomas Jefferson," *Southern Literary Studies* (Chapel Hill, 1927); Albert C. Baugh, "Thomas Jefferson, Linguistic Liberal," *Studies for William A. Read*, Nathanial M. Caffee, ed. (Baton Rouge, 1940); Thomas Fitzhugh, "Letters of Thomas Jefferson concerning Philology and the Classics," *Al. Bul. of the Univ. of Va.*, XI, XII (1918, 1919). The latter embraces the classics; see, in addition, Gilbert Chinard, "Thomas Jefferson as a Classical Scholar," *American Scholar*, I (March 1932) and Louis B. Wright, "Thomas Jefferson and the Classics," *Proc. of the Amer. Phil. Soc.*, LXXXVII (1943). Another aspect is treated in Mabel Morris, "Jefferson and the Language of the American Indian," *Modern Language Qtly.*, VI (1945). The taste of the poet its emphasized in John W. Wayland, "The Poetical Tastes of Thomas Jefferson," *Sewanee Review*, XVIII (July 1910), and Paul L. Haworth, "Thomas Jefferson, Poet," *Bookman*, XXXI (August 1910). Marie Kimball, *Jefferson: The Road to Glory*, takes a different view and also corrects Haworth's error in regard to "Lovely Peggy." The Thomas Jefferson Memorial Foundation exhibited in New York City the manuscript of the poem "Sir Valentine"; but see the *N.Y. Times*, January 11, 1929, for its attribution to Thomas Percy. This is only one example of erroneous claims.

Randolph G. Adams, "Thomas Jefferson Librarian," in his *Three Americanists* (Phila., 1939) is a superb essay. Also important for this aspect are William Peden, "Some Notes Concerning Thomas Jefferson's Libraries," *Wm. and Mary Qtly.*, 3rd Series, I (July 1944) and E. Millicent Sowerby, "Thomas Jefferson and His Library," *Publications of the Bibliographical Society of America*, L (1956). Adrienne Koch wrote a significant review of the latter's *Catalogue* in the *N. Y. Times Book Review*, September 7, 1952. Koch's *Philosophy of Thomas Jefferson* (N.Y., 1943) makes clear the larger importance of comprehending Jefferson's acquisition and management of books. William B. O'Neal is the editor of *Jefferson's Fine Arts Library for the University of Virginia, with Additional Notes . . .* (Charlottesville, 1956).

There is no major study of Jefferson the Lawyer. Marie Kimball's *Jefferson: The Road to Glory* places his reputation in this field on solid ground. Among the appreciations after 1900 are the following: Andrew J. Montague, "Jefferson as a Citizen of the Commonwealth of Virginia," *Memorial Edition*, V; Eugene L. Didier, "Thomas Jefferson as a Lawyer," *The Green Bag*, XV (April 1903); Randolph Bias, "Jefferson and Hamilton," *West Virginia Law Qtly.* (December 1926); Mary F. Lathrop, "Jefferson's Contribution to the Law of the West," *Report of the Thirty-third Annual Meeting of the Pennsylvania Bar Assn.* (Phila., 1927); John W. Davis, "Thomas Jefferson, Attorney at Law," *American Bar Assn. Journal*, XIII (January 1927). *Van Loon's Lives* (N.Y., 1942) contains a portrait of Jefferson as epicure, illustrated with recipes drawn from Marie Kimball's *Cook Book*. One of the best appreciations of Jefferson's "wholeness" will be found in Ezra Pound's "The Jefferson-Adams Correspondence," *No. Amer. Rev.*, CCXLIV (December 1937).

Charles Beard points up the need for a formula to comprehend Jefferson in his anniversary address at the University of Virginia, "Thomas Jefferson: A Civilized Man," published in the *Miss. Valley Hist. Rev.*, XXX (September 1943). Stuart P. Sherman sees the new departure represented by Nock's *Jefferson* in "Thomas Jefferson: A Revaluation," *Main Street*. Nock awaits a biographer, but his own *Memoirs of a Superfluous Man* (N.Y., 1943) and *Letters from Albert Jay Nock, 1924-1945*, Frank W. Garrison, ed. (Caldwell, Idaho, 1949) reveal the man.

Gilbert Chinard's discovery of Jefferson may be traced through his writings and publications of Jefferson's correspondence with French intellectuals. Important dissents to portions of his major work have been entered by A. J. Nock, "Mr. Thomas Jefferson," *Saturday Review of Literature*, V (January 11, 1930); James Truslow Adams, *The Living Jefferson*; Adrienne Koch, *The Philosophy of Jefferson*; and Elbert Thomas, *Thomas Jefferson, World Citizen* (N.Y., 1942). The contemporary interest in Jefferson's relations with France is evinced in the following: "Founder's Day in Paris," *Al. Bul. of the Univ. of Va.*, XII (July 1919); F. W. Garrison, "Jefferson and the Physiocrats," *The Freeman*, VIII (October 1923); Marie Kimball, "Unpublished Correspondence of

Madame de Staël with Thomas Jefferson," *No. Amer. Rev.*, CCVIII (July 1918) and "Jefferson's Farewell to Romance," *Va. Qtly. Rev.*, IV (July 1928); Dumas Malone, ed., *Correspondence between Thomas Jefferson and Pierre Samuel Du Pont de Nemours, 1798-1817* (Boston, 1930); Bernard Faÿ, *The Revolutionary Spirit in France and America* (N.Y., 1927); George H. McKee, *Th. Jefferson, Ami de la Révolution Française* (Lorient, 1928); Otto Vossler, *Die Amerikanischen Revolutionsideale in Ihrem Verhältnis zu den Eurapäischen Untersuch on Thomas Jefferson* (München, 1929). Robert R. Palmer offers an abstract of Vossler's neglected work in the *Wm. and Mary Qtly.*, XII (July 1955). Chinard returns to his theme in "Jefferson's Influence Abroad," *Miss. Valley Hist. Rev.*, XXX (September 1943).

Most of Marie Kimball's writings have been noticed. Fiske Kimball's "In Search of Jefferson's Birthplace," *Va. Mag. of Hist. and Biog.*, LI (October 1943) is important to her conception, as indeed is most of her husband's work. T. P. Abernethy's review of *The Road to Glory*, *La. Qtly. Rev.*, XIX (Spring 1943) highlights the significance of Mrs. Kimball's investigations of Jefferson's ancestry and early environment. Dumas Malone dwells on this theme in *Jefferson the Virginian* and in several articles, for example, "The Great Generation," *Va. Qtly. Rev.*, XXIII (Winter 1947) and "Jefferson Goes to School in Williamsburg," *ibid.* XXXIII (Autumn 1957). Two critical reviews which help to characterize Mrs. Kimball's later volumes are by Frederic R. Kirkland in the *Pa. Mag. of Hist. and Biog.*, LXXII (January 1948) and George Dangerfield in the *New Republic*, CXXIII (September 4, 1950).

Elizabeth Page's depiction of Jefferson in *The Tree of Liberty* (N.Y., 1939) may be compared with several other works of fiction, for example, Mary Johnston, *Lewis Rand* (Boston, 1908), S. Weir Mitchell, *The Red City* (N.Y., 1908), and Sonia Daugherty, *The Way of an Eagle* (N.Y., 1941). There are many juvenile biographies of which good examples are Gene Lizitzky, *Thomas Jefferson* (N.Y., 1933), Helen Nicolay, *The Boy's Life of Thomas Jefferson* (N.Y. 1933), and Vincent Sheean, *Thomas Jefferson, Father of Democracy* (N.Y., 1953). Sidney Kingsley's *The Patriots* (N.Y., 1943) and Paul Green's *The Common Glory* (Chapel Hill, 1948) are the only significant dramatic works. See also, however, the radio series, *The Jeffersonian Heritage*, Dumas Malone, ed. (Boston, 1953).

The history of the Jefferson Memorial may be traced through the *Cong. Record*, with supplementary documents, beginning with the 58th Congress, April 28, 1904. A résumé of the first phase is the *Report* of the House Library Committee, 62 Cong., 3 Sess., January 22, 1913. Several reports in the *N.Y. Times*, especially the feature article, "Jefferson Monument to Have Precedence," July 4, 1826, help to explain the revival of the project and John J. Boylan's connection with it. The memorial service for Boylan in the House of Representatives, May 30, 1939, throws some light on his contribution. Marquis Childs, "Mr. Pope's Memorial," *Magazine of Art*, XXX (April 1937) helps to characterize him. Several letters to Franklin D. Roosevelt in the archives at Hyde Park point up the Democratic expeetations of a Jefferson memorial: Edgar Lee Masters, December 24, 1933; Josephus Daniels, January 11, 1934; and William E. Dodd, December 17, 1938. The Jefferson National Expansion Memorial is of course debated and reported in Congress. The *St. Louis Post-Dispatch* is a key source; but see also the three-volume "Scrapbook" on the project in the library of the Missouri Historical Society. The United States Territorial Expansion Memorial Commission issued an elegant brochure, *Thomas Jefferson and the Pioneers to whom we owe our National Expansion* (n.p., n.d.). Paul W. Ward, "Washington Weekly," *Nation*, CXCII (March 4, 1936) deals with the shady side of the project.

The files of the Thomas Jefferson Memorial Commission, the Fine Arts Commission, and the Thomas Jefferson Bicentennial Commission, all in the National Archives, Washington, D.C., contain valuable information on the planning of the Jefferson Memorial. Additional papers are in the Roosevelt Library. The various phases of the controversy are aired in the *Cong. Record*, 73-75 Congress. See also the *Hearings* before the House Library Committee, 75 Cong., 1 Sess., on H. J. Res. 337; and the *Report* of the Memorial Commission, 75 Cong., 3 Sess., House Doc. 699. The *N.Y. Times, Washington Post,* and *Washington Star,* January 1937-December 1939 are full of information and discussion. Joseph Hudnut, "A Temple for Thomas Jefferson," *New Republic*, XCII (November 22, 1939) typifies the progressive criticism of the Pope plan. *Newsweek*, XIV (August 28, 1939) offers a summary of the Commission's troubles. The Commission of Fine Arts presents its side of the case in *Report to the Senate and the House of Representatives concerning the Thomas Jefferson Memorial* (Wash., 1939). Elbert Thomas's *Thomas Jefferson, World Citizen* and his address at Columbia University, April 21, 1948 (*Cong. Record*, 80 Cong., 2 Sess.) supply not always reliable information on the selection of inscriptions for the Memorial.

The files of the Thomas Jefferson Bicentennial Commission, in the National Archives, are the main source for comprehending the character and varied activities of the 1943 celebration. The files contain copies of most of the Commission's publications, minutes of its meetings, press clippings, and scattered correspondence. The Library of Congress retains records of its part in the Bicentennial; and the *Cong. Record*, 78 Cong., 1 Sess. is a repository of Jefferson address. The latter also reports the political hassle on Jefferson's meaning and the Commission's direction. Benjamin Fine's survey of American history is discussed in the *Record*, April 13; and Representative Kennedy reports on the same day a conversation with Sidney Kingsley. The reception of *The Patriots* may be gauged from comment in the *N.Y. Times*. February 7, April 2, June 2, 1943, and Norman Cousins's scathing review in the *Saturday Review of Literature*, XXVI (April 17, 1943).

The symposium edited by James Waterman Wise, *Thomas Jefferson, Then and Now, 1743-1943* (N.Y., 1943) provides a convenient cross section of American attitudes toward Jefferson, but this should be supplemented by items in national magazines and newspapers, for example: Donald C. Peattie, "Thomas Jefferson, Architect of Democracy," *Reader's Digest,* XLII (April 1943); "Thomas Jefferson, 1743-1943," *Life Mag.,* XIV (April 12, 1943); Allan Nevins, "Jefferson, Man for Our Times," *N.Y. Times Magazine,* February 21, 1943; "The Cult of Jefferson," *Commonweal,* XXXVII (April 9, 1943); Alben Barkley, Fourth of July Address, University of Virginia, *Vital Speeches,* IX (August 1, 1943); and the Jefferson number of *American Unity,* I (March-April 1943). The scholars' recognition of Jefferson may best be appraised in several symposia conducted by leading journals and learned societies: *Proc. of the Amer. Phil. Soc.,* LXXXVII (1943) gathers papers by Carl Becker, Gilbert Chinard, Louis B. Wright, Harlow Shapley, and others; *Ethics,* LIII (1943) has contributions from Claude Bowers, Herbert W. Schneider, Horace Kallen, Chinard, and others; the *Miss. Valley Hist. Rev.,* XXX (1943) prints articles by Chinard, George H. Knoles, Lynn W. Turner, Charles A. Beard, and Howard R. Marraro; and Chinard, Bowers, Dumas Malone, Bernard Mayo, Gerald Johnson, and Marie Kimball are represented in the Jefferson number of the *Va. Qtly. Rev.,* XIX (Spring 1943). Francis G. Wilson offers a dissenting opinion: "On Jeffersonian Tradition," *Review of Politics,* V (July 1943). William D. Grampp discusses Jefferson's reputation in the light of the Bicentennial in "Everyman His Own Jeffersonian," *Sewanee Review,* LII (January 1944). Douglass Adair has a useful discussion of Jefferson's reputation in "The New Thomas Jefferson," *Wm. and Mary Qtly.,* 3rd Series, III (January 1946). The verbatim transcript of the Library of Congress "Symposium on the Occasion of the Dedication of the Thomas Jefferson Memorial," April 13, 1943, is retained in the Library of Congress.

Elbert Thomas's views are amply stated in his book, but several articles and addresses included in the *Cong. Record,* 78 Cong., 1 Sess. and 80 Cong., 2 Sess. are also useful for understanding his viewpoint. Gilbert Chinard restates his opinion in "An American Philosopher in the World of Nations," *Va. Qtly. Rev.,* XIX (Spring 1943) and elsewhere. Claude Bowers treats a significant theme in "Thomas Jefferson and South America," *Bul. of the Pan-American Union,* LXXVII (April 1943). Roosevelt's last and undelivered address, "We Seek Peace—Enduring Peace," *Vital Speeches,* XI (May 1, 1945) embodies the "world citizen" idea of Jefferson.

Chinard's plea for a fuller edition of Jefferson's papers occurs in the Introduction to *Thomas Jefferson, Apostle of Americanism.* See also his statement in the *N.Y. Times,* January 22, 1930; A. J. Nock in "Mr. Thomas Jefferson," previously cited; and Maude H. Woodfin to Franklin D. Roosevelt, January 10, 1935, MS, Roosevelt Library. The files of the Bicentennial Commission shed light on the inception of the *Papers of Thomas Jefferson,* as do several letters in the Roosevelt Library. Julian P. Boyd's mimeographed "Report to the Thomas Jefferson Bicentennial Commission," September 25, 1943, is in the Commission files.

Boyd has described his connection with the project in a personal interview with me. The Introduction he wrote for the edition, along with the prefatory essay on "Editorial Method," provides a general view of the work. Boyd has written several independent essays which emphasize the importance of editorial scholarship to historical understanding; see, for example, " 'Gods Altar Needs Not Our Pollishings,' " *New York History*, XXXIX (January 1958). Lyman Butterfield, "The Papers of Thomas Jefferson," *American Archivist*, XII (1949) describes the editors at work and the magnitude of the project. Mina R. Bryan, "Thomas Jefferson Through the Eyes of His Contemporaries," *Princeton University Library Chronicle*, IX (1948), and Howard C. Rice, Jr., "Jefferson in Europe a Century and a Half Later," *ibid.* XII (1951) are interesting sidelights. Other sidelights are reported in the *N.Y. Times*, November 14, 1946, February 23, 1947, and April 13, 1947. The presentation ceremonies in Washington, D.C., May 17, 1950, are contained in the *Cong. Record*, 81 Cong., 2 Sess.

EPILOGUE

There are suggestive reflections on Jefferson's reputation and place in American life at mid-century in the following articles: Nathan Schachner, "Thomas Jefferson: The Man and the Myth," *American Mercury*, LXV (July 1947); Julian P. Boyd, "Thomas Jefferson Survives," *American Scholar*, XX (September 1951); Clinton Rossiter, "Which Jefferson Do You Quote?" *The Reporter*, XVII (September 15, 1955); and Dumas Malone, "Was Washington the Greatest American?" *N.Y. Times Mag.*, February 16, 1958.

The Jefferson Jubilee Pageant of the Democratic party is reported with comment in the *Christian Science Monitor*, May 11-19, 1951. Harry S. Truman draws Jefferson into political discussion therein and in several other speeches, which will be found in the *N.Y. Times*, February 20, 1948, April 15, 1951, and November 3, 1949. The latter speech at St. Paul raised the old question of the Louisiana Purchase; rejoinders in the *Christian Science Monitor*, November 5, 1949, and the *N.Y. Times*, November 6, 1949. Clarence Streit, a champion of world federation, puts a new face on a perennial subject in "Present-day Lesson of the Louisiana Purchase," reprinted in the *Cong. Record*, 83 Cong., 1 Sess. For General Dwight D. Eisenhower's political use of Jefferson, see the *Christian Science Monitor*, December 1, 1949, and September 27, 1952. Henry Wallace's speech accepting the presidential nomination of the Progressive party, *N.Y. Times*, July 25, 1948, states one view of Jefferson's relation to global problems. For Jefferson's demotion on the nation's postage and sundry other trivia, see Douglass Adair, "Trivia III," *Wm. and Mary Qtly.*, XII (April 1955).

The key works by Hofstadter, Hartz, Boorstin, Niebuhr, and Warren, all discussed, need no further citation. Warren describes "The Way It Was Written," in the *N.Y. Times Book Review*, August 23, 1953. Ralph H. Gabriel restates a traditional view in "Thomas Jefferson and Twentieth Century Rationalism," *Va. Qtly. Rev.*, XXVI (Summer 1950) and also in the second edition of his *Course of American Democratic Thought* (N.Y., 1956). Hans Morgenthau criticizes the Jeffersonian tradition in foreign policy: *In Defense of the National Interest* (N.Y., 1952) and, with Kenneth W. Thompson, *Principles and Problems of International Politics* (N.Y., 1950). President Sukarno's hymn to Jefferson is reported in the *N.Y. Times,* May 21, 1956. Louis M. Hacker, *Alexander Hamilton in the American Tradition* (N.Y., 1957) represents the renewed attempt to put Hamilton squarely in the tradition. The major work of the "new conservatives," Russell Kirk's *The Conservative Mind* (Chicago, 1953), is not favorable to Jefferson's reputation but it is much less favorable to Hamilton's.

No attempt is made here, or in the text, to examine Jefferson scholarship since the Bicentennial. The importance of Daniel Boorstin's *The Lost World of Thomas Jefferson* was quickly seized by George Dangerfield, reviewing it in the *New Republic,* CXIX (November 15, 1948). Dumas Malone's biography has been liberally showered with praise. Douglass Adair's sensitive appreciation appears in the *N.Y. Herald Tribune Book Review,* November 11, 1951. Recent scholarship accords with Malone's work in placing the emphasis on Jefferson's mind instead of his politics; but Claude Bowers restated his fixed view not long before his death in *Making Democracy a Reality: Jefferson, Jackson, Polk* (Memphis, 1954).

Bowers stresses Jefferson's concern for political and personal liberty; see his "Jefferson and Civil Liberty," *Atlantic Monthly,* CXCI (January 1953). Several addresses and articles by Julian P. Boyd are of particular significance for this aspect: "Thomas Jefferson and the Police State," *North Carolina Historical Review,* XV (April 1948); "Thomas Jefferson's Empire of Liberty," *Va. Qtly. Rev.,* XXIV (October 1948); "Subversive of What?" *Atlantic Monthly,* CLXXXII (August 1948); "The Relevance of Thomas Jefferson for the Twentieth Century," *American Scholar,* XXII (January, 1953). The *N.Y. Times,* March 28, 1956, reports John Gates's use of Jefferson at a crucial moment. The recent Southern revival of nullification is expounded by James J. Kilpatrick, *The Sovereign States* (Chicago, 1957), but Calhoun rather than Jefferson is the author's model. Senator Hubert Humphrey made an eloquent appeal for the Jefferson of human rights, as against the Jefferson of state rights, at the Democratic National Convention of 1948; see the *N.Y. Times,* July 15, 1948. An interesting controversy on Jefferson and academic freedom is discussed in detail, with the relevant documents, in Arthur E. Bestor's contribution, "Thomas Jefferson and the Freedom of Books," to *Three Presidents and Their Books* (Urbana, Ill., 1955). But a full-scale study of Jefferson and civil liberties is yet to be written.

INDEX

Abbott, Lyman, 269

Abdy, E. S., 184

Abelman v. Booth, 202-3

Abolitionism: and Declaration of Independence, 164, 172, 173-4; TJ's relationship to, 168, 171-3; and Protestant Christianity, 174; racial equality, 175-7; African colonization, 177-8; Slave Power concept, 178-80; miscegenation legend, 181-3, 186

Acton, Lord: on the Civil War, 211

Adair, Douglass: quoted, 455

Adams, Charles Francis: on Declaration of Independence, 201-2

Adams, Henry: quoted, 8, 173, 277, 291; his great *History*, 139, 270, 272, 280-91, 293, 319, 322, 402, 415, 417, 456; mentioned, 245, 279

Adams, Herbert Baxter: his *TJ and the University of Virginia*, 242, 292, 396

Adams, James Truslow: interprets "American Dream," 373; his *Living Jefferson*, 373-4

Adams, John: death and last words of, 3, 14, 458; eulogists' view of, 6-8, 11; his reputation, 13, 90; quoted on TJ, 157, 307; mentioned, 22, 32, 36, 97, 100, 103, 106, 108, 140, 144, 146, 149, 281, 300, 319, 362

Adams, John Quincy: and death of TJ, 4, 5; on political parties, 18, 20, 73; as President, 18-19, 23; TJ's opinion of, 19, 27; satirizes TJ, 22, 182; alienates Massachusetts Federalists, 27-8, 135; opinion of TJ, 28, 84, 85, 130, 135-9, 174, 177, 181; and

nullification, 59; and slavery, 173; mentioned, 20, 22, 32, 132, 281, 289

Adams, Randolph G.: quoted, 407

Adler, Cyrus: acquires Jefferson Bible, 301

African Repository, The, 178

Agar, Herbert: his interpretation of TJ, 365-6

Agassiz, Louis, 402

Agrarianism: in TJ's thought, 24-5; in Virginia Convention, 43-4; in Jacksonian ideology, 82, 84-5; in historical writing, 137, 138, 157, 284, 285, 315, 317-20, 321, 325-6, 327, 365-6; in pro-slavery ideology, 167, 168, 170; in George's philosophy, 258-9; in Southern Agrarianism, 363-6; mentioned, 201, 218, 255, 445

Agriculture: TJ and science of, 403, 405. *See also* Agrarianism

Agriculture Department, U.S.: and TJ, 361

Albany Argus: revives TJ's report on the Bank, 77; defends separation of church and state, 94; objects to Whig artifice, 105-6

Albany Journal, 105

Alderman, Edwin A.: and University of Virginia, 241; quoted on TJ, 242, 347, 393

Alexander Hamilton Memorial Association, 421

Alien and Sedition Laws, 65, 102, 202, 226, 297, 300, 457

Altgeld, John P.: quoted, 265

American Anti-Slavery Society, 173